God's Wisdom for Daily Living

A Devotional Bible Study based on the book of Proverbs

by Betty Miller

our love and blessings,
unlimited
Betty : Bud

www.BibleResources.org

God's Wisdom for Daily Living
A Devotional Bible Study
Based on the book of Proverbs

Published by
Christ Unlimited Publishing
P.O. Box 850
Dewey, AZ 86327

ISBN 1-57149-022-1

All Scripture quotations taken from
The King James Version of the Holy Bible (KVJ)
unless otherwise indicated

Printed and bound in the United States of America

Foreword

I have been privileged to observe the Holy Spirit revealing to Betty the truths of His Word, which He has set forth in this Daily Devotional.

Betty has said that the majority of the writing of this Devotional was the hardest writing she had ever done–and yet the easiest. By that statement, she meant that it was hard to discipline herself to spend two to three hours a day, for 365 days, to write, edit, and post the devotional. At the same time, it was also easy, because the Holy Spirit revealed to her what the teaching and prayer were to be for each day.

I thank God that He has allowed me to share such close love and partnership with Betty. I have said this before and know it to be true; that Betty has no personal ambitions, no personal ends to achieve. She has simply been doing the will of the Father in the writing of this anointed devotional. My prayer is that this devotional book becomes a classic for the ages, reaching many people with the wisdom of God.

May the Lord bless you daily with this devotional, as He has blessed us in being a part of His work.

Yours in Christ,

Pastor Bud Miller
January, 2008

Preface

The book of Proverbs was written to instruct the young and to guide them into a happy and prosperous life. Most of Proverbs (Chapters 1-24) is credited to King Solomon. Solomon's name means "Peace," and he is credited with writing two other books of the Bible including "Ecclesiastes" and "The Song of Solomon," or "The Song of Songs" as it's sometimes called. The book of Proverbs is the focus of this devotional.

Born in Jerusalem around 1000 BC, Solomon followed in the footsteps of his father and ruled Israel for about 40 years, from 970 to 930 BC. 1 Chronicles 29:26-28 tells us how Solomon became King: "David was king over the whole nation of Israel. He was the son of Jesse. He ruled over Israel for 40 years. He ruled for seven years in Hebron and for 33 years in Jerusalem. He died when he was very old. He had enjoyed a long life. He had enjoyed wealth and honor. His son Solomon became the next king after him." King David's legacy to his young son was to rule Israel with love and devotion to God.

In 2 Chronicles 1:7-12 we learn that God visited the young King: "That night God appeared to Solomon and said, 'What do you want? Ask, and I will give it to you!' Solomon replied to God, 'You showed faithful love to David, my father, and now you have made me king in his place. O Lord God, please continue to keep your promise to David my father, for you have made me king over a people as numerous as the dust of the earth! Give me the wisdom and knowledge to lead them properly, for who could possibly govern this great people of yours?' God said to Solomon, 'Because your greatest desire is to help your people, and you did not ask for wealth, riches, fame, or even the death of your enemies or a long life, but rather you asked for wisdom and knowledge to properly govern my people. I will certainly give you the wisdom and knowledge you requested. But I will also give you wealth, riches, and fame such as no other king has had before you or will ever have in the future!'"

In 1 Kings 4:29-31 we learn about Solomon's God-granted wisdom and fame: "God gave Solomon exceptionally much wisdom and understanding, and breadth of mind like the sand of the seashore. Solomon's wisdom excelled the wisdom of all the people of the East and all the wisdom of Egypt. For he was wiser than all other men, and his fame was in all the nations round about." He asked only for wisdom, but God granted Solomon so much more than that. The wise King then shared his great wisdom with the world through his writings and songs, originating over 3,000 proverbs and 1,005 songs during his lifetime. Now, thousands of years later, Solomon's Proverbs are still touching lives, since the Bible has been digitized and can be read by people all over the world via the Internet.

These daily devotions from the book of Proverbs were penned by Pastor Betty Miller. Betty, along with her husband, Pastor R. S. "Bud" Miller, were founders of the Bible.com website (which reaches millions of people every month and hosts the Bible in numerous versions and languages). They have now moved their ministry content to their newest website, **BibleResources.org**. They have served as pastors, teachers, and evangelists, with an apostolic/prophetic calling to proclaim the gospel through the Internet. Betty is a teacher of the Word of God, with a beautiful ability to present truth in a simple and understandable way. For each day of the year, a Scripture is provided from Proverbs, with a relevant mini-teaching for the day–often reflecting on additional Scriptures from the Bible. The devotionals always conclude with a heartfelt prayer.

Introduction

Knowing God's Wisdom is the Key to the Overcoming Life

A Personal Word from Betty Miller, January 2008

In our high-tech age, we are bombarded from every quarter to give our attention to something. Everyone has a message or a product they are promoting, and many of them are good and beneficial to humanity. However, over the year-end holidays, I found myself praying for the Lord to show me my priorities, as I only have so much time and energy. I want to stay focused on the things He feels are the most important things for me to accomplish at this time in my life.

What led me to pray this prayer was that my husband and I took a short sabbatical between Christmas and the New Year, and I faced the dilemma as to what I should do with this time. My "Things To Do" list was quite lengthy and included personal, business and ministry projects that were all screaming for my attention. Since I wear a number of "hats," (as I am sure you do also), it is not always easy to know what is the most important thing for me to do at any particular time.

I found the list of priorities in the Bible: "And thou shalt love the Lord thy God with all thy heart, and with all thy soul, and with all thy mind, and with all thy strength: this is the first commandment. And the second is like, namely this, Thou shalt love thy neighbour as thyself. There is none other commandment greater than these" (Mark 12:30-31).

The Lord has my heart, soul and mind, as that commitment was made long ago; but how can I love Him more with all of my strength? As Christians, we must all give an account of how we spend our time and energy, as well as our money. According to the above verse, God comes first above all others, which means I need to first give Him my time in prayer, meditation and the reading of the Word. As I do this, He will lead me by the Spirit as to what I am to do each day, and I will know how to love others properly. This also means that I must give him the first-fruits of my money, since money represents the energy and time we spend in labor (our strength).

Bud and I spent time seeking Him diligently, and the thing the Lord put on my heart to do during that time was to finish the edits for the devotional book, "God's Wisdom for Daily Living" that has been in progress for the last two years. Apparently, the Lord feels it is now time to share these writings with a larger audience. He spoke to my heart that as I gave my time to complete this book and share it with the body of Christ, He would give me the time and help to get the other things in my life done. He is so good! During this time, He furnished several other people to help in the editing process and with all the additional things it takes to get a book in print. We are self-publishing this book with a "print-on-demand" publisher, which allows us to pay for small batches at a time. Since we were unable to come up with the funds to do a hardback edition, we are launching with this paperback version instead, with the other goal still before us.

I started these devotionals back in 2004 and posted them daily on the Bible.com website. It was one of the hardest things I have ever done; and yet, the easiest. The hardest, as I had to yield to the discipline of devoting two hours daily to these writings for the period of 365 days. Yet, it was also the easiest, as the Holy Spirit met me in my writing studio each evening. As I sat down to read the scripture for that day's writing (with not a clue as to where that scripture would lead me in my composition), God would grace me to pen the wisdom that is contained in the book of

Proverbs. The words would just begin to flow, as the gift of writing that He bestowed upon me settled softly in my heart. I knew that the knowledge and wisdom I was gleaning from this book within the Holy Scriptures was not just for me, but for the extended family of God as well.

The "Thoughts for the Day" took various forms: one day it was a teaching, and the next day it was a sermon. One day would be a devotional meditation, and the next day would be a testimony. At times, I felt as if I penned things that were from the very heart of God Himself. I felt gratitude and a need to pray at the end of each devotional, so I thought I should include those prayers as well. The Holy Spirit inspired me to pray simple prayers from my heart that expressed my own need of change, as well as asking for the world around me to be changed.

Writing this book changed my life because of the treasure of wisdom I discovered in Proverbs. The real treasure is in knowing and loving Jesus, for He is ultimate Wisdom. If you decide to read this devotional, and you find just one gem that brings you into a closer relationship with Him, then my labor of love will bring me great joy. I will meet you daily through this book; but I also expect we shall have that Unseen Visitor with us, as this devotional was His idea.

His grateful handmaiden,

Betty Miller

God's Wisdom for Daily Living — ***Betty Miller***
January 1 — ***Day 1***

Proverbs 1:1-2 1 The proverbs of Solomon the son of David, king of Israel; 2 To know wisdom and instruction; to perceive the words of understanding.

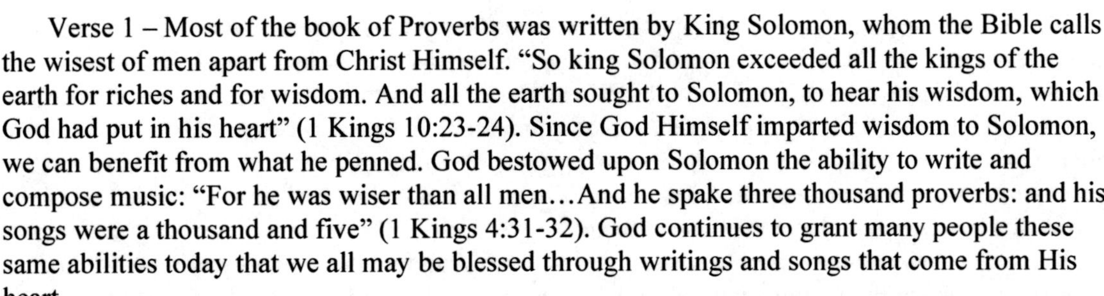

Verse 1 – Most of the book of Proverbs was written by King Solomon, whom the Bible calls the wisest of men apart from Christ Himself. "So king Solomon exceeded all the kings of the earth for riches and for wisdom. And all the earth sought to Solomon, to hear his wisdom, which God had put in his heart" (1 Kings 10:23-24). Since God Himself imparted wisdom to Solomon, we can benefit from what he penned. God bestowed upon Solomon the ability to write and compose music: "For he was wiser than all men…And he spake three thousand proverbs: and his songs were a thousand and five" (1 Kings 4:31-32). God continues to grant many people these same abilities today that we all may be blessed through writings and songs that come from His heart.

Solomon was endowed with both spiritual and practical wisdom. Wisdom is having insight into the true nature of things. It is being able to discern the mode of action that produces sensible results and having the understanding and knowledge to perceive what causes negative results. By the wisdom that God gives, we know *what* to do and *how* to do it. It enables us to avoid what results in destruction and to engage in what produces life and blessing.

Verse 2 – Wisdom is linked with instruction. To be wise, we must follow God's instructions recorded in the Holy Bible. If we ask the Lord for godly wisdom, He will give it, along with the ability to understand the Bible. We must know the Bible's Author to be able to understand the Bible's words. It will mean nothing to us without a relationship with Jesus Christ, God's Son. King Solomon gained wisdom because he had a relationship with God (2 Chronicles 1). We, too, can become wise, if we seek God with all our hearts and read the Book that He gave us.

Dear Father, I come to You in Jesus' name at the beginning of this new day, asking for Your wisdom that I may order my life, family, ministry, business, and all of my affairs according to Your Word. Please impart to me understanding of Your Word so that I will know how to do that which pleases You and produces blessing in my life and in the lives of all who know me. Thank You, Lord, for all the beautiful music and inspirational books, that You have blessed me to be able hear and read. Bless those who have been obedient over the years to share Your life through these avenues. They have made my life fuller and caused me to know You better. I ask this in the Name of Jesus. Amen.

Proverbs 1:3-4 3 To receive the instruction of wisdom, justice, and judgment, and equity; 4 To give subtlety to the simple, to the young man knowledge and discretion.

Verse 3 – Solomon, the author of most of Proverbs, sought instruction from God and became the wisest man of his day. Here we see that we can receive instruction in wisdom, justice, judgment, and equity by studying Proverbs. We all desire others to extend justice and equity to us; to judge and treat us fairly. However, a mark of maturity in Christ is respecting the rights of others while being willing to lay down our own rights. We must apply the Word of God to ourselves, as well as to those around us. This is what it means to live by the golden rule; to do unto others as you would have them do unto you.

Verse 4 – God promises to give wisdom to those who humble themselves in simplicity and become childlike in their approach to Him. We must not be prideful if we desire to receive knowledge from God. He gives instruction to the teachable; to those who depend on Him, and not upon their own human reasoning. This does not mean we should not use our minds, but that we are not to rely *only* upon our own logic and reasoning.

We need to invite God into our daily affairs so that we may have access to the mind of Christ, with His guidance and wisdom.

Dear Father, I come to You with a humble heart today, realizing that I need You in my life to help and guide me in all my ways. On my own, I cannot accomplish all the responsibilities that seem to be mine. Please show me my priorities and help me to lay down those things that are not really mine to do. Help me to trust You to take care of the things that I cannot change, and help me to work on those things that are my responsibility to change. I desire to walk in fairness with others. Help me to treat them today as I desire to be treated; realizing that I shall reap what I sow. If I sow seeds of kindness and equity, so shall I reap the same in return. Let me be more Christ-like today through the power of Your Holy Spirit. In the name of Jesus I pray. Amen.

Quotes About Forgiveness

God only asks us to make the decision to forgive; then He will supply us with the proper emotions and attitudes toward others. --Day 102

Though a Christian may sin and fall completely, as Peter did in denying Christ, he can still rise again. In Christ, there is complete forgiveness even for complete failure! --Day 253

We fail to appropriate God's grace when we don't forgive. Unforgiveness grows roots of bitterness in our hearts which defile us and others. --Day 291

God's Wisdom for Daily Living **Betty Miller**
January 3 ***Day 3***

Proverbs 1:5-6 5 A wise man will hear, and will increase learning; and a man of understanding shall attain unto wise counsels: 6 To understand a proverb, and the interpretation; the words of the wise, and their dark sayings.

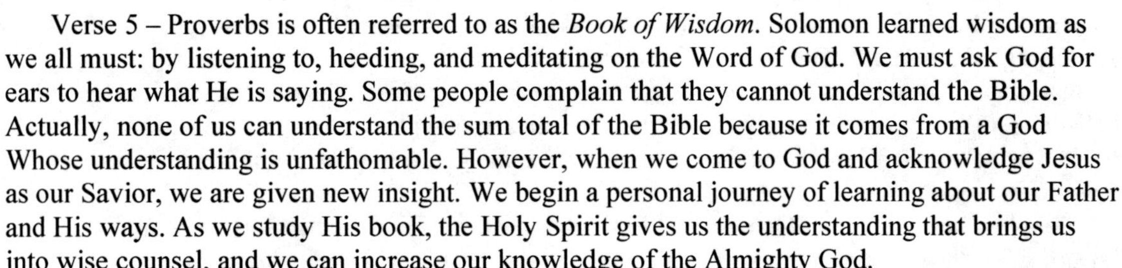

Verse 5 – Proverbs is often referred to as the *Book of Wisdom*. Solomon learned wisdom as we all must: by listening to, heeding, and meditating on the Word of God. We must ask God for ears to hear what He is saying. Some people complain that they cannot understand the Bible. Actually, none of us can understand the sum total of the Bible because it comes from a God Whose understanding is unfathomable. However, when we come to God and acknowledge Jesus as our Savior, we are given new insight. We begin a personal journey of learning about our Father and His ways. As we study His book, the Holy Spirit gives us the understanding that brings us into wise counsel, and we can increase our knowledge of the Almighty God.

Verse 6 – After over fifty years of studying the Bible, I am still awed when I read a verse I have read many times before, but never understood, and I am suddenly enlightened and can "understand a proverb" or a "dark saying." I realize that this enlightenment is due to my relationship with the One who inspired the Bible in the first place. He gives me something of His heart or mind, and my love for Him is deepened. We should always be grateful when God grants us revelation of His Word. Whenever we do not understand it, we should remember that we are called to trust Him anyway. Perhaps sometime later, having grown and matured in Christ, we can receive that understanding for which we have asked. In the meantime, we can certainly walk in the light of what we do comprehend.

Dear Father, in Jesus' Name, I thank You for every bit of understanding I have received from Your Word, the Holy Bible. I realize that it is by Your Holy Spirit that I am given the grace to understand this magnificent book. I thank You for the message of love that flows through its pages and penetrates my heart; a message that brings comfort and love, and also a message of correction when I need it. Lord, may I always yield to Your "course corrections" and line myself up with Your Word. I know that when I do, I become wiser for it, and I am blessed. Amen.

Proverbs 1:7 The fear of the LORD is the beginning of knowledge: but fools despise wisdom and instruction.

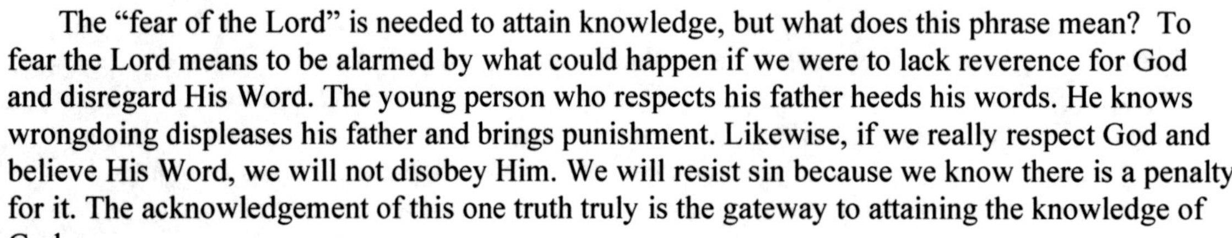

The "fear of the Lord" is needed to attain knowledge, but what does this phrase mean? To fear the Lord means to be alarmed by what could happen if we were to lack reverence for God and disregard His Word. The young person who respects his father heeds his words. He knows wrongdoing displeases his father and brings punishment. Likewise, if we really respect God and believe His Word, we will not disobey Him. We will resist sin because we know there is a penalty for it. The acknowledgement of this one truth truly is the gateway to attaining the knowledge of God.

People without a fear of God are rebellious and despise His instruction. They go about breaking His laws as if nothing will ever happen to them. The Bible refers to them as "fools." Because God is merciful, people do not usually face the consequences of their sins immediately. In time, however, all of us reap what we sow, as Galatians 6:7 tells us: "Be not deceived; God is not mocked: for whatsoever a man soweth, that shall he also reap."

The only way to stop the sowing and reaping process is to repent of our sins. The cleansing power of Christ can sterilize evil seeds we have sown. When we accept Jesus as our Savior, we do not have to pay the penalty for our sins because He paid it for us. We can escape sin's consequences. How wonderful this is! It is as if someone comes along and plows up the fields of our lives in which we had planted seeds of sin. In time, these would have sprouted and produced terrible consequences. Through Christ's love for us, our lives become like clean, plowed fields. We can now plant seeds of righteousness that produce abundant blessings that we can enjoy and share with others.

My Father, I am thankful that You came to save me from the consequences of my sins. I ask that You forgive me for every trespass I have committed in the weakness of my flesh. Help me today to resist the temptation to yield to any sin. I know I cannot do this in my own strength; but I call upon You to give me the power to overcome the desires of my flesh. Lord, I acknowledge my respect, fear, and awe of You. Deliver me from all foolishness. I know that You are all wise. I ask that You teach me Your ways so that I might walk in the path of blessing and be a blessing to all I meet today. I ask this in Jesus' name. Amen.

Proverbs 1:8-9 8 My son, hear the instruction of your father; reject not nor forsake the teaching of your mother; 9 For they are a (victor's) chaplet of grace upon your head, and the chains and pendants (of gold worn by kings) for your neck (AMP).

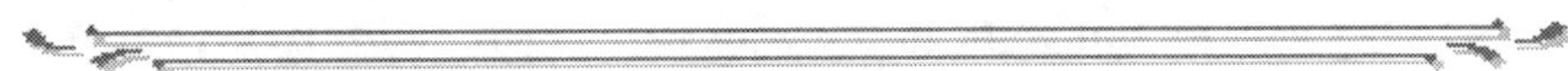

Verse 8 – One requirement for receiving wisdom is to heed the godly advice of our parents. This admonition is a facet of the Ten Commandments listed in Exodus 20: "Honour thy father and thy mother: that thy days may be long upon the land which the LORD thy God giveth thee." Notice that this commandment comes with a promise: if we honor our parents, we will have long life. We might wonder how this is true, but consider one possibility: young children failing to obey their parents can get into dangerous situations that could cost them their lives. Parents instruct their children to look both ways for oncoming traffic before crossing streets; a car could kill a child who does not obey these instructions.

Parents, being more experienced, can help their children avoid the same mistakes which they may have made. Even grown children can learn from their parents: how to raise children, how to manage financial affairs, how to find help with their occupations, for example. Christian parents possess even greater wisdom to pass on to their families. Those who know God's Word are in a position to pass godly advice on to their children. The children can become the recipients of a chain of blessings from their fathers and mothers.

Verse 9 – These blessings are described in today's verses as a victor's wreath, symbolic of walking as an overcomer in life; and a golden necklace, symbolic of prosperity and favor. If we are obedient children, we shall have these blessings. If we are godly parents, we shall be able to pass these blessings on to our children, who will in turn, be able to pass them on to theirs.

Dear Lord, I thank You for all the godly parents attempting to raise their children in Your nurture and admonition. Grant them Your wisdom as they guide their children in Your ways. Cause their children to submit to their leadership and to obey them, for this will save them from much suffering in life. Please heal the breaches in parent and child relationships. Put it into children's hearts to submit to their parents. Help parents to be patient and loving toward their children. Grant us love for one another in our homes and church families. In Jesus' name. Amen.

Proverbs 1:10-19 10 My son, if sinners entice you, do not consent. 11 If they say, Come with us, let us lie in wait for blood, let us wantonly ambush the innocent; 12 like Sheol let us swallow them alive and whole, like those who go down to the Pit; 13 we shall find all precious goods, we shall fill our houses with spoil; 14 throw in your lot among us, we will all have one purse: 15 my son, do not walk in the way with them, hold back your foot from their paths; 16 for their feet run to evil, and they make haste to shed blood. 17 For in vain is a net spread in the sight of any bird; 18 but these men lie in wait for their own blood, they set an ambush for their own lives. 19 Such are the ways of all who get gain by violence; it takes away the life of its possessors (RSV).

Verses 10-14 – God cares for His children. We do not need to go the way of sinners to attain our desires; for the Lord promises to grant them if we trust and obey Him (Psalm 37:1-4). Greed can lead to robbery and even murder. Gangs are rampant today because the above verses are unheeded by many people. Those of us with children are responsible to warn them of the dangers of following the wrong crowd. Birds of a feather flock together. If we do not desire to become like ungodly people, we must not be close friends with them. If we play with fire, we will be burned. Neither young, nor older people should entertain the notion that we can stay close to wickedness and not eventually do as the wicked do. If we do not resist evil, it will overtake us. Smaller sins eventually lead to bigger ones.

Verses 15-19 – It is not easy to live for Christ in an ungodly society. I praise God for the young people who are doing so. Becoming friends with ungodly people, however, is an enticement that Satan uses to ensnare Christians. He whispers that by becoming their friend, we can win them to Christ, but their influence usually overcomes the well-meaning person. I am not saying we should snub them, but that we should not become close friends with them. Doing so has been the downfall of many Christians. "Be ye not unequally yoked together with unbelievers: for what fellowship hath righteousness with unrighteousness? and what communion hath light with darkness? And what concord hath Christ with Belial? or what part hath he that believeth with an infidel? And what agreement hath the temple of God with idols? for ye are the temple of the living God; as God hath said, I will dwell in them, and walk in them; and I will be their God, and they shall be my people. Wherefore come out from among them, and be ye separate, saith the Lord, and touch not the unclean thing; and I will receive you" (2 Corinthians 6:14-17).

The best way to help ungodly people is to pray for them and live righteously before them. Witness to them, be kind to them, but do not yield to enticements to join their ways.

Dear Father, I come to You in Jesus' name, praying for people in all walks of life who are struggling with unrighteous relationships. Help them to live their lives pleasing to You. Deliver them from the fear of man, and give them the grace to cut all ties with those who would lead them into wickedness. Fill them with Your Spirit, that they will have the boldness to take a stand for truth. May we treat the ungodly with compassion, yet speak the truth in love, so as to help them. Give parents Your wisdom to help their teenagers resist the temptation around them, especially in inner cities where crime is rampant. Bless the workers You have sent to the inner cities. Provide for them and protect them as they work in the streets. Protect us all from evil and destruction. Help us to overcome evil with good, and be that light that shines in the darkness. Amen.

Proverbs 1:20-23 20 Wisdom cries aloud in the street; she raises her voice in the markets. 21 She cries at the head of the noisy intersections–in the chief gathering places–at the entrance of the city places she speaks: 22 How long, O simple ones and open to evil, will you love being simple? And the scoffers delight in scoffing, and (self-confident) fools hate knowledge? 23 If you will turn (repent) and give heed to my reproof, behold, I (Wisdom), will pour out my spirit upon you, I will make my words known to you (AMP).

Verses 20-21 – The author of all wisdom is the Lord God Himself. One of His names is WISDOM. The above Scripture is a picture of God's call to all men everywhere. In the typical city of ancient Israel, ordinary citizens were in its streets, businessmen were in its marketplaces, and leaders were found in the meeting places within the enormous gates of the city's surrounding walls. God calls people of every occupation, from ordinary citizens to highest officials, to heed Him and be saved. God, through His evangelists and servants, sends His gospel message to the marketplace and cities of the world.

Verses 22-23 – The Hebrew word for *simple* in these verses means "foolish, easily enticed, credulous, inexperienced.[1]" Therefore, we see that the Lord is telling us not to be foolish, but to apply His wisdom in all that we do. If we learn to be responsible and deal righteously, He will promote us to places of leadership. God desires to put us in positions of authority to help others learn His ways. He is using Christian businessmen today to bring godly principles into the market place. Any nation that aligns its economic principles with God's Word will prosper. The opposite is also true; nations failing to do this will not be blessed, but suffer poverty and economic failure. These same principles also apply to personal finances.

Dear Father, please give me wisdom in my personal affairs so that I might walk in Your blessings and prosperity and be able, in turn, to bless others. Lord, give us wise men in the places of authority to lead us as a nation. May Your wisdom be applied in the market places of our land and also to our economic situation at the highest levels. Give us wise men to rule over us; men who will be just and fair in their dealings; men of character. Thank You for teaching us Your ways and giving us the gift of the Holy Spirit. In the precious name of Jesus I pray. Amen.

[1] Wilson's Old Testament Word Studies, s.v. "simple"

January 8 ***Day 8***

**Proverbs 1:24-33 24 Because I have called, and ye refused; I have stretched out my hand,
and no man regarded; 25 But ye have set at nought all my counsel, and would none of my
reproof: 26 I also will laugh at your calamity; I will mock when your fear cometh; 27 When
your fear cometh as desolation, and your destruction cometh as a whirlwind; when distress
and anguish cometh upon you. 28 Then shall they call upon me, but I will not answer; they
shall seek me early, but they shall not find me: 29 For that they hated knowledge, and did
not choose the fear of the LORD: 30 They would none of my counsel: they despised all my
reproof. 31 Therefore shall they eat of the fruit of their own way, and be filled with their
own devices. 32 For the turning away of the simple shall slay them, and the prosperity of
fools shall destroy them. 33 But whoso hearkeneth unto me shall dwell safely, and shall be
quiet from fear of evil.**

Verses 24-27 – These verses are a serious warning to all who hate God's wisdom or refuse to yield to Him. God is very loving and compassionate; however, if we continually reject Him and His Word, we can reach a point where He will finally leave us alone. This is a frightening thought, of which the New Testament also warns us: "Therefore, as the Holy Spirit says, Today, if you will hear His voice, Do not harden your hearts, as in the rebellion (of Israel) and their provocation and embitterment (of Me) in the day of testing in the wilderness, Where your fathers tried (My patience) and tested (My forbearance) and found I stood their test, and they saw My works for forty years. And so I was provoked (displeased and sorely grieved) with that generation, and said, They always err and are led astray in their hearts, and they have not perceived or recognized My ways and become progressively better and more experimentally and intimately acquainted with them. Accordingly I swore in My wrath and indignation, They shall not enter into My rest. (Therefore beware,) brethren; take care lest there be in any one of you a wicked, unbelieving heart–which refuses to cleave to, trust in and rely on Him–leading you to turn away and desert or stand aloof from the living God" (Hebrews 3:7-12 AMP).

Verses 28-33 – The Lord makes it very clear that the following sins can bring us to the place where He will not answer us: failing to answer when He calls, failing to listen to His counsel, despising His correction and instruction, showing no fear of Him, backsliding from Him, and making prosperity one's primary goal. By doing these things, we sow rebellion, which will produce the fruit of destruction–and there will come a time when we will reap what we have sown (Galatians 6:6-7). With our own way comes bitter fruit. God promises that if we obey Him we shall dwell in safety. He wishes to bless us, but the choice is ours.

Dear heavenly Father, may I have the strength to resist temptation and always walk in Your ways. Lord, Your ways are not grievous, but given to help and bless me. May I realize this, and not rebel against Your restraints when I'm corrected. Give me grace to yield to Your Spirit and overcome the things that are not pleasing in Your sight. I know there is no temptation that I face that You have not made a way for me to escape and overcome. You are all-powerful, and I acknowledge my need for Your help in my time of trial. Thank You for Your promise of protection and freedom from fear. I am glad You are a caring Father who loves me. I ask these things in the name of Jesus. Amen.

Proverbs 2:1-5 1 My son, if thou wilt receive my words, and hide my commandments with thee; 2 So that thou incline thine ear unto wisdom, and apply thine heart to understanding; 3 Yea, if thou criest after knowledge, and liftest up thy voice for understanding; 4 If thou seekest her as silver, and searchest for her as for hid treasures; 5 Then shalt thou understand the fear of the LORD, and find the knowledge of God.

Verses 1-3 – If we desire to understand the "fear of the Lord," and discover a little of what He knows, we must do certain things; the most important of which is to *receive God's words and act on them*, by making Bible study an important part of our lives. As we study His Word and ask Him for understanding, it will come alive to us. Often while I am reading Scripture, the words suddenly seem to leap off the page and into my heart. Other times, I read a portion repeatedly without understanding, and ask the Lord to show me what it means. In this way, I am "lifting up my voice for understanding." Later, while reading that same passage, I suddenly understand it. Often the Holy Spirit brings to mind another verse that sheds light on it. Whenever God grants me understanding, I find that just knowing His Word is not enough; I must also obey it.

Verses 4-5 – If we seek knowledge from God as if searching for silver or hidden treasures, we will find it. Searching for treasure requires one to:

- Inquire where the treasure might be found
- Find a map to help in the search
- Gather tools for digging
- Find the right people to help in the search
- Dig!

I think we can see the spiritual application. We must realize that the Bible cannot be read as a common novel. It is a holy book granted to mankind, inspired by the Holy Spirit. It cannot be read with simply our natural eyes, nor studied with intellect alone. We must bring our hearts to God and ask Him to enlighten us; to give us spiritual ears to hear what He is saying. If we earnestly seek the Book's treasures in this way, we shall indeed find truth and gems of knowledge, like un-mined gold within its pages.

Dear Father God, I come to You in Jesus' name. Thank You for giving us the Bible, Your wonderful book. It is not only full of Your wisdom, but it is also Your love letter to mankind. Through it, the plan of redemption is revealed. You show us how we can find You, a loving God who gave His Son Jesus to die for us and redeem us from our sin and destruction. I am thankful that my name is written in the Book of Life. Help me today to be caring and loving, to share Your message with others. Give me understanding as I read the Bible; but most of all, give me grace to obey what You reveal to me in it. Amen.

Proverbs 2:6-7 6 For the LORD giveth wisdom: out of his mouth cometh knowledge and understanding. 7 He layeth up sound wisdom for the righteous: he is a buckler to them that walk uprightly.

Verse 6 – If we wish to be wise, we must read the Bible, which records the things that God has spoken. As we read His Word, we will receive knowledge and understanding from Him regarding any issue that we desire to know about.

When dealing with a problem we should do two things immediately: seek God in prayer, and search what the Bible says about it. After prayer, the Holy Spirit may speak to our heart concerning what we should do. He may bring a person to mind that will have the answer, or we may recall something that sheds light on our question. However, if we do not hear a direct answer from God in our spirits, many times we will find the answer by studying what the Bible says about it. A concordance or search engine on the Internet, such as the one found at Bible.com, can assist in finding verses on the topic in question.

Verse 7 – God "lays up" sound wisdom for us. This means it is available, but we must go and get it and not leave it in its storehouse. We are responsible for gaining wisdom by searching the Bible for it. This verse also mentions that the Lord is a buckler to those who walk uprightly. The Hebrew word for *buckler* means "shield."[2] God promises to protect us from harm when we obey Him and walk in His ways. This is only one of the many rewards that come from finding and walking in God's wisdom.

Dearest Father, I am grateful that You have given us the Bible with all its wisdom and knowledge, so that we do not get lost in life or overwhelmed by the problems that we face. I do thank You that for every problem we face, You will help me find the answer and overcome in the situation. Help me not only to be able to overcome my problems, but also Lord, help me to maintain the proper heart attitude as I work on the situations in my life that need changing. I know that I must react to my problems with Your love and in a way that is pleasing to You. Give me the grace to do that, as in my own strength, I am not able to approach many of my problems with a godly attitude. In Jesus' name. Amen.

[2] Wilson's Old Testament Word Studies

Proverbs 2:8 He keepeth the paths of judgment, and preserveth the way of his saints.

When we look at this scripture, we find that God keeps the *paths* (plural) of judgment. This reveals that there are two paths of judgment and that judgment is two-fold:

The Judgment of the Wicked: The wicked will be punished for their deeds; if not in this life, then certainly in hell. Those who refuse to accept Christ as Savior will pay the penalty for their sins. They will reap what they have sown. "But as for them whose heart walketh after the heart of their detestable things and their abominations, I will recompense their way upon their own heads, saith the LORD God" (Ezekiel 11:21). "Be not deceived; God is not mocked: for whatsoever a man soweth, that shall he also reap. For he that soweth to his flesh shall of the flesh reap corruption; but he that soweth to the Spirit shall of the Spirit reap life everlasting" (Galatians 6:7-8). We shall all appear before the Judgment Seat of Christ to be judged (2 Corinthians 5:10).

The Judgment of the Righteous: The righteous will be rewarded for their faithfulness. "Whoso despiseth the word shall be destroyed: but he that feareth the commandment shall be rewarded" (Proverbs 13:13). "But without faith it is impossible to please him: for he that cometh to God must believe that he is, and that he is a rewarder of them that diligently seek him" (Hebrews 11:6). We must all one day stand before the judgment seat of Christ. America's system of justice provides a picture of God's judgment. Defendants are brought to court to stand trial. Some are convicted of crimes and sentenced to death or imprisonment for their deeds. Others go to court to contest injustices, and are awarded settlements of money. Mistakes are often made in our system of justice, but we can trust God to judge all things fairly and righteously. If we have been wrongly judged or treated unfairly, God will eventually prove our innocence and properly reward us. Our greatest reward is living with Jesus eternally in heaven.

Today's verse also says that God preserves the way of the righteous, meaning that He protects and cares for His own. He will make a way out of our problems for us if there is no way out in the natural. The Lord delights in answering our prayers, even if a miracle is needed to do so. Remember: miracles are God's specialty!

Dear Father, thank You for Your love and concern for me. I was recently judged wrongly by some people that I love. It hurt, but I also hurt for them, as they believed a lie and now they no longer want this relationship. Lord, what do I need to learn from this experience? I confess that I wanted to defend my position, both to them and the other parties. I know however, that I must leave it to You, as You are the righteous Judge Who knows what really happened. Even if I defended myself, they could not hear it unless You revealed it to them. At this point, I shall leave all of this for You to repair. I will simply voice what You give me to share in this situation. I know those words will be gracious, since You are gracious. Thank You that I will be able to speak the truth in love, without justification or bitterness, and that this relationship will be restored at some point. I trust that as I keep Your commandments, You will keep my way. In Jesus' name I pray. Amen.

Proverbs 2:9 Then shalt thou understand righteousness, and judgment, and equity; yea, every good path.

To understand verse 9, we must look back to Proverbs 2:1: "My son, if thou wilt receive my words, and hide my commandments with thee..." Today's verse rests upon this condition. If we receive and treasure God's words, then we can understand righteousness, judgment, and equity and know the right path in which to walk. Let us consider the words *righteousness, judgment,* and *equity*: The Biblical definition of *righteousness* is "to be in right standing with God." There is only one way for us to be in right standing with God–we must accept Jesus as our Savior, and repent of our sins and receive God's pardon for them through what Jesus did on the cross. The moment we yield our lives to Christ, we become righteous, we come into *right standing* with God. In God's sight, we are as pure as His own Son, Jesus. This is a gift of God, and has nothing to do with what we have or have not done. The only requirement to maintain this righteousness is staying in right relationship with Christ *by faith.* We are not saved by works, but by grace. Good works are the fruit of salvation, but do not attain eternal life for us.

"But when the kindness and love of God our Savior appeared, he saved us, not because of righteous things we had done, but because of his mercy. He saved us through the washing of rebirth and renewal by the Holy Spirit, whom he poured out on us generously through Jesus Christ our Savior, so that, having been justified by his grace, we might become heirs having the hope of eternal life." (Titus 3:4-7 NIV).

Judgment, simply put, is a legal decree or sentence given by a judge. One day, God will judge every man by his deeds. Herein lies the most wonderful truth of Christianity. Anyone who accepts Jesus as Savior is judged to be righteous and will not be sentenced to hell, because the penalty for his sin was paid by Jesus. If we belong to God, we can boldly approach the Father through Jesus and ask for the things we need. We are accepted as righteous and our prayers are heard because of Him (Hebrews 4:16).

To practice *equity* means to be "fair, straight, or right."[3] When we trust God and obey His commandments, we will reap good from what we sow. However, because there is evil in the world, we will endure injustices. Although we may not always be treated fairly in this life, we can be sure that God will see that we receive fair and just rewards in the world to come.

Dearest Father, thank You for sending Jesus to die for my sins. I was a sinner and not worthy. Thank You that as I confess my sins, You are faithful to forgive and to consider me righteous in Your eyes. Since You have forgiven me, help me to forgive those who wrong me, as You taught us to do. I ask You to forgive our national sins of racism, greed, abortion, pornography, idolatry and others. Be merciful to us. We deserve judgment, but I ask that You send revival that we might turn from our wickedness and our land be spared. Help me to do my part to bring change. Although my life may only represent one drop of rain, there are many others who are rain drops too. Add each Christian's life and their godly influence to this sound of rain, until Your love and Your Word covers our dry and thirsty earth. In Your precious name I pray. Amen.

---

[3] Wilson's Old Testament Word Studies, s.v. "equity"

**Proverbs 2:10-15 10 When wisdom entereth into thine heart, and knowledge is pleasant
unto thy soul; 11 Discretion shall preserve thee, understanding shall keep thee: 12 To
deliver thee from the way of the evil man, from the man that speaketh froward things;
13 Who leave the paths of uprightness, to walk in the ways of darkness; 14 Who rejoice to
do evil, and delight in the frowardness of the wicked; 15 Whose ways are crooked, and they
froward in their paths.**

Verses 10-11 – God's Word imparts wisdom, which can deliver us from evil men. When His knowledge is pleasant to us, we receive discretion, which keeps us in many ways; one of which is replacing any desire to associate with wicked people or to speak *froward* things. *Froward* means contrary or adverse.

Verse 12 – If we obey God's wisdom, even people who speak wrongly of us will be unable to hurt us. We all face the temptation to retaliate when someone speaks against us. Answering ugly words with ugly words destroys many marriages. 1 Peter 3:8-11 advises this when others accuse or rail against us: "Finally, be ye all of one mind, having compassion one of another, love as brethren, be pitiful, be courteous: not rendering evil for evil, or railing for railing: but contrariwise blessing; knowing that ye are thereunto called, that ye should inherit a blessing. For he that will love life, and see good days, let him refrain his tongue from evil, and his lips that they speak no guile: let him eschew evil, and do good; let him seek peace, and ensue it."

We must ask the Lord to empower us to obey these instructions. We need His help to be kind to those who are unkind to us and to overcome evil with good. If we do not choose to obey God when tempted to enter into strife, we will become as heartless and evil as those who would persecute us.

Verses 13-15 – Those who leave the path of God's love to walk in darkness are blinded to the truth. This causes them to take the next step into evil and delight in their own and other's evil ways. Their ways become crooked, and that is why we call such people "crooks." By choosing the wrong path, they become lost. We must pray for those who are walking in wrong ways; especially for Christian brothers and sisters who fall into the trap of speaking wrongly against us. We must attempt to walk in peace and kindness regardless of their conduct. They may be guilty, but we will be guilty in a different way, if we retaliate. We must choose to walk in love.

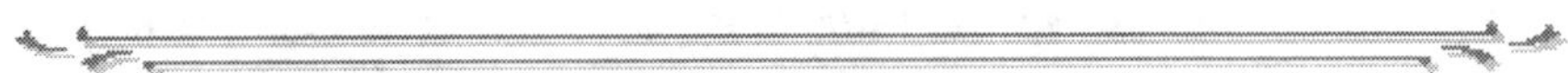

Father, I come to You in Jesus' name, desiring Your wisdom and knowledge. I want to walk in such a way that I can be kind to those who speak against me, truly seeking their good. I know that without the Holy Spirit I cannot do this; so please fill me with Your Spirit today. Let me be kind; change my heart from being argumentative and defensive. Help me to speak the truth in love, remembering that You will defend me. When I see the faults of others, help me to examine my own heart and motives. Please deliver us from those things that are not pleasing to You. I choose to be a peacemaker, not a troublemaker. I trust You to change whatever is in me and in those around me, which would cause us to engage in unkind speaking. I ask this in Jesus' name. Amen.

Proverbs 2:16-20 16 You will be saved from the loose woman, from the adventuress with her smooth words, 17 who forsakes the companion of her youth and forgets the covenant of her God; 18 for her house sinks down to death, and her paths to the shades; 19 none who go to her come back nor do they regain the paths of life. 20 So you will walk in the way of good men and keep to the paths of the righteous (RSV).

Verses 16-17 – Yesterday's devotional told us that if we hide God's Word in our hearts and obey Him, we will not fall into the snare of the enemy. Today's verses warn against the snare of immorality, and they are as applicable today as when first written. Many men have ruined both their reputations and lives by having sexual affairs. This has been demonstrated in recent decades in America in the lives of political and religious leaders. Dishonorable role models have left our nation and churches weakened; our young people disillusioned. God will forgive illicit affairs if one repents, but most people are not as forgiving. They remember them. A loose woman is unfaithful to her husband and forgets her covenant with God. She becomes ensnared with lust, and the devil incites her to flirt with men to lead them astray.

Verse 18 – This verse describes her house as sinking down to death. This is a picture of sin which carries the death principle (meaning that it releases those things that eventually lead to death). Sin always brings a curse. Our nation today is cursed with many painful and incurable sexually-transmitted diseases. At this writing, there are over 42 million people worldwide, who are living with AIDS/HIV, and this number continues to grow.[4] Many of these are children, born from infected mothers. This illustrates that one person's life of sin does not remain as an island to himself, but will eventually infect others, even the innocent.

Verse 19-20 – Those who are unfaithful cannot return to the paths of righteousness without God's help. The warning of Proverbs to men to stay pure is also applicable to women who would be tempted by lustful men. We must pray that our young people and nation return to the Biblical virtues of virginity and chastity before marriage and faithfulness to the marriage vows after wedlock. Fornication, adultery, and other sexual sins divide our homes and destroy the very heart of our nation, as well as the nations of the world.

Dear Father, forgive us for the many sexual sins that are committed on the earth. Help us to stay pure in a world of filth, and help those who struggle with pornography to break free from its bonds. Restore marriages that have been wounded through unfaithfulness; help them to forgive. For those who are involved in affairs, give them strength to break free. Restore wounded marriages with their original love. Cause those who are living together outside of marriage to recognize this as sin, and either marry or leave their sinful union. Deliver young people from temptation. Heal those who have repented; both emotionally and physically if they have contracted any sexual disease. Give us pure thoughts and deliver us from the evil of our day. Let us hide Your Word in our hearts so that we will not sin against You. Lord, if we are not guilty of any sexual sin, help us not to be critical of those who are. Let us help others by praying for them. In Jesus' name I pray. Amen.

[4] www.until.org

Proverbs 2:21-22 21 For the upright shall dwell in the land, and the perfect shall remain in it. But the wicked shall be cut off from the earth, and the transgressors shall be rooted out of it.

Verse 21 – These verses hold a wonderful promise of protection for God's people. The upright and the perfect will dwell in the land, and Satan cannot drive us from where the Lord places us. What makes a person upright and perfect? The Bible calls us *righteous* or *upright* when we have accepted the Lord Jesus as our Savior and walk in His will. *Perfect* speaks of our becoming like Jesus and our heavenly Father. When we read Matthew 5:48, where Jesus commanded "Be ye therefore perfect, even as your Father which is in heaven is perfect," we may think that there is no way that we can be perfect. The Lord, however, would never tell us to be what we cannot be. *Perfect* is better rendered as "mature." The Lord does not wish us to remain immature, walking in the flesh (our old, unregenerate nature) and doing what is unbecoming to His followers. He desires that we grow up into Christ, standing in His righteousness and not our own.

Verse 22 – This verse tells us that *the wicked* will be cut off (removed) from the earth–not the righteous. Psalm 24:1 says, "The earth is the LORD's, and the fulness thereof; the world, and they that dwell therein." Eventually only God and His people will inhabit the earth; the devil's followers will be removed. "The Son of man shall send forth his angels, and they shall gather out of his kingdom all things that offend, and them which do iniquity; and shall cast them into a furnace of fire: there shall be wailing and gnashing of teeth. Then shall the righteous shine forth as the sun in the kingdom of their Father. Who hath ears to hear, let him hear" (Matthew 13:41-43).

Jesus prayed, "Thy kingdom come. Thy will be done in earth as it is in Heaven." The Lord wishes to demonstrate His will and His Kingdom on this earth to all people through the lives of each of His children. He desires our light to shine in this dark world.

Dear heavenly Father, I want to be a light for You in this earth. Lord, we live in a dark world, and I desire that You shine in me that others may see Your light. Help me today to live perfectly toward You and walk in Your will. I know that when I do this, You will use me to help others. I know that while I am busy about Your business, You will keep me safe from all harm. Thank You for Your promise in Psalm 37 that says our seed shall be blessed. I am most blessed to have the promises of Your Word. May others also come to know that those same promises are for them and their families. In Jesus' name. Amen.

**Proverbs 3:1-2 My son, forget not my law; but let thine heart keep my commandments:
2 For length of days, and long life, and peace, shall they add to thee.**

Verse 1 – The first verse above gives us an admonition, while the second verse gives the result of keeping that admonition. What wonderful promises God gives us! If we do not forget His laws, but keep them in our hearts and obey them, they produce peace, long life, and days full of accomplishment–besides the many other things the Lord promises His people.

Over the years, I have heard people say things like "You never know when it will be your time to go" or "It may be God's will to take you home when you are young." Today's verses, and other verses, however, promise long life *if* we do certain things: "Because he hath set his love upon me, therefore will I deliver him: I will set him on high, because he hath known my name. He shall call upon me, and I will answer him: I will be with him in trouble; I will deliver him, and honour him. With long life will I satisfy him, and show him my salvation" (Psalm 91:14-16). "The fear of the LORD prolongeth days: but the years of the wicked shall be shortened" (Proverbs 10:27).

Verse 2 – God *desires* to bless us and our families with long life and peace. These promises are as available to us as are His many other blessings, but they are conditional. We must keep His Word in our hearts and appropriate His promises through faith and obedience. He has a wonderful purpose for every individual on earth and promises long life to fulfill them. However, we have an enemy who is determined to destroy us. Jesus spoke of Satan as a thief; he seeks to rob our families and us of the peace and long life that God promises (John 10:10). We must learn God's Word and walk in His ways to protect ourselves and our families from the enemy. One passage we can claim daily is Psalm 91. If we are in God's will, He will protect us, regardless of geographic location or circumstances. We could be in a war zone and still be safe; conversely, we could be in the safest place in the world and still have a fatal accident if we are *not* in His will, for then we are open to Satanic attack. The only safe place is in the will of God.

As we meditate on God's Word, and claim it by faith, we become overcomers in Christ, living abundant lives and fulfilling His purposes. Satan can take a Christian's life prematurely; however, the devil is ultimately defeated since we are promised eternal life in heaven.

Dear heavenly Father, I come in Jesus' name, thanking You for Your promises. Thank You especially for Your promise of peace in my life today. I thank You that when I am anxious or fearful, I can bring those fears to You, and You will remove them and give me Your peace. I appreciate Your promise of long life. Father, give my husband and me Your grace and health in our latter years that we may complete all that You have called us to do. Thank You for keeping us safe, even in the times we did not know it, and for placing protecting angels around my family, friends, and me. You are faithful to keep Your wonderful promises. May I remain strong in faith to receive and walk in them. Amen.

Proverbs 3:3-4 3 Let not mercy and truth forsake thee: bind them about thy neck; write them upon the table of thine heart: 4 So shalt thou find favour and good understanding in the sight of God and man.

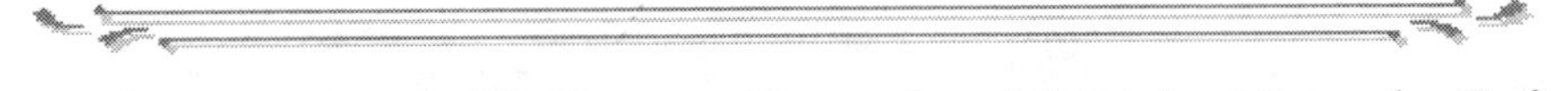

Verse 3 – Many "cause and effect" statements are found throughout Proverbs. Today's verses reveal that we find favor with God and man, if we allow mercy and truth to rule our hearts and lives. The Bible is God's Word; therefore, we are admonished to keep its truths in our hearts. John 14:6 also records that Jesus said "I am the way, the truth, and the life: no man cometh unto the Father, but by me." We must invite Jesus to dwell in our hearts, for He is the Truth. We will never find our way in this world until we allow the Holy Spirit, through Jesus, to lead and guide us. Life and truth are in Him. When we follow Him, we will keep His commandments, which are absolute truth. Jesus said "Heaven and earth shall pass away, but my words shall not pass away" (Matthew 24:35).

Humanistic teachings claim that there are no moral absolutes or absolute truth. These false doctrines have spread throughout the world. Humanism teaches that each man is his own guide and truth. We are told to do what "feels right" for us and to let others do what they "feel is right" for them. Right or wrong becomes whatever each individual decides it to be. This destructive teaching is wreaking havoc in our world. Without moral standards, there is no justice; each person becomes a law to himself. Proverbs 16:25 describes this kind of thinking: "There is a way that seemeth right unto a man, but the end thereof are the ways of death."

Verse 4 – If we desire God's favor, we must embrace His words and His ways. If we want man's favor, we must not only embrace the truth, but be merciful to people. We must not be legalistic about God's Word, but always have mercy in our hearts toward those who break the laws of God. The Lord tells us that if we desire to obtain mercy in our time of need, we must be merciful to those who fall short of the truth and hurt us. "Blessed are the merciful: for they shall obtain mercy" (Matthew 5:7).

Dear heavenly Father, I am so grateful that You have revealed Yourself to me. I want to walk in Your truth and keep Your words and commandments. I know that I cannot do this without the empowerment of the Holy Spirit, so fill me today with more of You. Help me to show mercy to all who need it, because I myself need Your mercy. Lord, deliver me from the temptation to be deceitful or dishonest in any way. May I be honest and truthful with everyone. Cleanse my heart of everything that is displeasing in Your sight. I desire Your mercy and truth that I might walk in favor with You and mankind. I pray in Jesus' name. Amen.

Proverbs 3:5-8 5 Trust in the LORD with all thine heart; and lean not unto thine own understanding. 6 In all thy ways acknowledge him, and he shall direct thy paths. 7 Be not wise in thine own eyes: fear the LORD, and depart from evil. 8 It shall be health to thy navel, and marrow to thy bones.

Verses 5-6 – "Leaning on our own understanding" does not mean we are not to use our minds. When we do not understand what is happening, we must trust the LORD to show us what to do. When we are tempted to blame God for trials, we must not yield to Satan's accusations against Him. Evil attacks against us or our families do not come from God but Satan, who is trying to discourage us. We must trust God to bring us through every trial. If we acknowledge Him, He promises to direct our paths and show us how to overcome every problem we encounter.

Verse 7 – We must not be "wise in our own eyes," but reverently respect the Lord. If we really believe that the Bible is true, we will leave our own ways and follow His. We will honor His Word and not treat it lightly, since we will fear the consequences of rejecting Him. The Bible tells us there is a heaven and a hell and that we will decide which will be our abode. We are invited to repent of our sins, accept Jesus as our Savior, and obey His law of love. To accept this invitation is to choose the way of heaven. If we reject it, our rebellion will take us to hell. A healthy fear and respect of God will help us to resist evil when we are tempted to sin.

Verse 8 – The navel marks where a baby's umbilical cord was once attached, reminding us that our mothers gave us life by nourishing us through the umbilical cord before we were born. Symbolically, this could represent God's life-bringing health to us as we are "attached" to Him. The Hebrew word for *navel* also means "nerve or muscle."[5] Following God brings health to our emotions and bodies. The phrase "marrow to thy bones" takes on strong implications regarding health in the light of modern medicine and biology: life-giving cells are created in the marrow of the bones and released to the body, and doctors even perform bone marrow transplants for the reversal of some fatal diseases.

Many helpful books are available on health, but the greatest advice on healthy living is found in God's Word. He desires to bless us with healthy minds, bodies and spirits. This complete health is obtained by allowing Jesus to rule every area of our lives.

Dear Father in heaven, I come to You in Jesus' name. Thank You for so many wonderful promises in Your Word. I come in humility, asking that You remove any prideful attitudes from my heart. I truly want to follow Your ways and serve You. Help me to trust You when things are going wrong, as much as when they are going right. I know that to walk in faith, I must believe that You will help me with my current problems even though I do not see a way at this time. You will make a way, since You will never fail those who come to You in faith. Thank You for good health; mentally and physically. I am so glad that my name is written in the Book of Life. Please use me to help others find the way to heaven. Amen.

[5] Wilson's Old Testament Word Studies, s.v. "navel"

Proverbs 3:9-10: 9 Honour the LORD with thy substance, and with the firstfruits of all thine increase: 10 So shall thy barns be filled with plenty, and thy presses shall burst out with new wine.

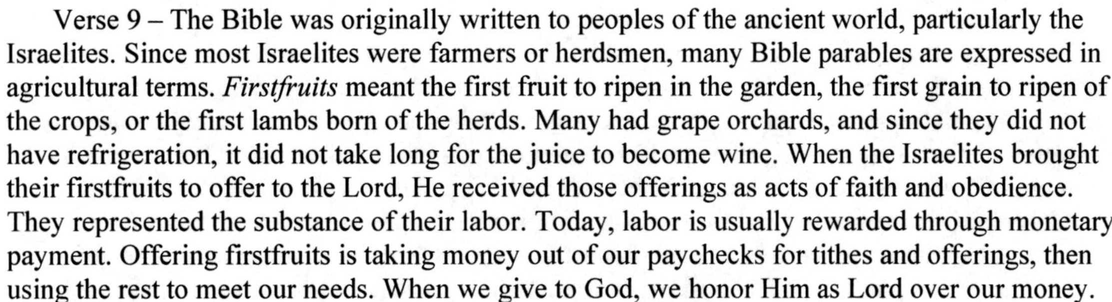

Verse 9 – The Bible was originally written to peoples of the ancient world, particularly the Israelites. Since most Israelites were farmers or herdsmen, many Bible parables are expressed in agricultural terms. *Firstfruits* meant the first fruit to ripen in the garden, the first grain to ripen of the crops, or the first lambs born of the herds. Many had grape orchards, and since they did not have refrigeration, it did not take long for the juice to become wine. When the Israelites brought their firstfruits to offer to the Lord, He received those offerings as acts of faith and obedience. They represented the substance of their labor. Today, labor is usually rewarded through monetary payment. Offering firstfruits is taking money out of our paychecks for tithes and offerings, then using the rest to meet our needs. When we give to God, we honor Him as Lord over our money.

Farmers kept grain to grind into flour as well as seed to plant the next crop. God expects us to keep some of our "seed" for bread, as well as some for sowing. Those who impulsively give it all away and then expect God to take care of them are violating this principle. Some people give away all their seed and have nothing to eat, while others eat all their seed and have nothing to plant or invest. We should have seed for both purposes.

In addition to our tithes or firstfruits for the Lord's work, we should also give to help others whenever the Lord directs. We must learn to give by the Spirit's direction, not allowing mere emotions or sympathies to direct us. Until these areas are renewed in us, Satan can still influence us through them. God is not always sympathetic with seemingly good causes. We should also not give mechanically, just because we have always given to a certain cause, but remain open to God's direction in our giving. Sometimes He may speak that we are not to give to a certain ministry we are used to supporting. He may desire us to give elsewhere. We need to be just as sensitive to God's "restraining voice" as to His "prompting" voice. However, we must remain compassionate in our giving. When we see those around us in obvious need we should not turn our backs on them, since we are called to be good Samaritans (Luke 10:30-37, 1 John 3:17).

Verse 10 – After we plant, we expect a harvest. In the same way, we can expect God to meet our financial needs when we have been obedient to give Him our tithes and offerings. "Give, and it shall be given unto you; good measure, pressed down, and shaken together, and running over, shall men give into your bosom. For with the same measure that ye mete withal it shall be measured to you again" (Luke 6:38). It is God's nature to give. Greed and stinginess are of Satan. If we are truly committed to God and walking in the Spirit, we will always desire to give. It will not be a burden, but a joy. If we are faithful in giving, we shall never lack anything that we really need; our "barns" will be filled with plenty. That is God's promise.

Dear Father, thank You for taking care of my needs today. Help me to always be faithful to give to Your work and to pray for those who are spreading the Gospel. Show me the places where You want me to give. I know we are to support our local churches, but help me also to give to missions and other projects that are laboring to help people come to know You. I know as I reach out and give, You will bless me. I thank You for the monetary blessings, so that not only will my needs be met, but I will have an abundance to help others in need. Help me to be generous in every good work, even as it was spoken of You, that You went about doing good. Amen.

Proverbs 3:11-12 11 My son, do not despise or shrink from the chastening of the LORD– His correction by punishment, or by subjection to suffering or trial; neither be weary and impatient and loathe or abhor His reproof. 12 For whom the LORD loves He corrects, even as a father corrects the son in whom he delights (AMP).

Verse 11 – To become wise, we must receive God's correction, or His *chastening*. We should pray for it so that we will remain on the right path; if we go astray we can be destroyed. God corrects His children as an earthly father does. A good father never injures his children when correcting them. He chastens to teach proper behavior so that they will avoid pain and trouble. It is important to understand that God does not send evil things into our lives in order to teach us. The Holy Spirit is our teacher and the Bible is our textbook. Students must learn from their teachers and textbooks to pass their tests. If one does not pay attention to instruction and refuses to study, he does not advance. He must *apply* what he hears. Likewise, we must obey the Holy Spirit's promptings and apply the Bible to our lives, in order to pass life's tests. If we are rebellious or ignorant of the Bible's teachings, we will suffer things that God never intended for us to suffer.

Verse 12 – A good father never does anything evil to his own child, but protects and cares for him. If his child should hurt himself, whether through ignorance or disobedience, he quickly comes to his aid. Our heavenly Father loves us and sent His Son to redeem us from the curse, not to put another one on us. The Bible tells us who the "troublemaker" is (the devil) and how to avoid his temptations and attacks.

Some people claim that they came to the Lord through tragedy. This may be true, but the devil, not God, devised the tragedy. God, in His grace, was there to help and deliver them in the midst of their troubles. Tragedies in themselves never save anyone; many lead to death, and those involved that do not know Jesus as Savior will endure eternity in hell. The Spirit of God brings us to salvation, not tragedy. "No man can come to me, except the Father which hath sent me draw him" (John 6:44). People are saved because the Holy Spirit leads others to pray for them.

We must never blame God for difficulties, but rather turn to Him and praise Him; not for the trouble, but for the fact that He is there to help us in the midst of it. Praise God that we can call upon Him to show us the way to overcome problems and grow spiritually in the process. Remember: He loves us and delights in us!

Dearest Father, I thank You for all the times You have corrected me. Please do not stop correcting me, even if I cry about my situation. Thank You for loving me enough to correct me and not allow me to continue in the wrong way. I am sorry that I sometimes complain of my trials. I want to rise above complaining and learn to trust You more. Help me to overcome the fears and doubts I feel when facing trouble. I want to come to the place when I am facing a test, that I will see the Your vastness and not the bigness of my problem. I know You love and care for me, so give me patience, grace and wisdom to overcome what the enemy brings against me. In Jesus' name I pray. Amen.

Proverbs 3:13-18 13 Happy is the man that findeth wisdom, and the man that getteth understanding. 14 For the merchandise of it is better than the merchandise of silver, and the gain thereof than fine gold. 15 She is more precious than rubies: and all the things thou canst desire are not to be compared unto her. 16 Length of days is in her right hand; and in her left hand riches and honour. 17 Her ways are ways of pleasantness, and all her paths are peace. 18 She is a tree of life to them that lay hold upon her: and happy is every one that retaineth her.

Verses 13-17 – The wisdom of God is better than any earthly treasure because it will not only produce prosperity, but prosperity which is gained honorably. Whoever gains wisdom is given the promise of long life, which only God can give, because life and death are in His hand.

Through the ages, men have sought to obtain happiness through riches. Many have even killed, in their search for gold and precious stones. However, in obtaining riches, they were still not fulfilled, because real peace only comes by knowing God. When we accept Jesus as our Savior, we are given a peace that passes understanding. It is a gift of God. The kind of peace and joy one receives from God is not based on circumstances, or how much wealth we might have. It is based on our relationship with Jesus. When we know Him, we have access to all things that we need in life.

Verse 18 – Wisdom is a "tree of life" and all who take hold of it experience joy. Since all the riches of wisdom are hidden in Christ (Colossians 2:3), Jesus is that "tree of life." His Word tells us how to take hold of and keep it. By embracing Christ, we experience His life in all we do. Scripture compares the "righteous" to trees planted by water. Trees with a continuous water supply will continue to grow. In the same way, all who commit themselves to the Lord and obey His Word will also continue to grow in Him.

Dear heavenly Father, I am thankful for all You have done for me. I appreciate the peace, love, and joy You have given me. Lord, money cannot buy these things. They come as virtues when we are "born again." Help me to walk in the Spirit, so that these fruits may grow daily. I wish to be more like You in all my ways. I seek Your wisdom because I need Your guidance and understanding in the affairs of my life. Strengthen me as I face challenges and circumstances daily that only You can give me the grace to bear and overcome. Thank You for the Scripture which says that when I am weak, You are strong. I claim Your strength today. In Jesus' name I pray. Amen.

Proverbs 3:19-20 19 The LORD by wisdom hath founded the earth; by understanding hath he established the heavens. 20 By his knowledge the depths are broken up, and the clouds drop down the dew.

Verse 19-20 – Today, as he has throughout history, man desires to know the origin of himself and the earth. Scripture states that the Lord God, in unsearchable wisdom, created the earth and all the galaxies, and that it was He who created man. The first chapter of Genesis tells us that God created first heaven, then the earth. In the following order, He made light, day and night, space, matter, energy, and time, along with the plants and animals, and His crowning creation: man and woman.

When I read this account, I appreciate the organization and order that is a part of God's wisdom, for it strikes me that everything was done in precisely the right order. First, God created the heavens and earth; then light and the cycle of day and night. Then He made the expanse and divided the waters. Next, He gathered the seas together, caused dry land to appear, and created vegetation on the earth, which must have light to grow. Then He created the sun, the moon and the stars. After that came the sea creatures and the birds; and then the land animals, which need vegetation to feed upon. Finally, He created man to rule over all He had made. In creating the sun, the moon and the planets, God set them in orbits so that they would not collide with each other. They rotate with exact precision and astronomers can calculate their alignments at any given time. This is but one example of the intricacy and orderliness of creation. The universe is full of visible evidence of God's wisdom.

We should pray for wisdom to know God's proper order for accomplishing His purposes in our lives. We may feel we have heard the Lord tell us to do something, as He is certainly calling people to serve Him at this hour, but we must know His *plan*, as well as His *call*. God's pattern is to call us to *be* before He calls us to *do*. Many babes in Christ are zealous to go into full-time ministry, but are unprepared for the task. Paul said of the Jews "they have a zeal of God, but not according to knowledge" (Romans 10:2). Faith and preparation should precede works. We must apply to our lives the knowledge of God's Word, which requires some time, before we can be effective ministers for Him. Real ministry flows from what Christ is doing in us, not from what we are trying to do for Him. We render a greater service through our "being" than through our "doing." It is a greater honor to be called to *be* something than to *do* something. True ministry is a natural part of our relationship with Jesus Christ. It naturally spills over onto others.

Dearest Father, I am grateful that You are a God of order and wisdom. Show me Your order in my every day affairs. I need my life and ways to be ordered by You. Lord, I live in a time where there is so much distraction. Let me not become caught up in the rush of society. Slow me down, and show me my priorities. Let me do the things that are most important to You. Let me not leave the important things of prayer and study of Your word undone. Forgive me when I neglect these things, because I run out of time and strength, having spent them on less important things. I know that if I put the things of God first, then I will have time for all the other important things in my life. Help me to work on "being" like You, instead of simply being busy doing things "for" You. I ask this in the name of Jesus. Amen.

Proverbs 3:21-24 21 My son, let not them depart from thine eyes: keep sound wisdom and discretion: 22 So shall they be life unto thy soul, and grace to thy neck. 23 Then shalt thou walk in thy way safely, and thy foot shall not stumble. 24 When thou liest down, thou shalt not be afraid: yea, thou shalt lie down, and thy sleep shall be sweet.

Verse 21 – If we are wise, we will keep God's laws and commandments from the heart. This is possible only as we rely on the power of the Holy Spirit and stay in close relationship with Jesus. Keeping God's words before our eyes (by studying the Bible) is one way in which we maintain a close relationship with Him. We keep sound wisdom and learn discretion by obeying His Word.

Verse 22 – Obeying God's Word brings life to our souls. The soul of man is made up of his mind, emotions, and will. Man is a spirit who has a soul and lives in a body. The body is only the house that holds the real man. The real person is the "spirit man." The Greek word for *spirit* is "pneuma," which also means "breath." The spirit man, unseen with the natural eye, is the true, inward man. It is made to rule over the realms of soul and body. It is the sphere of divine influence, referred to in Scripture as the heart of man. "But let it be the hidden man of the heart, in that which is not corruptible, even the ornament of a meek and quiet spirit, which is in the sight of God a great price" (1 Peter 3:4).

Verse 23 – The Lord promises us His grace to overcome in this life in addition to many other blessings. Among these are the blessings of safety and His grace to keep us from falling.

Verse 24 – The gift of sweet sleep is a wonderful blessing. Sleep for many people is not the peaceful state God intended it to be, but a restless one. Many are unable to rest at night because they fill their minds with unwholesome things through books, movies, and so forth during the day. Others are worried and anxious; life's cares keep them awake. Some experience tormenting dreams and nightmares. Many must even use prescription drugs in order to sleep. Although prescriptions may be a temporary help, we can have God's sweet sleep without them, if we ask Him to deliver us from the root problem which causes sleeplessness. "My son, forget not my law; but let thine heart keep my commandments" (Proverbs 3:1). God promises us sweet sleep. "I will both lay me down in peace, and sleep: for thou, LORD, only makest me dwell in safety" (Psalm 4:8). "The sleep of a labouring man is sweet, whether he eat little or much: but the abundance of the rich will not suffer him to sleep" (Ecclesiastes 5:12). "It is vain for you to rise up early, to sit up late, to eat the bread of sorrows: for so he giveth his beloved sleep" (Psalm 127:2).

Dear Father in heaven, I am so grateful to be Your child. Thank You for Your wonderful promises and Your encouraging words found in the Bible. I do want to walk in Your wisdom. Open my understanding to Your words, and then give me the grace to obey them. Help me to cast all my cares upon You when I am tempted to worry or fret over my problems. I do appreciate being able to lie down and have a restful night's sleep. Thank You also for soundness of mind and body. Help me to share with others about Your goodness this day. I ask in Jesus' name. Amen.

God's Wisdom for Daily Living ***Betty Miller***
January 24 ***Day 24***

Proverbs 3:25-26 25 Be not afraid of sudden fear, neither of the desolation of the wicked, when it cometh. 26 For the LORD shall be thy confidence, and shall keep thy foot from being taken.

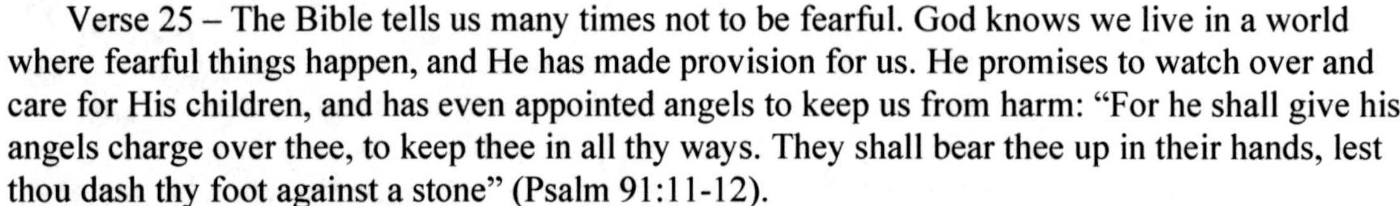

Verse 25 – The Bible tells us many times not to be fearful. God knows we live in a world where fearful things happen, and He has made provision for us. He promises to watch over and care for His children, and has even appointed angels to keep us from harm: "For he shall give his angels charge over thee, to keep thee in all thy ways. They shall bear thee up in their hands, lest thou dash thy foot against a stone" (Psalm 91:11-12).

We are living in the last days. Before the Second Coming of Christ, God will be dealing with the wicked. Many of them will be removed from the earth through judgments in the form of plagues, storms, earthquakes, and other catastrophes. (Not all who perish in these kinds of destructions are wicked, since many innocent souls can suffer too for various reasons). Today's verses charge us not to be fearful, but to have faith that our God will keep us, as well as our families, safe. We can be protected from these things if we stay close to the Lord and have faith in the protecting power of God, "under the shadow of His wings."

"He that dwelleth in the secret place of the Most High shall abide under the shadow of the Almighty. I will say of the LORD, He is my refuge and my fortress: my God; in him will I trust. Surely he shall deliver thee from the snare of the fowler, and from the noisome pestilence" (Psalm 91:1-3).

Verse 26 – Our confidence must not rest in the things of this world, but in the fact that our Father watches over us and keeps us from falling. That is what is meant by "keeping thy foot from being taken." Without God's protection we are apt to fall into the devil's snares. Satan uses many schemes to try to turn us aside from God's ways. If we pray, read our Bibles, and stay close to the Lord, he will not be able to "trip us up."

Dear Lord, I come to You in the name of Jesus. You know that at times I do experience fear. I am so glad that I can come to You in prayer. When I do, You remove the fear and give me the faith I need to trust You. Help me to trust You more. Thank You for Your angels watching over me and my loved ones. I am sure that when I get to heaven I will be amazed at the many things You protected me from in this life. Lord, have mercy on the lost and give them the opportunity to come to You and be spared from the awful judgments in this world and the world to come. Use me to share Your love with those around me. Thank You, Lord, for opportunities to witness to them. Give me the right words to speak, and prepare their hearts to receive those words. Amen.

Proverbs 3:27-29 27 Withhold not good from them to whom it is due, when it is in the power of thine hand to do it. 28 Say not unto thy neighbour, Go, and come again, and to morrow I will give; when thou hast it by thee. 29 Devise not evil against thy neighbour, seeing he dwelleth securely by thee.

Verse 27-28 – The Bible records much practical advice concerning finances, including instructions regarding payment of loans or services rendered. If we have enough money to reimburse a loan or pay for the work someone did for us, we should pay promptly and not put it off. Many friendships are strained if the borrower puts off paying back what was given to him as a temporary a loan. These verses say that if we have it, we must not turn our neighbor away and ask him to come back later.

How should we respond to situations in which we are asked to help someone? If we are able, we should help those in need, but this does not mean giving money to everyone that asks. There are many "con artists" in the world. Rather, these verses refer to neighbors and friends, meaning that we are to help those we know. We must always pray about what we are to give. Sometimes money is not the answer to someone's need. Instead, we may need to give of ourselves in time and effort to really help in the matter.

Although these verses do not refer to strangers, the Bible addresses this kind of giving also. My husband was a pastor for many years, and since our church building was located on a busy highway, we had many people come in and ask for our help. We always tried to help the best way we could. Many transients whose breath smelled of alcohol asked us for money. We knew that when they asked for money for food or gas, they would usually buy more alcohol. After praying about this problem, we came up with an answer. We arranged with a local restaurant and gas station near the church to pay for meals and gas for people who asked for money for these things. In this manner, we knew our money was helping them, not hurting them. Of course, we always prayed for them, too. Even if we cannot help by giving money, we can always pray for people. Prayer is a form of giving also.

Verse 29 – The Amplified Bible translates this verse this way: "Do not contrive or dig up or cultivate evil against your neighbor, who dwells trustingly and confidently beside you." We should always try to live peaceably with all men. We should especially strive for peace with our neighbors because we all need one another at times. In the future, we may be the ones asking for help instead of the ones called to give it. "If ye fulfil the royal law according to the scripture, Thou shalt love thy neighbour as thyself, ye do well" (James 2:8).

Dear Father, thank You for the book of Proverbs, in which there is so much good advice. Help me to take it to heart and apply it to my life. I see so much in this book about relationships. Lord, I know that, to be in a right relationship with You, I must be in a right relationship with my family, friends, and neighbors. Help me to be sensitive to the needs of others and to be a good neighbor. Help me to guard my mouth. Forgive me for having spoken unkindly about others at times. Lord, help me to be a generous giver and grant me Your discernment in giving. I ask You to empower me by Your Holy Spirit to truly love my neighbor as myself. In Jesus' name. Amen.

Proverbs 3:30-32 30 Strive not with a man without cause, if he have done thee no harm. 31 Envy thou not the oppressor, and choose none of his ways. 32 For the froward is abomination to the LORD: but his secret is with the righteous.

Verse 30 – We might phrase this admonition as "Don't start a fight without a reason." Some people just love to argue.

Verse 31 – Sometimes it seems that oppressors are better off than those seeking to do what is right. However, Psalm 37:1-9 tells us not to envy such people or choose to follow their ways:

> *"Fret not thyself because of evildoers, neither be thou envious against the workers of iniquity. For they shall soon be cut down like the grass, and wither as the green herb. Trust in the LORD, and do good; so shalt thou dwell in the land, and verily thou shalt be fed. Delight thyself also in the LORD; and he shall give thee the desires of thine heart. Commit thy way unto the LORD; trust also in him; and he shall bring it to pass. And he shall bring forth thy righteousness as the light, and thy judgment as the noonday. Rest in the LORD, and wait patiently for him: fret not thyself because of him who prospereth in his way, because of the man who bringeth wicked devices to pass. Cease from anger, and forsake wrath: fret not thyself in any wise to do evil. For evildoers shall be cut off: but those that wait upon the LORD, they shall inherit the earth."*

In time, the ungodly will perish, while those who wait upon the Lord and follow Him shall see the righteous desires of their hearts fulfilled.

Verse 32 – When the Bible speaks of a *froward* person, it refers to one who is crooked and perverse. It calls such people "an abomination to the Lord." This verse tells us of an advantage the righteous have over the wicked–the Lord shares His secrets with them. He knows the secrets of all hearts. When we are walking in God's will, the Holy Spirit will warn us if anyone tries to deceive us. This discernment will prevent us from being deceived by unscrupulous people and from becoming entangled with those who have wrong motives. 1 Corinthians 12:10 mentions this as the gift of "discerning of spirits." God not only shares His knowledge, but His hidden thoughts and feelings with those who love Him. This is the wonderful privilege of knowing God! God blesses us in so many ways. This is another reason why we should praise our Lord every day!

Dear heavenly Father, thank You for all Your wonderful gifts! I am especially thankful for the gift of discerning of spirits. Thank You for saving me from many bad situations I would have stepped into had it not been for Your warnings. I do thank You for spiritual eyesight. Lord, I pray today that I will always walk in Your way, and that I will seek to avoid strife and be a peacemaker. You said, "Blessed are the peacemakers." I need Your blessings today, and ask You to help me to be at peace with those around me. Help me to resolve my differences peacefully, according to Your will. I ask in the name of Jesus. Amen.

Proverbs 3:33-35 33 The curse of the LORD is in the house of the wicked: but he blesseth the habitation of the just. 34 Surely he scorneth the scorners: but he giveth grace unto the lowly. 35 The wise shall inherit glory: but shame shall be the promotion of fools.

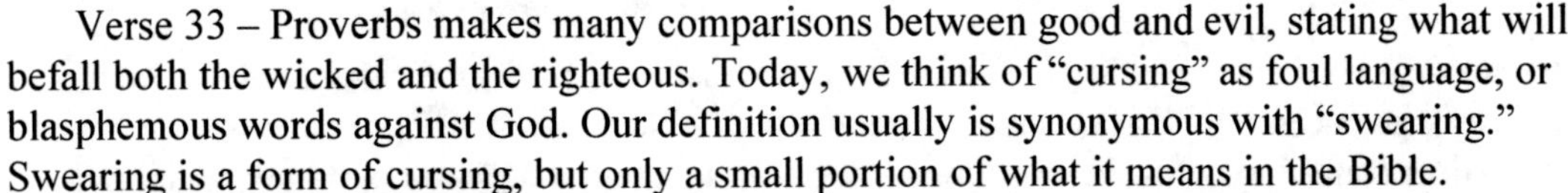

Verse 33 – Proverbs makes many comparisons between good and evil, stating what will befall both the wicked and the righteous. Today, we think of "cursing" as foul language, or blasphemous words against God. Our definition usually is synonymous with "swearing." Swearing is a form of cursing, but only a small portion of what it means in the Bible.

Biblically speaking, cursing is not only speaking evil of someone, but also invoking harm upon them. According to the Bible, evil comes upon a person under a curse. Evil circumstances, sickness, or tragedy occur in their lives. This evil is not coming from God, but rather, Satan. When we follow and obey God, we receive His blessings. Sin produces corruption in our lives and opens the door for curses to come upon us. If someone is sinning, he will reap the fruit of that sin. The wicked have a curse upon them because they are reaping what they have sown. "Be not deceived; God is not mocked: for whatsoever a man soweth, that shall he also reap. For he that soweth to his flesh shall of the flesh reap corruption; but he that soweth to the Spirit shall of the Spirit reap life everlasting" (Galatians 6:7-8). If we humble ourselves and repent of our sin, the Lord will free us from the bad things in our lives.

Verse 34 – God gives grace to the lowly. Grace is the power to overcome sin and lead a righteous life. The Bible calls those who scorn the way of the Lord "fools." The Biblical definition of a "fool" is one who is rebellious. Rebellion always brings us into shame.

Verse 35 – The wise are promised that they will inherit glory. The choice is ours: blessing or cursing, glory or shame.

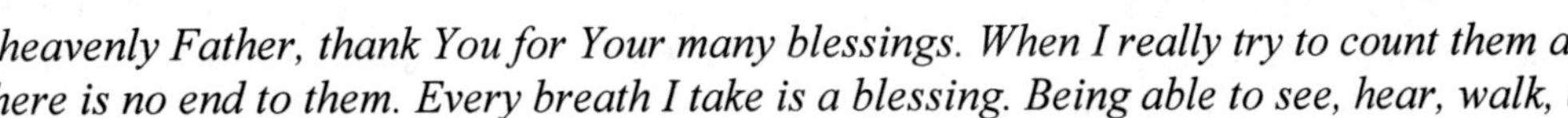

Dear heavenly Father, thank You for Your many blessings. When I really try to count them all, I find there is no end to them. Every breath I take is a blessing. Being able to see, hear, walk, and speak is a blessing. You have granted me blessings in the many friends and family that I have. I thank You for these and all the physical and material blessings I have. I do appreciate them, but they are overshadowed by Your blessings of peace, love, and joy that I have in my heart. Thank You for redeeming me from the curse of sin and death and for giving me eternal life. I am very grateful for what Jesus did for me on the cross. Lord, help me to live a Christian life before others, so that they might receive Your blessings too. In Jesus' name I pray. Amen.

God's Wisdom for Daily Living — ***Betty Miller***
January 28 — ***Day 28***

Proverbs 4:1-4: 1 Hear, ye children, the instruction of a father, and attend to know understanding. 2 For I give you good doctrine, forsake ye not my law. 3 For I was my father's son, tender and only beloved in the sight of my mother. 4 He taught me also, and said unto me, Let thine heart retain my words: keep my commandments, and live.

Verses 1-4 – These verses contain some important instructions for the present generation. Many children have become disrespectful of their father's instructions, as well as anyone else in authority. This creates havoc in society. I thank God for the Christian youth who are serving God and are respectful to their elders. These ones are making a difference in their circle of friends. But, at present, they are a minority. We should all remember to pray for our young people.

Throughout Scripture, children are admonished to obey their parents. The Bible also instructs fathers to be the right kind of parent. "Children, obey your parents in the Lord: for this is right. Honour thy father and mother; which is the first commandment with a promise; that it may be well with thee, and thou mayest live long on the earth. And, ye fathers, provoke not your children to wrath: but bring them up in the nurture and admonition of the Lord" (Ephesians 6:1-4).

Children are exposed to many ungodly influences through humanistic teachings, movies, television, music, and other things. As parents, we must teach them God's ways. Many parents think that taking their children to Sunday school is sufficient for their Christian training, but Sunday school should be only a supplement to teaching them at home. When I was young, most of the churches, schools, and homes of the West Texas town in which I was raised reinforced each other in teaching children moral values. It is sad today to see such a deterioration of society. We, as parents and grandparents, must be good examples to our children and grandchildren. We must talk about the Lord, read the Bible in our homes, and practice what it says, if we desire our children to be good Christians. "And thou shalt love the LORD thy God with all thine heart, and with all thy soul, and with all thy might. And these words, which I command thee this day, shall be in thine heart: And thou shalt teach them diligently unto thy children, and shalt talk of them when thou sittest in thine house, and when thou walkest by the way, and when thou liest down, and when thou risest up" (Deuteronomy 6:5-7).

If we obey the Lord, we–and our children–will be blessed. We are to pass the Bible's teachings down to our children just as our fathers passed them down to us. This spiritual inheritance will bless them more than any material thing we could ever leave them.

Dear Father in heaven, thank You for the youth of this nation who know You and are attempting to follow You and Your ways. I know it is not easy for them in a society such as ours. Give them grace and strength to live the Christian life and holy boldness to witness to their peers. Lord, help me as a parent and grandparent to be the kind of example that will inspire my children and grandchildren to want to know and follow You. Give my offspring respectful hearts for their elders and all those in authority, even as You have instructed. I pray that I will also have a respectful attitude for those in authority. Lord, even when those in authority may be wrong, give me the grace to honor the office they represent. Let me be an honorable example to the youth of our day. In Jesus' name I pray. Amen.

January 29 *Day 29*

**Proverbs 4:5-9 5 Get wisdom, get understanding: forget it not; neither decline from the
words of my mouth. 6 Forsake her not, and she shall preserve thee: love her, and she shall
keep thee. 7 Wisdom is the principal thing; therefore get wisdom: and with all thy getting
get understanding. 8 Exalt her, and she shall promote thee: she shall bring thee to honour,
when thou dost embrace her. 9 She shall give to thine head an ornament of grace: a crown
of glory shall she deliver to thee.**

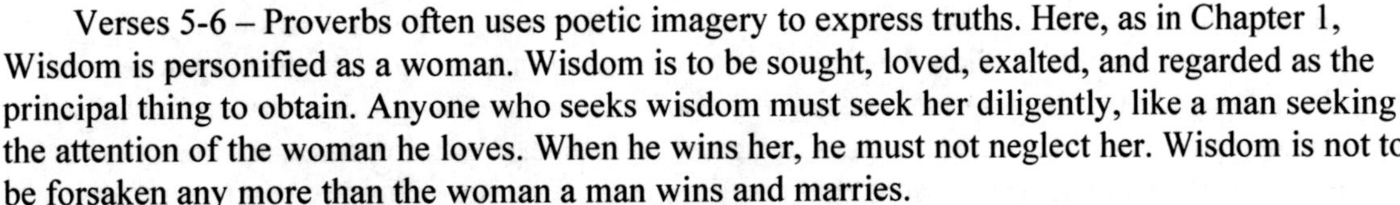

Verses 5-6 – Proverbs often uses poetic imagery to express truths. Here, as in Chapter 1, Wisdom is personified as a woman. Wisdom is to be sought, loved, exalted, and regarded as the principal thing to obtain. Anyone who seeks wisdom must seek her diligently, like a man seeking the attention of the woman he loves. When he wins her, he must not neglect her. Wisdom is not to be forsaken any more than the woman a man wins and marries.

The place to find wisdom is in God's Word. That is also where we shall be able to keep her and forsake her not. Many people ask to be kept in safety by God and pray to that end, yet prayer alone is not enough; we must find and keep the Word of God. If we do not forsake God's Word, but love it, then that very Word will preserve and keep us safe.

Verse 7-9 – Wisdom brings understanding. People who misunderstand God's will and purposes become easy targets for the devil. Satan easily talks some Christians out of their rightful inheritance. Because they have no faith, they cannot receive God's promises. That is why some Christians are overcomers and some are overcome. God does not love one of His children more than another. He loves us all equally, and is no respecter of persons (Acts 10:34-35). However, God is a respecter of His Word. A Christian who knows and applies the Word of God, has an advantage over one who does not. For example, if I read that Jesus died so that I might not only be saved, but also healed (Isaiah 53:4-3; John 1:2-3), I can appropriate healing by faith because God told me in His Word that He has provided healing for me, and He does not lie. However, if I have never studied those portions of the Bible, I may remain ill; deprived of my healing. This does not mean that God does not love me; it simply means that I am ignorant of that promise and may not even know to pray for healing.

We receive what we ask God for if we ask in faith according to His Word. Because some people do not seek the Lord diligently, they cannot spiritually hear what God has for them (Matthew 13:15-16). It is wise to study and obey God's Word; as we do, we shall receive grace for our circumstances and a crown of glory!

Dear Father, I am grateful for Your blessings. Thank You for opening my eyes to Your truths and Your many promises to me. I want to become wiser. So help me to understand the Bible better. Open my spiritual ears to hear the things I need to know at this time. I thank You for the knowledge that You have already given me, but I desire to know more, that I might know You better. I want to be closer to You than ever. Please give me the desire to pray and to read the Bible more. Forgive me when I neglect these two very important things. Thank You for the promise of health for me. I receive that promise so that I might be about Your business. How wonderful You are to me and all of Your children. Keep my family and friends in Your health and bless them, too. In Jesus' name I pray. Amen.

Proverbs 4:10-13 10 Hear, O my son, and receive my sayings; and the years of thy life shall be many. 11 I have taught thee in the way of wisdom; I have led thee in right paths. 12 When thou goest, thy steps shall not be straitened; and when thou runnest, thou shalt not stumble. 13 Take fast hold of instruction; let her not go: keep her; for she is thy life.

Verses 10-13 – Many of the instructions in Proverbs promote longevity of life. One of those teachings is that children obey their parents. Those who disobey may expose themselves to dangerous situations that can ultimately take their lives. Many young people think they are smarter than their parents; calling them "old-fashioned" and saying that they do not know what they are talking about. They do not recognize that with age comes something only time can produce: experience. In failing to take advantage of their elders' experiences, they miss opportunities to learn valuable lessons that can keep them from harm and prevent them from making the same mistakes that their elders made.

The warning to men to stay away from loose women (and women from lustful men) also brings long life if heeded. Those who remain chaste before marriage avoid emotional pain and the risk of sexually-transmitted diseases. Virgins enter marriage free from the emotional scars of previous relationships or the stigma of disease which they could transmit to their spouse.

Heeding the admonishment to avoid bad company also adds years to one's life. Getting involved with the wrong kind of people, and choosing their ways rather than the Lord's can lead to ruin and even death. It is true that there is "no honor among thieves." Members of the "wrong crowd" commit all kinds of crimes, including theft. If they steal from others, in time they will steal from you, even if they claim to be your friends. They can also stoop to murder, and you could be a victim of their anger and lack of morals.

These are but a few of the things that the Bible mentions we should avoid in order to obtain the promise of long life. In following God's instructions and applying godly wisdom, we will not stumble and fall, but will walk in the pathway of life. When we are determined to walk in God's ways, He watches over us, keeping us from the evils that Satan wants to bring upon us.

Dear Father, thank You for giving us instructions on how to have a long and good life. I know that when I ask You to watch over me and my loved ones, that You will hear and answer my prayers. You are such a wonderful Father! I am grateful for Your love and care. Please keep me on the pathway of life and warn me when I am straying. I do not want to get off the straight and narrow way. I realize that I can be blinded by my own desires and ideas, which may look good, but later prove to be otherwise. Help me today to not be discouraged by what seems like a delay in the answer to my prayers. I know as I continue to look to You in faith, You will prevail in my behalf. In Jesus' name, I pray. Amen.

Proverbs 4:14-19 14 Enter not into the path of the wicked, and go not in the way of evil men. 15 Avoid it, pass not by it, turn from it, and pass away. 16 For they sleep not, except they have done mischief; and their sleep is taken away, unless they cause some to fall. 17 For they eat the bread of wickedness, and drink the wine of violence. 18 But the path of the just is as the shining light, that shineth more and more unto the perfect day. 19 The way of the wicked is as darkness: they know not at what they stumble.

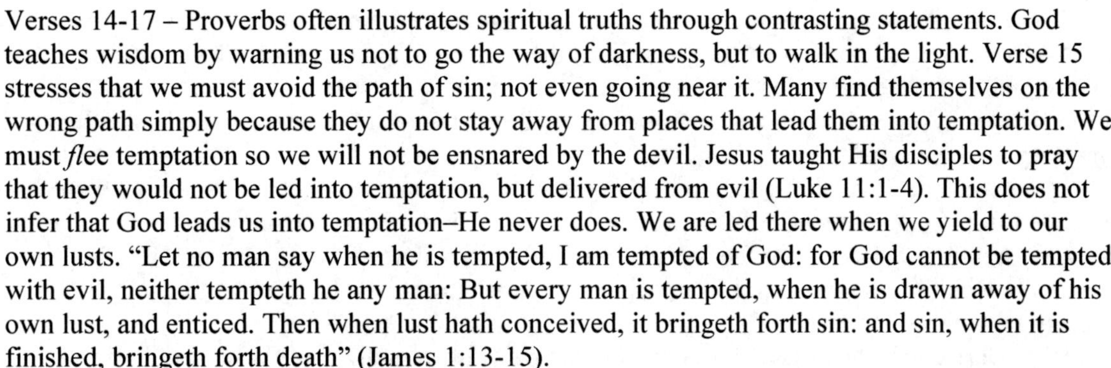

Verses 14-17 – Proverbs often illustrates spiritual truths through contrasting statements. God teaches wisdom by warning us not to go the way of darkness, but to walk in the light. Verse 15 stresses that we must avoid the path of sin; not even going near it. Many find themselves on the wrong path simply because they do not stay away from places that lead them into temptation. We must *flee* temptation so we will not be ensnared by the devil. Jesus taught His disciples to pray that they would not be led into temptation, but delivered from evil (Luke 11:1-4). This does not infer that God leads us into temptation–He never does. We are led there when we yield to our own lusts. "Let no man say when he is tempted, I am tempted of God: for God cannot be tempted with evil, neither tempteth he any man: But every man is tempted, when he is drawn away of his own lust, and enticed. Then when lust hath conceived, it bringeth forth sin: and sin, when it is finished, bringeth forth death" (James 1:13-15).

Verses 18-19 – The way of the wicked is darkness; those walking therein stumble and fall. Sin always activates the death principle; producing sickness, fear, poverty, strife, jealousy, and so forth. The way of the wicked is contrasted with the path of the just "which is as the shining light." The just can see where they are going. When we walk with Jesus, our path becomes brighter; every day we see more clearly to follow Him better.

Dearest Father, I am thankful for the light You have given me. Strengthen me to remain on the right path. I do pray for grace not only to resist temptation, but also to flee from it. I also pray for those who are struggling to get free from addictions or other sins. Deliver them from evil and help them to get back on track with You. Lord, help me not to criticize them but to be compassionate and lift them up in prayer until they are free. I do forgive them for the troubles that some of them have brought into my life. I know that if I did not have Your grace and mercy in my life, I could also be taken captive by the devil. Should I fall, Lord, I would want someone to be praying for me. So I ask that You be merciful to them, so that I also might obtain mercy when I need it. In Jesus' name I pray. Amen.

Proverbs 4:20-22 20 My son, attend to my words; incline thine ear unto my sayings. 21 Let them not depart from thine eyes; keep them in the midst of thine heart. 22 For they are life unto those that find them, and health to all their flesh.

Verse 20 – "Attend to my words" simply means to *pay attention* to my words. We can hear the Word of God with our physical ears without paying attention to it. "Incline thine ear" (verse 20) means to listen with our "spiritual ears" or "ears of our hearts." Many times after speaking to a multitude, Jesus is recorded as saying, "He that hath ears to hear, let him hear" (for example, Mark 4:2-9). He knew that no one can hear what the Spirit is saying unless we have a proper heart attitude; willing to hear Him. That is why those who do not know Jesus cannot understand the Bible. They may agree it is a book of history or literature, but cannot spiritually understand it until they are converted.

To be converted, we must come to God in humility, accepting that we are sinners who are separated from Him. We must turn from sin and give our lives to Jesus. Until we acknowledge our sins and ask forgiveness for the cause of our guilt, we will never be free from it. It will eventually lead us right into hell. It is not God's will that any should perish, "but that all should come to repentance" (2 Peter 3:9).

Jesus Christ, the Son of God, was nailed to the cross by ungodly men for no sin of His own. He was innocent of wrong–the only Man who was perfect and sinless. He willingly took our sins by accepting a death that He did not deserve. He was raised from the dead by His Father and given life and authority over the powers of darkness. God now imparts that same life and authority to all who will come to Him and receive His provision for their sin, for "...the blood of Jesus Christ his Son cleanseth us from all sin" (1 John 1:7).

Verse 21 – We should not only read God's Word diligently, but hide it in our hearts. If we desire to grow in faith and wisdom and be pleasing to God, we must apply His Word to everything in life.

Verse 22 – If we apply His word, we will experience true life. That life is not just a spiritual encounter, although spiritual rebirth is a glorious experience. By applying God's Word, we can also have physical health. The Lord wants to make us whole in spirit, soul, and body!

Dear heavenly Father, I am so glad that You gave Your Son, Jesus, so that I could know You and be saved. I do not understand why You did it, but I am very grateful for the gift of eternal life. I rejoice that my name is written in the Book of Life. Lord, I need to read and study Your Word more. Help me to give up the things that are robbing me of the time I need to be spending with You. I know that if I put prayer and Bible study first, then You will make a way for me to take care of all my pressing responsibilities. Things just go better when I take time to spend with You. I also thank You for health in my body. I am grateful that You are not only my Savior, but my Healer as well. I ask for health and strength today that I might serve You and those around me. In Jesus' name, I pray. Amen.

**Proverbs 4:23-27 23 Keep thy heart with all diligence; for out of it are the issues of life.
24 Put away from thee a froward mouth, and perverse lips put far from thee. 25 Let thine
eyes look right on, and let thine eyelids look straight before thee. 26 Ponder the path of thy
feet, and let all thy ways be established. 27 Turn not to the right hand nor to the left:
remove thy foot from evil.**

Verse 23 – Proverbs is a wonderful book from which to teach our children the wisdom to become overcomers. This verse goes to the very heart of what determines our destinies; the "issues of life" that come from our hearts. We are born in wickedness, having inherited a sin nature from our forefathers, beginning with Adam. It will destroy us unless we come to Jesus for a heart cleansing. "Not that which goeth into the mouth defileth a man; but that which cometh out of the mouth, this defileth a man" (Matthew 15:11).

Verse 24 – We are commanded to guard our hearts; to be cautious of what we embrace and take into our spirits, and to stop speaking things that are not right. Obedience in these two areas determines the kind of life we have on earth. "For as he thinketh in his heart, so is he…" (Proverbs 23:7a). We must put away a froward tongue and stop gossiping, lying, criticizing, and so forth. Through this sort of talk, we can release curses upon others. Eventually, we will receive them back upon ourselves, because we reap what we sow.

"And the tongue is a fire, a world of iniquity: so is the tongue among our members, that it defileth the whole body, and setteth on fire the course of nature; and it is set on fire of hell. For every kind of beasts, and of birds, and of serpents, and of things in the sea, is tamed, and hath been tamed of mankind: But the tongue can no man tame; it is an unruly evil, full of deadly poison. Therewith bless we God, even the Father; and therewith curse we men, which are made after the similitude of God. Out of the same mouth proceedeth blessing and cursing. My brethren, these things ought not so to be" (James 3:6-10). We will be unable to tame our tongues unless we allow Jesus to help us, for our "mouth problem" is actually a heart problem. To correct it, we must ask the Lord to cleanse our hearts. We must speak God's Word over ourselves and others.

Verses 25-27 – Notice that not only is the heart mentioned, but the mouth, the eyes, and feet. To live righteously and walk in God's blessing and wisdom, we must make a total commitment and serve God with all of our hearts, minds, and physical beings.

Dear Lord, I realize I have been guilty of not guarding what has gone into my heart. Forgive me, Lord, for this sin. I have also been guilty of allowing the wrong things to come out of my mouth at times. Also, please forgive me of the things that I have spoken that have come from a wrong heart attitude. Lord Jesus, I would like to make the words of a worship song my prayer today: "Change my heart, O God, make it ever true. Change my heart, O God, may I be like You. You are the Potter, I am the clay. Mold me and make me, this is what I pray"[6] in Jesus' name. Amen.

[6] (Eddie Espinosa) Mercy/Vineyard Publishing

Proverbs 5:1-13 1 My son, attend unto my wisdom, and bow thine ear to my understanding: 2 That thou mayest regard discretion, and that thy lips may keep knowledge. 3 For the lips of a strange woman drop as an honeycomb, and her mouth is smoother than oil: 4 But her end is bitter as wormwood, sharp as a twoedged sword. 5 Her feet go down to death; her steps take hold on hell. 6 Lest thou shouldest ponder the path of life, her ways are moveable, that thou canst not know them. 7 Hear me now therefore, O ye children, and depart not from the words of my mouth. 8 Remove thy way far from her, and come not nigh the door of her house: 9 Lest thou give thine honour unto others, and thy years unto the cruel: 10 Lest strangers be filled with thy wealth; and thy labours be in the house of a stranger; 11 And thou mourn at the last, when thy flesh and thy body are consumed, 12 And say, How have I hated instruction, and my heart despised reproof; 13 And have not obeyed the voice of my teachers, nor inclined mine ear to them that instructed me!

Verses 1-13 – One of the miraculous things about the Bible is its relevancy for us today. Generations pass, cultures come and go, but man's issues and problems remain the same. (I use *man* in the dictionary sense of "the human race," including women. Though the above warning is addressed to a son by his father, it equally applies to daughters.) Sin in his heart has been man's downfall since Adam and Eve committed the first transgression.

There is an ungodly emphasis on sex all over the world. The world is filled with those who have experienced the progression of events outlined above. They are lured by temptation; but however sweet a temptress' kiss, it will have a bitter end. It is better to deny unholy pleasure for the moment in exchange for eternal reward. Moses is an example of this, as he gave up the pleasures he could have had as a prince of Egypt and chose rather to suffer with God's people (Hebrews 11:24-26). He was able to do this because he had an eternal perspective.

The devil destroys many marriages because the above advice is not heeded. Many great men have lost their honor when their illicit affairs were exposed. They may still have their marriages if they have forgiving mates, but their names are forever blighted. Others have lost families, positions, and even their health. Yielding to immoral appetites in one area causes a man to sin in other areas, leading him in a downward spiral. Sin begets sin, and sin brings corruption and death.

Sin, like righteousness, is progressive. Daily, we become either more wicked by serving sin, or more like the Lord by serving Him. God doesn't want us to waste our lives but tells us very clearly that it is our choice. "...I have set before you life and death, blessing and cursing: therefore choose life, that both thou and thy seed may live" (Deuteronomy 30:19b).

Dear Father, thank You for Your instructions in the Bible. Give me grace and humility to accept Your advice and correction. I know when You instruct me, it is for my good. I pray for those in our nation that have gone through divorce. This has wounded our nation, because many of our children do not have their fathers, and some do not even have their mothers. Second marriages carry wounds from the previous ones. Lord, heal these marriages and homes. Forgive the adultery and fornication that has led to many of these marriage breakdowns. Forgive the young people who are living together. Many of them do not even know this is wrong, because society has embraced it as acceptable behavior. Please restore love in our families and heal our homes. In Jesus' name I pray. Amen.

**Proverbs 5:14-23 14 [The extent and boldness of] my sin involved almost all evil in the
estimation of the congregation and the community. 15 Drink waters out of your own cistern
[of pure marriage relationship], and fresh, running waters out of your own well. 16 Should
your offspring be dispersed abroad as water-brooks in the streets? 17 [Confine yourself to
your own wife] let your children be for you alone, and not the children of strangers with
you. 18 Let your fountain–of human life–be blessed [with the rewards of fidelity], and
rejoice with the wife of your youth. 19 Let her be as the loving hind and pleasant doe
[tender, gentle, attractive]; let her bosom satisfy you at all times; and always be transported
with delight in her love. 20 Why should you, my son, be infatuated with a loose woman,
embrace the bosom of an outsider, and go astray? 21 For the ways of man are directly
before the eyes of the LORD, and He [Who would have us live soberly, chastely and godly]
carefully weighs all man's goings. 22 His own iniquities shall ensnare the wicked, and he
shall be held with the cords of his sins. 23 He will die for lack of discipline and instruction,
and in the greatness of his folly he will go astray and be lost (AMP).**

Verses 14-15 – Using poetic symbolism, today's verses teach the principle of monogamy and warn of the destruction that adultery produces. Marriage is likened to a cistern of water. Water quenches thirst and is a good symbol of a love relationship. We all thirst for intimacy. True refreshment in marriage is born out of intimacy between a man and wife. The Song of Solomon also refers to the exclusivity of the marriage relationship, likened to a secret garden. Solomon described his beloved as a sealed fountain; closed to all others, but open to him–a "fountain of gardens, a well of living waters, and streams from Lebanon" (Song of Solomon 4:12,15). A third party's intrusion spoils the "water." The cistern of love that refreshes husband and wife becomes bitter, affecting the relationship and all the family.

Verses 16-17 – Adultery can produce illegitimate children, and a breakdown of the family. The verses above extol the joy that can be had within the unbroken family unit, ideally composed of a man, his wife, and their offspring.

Verses 18-23 – At times, the delight in the spouse of one's youth can slip away. The enemy then tries to tempt people to quench their thirst in the embrace of an outsider. While reading this, you may be facing the temptation to embrace someone outside of your marriage. These verses warn of the consequences of unfaithfulness. We should take them to heart. The final picture of the adulterer is one of being tied up in his own sins. Like an animal that falls into a trap, it cannot escape. He will die. In marriage, as in everything else in life, the stakes are high. We choose peace and joy by obeying God's precepts, or pain and confusion by following the lusts of our flesh. By God's grace, let us choose to do right–not only for our own sakes, but for our children's.

Father, I thank You for Your grace; that when we are tempted, You help us to overcome. I pray for all who are facing temptations and are struggling to do what is right. Lord, have mercy on them. Show them the way of escape, and give them strength to follow it. I pray for marriages that are suffering from adultery and are on the brink of collapse. Please comfort those who have been wounded; both those who have been betrayed, and those who have committed adultery. I pray for healing in their relationship and for the children, and the grace for true repentance and forgiveness. Only You can restore these broken relationships, and I ask for You to show yourself mighty on behalf of all who call on You with a sincere heart. In Jesus' Name I pray! Amen

Proverbs 6:1-5 1 My son, if you have become security for your neighbor, if you have given your pledge for a stranger or another, 2 You are snared with the words of your lips, you are caught in the speech of your mouth. 3 Do this now (at once and earnestly), my son, and deliver yourself, when you have put yourself in to the power of your neighbor; go, bestir and humble yourself, and beg your neighbor (to pay his debt and release you). 4 Give not sleep to thine eyes, nor slumber to thine eyelids. 5 Deliver thyself as a roe from the hand of the hunter, and as a bird from the hand of the fowler (AMP).

Verses 1-3 – Becoming *security* for someone means to co-sign his bank loan; a practice that destroys many friendships. Although the borrower may have good intentions, he may be unable to pay his note. Does this mean we should not help those who ask? Certainly not! However, many people request loans to live beyond their means, rather than just for emergency help. Often, it becomes too difficult for them to continue their payments. Whoever became security for them will be held accountable to pay their debt. It is not wisdom to co-sign a note for people who are not practicing financial Biblical principles.

By signing an agreement, we are giving our word; and this is a serous thing before God and man. We all have "sworn to our own hurt" at times (Psalm 15:4). Often, after committing to something, I have wished that I hadn't, because it was difficult to keep my word. God expects His children to keep their word just as He keeps His. We should always take every agreement that we sign very seriously. If we become security for someone, we must keep our promise to pay that person's debt if he is unable to do so, because we have given our word. "Whatever your lips utter you must be sure to do, because you made your vow freely to the LORD your God with your own mouth" (Deuteronomy 23:23).

Verses 4-5 – It is dangerous to become surety for someone. Anyone ensnared by this is exhorted to earnestly find a way to legally escape it. He should make every effort to escape, even as a deer runs for its life from a hunter, or a bird flees a trap set for it. Ignoring the danger of this monetary trap can lead to the financial ruin of the lender.

No one knows what the future holds; therefore, it is unwise to accept responsibility for another's debt. If you have done this, verse 3 gives some good advice. First, humble yourself before God, confessing your mistake. Ask Him to make a way for you to get out of the situation without destroying your relationship with the one for whom you have become security. Then, humble yourself before that person and ask to be released from financial bondage. Being responsible for someone's debt puts you in his power. However, if you are wealthy and it would not hurt you to repay the loan, you may want to help give him a fresh start. The important thing is to seek God's guidance in these matters.

Dear Father, I am thankful that You care about the practical matters in this life. I am asking for Your wisdom and guidance in our financial affairs, as well as all areas of our lives. Father, I ask You to be Lord over our finances. Please help my husband and I to put all of our financial affairs in Divine order. I ask for a generous heart to give when You tell me to give, but I also ask for wisdom and grace to restrain from giving, when I should not give to certain individuals. You know my heart, please remove the wrong ideas I might have in the area of finances and let me have the mind of Christ in all of our financial dealings with others. In Jesus' name I pray. Amen.

Proverbs 6:6-11 6 Go to the ant, thou sluggard; consider her ways, and be wise: 7 Which having no guide, overseer, or ruler, 8 Provideth her meat in the summer, and gathereth her food in the harvest. 9 How long wilt thou sleep, O sluggard? when wilt thou arise out of thy sleep? 10 Yet a little sleep, a little slumber, a little folding of the hands to sleep: 11 So shall thy poverty come as one that travelleth, and thy want as an armed man (AMP).

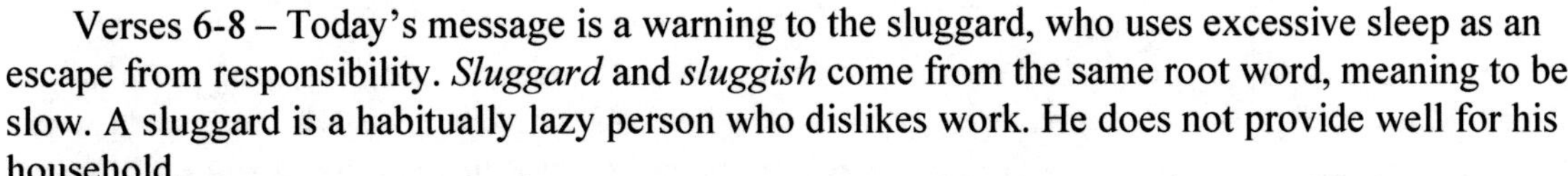

Verses 6-8 – Today's message is a warning to the sluggard, who uses excessive sleep as an escape from responsibility. *Sluggard* and *sluggish* come from the same root word, meaning to be slow. A sluggard is a habitually lazy person who dislikes work. He does not provide well for his household.

We are told to be wise like the ant, one of God's hardest-working creatures. Without a supervisor, ants work hard. Some people only work when they have to. Ants gather food in the summer and harvest season, so that when winter arrives they have plenty to eat. We all experience "summer seasons" of plenty in life during which we should diligently save so that we may have plenty in "winter seasons" of lack. The old saying "make hay while the sun shines," fits with these verses.

Verses 9-10 – Here we are given an idea of what the Holy Spirit might say to a lazy person: "How long will you sleep? When are you going to get up and go to work?" and an idea of how the devil might tempt him: "Just a little more slumber; fold your hands, rest on your pillow and go to sleep." Let us wake up and get to work! There are things to be done in life; things we need to do for our families, and things waiting to be done for the Lord. Let us ask God for His strength to do them. Jesus declared that He must do the work of His Father, and went about doing good (John 9:4, Acts 10:38). Let us also be about His business.

Verse 11 – Indolence leads to poverty. Poverty, like a traveler making his way on foot, comes slowly, but surely. The sluggard may live for a while without seeing the results of his laziness, especially if he has inherited wealth. However, like a robber who has marked out the house of a rich man, poverty will suddenly strike, depriving the sluggard of luxuries and necessities alike. The Bible teaches us that we are to all work. We are to provide for ourselves and our families so that we may be able to eat. "For even when we were with you, this we commanded you, that if any would not work neither should he eat" (2 Thessalonians 3:10).

Dearest Father, thank You for giving me a job. Forgive me if I complain at times, for all the work it involves. I am thankful that I can work, and that the devil does not have me in the trap of indolence. I need Your strength to do all that You require of me. Lord, I know people who are lazy and I lift them up in prayer. I do not know why they refuse to take their responsibilities, but I do know that my criticism will not help them. Instead, I pray for them to overcome their irresponsibility, and that they will find a reason to get up and go to work. Lift the discouragement from them. Give them a desire to pursue the right things in their lives. Help us all to labor in the kingdom of God. In Jesus' name I pray. Amen.

Proverbs 6:12-15 12 A worthless person, a wicked man is he who goes about with a perverse (contrary, wayward) mouth. 13 He winks with his eyes, he speaks by shuffling or tapping his feet, he makes signs (to mislead and deceive) and teaches with his fingers. 14 Willful and contrary in his heart, he devises trouble, vexation and evil continually; he lets loose discord, and sows it. 15 Therefore upon him shall the crushing weight of calamity come suddenly; suddenly shall he be broken and that without remedy (AMP).

Verse 12 – Today's verses characterize the charlatan. A "perverse mouth" belongs to a "slick talker." Many slick talkers lie convincingly to cheat others out of their money through scams and dishonest operations. Many evil people prey on Christians because they are good-hearted. I have even heard wicked men say that Christians are gullible and believe anything. We should ask the Lord to help us discern when someone is trying to cheat us so that we will not be taken advantage of. We should not allow ourselves to be pressured into giving or buying something without first asking the Holy Spirit to guide us.

The Bible warns of charlatans; false prophets that pretend to be Christians. Just because one comes in Jesus' name does not guarantee that he is truly His. "Beware of false prophets, which come to you in sheep's clothing, but inwardly they are ravening wolves. Ye shall know them by their fruits. Do men gather grapes of thorns, or figs of thistles? Even so every good tree bringeth forth good fruit; but a corrupt tree bringeth forth evil fruit. A good tree cannot bring forth evil fruit, neither can a corrupt tree bring forth good fruit. Every tree that bringeth not forth good fruit is hewn down, and cast into the fire. Wherefore by their fruits ye shall know them" (Matthew 7:15-20). The Lord instructs us to examine someone's fruit to discern who he is really serving. Some good questions are: Would Jesus act this way? Would He do this? If he does not behave in a godly manner, he is, at best, not walking in the Spirit; at worst, he is an emissary of the devil.

Verse 13 – A charlatan might use a lot of body language to express himself. He will often work with partners whom he signals by certain actions to cheat people. This is seen many times in gambling halls and casinos. Christians should not go to these places unless called there by God to share the Gospel. Gambling is an addiction that brings loss.

Verses 14-15 – Wicked men sow discord and mischief among their acquaintances. They will, in the end, be overtaken and broken by calamity. Calamity will come suddenly and unexpectedly; there will be no way out of it or any remedy for it. We must ask the Lord to keep us from getting involved with people of this sort, and from falling into gambling or any other trap that would allow the enemy to rob us.

Dear heavenly Father, I thank You for keeping me from evil people who would be set on destroying me or my family. I need your discernment to help me to know when I should and should not give. I want to be generous, but I do not want the enemy causing me to waste my money. Lead me by Your Spirit to know the things I should and shouldn't do. Lord, I pray for my Christian brothers and sisters who are addicted to gambling. Help them to get free. Show them that the lottery is not the answer to their financial problems. Teach them how to manage their monetary affairs according to the Word of God. When we do that, we are promised blessings from You. In the name of Jesus, I pray. Amen.

Proverbs 6:16-19 16 These six things doth the LORD hate: yea, seven are an abomination unto him: 17 A proud look, a lying tongue, and hands that shed innocent blood, 18 An heart that deviseth wicked imaginations, feet that be swift in running to mischief, 19 A false witness that speaketh lies, and he that soweth discord among brethren.

Verses 16-19 – God's hatred is directed against evil, beginning with a proud look. Haughtiness and arrogance have been the downfall of many. Pride causes one to overestimate oneself and underestimate others. Those who allow it to dominate their heart open the door to many other sins, causing major self-deception (Proverbs 16:18). Without a submissive heart, we cannot be guided by the Holy Spirit.

Next is a lying tongue. Recent surveys show that most Americans lie on a regular basis. Many lie because they either fear the consequences of the truth being known, or they are too proud to admit the truth. God highly values truthfulness. It may be difficult to admit our sins, but God is merciful to those who confess. Jesus' story of the Pharisee and the sinner (Luke 18:9-14) illustrates this.

God hates murder, but lists pride and lying as being ahead of it! Before someone commits murder, he yields to the sins of pride and lying. God hates the shedding of innocent blood, yet sees it shed every day. Not only are people shot down and killed, but innocent babies are murdered in the womb by abortion, mainly because of the selfishness of their parents.

Fourth, is a wicked imagination, giving birth to such evils as pornography. Our world is full of filthiness because of this. No wonder God hates it. Billions of dollars are spent on it each year, and it ruins millions of lives by embedding evil images in the minds of those who view it. Only God can free people from the bondage of pornography.

Fifth, is being quick to do mischief. While God is merciful to those who attempt to resist evil but fall into it, He hates the practice of those who throw restraint to the wind. The image here implies enjoyment and adeptness in wrongdoing, and alertness to take every opportunity to do evil.

Sixth, is bearing false witness. Lying about what one has witnessed is a serious sin before God and a crime in the eyes of man. Gossip is a second cousin to this sin. Stories are repeated not on the basis of truth, but simply because they speak evil about someone.

Last on God's list is a sin often committed in the church; that of sowing discord among the brethren. We are to love one another. God hates it when we fail to practice love as He commanded. Notice that He hates the first six sins, but that all seven are an abomination to Him. An *abomination* is something God abhors with extreme disgust. Let us not be guilty of doing anything that He detests. Let us cry out for deliverance, if we are guilty of any of these sins. God loves us and will free us if we come to Him with an honest heart.

Dear heavenly Father, I do not ever want to grieve Your heart by my actions. Help me to overcome all sin in my life. Lord, I especially do not want to ever partake in any of the sins you hate. I realize that our nation is guilty of these sins as a whole. Please forgive us and lead us to repentance. I know if we do not repent, judgment will surely come upon us in greater degrees. Help me to do my part in changing the world around me. Help me to share the gospel with all who have not heard. Lord, allow me to walk in love toward my brothers and sisters in Christ. I ask this in Jesus' name. Amen.

February 9 ***Day 40***

Proverbs 6:20-22 20 My son, keep your father's (God given) commandment, and forsake not the law of (God) your mother (taught you). 21 Bind them continually upon your heart, and tie them about your neck. 22 When you go, (the Word of your parents' God) it shall lead you; when you sleep, it shall keep you, and when you waken, it shall talk with you (AMP).

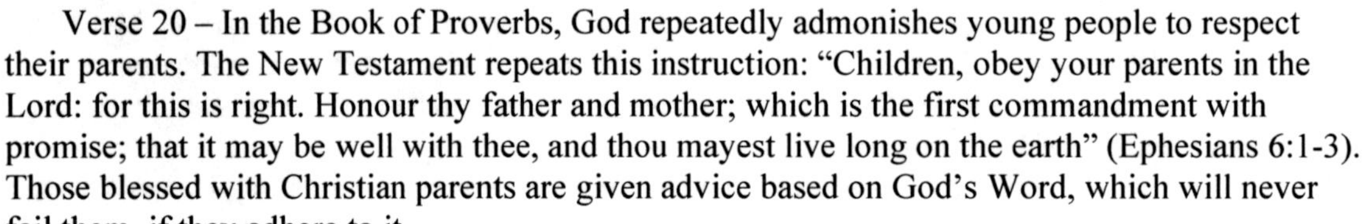

Verse 20 – In the Book of Proverbs, God repeatedly admonishes young people to respect their parents. The New Testament repeats this instruction: "Children, obey your parents in the Lord: for this is right. Honour thy father and mother; which is the first commandment with promise; that it may be well with thee, and thou mayest live long on the earth" (Ephesians 6:1-3). Those blessed with Christian parents are given advice based on God's Word, which will never fail them, if they adhere to it.

Verse 21 – The admonition to "bind them continually upon your heart" means to heed God's Word; meditating on Scripture. Meditation requires one to ponder or think about the meaning of a particular scripture. The word "meditate" in Hebrew comes from the same root word that has the meaning of a cow chewing her cud. A cow grazes to take in food, and later brings the grass from its first stomach back to its mouth to slowly and thoroughly chew it. Similarly, we take in truth when we read or hear something that God makes alive to us; and through meditating on it, we consider how to apply it to our lives.

What does it mean to "tie the Word about the neck?" Scarves or bandanas tied about our necks are noticed; they are not hidden. The influence of God's Word in our lives should not be hidden either, but it should stand out. The affect of His Word should adorn our lives like a necklace. People should see that something is different about us. The Bible tells us not to hide our light. "Let your light so shine before men, that they may see your good works, and glorify your Father which is in heaven" (Matthew 5:16).

Verse 22 – God's Word can guide us by day and keep us safe at night. If we heed it, we will not be sleeping in places that would cause us to sin or to go astray. In today's vernacular, we will not be "sleeping around." One of the ways in which the Holy Spirit often speaks to us is by bringing to mind the words of godly people. Let us listen to what the Lord says to us and obey Him so that we will walk in blessing and safety.

Dear heavenly Father, I am grateful that You speak to us in many different ways. Thank You for using our elders to speak to us. Help me not only to hear what You are saying, but to also obey what You are saying. Help me to also spend more time studying and meditating on Your Words in the Bible. I know that as I do this, I will have the answers to my problems. I also thank You for encouraging me in Your Word. Lord, bless my family and friends today and may they hear a Word from You. Speak to all of us so that we might be led by the Spirit of God today. I ask in the name of Jesus. Amen.

Proverbs 6:23-29 23 For the commandment is a lamp; and the law is light; and reproofs of instruction are the way of life: 24 To keep thee from the evil woman, from the flattery of the tongue of a strange woman. 25 Lust not after her beauty in thine heart; neither let her take thee with her eyelids. 26 For by means of a whorish woman a man is brought to a piece of bread: and the adulteress will hunt for the precious life. 27 Can a man take fire in his bosom, and his clothes not be burned? 28 Can one go upon hot coals, and his feet not be burned? 29 So he that goeth in to his neighbour's wife; whosoever toucheth her shall not be innocent (AMP).

Verse 23 – Obedience to the commandments of the Lord is like walking by the light of a lamp shining in a dark night. If we went out walking at night without a light, we would stumble and fall. No one can go very far without a light to guide them. Even sailors use the light of the stars to navigate on the seas. God's Word is the guiding light of our lives.

Verses 24-26 – Obeying God's Word keeps a man from being ensnared by evil women. The adulteress impoverishes the precious life of a man. An evil women entices him with alluring dress, provocative looks, and flattery. Satan easily ensnares a man if he can get him to engage in conversation with her. These verses apply to women as well as to men. Naïve women can be led astray by lustful men in the same way.

Verses 27-28 – A man cannot expose himself to great temptation and expect not to fall. Whoever thinks that a fling with a prostitute is harmless is deceived. A man cannot give in to this type of sin and not expect it to hurt him. It is like holding fire to his chest; it brings physical, emotional, and spiritual damage. To avoid sin, a man must flee its enticement. He does this by avoiding situations where he knows he would be tempted to commit fornication. "Flee fornication. Every sin that a man doeth is without the body; but he that committeth fornication sinneth against his own body" (1 Corinthians 6:18).

Fornication is any illicit sexual act. The Greek word for a fornicator is *pornos*, the root of our word pornography. Anyone tempted to indulge in pornography must flee it. Some ways to do this are: destroy all pornographic materials owned; avoid places that sell pornographic material; install a computer program to block pornographic emails. Those trapped in this bondage can be freed by the power of the Holy Spirit. God is forgiving, and will bring deliverance but it is best to never fall into this trap in the first place.

Verse 29 – What is true of fornication is true of adultery. Adultery is defined as a sexual act a married person commits outside of marriage. The Bible says that a man that has intercourse with any woman besides his own wife is guilty of adultery. This sin brings evil consequences and a troubled conscience that tortures the emotions.

Dear heavenly Father, thank You for addressing these issues in Your Word. We do not have to wonder what Your position is about the sexual issues in life. You have made it very clear. Help us, as parents and leaders, to address these issues so that our young people will not be influenced by the ungodly standards of society. Father, I pray for those who are caught in the addiction of pornography and illicit affairs. Please set them free. Have mercy on them and show them the way out. Lord, keep my mind and my heart pure in an age when sexual filth is everywhere. Protect my children, and grandchildren also, from the evils of this day. I ask this in Jesus' name. Amen.

Proverbs 6:30-35 30 Men do not despise a thief, if he steal to satisfy his soul when he is hungry; 31 But if he be found, he shall restore sevenfold; he shall give all the substance of his house. 32 But whoso committeth adultery with a woman lacketh understanding: he that doeth it destroyeth his own soul. 33 A wound and dishonour shall he get; and his reproach shall not be wiped away. 34 For jealousy is the rage of a man: therefore he will not spare in the day of vengeance. 35 He will not regard any ransom; neither will he rest content, though thou givest many gifts.

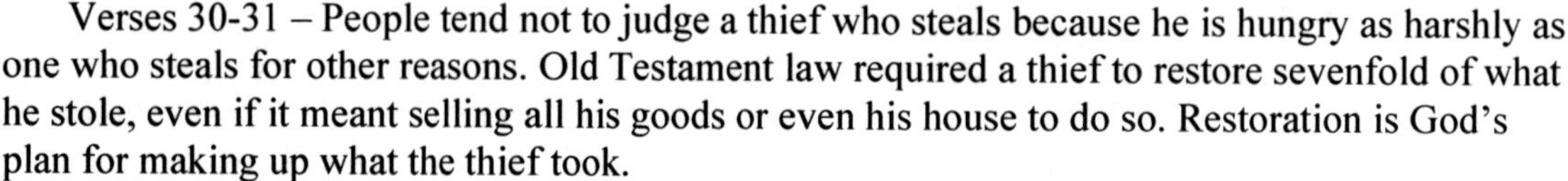

Verses 30-31 – People tend not to judge a thief who steals because he is hungry as harshly as one who steals for other reasons. Old Testament law required a thief to restore sevenfold of what he stole, even if it meant selling all his goods or even his house to do so. Restoration is God's plan for making up what the thief took.

Verses 32-33 – While thievery can impoverish a man, adultery can destroy his very soul. The Old Testament sentence for adultery was death (Leviticus 20:10). Many murders have been committed by both men and women over the sin of adultery. When a husband discovers a man having an affair with his wife, he may attack him in his rage and jealousy. An adulterer is often physically wounded or murdered. He can also be publicly dishonored. This was demonstrated in America when a president, some congressional leaders, and even some religious leaders were found guilty of adultery some years ago. Their reproach has not been wiped away, and it will be remembered in history books. If they repent, the Lord will forgive them, but most people will never forget.

Verses 34-35 – Gifts, bribes, or settlements can never compensate for the damage done by adultery. A husband will demand all the punishment the law can give. Some angry husbands will never be content with an apology or even legal action, but they will be bent on destroying the guilty party. The Bible is very clear: anyone that desires honor must resist the deadly sin of pursuing an affair with a married person, as the outcome could be deadly.

Dear heavenly Father, I come to You in Jesus' name, asking that You forgive us as a nation for the terrible sin of adultery. Lord, we are paying a dear price for disobeying Your instructions with regard to the sanctity of marriage. Forgive us for the affairs, the lust and selfishness, the lying, the cheating, and the "running around." These things have led to divorce and broken homes. Our children are suffering because so many do not have two parents to guide them. Please have mercy on us and restore our families. Help us to live for You, rather than for our own selfish desires. I pray for the marriages that are under attack right now, and ask that You heal these strained relationships. Amen.

God's Wisdom for Daily Living — *Betty Miller*
February 12 — *Day 43*

Proverbs 7:1-3 1 My son, keep my words, and lay up my commandments with thee. 2 Keep my commandments, and live; and my law as the apple of thine eye. 3 Bind them upon thy fingers, write them upon the table of thine heart.

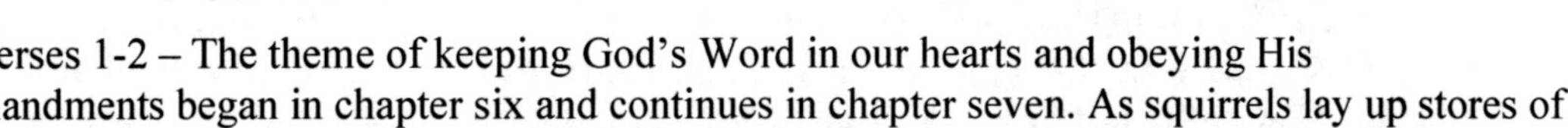

Verses 1-2 – The theme of keeping God's Word in our hearts and obeying His commandments began in chapter six and continues in chapter seven. As squirrels lay up stores of nuts in autumn so they will have food to get them through the winter, we need to "lay up" the Word of God in our hearts for the winter seasons of life.

When Jesus was tempted in the wilderness, He overcame the devil by answering him with Scripture. If we do not know the Bible, the devil can take advantage of us in times of temptation and rob us of our inheritance. James 4:7 says: "Submit yourselves therefore to God. Resist the devil, and he will flee from you." We resist Satan by choosing to believe the Word and speaking against his lies. Speaking Scripture will cause the devil to flee. We need to speak those verses that pertain to what the enemy is trying to do against us. If we do not know what the Word says about our circumstances, we can be defeated (Hosea 4:6b).

Let us say, for example, that the devil tempts us to sin; however, we repent and receive forgiveness. Later, someone we love needs prayer for their healing. The devil does not want us to pray for people to be healed, so he might begin to drop thoughts in our minds such as this: "You cannot ask God to heal your loved one because you committed a terrible sin! You are not righteous. You are being punished because of your sin." If we know God's Word, we will recognize two lies here. We will know that "If we confess our sins, [God] is faithful and just to forgive us our sins, and to cleanse us from all unrighteousness" (1 John 1:9), and that He will then answer our prayers when we pray according to His will. We will also know that the Lord desires all to be healed since Jesus went about healing all that were sick (Acts 10:38). Thus, we will know that our loved one's illness is not God punishing us, but the devil's attempt to steal, kill, and destroy. We have authority over him in the name of Jesus; and should never hesitate to pray for our loved one to be healed.

Verse 3 – Information was recorded differently in Biblical times than today. People wrote on tablets made of clay, slate, or something similar; thus the phrase, "write them upon the table of thine heart." We are to engrave God's word upon our hearts; to memorize it, to know it by heart. "Bind them upon thy fingers" has the same kind of meaning. We must keep God's Word close at hand so we can read it, know it, and most importantly–live it!

Dearest Father, thank You for giving me the Bible so I can understand Your ways. I also appreciate You giving me understanding when I read and study it. Help me to live my life in accordance with Your Word. Please warn me when I am straying so that I can stay right on course with You. Help me to be disciplined to study the Bible daily. I need this discipline in my prayer life, too. Please guide me as I read, and guide my prayers so that I might pray for the things that are on Your heart. I ask this in the name of Jesus. Amen.

Proverbs 7:4-27 4 Say unto wisdom, Thou art my sister; and call understanding thy kinswoman: 5 That they may keep thee from the strange woman, from the stranger which flattereth with her words. 6 For at the window of my house I looked through my casement, 7 And beheld among the simple ones, I discerned among the youths, a young man void of understanding, 8 Passing through the street near her corner; and he went the way to her house, 9 In the twilight, in the evening, in the black and dark night: 10 And, behold, there met him a woman with the attire of an harlot, and subtle of heart. 11 (She is loud and stubborn; her feet abide not in her house: 12 Now is she without, now in the streets, and lieth in wait at every corner.) 13 So she caught him, and kissed him, and with an impudent face said unto him, 14 I have peace offerings with me; this day have I payed my vows. 15 Therefore came I forth to meet thee, diligently to seek thy face, and I have found thee. 16 I have decked my bed with coverings of tapestry, with carved works, with fine linen of Egypt. 17 I have perfumed my bed with myrrh, aloes, and cinnamon. 18 Come, let us take our fill of love until the morning: let us solace ourselves with loves. 19 For the goodman is not at home, he is gone a long journey: 20 He hath taken a bag of money with him, and will come home at the day appointed. 21 With her much fair speech she caused him to yield, with the flattering of her lips she forced him. 22 He goeth after her straightway, as an ox goeth to the slaughter, or as a fool to the correction of the stocks; 23 Till a dart strike through his liver; as a bird hasteth to the snare, and knoweth not that it is for his life. 24 Hearken unto me now therefore, O ye children, and attend to the words of my mouth. 25 Let not thine heart decline to her ways, go not astray in her paths. 26 For she hath cast down many wounded: yea, many strong men have been slain by her. 27 Her house is the way to hell, going down to the chambers of death.

Verses 4-27 – Proverbs records a detailed description of how a young man is seduced by a prostitute. Verse 4 begins by telling him to get wisdom and an understanding of the "women" that he should pursue. Wisdom will make a wonderful "sister" and understanding a great "aunt" that will give the good advice that he needs. Their counsel will keep him from sin, because they have true love and concern for him.

The ways of the seductress presents an analogy of Satan's attempts to lure the believer into his clutches. The devil has an arsenal of temptations and exploits our weaknesses. Just as the adulteress used what smelled, looked, tasted, and felt good to lure the young man, so the devil uses these same means to tempt us. While dangling his bait, he may often say something like the adulteress' words in verses 19 and 20: "Jesus will not return for a while. You have plenty of time to indulge in sin before He comes back!" Beware of the enemy's flattering words.

This portion of Scripture reminds us that "...many strong men have been slain by her." In other words, we cannot count on our own strength to resist temptation. At some point we will fall, unless we humbly call out to God for the grace to overcome in our struggles.

Dear Father, thank You for giving me the power to overcome the schemes of the devil. I pray for all the young men that I know, that they might be kept from the ways of harlots. I also pray for those who are trapped in the bondage of prostitution. I know that You love them and want to free them from sin. Help these women to cry unto You for deliverance. Wash them clean by Your blood. Keep us in Your hand and protect our children and grandchildren. In Jesus' name. Amen.

**Proverbs 8:1-11 1 Doth not wisdom cry? and understanding put forth her voice? 2 She
standeth in the top of high places, by the way in the places of the paths. 3 She crieth at the
gates, at the entry of the city, at the coming in at the doors. 4 Unto you, O men, I call; and
my voice is to the sons of man. 5 O ye simple, understand wisdom: and, ye fools, be ye of an
understanding heart. 6 Hear; for I will speak of excellent things; and the opening of my lips
shall be right things. 7 For my mouth shall speak truth; and wickedness is an abomination
to my lips. 8 All the words of my mouth are in righteousness; there is nothing froward or
perverse in them. 9 They are all plain to him that understandeth, and right to them that
find knowledge. 10 Receive my instruction, and not silver; and knowledge rather than
choice gold. 11 For wisdom is better than rubies; and all the things that may be desired are
not to be compared to it.**

The book of Proverbs tells us to get wisdom, but where do we find it and what exactly is it? The dictionary[7] lists these definitions for wisdom: "(1) the quality of being wise; power of judging rightly and following the soundest course of action; good judgment; (2) learning; knowledge; the wisdom of the ages (3) wise discourse or teaching."

Verses 1-4 – Since God has always existed, He has all knowledge. His wisdom truly is the "wisdom of the ages." Using poetic imagery, Proverbs contrasts godly wisdom (pictured as a righteous woman), with worldly wisdom, (pictured as a wicked whore at the end of chapter nine).

Wisdom offers a righteous path to follow. She is not hard to find. She is crying out in the "gates." In Biblical times, most cities had thick walls built around them and huge gates to close at night to keep out enemies. Near the open gates, was the meeting place of the city's elders. They presided over the city's affairs, even as members of city councils do today, watching what came into the city and marketplace and making judgments on safety, commerce, and legal matters.

One way that a young Christian "seeks wisdom in the gates" today is by going to his elders for godly advice. They can help guide him in the right path for his life. God has sent the Bible and His preachers into the world so that all may hear His wisdom. Finding wisdom is not hard, but heeding it can be hard unless we surrender to God.

Verses 5-11 – We will understand what God is saying to us, if we seek Him with all our hearts. He will make His will very clear to us. His instruction is better than silver. His knowledge is better than gold, His wisdom is better than rubies. All the earthly riches we could possibly desire cannot compare with God's wisdom. The Bible contains God's wisdom, and through Jesus, we can find our needed answers. He is the Creator of the world and more precious than all its wealth. By seeking Him and heeding the Bible, we find wisdom.

Father, I am thankful for everything You have provided for us. I need Your wisdom and guidance every day. Each new day brings situations that I must lean on You for help. You are faithful in meeting those needs. Thank You for the people You send into my life to help and strengthen me. Many of them have "words of wisdom" that are invaluable in helping me overcome my present problems. Thank You for the church elders who have graced my life with Your wisdom as well. May I heed godly counsel and esteem those who share it. I ask this in the name of Jesus. Amen.

---

[7] Webster's New World Dictionary of the American Language, Second college edition

Proverbs 8:12 I wisdom dwell with prudence, and find out knowledge of witty inventions.

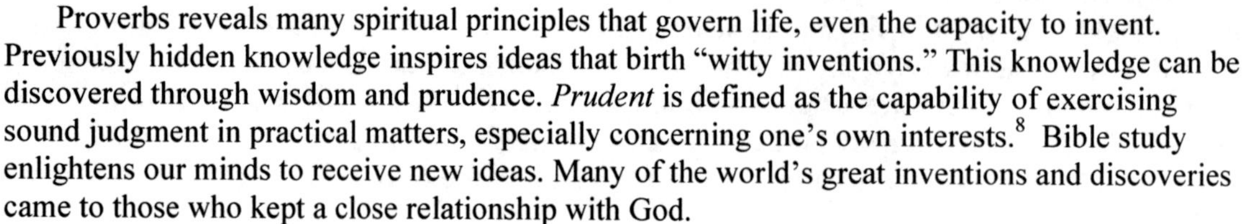

Proverbs reveals many spiritual principles that govern life, even the capacity to invent. Previously hidden knowledge inspires ideas that birth "witty inventions." This knowledge can be discovered through wisdom and prudence. *Prudent* is defined as the capability of exercising sound judgment in practical matters, especially concerning one's own interests.[8] Bible study enlightens our minds to receive new ideas. Many of the world's great inventions and discoveries came to those who kept a close relationship with God.

The tremendously talented George Washington Carver was the child of slaves. He invented more than 300 products from the peanut, 118 from the sweet potato, and 75 from the pecan. His discoveries increased the South's income by millions of dollars. Concerning his "witty inventions" he wrote the following:[9] *"The secret of my success? It is simple. It is found in the Bible. I prayed that my life and work had helped in a small way to make the world peaceful and make [God] happy."*

Sir Isaac Newton, a devout Christian of the 1600's, was another great scientist. He discovered how the universe holds together through the force of gravity, developed the branch of mathematics known as calculus, and discovered secrets of light and color. He is described as one of the greatest names in the history of human thought. How did he discover so many "witty inventions?" The key to his success is found in these quotes:[10] *"I have a fundamental belief in the Bible as the Word of God, written by men who were inspired. I study the Bible daily"* and *"Atheism is so senseless. When I look at the solar system, I see the earth at the right distance from the sun to receive the proper amounts of heat and light. This did not happen by chance."*

Christopher Columbus's greatest discovery was not the New World, but the discovery of God's ways. He desired to explore the world to find new lands and proclaim Christ to the peoples there. This little-known fact was the motivation behind his adventurous life. An excerpt from one of his letters reveals his faith:[11] *"At this time I read and studied all kinds of literature: cosmography, histories, chronicles, and philosophy and other arts, to which our Lord opened my mind unmistakably to the fact that it was possible to navigate from here to the Indies, and He evoked in me the will for the execution of it...Who would doubt that this light did not come from the Holy Spirit...which comforted with rays of marvelous clarity and its Holy and Sacred Scriptures."*

From these examples of great men, we see that they gained insight from God through studying the Bible. Some secular historians omit any mention of the commitment to God that made these men successful. Our children are denied the right to know the full story in their history books. They need to know that "witty inventions" are possible because of the wisdom that God gives.

---

[8] Webster's New World Dictionary of the American Language, Second college edition
[9] Collins, David A Man's Slave Becomes God's Scientist: George Washington Carver (Mott Media, 1981)
[10] Tiner, John Hudson Isaac Newton, Inventor, Scientist and Teacher (Mott Media, 1981)
[11] Rhodes, Bennie Adventurer of Faith and Courage: Christopher Columbus (Mott Media, 1981)

Dear Father, thank You for the great men that You have used to bring us to this place in time. I pray that the true God of the Bible will be known in all the nations of the world. Lord, may we in the United States, bring the Bible and prayer back into our schools. Without this influence some of our children are becoming murderers and our schools are not safe. Our nation was founded as a Christian nation; may we not deny You in our schools, businesses, and homes. Lord, comfort all those families who have lost their children due to the violence in our schools, and forgive us for not raising our families in the nurture and admonition of the Lord. Help me to bring the light of Your Word to all, and change this world for the better. In Jesus' name, I pray. Amen.

Quotes about the Bible

We must know the Bible's Author to be able to understand the Bible's words. --Day 1

We must realize that the Bible cannot be read as a common novel. It is a holy book granted to mankind, inspired by the Holy Spirit. --Day 9

God does not love one of His children more than another. He loves us all equally, and is no respecter of persons. However, God is a respecter of His Word. A Christian who knows and applies the Word of God, has an advantage over one who does not. --Day 29

One of the miraculous things about the Bible is its relevancy for us today. Generations pass, cultures come and go, but man's issues and problems remain the same. --Day 34

Knowing only portions of the Word can cause us to become unbalanced. We must seek to know the whole truth and be completely surrendered to the will of God for us to be victorious Christians. --Day 133

Those opposing the Bible do not realize they are opposing the very influences that make life pleasant, for God is light and His light brings revelation, which liberates people. --Day 338

If we do not study the Bible, we will end up learning God's ways the hard way–through the pain of trial and error. However, if we apply God's Word to our lives, He will be a shield for us. --Day 343

Proverbs 8:13 The fear of the LORD is to hate evil: pride, and arrogancy, and the evil way, and the froward mouth, do I hate.

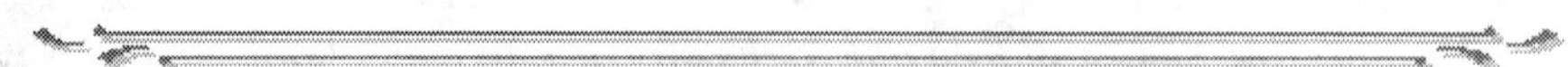

Proverbs gives us a good explanation of what the "fear of the Lord" is. Some people are confused by this concept when they see in the New Testament, that "There is no fear in love; but perfect love casteth out fear: because fear hath torment..." (1 John 4:18).

To reconcile these seemingly opposing truths, we must understand what it means to fear the Lord. The Hebrew noun *yir'âh* comes from the verb *yârê'*, "...to venerate, reverence.[12]" It means to be humble toward God, because we acknowledge His power and authority. A small example of this would be the sort of reverence we have toward our parents. We should respect what our parents say. If our father warns us of the danger of smoking, we will not rebel against him. We will fear the consequences of what might happen to us if we get addicted to cigarettes. This is a healthy fear that protects us; it does not torment. Likewise, fearing the Lord means we respect His Word and apply it to our lives.

We read that "perfect love casteth out fear." If we love God and desire to please Him, we will want to obey Him. If we do not disobey Him, we have nothing to fear. This does not mean we must be perfect, since we all fail God at times, but because of our love for God, we strive to obey Him perfectly. When we fail, we must confess our guilt to God, or the devil will be able to torment us. "If we confess our sins, he is faithful and just to forgive us our sins, and to cleanse us from all unrighteousness" (1 John 1:9).

If we fear the Lord, we will hate evil. We will ask Him to deliver us from arrogance and a perverse mouth. If we tolerate evil in our lives, we do not fear God. We may think that God is overlooking wrong attitudes if we are not immediately punished for them. We need to realize that God is being merciful, giving us time to repent so that our sins do not activate the principle of sowing and reaping (Galatians 6:7-8). The fear of the Lord turns us from sin. It causes us to seek His help to resist evil, and it stirs within us a desire to walk in the truth.

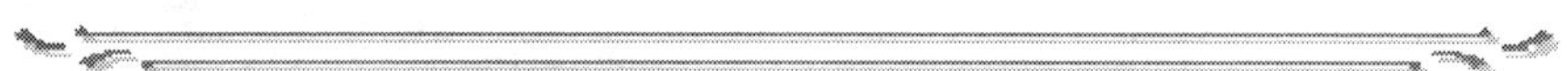

Dear Father, thank You for Your love and patience, helping me overcome the things in my life that are not pleasing to You. I realize that I cannot do this without the help of the Holy Spirit. I am calling on You to empower me to be an overcomer and help me to come to the place that I love You so much, that I will never want to hurt You by going my own way. I humbly ask You to remove all pride and rebellion from my heart. Cleanse me, and may I always have the "fear of the Lord" in my heart. I ask this in Jesus' name. Amen.

[12] Strong's Exhaustive Concordance of the Bible, Hebrew and Chaldee Dictionary

Proverbs 8:14 Counsel is mine, and sound wisdom: I am understanding; I have strength.

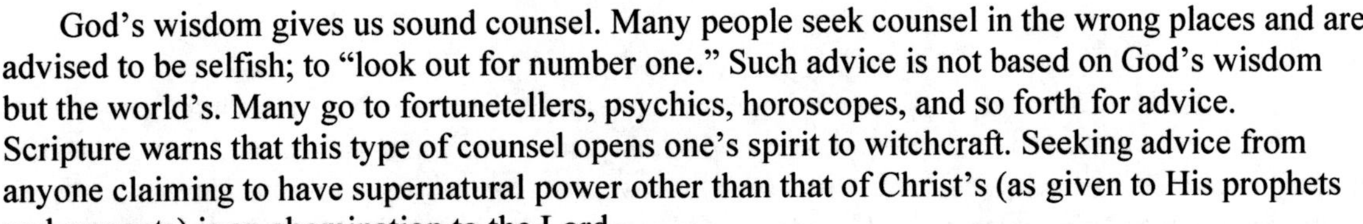

God's wisdom gives us sound counsel. Many people seek counsel in the wrong places and are advised to be selfish; to "look out for number one." Such advice is not based on God's wisdom but the world's. Many go to fortunetellers, psychics, horoscopes, and so forth for advice. Scripture warns that this type of counsel opens one's spirit to witchcraft. Seeking advice from anyone claiming to have supernatural power other than that of Christ's (as given to His prophets and servants) is an abomination to the Lord.

"There shall not be found among you any one that maketh his son or his daughter to pass through the fire, or that useth divination, or an observer of times, or an enchanter, or a witch, or a charmer, or a consulter with familiar spirits, or a wizard, or a necromancer. For all that do these things are an abomination unto the LORD: and because of these abominations the LORD thy God doth drive them out from before thee. Thou shalt be perfect with the LORD thy God. For these nations, which thou shalt possess, hearkened unto observers of times, and unto diviners: but as for thee, the LORD thy God hath not suffered thee so to do. The LORD thy God will raise up unto thee a Prophet from the midst of thee, of thy brethren, like unto me; unto him ye shall hearken" (Deuteronomy18:10-15).

The above scriptures mention several wicked things that the nations of Canaan practiced. They sought counsel from divination, astrology (observing the times), enchanters or witches, the dead (necromancy), and séances (consulting with familiar spirits). They even burned their children as sacrifices to idols.

God commands that we seek counsel from Him, not demonic sources. He desires to direct us and give us His understanding. In Him alone are wisdom and strength. Moses, inspired by the Holy Spirit, told Israel to heed the Prophet whom God would raise up after him (Deuteronomy 18:15). That Prophet is Jesus.

We are also told that the way to overcome is not to rely on our own strength and wisdom, but to look to God for His counsel and advice–and the strength to obey Him. When we feel we cannot possibly do or face something, we can rely upon His promise to give us the strength to accomplish it. One of the best verses to claim for strength is Philippians 4:13: "I can do all things through Christ which strengtheneth me." Ephesians 6:10 tells us to "...be strong in the Lord, and in the power of his might." It does not say to be strong in *our* strength, but "in the Lord, and in the power of his might." We can rely on God for all we need. We can trust Him to enable us to follow His counsel. In so doing we will walk in strength and victory!

Dear Father in heaven, I thank You for guiding me this far, and I trust You to continue to show me the right path to take and the right things I should do. I am asking for Your wisdom and counsel in all that I do. You are all wise and I can trust Your advice. I need You, in every area of my life. Please give me the strength I need daily, as I work and serve You. I also ask that You touch my family, friends, and all of my loved ones. Lord, also touch each one who reads this prayer that they may feel Your love and strength in their life today. Bless all of those whom You have placed in my life. I ask this in Jesus' name. Amen.

Proverbs 8:15-17 15 By me kings reign, and princes decree justice. 16 By me princes rule, and nobles, even all the judges of the earth. 17 I love them that love me; and those that seek me early shall find me.

Verses 15-16– Our study in Proverbs continues to emphasize the value of having God's wisdom. These verses tell us that good rulers will rule justly, using sound wisdom. A student of history knows that since Christ's resurrection the most prosperous kingdoms and nations have been those whose leaders exerted a Christian influence over their people. Historically, when true Christianity came to a region, those practicing Christ's commands began to help the poor and oppressed. Many present-day universities, hospitals, and orphanages were founded by those who desired to demonstrate Christ's love to a needy world. God always desires to help the weak and afflicted. Ungodly societies destroy their feeble, helpless, or otherwise "burdensome" members.

I pray that the ungodly practice of abortion will cease in all nations which legally allow and encourage it. Abortion adversely affects all of society. It runs completely against a basic respect for human life. The more we harden our hearts to protecting the sanctity of human life, the more susceptible we become to violent crimes against humanity. The consequence of murder is "a life for a life." Many lives will be lost in any nation that practices abortion unless the people repent. "...the land cannot be cleansed of the blood that is shed therein, but by the blood of him that shed it" (Numbers 35:33b). Despite what those who believe in abortion rights claim, most abortions are not done to protect the mother's life, but rather to allow the mother and father to escape their responsibility of caring for the little life that they created. Most abortions are sought out of selfishness: the parents do not want a child interfering with their plans. The Bible teaches that we must overcome selfishness, not encourage it.

Verse 17 – The Lord loves those who love Him. Love for God is shown by loving one another and keeping His commandments. If we desire God's love and favor, we must seek Him "early," before our nations are faced with severe judgment. We must turn back to God and obey His commandments.

Dear Father, please forgive the sin of murder in our nation and the world. Murder begins with the sins of lust and selfishness. Deliver Your people from these sins. Help me, Lord, to overcome my own selfishness, and be willing to lay down my wants for the sake of the kingdom of God. Help me to think of others and their needs, and not concentrate so much on my own needs. I thank You for taking care of my needs, so that I can help and bless others. I pray for the leaders of our nation. Give them wisdom. Protect them from harm. Give them strength and health. Turn our nation back to the Christian principles that it was once founded upon. Thank You, Lord, for being merciful to all of us. In Jesus' name I pray. Amen.

Proverbs 8:18-21 18 Riches and honour are with me; yea, durable riches and righteousness. 19 My fruit is better than gold, yea, than fine gold; and my revenue than choice silver. 20 I lead in the way of righteousness, in the midst of the paths of judgment: 21 That I may cause those that love me to inherit substance; and I will fill their treasures.

Verses 18-20 – Whoever possesses God's wisdom will receive both honor and blessing. Portions of the church are divided on whether Christians can expect material blessings from God. The Bible clearly indicates that poverty does not come from Him; He is a God of abundance. He has never disapproved of His people receiving riches, but He is against the sins that many people embrace with wealth: greed, hoarding, and selfish indulgence.

Notice that godly wisdom brings not only wealth, but righteousness. God honors those who seek His direction for the use of their resources. Godly men look for ways to bless others and support ministers who are spreading the Gospel. They are not consumed with extravagance, but are satisfied with a modest lifestyle. The man whom God makes rich is different from the worldly rich man. The godly man trusts God, because he knows where his wealth comes from. He is aware that, but for God, he would own nothing and could lose everything if he turned away from Him (Deuteronomy 8:18). He does not consider his wealth his own and is not troubled about losing it. He acknowledges God's ownership of his wallet and his very life. Knowing that he is only a steward, he listens to the Holy Spirit to learn where his money should go. He is ready, if the Lord asks him, to give it all away.

God is a loving Father who desires to bless His people. He wants us to have the same generous heart that He does. How much should we give? We should keep some money as seed for bread, but also give some back to God for the Gospel. In the Bible, we find that God required His people to give a tithe (ten-percent, or the firstfruits) of their increase. That is a good starting point; however, the truly wealthy man will desire to give God more as he is entrusted with more. I read of a very wealthy man who gave huge sums of money to the work of the Kingdom. This man reversed God's requirement: he gave ninety-percent to God and lived on ten-percent.

Verse 21 – Some of us may be struggling to make a living. The Lord has much to say about finances and giving. We can get out of financial bondage by following His wisdom. When we give of what we have: our time, prayers, possessions and money, He has a way of meeting our needs and multiplying it back to us so that we can give again. As we help each other, we find our treasuries being filled. As God's obedient children, we receive true inheritance; not merely material things, but the treasures of heaven that cannot be bought. Only Jesus can give us faith, peace, love, joy, health and eternal life.

Dearest Father, how grateful I am for all You have given me. I have never lacked. Yes, I have had to wait for certain things that did not come in my time, but You have always come through. I thank You, that You truly have made us wealthy. I have a home, an automobile, clothes, and wonderful appliances that wash and dry our clothes and do the dishes. This gives me more time to seek You and reach out to others. Thank You for these blessings. I am also grateful for all the wonderful friends You have given me and my mate. Thank You for the people who pray for us and help us get the gospel out. Most of all, I am thankful for You and Your love and that my name is written in the Book of Life. I pray in the wonderful name of Jesus. Amen.

Proverbs 8:22-31 22 The LORD possessed me in the beginning of his way, before his works of old. 23 I was set up from everlasting, from the beginning, or ever the earth was. 24 When there were no depths, I was brought forth; when there were no fountains abounding with water. 25 Before the mountains were settled, before the hills was I brought forth: 26 While as yet he had not made the earth, nor the fields, nor the highest part of the dust of the world. 27 When he prepared the heavens, I was there: when he set a compass upon the face of the depth: 28 When he established the clouds above: when he strengthened the fountains of the deep: 29 When he gave to the sea his decree, that the waters should not pass his commandment: when he appointed the foundations of the earth: 30 Then I was by him, as one brought up with him: and I was daily his delight, rejoicing always before him; 31 Rejoicing in the habitable part of his earth; and my delights were with the sons of men.

Verses 22-30 – This portion of Scripture is a poetic description of Wisdom's role in creation. The Lord possessed Wisdom "before His works of old." Wisdom is eternal; "from everlasting." She existed in the beginning. These verses hint that Wisdom is a Person; Jesus, the Son of God (Colossians 2:3). The New Testament refers to God as love; and here, Jesus is referred to as "Wisdom." As we follow the ways of wisdom, we are following the ways of Christ.

These verses harmonize with the Genesis creation record, which some of the scientific community tries to replace with theories that are even harder to believe! Many of these theories, however, are being proved false; as evidence is brought to light that gives credence that the Biblical account of creation is true. It is foolish to believe that the earth "just happened," originating from a condensed pinpoint of matter that one day exploded in a "big bang;" and the resulting chaos just happened to fall into meticulous order.

The design of creation gives clearer evidence of a Creator than the structure and design inside of a computer. No chance encounter with a passing star set our solar system in perfect order. God is the wise Master Designer who created the solar systems and set the planets to rotate in exact orbits. God positioned the earth at precisely the right distance from the sun. He created mountains, lakes, forests and fields and set the oceans' boundaries by His command (Job 38:11). We need not worry about the earth entering into an ice age, because the scripture says, "While the earth remaineth, seedtime and harvest, and cold and heat, and summer and winter, and day and night shall not cease" (Genesis 8:22).

Verse 31 – The most delightful thing God created was human beings. He fashioned man, the height of His creation, in His own image. He desired a race of beings with whom He could fellowship. He has continued His creation of man with each individual born through the ages since Adam and Eve. It delights His heart to commune with each of His children daily.

Father, I am blessed to be Your child. I appreciate Your handiwork in creation. I am in awe that You made it all for mankind so that we might be blessed in it. Thank You for the beauty of the mountains, the glorious sunsets and the blue skies with those patches of little white clouds on a nice day. Thank You for eyes to see Your great artistry in the earth. Forgive me when I am tempted to complain about anything. I have nothing to complain about when I have the Creator of the universe as my Father and friend. May I be a good friend to You and serve You faithfully every day of my life. Use me today to bless and help others. I ask this in Jesus' name. Amen.

Proverbs 8:32-36 32 Now therefore hearken unto me, O ye children: for blessed are they that keep my ways. 33 Hear instruction, and be wise, and refuse it not. 34 Blessed is the man that heareth me, watching daily at my gates, waiting at the posts of my doors. 35 For whoso findeth me findeth life, and shall obtain favour of the LORD. 36 But he that sinneth against me wrongeth his own soul: all they that hate me love death.

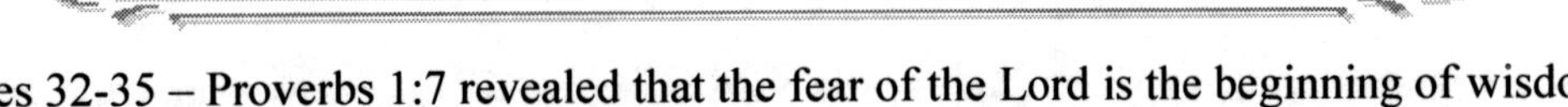

Verses 32-35 – Proverbs 1:7 revealed that the fear of the Lord is the beginning of wisdom. Proverbs 1:8 named the next step on the path of wisdom: listening to instruction. It has been mentioned in every chapter since, and again here. In school, we discover that if we do not pay attention to the teacher's instruction, we fail the tests. Similarly, if we refuse the Bible's instruction, we will be unable to pass life's tests. The opposite is also true: we are blessed if we diligently heed His instruction. We must seek the Lord every day to find His favor and the path of life.

Verse 36 – When we sin against God, we not only hurt ourselves but actually invite Satan to bring the death principle into some part of our lives. A principle is "a comprehensive and fundamental law."[13] Sinning against God activates the death principle set down in Ezekiel 18:4, "...The soul that sinneth, it shall die" and Romans 6:23a, "For the wages of sin is death." Death claims not only the physical body but the inner being. Sickness, fear, depression, misfortunes, and so on, are effects of activating the death principle.

There are two kinds of sins: sins of commission (doing what is wrong) and sins of omission (failing to do what is right). "Therefore to him that knoweth to do good, and doeth it not, to him it is sin" (James 4:17). Many Christians do not realize that failing to pray and read the Bible is sin. I have heard many Christians remark: "I don't understand why this is happening to me. I haven't done anything!" This is often true! They have not been praying. They have not been reading their Bibles. They have not been seeking God. They truly have not done the things they should have been doing. They may not have committed overt sin to open a door to the enemy, but they sinned by failing to do what would have stopped him. "Finally, my brethren, be strong in the Lord, and in the power of his might." We must put on the whole armor of God which is listed in Ephesians 6:13-17. Satan is out to destroy our souls and we must take action to prevent him from overcoming us.

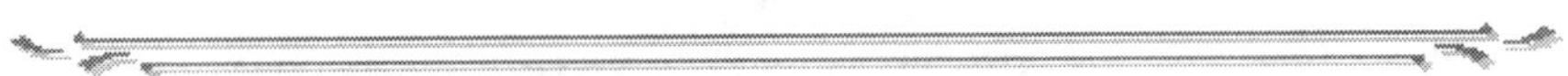

Dear heavenly Father, I bless Your wonderful name! Thank You for being merciful and patient with me. I have failed You many times, and yet You heard my prayers of repentance and have kept me in Your favor. I love you, Lord. Help me to continue in Your way, even through hard times. I know the devil's way is harder. With You, we can overcome anything. Lord, bless Your people today and forgive us all. Keep us from the wicked one and let us remember that the Greater One lives in us, so we are never to fear the enemy. Thank You for giving us all overcoming faith. I ask in the name of Jesus. Amen.

---

[13] "Principle." Merriam–Webster Online Dictionary. 2004 http://www.merriam–webster.com (22 November 2005).

God's Wisdom for Daily Living — *Betty Miller*
February 22 — *Day 53*

Proverbs 9:1-5 1 Wisdom hath builded her house, she hath hewn out her seven pillars:
2 She hath killed her beasts; she hath mingled her wine; she hath also furnished her table.
3 She hath sent forth her maidens: she crieth upon the highest places of the city, 4 Whoso is
simple, let him turn in hither: as for him that wanteth understanding, she saith to him,
5 Come, eat of my bread, and drink of the wine which I have mingled.

These verses contain a powerful message. Wisdom, personified as a woman, calls us to her banquet of "best things," in contrast to the foolish woman mentioned later in chapter 9, who calls the simple to drink "stolen waters." Here, as in chapter 8, wisdom is more than a trait or quality. It is a symbol of Jesus, who is also referred to as the *rose of Sharon* and the *lily of the valleys*, the One who brings us to His banqueting table (Song of Solomon 2:4).

Wisdom has built a house; Jesus tells us how to build ours. These "houses" do not mean our physical residences, but our spiritual houses (Matthew 7:24-27). The storms of life come against the houses of both the wise and foolish, but only those of the wise remain standing after being battered. The wise are those who obey God's Word, putting into practice what they learn. The foolish hear His Word, but do not act on what they hear. If we desire our "financial houses," "career houses," and families to withstand life's storms, we must keep the commandments of God pertaining to each.

Verse 1 – In Scripture, numbers are not simply digits used in arithmetic; as all Hebrew names and numbers have meanings. What does it mean when it says that Wisdom has "hewn out her seven pillars?" A carpenter knows that pillars in a house are the support beams. The seven pillars in Wisdom's house symbolize that the house has perfect support, because symbolically the number seven stands for perfection or completeness. When the structure of our lives rests upon Biblical principles, our building is not in vain. "Except the LORD build the house, they labour in vain that build it..." (Psalm 127:1).

Verses 2-5 – The remainder of these verses describe the banquet that Wisdom has prepared. She has butchered her meat and set her table with wine. She invites those who will listen to "come and dine." This is a picture of Jesus' invitation to come and eat of His bread (understand His Word) and drink of His wine (receive the Holy Spirit). This invitation is still going out from the Master today.

Dear heavenly Father, how grateful I am that You have given us such wonderful things to feast upon. It is a blessing to understand Your Word and know Your presence. I need Your help in building and setting in order the things in my life. Give me wisdom for the task. I also need Your love and strength to carry out those things that You have spoken to me to do. Lord, I want to be a blessing today, as I labor in Your kingdom. Help me to represent You well, and to be good and kind to all of those in my house and office, and all that I meet. Thank You for Your love and watchful care over me, my family and my loved ones. Bless Your people all over the world. I ask in the name of Jesus. Amen.

Proverbs 9:6-9 6 Forsake the foolish, and live; and go in the way of understanding. 7 He that reproveth a scorner getteth to himself shame: and he that rebuketh a wicked man getteth himself a blot. 8 Reprove not a scorner, lest he hate thee: rebuke a wise man, and he will love thee. 9 Give instruction to a wise man, and he will be yet wiser: teach a just man, and he will increase in learning.

Verse 6 – Scripture uses the word "fool" to describe those who lack moral reason and righteousness. Because the foolish are rebels, the Lord tells us to forsake foolish people and their ways, and to follow Him in understanding.

Verses 7-8 – If we try to correct a scornful man, he will hate us for reproving him. He will reject our advice and turn on us; hurling a deluge of hateful words and abuse. This is also true of the wicked man. Scorners, mockers, and scoffers are prideful and impudent, and therefore not teachable. They resent anyone telling them what to do. They will try to humiliate anyone who tells them the truth or tries to correct them.

Because they are not ready to hear correction or repent, the best way to deal with scorners is to pray for them until the Lord softens their hearts. We need discernment to know when it is wise to share the truth in love and when it is best to keep quiet and pray. Only God knows when a person is ready to hear. We need to remember this in witnessing to people. Luke 8:11-15 likens the Word of God to seed and a person's heart to the soil in which it is planted. Sometimes the words we share with people will "plow the ground" of the heart, while at other times they will be planted like seed. Someone else may come along later and water the seed of truth we have planted in a person. Still later, the Lord may send a different person to reap the harvest when it is ready, and lead that person to Christ.

Verse 9 – A wise man is teachable. He learns from his mistakes because he does not allow pride to keep him from receiving correction. He is happy to receive a "course correction" and will love those who help him see the truth and avoid a problem. He appreciates the fact that he has gained new understanding because he has a teachable spirit. This kind of man or woman grows wiser and wiser.

Dear heavenly Father, thank You for giving us the Bible, so that we can study Your words and grow in wisdom. I appreciate Your correction. Thank You for giving me a teachable spirit. Lord, also give me discernment as to when I need to open my mouth and speak the truth, and when I need to be silent and just pray. Give me the holy boldness to speak up when You tell me that someone needs a Word or prayer. I want to let my light shine so that others might know that You are a real and loving God. I give You my life afresh today. Strengthen me to be what You want me to be. I ask this in Your son Jesus' name. Amen.

God's Wisdom for Daily Living ***Betty Miller***
February 24 ***Day 55***

Proverbs 9:10-12 10 The fear of the LORD is the beginning of wisdom: and the knowledge of the holy is understanding. 11 For by me thy days shall be multiplied, and the years of thy life shall be increased. 12 If thou be wise, thou shalt be wise for thyself: but if thou scornest, thou alone shalt bear it.

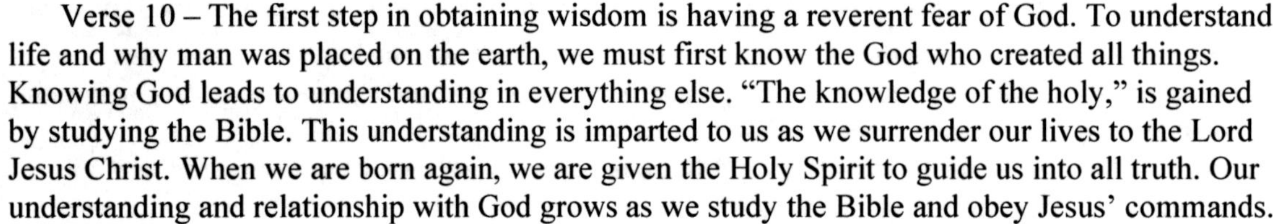

Verse 10 – The first step in obtaining wisdom is having a reverent fear of God. To understand life and why man was placed on the earth, we must first know the God who created all things. Knowing God leads to understanding in everything else. "The knowledge of the holy," is gained by studying the Bible. This understanding is imparted to us as we surrender our lives to the Lord Jesus Christ. When we are born again, we are given the Holy Spirit to guide us into all truth. Our understanding and relationship with God grows as we study the Bible and obey Jesus' commands.

Verse 11 – If we walk in God's wisdom by applying what the Bible teaches to our lives, we are promised certain blessings. One is that "our days shall be multiplied" and the years of our lives increased. The word *multiply* in Hebrew can mean "to enlarge.[14]" One might say that our days and years will be more profitable. It is amazing what we can do in a day by giving it to the Lord. We are able to accomplish things that would be impossible without His help and strength. When our priorities are focused on Him, our days and years bear much fruit for His Kingdom.

Many people look back on their lives with remorse, feeling they were wasted. They do not have anything to show for their contribution to the world, nor do they have many heavenly rewards to look forward to. If we wisely serve the Lord, we will not find ourselves in that state. At the end of our lives, when it is time to meet the Master, we can look forward to a greeting like that of Matthew 25:23: "Well done, good and faithful servant; thou hast been faithful over a few things, I will make thee ruler over many things: enter thou into the joy of thy Lord."

Verse 12 – Wisdom has its own reward. If we scorn it, we only hurt ourselves. God gave us free will. He will not force us to make the right choices. What we do with our lives is our own decision. If we ignore God and His wisdom, we will suffer the consequences and reap what we sow. However, on the positive side, if we yield to the will God and ask for His help to lead a righteous life that is full of wisdom, He will grant our request. As we follow and obey Him, He will bless us, fulfilling the promises He has given in the Bible.

Dearest Father, our greatest wealth is Your blessing. You give us so many things that the world does not have. As Your children, we are promised peace in the storm, provision when we have nothing, love for those who persecute us, joy in the face of grief, forgiveness for our sins and so many more promises. I am so grateful for Your blessings. I want to be a blessing to those around me. Help me remain strong in the faith for all things I am believing You for; especially remember our family members who have strayed away from You. Forgive them and draw them back to Your side with cords of love. Remember those whom I daily keep on my prayer list and meet their needs this day. Thank You for saving me and healing me. I ask this in the name of Jesus. Amen.

[14] Strong's Exhaustive Concordance of the Bible, Hebrew and Chaldee Dictionary

God's Wisdom for Daily Living — ***Betty Miller***
February 25 — ***Day 56***

Proverbs 9:13-18 13 A foolish woman is clamorous: she is simple, and knoweth nothing. 14 For she sitteth at the door of her house, on a seat in the high places of the city, 15 To call passengers who go right on their ways: 16 Whoso is simple, let him turn in hither: and as for him that wanteth understanding, she saith to him, 17 Stolen waters are sweet, and bread eaten in secret is pleasant. 18 But he knoweth not that the dead are there; and that her guests are in the depths of hell.

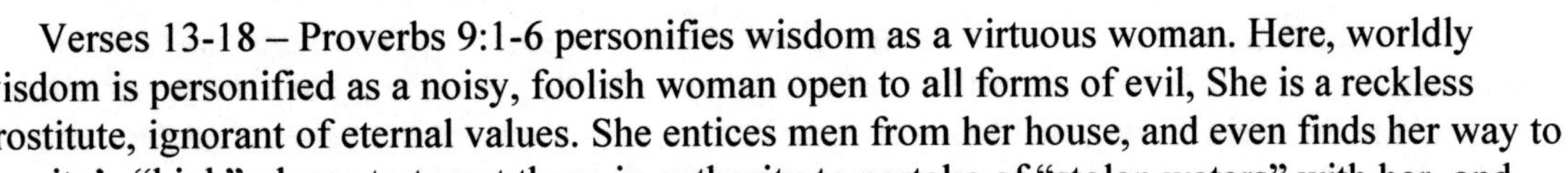

Verses 13-18 – Proverbs 9:1-6 personifies wisdom as a virtuous woman. Here, worldly wisdom is personified as a noisy, foolish woman open to all forms of evil, She is a reckless prostitute, ignorant of eternal values. She entices men from her house, and even finds her way to the city's "high" places to tempt those in authority to partake of "stolen waters" with her, and "bread eaten in secret." Those who lack understanding are easily persuaded to follow her. Unless they repent, they will end up in hell, along with the others who embraced this spiritual whore.

The deeds of wicked women are recorded in the Bible to teach us the consequences of sin. One of the most wicked was Jezebel, a relentless woman of strong will and intellect (1 Kings 16-21; 2 Kings 9). She was an ardent idolater, practiced witchcraft, and sought to convert Israel to Baal worship. She seems to have lacked all the nobler feminine qualities. She prostituted her gifts for evil and her talents became a curse. Persuasive, she misdirected her influence. Resolute, she used her strength to destroy a king and pollute a nation. Proud and merciless, she perpetrated many evil schemes, such as the murder of an innocent man to satisfy her husband's whim for the man's property. Her own life ended tragically, as she reaped what she had sown.

Jezebel was domineering and controlling. Like a puppet in the hands of his wife, spineless Ahab did not resist her schemes. Possibly, he was more luxury-loving and sensual than cruel, but being weak and passive, he acted against his conscience under the control of his wife, who mocked what scruples he had. Many women are prone to this "Jezebel spirit." They want to rule their husbands and are determined to have their own way. Men can act like "Jezebels" too, if they have a domineering attitude over their wives. True submission in marriage means that both husband and wife first submit to the Lord, then to one another in love.

Women who are in obedience to God, can have a godly influence on their husbands and change the whole atmosphere of their homes with love and prayer. It would be quite revealing to take inventory of how many men have come to know Jesus because of the faith of a woman. I'm sure that millions of men have been saved as a direct result of the prayers of a mother, a wife, or a fiancée. "Jezebels" can lead the men in their lives astray, but godly women can bring the men in their lives to Him.

Dear Father, thank You for Your love for me today. I am blessed with a wonderful godly husband and I am most grateful. Lord, I pray for those who are having problems in their marriages. Help them to yield their desires to You and seek first to please You. Give them grace to love with Your love. You love us even when we are unlovely. Help us all to love one another with the love of God. Give us the kind of love that allows us to forgive all past hurts and wounds. Your love is patient and kind; it endures all things. Give us the grace to stand up against all domineering and controlling spirits by speaking the truth in love. Lord, fill us with Your Spirit today so that we can overcome evil with good. I ask this in Your name. Amen.

February 26 — *Day 57*

Proverbs 10:1 The proverbs of Solomon. A wise son maketh a glad father: but a foolish son is the heaviness of his mother.

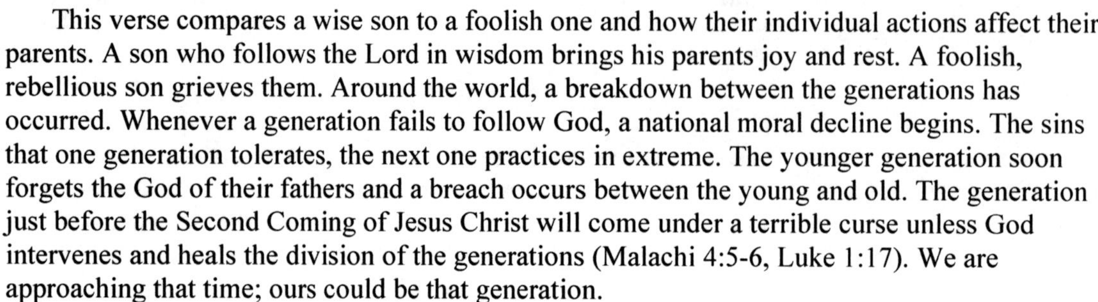

This verse compares a wise son to a foolish one and how their individual actions affect their parents. A son who follows the Lord in wisdom brings his parents joy and rest. A foolish, rebellious son grieves them. Around the world, a breakdown between the generations has occurred. Whenever a generation fails to follow God, a national moral decline begins. The sins that one generation tolerates, the next one practices in extreme. The younger generation soon forgets the God of their fathers and a breach occurs between the young and old. The generation just before the Second Coming of Jesus Christ will come under a terrible curse unless God intervenes and heals the division of the generations (Malachi 4:5-6, Luke 1:17). We are approaching that time; ours could be that generation.

Today Satan tries to destroy families through the sins of the fathers as well as the sins of the sons. Families will be mended only when both fathers and sons turn back to God. ("Fathers and sons" encompasses mothers and daughters as well; I believe it also includes "church fathers" and their "spiritual sons" since there has been much division in the church as well.) God desires both families and churches to walk in His love and unity. The curse of strife and division can be mended, if we seek the Lord and walk in His love and forgiveness. "And he shall go before him in the spirit and power of Elias, to turn the hearts of the fathers to the children, and the disobedient to the wisdom of the just; to make ready a people prepared for the Lord" (Luke 1:17).

According to Malachi 4:6 and Luke 1:17, healing must begin with the fathers. Being more mature, parents must reach out to rebellious children with forgiveness, prayer, and love. God will show us how to mend broken relationships as we seek Him. We who are parents must have patience and faith that the Lord will bring our natural and spiritual children back to Himself. God promises that our children will be delivered and blessed: "Though hand join in hand, the wicked shall not be unpunished: but the seed of the righteous shall be delivered" (Proverbs 11:21). "I have been young, and now am old; yet have I not seen the righteous forsaken, nor his seed begging bread. He is ever merciful, and lendeth; and his seed is blessed" (Psalm 37:25-26).

Dear heavenly Father, I thank You for Your love and care. Today I pray for families and churches that have suffered division and broken relationships. Forgive the selfishness of those who have refused to maintain fellowship and are in rebellion. Give both those who have been wounded by rebellious children, and those who have been mistreated by parents and elders, the grace to forgive. Heal those who are hurting because of church splits and bring reconciliation. Deliver those who have been taken captive by the enemy's lies. May Your love and truth prevail. Please show those contemplating divorce that You can bring healing and restoration to their marriages. Thank You for the miracles that will turn the hearts of the fathers to the children. In Jesus' name I pray. Amen.

Proverbs 10:2-3 2 Treasures of wickedness profit nothing: but righteousness delivereth from death. 3 The LORD will not suffer the soul of the righteous to famish: but he casteth away the substance of the wicked.

Verse 2 – The riches that belong to the wicked will not deliver them from death. At some point, every man comes to the end of himself, and realizes that money cannot buy the things that really matter. Riches follow no one to the grave, and there is only one way to escape the punishment of hell waiting on the other side–it is through Jesus Christ. He took our sins and punishment upon Himself on the cross. If we repent and accept Him as Savior, we will not face hell, but rather live with Him in heaven. God's original plan for man did not include death or hell. Hell was created for Satan and his evil angels (Matthew 25:41). Men are going there because they are deceived into following Satan's ways.

No man can attain the righteousness which delivers one from hell outside of receiving the righteousness of Christ. This is a sin-cursed world. We are all born into sin. We do not have to remain in sin, however. If we ask God to help us forsake our sins, He will. The only redemption for any of us is in Christ. We must ask Jesus into our hearts and allow Him to live His life through us; then we will have His righteousness and can live an overcoming life. When we accept Jesus as our Lord, death holds no fear for us, because He conquered death and hell by rising from the dead. As His children, we have been given victory over the devil and no longer have to live in fear, sickness, poverty, or any other curse.

Verse 3 – As God's righteous people, our souls need never be famished. If we come with a humble heart and ask Him to meet our needs, He promises to provide. He gives strength to the weary; courage to the fearful; healing to the sick; peace to the angry; comfort to the wounded; guidance to the troubled and the list goes on and on. The world knows nothing about the wondrous things God freely gives His children–things no amount of money can buy!

Many people lose their riches because they are not serving God, who "casts away the substance" of the wicked. Sometimes, through loss, people will turn to God. The Lord does not desire us to come to Him this way, but rather, simply to surrender to His will. When we do, worldly riches will mean nothing to us compared to the riches that we will find in Christ. "Again, the kingdom of heaven is like unto a merchant man seeking goodly pearls, who, when he had found one pearl of great price, went and sold all that he had, and bought it" (Matthew 13:45-46).

Dear heavenly Father, You truly are " the Pearl of Great Price. " I am so glad that I found You. There is nothing in this world that compares to Your beauty! Lord, even the times in my life that have been the most difficult, I have never doubted Your love for me, as You have always been there. I have not understood everything that has happened, but I really do not have to understand everything. I trust that You know what is best for me. As I yield to You, You will show me how to overcome all the troubling things that confront me. Show me how to overcome the attacks of the enemy. Thank You for delivering Your people. Bless and strengthen them. In the name of Jesus I pray. Amen

Proverbs 10:4-5: 4 He becometh poor that dealeth with a slack hand: but the hand of the diligent maketh rich. 5 He that gathereth in summer is a wise son: but he that sleepeth in harvest is a son that causeth shame.

Verse 4 – These verses deal with the practical matter of our work ethic. One will become poor if he deals with a "slack hand," that is, to be remiss about the things that we have charge over and "slack off." Many people have this type of approach to their work. They do the least amount of work that they can do without jeopardizing their jobs. These people will always have to accept lesser-paying jobs because they will never be promoted.

"Servants, be obedient to them that are your masters according to the flesh, with fear and trembling, in singleness of your heart, as unto Christ; not with eyeservice, as menpleasers; but as the servants of Christ, doing the will of God from the heart; with good will doing service, as to the Lord, and not to men: knowing that whatsoever good thing any man doeth, the same shall he receive of the Lord, whether he be bond or free. And, ye masters, do the same things unto them, forbearing threatening: knowing that your Master also is in heaven; neither is there respect of persons with him" (Ephesians 6:5-9).

In the scripture above, employees would be in the "servant" (performing services) position, while the boss would be in the "master" position. Paul gives instructions for both. Employers are accountable to God for their treatment of their employees. Employees are to submit to an employer's orders unless it requires immoral action. We must not work simply to please our employers, but more importantly, to please our Lord. If we have this attitude, God, who sees our labor and desire to please Him, will reward us. Sometimes employers are unfair and do not appreciate good workers enough to raise their salaries. If we feel that we are being mistreated, we must take our case to God. He will defend us and show us what to do. However, we must keep our hearts right and not speak ill of our employer to fellow-workers. We should pray for those in authority and allow the Holy Spirit to help us to deal with problems on the job in a godly way.

Verse 5 – Every farmer who has a son would desire him to be like the wise son in this verse. This son does not slack off in the summer, but works to help gather in the harvest. A lazy son who sleeps during this very critical time certainly brings shame to his family by failing to do his part. If his father does not have enough workers, his laziness could cause the loss of the harvest and bring poverty to the whole family. We can apply this spiritually also. Our heavenly Father asks His children to help Him bring in a harvest of souls for His kingdom. We have only a small window of time to get the job done for our Father. We must not slumber, but toil while we can, for a time is coming when we cannot labor (John 9:4). We do not want to be sons who bring their Father shame.

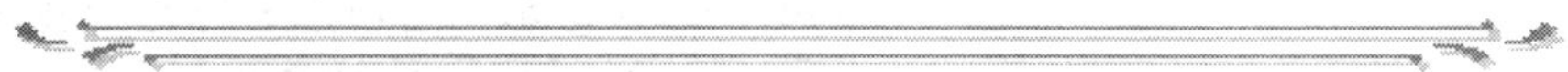

Dear Father, thank You that I am able to work. You know that I get weary at times, but each time I call on You for strength, I am able to complete my daily tasks. I pray for kindness to come to the work places of the world. Let there be righteousness in the market place. May we all work to please You and bring glory to Your name. Help us to also find our place in Your Kingdom, so that we might help to bring in the harvest of souls that need You. Let us pray, give our money to send others to the mission-field, or go ourselves. Empower all of us to do our part to see that people come to Christ. Let us work while it is day. I ask this in Your name. Amen.

Proverbs 10:6-11 6 Blessings are upon the head of the just: but violence covereth the mouth of the wicked. 7 The memory of the just is blessed: but the name of the wicked shall rot. 8 The wise in heart will receive commandments: but a prating fool shall fall. 9 He that walketh uprightly walketh surely: but he that perverteth his ways shall be known. 10 He that winketh with the eye causeth sorrow: but a prating fool shall fall. 11 The mouth of a righteous man is a well of life: but violence covereth the mouth of the wicked.

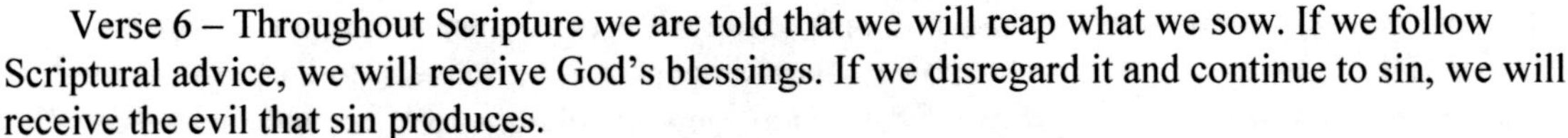

Verse 6 – Throughout Scripture we are told that we will reap what we sow. If we follow Scriptural advice, we will receive God's blessings. If we disregard it and continue to sin, we will receive the evil that sin produces.

Verse 7 – People remember what kind of things we do in life. History records the deeds of the wicked and the just, as does the Bible. This verse tells us that we will remember fondly the deeds of just people and bless them, while the names of wicked men leave a rotten memory. Even in families, honorable members are recalled with admiration, while shame attends the memory of the "black sheep." We should take inventory of our lives and ask ourselves what kind of legacy we are leaving behind us.

Verses 8-9 – Those who walk according to God's Word take sure steps, since they are led by God's Spirit. Fools fall because they do not walk uprightly; those who pervert their lives eventually will be found out. We are known by our deeds (Proverbs 20:11). Many Christians say the right things, but their lives reveal that they do not "walk the talk." Jesus describes them in Matthew 15:8: "This people draweth nigh unto me with their mouth, and honoureth me with their lips; but their heart is far from me."

Verses 10-11 – Winking is often a signal that one is teasing or flirting. As used in verse 10, it indicates insidious designs toward someone. This kind of winking is done with impure intentions. Crafty people are often successful in their schemes against the naïve. By contrast, the plans of fools usually fail and they themselves are ruined. A "prating fool" boasts idly, damaging both his own and others' lives. The word, "prating" means one who chatters foolishly and is an idle "blabber mouth." It is emotional violence to speak ugly things about others. Scripture warns us to guard our mouths and speak only what is edifying, for we reap the effects of our words. "A man's belly shall be satisfied with the fruit of his mouth; and with the increase of his lips shall he be filled. Death and life are in the power of the tongue: and they that love it shall eat the fruit thereof" (Proverbs 18:20-21). Let us speak what brings life, and not what brings curses and death.

Dear heavenly Father, I love You today and am grateful for all of Your goodness to me. Please forgive me when I have not spoken kindly of others. Help me to guard my mouth from speaking any kind of evil. May the words of my mouth and the meditations of my heart be acceptable in Your sight. I cancel all words that I have spoken that do not agree with the Word of God. I also cancel all evil words that have been spoken against me, my family, or ministry. Lord, please forgive those who would speak amiss against us. May Your people be careful to guard their tongues. Help us all to speak Your words and to be gracious and kind to one another. I ask this in the Holy name of Jesus. Amen.

God's Wisdom for Daily Living | ***Betty Miller***
March 2 | ***Day 61***

Proverbs 10:12-14   12 Hatred stirreth up strifes: but love covereth all sins. 13 In the lips of him that hath understanding wisdom is found: but a rod is for the back of him that is void of understanding. 14 Wise men lay up knowledge: but the mouth of the foolish is near destruction.

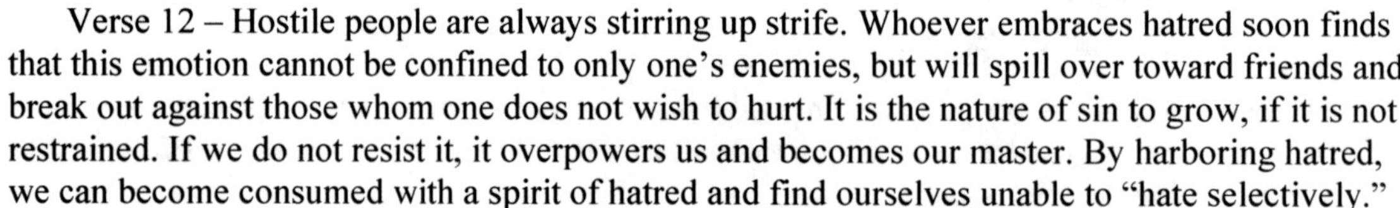

Verse 12 – Hostile people are always stirring up strife. Whoever embraces hatred soon finds that this emotion cannot be confined to only one's enemies, but will spill over toward friends and break out against those whom one does not wish to hurt. It is the nature of sin to grow, if it is not restrained. If we do not resist it, it overpowers us and becomes our master. By harboring hatred, we can become consumed with a spirit of hatred and find ourselves unable to "hate selectively."

Those who choose to love and forgive others will not be mastered by sin. We can conquer hateful thoughts by asking the Lord to enable us to love those who mistreat us. We cannot do this ourselves: only the Holy Spirit can empower us to overcome hatred. We can receive it as a miracle of love. As we grow in Him, we will not want to expose people's sins but rather cover them. Digging up and exposing the sins of others has always been a popular pastime of the ungodly. Gossip-mongers usually do this for political reasons. Many good people in the public eye are censured unmercifully for past mistakes. I do not refer to corrupt leaders who openly sin; they reap what they sow and their own sins "find them out."

Verse 13 – Those who lack understanding will feel the "rod of correction." In early times, wicked deeds were punished by public beatings. A rod is a stick or staff. Every sin carries a penalty. The greater the sin, the greater the penalty. Jesus died on the cross to pay the penalty for our sins. All of us deserve to be sentenced to hell, and without Christ's sacrifice, all of us would be. By repenting, asking for His forgiveness and inviting Him into our hearts, we can escape hell and gain a home in heaven.

Verse 14 – Hosea 4:6 says: "My people are destroyed for lack of knowledge." If we wish to be wise, we will store up knowledge. Many Christians foolishly speak evil and bring destruction into their lives because they do not know God's Word. We should not allow negative things, contrary to God's Word, to come out of our mouths.

Dear Father in heaven, I thank You today for my salvation. Thank You for delivering me from evil and filling me with Your love. Help me to witness to those around me about Your love. Give me the grace to always be kind, even when others are rude. Help me not to repeat the sins of others, but rather cover them with prayer, lest I am also tempted. Forgive our nation for its taste for gossip and its unsavory thirst for finding out evil about others. May we cover one another's sins in mercy and prayer, that we may rise to an honorable national life. Lord, You said You would deal with the wicked. We do not have to do it. You said vengeance was Yours; because You are just, You will see to it that we are eventually treated fairly, if we pray and trust You. Give us grace to do this. In Jesus' name I pray. Amen.

Proverbs 10:15-17 15 The rich man's wealth is his strong city: the destruction of the poor is their poverty. 16 The labour of the righteous tendeth to life: the fruit of the wicked to sin. 17 He is in the way of life that keepeth instruction: but he that refuseth reproof erreth.

Verse 15 – Some are born into wealth, others into poverty. Neither condition can prevent someone from serving God. Some think that a rich person cannot serve God because "money is the root of all evil." This is an inaccurate quote of 1 Timothy 6:10, which actually says that "...the *love* of money is the root of all evil..." (my emphasis).

Sin is not in things, but in the heart of man. Money is simply a medium of exchange. Used correctly, it can further God's work. The spirit of mammon and the love of money, however, ruin many people. 1Timothy 6:17-19 warns the wealthy not to trust in riches or become arrogant. While they may enjoy what money can buy, they are charged to use their wealth properly; to distribute riches to those in need and to the work of the Gospel. They are to store up eternal rewards–to obtain true riches, which cannot be bought. Jesus said, "If therefore ye have not been faithful in the unrighteous mammon, who will commit to your trust the true riches?" (Luke 16:11).

What are the "true riches?" The true riches are the righteousness, godliness, faith, love, patience and meekness mentioned in 1 Timothy 6:10-12.

Verse 16 – Because God's blessings always follow His obedient children, one can rise above one's lot in life even if born into poverty. Wherever the Gospel is preached, those who come to know Christ will begin to overcome poverty, filth, and ignorance. Poverty is not from God, but we can at times be subject to it. Even so, every Christian is promised the provision of his needs. The poor may ask God for daily bread; the rich, guidance in all the responsibilities that come with wealth. We can grow in Christ to the point where we can say with Paul "I have learned, in whatsoever state I am, therewith to be content. I know both how to be abased, and I know how to abound: every where and in all things I am instructed both to be full and to be hungry, both to abound and to suffer need. I can do all things through Christ which strengtheneth me" (Philippians 4:11-13).

Verse 17 – To walk in the way of life, we need God's instruction and must be reproved at times to avoid what leads to ruin and poverty. Some lose their riches and must work their way out of poverty. Those in this situation need to ask God why it happened; if making money had become more important than serving Him. We should all have a teachable spirit so that God can correct us and we can walk in victory.

Dear heavenly Father, You are very gracious to all of Your children. Thank You for the material blessings You have given us in the United States. Help us to be good stewards over these things and to use them wisely. Help us to be generous; giving to the people and the works You would like us to help. Help us not to get so busy enjoying our blessings that we forget the One who gave them to us. Deliver us from the spirit of mammon and the love of money. Lord, help me not to base my decisions on whether or not I have the money to do something, but rather on whether it is Your will for me to do it. I know if it is Your will for me to do something, You will supply the means, if I trust and obey You. Thank You for the faith to do Your will. I ask this in the name of Jesus Christ. Amen.

Proverbs 10:18-21 18 He that hideth hatred with lying lips, and he that uttereth a slander, is a fool. 19 In the multitude of words there wanteth not sin: but he that refraineth his lips is wise. 20 The tongue of the just is as choice silver: the heart of the wicked is little worth. 21 The lips of the righteous feed many: but fools die for want of wisdom.

These verses deal with the words that we speak. Notice the words listed in reference to speaking: lips, lying, utterances, words, and the tongue.

Verse 18 – Scripture refers to slanderers as foolish. Those who hide feelings of hatred, and then lie about it, are also fools. The things we "say" and the things we "pray" will either bless, or harm others. James 3:2-10 tells us how deadly the tongue can be. Unless we allow the Lord to help us control our mouths, we can be guilty of cursing others.

Verse 19 – Those who speak continuously will end up sinning, because they do not take time to ponder what they should say. Incessant speech is a way of monopolizing attention and a sign of selfishness. Incessant talkers usually have problems with unrestrained emotions. They speak out of the soulish realm instead of allowing the Spirit to guide what they say. If they are angry, everyone knows about it. If they do not feel well, they describe every symptom. If they have problems, they recount them in detail. These troubled souls need to ask the Lord to help them to take the advice found in Proverbs to be prudent; to guard what they say and restrain themselves from speaking so much.

Verse 20 – Those who ask the Lord to fill their mouths with wise, kind, and edifying things will be a blessing to all. Their speech will lift others up, and everyone around them will love to talk to them. Those who encourage others never lack friends. Words of truth spoken in love are valuable, like choice silver. By contrast, the wicked, who are out of harmony with God, will speak things from their corrupt hearts that are of little value.

Verse 21 – Righteous people, through spoken or written words, feed many people's souls. Praying for those who are angry, depressed, or gossipers releases the Holy Spirit to change them. Fools die for lack of understanding and heart. This is all the more reason to pray for them, so they will have a chance to repent and be touched by the Lord.

Dear Father, thank You for Your goodness to us. We are so grateful for Your patience. Help us to have the same grace toward those who trouble us. Help me to speak gracious and kind things about others. When Isaiah had a vision of Your holiness, he cried out, "Woe is me! I am undone; because I am a man of unclean lips, and I dwell in the midst of a people of unclean lips; for mine eyes have seen the King, the Lord of hosts." Forgive us all for the unclean things we have said that have not pleased You, and for hurting one another with unkind words. Please purify our hearts of the things that are unholy; for our lips have voiced the sin that resides there. Remove those things and cleanse us from all evil. I ask this in the name of our Lord Jesus Christ. Amen.

Proverbs 10:22-26 22 The blessing of the LORD, it maketh rich, and he addeth no sorrow with it. 23 It is as sport to a fool to do mischief: but a man of understanding hath wisdom. 24 The fear of the wicked, it shall come upon him: but the desire of the righteous shall be granted. 25 As the whirlwind passeth, so is the wicked no more: but the righteous is an everlasting foundation. 26 As vinegar to the teeth, and as smoke to the eyes, so is the sluggard to them that send him.

Verse 22 – God grants prosperity without sorrow to those who obey Him. Rich people who fail to share their wealth find sorrow attached to it, for they fear losing it. Fear has torment and is a form of sorrow. So is loneliness. The rich are surrounded by many people, but few friends. Their money attracts swindlers and those looking for a free ride. They often buy friends, and their wealth can replace God in their hearts. It then becomes a curse, robbing them of peace and joy.

Verse 23 – Some time ago, my husband and I visited a coastal city under hurricane warning. We stayed indoors and turned on the television. News reporters tracking the storm interviewed a crowd of people drinking and having a "hurricane party" on a nearby island. Everyone was warned to leave the island, since the hurricane was expected to strike there before hitting the mainland. One drunken young man made sport of the situation. Scoffing at the warnings, he boasted that he was not afraid of a windstorm. One reporter stayed on the island and filmed the terrifying effects of the hurricane as it hit the hotel. Large windows facing the ocean were suddenly blown in by fierce winds. The explosion of glass and water sent the partygoers and the reporter running to the basement for cover. In the last shots filmed, I noticed the young man who had dismissed the storm, running in terror. The thing he had scoffed at had become a reality that he could not control. He was the epitome of a self-confident fool. A worse predicament than that young man's awaits those who mock God. Eventually, they will face His wrath, and not the fury of a mere hurricane. God warns man to leave his sin before he is judged for it, just as the people were warned to leave the island before the hurricane struck. The wise will submit to God now.

Verses 24-26 – To walk in rebellion is to walk in Satan's territory and make ourselves easy targets. God is not punishing us when things go wrong; it is the result of our walking away from His protection. To step back under it, we must repent, but even then, fear may torment us. If we submit to God and resist the devil, then he must flee, and we can walk in God's grace (James 4:7-8). As a tornado destroys everything in its path, Satan destroys the wicked. The righteous, however, will stand through life's storms because Jesus Christ is their firm foundation (Romans 6:23). No one wants to send a sluggard (lazy person) to do a job. God does not choose such a person for His work either. If we desire to be used of God, we must learn how to work well for people. God commissions faithful people who do not shirk responsibility.

Dear Father, thank You for giving me such good advice in the Bible. Please give me the grace to heed it. Help me to do a good job at each task that is before me. I want the works of my hands to glorify You. Please keep Your hand of protection on me and my loved ones. I pray for all who read this devotional, that You will protect and guide them. Reveal Yourself to them in a deeper way. Heal and bless each of them this day. Give me the grace to overcome the things that are not pleasing to You. You are so good to me! I am thankful for the wonderful work that You are doing in my life and among Your people all over the world. In Jesus' name I pray. Amen.

March 6 *Day 65*

Proverbs 10:27-30 27 The fear of the LORD prolongeth days: but the years of the wicked shall be shortened. 28 The hope of the righteous shall be gladness: but the expectation of the wicked shall perish. 29 The way of the LORD is strength to the upright: but destruction shall be to the workers of iniquity. 30 The righteous shall never be removed: but the wicked shall not inhabit the earth.

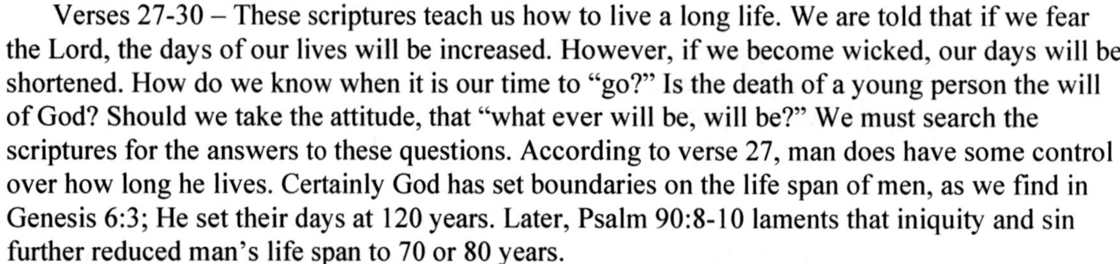

Verses 27-30 – These scriptures teach us how to live a long life. We are told that if we fear the Lord, the days of our lives will be increased. However, if we become wicked, our days will be shortened. How do we know when it is our time to "go?" Is the death of a young person the will of God? Should we take the attitude, that "what ever will be, will be?" We must search the scriptures for the answers to these questions. According to verse 27, man does have some control over how long he lives. Certainly God has set boundaries on the life span of men, as we find in Genesis 6:3; He set their days at 120 years. Later, Psalm 90:8-10 laments that iniquity and sin further reduced man's life span to 70 or 80 years.

When God created man, His plan was that we live forever. However, when Adam and Eve disobeyed God, it brought death not only to them, but to all people born after them. Though Adam sinned, God had a plan to redeem his offspring. He sent His Son Jesus Christ to live a sinless life, and through the sacrifice of His death on the cross for man's sins, we can receive eternal life as God intended. When we receive Him as our Savior, we are no longer subject to the death principle that works in the lives of others. We are now partakers of "abundant life" (John 10:10).

The first few generations of men lived very long lives. In fact, they lived to be hundreds of years old. Methuselah, the oldest man in the world, lived 969 years. Adam lived to be 930 years old (Genesis 5:3-4). Because these men were created and placed in a perfect world, it took some time for sin to increase to the point where God reduced their life span (Genesis 6).

Psalm 91:14-16, Ephesians 6:1-3, and Deuteronomy 30:17-20 all support the view that long life is our portion as a child of God. If the devil tries to come against us with sickness, we can call on God and He will save us and extend our life. The Bible tells of two men who never died physically: Enoch (Genesis 5:23-24) and Elijah (2 Kings 2:11). There is even the possibility of escaping death, if we live an obedient life and have the faith that they did. In fact, there *will* be a generation at the coming of the Lord who will not experience death, but will be changed at the twinkling of an eye and caught up with Christ. We may be that generation that will overcome the last enemy of death (1 Corinthians 15:51-55).

With all these verses in mind, we can see that sin cuts our lives short, while righteousness increases our days.

Dear heavenly Father, thank You for the many promises that You have given to us in the Bible. Thank You for watching over us and our children and grandchildren, and giving us all a long life. Lord, give me the grace to live my life in accordance with Your Word. Forgive me of my sins and keep me from temptation. Strengthen me to do things that please You. I want to be a blessing to others, so help me to be sensitive to those around me who might need my help and encouragement. Thank You for guiding me in the right way, and please give me the willingness to always do Your will. I ask this in the name of Jesus. Amen.

Proverbs 10:31-32 31 The mouth of the just bringeth forth wisdom: but the froward tongue shall be cut out. 32 The lips of the righteous know what is acceptable: but the mouth of the wicked speaketh frowardness.

Verses 31-32 –When I was young, children would often quote the saying: "Sticks and stones may break my bones, but words will never hurt me." After studying the Bible, I realize that this old adage is not true. Derogatory names and harsh words *are* harmful, both to the person addressed and the speaker. Words are powerful. Lawyers use powerful words to build cases. Our nation's laws consist of volumes of words. National treaties are formed by words. Words announce the daily news and enable us to communicate with each other. God used words to create the universe, speaking everything into existence (Genesis 1). The Bible is the Word of God. Jesus Himself is referred to as the living Word (John 1:1). Words are powerful!

God's Word has much to say about how we should speak. Biblically, praying for God's blessing or speaking good and uplifting words to someone is referred to as blessing. Speaking evil against someone or wishing ill toward them is referred to as cursing. "Curse words" or "cussing" originated from speaking evil words. Profanity is using God's Name in vain or speaking irreverently of Him. It ranges from mild expletives to horrible blasphemies. Society accepts foul language as normal. Popular films and television programs depict it as a way to vent anger or verbally assault others. Such use demonstrates that cursing is wrong because it demeans others. Jesus said that cursing points to evil in the heart. It is common today for both men and women to curse and never consider it as an indication of evil in their hearts. They view it as inconsequential, as something everyone does. Scripture teaches that this "little" matter of cursing and using God's Name in vain defiles the whole person.

Have you ever wondered why people do not use the names of gods of other religions when they curse? The names that the devil hates are "God" "Christ" "Jesus Christ" and "Jesus." Terms about hell and heaven are also used in derogatory ways. The very misuse of these words proves the existence of God and the reality of a heaven and hell. Neither adults nor children should use bad language, if we are to be like our Lord. We do not have to use curse words to emphasize our intentions (Colossians 3:8; Matthew 5:37).

Proverbs states that God accepts the words of the righteous, but the words of the wicked will one day be cut off, along with those who speak them. "Let the words of my mouth, and the meditation of my heart, be acceptable in thy sight, O LORD, my strength, and my redeemer" (Psalm 19:14).

Dear Father, thank You for all that You have done for me. Please forgive me for failing You. I want my words to be like Yours. You never speak unkindly. You are gentle and loving. Your Words are always the truth. We can depend on You and trust that what You say is the truth. You never lie. Lord, may my "word" be good. Help me not to give it lightly. When I tell someone that I will do something, remind me, if I fail to keep my word so I can make it right. In our society, it seems that so many, especially in the business world, are very careless about their words. Help me to be a witness for You as one who keeps my word even as You do. In the name of Jesus I pray. Amen.

Proverbs 11:1-3 1 A false balance is abomination to the LORD: but a just weight is his delight. 2 When pride cometh, then cometh shame: but with the lowly is wisdom. 3 The integrity of the upright shall guide them: but the perverseness of transgressors shall destroy them.

Verse 1 – In Biblical times, much of the trade was done by weighing items on a pair of scales. While the item to be purchased was placed on one of the trays, the other tray held a corresponding weight and when the scales were balanced the amount could be determined. Since the item was sold by quantity, and the price was determined by weight, a fair and equitable price was established. However, just as we have crooks today, there were traders who tampered with the weights causing the customer to pay for more than they actually were getting. The weights were unjust, which resulted in a false balance or standard. The Lord says that a false balance is an abomination to Him because it is cheating. Our God is a just God, so He loves justice and equity. He wants all of His children to be fair and just too, and never cheat each other in any way.

Cheating is a major problem in America. Students cheat on tests, and fail to gain the knowledge that their diplomas say they have. Citizens cheat when filing income taxes, leaving others with their share of the tax burden. Businessmen cheat by overcharging for an item, making its market price unstable. Many cheat by making contracts in their favor rather than contracts equitable for both parties. Adults cheat on their spouses by having affairs. Children cheat to win games. No one likes to be cheated, but just about everyone has cheated at some time or other and been cheated in some way. The only remedy is asking the Lord to forgive us and cleanse us of dishonesty. "If we say that we have no sin, we deceive ourselves, and the truth is not in us. If we confess our sins, he is faithful and just to forgive us our sins, and to cleanse us from all unrighteousness" (1 John 1:8-9). After we receive His forgiveness, we must ask anyone whom we have cheated or defrauded to forgive us and restore what we took wrongfully.

We must forgive those who have taken advantage of us. "For if ye forgive men their trespasses, your heavenly Father will also forgive you: but if ye forgive not men their trespasses, neither will your Father forgive your trespasses" (Matthew 6:14). We are told to pray for them (Matthew 5:44-45) and to overcome evil with good (Romans 12:19-21). By harboring unforgiveness in our hearts, we become bitter. This attitude will destroy us. We must learn to give our hurts to Jesus and ask Him to forgive those who wrong us. He is their judge, as He is ours, and He judges all people with equity. He alone can see what really happens in every situation and see the motives of our hearts. He is the final Judge of men's affairs. "...Shall not the Judge of all the earth do right?" (Genesis 18:25).

Verses 2-3 – If we take a humble position, we will gain wisdom. But if we remain proud and arrogant, it is to our shame. Integrity will guide us if we walk in it, but perversity (going one's own way) destroys us. Integrity lifts a person up.

Dear Father, thank You for the love and forgiveness that You show us daily. Help us to overcome any sin that the enemy tempts us to engage in. Thank You for forgiving us for the times we fail You. We also forgive those who have hurt us and sinned against us. May they come to repentance so that that they might know Your forgiving love. We all need Your love and mercy. Be merciful to our families and our friends. Watch over them and keep them from harm. Guide us daily in the right path so that we do not stray from the straight and narrow. In Jesus' name I pray. Amen.

Proverbs 11:4-6 4 Riches profit not in the day of wrath: but righteousness delivereth from death. 5 The righteousness of the perfect shall direct his way: but the wicked shall fall by his own wickedness. 6 The righteousness of the upright shall deliver them: but transgressors shall be taken in their own naughtiness.

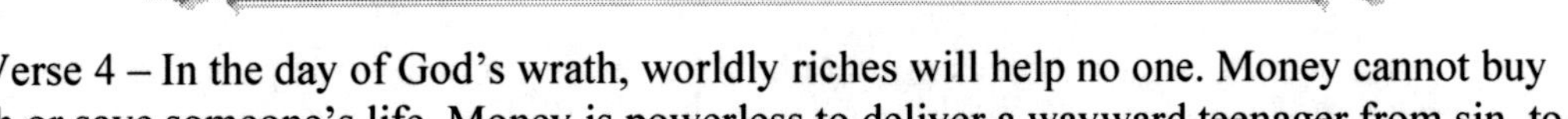

Verse 4 – In the day of God's wrath, worldly riches will help no one. Money cannot buy health or save someone's life. Money is powerless to deliver a wayward teenager from sin, to buy peace for our souls when fear surrounds us, to preserve a marriage, or keep a soul from hell. Only God can provide these things. The Bible says we are to seek the true riches of God, not the riches of this world.

God desires to bless us with material things, but we must seek God for Himself, not for what He can give us. Jesus said, "Therefore take no thought, saying, What shall we eat? or, What shall we drink? or, Wherewithal shall we be clothed? (For after all these things do the Gentiles seek:) for your heavenly Father knoweth that ye have need of all these things. But seek ye first the kingdom of God, and his righteousness; and all these things shall be added unto you" (Matthew 6:31-33).

We should be more concerned about having God's righteousness than material things. It is certainly right to ask the Lord for our daily needs since Jesus Himself prayed as a model for us "give us this day our daily bread" (Mathew 6:11). However, our focus should be on seeking His kingdom first. God knows that we need the things of this world because we live in it. He delights to bless us, even as we like to take care of our children and bless them. When we seek God first, He supplies our needs in beautiful ways.

Verses 5-6 – God directs the upright in Christ and delivers them, but the wicked reap what they sow. God does not bring evil upon us–we bring it upon ourselves through our own sin and waywardness. By moving out of God's will, we move into the enemy's territory and make ourselves vulnerable to the attacks of the devil. God sees the future. He knows better than we do what is best for us. In every situation we face, we must be willing to do whatever the Lord directs us to do. This is what it means to be totally committed to His will.

We are often tempted to cling to possessions for security, but the only safe place for us is in God's hands. Situations change. The things we cling to will be lost, if we refuse to give them to the Lord. Satan, the thief, can gain access to whatever does not belong to God, but he has no right to anything that we turn over to God. God is a good Father. If He asks us to let go of a thing, it is only because He wishes to give us something better and wants us to trust Him. His riches are valuable beyond anything the world contains.

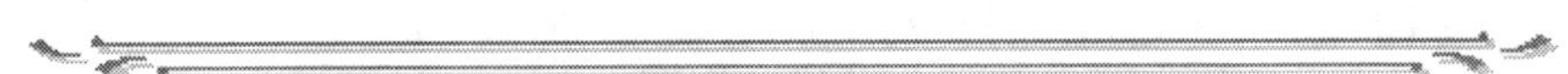

Dear heavenly Father, I am so thankful that You are my Father. You are so kind and patient with me. I want You to work in my life and set me free from all weakness and sin. Cleanse and deliver me from all that offends You. Give me a forgiving heart toward those who have hurt me. I want Your nature to be formed in me. I offer my life to You again today–to die to my own way and live to Yours. I know You have the plan that is best for me and that You will give me the grace and faith to walk in it. Fill me with Your love today and use my life to bring glory to You. I ask this in the name of Jesus. Amen.

Proverbs 11:7-9 7 When a wicked man dieth, his expectation shall perish: and the hope of unjust men perisheth. 8 The righteous is delivered out of trouble, and the wicked cometh in his stead. 9 An hypocrite with his mouth destroyeth his neighbour: but through knowledge shall the just be delivered.

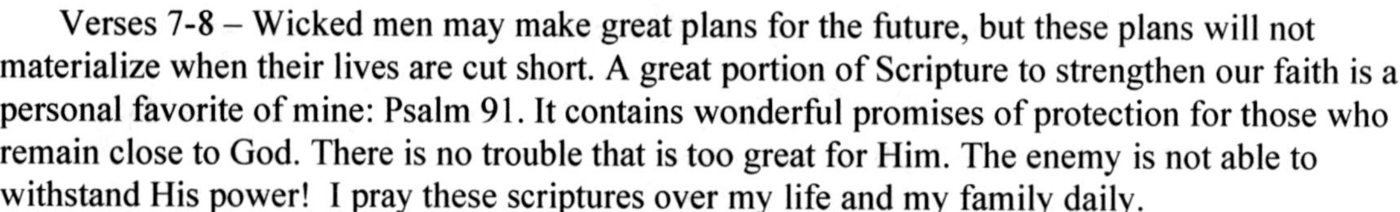

Verses 7-8 – Wicked men may make great plans for the future, but these plans will not materialize when their lives are cut short. A great portion of Scripture to strengthen our faith is a personal favorite of mine: Psalm 91. It contains wonderful promises of protection for those who remain close to God. There is no trouble that is too great for Him. The enemy is not able to withstand His power! I pray these scriptures over my life and my family daily.

Verse 9 – Gossips are hypocrites. They criticize others, yet they themselves are guilty of great evil, destroying a person's reputation by repeating things that may or may not be true. Even truthful things become distorted by repetition. When I was young, we used to play a game called "Gossip." Someone whispered something to the person seated next to them, who in turn told what they had heard to the next person and so on. The last person in the circle related what they had heard aloud. Everyone would laugh, since what was said was usually very different from what was originally whispered. This truly illustrates what happens when people gossip. Things become distorted and perverted, the more they are repeated.

People love gossip. They buy tabloids that print disgraceful things about well-known people. This is displeasing to God, Who tells us in Psalm 34:13-14, "Keep thy tongue from evil, and thy lips from speaking guile. Depart from evil, and do good; seek peace, and pursue it" and in 1 Peter 3:10-11, "For he that will love life, and see good days, let him refrain his tongue from evil, and his lips that they speak no guile: let him eschew evil, and do good; let him seek peace, and ensue it." Proverbs 15:1-4 says, "A soft answer turneth away wrath: but grievous words stir up anger. The tongue of the wise useth knowledge aright: but the mouth of fools poureth out foolishness. The eyes of the LORD are in every place, beholding the evil and the good. A wholesome tongue is a tree of life: but perverseness therein is a breach in the spirit."

The knowledge of the Lord can deliver us from every troublesome situation, even destructive gossip. We have an advantage over others because we are God's children, and can receive His instruction in harmful situations. By following His advice, we can overcome anything that the enemy would try to do to hurt us. We can walk in victory at all times, because the Holy Spirit lives within us.

Dear Father, thank You for this day. I find that many of my days are challenging because I must deal with certain unpleasant people. Help me to be gentle and not respond in the wrong way to those who say things that bother me. I need Your compassion. Help me to pray for them instead of criticizing them. Also, Lord, I find that I often try to justify my position, when it would be better if I simply let You defend me. Help me to guard my tongue. Use my words to be a blessing to others. Help me to overcome the temptation to speak evil about anyone. Especially help me to be kind to members of my family and those in the workplace so that we may live and work in peace and harmony. I ask this in the name of Jesus. Amen.

God's Wisdom for Daily Living *Betty Miller*
March 11 *Day 70*

Proverbs 11:10-11 10 When it goeth well with the righteous, the city rejoiceth: and when the wicked perish, there is shouting. 11 By the blessing of the upright the city is exalted: but it is overthrown by the mouth of the wicked.

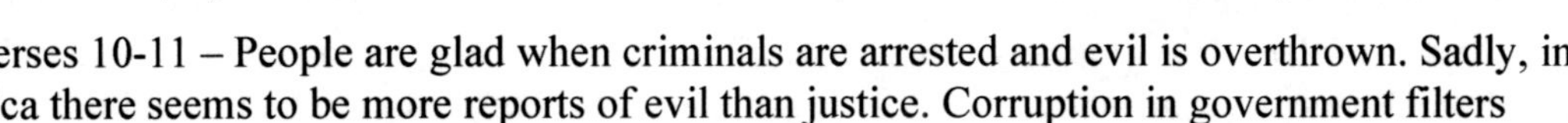

Verses 10-11 – People are glad when criminals are arrested and evil is overthrown. Sadly, in America there seems to be more reports of evil than justice. Corruption in government filters down to all levels of society. Truly, no man is an island; our individual actions affect those around us. Each of us influence the world for good or evil by our deeds.

In countries governed by democracy, citizens have a responsibility to elect qualified, morally-upright leaders to governmental posts. Satan wants to keep godly people from voting so that corrupt officials will be elected. If we do nothing, we aid the enemy in helping ungodly people become the leaders of our nations. Only Judgment Day will reveal how many opportunities to change things for the better were lost because of apathy.

1 Timothy 2:1-3 expresses God's concern for the leaders of governments: "I exhort therefore, that, first of all, supplications, prayers, intercessions, and giving of thanks, be made for all men; For kings, and for all that are in authority; that we may lead a quiet and peaceable life in all godliness and honesty." Since the Lord charges us to pray for our leaders, should we not assume that He expects us to use every opportunity to assist in electing candidates who are most likely to promote peace and righteousness? Jesus told the Jews of His day, "Render therefore unto Caesar the things which be Caesar's, and unto God the things which be God's" (Matthew 22:21). Caesar was the title of the Roman emperors. Jesus was telling them to pay taxes as well as to support God's work.

Good citizens do not leave the operation of government to ungodly men if they have the opportunity to change things. If we have been given the opportunity to vote, we should fulfill that responsibility as well as paying our taxes. We do not realize how great a privilege it is to have a voice in the selection of the leaders and the laws that govern our land. If we were to live for awhile under one of the dictatorships in the world, we might be more thankful for this privilege.

We are accountable to God for how we vote, and we should accept our civil duties along with our Christian ones. We need to spend time studying and praying about the issues in order to vote wisely for the best candidates and the right issues. One vote does make a difference. As Christians, our lives should make a difference in our circle of influence. Let us live righteously wherever we are, so that our nations will be changed. "Righteousness exalteth a nation: but sin is a reproach to any people" (Proverbs 14:34).

Dear heavenly Father, thank You for all the blessings that You have given us this day. Even when we face troubles, we know we can face them with Your guidance to solve them. Thank You for the promise that You are with us in everything. I love and appreciate You, Lord. You are very kind and merciful to us. Help me to live a righteous life before those whom You have allowed me to influence. May I never bring reproach upon You. Help me to change my little corner of the world for the better through Your power and help. I humbly ask this in Your Son Jesus' name. Amen.

Proverbs 11:12 He that is void of wisdom despiseth his neighbour: but a man of understanding holdeth his peace.

Proverbs is a great book for helping us to learn how to have good relationships with people. *Who is my neighbor?* We generally think of neighbors as those who live near us. The Bible's definition of "neighbor" certainly includes this, but also reaches farther to include all of those with whom our lives come into contact. If we turn to Luke 10:25-29, we will read how Jesus defined who is our neighbor, by sharing a parable. In this story, we hear about a traveler who was assaulted by thieves, and left nearly dead beside the road. A priest who was passing by saw the man, but went on the other side of the road so that he would not have to help him. Another religious man, a Levite, came by and did the same thing.

Finally, a Samaritan came along. Samaritans were outcasts. The Jews wanted nothing to do with them. Despite the hospitality between the Jews and his own people, the Samaritan man had compassion for the injured Jew, tended his wounds, and brought him to an inn to be cared for at his own expense. He had more compassion than the hypocrites who claimed to be followers of God. After relating this parable, Jesus asked the lawyer, "Which now of these three, thinkest thou, was neighbour unto him that fell among the thieves?" The lawyer replied, "He that showed mercy on him." Jesus then told him, "Go, and do thou likewise" (Luke 10:36-37).

Having established who our neighbor is, let us refer to the Ten Commandments for further instruction on how to properly relate to our neighbors: "Thou shalt not bear false witness against thy neighbour. Thou shalt not covet thy neighbour's house, thou shalt not covet thy neighbour's wife, nor his manservant, nor his maidservant, nor his ox, nor his ass, nor any thing that is thy neighbour's" (Exodus 20:16-17). If we respect someone, we do not lie about him or covet what is his. To do either is to despise him. We must not allow ourselves to covet those things that belong to others. God has a bounteous supply for all of His children. If we seek Him, He will bestow upon us our own special blessings.

Today's verse tells us that if we despise our neighbor, we lack wisdom. We should hold our peace if we have a misunderstanding with a neighbor. This simply means that if we should become angry with a neighbor, we must not despise him by saying negative things about him, but deal with him in love and try to work out any problems with him.

Dear heavenly Father, thank You for being so loving and kind to us. You are full of mercy and want so much to bless each of us who are called by Your name. Forgive us for the times we have failed to be the "Good Samaritan." We know that, at times, we all have "walked on the other side of the road" because we were selfish and simply did not want to get involved in helping others. Help me to use whatever talents and abilities I have to be a good and faithful servant at my job, at home, and in whatever situation I may find myself. Help me to treat others as I want to be treated. Lord, grant my physical body the energy and strength for the daily tasks before me. In Jesus' name I pray. Amen.

Proverbs 11:13-15 13 A talebearer revealeth secrets: but he that is of a faithful spirit concealeth the matter. 14 Where no counsel is, the people fall: but in the multitude of counsellors there is safety. 15 He that is surety for a stranger shall smart for it: and he that hateth suretiship is sure.

Verse 13 – Proverbs is packed with wonderful bite-size truths that are practical for everyday living. In these verses, we are given some gems of wisdom in avoiding relationship problems.

Those who cover others' sins and conceal questionable matters that would harm others have a faithful spirit. Those who blab everything they hear are gossips. Many years ago when I was young and had fully surrendered to the Lord, my eyes were opened to the fact that I was guilty of gossip. At that time, I was also in bondage to tobacco. To my surprise, rather than first freeing me from smoking, the Lord dealt with my gossip. I often reflected on this and wondered why He had not dealt with me about smoking first, since it was a more obvious sin. One day He quietly spoke to my heart that what had been coming out of my mouth had been more damaging to my Christian walk than my smoking. He was not excusing my smoking, because He did correct that too. However, He was showing me that what we speak is powerful for either destruction or good. Proverbs 18:21 says that death and life are in the power of the tongue.

Much of what we reap in life can be traced directly to things we have spoken. Normally, we talk about a matter before acting on it. If we allow the Holy Spirit to guide what we think and say, our lives will produce good fruit and bless others. It all begins with speaking and praying God's Word.

Verse 14 – The Word of God cautions us not to make major decisions without godly counsel. Having several counselors consider a situation and pool their experience is a safer approach to important situations. Of course, these should be godly and experienced counselors. They could be church elders, Christian businessmen, or grandparents, etc. Worldly counselors do not have access to the wisdom of God. Even their joint contributions can be wrong. Seeking God's guidance should always be first and foremost.

Verse 15 – We are instructed not to guarantee a loan for strangers. To be surety for someone means giving security for the repayment of a loan, or a pledge to pay the debt if the party fails to pay it. We are told that if we do this for a stranger or someone we do not know that well, we end up "smarting," or hurting for it. Those who have the audacity to ask someone they do not know to be surety for them, usually do not possess the character to repay the debt. It is better to hate this kind of dealing, so that we will not be stuck with someone else's debt. There are better ways to help strangers with legitimate needs.

Dear Father, thank You for delivering me from so many things! I am so grateful that I am free of those things that were destroying me. Help me to be patient with those around me who are struggling with sin. Remind me to pray for them; and not talk about them wrongly. Lord, I need Your counsel, as I have many decisions to make and I do not want to make the wrong ones. Help me to recognize and appreciate godly advice that comes from others. I humble myself, and ask that You lead me in Your ways. I pray for my brothers and sisters as well. May we submit to Your will in all things. I ask in Jesus' name. Amen.

Proverbs 11:16-20 16 A gracious and good woman wins honor [for her husband], and violent men win riches but a woman who hates righteousness is a throne of dishonor for him. 17 The merciful, kind, and generous man benefits himself [for his deeds return to bless him], but he who is cruel and callous [to the wants of others] brings on himself retribution. 18 The wicked man earns deceitful wages, but he who sows righteousness (moral and spiritual rectitude in every area and relation) shall have a sure reward [permanent and satisfying]. 19 He who is steadfast in righteousness (uprightness and right standing with God) attains to life, but he who pursues evil does it to his own death. 20 They who are willfully contrary in heart are extremely disgusting and shamefully vile in the eyes of the Lord, but such as are blameless and wholehearted in their ways are His delight! (AMP).

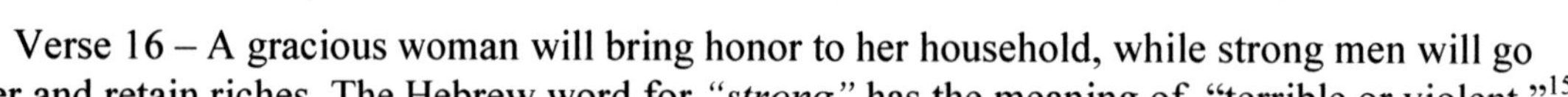

Verse 16 – A gracious woman will bring honor to her household, while strong men will go after and retain riches. The Hebrew word for *"strong"* has the meaning of "terrible or violent."[15] The wicked will go to any extreme both to obtain and hold on to wealth.

Verse 17 – A merciful man benefits himself as well as others; his deeds will return to bless him. The cruel bring trouble to themselves and their families. Those who are callous to others will bring retribution upon their own heads. We should remember the Golden Rule: "And as ye would that men should do to you, do ye also to them likewise" (Luke 6:31), or, do unto others as you would have them do unto you.

Verses 18-19 – The wicked person despises righteousness and thinks he is clever, but sin is deceitful. What looks valuable and pleasurable now will crumble. He will find he has pursued his own death. Those who sow righteousness, however, will have a sure reward. "Be not deceived; God is not mocked: for whatsoever a man soweth, that shall he also reap. For he that soweth to his flesh shall of the flesh reap corruption; but he that soweth to the Spirit shall of the Spirit reap life everlasting. And let us not be weary in well doing: for in due season we shall reap, if we faint not." (Galatians 6:7-9). "Sow to yourselves in righteousness, reap in mercy; break up your fallow ground: for it is time to seek the LORD, till he come and rain righteousness upon you" (Hosea 10:12). Verse 19 continues to admonish us that righteousness leads to life, while a life of evil will lead to death.

Verse 20 – The Lord loves His children very much. I believe one of God's primary reasons for creating man was so that He could fellowship with him. When we obey and fellowship with Him, it brings Him great delight. God loves it when we take time to talk to Him in prayer. He also delights in sharing His heart with us regarding the people and things He is concerned about. He desires to use us to bring change. May we all bring Him much delight!

Dear Father in heaven, thank You for the opportunity to serve You! Please grant us the strength daily to do Your will. Lord, we are weak, but You are strong! Enable us to serve You with all our hearts, minds and souls. Lord, keep us from evil and fill us with Your Holy Spirit. Thank You for empowering us to do all that You call us to do. Bless Your people everywhere. I ask this in Jesus' name. Amen.

[15] Strong's, s.v. "strong"

Proverbs 11:21-23 21 Though hand join in hand, the wicked shall not be unpunished: but the seed of the righteous shall be delivered. 22 As a jewel of gold in a swine's snout, so is a fair woman which is without discretion. 23 The desire of the righteous is only good: but the expectation of the wicked is wrath.

Verse 21 – The book of Proverbs is continually pointing out the contrast between good and evil. It points out how the results of each of these lives affects them personally and those around them. The first half of this verse tells us that even if two people are walking together and holding hands, if one is evil and the other righteous, the wicked will not be spared judgment, just because they are close to a righteous person. In a marriage where one of the partners is a Christian while the other is not, this verse reminds us that the Lord will judge each one separately, on their own merits. Many times, a wayward spouse or child will think that the prayers of their family members will be enough to prevent them from facing any judgment. While it is true that prayers said for the backsliders will certainly give them extra time to repent, each one who is wicked or unrepentant will have to face a day of reckoning.

Women or men who marry a mate who does not know the Lord are getting into a situation that they will regret, as the Scripture warns us not to become "unequally yoked." 2 Corinthians 6:14-16 says: "Be ye not unequally yoked together with unbelievers: for what fellowship hath righteousness with unrighteousness? and what communion hath light with darkness? And what concord hath Christ with Belial? or what part hath he that believeth with an infidel? And what agreement hath the temple of God with idols? for ye are the temple of the living God; as God hath said, I will dwell in them, and walk in them; and I will be their God, and they shall be my people."

These scriptures apply to other relationships too, such as close friends, business partners, etc. We should pray diligently before entering into any kind of partnership, and heed the advice of not becoming unequally yoked, if the other party does not know the Lord.

The last half of this verse is a wonderful promise for Christian parents for their children's welfare. If our seed (our children) stray from God's ways, we can pray. The prayers and confessions of parents can greatly affect their children's lives. We should always stand in faith for them and never speak evil of them, even if they fall into Satan's snares. The Lord will hear our prayers and deliver our children as this verse promises.

Verse 22 – Indiscretion is the lack of "taste, judgment, [or] reason." It results in failing to act and speak properly. Proverbs paints the humorous picture of a pig with a gold ring in its snout as the description of a lovely woman (a beautiful looking jewel); yet a pig (her behavior) is wearing it. Although a woman can be attractive, without the beauty of the inward life, she is like the unclean hog.

Verse 23 – The desire of the consistently righteous is only for good and brings good to them, but the evil expectations of the wicked bring them God's and man's wrath. The Lord promises that He will give those who follow Him the desire of their hearts. "Delight thyself also in the LORD; and he shall give thee the desires of thine heart. Commit thy way unto the LORD; trust also in him; and he shall bring it to pass" (Psalm 37:4-5).

Dear heavenly Father, thank You for being so good to us. When I count my blessings, they are many! Lord, as I daily seek You, may I always be willing to change those things that are not pleasing to You. I know if I surrender them to You, You will empower me to overcome the things that are not like You. Help all of us who are called by Your name so that we might reflect Your love to a world that needs You so much. Thank You for Your strength to carry out Your will daily. I thank You that You promised never to leave me, nor forsake me! I am not alone. I love You, Lord. In the name of Jesus I pray. Amen.

Quotes About Christian Character

Godly character is the greatest asset that anyone can have. It cannot be purchased. --Day 76

In God's Kingdom, the way up is down; the way to lead is to serve; the way to receive is to give; the way to gain is to give up; and the way to live is to die. --Day 86

Everything we say and do affects our character and relationships. God desires us to be faithful in little matters so we will be trustworthy in great ones. --Day 195

If we are in right standing with God, we will then be in right standing with men, as the Lord will always lead us to do the right thing in relation to others. --Day 209

Physical beauty is temporary, but the spiritual beauty of a good character will endure into eternity. --Day 365

Quotes About Making Judgments

The Lord will judge all men fairly, as He knows what really happened in every situation. He sees the motives of men's hearts, and is the final judge of all. --Day 188

We all must make judgments in life. Some Christians mistakenly believe that we should not judge others at all; but that is not what scripture teaches. Jesus did not say we should never judge, but rather, told us *how* to judge. --Day 258

Proverbs 11:24-26 24 There are those who (generously) scatter abroad, and yet increase more; there are those who withhold more than is fitting or what is justly due, but it tends only to want. 25 The liberal person shall be enriched, and he who waters shall himself be watered. 26 The people will curse him who holds back grain (when the public needs it); but a blessing (from God and man) is upon the head of him who sells it (AMP).

Verses 24-26 – The Bible tells us that the way to receive is to give. Many attain wealth by saving their money, but they may lose it, if they fail to apply another Biblical financial principle–giving. When we give to God's work, we sow seed which will produce a crop of blessing. "But this I say, He which soweth sparingly shall reap also sparingly; and he which soweth bountifully shall reap also bountifully. Every man according as he purposeth in his heart, so let him give; not grudgingly, or of necessity: for God loveth a cheerful giver. And God is able to make all grace abound toward you; that ye, always having all sufficiency in all things, may abound to every good work: (As it is written, He hath dispersed abroad; he hath given to the poor: his righteousness remaineth for ever. Now he that ministereth seed to the sower both minister bread for your food, and multiply your seed sown, and increase the fruits of your righteousness;) Being enriched in every thing to all bountifulness, which causeth through us thanksgiving to God" (2 Corinthians 9:6-11).

Isaiah 55:10-11 shows us the sure fact that God's Word always accomplishes what He desires it to accomplish. It also reveals that God commands the weather, causing the earth to produce seed in order for man to plant some of it and use some of it for food. The Lord gives us money for the same purpose that He gives farmers seed: to supply our needs ("bread to the eater") and to enable us to help others ("seed to the sower.") Sowing and reaping are important Biblical principles. Some Christians fail to give because of fear that they will not have enough for themselves. Others fail to give because of selfishness, wanting to spend their money on other things. They think it is wise to keep their money for themselves, but they are only following the world's wisdom. Satan is the god of this world; and unbelief, fear, and selfishness are his ways. God is love and He gives liberally to all men. As we walk in faith, we learn to trust God. Giving our tithes and offerings can be a sacrifice, but God is always faithful to provide for us when we trust and obey Him.

If we are truly walking in the spirit, we will always have the desire to give because it is the nature of God to give. Greed and stinginess are from Satan. If we are truly committed to God, giving will not be a burden, but rather a joy.

Dear Father in heaven, thank You for the blessings You have given to me. Help me to be sensitive to give at Your direction. Let me be a blessing to others, as You have blessed me. Thank You for all the help You have sent to this ministry. I am grateful for those who give of their finances. Please bless each of them, in the form of their need. Bless those who give in other ways, too. I am so grateful for the ones who take time to pray for us. Thank You for rewarding us in heaven for giving to Your work here on earth. Our greatest rewards will come when we get to meet those who were touched by Your Spirit because we reached out to them. I know that if we obey You in our giving that we shall never lack. Thank You for providing for all of Your children. In Jesus' name I pray. Amen.

Proverbs 11:27-28 27 He that diligently seeketh good procureth favour: but he that seeketh mischief, it shall come unto him. 28 He that trusteth in his riches shall fall: but the righteous shall flourish as a branch.

Verse 27 – The book of Proverbs continues to instruct us on how doing good brings blessings, while seeking mischief brings us trouble. If we listen to this advice, we will find favor with God and man. The New Testament lists having a good report from those "without" (those who are not Christians) as a requirement for the office of a bishop (an overseer). The Lord is calling men and women to be leaders in His kingdom; and to qualify we must be good witnesses to those who are in the world. "Moreover he (a bishop) must have a good report of them which are without; lest he fall into reproach and the snare of the devil." (1 Timothy 3:7).

Verse 28 – There is no security in this world except in God. God's people are promised that they will flourish in spite of what is going on around them, as they have the life of God in them. He will sustain them in any economy and circumstance. Many rich men are miserable because a crumbling economy has stripped them of the profits of many years of work. James 5:1-5 says that wicked men will lose the riches they heap up in the last days before the return of the Lord. If we have been depending on the things of the world for security, we need to turn to God and trust Him to care for us.

"And I will shake all nations, and the desire of all nations shall come: and I will fill this house with glory, saith the LORD of hosts. The silver is mine, and the gold is mine, saith the LORD of hosts. The glory of this latter house shall be greater than of the former, saith the LORD of hosts: and in this place will I give peace, saith the LORD of hosts" (Haggai 2:7-9).

The Lord will have a people who seek Him and His righteousness, and they will have His blessings (Psalm 112:1-3). Every Christian should be a priest and a minister, sharing the Gospel at home, the workplace, and every sphere of influence.

A day is coming when the wealth of the wicked will be given to the righteous (Proverbs 13:22), who will use it to take the Gospel to the whole world before the Lord's Second Coming. Please note that these people will not be seeking the blessings of God, but will be seeking the God of blessings! They will desire to be sanctified and made Christ-like in character, above all material blessings. Proverbs 11:28 says they will flourish like a branch and the prophecy of Isaiah 61:3-9 will be fulfilled in them. Godly character is the greatest asset that anyone can have. It cannot be purchased. May we all prepare for that day by asking Him to cleanse us and establish us in His righteousness.

Dear heavenly Father, what a wonderful time we live in...the days just before your second coming. Thank You that You have chosen me and my brothers and sisters for this great day. May we prepare our hearts before You so that we will not fail to accept the call that is on each of our lives. We are all called to serve You. Some presently have the high honor of raising their children in the nurture and admonition of the Lord, while others are businessmen who are ministering to their flocks (employees). We are all servants of the most High and it matters not what our vocation is, since our true vocation is to minister Your love and Word wherever we are. May we each be faithful so that You truly will be glorified. I ask this in the name of Jesus. Amen.

God's Wisdom for Daily Living — ***Betty Miller***
March 18 — ***Day 77***

Proverbs 11:29-31 29 He that troubleth his own house shall inherit the wind: and the fool shall be servant to the wise of heart. 30 The fruit of the righteous is a tree of life; and he that winneth souls is wise. 31 Behold, the righteous shall be recompensed in the earth: much more the wicked and the sinner.

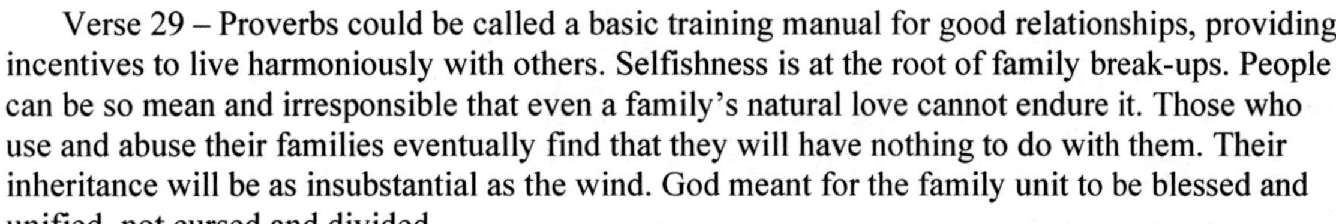

Verse 29 – Proverbs could be called a basic training manual for good relationships, providing incentives to live harmoniously with others. Selfishness is at the root of family break-ups. People can be so mean and irresponsible that even a family's natural love cannot endure it. Those who use and abuse their families eventually find that they will have nothing to do with them. Their inheritance will be as insubstantial as the wind. God meant for the family unit to be blessed and unified, not cursed and divided.

The last half of this verse tells us that those who are fools will end up serving those who are wise. In the Old Testament, the word for "fool" usually refers to one who is sinful, rebellious, and practices folly. The foolish are irresponsible and careless. Because of these traits, they are not able to obtain a good position in this life and they end up working in a servant capacity. This is not to say that servant jobs are inferior. Many successful businessmen and women took servant jobs so that they could go to college, which made it possible for them to obtain a better job. Others worked their way from the bottom of a company until they were promoted to the top. Hard work is something that a fool will avoid, since his aim is for immediate gratification. That is why he will never attain a better status but will have to be under someone else's supervision as a servant.

Verse 30 – As the fruit of the tree of life in the Garden of Eden gave eternal life, so the fruit of the Spirit in a Christian's life should lead others to eternal life in Christ. Each of us is an influence for good or evil–the choice is ours. If everyone claiming to be a Christian truly lived according to Christ's commands, we could quickly win the whole world for Christ. It breaks God's heart to see His children behave like unbelievers. His desire is that we be "fishers of men." If we are wise, we will make soul-winning a priority in our lives (Daniel 12:3). We can do this by praying for and witnessing to those who do not know Christ and by supporting ministries that do so.

Verse 31 – Because we reap what we sow, we do not have to wait until we get to heaven to receive rewards. By sowing righteousness, we shall have rewards in this life as well as in heaven. One of heaven's greatest rewards will be meeting those for whom we prayed or helped lead to Christ. Every soul whom we lead to Christ will be eternally grateful for our witness. This should inspire us to pray, witness, and give.

Dear heavenly Father, thank You for those who have prayed for me over the years. Although we do not know many of the people whom You have had to pray for us, we are thankful for those prayers, and we know that we will meet those people in heaven. Help us to be faithful to intercede for others who may be needing special prayer this very day. What a wonderful privilege to pray for others. Increase our prayer life, as this is the way you have designed to channel blessings to the earth. Prayer is an act of love, so may I love others today in this manner. Bless your faithful saints who have prayed and stood in faith to see their family members come home to You. I ask this in the blessed and holy name of Jesus. Amen

Proverbs 12:1-3 1 Whoso loveth instruction loveth knowledge: but he that hateth reproof is brutish. 2 A good man obtaineth favour of the LORD: but a man of wicked devices will he condemn. 3 A man shall not be established by wickedness: but the root of the righteous shall not be moved.

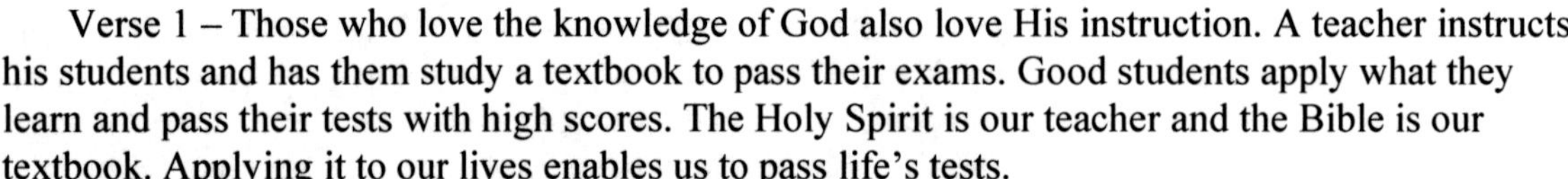

Verse 1 – Those who love the knowledge of God also love His instruction. A teacher instructs his students and has them study a textbook to pass their exams. Good students apply what they learn and pass their tests with high scores. The Holy Spirit is our teacher and the Bible is our textbook. Applying it to our lives enables us to pass life's tests.

With instruction also comes reproof. God corrects us as any good teacher does; bringing to light the mistakes made in the lesson and the misunderstandings that caused the error. Because good students desire to master their lessons, they value correction. We should be grateful that the Lord corrects us when we stray from His will. Hebrews tells us that He deals with us as a Father deals with a son (Hebrews 12:5-11). Disobeying Him and doing things our own way ends in suffering and heartache. The Lord loves His children very much. If we yield to His way when we do get into trouble, He will show us the way out of it.

Verse 2 – God does not send illness or tragedy to us to teach us; these come from Satan. Throughout the Gospels, we find that Jesus never called for illness or evil to come upon anyone. He always freed people from oppression and healed the sick. He refused no one who came to Him for healing. We suffer evil things because sin gives the devil the right to torment us. Jesus came to redeem us from sin and deliver us from the devil's oppression. When we accept Christ, we experience His favor in our lives. Only those who refuse to repent are condemned, because they refuse to come to Him for deliverance.

Verse 3 – No one can be established by wickedness. The wicked are unstable, "like the troubled sea, when it cannot rest, whose waters cast up mire and dirt. There is no peace, saith my God, to the wicked" (Isaiah 57:20-21). The righteous, however, are like a tree whose deep roots firmly anchor it in the earth and find underground water. Such a tree is neither moved by storms nor harmed by droughts (Jeremiah 17:7-8; Psalm 1:3).

Dearest heavenly Father, I am thankful for the love and favor You have given me. Thank You for the times You have corrected me, even though it was not pleasant. I know You love me enough to not allow the enemy to destroy me. Please continue to do Your work in my heart, as I want to become like You. Remove those things that offend You and forgive me when I fail You. I am grateful that I can call on Your mercy and grace when I am in trouble, and that You hear me and rescue me. Give me a love for prayer and the Word of God, so that my steps will not falter and I can walk in Your will. Fill me with Your love this day so that I may bless those around me. I ask in Jesus' name. Amen.

Proverbs 12:4 A virtuous woman is a crown to her husband: but she that maketh ashamed is as rottenness in his bones.

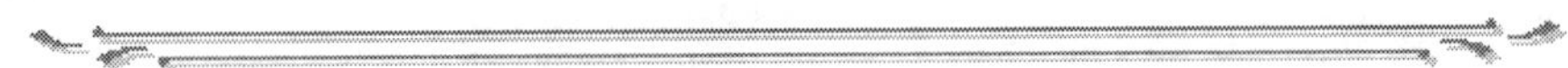

A wife of good character brings honor to her husband, while an ungodly woman brings him trouble. Because a man and woman become one in marriage, an ungodly woman undermines a man's well-being in the way a bone disease would undermine his health. The expression, "rottenness in his bones" simply means that he suffers with a lot of pain.

The creation account reveals that God made Adam from the dust of the ground.[16] He later put him in a deep sleep and removed a rib, from which He made Eve. Adam recognized Eve as being literally "bone of his bones and flesh of his flesh." Scripture uses the phrase "one flesh" for the first time to express the union of man and woman in marriage in Genesis 2:23-24: "And Adam said, This is now bone of my bones, and flesh of my flesh: she shall be called Woman, because she was taken out of Man. Therefore shall a man leave his father and his mother, and shall cleave unto his wife: and they shall be one flesh." Paul also uses the phrase "one flesh" in Ephesians 5:28-31 in speaking of a man and woman joined together in marriage: "So ought men to love their wives as their own bodies. He that loveth his wife loveth himself. For no man ever yet hated his own flesh; but nourisheth and cherisheth it, even as the Lord the church: for we are members of his body, of his flesh, and of his bones. For this cause shall a man leave his father and mother, and shall be joined unto his wife, and they two shall be one flesh."

If one partner acts dishonorably, it brings shame to both. If honor comes to one, both receive honor. If one suffers in illness, both suffer: one physically, one emotionally. Christian marriages should reflect God's love; the husband should lay down his life for his wife as Jesus laid down His life for the Church. The wife should honor her husband as the Church honors and respects Christ as her Head. The woman is the glory of the man (I Corinthians 11:7); she reflects her husband's qualities. When she is loved and cared for by her husband, it shows in her life.

Husbands or wives who say negative things about their mates hurt themselves, for they attack their own flesh. Many marriages have an unstable foundation because the couple selfishly looks for what their mate can give them, rather than for ways to give to their mate. Those who treat their partners as their personal servants or attempt to control and dominate them, disobey the command to love one's spouse. Spouses should build each other up by honoring and preferring each other. Those who sow selflessness, respect, and thoughtfulness in their marriages will reap blessings. There is no lack of love in a marriage in which the individuals serve each other.

Father, thank You for my wonderful mate. Help me to be the kind of person who will always bring honor to my mate and to You. Help me to guard my mouth and speak edifying things. Forgive me, as sometimes in my frustration with my problems, I air them in the wrong way. I know my mate kindly listens to me, but help me not to speak things that should just be taken to You in prayer. I pray for all marriages in the Body of Christ today and ask that You strengthen each of them. May we all be filled with Your love daily so that we can become the kind of mates we should be. Amen.

---

[16] The Amplified Bible makes this notation at Genesis 2:7: "The same essential chemical elements are found in man and animal life that are in the soil. This scientific fact was not known to man until recent times, but God was displaying it here."

Proverbs 12:5-7 5 The thoughts of the righteous are right: but the counsels of the wicked are deceit. 6 The words of the wicked are to lie in wait for blood: but the mouth of the upright shall deliver them. 7 The wicked are overthrown, and are not: but the house of the righteous shall stand.

Verse 5 – The book of Proverbs contrasts the thoughts and words of the righteous with those of the wicked. Looking at these verses carefully, we notice the progression of both sin and righteousness. Both of them first proceed from the heart. Next, they become thoughts in the mind, and finally are manifested in our actions. Sin begins in a man's heart; first, a man will have thoughts about the sin, then his mouth will speak of those sins, and finally he will actually commit those sins. The same is true of righteousness; it also proceeds from the heart, and forms righteous thoughts. As a man speaks of those thoughts, he will finally act upon them and bring them forth as righteous deeds.

Jesus confirms this in Mark 7:20-23: "And he said, That which cometh out of the man, that defileth the man. For from within, out of the heart of men, proceed evil thoughts, adulteries, fornications, murders, Thefts, covetousness, wickedness, deceit, lasciviousness, an evil eye, blasphemy, pride, foolishness: All these evil things come from within, and defile the man."

The Bible tells us that all people have the tendency to sin. How can we have a change of heart and be free from sin? We can be free only by being born again. We must confess our sins to God, acknowledge that Jesus Christ died in our place to pay the penalty for our sins, ask His forgiveness, and invite Him to come into our lives and give us new hearts. As we surrender our lives to God, the Holy Spirit breaks sin's power over us. "...So you also must consider yourselves dead to sin and alive to God in Christ Jesus. Let not sin therefore reign in your mortal bodies, to make you obey their passions. Do not yield your members to sin as instruments of wickedness, but yield yourselves to God as men who have been brought from death to life, and your members to God as instruments of righteousness" (Romans 6:9-13 RSV).

Verse 6 – Though the wicked plot murder, the righteous can prevent it through prayer. Speaking God's protection over a situation can destroy the plans of the wicked and establish the righteous. "No weapon that is formed against thee shall prosper; and every tongue that shall rise against thee in judgment thou shalt condemn. This is the heritage of the servants of the LORD..." (Isaiah 54:17a). Psalm 91 contains many promises of God's protection that we can pray aloud for others or ourselves.

Verse 7 – To walk in righteousness so that our "houses will stand," we must keep our minds on the things of God; guarding our hearts. As we saw above, sin is produced in the heart. Satan tries to enter through our "eye and ear gates." We must be careful of what we expose ourselves to on television, the Internet, and in books. Parents should monitor these, along with video games and music. It is not a sin to have an evil thought; it is sin to consider it and dwell upon it. We can resist evil thoughts with God's Word (James 4:6-7). For instance, if tempted to covet, we can resist it by remembering the commandments not to covet (Exodus 20:17) and to be content with what God has given us (Hebrews 13:5). We can also remember that the Lord desires to bless all His children: He will bless us in due time if we are not jealous of others.

Dear Father God, I am grateful for all the times that Your hand of protection has been over my family. Thank You! Help me to keep my thoughts on good things and take those things out of my heart that are not like You. Forgive me when I dwell upon wrong thoughts and fail to resist the devil immediately. I do want a clean heart and a pure mind. Help me to resist the evil that is in the world and keep my thoughts on edifying things. Lord, I pray for all the Christian parents who are raising their children in this crooked generation. Give them wisdom and love as they instruct their children in Your ways. Remove rebellion from the hearts of people whose thinking is perverted. Protect our children in the schools and on the streets. Have mercy on us and give us Your grace to be good examples to our children and young people we know. In Jesus' name I ask. Amen.

Quotes About Salvation and Healing

There is only one way for us to be in right standing with God–we must accept Jesus as our Savior. --Day 12

When we accept Jesus as our Lord, death holds no fear for us, because He conquered death and hell by rising from the dead. As His children, we have been given victory over the devil and need no longer walk in fear, sickness, poverty, or any other curse.
--Day 58

The Greek meaning of *salvation* includes deliverance from sin, sickness, danger, lack, and poverty. Jesus came to save us from our sin and its effects upon us both in this life as well as eternity.
--Day 111

When we belong to Christ, we do not have to be afraid when facing death. He who has conquered death is with us as we make the transition from this life to heaven. --Day 112

When we give our lives to the Lord, we take His name. We then have access to all that belongs to Jesus. We can ask anything in His Name and receive it. When we have this kind of relationship, we will not ask for the wrong things, but only for those things that are according to His will. --Day 159

God does not want us to keep our sicknesses any more than He wants us to keep our sin. If He paid for it on the cross, we do not have to bear it today. --Day 306

Proverbs 12:8-9 8 A man shall be commended according to his wisdom: but he that is of a perverse heart shall be despised. 9 He that is despised, and hath a servant, is better than he that honoureth himself, and lacketh bread.

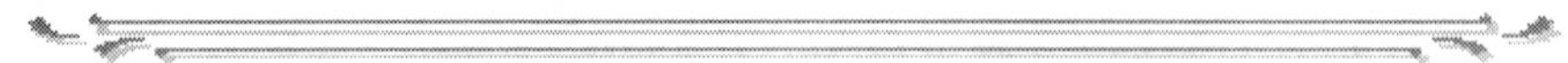

Verse 8 – The wise will be commended for their wisdom, while those who practice perverse deeds will be despised. Society at large praises the good deeds of people and condemns their evil deeds. Jesus Himself was known as One who went about doing good (Acts 10:38). As God's children, we also should be known for good deeds.

Verse 9 – One who works to support himself may not be highly esteemed by the world, but is better off than someone that considers himself important, and yet is too poor to buy food. Such a man is too proud to ask for help when he needs it. We all need the help of others at times. Even the wealthiest man must depend on other people. We came into the world as helpless babies, needing someone to care for us. God created us to need Him first of all, and then to need each other. Men need women, women need men, children need their parents and older people need younger ones to help and care for them as they age.

For many people, giving is easier than receiving. We should learn to do both, just as the Apostle Paul did. He supported himself and those with him (Acts 20:34) and later, while in prison, was supported by others (Philippians 2:25). We must learn not to be too proud to admit our needs and receive help, and also to be willing to help with the genuine needs of others.

We should not stop at just providing for our families; we should also help those on the outside. Giving to God's work spreads the good news of Jesus Christ to the world. When people's hearts are changed, they find permanent solutions to their problems. We can feed the poor, but they will remain poor unless they change their ways. There is a saying: "Give a man a fish and you feed him for a day. Teach a man to fish and you feed him for a lifetime."

When people are born again and obey God, He can lead them out of their bondage and poverty. "But this I say, He which soweth sparingly shall reap also sparingly; and he which soweth bountifully shall reap also bountifully. Every man according as he purposeth in his heart, so let him give; not grudgingly, or of necessity: for God loveth a cheerful giver. And God is able to make all grace abound toward you; that ye, always having all sufficiency in all things, may abound to every good work…" (2 Corinthians 9:6-9).

Dearest Father, thank You so much for all the good things You have done for me! Help me to always have a grateful heart, even when I do not see an immediate answer to my prayers. I know You will never leave me nor forsake me. Give me a servant's heart so that I might always be willing to serve others. Lord, help me to be humble enough to ask for help when I need it. May all Your children have generous hearts, that we might change the world for the better. Thank You for Your daily provision and use me to provide for others. Even if I do not have enough money to give to all to whom I would like to give, I know I can always give by praying or speaking an encouraging word to those around me. Help me to give of the things I possess. I ask in Jesus' name. Amen.

God's Wisdom for Daily Living *Betty Miller*
March 23 *Day 82*

Proverbs 12:10-11 10 A righteous man regardeth the life of his beast: but the tender mercies of the wicked are cruel. 11 He that tilleth his land shall be satisfied with bread: but he that followeth vain persons is void of understanding.

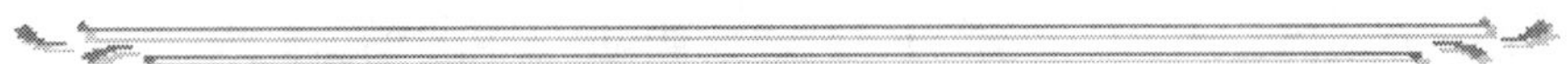

Verse 10 – A righteous man cares for his animals, unlike the wicked who is cruel even when he thinks he is being kind. Does God care how we treat animals? Does He respond to the fearful mewing of a motherless kitten or the exhaustion of a donkey staggering under a far too heavy load? Does He care about animals bred in cramped quarters and exploited for profit? Does He care that cocks and dogs are encouraged to fight to the death for a bet; or that bulls are repeatedly stabbed, and then killed for applause in the studied pageantry of man against beast? Yes, He cares, and so should we. In Genesis, He commanded Noah to make an ark big enough to hold two of every kind of creature so that they would not be made extinct by the flood. He made animals for man's enjoyment and never intended the abuse that we see today of these wonderful creatures.

The Bible actually has much to say regarding animal abuse. In the beginning, God put the earth and its wonderful creatures under human authority, entrusting them to man's care (Genesis 1:26). Our sinful nature, however, causes us to abuse them, sometimes unknowingly. God expects Christians, above all others, to care for creation. Exploiting or abusing any part of it shows disrespect for God Himself and it does not reflect His character, but the evil one's. Several Old Testament laws instructed the Israelites in the care of animals. The Sabbath day was designed to give man and his animals rest (Exodus 20:10). The Israelites were instructed to help their friends and enemies get their oxen or donkeys back up on their feet if they fell down in the road, or beneath burdens too heavy for them (Exodus 23:5; Deuteronomy 22:4). Animals were also to be allowed to eat as they worked (Deuteronomy 25:4). Finally, God says to us in Proverbs 27:23 (NIV), "Be sure you know the condition of your flocks, give careful attention to your herds."

Verse 11 – This verse tells us that if a man works and takes care of his land, it will provide him with food. Men not only abuse animals but also abuse the earth through overuse. The Israelites were instructed to keep a Sabbath year of rest for the land. It was to lie fallow so that the poor and wild animals could eat from it (Exodus 23:11; Leviticus 25:7). The earth is a gift from God to man and we are to manage it properly. If abused, it produces inferior crops. If a man takes care of his land, it produces a harvest providing the bread that he needs. Whoever follows useless pursuits and neglects his land or responsibilities lacks an understanding of the principle of stewardship. Christians should lead the way in ecology that is Bible-based.

Dear Father, thank You for the beautiful creation of the animal world. I am personally thankful for the wonderful pets and animals I have had throughout my life. They have been a great joy to me. I pray for their safety and health. I also pray that men will care for the animals in this world properly. Change the hearts of men that are guilty of exploiting animals all over the world. Bless the creatures of the sea, the birds of the air, the domestic and wild animals. It will be a blessing when Your kingdom arrives in this earth, and the they will no longer fear man and the lamb and the lion will lie down together. In the meantime, help us all to do our part in caring for Your magnificent creation; the animals and plants, the sea and the land. In Jesus' name I pray. Amen.

Proverbs 12:12-15 12 The wicked desireth the net of evil men: but the root of the righteous yieldeth fruit. 13 The wicked is snared by the transgression of his lips: but the just shall come out of trouble. 14 A man shall be satisfied with good by the fruit of his mouth: and the recompense of a man's hands shall be rendered unto him. 15 The way of a fool is right in his own eyes: but he that hearkeneth unto counsel is wise.

These verses tell us that the righteous are delivered from trouble, while the wicked are snared by their own transgressions.

Verse 12 – Wicked men desire the things that evil men catch in their net. The righteous are different; their lives produce fruit that benefits others because they are rooted and grounded in God's love (Ephesians 3:16-19).

Verses 13-14 – Most people do not realize that the things they speak, whether positive or negative, will affect their lives. We all know people who are habitual complainers, always confessing a scenario of bad things that could happen. Many of these bad things do happen to them, because they are not walking in faith. On the other hand, those who voice a positive confession of faith in the face of their troubles are an inspiration to others and many are granted miracles to overcome the obstacles in their lives.

A Biblical confession is not to be confused with the "positive confession" taught by success propagators. Positive confessions are aimed at promoting self, not the kingdom of God. They usually claim worldly wealth and personal success. Success propagators' confessions are based on selfishness and the misuse of Scripture, rather than on truth.

Confessing God's Word will empower us to do His will. We must be careful to claim scriptural promises not only for what we desire, but for what the Lord desires for us. God desires to bless us, but desires even more to cleanse us. He is more interested in our eternal character than our temporary comfort. We must be as faithful to claim God's promises for cleansing from what offends Him, as for healing or material blessings.

Verse 15 – The wise seek the counsel of God's Word. We must learn not to merely give our own opinions about things, but to speak what God's Word says. We easily quote what men have to say on a subject, often believing their words, even if they contradict the Bible. We may hesitate to quote what God says because the devil persuades us that to do so in our circumstances would be lying. Satan wants us to look at our circumstances rather than God's Word. Circumstances, however, are subject to change, and one of the things that cause them to change is confessing God's Word over them (Romans 4:17).

Dear Father in heaven, I am grateful for Your constant provision. You have never failed me and I know that You never will. You are a faithful God and I ask You to help me to trust You before my answer arrives. Lord, You are my source, and I know as I continue to look to You, I never need worry about how You will provide. I just know that You will. Guard my mouth and remind me to speak what Your Word says about my situation. Deliver me from every vestige of fear, and fill me with Your Holy Spirit so that I will always walk in faith. Lord, I also pray that all my brothers and sisters in the family of God will also be granted this favor. May we each fulfill Your will in our lives. In Jesus' name I pray. Amen.

God's Wisdom for Daily Living **_Betty Miller_**
March 25 **_Day 84_**

Proverbs 12:16-19 16 A fool's wrath is presently known: but a prudent man covereth shame. 17 He that speaketh truth showeth forth righteousness: but a false witness deceit. 18 There is that speaketh like the piercings of a sword: but the tongue of the wise is health. 19 The lip of truth shall be established for ever: but a lying tongue is but for a moment.

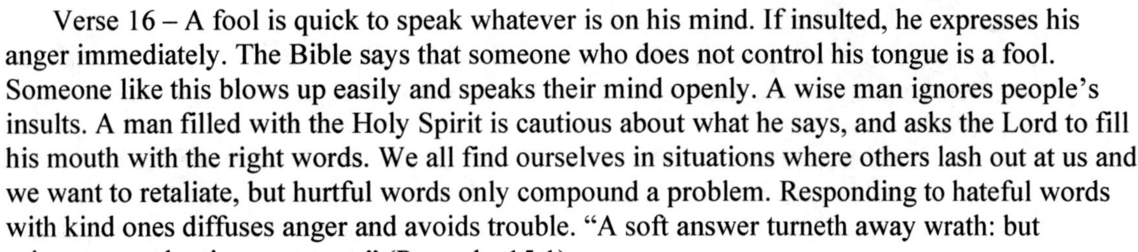

Verse 16 – A fool is quick to speak whatever is on his mind. If insulted, he expresses his anger immediately. The Bible says that someone who does not control his tongue is a fool. Someone like this blows up easily and speaks their mind openly. A wise man ignores people's insults. A man filled with the Holy Spirit is cautious about what he says, and asks the Lord to fill his mouth with the right words. We all find ourselves in situations where others lash out at us and we want to retaliate, but hurtful words only compound a problem. Responding to hateful words with kind ones diffuses anger and avoids trouble. "A soft answer turneth away wrath: but grievous words stir up anger…" (Proverbs 15:1).

Being angry is not a sin. God Himself is angered by injustice, murder, and every other kind of wickedness. God hates sin because it destroys the people He created. We *should* be angry at the evil we see in the world. However, we must not hate wicked people, but rather their deeds and the source of evil. Satan and his demons, not people, are the real enemies. We must love sinners and pray that they will come to the knowledge of Christ and abandon their evil ways.

We are to confess our unrighteous anger to the Lord, and ask Him to deal with unjust situations, as He helps us to walk in righteousness and speak truth. God tells us to "Be ye angry, and sin not: let not the sun go down upon your wrath: Neither give place to the devil" (Ephesians 4:26-27). Many psychologists advise people to vent their anger by throwing something or shouting in a closed room. While this might temporarily help to relieve pressure, without the Lord, it will never get to the root of the problem. We must forgive those with whom we are angry and cry out to the Lord that His love and grace will prevail in the matter. Sometimes the Lord will lead us in an emotional release by crying, wailing, or even shouting in prayer at times. We must trust God to make things right for us, as we resist yielding to anger, resentment, or bitterness.

Verses 17-18 – We can bring wounding or healing with our mouths. How destructive and hurtful words can be! Proud or thoughtless words can pierce and wound the soul as deeply as a sword can pierce and wound the body. But those with godly wisdom release God's healing to inner wounds through their words of blessing.

Verse 19 – What we say will be established if we are honest and speak the truth in love. Liars may deceive others for a time, but eventually one's sin finds one out. Numbers 32:23b says, "…And be sure your sin will find you out." In the end, truth will triumph, for it is stronger than any lie.

Dear heavenly Father, I am grateful for Your love and mercy in my life. I thank You that You were patient with me when I failed and lost my temper in times past. I am grateful that I have now been delivered from resentment and an unrestrained temper. May I be gracious to those who are still having problems in this area. Lord, deliver all Your people from lying and anger so that we may truly love others. Give us Your love for one another so that the world will see us walking hand in hand. May they know and believe that You are real. I ask in the name of Jesus. Amen.

God's Wisdom for Daily Living — ***Betty Miller***
March 26 — ***Day 85***

Proverbs 12:20-22 20 Deceit is in the heart of them that imagine evil: but to the counsellors of peace is joy. 21 There shall no evil happen to the just: but the wicked shall be filled with mischief. 22 Lying lips are abomination to the LORD: but they that deal truly are his delight.

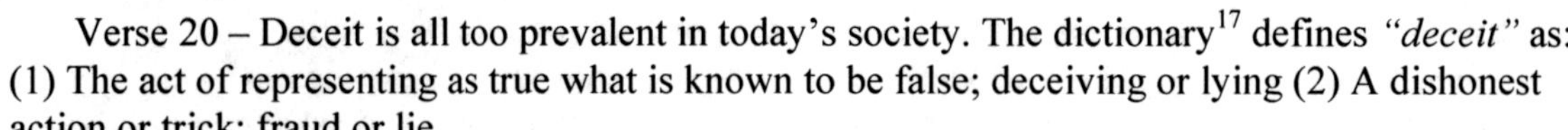

Verse 20 – Deceit is all too prevalent in today's society. The dictionary[17] defines *"deceit"* as: (1) The act of representing as true what is known to be false; deceiving or lying (2) A dishonest action or trick; fraud or lie.

Those who practice deceit have evil imaginations. Greed motivates them to seek personal gain at another's expense; and fraudulent schemes abound today. Covetousness (desiring what belongs to another) is idolatry (Colossians 3:5). Swindlers avoid honest work and take advantage of others' weaknesses. Seeking to make money without working for it is unrighteous (2 Thessalonians 3:10). Our character is built through honest work. Anyone claiming to be a Christian while swindling others brings disrepute to the church. In fact, we are told not to even fellowship with brothers and sisters in the Lord who are dishonest, immoral and greedy. "But now I have written unto you not to keep company, if any man that is called a brother be a fornicator, or covetous, or an idolator, or a railer, or a drunkard, or an extortioner; with such an one no not to eat" (1 Corinthians 5:11).

Promoters of peace will have joy. Jesus said, "Blessed are the peacemakers: for they shall be called the children of God" (Matthew 5:9). We are blessed when we pursue peace and counsel others to walk in peace. We promote peace between God and man by sharing the Gospel. There is great joy in bringing others to Christ and helping them live godly lives.

Verse 21 – Ultimately no evil, misfortune, or calamity shall overcome the righteous, whereas the wicked will be filled with these things. Looking at this verse we may not believe it, because we or other Christians we know, have gone through many kinds of evil, misfortune and calamity. However, in this world, we may suffer some of the things that people who do not know the Lord suffer; but the difference is that we go *through* them and are not destroyed by them. Our eternal state in Christ causes us to overcome all evil that the devil may try to bring our way. "These things I have spoken unto you, that in me ye might have peace. In the world ye shall have tribulation: but be of good cheer; I have overcome the world" (John 16:33).

Our life in Christ enables us to overcome all the evil and suffering that Satan may try to bring our way. We are more than conquerors through our Lord Jesus Christ (Romans 8:37-39; Isaiah 54:17a). For those without faith, suffering has no benefit. The fate of the wicked is ruin, which their own wicked deeds bring upon them.

Verse 22 – The fate of the wicked is different, as their own wicked deeds bring them down. They are ultimately destroyed–either in this life on earth or the life to come in hell. They are filled with mischief and deceit. Their lying lips are extremely disgusting and hateful to the Lord, but He delights in those who speak and act honestly. God cannot lie and hates lying. Lying is on the list of seven things that God hates in Proverbs 6:17. We must guard ourselves against it.

Dear Father God, thank You for Your love. You have been very patient and merciful to me, and I

[17] Webster's New World Dictionary of the American Language, Second college edition

need to extend that same love and mercy towards others. I ask You to remove all deceit from my heart and cleanse me so that I might have a pure heart before You. Deliver this nation from deceit and lying. Help us to keep our word, and restore truth to our land. We desire truth to abide in our homes, businesses and governments. I also ask that You give me an overcoming spirit so that I will not walk in fear. Help me to trust You, even when circumstances would cause me to doubt at times. Please deliver me from doubt and unbelief in every area of my life. I ask in Jesus' name. Amen.

Quotes About Wisdom

Wisdom is having insight into the true nature of things. It is being able to discern the mode of action that produces sensible results. --Day 1

By the wisdom that God gives, we know what to do and how to do it. It enables us to avoid what results in destruction and to engage in what produces life and blessing. --Day 1

We must not be prideful if we desire to receive knowledge from God. He gives instruction to the teachable; to those who depend on Him, and not their own human reasoning. --Day 2

Anyone who seeks wisdom must seek her diligently, like a man seeking the attention of the woman he loves. --Day 29

A wise man is teachable. He learns from his mistakes because he does not allow pride to keep him from receiving correction. Like a pilot flying in fog, he is happy to receive a "course correction" and will love those who help him see the truth and avoid a problem. --Day 54

The Bible tells us that we should *prove* all things, not *believe* all things. --Day 105

True wisdom, like all the great things of God, is something that any of us can attain if we are willing to humble ourselves. --Day 148

Proverbs 12:23-24 23 A prudent man concealeth knowledge: but the heart of fools proclaimeth foolishness. 24 The hand of the diligent shall bear rule: but the slothful shall be under tribute.

Verse 23 – Prudent people are reluctant to display their knowledge. Men of character display a humble spirit, but a self-confident fool brags about what he knows and does.

Verse 24 – A diligent person will rise to a place of authority over others, but a lazy person will be forced to labor under someone else. Diligence is a required quality in those desiring to enter ministry. Another requirement for leadership is a servant's heart, for the Lord calls leaders to serve Him by serving others. In God's Kingdom, the way up is down; the way to lead is to serve; the way to receive is to give; the way to gain is to give up; and the way to live is to die.

Many Christians never attain victory in Christ because they fail to embrace the message of the cross: "Then said Jesus unto his disciples, If any man will come after me, let him deny himself, and take up his cross, and follow me. For whosoever will save his life shall lose it: and whosoever will lose his life for my sake shall find it" (Matthew 16:24-25). (See also Mark 10:43-45 and Luke 14:27.). Too often, the emphasis from American pulpits has been on what God can do for us. Some think God is supposed to serve them, as though He is some sort of bell boy. Their prayers amount to telling God what He should do for them. God desires to bless us, but blessings follow our making a total commitment to Him. There are two things the church must do to be victorious: we must embrace God's Lordship and die to our ways; and we must exercise our authority in Christ over the kingdom of darkness. We must submit to God, by putting our old nature to death, and then we must resist the devil, who will then flee from us. "Submit yourselves therefore to God. Resist the devil, and he will flee from you. Draw nigh to God, and he will draw nigh to you. Cleanse your hands, ye sinners; and purify your hearts, ye double minded. (James 4:7-8). We cannot have victory over sin and sickness unless we practice both of these things.

There is a great deal of teaching on ruling and reigning with Christ, and rightly so. We are approaching the millennial reign of Christ. We, His saints, will reign with Him, and must therefore embrace a Kingdom mentality. However, there are prerequisites for reigning with Christ: complete surrender to Him and total obedience to the laws of His Kingdom. If we cannot rule over sin in our individual lives, how shall we reign over nations in His Kingdom? Jesus was first the *Lamb of God* before He demonstrated His role as the *Lion of Judah*. He came first as a sacrificial "Lamb" but He is coming again as a "Lion" who will rule with a rod of iron and judge every person on earth. If we do not take up our crosses as our King and Master did, we will be unfit to reign with Him when He returns. If we yield to the Lord now, we shall reign with Him in the future. Praise the Lord!

Dear heavenly Father, I come to You with a thankful heart for all that You have done for me. I really cannot thank You enough. I do want to continue to be one of Your faithful servants. I rely on You to fill me with Your love and strength every day in order to obey and serve You. Help me to share Your love with all those to whom You allow me to be a witness. Lord, help me to overcome the sin and weaknesses that hinder Your work in my life. I do ask for the grace to die to my ways and live unto Yours. Help me to be diligent in all the things You have commissioned me to do. May I reflect Your glory and love to all who know me. I ask in Jesus' name. Amen.

Proverbs 12:25-26 25 Heaviness in the heart of man maketh it stoop: but a good word maketh it glad. 26 The righteous is more excellent than his neighbour: but the way of the wicked seduceth them.

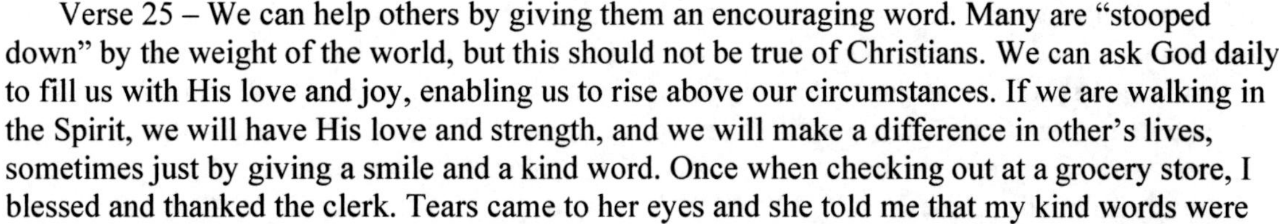

Verse 25 – We can help others by giving them an encouraging word. Many are "stooped down" by the weight of the world, but this should not be true of Christians. We can ask God daily to fill us with His love and joy, enabling us to rise above our circumstances. If we are walking in the Spirit, we will have His love and strength, and we will make a difference in other's lives, sometimes just by giving a smile and a kind word. Once when checking out at a grocery store, I blessed and thanked the clerk. Tears came to her eyes and she told me that my kind words were the nicest thing anybody had said to her all day. We never know when our kindness might change someone's entire day.

Verse 26 – The righteous man has a good influence on his neighbors by the example he sets. The ungodly man leads others astray. In almost every neighborhood, there is a particular family that stirs up strife and trouble. We must pray for these families, reach out to them, and try to overcome evil with good. With Christ's help, we can have a positive influence in our neighborhoods and change the atmosphere of our communities.

Being separate from the world (2 Corinthians 6:17) does not mean never becoming involved in politics or civic affairs. If every Christian followed this reasoning, government and administrative positions would be left to immoral people and sinners. Being separate means no longer participating in the selfish, unclean ways and practices of the world.

We are called to be salt and light in the world (Matthew 5:13-16). Salt causes food to taste better and is used as a preservative. Mixed with water, it forms a cleansing saline solution. Salt generates thirst so that we drink more water. It is essential to the human body. The analogy is clear: Christian beliefs improve life and our presence preserves the world from moral decay. The righteousness of Christ makes us the salt of the earth, which when combined with the living water of the Holy Spirit, makes our witness produce a cleansing effect upon sin-sick souls and society. A true Christian witness creates a spiritual thirst in others to know Jesus Christ. As Christians, we must share the "good news" with this world, which is dying for truth and light to be revealed. We must not utter empty phrases and be like salt that is no longer salty: such a witness is worthless. Our light shines by the good deeds that we do. Living out what we say we believe brings glory to our heavenly Father. Jesus said, "And I, if I be lifted up from the earth, will draw all men unto me" (John 12:32). If we "lift up" Jesus, people will be drawn unto Him. This is how we shall bring glory to our Father who is in Heaven.

Dear heavenly Father, I appreciate You and I want my life to glorify You. Fill me today with Your Holy Spirit so that I might bring encouraging words to others. Lord, I have been down at times in my life and I am so grateful for my brothers and sisters who came to me with faith and encouragement. They lifted me up, and today I want to lift them up. You know each of them and exactly what they are going through at this time. Bless them and meet their needs, even as You used them to meet my needs in the trying times of my life. May we all be good witnesses for You and never lose our "saltiness." Shine on us that we may reflect Your glory. I ask in Jesus' precious name. Amen.

Proverbs 12:27 The slothful man roasteth not that which he took in hunting: but the substance of a diligent man is precious.

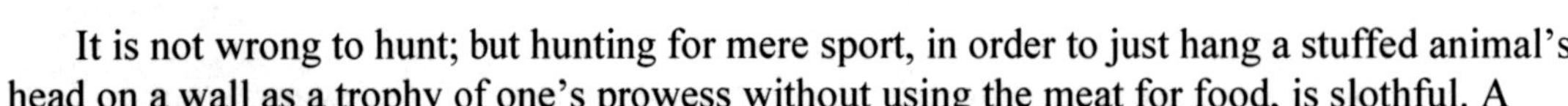

It is not wrong to hunt; but hunting for mere sport, in order to just hang a stuffed animal's head on a wall as a trophy of one's prowess without using the meat for food, is slothful. A diligent man considers game a precious possession providing food for his family's table.

While some people wastefully destroy animals, others consider it evil to kill them for food and become vegetarians. This is a nobler viewpoint, but the Bible does not forbid killing animals for food at this time. In the beginning, man was given a vegetarian diet of fruit, grains, vegetables, and seeds (Genesis 1:29-30, NIV). Apparently, all creatures of the earth were herbivores until after the great flood. This could have been one of the reasons that Noah was able to easily gather them into the ark and that they did not attack each other while in it. After the Flood, God blessed Noah and his sons and told them, "Everything that lives and moves will be food for you. Just as I gave you the green plants, now I give you everything" Genesis 9:3, NIV). God had already established the difference between clean and unclean animals in Genesis 8:20, and now told them that they could eat all clean animals as well as plants and fruit. He also told Noah that the animals would now fear man; something that apparently did not exist in the pre-flood world.

A possible clue to why God saw fit to allow some of His creatures to feed upon others after the Flood is that it somehow changed the order of things. God had created a perfect world. Earth's atmosphere and vegetable life had provided a perfect environment and perfect nutrition for man and animals. This perfect earth was first cursed because of man's sin and destroyed when man's wickedness reached its fullness. After the flood, Noah and his family began all over again like Adam and Eve, but in an imperfect world. Perhaps God allowed the eating of meat–so familiar a part of our existence today–because the original order of things had now changed due to the influence of sin in the world.

By choosing to sin, man lost his position of authority over God's creation. The loss of man's proper position on earth caused the rest of creation to lose its proper position. Creation has now been tainted by the wicked one's perverted character. Certain animals and humans now prey upon each other.

This will change. We will all be able to truly enjoy the earth when Jesus returns. He will restore it to what He originally planned it to be, when He reigns during the millennium (Isaiah 11:6-9). The animals will once again eat plants and not each other. Man will enjoy the original foods that God made for him without any desire to hunt or kill. Satan will no longer be loose on earth, and all creation will be free from the atrocities of sin. All the earth groans and waits for the day when Christ will return as King.

Dear heavenly Father, thank You for creating animals. You made so many magnificent creatures. Your diversity is astounding. Some animals are such a delight to watch. We can learn from so many of them. Your domesticated animals are such a joy to us, while the wild ones challenge us to observe their ways and learn about them. Thank You that You made them for man's enjoyment and use. Since many of them are directly dependant upon us, help us to be good stewards over them. Lord, protect the endangered beasts of the earth which are hunted by poachers for the wrong reasons. May our prayers create a spiritual ark for the preservation of Your animals,

especially the ones that are near extinction. Give us Your heart for the animals that You created. I ask in Jesus' name. Amen.

Quotes About Marriage

Many marriages have an unstable foundation because the couple selfishly looks for what their mate can give them, rather than for ways to give to their mate. --Day 79

The Lord calls us to be as courteous to our mates as to any sister or brother in Christ. We should be kind to one another, and think about saying and doing nice things that edify our spouses and build our marriages. --Day 115

There are worse things than being single. One of these is to be out of God's will by compromising and marrying someone who does not feel the same way we do about the Lord. --Day 122

We must choose the one with whom we will spend our lives with great care. Any character flaws we notice in someone (including ourselves) before marriage will be amplified afterwards. --Day 278

Quotes About Ministry

Real ministry flows from what Christ is doing in us, not from what we are trying to do for Him. --Day 22

Every Christian should be a priest and a minister, sharing the Gospel at home, the workplace, and every sphere of influence.
--Day 76

If everyone claiming to be a Christian truly lived according to Christ's commands, we could quickly win the whole world for Christ. --Day 77

Proverbs 12:28 In the way of righteousness is life; and in the pathway thereof there is no death. Proverbs 13:1 A wise son heareth his father's instruction: but a scorner heareth not rebuke.

Verse 28 – Righteousness, as we saw in Day 12, is found only in Christ. To follow Christ is to walk in the way of life. This refers not only to physical life but also to the *principles* of life; the thoughts, words, and deeds that line up with God's ways. Those which do not line up with His ways lead to death. The fall of man in the Garden of Eden put the death principle into effect for all people. Sickness is one of the results of the fall, an example of the death principle in action. Another example is depression. Interestingly, many English words associated with the death principle begin with the letter *"D,"* such as discouragement, disease, disappointment, disillusionment, despondency, doubt, and despair, not to mention the one behind the *"deadly D's"*–the devil himself.

We need to be careful to think and do what will activate the life principle. For instance, when we praise God, depression is driven away; when we pray in faith, discouragement lifts; when we stand on healing scriptures, sickness leaves; when we sing and worship God, joy fills our hearts. Jesus promised us abundant life (John 10:10). If we are not experiencing it, we need to commit ourselves totally to God and ask Him to fill us with the Holy Spirit so that we can walk in the Spirit and receive all that He has for us.

Verse 1 – One of the Ten Commandments states that if we want a long and happy life, we must honor our parents (Deuteronomy 5:16). If we are wise, we will not only obey the instruction of our earthly fathers, but also our spiritual fathers. Keeping God's Word in our hearts produces blessings of health and long life. What is in our hearts will surface and come out of our mouths. From computer terminology we have the acronym *GIGO*: *garbage in, garbage out.* If we put "garbage" in our spirits, garbage will come out; especially when we are under pressure.

Rebellion toward authorities reveals a heart problem. A rebellious son's refusal to accept his father's correction is his downfall. Those who refuse things that bring life are left to reap the destruction they sow in their lives. The Lord desires to bless all His children, but we cannot be blessed if we insist upon our own way. If we refuse to obey God, we will eventually find ourselves in a distressing place. For sinners without Christ that place will be hell. For rebellious Christians, that place will be a type of hell now. There are many agonies in the hells created by disobedience; the deepest being the loss of fellowship with God. The only safe place in this world for any of us is the center of God's will. Let us choose to walk on the path of life, not death.

Dear Father, thank You, as always, for Your abundant blessings. I may never know until I reach heaven how many times You have had Your angels protect me from the wicked one. I appreciate Your watching over my loved ones and me. Lord, I pray this day for all of the backsliders. Draw them back to Yourself. Forgive them and be merciful to them. Thank You that Your mercy endures forever. Lead us not into temptation, but deliver us from the evil one. Thank You for correcting me when I have missed You in some way. I do want to stay on the path of life. Please keep all Your children in the path of holiness and righteousness. I ask in Jesus' name. Amen.

Proverbs 13:2-3 2 A man shall eat good by the fruit of his mouth: but the soul of the transgressors shall eat violence. 3 He that keepeth his mouth keepeth his life: but he that openeth wide his lips shall have destruction.

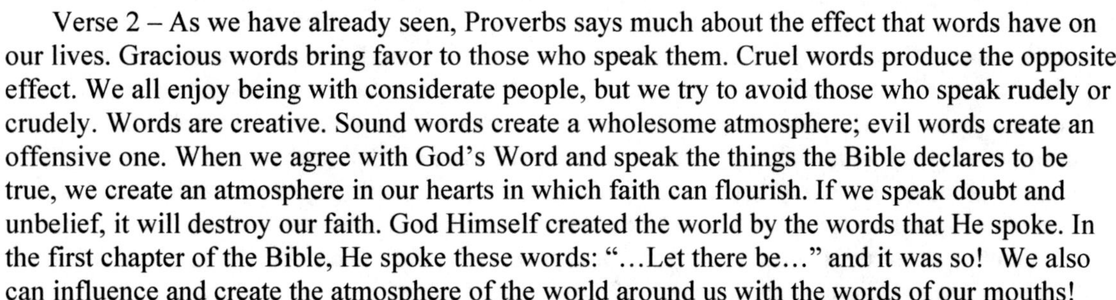

Verse 2 – As we have already seen, Proverbs says much about the effect that words have on our lives. Gracious words bring favor to those who speak them. Cruel words produce the opposite effect. We all enjoy being with considerate people, but we try to avoid those who speak rudely or crudely. Words are creative. Sound words create a wholesome atmosphere; evil words create an offensive one. When we agree with God's Word and speak the things the Bible declares to be true, we create an atmosphere in our hearts in which faith can flourish. If we speak doubt and unbelief, it will destroy our faith. God Himself created the world by the words that He spoke. In the first chapter of the Bible, He spoke these words: "...Let there be..." and it was so! We also can influence and create the atmosphere of the world around us with the words of our mouths!

Things do not come out of our mouths accidentally; they reveal what is already in our hearts though we may have been unaware of their presence. Expressions of jealousy, falsehood, fear, doubt, hatred, resentment, pride, selfishness and so forth reveal those very things to be in our hearts (Matthew 12:34-37). We all say things that we wish we could take back. When we do speak wrong things, we should repent and ask God to cleanse our hearts. Each time that we repent of the sin in our hearts and correct our speech it makes a difference. We will soon find good things coming out of our mouths more often than evil things.

Verse 3 – If we allow the Holy Spirit to direct our lives and ask Him to fill our mouths with His Word, we shall "keep our mouths" and live abundant lives. "And Jesus answered him, saying, It is written, That man shall not live by bread alone, but by every word of God" (Luke 4:4). We enter into life by speaking and living God's Word (Matthew 19:17). We can rest assured that what God has said is true. God's words are eternal and will never pass away. "Heaven and earth shall pass away: but my words shall not pass away" (Mark 13:31). He cannot lie. If we align our words with His, we shall be blessed. Allowing just anything to come out of our mouths brings destruction. Let us ask God to help us keep our mouths from saying wrong things, even as David did in the Psalms: "Set a watch, O LORD, before my mouth; keep the door of my lips" (Psalm 141:3).

Dear heavenly Father, I praise You for Your abundant love and mercy toward us! Thank You for being patient with me as I am learning not to say things that would hurt You or others. I do ask that You help me to guard my lips from saying unkind things. Lord, even as David prayed these words in Psalm 19:14, I ask that they be my prayer also: "Let the words of my mouth, and the meditation of my heart, be acceptable in thy sight, O Lord, my strength, and my redeemer." Help us all, as Your children, to say edifying things about one another. Thank You for the abundant life that is ours as we hear, speak and obey the Words of God. I ask this in the name of Jesus. Amen.

April 1 *Day 91*

Proverbs 13:4-6 4 The soul of the sluggard desireth, and hath nothing: but the soul of the diligent shall be made fat. 5 A righteous man hateth lying: but a wicked man is loathsome, and cometh to shame. 6 Righteousness keepeth him that is upright in the way: but wickedness overthroweth the sinner.

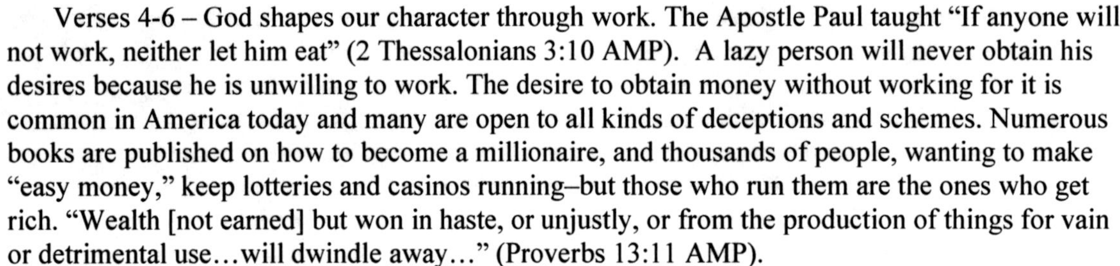

Verses 4-6 – God shapes our character through work. The Apostle Paul taught "If anyone will not work, neither let him eat" (2 Thessalonians 3:10 AMP). A lazy person will never obtain his desires because he is unwilling to work. The desire to obtain money without working for it is common in America today and many are open to all kinds of deceptions and schemes. Numerous books are published on how to become a millionaire, and thousands of people, wanting to make "easy money," keep lotteries and casinos running–but those who run them are the ones who get rich. "Wealth [not earned] but won in haste, or unjustly, or from the production of things for vain or detrimental use…will dwindle away…" (Proverbs 13:11 AMP).

Others treat the stock market like a casino, and they suffer for it. Followed properly, the basic principle upon which the stock market operates is not wrong. Simply put, entrepreneurs and investors meet each other's needs to their mutual benefit. Entrepreneurs need capital to market their ideas and those with liquid assets need good places to invest. Each party profits by meeting the other's need; one performs a profitable work and the other funds it. Unfortunately, the stock market operates mostly on greed, not a desire for mutually-beneficial arrangements.

Putting money into the stock market is not wrong if one does the proper research. Scripture speaks of investing our money wisely. However, it is never wise to borrow money on a credit card to make an investment. Many people have done this to invest in so-called "hot" stocks. To invest in a company on a hunch or a tip on what looks like a winner is to "play the stock market" as if it were a lottery. This is not investing wisely. Before investing in a company, we ought to know its history; how its employees are treated; whether its owners are honest and trustworthy; whether its policies are based on Biblical principles; what its owners' alliances are, etc. Many people unknowingly invest in companies that are run on ungodly principles, whose directors do not really care if they hurt investors.

We should flee from any form of deceit, including gambling, unrighteous business deals, and questionable stock investments–activities that promote or operate on greed. We live in uncertain times; even good investments have risks. Christians should not look to stock market investments for future security. Our real security is in the keeping power of Jesus Christ.

Dear Father, thank You for Your daily provision. You have been gracious to provide for me and my family. I am truly grateful. I pray for those today who may have been caught up in the deception of trying to obtain wealth in the wrong way. Deliver and guide them in Your ways. Teach us to use our money wisely; to give when You speak to us to give and to help when there is a need. Deliver Your children from greed and lust. Take anything out of my heart that would keep me from following You completely. Keep us from evil. I ask in the name of Jesus. Amen.

Proverbs 13:7-9 7 One man considers himself rich, yet has nothing (to keep permanently); another man considers himself poor, yet has great (and indestructible) riches. 8 A rich man can buy his way out of threatened death by paying a ransom, but the poor man does not even have to listen to threats (from the envious.) 9 The light of the (uncompromisingly) righteous (is within him; it grows brighter and) rejoices; but the lamp of the wicked (furnishes only a derived, temporary light and) shall be put out shortly (AMP).

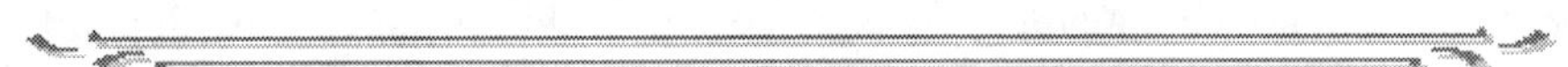

Verse 7 – This verse compares a rich and poor man; distinguishing between true riches and worldly wealth. True riches are found in Christ, while the wealth of this world is simply temporary ownership of money and things. A man may accumulate great wealth in this life, but he will not be able to take any of it with him when he dies. Jesus told a parable about a wealthy man who had such a large harvest he ran out of room to store it. He tore down his barns, built bigger ones, and congratulated himself: "Soul, thou hast much goods laid up for many years; take thine ease, eat, drink, and be merry. But God said unto him, Thou fool, this night thy soul shall be required of thee: then whose shall those things be, which thou hast provided? So is he that layeth up treasure for himself, and is not rich toward God. And he said unto his disciples, Therefore I say unto you, Take no thought for your life, what ye shall eat; neither for the body, what ye shall put on. The life is more than meat, and the body is more than raiment" (Luke 12:19-23).

Verse 8 – One benefit of being poor is that there is never a fear of being held for ransom! A spiritual analogy can be drawn. If we remain "poor" before God, claiming nothing as our own and recognizing that we are mere stewards of it, we will not worry about losing our possessions. How can we lose what is not ours? I take the position that everything I have belongs to God; Satan has no authority to take any of it. When the Lord tells me to give something away, I do so without a second thought. I refuse, however, to let the devil rob me of anything God has given me. I want to be a good steward and will fight the enemy if he tries to steal anything in my possession.

As a young shepherd tending his father's sheep, David overcame a lion and a bear on separate occasions. He risked his life to be a good steward of his father's sheep. We must have the same attitude; through prayer, fighting to keep the enemy from destroying our children, mates, homes, businesses, ministries, and even our lives. The enemy comes to kill, steal and destroy, but Christ came to give us abundant life (John 10:10-11). However, we must contend for it using our faith and God's Word against the enemy.

Verse 9 – The light of the righteous grows brighter each day, but the light of the wicked will be put out. The choice is ours: to walk in the guidance of God's light, or to walk in the darkness of hell.

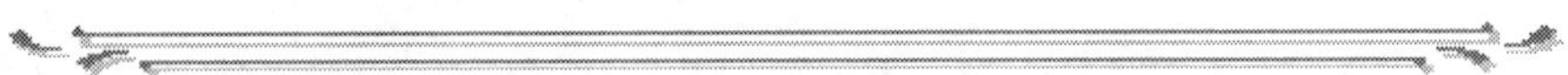

Dearest Father, I appreciate Your counsel and guidance. Thank You for Your love and care over me and my family. I desire Your riches above all the riches in this world. Strengthen me so that I will always obey You. I want Your righteousness first and foremost in my life. Cleanse me of the things that would prevent me from receiving all that You desire to do in me. Lord, help me, when I am under attack, to be as bold and courageous as David. I know that through the power of the Holy Spirit, I can do all things. I declare I will not be robbed of anything that You have entrusted to my care. Give me the grace to prevail over the enemy when he attempts to rob me. I ask this in the mighty name of Jesus. Amen.

Proverbs 13:10-12 10 Only by pride cometh contention: but with the well advised is wisdom. 11 Wealth gotten by vanity shall be diminished: but he that gathereth by labour shall increase. 12 Hope deferred maketh the heart sick: but when the desire cometh, it is a tree of life.

In these verses, we find three precious gems of wisdom: how to avoid contention, how to prosper financially, and how the results of answered prayer will produce growth and life.

Verse 10 – Unyielding pride always produces strife. To live peaceably, we must be humble. not thinking of ourselves as better than others. To be right about the facts, and yet act in a wrong way is still not right. As God's children, we must always act as He would have us act (1 Peter 5:5-7). This is not to say we should always defer to others or be a "door mat." Sometimes, it is harder to face people by speaking the truth in love, as we would rather avoid a difficult confrontation. When we find ourselves in disagreement, we should ask God how He would have us respond, no matter what our personal feelings. If we feel we are being treated unfairly, the best way to seek justice is to forgive, and treat others as we wish to be treated. When we pray for the good of others, God will defend us. We should never pray for evil to come to those who oppose us. Such a prayer does not come from God's heart. By blessing our enemies in our thoughts and prayers, we overcome evil with good (Romans 12:19-20).

Verse 11 – Obtaining money quickly does not develop character, which comes with patience and hard work. Those lacking character soon waste their money. Wealth gained by the sale of goods of a detrimental nature, such as drugs and pornography, will not last either. Wealth that is obtained at the expense of another's harm will dwindle away. History has recorded the deeds of some very wealthy men who gained their wealth by exploiting others. At the end of their lives, they were left as paupers.

Verse 12 – The last gem in our study tells us that when something we have set our heart on does not come to pass, we can become heart-sick. If disappointment comes over and over again, hope is soon lost. However, when a person receives the desire of his heart, it produces great joy, like a tree of life. A healthy tree grows bigger and stronger each year. So it is, when we receive things that we have prayed for and desired. As Christians, we should never yield to discouragement or despair, because the One Who is Hope lives in us. We must remember God has a perfect time to answer our prayers. We must learn not to depend on people or circumstances for encouragement but on the Lord. We must be like David who sought encouragement from God when threatened by his own men. "And David was greatly distressed...but David encouraged himself in the LORD his God" (1 Samuel 30:6).

Dear Father, thank You for Your strength when I am tempted to become discouraged in certain situations. I am so encouraged when You answer my prayers. You truly are a faithful God Who hears and answers us. I am amazed when I have totally forgotten a prayer that I prayed years ago and suddenly it comes to pass. Lord, please encourage my brothers and sisters and answer their prayers that have been prayed according to Your will. Send hope to those who need it and give them faith to believe You for their answers. Help me to respond in the manner that You would, to those who disagree with me. Fill me with Your love, and empower me with Your Holy Spirit to do Your will in every situation. I ask this in the name of the Lord, Jesus Christ. Amen.

Proverbs 13:13-16 13 Whoso despiseth the word shall be destroyed: but he that feareth the commandment shall be rewarded. 14 The law of the wise is a fountain of life, to depart from the snares of death. 15 Good understanding giveth favour: but the way of transgressors is hard. 16 Every prudent man dealeth with knowledge: but a fool layeth open his folly.

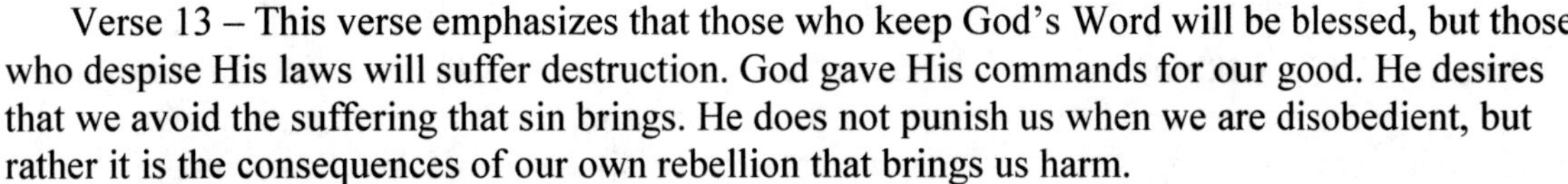

Verse 13 – This verse emphasizes that those who keep God's Word will be blessed, but those who despise His laws will suffer destruction. God gave His commands for our good. He desires that we avoid the suffering that sin brings. He does not punish us when we are disobedient, but rather it is the consequences of our own rebellion that brings us harm.

A good parent warns a child not to touch a hot stove. It is not the parent's fault if the child disobeys. Even so, if the child is accidentally burned, his father immediately takes care of him. He may scold the child for disobeying, but he is sensitive to his pain. It is the same with God. He does not cause hurtful things to happen in our lives. Would a good earthly parent make their child touch a hot stove? We bring the painful results of sin upon ourselves. When we disobey, He is still with us to help us when we cry out to Him.

Verses 14-15 – The wisdom in God's Word brings life, enabling us to resist the devil's attempts to draw us into snares leading to death. Good understanding wins us favor and causes life to go more smoothly. Life is difficult for transgressors; yielding to sin fills their lives with problems and pain. Obeying God is not hard; it is the way of the sinner that is hard. God empowers us to obey Him by giving us the Holy Spirit so that sin will not have dominion over us (Romans 6:14).

Verse 16 – Prudent people prosper because they do not commit to things or express opinions until they are sure of the facts. Fools flaunt their ignorance because they cannot keep quiet. Many times a criminal is caught because he simply had to boast to someone of his evil deeds and thus provided a witness to help convict him. If we are wise, we will walk in the knowledge of God; it will keep us from foolish mistakes.

Dear heavenly Father, I do thank You that You have given us Your Word and wisdom. Help us to walk in Your ways so that we will avoid the traps of the enemy. Lord, I am thankful that by following Your commandments, You have prevented the devil from harming me. I ask for Your protection over all of Your children. Lord, help me today to walk in love and be a good witness to all that I come in contact with. Help me to be sensitive to Your Spirit and respond to the things You ask me to do. Give me the courage and strength to do all that You ask of me. I ask this in the name of Jesus. Amen.

Proverbs 13:17-21 17 A wicked messenger falleth into mischief: but a faithful ambassador is health. 18 Poverty and shame shall be to him that refuseth instruction: but he that regardeth reproof shall be honoured. 19 The desire accomplished is sweet to the soul: but it is abomination to fools to depart from evil. 20 He that walketh with wise men shall be wise: but a companion of fools shall be destroyed. 21 Evil pursueth sinners: but to the righteous good shall be repayed.

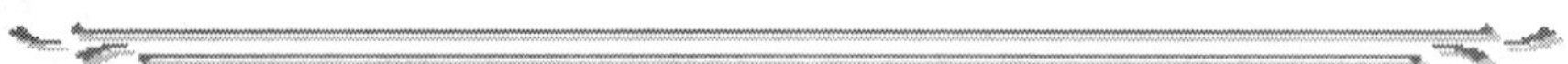

Verses 17-18 – Faithfulness is an attribute that many people lack today. A faithful employee abides by company rules and heeds correction. This makes him a valuable asset in forming a healthy company and brings him honor and promotion. A faithless employee falls into mischief that hinders his job performance. A rebellious employee refuses instruction. This usually costs him his job, resulting in poverty and shame.

Verse 19 – Accomplishment brings a satisfaction rarely experienced by the person who seldom finishes a project. Procrastination stops many people from accomplishing their goals (Ecclesiastes 11:4). It is also a very subtle sin. Satan encourages procrastination with perfectly good-sounding reasons which usually involves one's immediate comfort. Those who entertain procrastination usually have good intentions of accomplishing their goals–just at a later time, which never comes. Persevering when we do not feel like doing something is a godly trait we must develop to become overcomers in Christ. Perhaps you have heard the old saying; the highway to hell is paved with good intentions. God deals with people's hearts, asking them to surrender to His will, yet many resist, thinking they will yield at a later time when they feel like it. We are warned not to turn from God when He speaks (Hebrews 12:25).

Fools refuse to repent. To even consider giving up the evil things upon which they set their hearts is an abomination to them. Let us not be foolish. Let us not procrastinate, if we need to repent or perform any responsibility. God will strengthen us to accomplish any task if we ask Him to do so.

Verse 20 – We have heard the expression, "birds of a feather flock together." To grow in wisdom, we should select wise friends and associates. Their input can rightly direct us so that we succeed in our endeavors and avoid many difficulties. If we choose the company of foolish and rebellious people, we will face destruction. Those who are wise want to be around those who are wise, while the foolish desire the company of fools.

Verse 21 – Evil things follow evil people, but if we seek God in faith, we are promised the rewards of the righteous. We must, however, seek God diligently and not half-heartedly. "But without faith it is impossible to please him: for he that cometh to God must believe that he is, and that he is a rewarder of them that diligently seek him" (Hebrews 11:6).

Father, I praise You for Your goodness. I am blessed to know and follow You. Help me to make wise decisions in all the things that I daily face. Give me Your love for all that I meet. Help me not to procrastinate in the responsibilities that are before me. I need Your guidance to know the things that should be my priorities, as sometimes I do not know what needs to be taken care of first. Give me the strength I need to perform my many tasks. Help me to demonstrate Your nature in all my daily activities at home and at my workplace. I ask this in the name of Jesus Christ. Amen.

Proverbs 13:22-23 22 A good man leaves an inheritance (of moral stability and goodness) to his children's children, and the wealth of the sinner (finds its way eventually) into the hands of the righteous, for whom it was laid up. 23 Much food is in the tilled land of the poor, but there are those who are destroyed because of injustice (AMP).

Verse 22 – Material blessings are part of God's plans for His children. However, He encourages us to seek Him and His righteousness first, and then blessings follow as a result of our obedience. His Word also teaches us to give. Giving from what God has entrusted to us activates the law of sowing and reaping; God multiplies our giving back to us in answer to our needs.

Leading a godly life before our families and teaching them God's Word is the greatest inheritance we can leave them. God watches over those who are faithful and righteous. When they have needs, He will at times divert the wealth of the wicked to them. He does this in different ways. The Egyptians had oppressed the Israelites with slavery for many years, but when God led the Hebrews out of Egypt through Moses, He settled the books by causing the Egyptians to give of their silver, gold, and clothing to His own people (Exodus 12:36).

Verse 23 – The poor would have much food if their land was worked properly, but they are usually uneducated. Because they do not know how to make their land fully productive, they barely make a living. Wicked men recognize the potential for gain from the poor and exploit them. Their destruction through injustice is very evil in God's sight.

God sends missionaries into spiritually and physically impoverished places that the people might learn His ways. Bringing the Gospel to the poor so that they might have eternal life is the most important goal. Most missionaries, however, also teach practical things to improve people's lives, such as agricultural techniques, reading and writing, and sanitary practices (many of the diseases in remote areas are caused by contaminated drinking water and are preventable). The Lord does not desire people to remain ignorant. We are called not only to preach the Gospel, but to teach principles that save lives.

The Bible is filled with spiritual and practical principles. It discusses such topics as nutrition, sanitation, land conservation, animal husbandry, social etiquette, government administration, ecology, and family structure. Whenever we seek God's answer to a problem, we will find that the Bible has something to say regarding it. That is why it is so important to read the Bible daily.

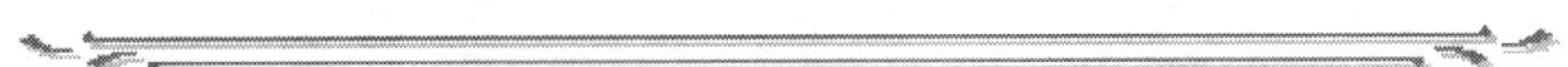

Dearest Father, I am thankful for Your love and the opportunity to serve You. I truly want to leave my children and grandchildren a godly inheritance. I pray that they will each be guided by You and that they will remain in Your will. May they serve and follow You. Protect them from evil. Lord, filter out the humanism of this world so that it does not enter into their thinking patterns; may they be influenced by godly thinking instead. May Your Words be spread to the world's poor so that they might be set free from all bondage and come into the knowledge of the Lord. Use all of us who are Christians to reach out to the impoverished and hurting and share Your ways with them. I ask this in the name of Jesus. Amen.

God's Wisdom for Daily Living — ***Betty Miller***
April 7 — ***Day 97***

Proverbs 13:24 He who spares his rod (of discipline) hates his son, but he who loves him diligently disciplines and punishes him early (AMP).

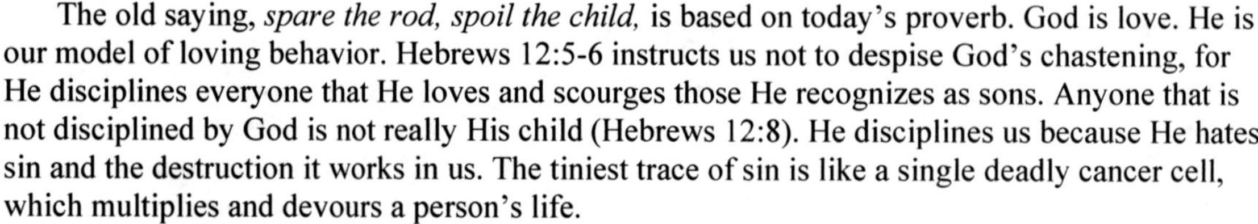

The old saying, *spare the rod, spoil the child,* is based on today's proverb. God is love. He is our model of loving behavior. Hebrews 12:5-6 instructs us not to despise God's chastening, for He disciplines everyone that He loves and scourges those He recognizes as sons. Anyone that is not disciplined by God is not really His child (Hebrews 12:8). He disciplines us because He hates sin and the destruction it works in us. The tiniest trace of sin is like a single deadly cancer cell, which multiplies and devours a person's life.

Just as God's discipline demonstrates His love for us, we also demonstrate our love for our children by disciplining them. Those who love their children view them as among God's most important blessings to them. They prize their children and are careful to teach and equip them not only to live in the world, but also to live for eternity.

Parents that love themselves more than their children either provide no discipline at all or discipline that is slack or inconsistent. There are numerous symptoms of self-love in our societies. These symptoms are displayed in fathers or mothers that abandon their families to "find themselves;" in parents that value their career advancement, money, or material things above spending time with their children; in spouses that cheat on their partners and destroy their family for the sake of their own pleasure. Selfishness is seen in those who think that disciplining their children too much of an effort (requiring too much time, energy, and attention); and also in those who have "more important" things to do.

In order to discipline one's child, one must discipline oneself. Parents who do not discipline themselves to curb their selfishness have no interest in disciplining their children. Selfishness is at the root not only of many parents' pursuit of pleasure and self-aggrandizement, but also various substance addictions. Jesus said that in the last days the love of many would grow cold because lawlessness would abound (Matthew 24:12). The widespread use of drugs throughout many nations of the world has given rise to a type of lawlessness perhaps unparalleled in history. Families are at the foundation of every nation; but the heads of many families–the parents–have become shockingly lawless. Drug-addiction causes frightening numbers of parents to murder their children by abuse or abortion, or to neglect, or abandon them. One of the most fundamental forms of love: that of a parent for a child, has grown cold in our generation.

Dear Father in heaven, thank you for my children and my grandchildren. I have learned so much over the years through the parenting process. I have failed so many times, but You have been there to pick me up and help me overcome the things that came against me and my children. Lord, being a parent is a challenge. Only with Your help and love can we be the kind of parents that You call us to be. I pray for all mothers and fathers who are seeking You for help with their families. Grant Your help and favor to them. Give them your love, wisdom and patience in dealing with their children. May all Christians be the godly parents You call them to be, and may their children be loving and obedient so that we all have happy and blessed homes. I ask this in the name of the Lord Jesus Christ. Amen.

Proverbs 13:25 The righteous eateth to the satisfying of his soul: but the belly of the wicked shall want.

Jesus taught us to pray for our daily bread (Mathew 6:9-13). He promises that those who obey Him will not lack food, and neither will their children (Psalm 37:25-26). God keeps this promise even by going to extreme and supernatural measures to do so. When the prophet Elijah hid by a brook from the evil king Ahab, God provided for him by causing ravens to bring him food every day (1 Kings 17:2-6). On two separate occasions, Jesus multiplied a very small amount of food to feed huge crowds. The first time, He multiplied five loaves of bread and two fish to feed a crowd of over 5,000 that had been with Him all day (Matthew 14; Mark 6; Luke 9; John 6). The second time, a crowd of over 4,000 had stayed with Jesus for three days while He healed their sick and taught them. Concerned lest they faint on the way home, He multiplied seven loaves of bread and a few fish. As before, the entire crowd was filled (Matthew 15:32-38 and Mark 8:1-9).

These accounts of God's miraculous provision show His love. His miracles have continued throughout history. My husband and I have personally experienced His provision: A number of times we had a large crowd, but not enough food. Each time, He honored our prayers and multiplied our food so that everyone could eat. We have also heard testimonies of God's provision from others. Here are two of them:

A missionary in South America ran out of provision when funds from her homeland did not arrive on time. She and her daughter came to the last of their food and cried out to God. The next day, a plant sprang up in their back yard and to their amazement, the same day bore full-grown squash. They ate squash for three days, and then the plant wilted and died. That evening, the missionary's landlord came to her door with several sacks of food he thought she needed. He said that God had been speaking to him to bring them for the three previous days! The food he gave her lasted until her support came from home.

Another amazing account of God's provision was given by a Chinese Christian and it occurred many years ago. A group of Christians who were meeting secretly to study God's Word were discovered by the authorities. They were forced to go hungry for many days. In their hunger, they sought the Lord for food. As they stood praying, they suddenly began to testify to one another that they felt like they had just sat down and finished a full meal. None were hungry. The Lord supernaturally sustained them until provision came.

Experiencing God's faithfulness strengthens our faith! He does not want us to worry about where the necessities of life will come from. He promises that if we seek His kingdom and His righteousness first, He will provide everything we need (Matthew 6:31-33).

Dear Father in heaven, thank You for Your promise of daily provision. You have always been faithful to supply all of our needs. Lord, help me to be sensitive to the needs of others, and share with them the things that You have blessed me with. Help me not to forget the poor and the hungry. I pray for people who are suffering in famine and war. Send the food and help to keep them alive, so that they might find eternal life through Christ if they do not know You. Empower us to reach out to the world with help and the Word of God so they will come to know You and Your love. I ask in the name of the Lord Jesus. Amen.

God's Wisdom for Daily Living — *Betty Miller*
April 9 — *Day 99*

Proverbs 14:1-2 1 Every wise woman builds her house, but the foolish one tears it down with her own hands. 2 He who walks in uprightness reverently and worshipfully fears the LORD, but he who is contrary and devious in his ways despises Him (AMP).

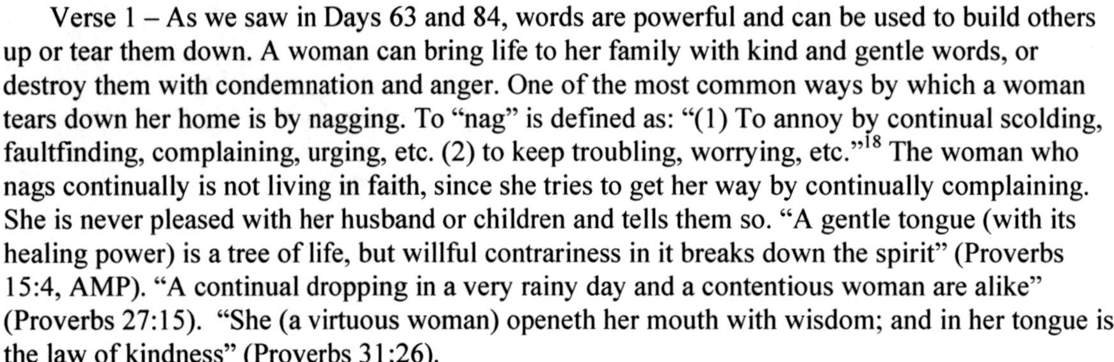

Verse 1 – As we saw in Days 63 and 84, words are powerful and can be used to build others up or tear them down. A woman can bring life to her family with kind and gentle words, or destroy them with condemnation and anger. One of the most common ways by which a woman tears down her home is by nagging. To "nag" is defined as: "(1) To annoy by continual scolding, faultfinding, complaining, urging, etc. (2) to keep troubling, worrying, etc."[18] The woman who nags continually is not living in faith, since she tries to get her way by continually complaining. She is never pleased with her husband or children and tells them so. "A gentle tongue (with its healing power) is a tree of life, but willful contrariness in it breaks down the spirit" (Proverbs 15:4, AMP). "A continual dropping in a very rainy day and a contentious woman are alike" (Proverbs 27:15). "She (a virtuous woman) openeth her mouth with wisdom; and in her tongue is the law of kindness" (Proverbs 31:26).

We can see from these verses that we can build up our husbands and children with kind words, or we can destroy them with words of condemnation. Good and gentle words bring life to others, while words spoken in anger will tear down those around us. What if our spouse or others around us are saying unkind things to us? Are we justified in returning railing words back to them? Here is what the Scripture tell us.

Verse 2 – If we desire to see good days and our prayers answered, we must guard our tongues from speaking evil, including returning evil for evil. We might think we are justified to return angry words, but 1 Peter 2:21-23 and 3:8-12 tell us that we are not justified to return railing for railing. Responding kindly to an angry person requires the enabling of the Holy Spirit. Many times, I have called on the Lord to help me rightly respond to those who are opposing me. Without His help, I could not have responded properly. If we ask Him, He will enable us to respond with loving words rather than anger. We should take our hurt and frustration to the Lord, asking Him to fill us with the Holy Spirit so that we can overcome evil with good (Romans 12:21). With His love and power we can respond in a godly way to all that come against us.

Pride and fear usually keep us in bondage to our old ways. If we humble ourselves and ask God to deliver us from these sins, we can overcome through Christ; and build up instead of tear down those around us with our words.

Dear Father, thank You for Your love and grace that empowers me to overcome the fear and pride that comes against me. I humble myself before You, asking You to be merciful to me and all of my family. We need Your love so that we can overcome evil with good. Help each of us in our families and jobs to be more like You. Give us patience and forbearance with one another. Let us be gentle and kind to all; especially in our own homes. Help us guard our mouths so that we speak gracious things about one another. Help us to build up each other and never tear down. I ask this in the name of Jesus Christ, our Lord in whose steps we desire to follow. Amen.

---

[18] Webster's New World Dictionary of the American Language, Second college edition

God's Wisdom for Daily Living — *Betty Miller*
April 10 — *Day 100*

Proverbs 14:3-5 3 In the mouth of the foolish is a rod of pride: but the lips of the wise shall preserve them. 4 Where no oxen are, the crib is clean: but much increase is by the strength of the ox. 5 A faithful witness will not lie: but a false witness will utter lies.

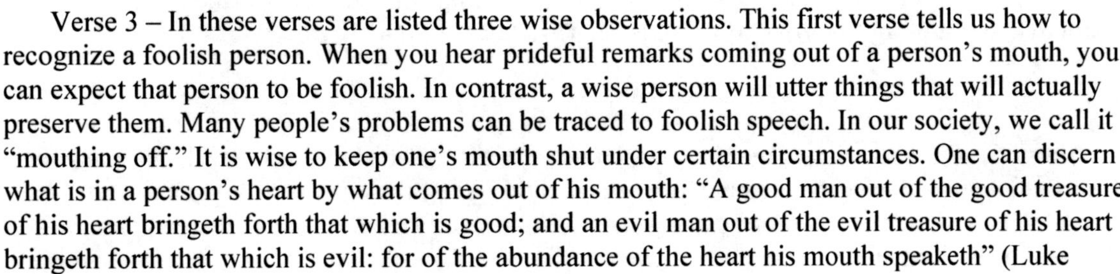

Verse 3 – In these verses are listed three wise observations. This first verse tells us how to recognize a foolish person. When you hear prideful remarks coming out of a person's mouth, you can expect that person to be foolish. In contrast, a wise person will utter things that will actually preserve them. Many people's problems can be traced to foolish speech. In our society, we call it "mouthing off." It is wise to keep one's mouth shut under certain circumstances. One can discern what is in a person's heart by what comes out of his mouth: "A good man out of the good treasure of his heart bringeth forth that which is good; and an evil man out of the evil treasure of his heart bringeth forth that which is evil: for of the abundance of the heart his mouth speaketh" (Luke 6:45).

"These men are grumblers and faultfinders; they follow their own evil desires; they boast about themselves and flatter others for their own advantage" (Jude 1:16 NIV).

Verse 4 – The second observation has to do with labor. The lesson we can learn from this proverb is that if we desire to have an increase in any of our endeavors, it will take strength and labor, and it will also call for provision for the animals (the workers). One must provide feed for his oxen in the crib (feeder) so that they can eat well and perform properly. Also, the stall of the oxen will require a cleaning, if they are kept around to do any work. Work is not always pleasant, and is sometimes messy before the job gets completed. The modern work ethic is somewhat distorted in some people's minds, since some believe that work should never be unpleasant! With this kind of attitude, very little work would be accomplished. The Bible tells us that whatever we are working at, we should give it our best effort and work as unto Him, and not men. If we do this, God Himself will reward us: "Servants, be obedient to them that are your masters according to the flesh, with fear and trembling, in singleness of your heart, as unto Christ; Not with eyeservice, as menpleasers; but as the servants of Christ, doing the will of God from the heart; With good will doing service, as to the Lord, and not to men: Knowing that whatsoever good thing any man doeth, the same shall he receive of the Lord, whether he be bond or free" (Ephesians 6:5-8).

Verse 5 – This last verse refers to liars. A liar does not make a good witness, since he will lie to cover his own guilt. In contrast, a faithful witness will tell the truth even if it does not benefit him. Truthfulness should be found in all of God's children. We are to be witnesses to the world and if we are dishonest, we destroy that witness.

Dear heavenly Father, thank You for Your love and patience with all of us as Your children. We ask You to deliver us from pride and foolishness and give us Your wisdom. Give us the strength to do all that is before us each day. May we do our work as unto You and not unto men. May our labors count for something. Let us lead good and pure lives before those with whom we live and work. Lord, deliver us from the temptation to lie. May truthfulness always be found upon our tongues. Help me to be a good witness to all that I come in contact with. I ask this in the name of Jesus. Amen.

Proverbs 14:6-9 6 A scoffer seeks Wisdom in vain (for his very attitude blinds and deafens him to it), but knowledge is easy to him who (being teachable) understands. 7 Go from the presence of a foolish and self-confident man, for you will not find knowledge in his lips. 8 The wisdom of the prudent is to understand his way, but the folly of (self-confident) fools is to deceive. 9 Fools make a mock at sin, and sin mocks the fools (who are its victims) –a sin offering made by them only mocks them (bringing them disappointment and disfavor); but among the upright there is the favor of God (AMP).

Verse 6 – Proverbs encourages us to seek God's wisdom, which only the teachable can gain. We must come to God with a humble heart and a child-like attitude if we desire to know the secrets of His Kingdom. "Verily I say unto you, Whosoever shall not receive the kingdom of God as a little child, he shall not enter therein" (Mark 10:15). "Draw nigh to God, and he will draw nigh to you..." (James 4:8). This means that we are to be "child-like," (not "childish") in our approach to God. We are to come to God trusting Him with a child-like trust. Defiant scorners can neither know God's ways nor find answers to their questions. Applying the Word of God to our adverse circumstances is what is needed if we are to have the victory.

Verses 7-8 – We are admonished to depart from the foolish and self-confident man, since he will not listen to words of wisdom. It is important to seek godly counsel regarding our problems because the only way we can overcome them is to apply what the Bible says about them. A prudent man understands which is the right way to go, and can give wise advice. Knowledge should not be sought from rebellious, self-confident men; they only have worldly answers. Their advice is deceptive, because it does not contain the truth. Applying the Word of God to our adverse circumstances is what is needed if we are to have the victory.

Verse 9 – A fool mocks at sin; but ultimately sin will mock the fool. He considers standards of right and wrong to be outdated, and he jokes about them. He seeks temporary relief from his problems, but permanent answers are found only through Jesus Christ. Sin prevents him from finding eternal life and true answers to his problems. Men will reap what they sow in eternity, if not in this life. When we repent of our sins and turn from our wicked ways, our faith in Jesus Christ will deliver us from the destruction we deserve.

Those who follow Christ find God's favor, which cannot be bought through religious rituals. What is God's favor? God's favor is experienced when we find His peace in the midst of our storms; His provision for all our needs; His strength when we are weary; His healing when we are sick; His protection when we are threatened; His love when we are lonely. It is something money cannot buy. Many times in my life when I prayed for the money to meet a need, God gave me favor instead, so that I was given more time to take care of the bill or even had it cancelled. We are most blessed as His children to have access to His favor.

Dearest Father, thank You for Your favor in my life. I do not ever want to take it for granted. You have provided abundantly and I am thankful for all of my blessings. I desire to keep a "child-like" attitude so that I can learn more about You and Your kingdom. Thank You for love and strength for each day. I know that You will make a way for me to walk in victory today. I appreciate Your goodness toward me and those who I am praying for. Bless all of my loved ones. I ask this in the name of Jesus Christ. Amen.

God's Wisdom for Daily Living — ***Betty Miller***
April 12 — ***Day 102***

Proverbs 14:10-11 10 The heart knoweth his own bitterness; and a stranger doth not intermeddle with his joy. 11 The house of the wicked shall be overthrown: but the tabernacle of the upright shall flourish.

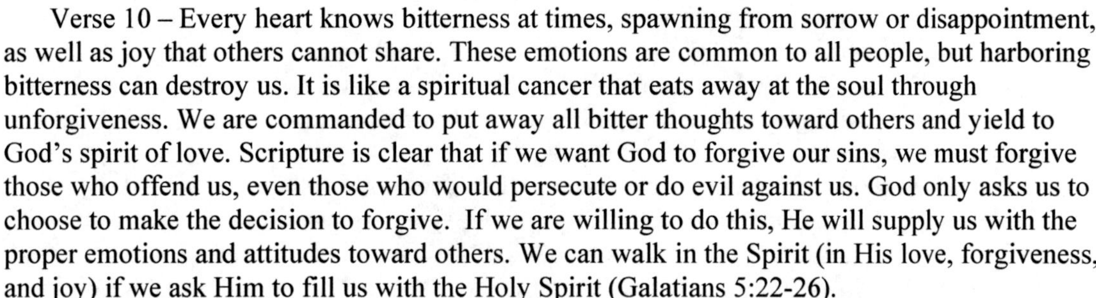

Verse 10 – Every heart knows bitterness at times, spawning from sorrow or disappointment, as well as joy that others cannot share. These emotions are common to all people, but harboring bitterness can destroy us. It is like a spiritual cancer that eats away at the soul through unforgiveness. We are commanded to put away all bitter thoughts toward others and yield to God's spirit of love. Scripture is clear that if we want God to forgive our sins, we must forgive those who offend us, even those who would persecute or do evil against us. God only asks us to choose to make the decision to forgive. If we are willing to do this, He will supply us with the proper emotions and attitudes toward others. We can walk in the Spirit (in His love, forgiveness, and joy) if we ask Him to fill us with the Holy Spirit (Galatians 5:22-26).

Verse 11 – The house of a wicked man shall fall, while the tabernacle (house) of the upright shall flourish. The influence of the wicked hurts those around him. When he falls, those of his house are also ruined. That is why Scripture admonishes us to choose mates, business partners, and friends carefully. If they are wicked, we will suffer by our association with them. If we make godly alliances, we will be blessed and prosper.

Marriage should be directed by the Holy Spirit. Young people should carefully seek the Lord concerning their future life partner. Many choose a mate based on emotions or lust, and later they suffer because their spouse lacks character. God's character defines what love is because He is love. 1 Corinthians 13 beautifully describes real love: it gives without expecting to receive, it is forgiving and patient, it is gentle and kind; it waits; it sacrifices. A Christian's love for another is based on commitment. Emotions should always follow, never direct, the decision-making process. Those who allow their unsanctified emotions to rule them cannot be victorious Christians because our emotions should be ruled by our spirit man, and not the other way around. God knows what is best for us. If we trust Him, He will not fail us regarding this or any other important decision.

The house of the righteous will flourish because Christ is Lord over their home. My husband and I have been married for over thirty years and have never had a hateful argument. Most people are shocked at this statement! Naturally, we have disagreed about things, but we knew the Lord at the start of our married life and learned the Biblical way to settle disagreements. When we disagree, we both seek the Lord. We ask Him to be our referee and show us who is right about the matter. Sometimes one and sometimes both of us are wrong; and sometimes the Lord has an entirely different solution to our problem. We simply ask God to show us His mind. He has never failed to show us what to do when our opinions differ. We thank God that He is Lord of our house!

Dearest Father, thank You for the godly mate that You gave me. I am most appreciative. Help me to be the supportive person that my mate needs. Forgive me when I fail to live up to the things that a Christian should exemplify. Lord, help me to be the person I should be in all of my relationships with others. I thank you for a forgiving heart when I feel I have been wronged by anyone. Fill me with Your Holy Spirit and Your love every day so that those in my house will always be blessed. I ask this in the name of Jesus. Amen.

God's Wisdom for Daily Living ***Betty Miller***
April 13 ***Day 103***

Proverbs 14:12 There is a way which seemeth right unto a man, but the end thereof are the ways of death.

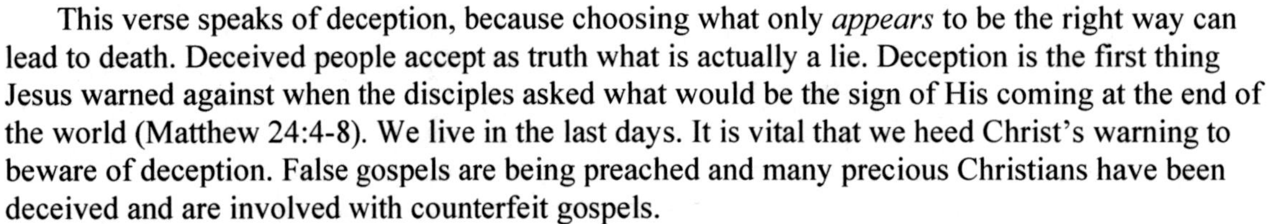

This verse speaks of deception, because choosing what only *appears* to be the right way can lead to death. Deceived people accept as truth what is actually a lie. Deception is the first thing Jesus warned against when the disciples asked what would be the sign of His coming at the end of the world (Matthew 24:4-8). We live in the last days. It is vital that we heed Christ's warning to beware of deception. False gospels are being preached and many precious Christians have been deceived and are involved with counterfeit gospels.

Man is a spiritual being created to worship God. If he does not worship God, he will worship something else; whether the demons of false religion, money, relationships, or his own intellect. Religion is Satan's counterfeit of the knowledge of God. True faith is not following a set of rules; it is a way of life that flows out of a relationship with God. Satan uses religion to enslave billions worldwide. The strands of truth woven into false religion make them sound convincing, and many even mention Jesus. Satan does not mind this as long as the truth about Jesus is not taught. Many cults deceive people through demonic feats, taking advantage of man's craving for the supernatural.

Participation in false religions represent the earnest attempt of millions of people to fulfill deep and legitimate needs of the human spirit which many seem not to have found in established churches (Matthew 7:13-14). One of the most dangerous lies is that all religions lead to heaven; that no matter which god you serve: whether it be the Hindu, Muslim, Buddhist or Christian deity, it is really all the same. This is a false teaching. The Bible tells us there is only one way to heaven: that is by believing upon the Lord Jesus Christ. All other gods and religions are false. "Jesus saith unto him, I am the way, the truth, and the life: no man cometh unto the Father, but by me." (John 14:6).

Whoever accepts Jesus as Savior is assured of eternal life. The Holy Spirit will always attempt to lead people out of the bondage of false religion. God will answer the prayer of any honest seeker. We should not condemn, but love and pray for anyone whom we know is involved in a false religion. Satan has blinded them, but God loves them and desires that they come to the knowledge of the truth. Within Christianity, God's church is not a particular denomination or building. The true church is made up of all believers in Christ from all ages, and the true Kingdom of God is within. Satan seeks to lead people down any path except the one that leads to life in Christ.

Dear heavenly Father, thank You that my name is written in the Book of Life. Lord, I pray for all who do not know You as the true and living God. Reveal Yourself to them so that they too might have eternal life. Deliver those who are in any form of deception that keeps them from knowing You. Father, I also ask that You keep me free from error. Deliver me from all pride and deception. Lord, reveal Yourself to all those who sincerely desire to know the true God. Please bless and keep my family and friends in the path of truth. I ask this in the name of Jesus, our Savior. Amen.

Proverbs 14:13-14 13 Even in laughter the heart is sorrowful; and the end of that mirth is heaviness. 14 The backslider in heart shall be filled with his own ways: and a good man shall be satisfied from himself.

Verse 13 – Laughter is an emotion, and it proceeds from the soul of man. When a man's soul is unredeemed, he can laugh with temporary amusement but still be miserable at heart. The world is amazed that Christians can maintain a spirit of joy even in great suffering. This is because the joy that the Lord gives to His saints is not dependant on circumstances, but upon abiding in Christ. The power of the Holy Spirit can sustain us in our severest trials.

Verse 14 – Those who slide away from God, back to their old lifestyles, are filled with their own ways instead of the Holy Spirit. When trials come, they have no reserves of inner strength to draw upon, and many are destroyed for lack of faith. It is important to stay alert and not slack off in our pursuit of God. We must use our time wisely when things go well and study God's Word, storing up His truths in our hearts (2 Timothy 2:15).

Ignorance causes much suffering in the natural and the spiritual. I can think of a perfect example of this truth. Some years ago, my husband Bud and I made a journey to India and visited a small church. Every family attending this church was afflicted with dysentery. When we asked the mothers to bring forward the children ill with fever, almost the whole church came forward. We prayed and rebuked the fever in Jesus' name. Instantly the children who were hot with fever were restored to their normal temperature. We rejoiced in the goodness of God, as we had remembered how Jesus prayed and rebuked the fever from Peter's mother-in-law and she was healed (Matthew 8:14-17).

The next day, we were visiting the pastor. One of his children, who had been healed the night before, became feverish again. As we prayed, the Holy Spirit revealed that we needed to deal with the root of the illness. After asking the pastor several questions, we learned that the water and sewer pipes of the houses were laid side by side. Because the pipes were leaking and the joints were improperly sealed, sewage was contaminating the drinking water. Lack of knowledge had brought disease to that entire church. We told the pastor to boil all the drinking water and to have the church families to do likewise. Through the knowledge given by the Holy Spirit to find the root of the problem, and the practical knowledge of how to purify water, the families were spared continued illness.

Lack of spiritual knowledge causes spiritual illnesses. We must study and obey God's Word to overcome life's problems and walk victoriously in the Lord.

Dear Father, thank You for the joy that You have given me. I do not want to take the fruit of the Spirit for granted. I am blessed to experience Your love, joy and peace, especially in the middle of my trials. Truly, You give us peace that passes understanding. Please give me a continued love for Your Word and a desire to study it faithfully. I also need the grace to apply it in my daily life. Help Your people to esteem Your Word and honor You by keeping it. May we all declare as David did in Psalm 119:11, "Thy word have I hid in mine heart, that I might not sin against thee." I ask in the name of Jesus Christ. Amen.

Proverbs 14:15-18 15 The simple believeth every word: but the prudent man looketh well to his going. 16 A wise man feareth, and departeth from evil: but the fool rageth, and is confident. 17 He that is soon angry dealeth foolishly: and a man of wicked devices is hated. 18 The simple inherit folly: but the prudent are crowned with knowledge.

Verse 15 – The Hebrew word for *simple* in verses 15 and 18 means "foolish, easily seduced."[19] The simple believe anything; the wise examine a matter before committing to it. The Bible tells us that we should prove all things, not believe all things. Society is flooded with things that appear harmless. We cannot be overcomers until we learn to "test" or "prove" the issues of this life (1Thessalonians 5:21). Jesus warned of false teachers and gave guidelines for detecting them (Matthew 7:15-23). Just because someone prophesies, casts out devils, or does miracles in Christ's name does not mean that he is from God. Jesus said we would know false prophets by their *fruits* (by whether or not they live godly lives). This fruit of the Spirit is listed in Galatians 5:22-23.

While we are admonished to be careful, some become closed to some beautiful Biblical truths in the name of caution. We are told to prove all things; neither rejecting something because it is strange or new, nor receiving anything until we have proved it against God's Word. All Christians agree that our standard is the Bible. God gave us this book as a gauge so that we could know whether something is good or evil, truth or error, right or wrong (2 Timothy 3:16-17).

Not only are we to "test" the spirits in men, but we are to do the same with any supernatural manifestations that we might experience. Today, when the world is being exposed to so many false things, we need to be careful not to expose our spirits to false dreams, visions, revelations, prophecies, or voices. The Word of God definitely teaches that God can manifest Himself in any of these things, but we are not to blindly accept everything that comes in the name of Jesus. We need to test or prove these also. One of Satan's greatest devices is to counterfeit the real things of God and come to us disguised as the working of the Holy Spirit. How do we test these things? Let us look to God's Word, as there is always wisdom there to show us what is truth.

Verses 16-18 – Those who are wise will reverence God and turn away from evil. Fools are arrogant, quick-tempered, and reap folly as their portion. The wise gain knowledge from God and lead overcoming lives. God's ways are pure, peaceable, and full of good works. The devil inspires strife and envy. We must prove all things, checking to see if they agree with Scripture and if they produce good fruit. Only then can we accept it.

Dear Father, thank You for Your wisdom and guidance each day. It is so exciting to walk in Your ways. I do appreciate the unexpected blessings that You bring my way each day. Thank You for the wonderful people You have brought in my life. Give me discernment to recognize those things that are not of You, and have the spiritual eyesight to see things that are of the enemy so that I might not be fooled by him. Keep me from anger and help me to know Your will so that I can follow You closely in all of my ways. Bless my family and friends and keep them from the wicked one also. I ask this in the name of Jesus Christ. Amen.

[19] Wilson's Old Testament Word Studies, s.v. "simple"

Proverbs 14:19 The evil bow before the good; and the wicked at the gates of the righteous.

In ancient times, people acknowledged a man's superiority by bowing to him. In this verse, we are told how evil men cannot prevail against righteous men. Eventually they will surrender or bow before them. The wicked will stand before the gates of the righteous, but they will not be able to gain entrance into their safe domain. Gates are "portals" or 'entry ways" into someone's territory. The righteous in Christ have the covenant promise of protection. Christians who claim that protection by faith will be in a place of safety. The enemy cannot enter in at our gates. We can claim protection over our hearts, our minds, our bodies and our homes. In fact, the Scriptures tell us that safety is not in any natural provision that we make, but is really in the Lord: "The horse is prepared against the day of battle: but safety is of the LORD" (Proverbs 21:31).

Christians who claim God's protection and walk with Him, will dwell in safety. We can claim protection over our hearts, minds, bodies, and homes. This does not mean that we should not make preparations for emergencies or battles. Proverbs 21:31 tells us to use wisdom by preparing for the future. However, we must understand that our real safety is in the Lord. The Bible records many battles in which God's people were greatly outnumbered by their enemies. Whenever their leaders sought the Lord for His battle plans, they would prevail. We should remember that one person with God equals a majority! Jonathan, David's friend in the Old Testament, knew this truth: "And Jonathan said to the young man that bare his armour, Come, and let us go over unto the garrison of these uncircumcised: it may be that the LORD will work for us: for there is no restraint to the LORD to save by many or by few" (1 Samuel 14:6).

Numbers cannot help us, nor can lack prevent us from accomplishing anything that God calls us to do. We must remember His sufficiency! God enabled Samson to prevail over a thousand of his enemies with a makeshift weapon; the jawbone of an ass (Judges 15:15). David was a man of God who "inquired of the Lord" before every battle. Each time he received God's plan and obeyed it, he won the battle (1 Samuel 23:1-5).

Like the Philistines, our enemy, the devil, comes to rob us and our families. We should do as David did and inquire of the Lord as to what we should do to overcome him. The key to safety is maintaining a close relationship with the Lord. This enables us to hear His battle plans. Psalm 91 is one of my favorite chapters of the Bible. I claim its promises every day for myself and my loved ones. I encourage you to do likewise. This Psalm should cause every believer to trust in God's power to keep us.

Dear heavenly Father, thank You for Your promise of protection from the enemy, and for the many times that I have been spared from the evil plans of the devil. I appreciate Your angels watching over me and my loved ones. I am grateful that no weapon formed against me prospers. Lord, I submit to You, knowing that when I resist the enemy, he must flee from me. Thank You for answering me when I am in trouble and showing me how to overcome every problem that I face. Lord, help all of Your people to know the promise of Your power to keep us from harm. Strengthen our faith to trust You in all of our ways. Amen.

April 17 *Day 107*

Proverbs 14:20-21 20 The poor is hated even of his own neighbour: but the rich hath many friends. 21 He that despiseth his neighbour sinneth: but he that hath mercy on the poor, happy is he.

Verse 20 – The fact that the poor are hated even by their own neighbors explains why there is often so much violence in poor neighborhoods. The Bible calls poverty a curse. It breeds many problems, such as filth and sickness. In many areas, the poor do not have access to buy healthy foods, their poor nutrition results in poor health. It is demoralizing to live in a poverty-stricken region. Poverty crushes any hope for improvement. Depressed people stop trying to better themselves. This breeds irresponsibility, which becomes a hotbed for rebellion. Or in some cases, the poverty is so extreme that total exhaustion and starvation strips the people of any desire or hope for life. The only way to break the cycle of poverty is to bring the gospel to the poor, and support those ministries that will bring the needed provisions to those who lack them. We can be redeemed from poverty and anything else that misrepresents God to the world. God blesses His people when they follow and obey Him (Deuteronomy 28:1-6).

We are incapable of keeping God's commandments by ourselves; we can only keep them by the enabling of the Holy Spirit. If we rebel and go our own way, the law of sowing and reaping will bring a curse upon us. Poverty is a part of that curse. Money is not the answer to poverty, since it only takes care of the surface problems. As the American government has discovered; throwing money at the problem through welfare programs only compounds it. Money never solves the root problems of hatred, violence, irresponsibility, or fear. Only a change of heart that comes from knowing Christ can accomplish that. When hearts are not changed, the curse continues (Deuteronomy 28:15-20).

Verse 21 – The rich man has many friends; but love for his money and what it can obtain for them, is at the heart of many of these friendships. The rich man's money can also make him proud, causing him to sin against God, his fellow man, and himself. Christ owns the earth and the entire universe. He gave up His position of supreme power and wealth and became poor to save us, that we might become rich in His blessings (2 Corinthians 8:9). Those who are merciful to the poor are happy and blessed, for they follow in the steps of Jesus Himself.

Dear Father, I am so grateful that I know You. You have blessed me greatly; I am thankful for Your goodness. Strengthen me to walk daily in obedience to Your commandments. Lord, help me also to be sensitive to the needs of others. I desire to be a giver; to reach out to the poor. Help me not to ever demean or look down on those who are less fortunate than I, but rather let me give them hope and encouragement. Help me to trust You for daily provision and to give of those things that I do have. I can always share a smile, encouragement, faith, love, and prayers with others. I ask this in the name of Jesus. Amen.

Proverbs 14:22-25 22 Do they not err that devise evil? but mercy and truth shall be to them that devise good. 23 In all labour there is profit: but the talk of the lips tendeth only to penury. 24 The crown of the wise is their riches: but the foolishness of fools is folly. 25 A true witness delivereth souls: but a deceitful witness speaketh lies.

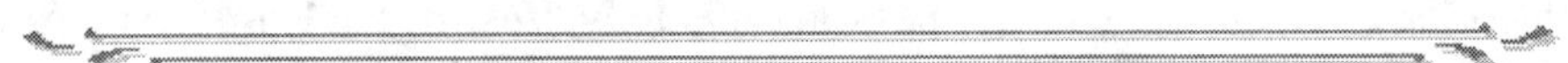

Verse 22 – Evildoers bring evil on themselves, but the Lord shows loving-kindness to those who are good to others. As we have seen in other lessons, Jesus "went about doing good" (Acts 10:38). Good works flow out of our relationship with God. The more we know Him, the more we love Him and allow His Spirit to change us. This enables us to do more good works, followed by more of His mercy and truth, and so on; an endless cycle of blessing!

Verse 23 – The principle of sowing and reaping is easily seen in the area of work. Those who work hard will have a profit for their labor. Those who waste their time will end in poverty. I have known people who talked about certain things they wanted to do, but because they did not invest the time and work needed, they never accomplished their desires. They were talkers, not doers. I hear many Christians talk about increasing their prayer life, but most never seem to actually do it. I have failed in this area myself. I remember a time when I was going through many difficult trials and facing new problems daily. The Lord spoke something to my spirit that I have never forgotten, He said: "If you prayed about your problems as much as you talk about your problems, you would not even have the problems." We must diligently work at maintaining a healthy prayer life; it does not come easily.

Verse 24 – This verse speaks of the wise as wearing a crown of riches. A wise man's wealth is his wisdom. We are rich indeed when we have the wisdom of God. With His wisdom, nothing is impossible to us. We noted in Day 1 that wisdom is the ability to discern the soundest course of action in a situation. This is a true gift, a priceless "crown of riches;" for wise decisions lead to abundant life (John 10:10).

Verse 25 – Those who speak truth can save lives. This can happen in court cases; the charge against an innocent person can be dropped because of the truthful testimony of a witness. A faithful witness is also one who shares the truth about Jesus with others. The Bible itself is a faithful witness of Christ (John 5:39); its truths can save people. A deceitful witness, whether in a courthouse or preaching a false doctrine, endangers others. Spreading lies has destroyed many people. We should not believe everything we hear, but bring all things to God in prayer and measure them against His Word. Jesus Himself is the truth (John 14:6); we can trust Him to let us know what is truth and what is a lie.

Dear heavenly Father, I am thankful for Your mercy and truth each day. Thank You for forgiving me and being patient with me when I fail. I ask for the desire to be more diligent in my prayer life. I need help in my own life and I also need the burden to pray for others who need Your help. I lift up my brothers and sisters and ask that You would minister to each of them in the area of their lives where they have the greatest need. Encourage those who are weary, give faith to those who are losing hope, grant strength to the weak and health to the sick. Bless Your children and keep us from evil. In the name of Jesus I pray. Amen.

Proverbs 14:26-27 26 In the fear of the LORD is strong confidence: and his children shall have a place of refuge. 27 The fear of the LORD is a fountain of life, to depart from the snares of death.

Verse 26 – Many verses in Proverbs speak about a holy "fear of the Lord." The Amplified Bible sheds light on this phrase: "In the reverent and worshipful fear of the LORD is strong confidence." Those who reverence the Lord believe His word. We have already seen in Day 55 that the fear of the Lord is the beginning of wisdom. Respect and understanding of God produces a desire in us to obey Him. Keeping God's Word brings us under His protection; those who fear Him are promised a long life, strong confidence, and refuge.

Verse 27 – The worshipful fear of God is like a fountain of life. By walking in His path we avoid the traps leading to death. What is true worship? Some equate singing songs with worship. One can worship God while singing, but singing alone does not mean that one is worshipping. It is the voice of the heart that God hears, not just the words of the song. The highest form of worship is obedience. God has a name for those who draw near to Him with their lips but not their hearts: "Ye hypocrites, well did Esaias prophesy of you, saying, This people draweth nigh unto me with their mouth, and honoureth me with their lips; but their heart is far from me…" (Matthew 15:7-9).

The heart of man speaks louder to God than his words. God considers men's hearts, and is not influenced by outward appearances. When told to anoint a king to replace Saul from among Jesse's sons, Samuel was impressed with the fine appearance and stature of the eldest, but the LORD told Samuel, "…Look not on his countenance, or on the height of his stature; because I have refused him: for the LORD seeth not as man seeth; for man looketh on the outward appearance, but the LORD looketh on the heart" (1 Samuel 16:7).

Without God, all men's hearts are wicked and deceitful. We must be "born again," to get a new heart, so that we have the Holy Spirit, and are made able to obey the Lord. We can align our words with His Word, making them acceptable to Him. David knew it would require God's strength and redemption to make his heart's meditations and the words he spoke acceptable to Him. This is true of us too! We need to make David's prayer our own: "Let the words of my mouth, and the meditation of my heart, be acceptable in thy sight, O LORD, my strength, and my redeemer" (Psalm 19:14).

Dear heavenly Father, thank You for Your many promises of blessings. I am thankful that You are my refuge and I can run to You when I am in trouble. I am also grateful that You keep me from the traps of the devil. Lord, I do love You, and I ask that You cleanse my heart from any thing that is not like You. Strengthen me to walk in a worthy way before You and my fellow men. Restore the "fear of the Lord" to Your people today. Forgive us when we have become too casual about the things of God. Instill in us a reverential fear of Your Holy Name and Word. I ask this in Jesus' name. Amen.

God's Wisdom for Daily Living ***Betty Miller***
April 20 ***Day 110***

Proverbs 14:28-30 29 In the multitude of people is the king's honour: but in the want of people is the destruction of the prince. 29 He that is slow to wrath is of great understanding: but he that is hasty of spirit exalteth folly. 30 A sound heart is the life of the flesh: but envy the rottenness of the bones.

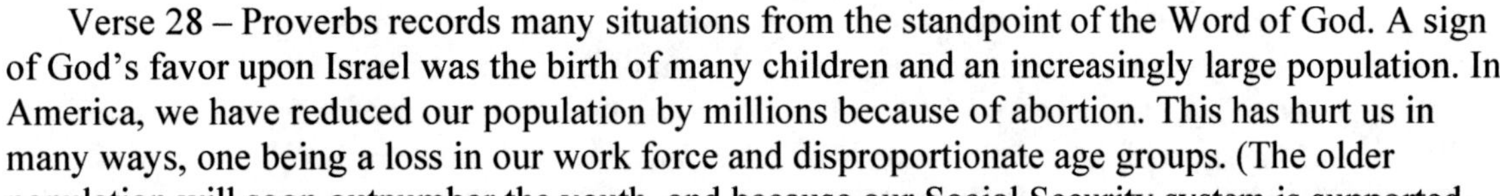

Verse 28 – Proverbs records many situations from the standpoint of the Word of God. A sign of God's favor upon Israel was the birth of many children and an increasingly large population. In America, we have reduced our population by millions because of abortion. This has hurt us in many ways, one being a loss in our work force and disproportionate age groups. (The older population will soon outnumber the youth, and because our Social Security system is supported by new workers enrolling in it, this means there will not be enough contributions to support it).

However, the greatest damage to our country is the curse of death that is upon it because of abortion. Because millions of innocent babies have been murdered, we will reap what we have sown. We are told in Genesis 9:6-7 and Deuteronomy 27:25 that the penalty for shedding innocent blood is that we will experience the shedding of blood in our nation.

Any country with a small population has difficulty in defending itself and is deprived of the talents that many people contribute and inspire in others. Evil kings can rule so badly that their own people will flee the country and strangers will not want to settle in it. A king without the support of his people cannot maintain his position. If a ruler does not have his people behind him, it will eventually be to his destruction.

Verse 29 – Whoever is slow to become angry is a man of understanding. The quick-tempered man exposes his own folly. He says and does many foolish things, and some may not be correctable (Proverbs 14:17a). Hateful, angry words can devastate others and cannot be taken back. Only God can deliver someone from a bad temper and heal the wounds that he has inflicted on others. God will do this for us if we ask Him.

Verse 30 – Doctors have discovered that many physical ailments are due to problems in the soul. Patients who replace negative attitudes with positive ones recover dramatically. The physical body can express envy, anger, and unforgiveness in the form of various diseases. Yielding to anger drains us of energy we could have used productively, whereas walking in love, faith, and forgiveness produces peace of mind and health. Self-control is a fruit of the Spirit. It develops in us as we allow the Holy Spirit to change us. We must ask the Lord to help us to restrain our anger. "Wherefore, my beloved brethren, let every man be swift to hear, slow to speak, slow to wrath: For the wrath of man worketh not the righteousness of God" (James 1:19-20).

Dear Father, thank You for Your grace that abounds in my life. I am most appreciative for Your daily provisions. Help me to overcome the character flaws in my life. May I be angry at the things You are angry about, but I do not want to be angry in my own wrath. Remove that kind of anger from my life and give me patience with all men. I want to be controlled by Your Holy Spirit. Forgive us, as a nation, for all the innocent blood we have shed through millions of abortions. Have mercy on us and make a way for us to stop this horrible murdering of innocent babies. I ask in the merciful name of Jesus. Amen.

Proverbs 14:31 He that oppresseth the poor reproacheth his Maker: but he that honoureth him hath mercy on the poor.

Throughout Scripture, God expresses His love and concern for the poor: "If there be among you a poor man of one of thy brethren within any of thy gates in thy land which the LORD thy God giveth thee, thou shalt not harden thine heart, nor shut thine hand from thy poor brother: But thou shalt open thine hand wide unto him, and shalt surely lend him sufficient for his need, in that which he wanteth" (Deuteronomy 15:7). "I know that the LORD will maintain the cause of the afflicted, and the right of the poor" (Psalm 140:12). "The Spirit of the Lord is upon me, because he hath anointed me to preach the gospel to the poor…" (Luke 4:18a).

The Lord is interested in every soul. His nature is to seek and help the poor, and He commands His children to do likewise. When we treat the poor with equity, we honor God. In giving money or material things to the needy, or reaching out with His love in other ways, it creates opportunities to lead people to Christ by demonstrating His love to them. The Greek meaning of the word, "salvation" includes deliverance from sin, sickness, danger, lack, and poverty. Jesus came to save us from our sin and its effects upon us both in this life, as well as eternity. He came to redeem us not only from our sin, but our sickness and poverty as well. "For ye know the grace of our Lord Jesus Christ, that, though he was rich, yet for your sakes he became poor, that ye through his poverty might be rich" (2 Corinthians 8:9).

As God's children, we are promised abundance in both material things as well as spiritual things, which are far more valuable. The Lord wants to bless us so that we can bless others. How can we give to others if we ourselves are poor? We must learn how to receive God's blessings so that we can pass them on to others. Helping the needy, the poor, the sick, or prisoners is the same as giving to the Lord Himself and He shall reward us. To ignore or reject them is to reject Christ, for which He will reject us. "And the King shall answer and say unto them, Verily I say unto you, Inasmuch as ye have done it unto one of the least of these my brethren, ye have done it unto me. Then shall he say also unto them on the left hand, Depart from me, ye cursed, into everlasting fire, prepared for the devil and his angels: For I was an hungred, and ye gave me no meat: I was thirsty, and ye gave me no drink: I was a stranger, and ye took me not in: naked, and ye clothed me not: sick, and in prison, and ye visited me not. Then shall they also answer him, saying, Lord, when saw we thee an hungred, or athirst, or a stranger, or naked, or sick, or in prison, and did not minister unto thee? Then shall he answer them, saying, Verily I say unto you, Inasmuch as ye did it not to one of the least of these, ye did it not to me. And these shall go away into everlasting punishment: but the righteous into life eternal" (Matthew 25:40-46).

Dear Lord, thank You for Your sacrifice on the cross to save me from my sin and deliver me from the curse of sickness and poverty. Please strengthen me to use the blessing of health to serve You and Your people. Direct me in my giving so that I might help those who are hurting and needy. Guide me in giving to those ministries that are making a difference in the world. Lord, help me to be sensitive to the cries of the poor and not to turn a deaf ear to any that I am able to help. May all of Your children rise above selfishness, and as a corporate body reach out to the world of needy people. Strengthen us all for that task. I ask in the name of Jesus Christ. Amen.

Proverbs 14:32-33 The wicked is driven away in his wickedness: but the righteous hath hope in his death. 33 Wisdom resteth in the heart of him that hath understanding: but that which is in the midst of fools is made known.

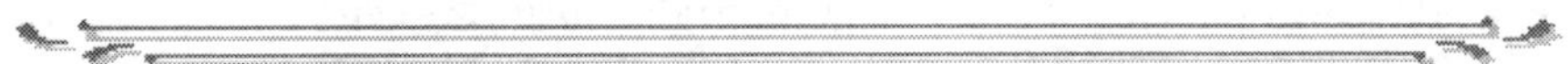

Verse 32 – The wicked person is destroyed by his own evil doings, since men reap what they sow. The righteous have an entirely different fate. When we belong to God and are "born again," we do not have to be afraid when we face death. The One who has conquered death is with us, as we make the transition from this life to heaven. The most wonderful promise that belongs to every Christian is that we shall not taste death. Yes, our body dies, but the spirit of every believer in Jesus Christ lives on, and will meet Jesus and their loved ones who knew Him in heaven. Then, at the resurrection of the dead, we shall rise and receive our new immortal bodies.

"Behold, I shew you a mystery; We shall not all sleep, but we shall all be changed, In a moment, in the twinkling of an eye, at the last trump: for the trumpet shall sound, and the dead shall be raised incorruptible, and we shall be changed. For this corruptible must put on incorruption, and this mortal must put on immortality. So when this corruptible shall have put on incorruption, and this mortal shall have put on immortality, then shall be brought to pass the saying that is written, Death is swallowed up in victory. O death, where is thy sting? O grave, where is thy victory? The sting of death is sin; and the strength of sin is the law. But thanks be to God, which giveth us the victory through our Lord Jesus Christ" (1 Corinthians 15:51-57).

During His ministry on earth, Jesus had the power to raise the dead, as seen in the story of Lazarus (John 11:21-45); but at some point those raised from the dead, died again. Jesus just saved them from premature death. Many have been raised from the dead throughout history by Spirit filled believers; however, only One was resurrected from the dead and that was Jesus Christ! By His own death and resurrection, Jesus conquered death and hell for all who believe on Him. The resurrection of the remainder of the dead will not occur until Christ returns to the earth to judge them. For Christians there is no longer any fear in death, because its power is broken through the death and resurrection of Jesus Christ. Praise God!

Verse 33 – God's wisdom resides within those who belong to Him. Because of this, we have access to His wisdom and knowledge for the answer to any problem. Self-confident fools will eventually show themselves as such; for what is in a man will at some time or other surface for others to see. All who desire to know Christ do not need to remain foolish and self-confident. If we seek Him, He will give us the power to follow and obey Him. We will not need to fear death or hell, for those who know Christ and love God have the promise that they will be with Him eternally.

Dear heavenly Father, thank You for the promise of eternal life. I am so thankful that my name is written in the Book of Life. Lord, I pray that each and every member of my family comes to know You and the power of Your resurrection life. Thank You, that as Christians, when it is our time to cross over into heaven, we do not have to fear. Death is the last enemy we shall face, and because You have overcome death and hell, we will not even feel its sting. Lord, we are grateful for the promise that we shall once again see all of our loved ones that are in Christ, because they live in You. Comfort those who have lost loved ones with the knowledge that they shall indeed see them and love them once again in our heavenly home. I ask this in Your Son Jesus' name. Amen.

Proverbs 14:34 Righteousness exalteth a nation: but sin is a reproach to any people.

In this verse, Proverbs points out that corporate righteousness exalts a nation, while corporate sin brings reproach. Every blessing comes directly or indirectly from God's grace. It grieves the heart of God, that instead of being grateful for all the blessings God has bestowed upon mankind, many blame Him for the problems in the world. They do not understand that sin has created the problems.

Keeping God's Word brings blessing. Some nations, though they follow false religions, are blessed in some aspects of their society because they practice scriptural principles. Many people do not realize what tremendous things Christianity has accomplished for the betterment of our lives, especially here in the United States. Many here enjoy a good life with abundance, not realizing that they owe our prosperity and freedom to a book that many are taught to despise–the Bible. Many of our founding fathers were godly men who used Biblical principles to construct the Constitution and the Declaration of Independence. Any unbiased historian knows that the Bible has had a much greater influence in the shaping of our nation than what is currently being taught in our schools.

When the Bible's influence is strong, it affects a culture in positive ways. When a society rejects Biblical principles, evil will be reflected in its cultural choices. We see this today worldwide, as both young and old people are embracing things that are unbiblical. Choice of dress, food, music, and entertainment are all reflections of how we embrace or reject God's Word. Rebellious, anti-Christian music, for example, has become firmly established in society, despite its dangerous influences of encouraging lust, sexual promiscuity, suicide, rebellion against authority, and so forth.

We must repent and return to righteousness so that our nations will be exalted. Sin brings reproach to us–individually and corporately. "God be merciful unto us, and bless us; and cause his face to shine upon us; Selah. That thy way may be known upon earth, thy saving health among all nations. Let the people praise thee, O God; let all the people praise thee. O let the nations be glad and sing for joy: for thou shalt judge the people righteously, and govern the nations upon earth" (Psalm 67:1-5).

Dear Father God, thank You for this nation. May I be one who is a righteous influence to those around me; affecting society for good. Lord, bring revival to our land and turn sinners to the gospel so that they might be saved. Deliver our children from the Satanic influences in society. Please protect them from the evil one and show them the way of the Lord. Help me to be a good example to young people and influence them to follow You. Forgive us of our national sins of lust, materialism, pride, witchcraft, murder, lying, abortion, and sexual sins. Deliver us from evil. I ask this in the name of Jesus Christ. Amen.

God's Wisdom for Daily Living — *Betty Miller*

April 24 — ***Day 114***

Proverbs 14:35-15:1 35 The king's favour is toward a wise servant: but his wrath is against him that causeth shame. 1 A soft answer turneth away wrath: but grievous words stir up anger.

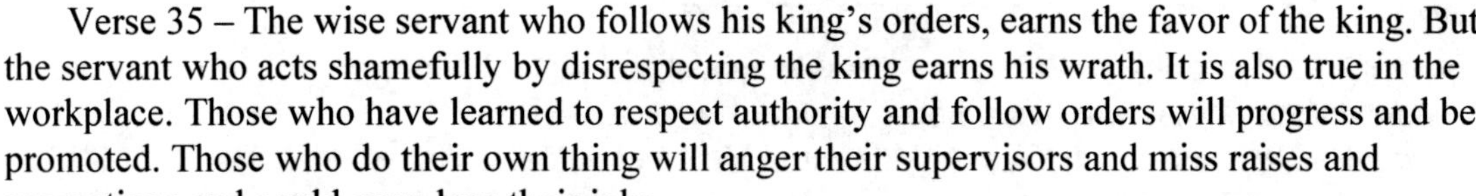

Verse 35 – The wise servant who follows his king's orders, earns the favor of the king. But the servant who acts shamefully by disrespecting the king earns his wrath. It is also true in the workplace. Those who have learned to respect authority and follow orders will progress and be promoted. Those who do their own thing will anger their supervisors and miss raises and promotions and could even lose their jobs.

The Lord expects us to respect those in authority over us. Without this honor and obedience, anarchy and rebellion will set in and confusion and disorder will be the result. The Lord expects the worker (servant) to honor his boss and work for him as unto the Lord. He also expects the boss (master) to be kind to his workers and not threaten them. The Lord is the one who will repay both master and servant (Ephesians 6:5-9).

We are to work with a submissive spirit. Sometimes people who appear to be submissive are only "going through the motions," while, inwardly they are resenting their positions. Of course, there are limits to submission; it should always be "as unto the Lord." As we submit to God first, He will resolve any problems involving submission to others. God never expects us to submit to anything that is immoral or contrary to His Word. If an authority were to ask us to lie for them, we would have to refuse; but even then, we can refuse with a proper attitude.

Verse 1 – As this verse says, "A soft answer turneth away wrath: but grievous words stir up anger." Extremes in submission have caused confusion in the body of Christ. Those who refuse to submit to authority are just as out of balance as those who submit to every dictate from those they feel are their superiors. We must submit to the leadership of the Holy Spirit to direct us in all areas. This requirement has been greatly abused by church authorities. Some pastors are dictators, while others are so permissive that church order is lost, resulting in chaos. There are always those who tend to be hard and dogmatic in handling the truth. While there must be respect for leadership in the body of Christ, a legalistic approach brings bondage, which is contrary to God's will. Paul's letter to the Galatians reprimanded them for leaving the simplicity of the Gospel by adding strict rules and regulations to it. Submission is required of God's people, but never to the point that leaders become dictators.

True pastors and leaders–the ones God chooses to guide His people–do not dictate, but lead His flock in love and by example. "Neither as being Lords over God's heritage, but being ensamples to the flock" (1 Peter 5:3). If you have been unable to find leaders like this in your area, ask the Lord to lead you to someone who has a heart like His.

Dear heavenly Father, I thank You for the godly men and women that You have put in my life to teach me Your ways, that I may learn submission. I desire to always walk in humility, and not always insist on my way. I know at times, that I may be right about something, but please help me to maintain a submissive spirit while discussing those kinds of issues. Deliver me from pride and anger. May issues be resolved by You having Your way in situations, and not my way or the other person's way. May You always be glorified in my workplace, home, and everywhere that I find myself. I ask in the name of the Lord Jesus Christ. Amen.

Proverbs 15:2-4 The tongue of the wise utters knowledge rightly, but the mouth of the [self-confident] fool pours out folly. The eyes of the Lord are in every place, keeping watch upon the evil and the good. A gentle tongue [with its healing power] is a tree of life, but willful contrariness in it breaks down the spirit (AMP).

Verse 2 – All throughout Proverbs we are admonished to guard what we say, because what comes out of our mouths will determine if we are wise or foolish.

Verse 3 – No one can hide from God because He "sees all" and "knows all." The Lord is omnipresent (present everywhere) and omniscient (knows all things). No one can hide a word or deed from Him. That the unsaved do evil without restraint is understandable, since they do not know God. But many Christians act as if God were on vacation and not watching all they do. If we really believe that He hears our conversations, would we speak to family and friends the way we do?

Speaking critically to and of one's spouse is one of the things that erodes a marriage. Consistent use of negative words and critical comments will lead to destruction of the marriage, which can escalate to divorce. The threat of divorce should never be used to manipulate a spouse. Using divorce as a threat is like speaking murder to the marriage.

Words can accumulate in the spirit and cause one to react lovingly or hateful by what is spoken. The Bible warns each spouse not to return "railing for railing" but "blessing for a railing." As kind words are returned this stops the cycle of "railing for railing." "Likewise, ye husbands, dwell with them according to knowledge, giving honour unto the wife, as unto the weaker vessel, and as being heirs together of the grace of life; that your prayers be not hindered. Finally, be ye all of one mind, having compassion one of another, love as brethren, be pitiful, be courteous: Not rendering evil for evil, or railing for railing: but contrariwise blessing; knowing that ye are thereunto called, that ye should inherit a blessing. For he that will love life, and see good days, let him refrain his tongue from evil, and his lips that they speak no guile: Let him eschew evil, and do good; let him seek peace, and ensue it (1 Peter 3:7-11).

We are admonished in the Bible to seek peace and do good. We should never take our anger out on anyone, especially our mates. We are to give our anger to Jesus and ask Him to remove it, replacing it with His forgiveness, love, and patience. Often, after people get married, they cease to be courteous to one another, becoming rude and unmannerly. The Lord calls us to be as courteous to our mates as to any sister or brother in Christ. We should be kind to one another, and think about saying and doing nice things that edify our spouses and build our marriages. Let us be as a tree of life, our tongues producing words that nourish and delight the souls of others.

Father, I am thankful that You are "all-seeing" and "all-hearing." It brings me great comfort to know You are watching over me at all times, and that You hear my every word and prayer. You are a wonderful Father who not only loves me, but the whole world! Thank You for being concerned about the little things that concern me, as well as the things that I perceive as big. Lord, I know that my concerns are never too small to miss Your attention, nor are they so big that You cannot take care of them because You are size less! You are GOD! May this truth be planted strongly in my spirit and in those whom I pray for. Meet the needs of the thousands of people who write to us for prayer, according to Your will. Let each of them know how much You love and care for them. I know that You will come and save them! I ask this in Jesus' name. Amen.

Proverbs 15:5 A fool despiseth his father's instruction: but he that regardeth reproof is prudent.

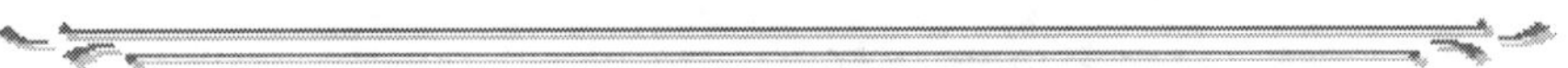

If we love our earthly fathers, we respect and obey them. As adults, we are grateful that they disciplined us out of love and protection. These things are true not only of our relationships with our natural fathers, but also of our heavenly Father. To enter the Kingdom of God, we must have a child-like heart of trust, knowing that He loves us far more than any earthly father could and that His instructions are for our good. We are blessed when we remain teachable, with child-like faith and yield to our Father's correction. "But Jesus called them unto him, and said, Suffer little children to come unto me, and forbid them not: for of such is the kingdom of God. Verily I say unto you, Whosoever shall not receive the kingdom of God as a little child shall in no wise enter therein" (Luke 18:16-17).

Jesus is our supreme example of obedience, desiring to please His Father at all times. He never did anything except what His Father desired Him to do. He was obedient to the point of death, yielding Himself to the cross. The sacrifice of the perfectly obedient Son of God, made it possible to save many disobedient sons.

Obedience is the evidence that we are true disciples of Christ. Jesus said, "If ye love me, keep my commandments" (John 14:15). For most Christians, learning submission to Our Father's will is the hardest lesson to learn, but if we rebel at His leading, we will suffer for our disobedience. God never wants us to be hurt or suffer at Satan's hand, but if we disobey God, we may reap the consequences of our own sin. The Bible gives numerous warnings that obedience brings blessing and disobedience leads to destruction: "Come now, and let us reason together, saith the LORD: though your sins be as scarlet, they shall be as white as snow; though they be red like crimson, they shall be as wool. If ye be willing and obedient, ye shall eat the good of the land: But if ye refuse and rebel, ye shall be devoured with the sword: for the mouth of the LORD hath spoken it" (Isaiah 1:18-20).

Cleansing and forgiveness are available to us when we come to Christ. Our sins, which have left a deep stain upon our souls, will be forgiven and our souls cleansed. As new creatures in Christ, we are made as white as snow. Many suffer under the burden of guilt for their sins. This is unnecessary, because "If we confess our sins, he is faithful and just to forgive us our sins, and to cleanse us from all unrighteousness…" (1 John 1:9-10a).

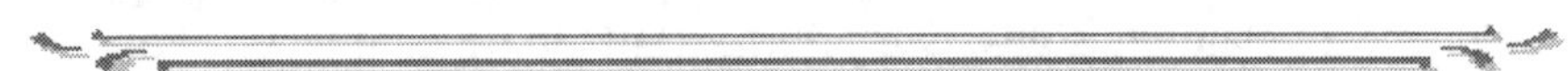

Dearest Father, thank You for loving me so much that You sent Your Son to die for my sins. I do not understand a love like that, but I am eternally grateful for it. I also appreciate Your hand of correction in my life. I know without it, I would have gone astray and the enemy would have destroyed me. Lord, help us to be obedient to Your will. Give us a greater desire to serve You and others. Keep us from the evil one. Bless our loved ones and keep them in Your hand. I ask this in the name of the Lord Jesus Christ. Amen.

Proverbs 15:6-7 6 In the house of the righteous is much treasure: but in the revenues of the wicked is trouble. 7 The lips of the wise disperse knowledge: but the heart of the foolish doeth not so.

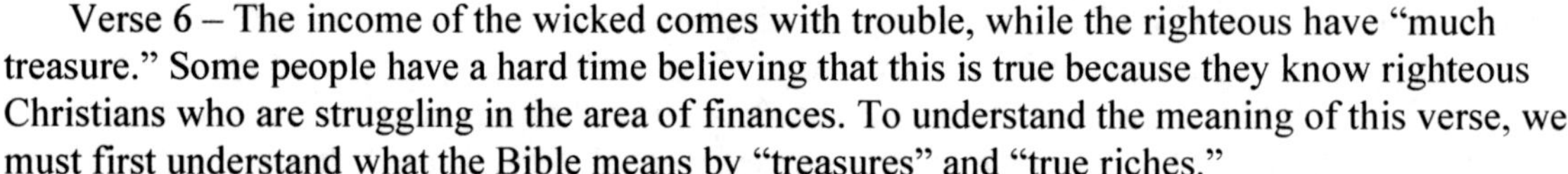

Verse 6 – The income of the wicked comes with trouble, while the righteous have "much treasure." Some people have a hard time believing that this is true because they know righteous Christians who are struggling in the area of finances. To understand the meaning of this verse, we must first understand what the Bible means by "treasures" and "true riches."

Money cannot buy health or save someone's life. The Bible says that we are to seek the true riches of God, not the riches of this world. His riches are things that money cannot buy. How can money deliver a wayward teenager from drugs and sin? How can money buy peace in our souls in the face of fear all around us? How can money save a soul from hell? Only God's riches are available to do these things. We are truly rich when we have faith in God.

Certainly God does want to bless us with material things, but it will be Him that we are seeking when these things come, not the things themselves. Many today are seeking God for what He can do for them, instead of asking God how they can serve Him. We cannot seek mammon and God at the same time.

"If therefore ye have not been faithful in the unrighteous mammon, who will commit to your trust the true riches? And if ye have not been faithful in that which is another man's, who shall give you that which is your own? No servant can serve two masters: for either he will hate the one, and love the other; or else he will hold to the one, and despise the other. Ye cannot serve God and mammon." (Luke 16:11-13).

"Lay not up for yourselves treasures upon earth, where moth and rust doth corrupt, and where thieves break through and steal: But lay up for yourselves treasures in heaven, where neither moth nor rust doth corrupt, and where thieves do not break through nor steal: For where your treasure is, there will your heart be also" (Matthew 6:19-21).

"Therefore take no thought, saying, What shall we eat? or, What shall we drink? or, Wherewithal shall we be clothed? (For after all these things do the Gentiles seek:) for your heavenly Father knoweth that ye have need of all these things. But seek ye first the kingdom of God, and his righteousness; and all these things shall be added unto you" (Matthew 6:31-33).

Verse 7 – The lips of the wise share godly knowledge, claiming the promises of God. However, claiming only material things is foolish. Many today are heard claiming cars and houses, but seldom heard claiming souls. Our priorities should be right when claiming and confessing. The Lord's greatest desire is for us to grow in Him and to bring others to the knowledge of His love. He will take care of our needs if we seek Him first.

Dear Father, we come to You in Jesus' most precious name, thanking You for Your love for us. You see where our lives are not in balance in the area of material things. We ask that You reveal those areas to us and help us to walk in the path of righteousness and balance. Deliver us from any lust for the things of this world and give us a vision of the rewards that await us in the world to come. Let us not worry about finances, but rather cast all of our cares upon You, for You care for us. Heal us today, spirit, soul, and body, so that we might serve You by walking in a victorious Christian life. Let our lights shine so that others might truly see Your love in us. In Jesus' name we pray, Amen.

Proverbs 15:8-9 8 The sacrifice of the wicked is an abomination to the LORD: but the prayer of the upright is his delight. 9 The way of the wicked is an abomination unto the LORD: but he loveth him that followeth after righteousness.

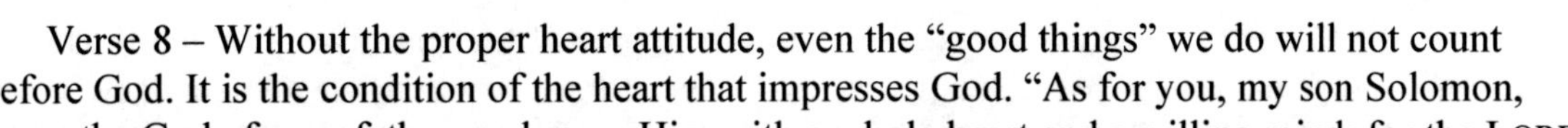

Verse 8 – Without the proper heart attitude, even the "good things" we do will not count before God. It is the condition of the heart that impresses God. "As for you, my son Solomon, know the God of your father, and serve Him with a whole heart and a willing mind; for the LORD searches all hearts, and understands every intent of the thoughts. If you seek Him, He will let you find Him; but if you forsake Him, He will reject you forever" (1 Chronicles 28:9 NASB).

Many voice a love for God, but deny Him by their compromised lifestyles. A man cannot live in two worlds, nor can he serve two masters. Ultimately, he will choose one over the other, even as Jesus declared in Matthew 6:24. If we are not on fire with a love for God that causes us to live in close relationship and in obedience with Him, we are lukewarm and need to repent. Many people are spiritually blind, because they are rich in the world's goods and do not line their perspectives up with God's truth. They are "naked" because they do not have His eyesight nor cover themselves with His righteousness (Revelation 19:8).

The Lord will not accept the sacrifices of the wicked, nor will He hear their music. Their worship songs are just noise to Him because their hearts are not right before Him: "I hate, I reject your festivals, Nor do I delight in your solemn assemblies. Even though you offer up to Me burnt offerings and your grain offerings, I will not accept them; And I will not even look at the peace offerings of your fatlings. Take away from Me the noise of your songs; I will not even listen to the sound of your harps. But let justice roll down like waters And righteousness like an ever-flowing stream" (Amos 5:21-24 NASB)

Verse 9 – While the way of the wicked is an abomination to the Lord, He loves those who follow after righteousness. We must be totally committed to God's will if we are to be overcomers. A compromised life style brings judgment upon us and it will ultimately destroy our relationship with the Lord. However, if we remain steadfast, and follow the Lord daily, we will bring joy to His heart and be blessed.

Father God, I am thankful that You give me spiritual eyes to see, so that I do not go astray on the wrong path. I do ask You to forgive me for my sins and shortcomings. Change those things in my life that are not like You. Help me to be obedient to Your will for my life. Give me the strength to obey all that You require of me. Lord, I pray for my friends and family, that they too, would follow You and obey Your will. Keep Your hand of protection over us all, and give us light on our path, that we may follow in the way of righteousness. I ask this in the name of the Lord Jesus Christ. Amen.

Proverbs 15:10-12 There is severe discipline for him who forsakes God's way, and he who hates reproof will die (physically, morally and spiritually). 11 Sheol (the place of the dead) and Abaddon (the abyss, the final place of the accuser Satan) both are before the LORD; how much more then the hearts of the children of men? 12 A scorner has no love for one who rebukes him, neither will he go to the wise (for counsel) (AMP).

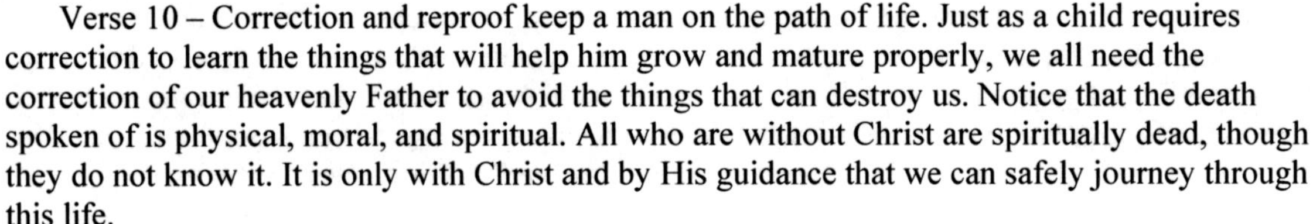

Verse 10 – Correction and reproof keep a man on the path of life. Just as a child requires correction to learn the things that will help him grow and mature properly, we all need the correction of our heavenly Father to avoid the things that can destroy us. Notice that the death spoken of is physical, moral, and spiritual. All who are without Christ are spiritually dead, though they do not know it. It is only with Christ and by His guidance that we can safely journey through this life.

"And you hath he quickened, who were dead in trespasses and sins: Wherein in time past ye walked according to the course of this world, according to the prince of the power of the air, the spirit that now worketh in the children of disobedience: Among whom also we all had our conversation in times past in the lusts of our flesh, fulfilling the desires of the flesh and of the mind; and were by nature the children of wrath, even as others. But God, who is rich in mercy, for his great love wherewith he loved us, Even when we were dead in sins, hath quickened us together with Christ, (by grace ye are saved;)" (Ephesians 2:1-6).

Verse 11 – If hell and the place of the dead are clearly visible to God, how much more are men's hearts visible to Him? We may be able to deceive people into thinking that we are good Christians, but God sees our hearts. If we are not walking in the truth, He knows it. We will reap what we sow. If we belong to Christ, our lives should show it.

Verse 12 – Fools despise correction and their pride keeps them from coming to the wise ones for guidance. Their lusts and desires lead them. If they do not repent and turn to Jesus, their end will be hell. The Lord does not desire that anyone should perish, but because He has given each of us the gift of free will, we choose whom we serve, either God or Satan. We may think we can choose to serve ourselves, but this is *not* an option. If we serve self, we are really serving Satan. God has given us, His children, the task of sharing the Gospel with those around us, so that they will have the opportunity to accept Christ as their Savior and escape hell (2 Peter 3:9). May we welcome the Lord's correction so that we will not open the door for Satan to attack us through our own rebellion and sin. May we also pray for and witness to the lost so that they may be saved and escape the torments of hell.

Dear Father, thank You for being so good to me. Deliver me of any rebellion that would cause me to ignore Your leading in my life. Strengthen me, so that I will always be an obedient child. I appreciate Your patience toward me. Give me patience with those around me who do not know You. Let me share the gospel in love with each of them. Thank You for delivering me from hell. I am grateful for the promise of Your presence with me in this life and the promise of heaven to come. Lord, watch over all of Your children and keep us from evil. I ask this in the name of Jesus. Amen.

Proverbs 15:13-14 13 A merry heart maketh a cheerful countenance: but by sorrow of the heart the spirit is broken. 14 The heart of him that hath understanding seeketh knowledge: but the mouth of fools feedeth on foolishness.

Verse 13 – One can tell the condition of a person's heart by looking at his countenance (his facial appearance). We all know when people are happy; we can tell by the sparkle in their eyes, their smile and their cheerful countenance. When they are old, happy people have "smile wrinkles" instead of those caused by frowning. Facial expressions reveal a lot about a person. Even children will speak up when they observe an unkind face, and they might say, "That is a mean man!"

Sorrow in the heart can also be read on the face. When we are troubled, we've probably heard someone ask us what was wrong. We all experience things in life that break our hearts. If sorrow of heart continues indefinitely, it can break our spirits. How can we recover from heartbreak? We must give the situation to the Lord and ask Him to heal our grief. If we have lost a loved one, we can enjoy the good memories, but we must not allow the enemy to torment us with prolonged grief. God can fill the emptiness from the loss of a mate, a child, a friend, or anything else. Jesus died, not only to give us eternal life, but abundant life now. Since He Himself bore all of our iniquities, pains, sicknesses, griefs, and sorrows, we do not have to bear them. We can receive our healing and deliverance by faith.

"Surely he hath borne our griefs, and carried our sorrows: yet we did esteem him stricken, smitten of God, and afflicted. But he was wounded for our transgressions, he was bruised for our iniquities: the chastisement of our peace was upon him; and with his stripes we are healed. All we like sheep have gone astray; we have turned every one to his own way; and the LORD hath laid on him the iniquity of us all" (Isaiah 53:4-6).

Verse 14 – Those who have godly understanding always want to learn more about God and His ways. We can ask Him for knowledge to overcome every trial we face. God is bigger than our grief, pain, and any problem that we will ever face. He is always there to help us to overcome anything the enemy is trying to do. He will rescue us in our time of need. However, we must not be like the fool who feeds on his own folly, continually airing his troubles and blaming others (including God) for his circumstances. People like this feed on self-pity. When sorrow overwhelms us, we need to remember the little phrase, "this too, shall pass." God is eternal and He has good plans for our futures.

Dear Father, I thank You for always being there for me no matter what I face. I can honestly say that You have never failed me, even in my most intense trials. I have not always understood why I was going through certain things; however, I do not have to understand. You are God, and You are in control, in spite of my lack of understanding. I know that all You require of me is to trust You and look to You in faith, and You will come and save me and bring me an answer. You always have and You always will, because You are faithful. You never fail any of us who look to You. I have failed You, Lord, by my doubt and unbelief at times, but You have never failed me. Help us to trust You more. I ask this in the name of Jesus Christ. Amen.

Proverbs 15:15 All the days of the desponding afflicted are made evil (by anxious thoughts and foreboding), but he who has a glad heart has a continual feast (regardless of circumstances) (AMP).

Bad experiences do not have to produce a bad attitude. Some people allow circumstances, instead of the Holy Spirit, to rule them. We can choose how to react to our circumstances. A person who has the joy of the Lord can endure and overcome all adverse circumstances without losing their peace, because God's joy (which is not dependant upon outward circumstances) comes from the spirit inside a person. Some people, all the days of their lives, will experience evil days because they never have learned to overcome the devil's attacks of evil, fear, worry and depression.

God's joy is like a well within us. To get it flowing, we need only "prime the pump." The best way to overcome despondency and worry is to start praising God for His many blessings. Instead of focusing on negatives, we can activate our faith and joy by turning our attention to God's goodness. Many times, when I have been tempted to get depressed, I just start singing this little chorus: 'Count your blessings, name them one by one; count your blessings, see what God has done!" Recalling God's blessings and thanking Him for them reminds me that He is the Almighty God with whom nothing is impossible! Praise is a wonderful way to dispel depression or fear.

1 Thessalonians 5:18 says, "In everything give thanks: for this is the will of God in Christ Jesus concerning you." Now let us notice the Scripture says to praise God *in* everything, not *for* everything. Not everything that happens to us is God's will, but it is God's will that we always be thankful. We should not praise God *for* tragedies or sickness, yet we should praise Him in the midst of every situation. Evil things do not come from God; He is not the author of sickness, sin, or sorrow. The devil, who is *not* omnipresent, must have armies of demons to carry out his evil work against humanity. The devil is the one who sends such things and then tries to get us to blame God for them!

When we praise God, Satan flees, because God inhabits the praises of His people (Psalm 22:3). Psalms is a wonderful book of songs and praises to the Lord. Psalms 29, 30, 34 and 103 are very uplifting. Meditating upon and reading psalms of praise aloud to the Lord will lift our hearts from despair. Praise can bring about our answers, for the Lord loves to fellowship with those having grateful hearts. His nature is one of joy, and He desires to fill us with His joy. We are surrounded by His blessings every day. We have so much for which we should be thankful. Christ's sacrifice for our sins on the cross, is reason enough for us to gratefully praise Him forevermore!

Dear heavenly Father, I am so thankful to be called a child of God. Forgive me when I fall into the devil's trap of complaining or worrying. Help me to cast my cares upon You, for I know that You care for me. Help me also not to allow contrary circumstances to get me down, but rather, remember that I serve a mighty God who is greater than my circumstances. I love and worship You, no matter what the devil is trying to do. I want you to know that I love You, and Lord, I know You love me. When I think of all the things You have done for me over the years, I am truly grateful. Fill me daily with Your joy, peace, and love so that I might serve You with a merry heart. I ask this in the name of the Lord Jesus. Amen.

Proverbs 15:16-17 16 Better is little with the fear of the LORD than great treasure and trouble therewith. 17 Better is a dinner of herbs where love is, than a stalled ox and hatred therewith.

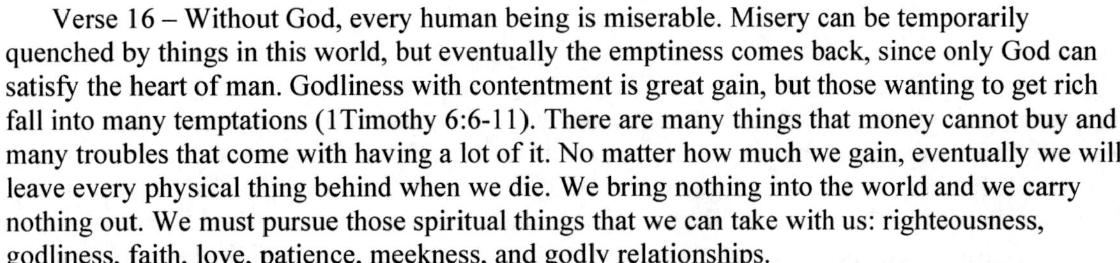

Verse 16 – Without God, every human being is miserable. Misery can be temporarily quenched by things in this world, but eventually the emptiness comes back, since only God can satisfy the heart of man. Godliness with contentment is great gain, but those wanting to get rich fall into many temptations (1Timothy 6:6-11). There are many things that money cannot buy and many troubles that come with having a lot of it. No matter how much we gain, eventually we will leave every physical thing behind when we die. We bring nothing into the world and we carry nothing out. We must pursue those spiritual things that we can take with us: righteousness, godliness, faith, love, patience, meekness, and godly relationships.

We should here note again that the *love* of money (not money itself) is the root of evil. We all need money, but for Christians, it is simply a medium of exchange that we use to take care of our families and ourselves and to spread the Good News of Jesus Christ.

Verse 17 – It is better to share a small, inexpensive meal with someone you love than to live with someone who is full of hate, even though they may have an ox in the stall being fattened up for a big dinner. We can make bad choices regarding marriage partners, if we allow money to influence our decision. Having love in a marriage is more important than having money.

Godly character should be the deciding factor in choosing a mate. A Christian should seek the will of God first, and allow the Lord to bless them with His choice. If marriage with a particular person cannot glorify the Lord, then it would be better to remain alone. There are worse things than being single. One of them is to be out of God's will by compromising and marrying someone who does not feel the same way we do about the Lord. Marriage is the second major choice we make in our lives; rushing into it can be disastrous. We should enter into it with much prayer.

Of course, the most important decision of our lives, is our decision to follow the Lord. This is not just a one-time declaration, but a daily determination to follow Jesus. Just as it is better to have little of this world's possessions and to have the Lord, than to have great treasures without Him, so it is better to have a godly, loving mate with little of this world's pleasures, than to live with someone who lacks godly character. If we honor God in every part of our lives and every decision we make, He will bless us. "But seek ye first the kingdom of God, and his righteousness: and all these things shall be added unto you" (Matthew 6:33).

Father God, I am so blessed to have You in my life. Thank You for loving and giving me eternal life. I am so grateful to have a godly mate who is loving and kind. You have blessed us with a good family. We are thankful for loving children and grandchildren. We have also been blessed with many wonderful friendships that have grown stronger over the years in the love of God. How blessed we are with friends that have demonstrated their love over and over again. Lord, help us to be the same kind of friends to them. Our family and friends are our true treasures in life. Keep them under Your protection and bless each of them. Bless the many people whom we have not met who pray for us and support this ministry. We are thankful for each of them and look forward to meeting them one day, if not in this life, in the life to come. I ask this in the name of the Lord Jesus. Amen.

God's Wisdom for Daily Living — ***Betty Miller***

May 3 — ***Day 123***

Proverbs 15:18-21 18 A wrathful man stirreth up strife: but he that is slow to anger appeaseth strife. 19 The way of the slothful man is as an hedge of thorns: but the way of the righteous is made plain. 20 A wise son maketh a glad father: but a foolish man despiseth his mother. 21 Folly is joy to him that is destitute of wisdom: but a man of understanding walketh uprightly.

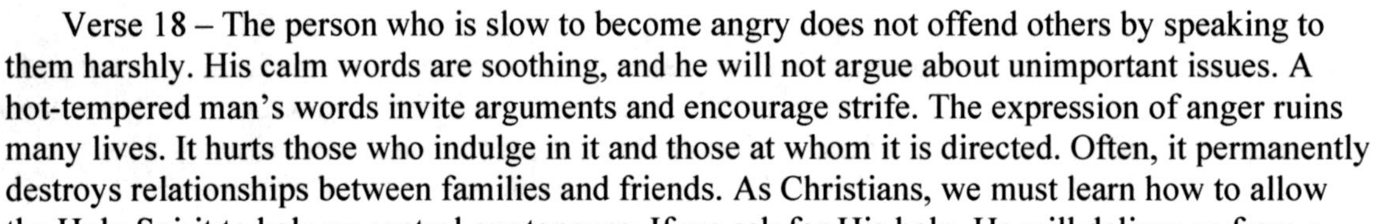

Verse 18 – The person who is slow to become angry does not offend others by speaking to them harshly. His calm words are soothing, and he will not argue about unimportant issues. A hot-tempered man's words invite arguments and encourage strife. The expression of anger ruins many lives. It hurts those who indulge in it and those at whom it is directed. Often, it permanently destroys relationships between families and friends. As Christians, we must learn how to allow the Holy Spirit to help us control our tongues. If we ask for His help, He will deliver us from a spirit of anger.

Verse 19 – The way of the slothful person is difficult. Ignoring one's responsibilities carries a penalty. The sluggard actually makes more work for himself by trying to avoid work. For example, failing to keep good records of bank transactions can result in writing a check for monies that one does not have. This leads to fines and can become a criminal offence, if the overdrawn amount is large enough. At the very least, it gives one a bad reputation. The righteous person avoids such confusion, trouble, and the waste of time and money. Thus, his path is plain, unblocked by thorny problems.

Verse 20 – There are many people today who dishonor their parents. A common way that they do this is by simply ignoring their parents or grandparents, being too selfish to make time to visit or remember them. It is painful for good parents to realize that their children are selfish. It is also displeasing to God, who issues this command: "Honour thy father and thy mother: that thy days may be long upon the land which the LORD thy God giveth thee" (Exodus 20:12). If they do not repent, these children may find themselves in a similar situation, enduring the same heartbreak later in life. We reap what we sow.

Verse 21 – Fools take pleasure in going their own way. However, any path that is not God's way ends in death (Proverbs 14:12). We all choose how we will walk through life. The wise look to God and find the straight and narrow way of blessing.

Dear Father, I thank You for showing me daily the path of righteousness and helping me to walk on it. Deliver me from every angry thought so that those thoughts do not become deeds. I desire to have a clean heart and mind. Lord, grant me the strength to perform my responsibilities toward all men; and most of all to take care of my responsibilities in the kingdom of God. Help me to make this world a better place to live. Lord, fill me with Your spirit so that I can love all men with the love of God. Thank You for your loving kindness toward me and my family. I ask this in the name of Jesus Christ. Amen.

Proverbs 15:22-24 22 Where there is no counsel, purposes are frustrated, but with many counselors they are accomplished. 23 A man has joy in making an apt answer, and a word spoken at the right moment, how good it is! 24 The path of the wise leads upward to life, that he may avoid the gloom in the depths of Sheol (AMP).

Verse 22 – For a project to be accomplished, good counsel is a must. In fact, in larger projects, a multitude of counselors is better than one man. Team work is vital for a large vision to be accomplished. A good counselor weighs the pros and cons of a situation and either suggests the best way to accomplish a project or offers corrections to it. With the help of many counselors, goals and purposes will be completed. Each department will have sound suggestions to establish the vision.

For personal problems, one godly counselor basing his advice on what the Bible teaches could help immensely. The key to solving personal problems is discovering what the Bible says about our situation and applying that truth to our lives. Since God's Word never fails, we are assured of resolving and overcoming our difficulties. Since the Bible has a multitude of godly counsel about all of life's problems, we can find our needed answers within its pages.

We should be careful about seeking just any counsel, and we should pray to find the right person to talk to. Worldly counselors can hurt a believer's walk with God since their advice is not necessarily scriptural. Worldly advice is generally based on selfishness, pride, and lust. Many worldly counselors actually encourage selfishness, because humanism teaches people to look out for themselves first. Certainly, we should take care of ourselves, but not at the expense of violating our moral values. "Love not the world, neither the things that are in the world. If any man love the world, the love of the Father is not in him (1 John 2:15).

Verse 23 – A man who has a good answer for someone's problem will receive great joy out of sharing it with them. It is always a blessing to help someone by giving advice that keeps them from being destroyed or overwhelmed by his or her problems.

Verse 24 – God's wisdom is a pathway that leads us upward to life in Him. Worldly wisdom is the lower path that leads to hell. God always wants to lift us up higher on His path. The devil wants to bring us down to where he is. The Lord desires us to avoid Satan's traps and snares, so that we can walk in the ways of God and be blessed.

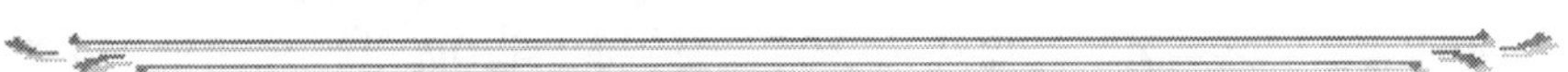

Father, I am ever so grateful to have access to a reservoir of wisdom, counsel, and guidance in knowing You. I know that when I have a problem I can ask You how to solve it, and You always have the perfect answer. Thank You for sending my answers in a variety of ways, and through many different people. I have been very blessed by the family of God, as they have reached out to us in so many ways. I appreciate the prayers of Your people. I also thank You for those who help us financially in this ministry. Bless each one who gives. I thank You for my brothers and sisters in Christ. Bless them all and meet their needs. I ask this in the name of Jesus. Amen.

Proverbs 15:25-27 25 The LORD tears down the house of the proud, but He will make secure the boundaries of the (consecrated) widow. 26 The thoughts of the wicked are shamefully vile and exceedingly offensive to the LORD, but the words of the pure are pleasing words to Him. 27 He who is greedy for unjust gain troubles his own household, but he who hates bribes will live (AMP).

Verse 25 – God protects the humble widow who looks to Him, and secures her borders. The prideful man will reap what he has sown, as God will allow his house to be destroyed. God treats all men fairly. Though He is not partial toward individuals, He is partial to His Word. Faith and obedience to God's Word brings us His favor, no matter who we are or where we come from. "Then Peter opened his mouth, and said, Of a truth I perceive that God is no respecter of persons: But in every nation he that feareth him, and worketh righteousness, is accepted with him" (Acts 10:34-35). His promises are to "whosoever will" (Revelation 22:17). This means that anyone who desires to come to God through Jesus will be accepted. It does not matter if we are rich or poor, male or female, black or white. God will accept us because He made us and loves us. The only condition is that we come to Him with a humble heart, acknowledging our need for Him to save us.

Verse 26 – God knows our thoughts and words. The thoughts of the wicked are extremely offensive to God. He is holy and pure, and He desires His children to walk in holiness and purity as well. When He hears us speaking good words, it is pleasing to Him. Just as we, as parents, are pleased to hear our children speak good things, so our heavenly Father is pleased when our words and actions are right.

Verse 27 – The greedy bring trouble to their households. Everyone in a family suffers when one member does not walk in God's ways. If that person is the father, he brings problems down upon the whole household. A greedy man can be so preoccupied with making money that he neglects his wife and children, or selfishly keeps his money for himself and gives little to his family.

A greedy man is susceptible to compromise. Those wanting favors from others learn to manipulate them with gifts or money. A greedy man falls into this trap easily. This is why one of the qualifications for the office of a deacon in the New Testament is that he not be greedy for money gained unjustly (1 Timothy 3:8-9). To please God, we must allow Him to deal with any greediness within us and resist anything that even looks like a bribe. Otherwise, we can be manipulated by evil men and violate our conscience.

Dear heavenly Father, thank You for all the good things that You have given me. I want to be like You, so help me do those things that bless You. May my thoughts and deeds be pleasing to You. Deliver me from the evil temptations that would cause me to fall from Your grace. Lord, set me free from all pride, greed, and fear. Let me be like You and treat all men fairly and justly. Keep me from manipulation, so that I obey You, no matter what the cost to me personally. Help me to always do the right thing, and may the meditations of my heart be pleasing to You. I ask this in the name of the Lord Jesus Christ. Amen.

Proverbs 15:28-29 28 The heart of the righteous studieth to answer: but the mouth of the wicked poureth out evil things. 29 The LORD is far from the wicked: but he heareth the prayer of the righteous.

Verse 28 – The righteous are not quick to answer, but ponder how they should reply. The wicked allow the evil stored in their hearts to pour out of their mouths, not caring if they sin. Having an evil thought is not a sin; it is not a sin to be tempted. It *is* sin, however, to act out the evil thought in our imaginations, even if we never act it out in reality (Matthew 5:27-28). This is why pornography and masturbation are affairs of the mind. Our minds are a spiritual battleground. A thought is like a seed. If watered with our thoughts and attention, it grows and bears fruit. This is why it is so important to submit our minds to God and resist the devil, "...bringing into captivity every thought to the obedience of Christ" (2 Corinthians 10:5).

We *can* gain the victory over evil thoughts! First, we must submit to God, asking Him to cleanse our minds. Next, we must cleanse our hands; getting rid of anything that supplies our evil thought life, and replace all such things with God's Word and whatever is noble and wholesome (Philippians 4:8). Finally, when the devil tempts us, we must resist, using Scripture. When we choose what is right, the Holy Spirit will empower us. As we draw close to God, He will draw close to us (James 4:8), enabling us to break free of sin's bondage. We must not be discouraged if it takes some time before we are free. God never becomes impatient, no matter how many times we confess the same sin while struggling against it.

Verse 29 – The Lord hears the prayers of His children. Our Father loves us. When we fall into sin, He desires that we call upon Him, that He may deliver us. We must not allow the enemy to discourage us from coming to God when we have fallen, but immediately repent, receive God's forgiveness, and go on with the Lord. The devil seeks to keep us out of fellowship with our Father by making us feel unworthy of forgiveness. He is cruel, first tempting us to sin, and then tormenting us. He tells us that we are unworthy of God's grace after God has been so patient with us. Satan then continues his assault by telling us that God is angry and we have no right to communicate with Him. It is vital that we recognize Satan's lies. Our guilty consciences will agree with the devil, so we must also reject our feelings. If we have asked God to forgive us, then we must choose to believe the truth that we are forgiven and that even when we fail, God is on our side. When we sin, we must run *to* Him, not *away* from Him. God's mercy endures forever. It is new every morning and is greater than our sin! "If we confess our sins, he is faithful and just to forgive us our sins, and to cleanse us from all unrighteousness" (1 John 1:9). "I acknowledged my sin unto thee, and mine iniquity have I not hid. I said, I will confess my transgressions unto the LORD; and thou forgavest the iniquity of my sin" (Psalm 32:5).

Dear Father, thank You for Your abundant love and mercy that You have shown to us. I have needed Your mercy on many occasions. When I call out to You, asking for forgiveness, You have never failed to reach down and restore me. I am grateful for Your unchanging love. Help me to be like You, showing mercy and love to those around me, even when they fail me. Cleanse me from all unrighteousness in my heart. May Your love manifest itself in the body of Christ, so that we truly love and serve one another. I ask this in the name of Jesus. Amen.

Proverbs 15:30-33 30 The light in the eyes (of him whose heart is joyful) rejoices the heart of others, and good news nourishes the bones. 31 The ear that listens to the reproof [that leads to or gives] life will remain among the wise. 32 He who refuses and ignores instruction and correction despises himself, but he who heeds reproof gets understanding (AMP).

Verse 30 – This verse states that the facial countenance reflects the attitude of the soul. One who has the joy of the Lord in their heart will have light in their eyes and a glow on their face. Another way to say this would be that a person who has the joy of the Lord will have a twinkle in their eyes and will be aglow with the Spirit of the Lord. Joy brings health to the body as well as to the soul, so we receive a health benefit by maintaining a joyful attitude. "Be not wise in thine own eyes: fear the LORD, and depart from evil. It shall be health to thy navel, and marrow to thy bones" (Proverbs 3:7-8). "Making the bones fat" or "It shall be health to the marrow of thy bones" refers to a healthy immune system that produces healthy blood. Life, the Bible says, is in the blood (Leviticus 17:11). A strong immune system is produced by the healthy blood created by healthy bones. The medical profession has now recognized and proven that laughter releases certain hormones that bring a health benefit to the body. The joy of the Lord helps keep us healthy and makes us a blessing to others, because joyful people bring joy to others. Proverbs 17:22 says, "A merry heart doeth good like a medicine: but a broken spirit drieth the bones."

Verses 31-32 – One of the ways to obtain wisdom is to yield to reproof that comes from the Spirit of the Lord. We need to ask the Lord to reveal any hidden sin in our hearts. When we allow Him to show us those areas needing correction, and we yield to that correction, we will grow in the wisdom of the Lord. Stubborn attitudes cost us dearly. To remain in the company of the wise, we must yield to their advice–and who is wiser than the Lord? Everyone who heeds reproof gains understanding. God desires the best for us. He corrects us for our good, so that we will abandon what hurts us.

Verse 33 - The Lord instructs those who reverently and worshipfully fear Him, honoring those who approach Him in an attitude of humility. He will give them grace and mercy in any situation they may find themselves. "...God resisteth the proud, but giveth grace unto the humble. Submit yourselves therefore to God. Resist the devil, and he will flee from you. Draw nigh to God, and he will draw nigh to you. Cleanse your hands, ye sinners; and purify your hearts, ye double minded" (James 4:6-8)." By keeping a proper attitude toward God, we will be a blessing to others as we maintain an attitude of joy.

Father God, I am grateful for Your lovingkindness. I appreciate Your grace and mercy in my life. When I come to You asking for forgiveness of my sins, I can feel Your mighty power cleansing me. I want You to correct me when I need it, as I do not want to get off of the path of holiness. Use me to reach out to others with the same love You have shown me. Guide me today in the things that I should do. Sometimes I feel overwhelmed with so many things to do. I am trusting You to show me what my priorities are and that You will give me the grace and strength to do them. Make me an instrument of Your love today. I ask this in the name of Jesus. Amen.

Proverbs 16:1-3 1 The preparations of the heart in man, and the answer of the tongue, is from the LORD. 2 All the ways of a man are clean in his own eyes; but the LORD weigheth the spirits. 3 Commit thy works unto the LORD, and thy thoughts shall be established.

Verse 1 – When a man has the heavenly Father's heart, he orders his speech to reflect God's wisdom. As His children, we prepare ourselves to receive from Him by filling our hearts with His Word. Reading the Bible renews our minds, changing our carnal thinking to godly thinking.

God's Word cleanses us like water, washing our minds clean (Ephesians 5:26-27). We must not only meditate on God's Word, but also ask Him to help us apply it to our lives. God's Word is full of power and able to change us, as we call upon Him in faith to help us obey it. "For the Word that God speaks is alive and full of power-making it active, operative, energizing and effective; it is sharper than any two-edged sword, penetrating to the dividing line of the breath of life (soul) and (the immortal) spirit, and of joints and marrow (that is, of the deepest parts of our nature) exposing and sifting and analyzing and judging the very thoughts and purposes of the heart" (Hebrews 4:12 AMP).

Verse 2 – Without God's light, man always thinks himself to be pure. He is unable to perceive that his thoughts or deeds are wrong. God sees the thoughts and intents of men's hearts and weighs our spirits, revealing Himself to those searching for the truth. Without God, man walks in ways that seem right but which actually lead to death (Proverbs 14:12). He will perish, unless he gives his life to God and follows Him.

Verse 3 – As we commit our works wholly to the Lord, He causes our thoughts to come into agreement with His will. Our plans will then succeed, because they are His plans. When I am in doubt about what to do in a situation, I ask God to make my thoughts and feelings about it stronger if they are from Him. If they are not from Him, I ask that He will remove them from my mind and replace them with His thoughts. We must not be led by circumstances or by emotions;, but by the Holy Spirit's guidance. The sons of God are led by the Spirit of God. Our thoughts, circumstances, and emotions should line up with what the Spirit has revealed to us. He leads; we follow. "Therefore, brethren, we are debtors, not to the flesh, to live after the flesh. For if ye live after the flesh, ye shall die: but if ye through the Spirit do mortify the deeds of the body, ye shall live. For as many as are led by the Spirit of God, they are the sons of God" (Romans 8:12-14).

If we strive to please God, we will not live to please our flesh. When we allow the Holy Spirit to guide us, we are promised success in whatever we do. Our all-wise Father in heaven will not allow His sons and daughters to be defeated, if we follow the ways of the Lord and desire to please Him.

Dear heavenly Father, thank You for Your promise of wisdom and guidance. Help me to overcome my carnal desires and live to glorify You in all of my ways. Fill me with the Holy Spirit daily, so that I can walk in Your power to overcome those things that the devil uses to try and defeat me. Lord, cleanse my heart and mind of the things that do not agree with Your Word. Please bless Your people everywhere; my brothers and sisters in all the nations of the world. Meet their needs, as well as ours, so that we can share the gospel with others who need You. I ask this in the name of Jesus Christ. Amen.

Proverbs 16:4 The LORD hath made all things for himself: yea, even the wicked for the day of evil.

God is the Creator of all things, and He has created man and angels with a free will, therefore allowing wickedness to exist. Through the ages, people have struggled to understand why He created the devil who has caused so much suffering. We must realize that God never desired evil to exist. He created angels as sinless beings and gave them the ability to make moral choices. Ezekiel 28:15 records that God created Satan, originally called Lucifer, without sin. Lucifer was full of wisdom and perfect in beauty; he was the anointed cherub who walked upon the holy mountain of God. Despite these honors, he was not content with his position. Corrupted by pride, he attempted to usurp God's authority. By his own choice, he became evil. He desired God's throne and set his will against God's. Five times he said *"I will"* in Isaiah 14:13-14: "...For thou hast said in thine heart, I will ascend into heaven, I will exalt my throne above the stars of God: I will sit also upon the mount of the congregation, in the sides of the north: I will ascend above the heights of the clouds; I will be like the most High..."

The Lord never meant for evil to exist. It is simply the opposite of good. For evil to exist, someone has to exercise their free will to choose to do evil. It is simply the corruption of goodness, and came into existence through Lucifer's choice to sin. He is now called Satan, which comes from a Hebrew word signifying an adversary, an enemy, an accuser. He opposes God's plans; is the enemy of men (especially God's people); and attempts to overthrow God's kingdom on earth. We gain a glimpse of his evil knowledge, strength, glitter, and inevitable end from Ezekiel 28:12-19 and the above passage in Isaiah.

Eastern religions claim that the powers of good and evil are equally balanced. This is a lie. Satan's power is *not* equal to God's. God's omnipotence is inconceivably greater than any power that He originally delegated to the angels. We must remember, however, that although these supernatural beings are limited, they still have power and can use it for evil. Satan is still the dark prince, a fallen angel who is the god of this world today. He still rules over evil spirits, human beings, and even nations that choose the same path of rebellion against God that he himself chose.

Anyone who is ignorant of Satan and his devices will inevitably become his victim. Those who are filled with the Spirit of God, however, have no need to fear him. Jesus Christ defeated him at the cross (Hebrews 2:14). Jesus said, "I am he that liveth, and was dead; and, behold, I am alive for evermore, Amen; and have the keys of hell and of death" (Revelation 1:18). We now have authority over him through Christ (Luke 10:19). Though the earth is Satan's present abode, he will be brought down to hell. Whoever refuses to repent of the same choice and rebels against God like Satan did, will ultimately share his torment in the lake of fire.

Dear heavenly Father, I am thankful that You have set me free from the power of sin, through the death, burial, and resurrection of Jesus Christ. You have given us power over the devil. Let us be faithful to exercise our authority and not allow him to come and rob from us. Lord, You made the earth and called it good, and we now can look around and see the things that the devil has done to make it bad. Help each of us, as Christians, to do our part to change this world by overcoming evil with good, and reversing the things that the devil has done. I ask this in Jesus' name. Amen.

Proverbs 16:5-7 5 Every one that is proud in heart is an abomination to the LORD: though hand join in hand, he shall not be unpunished. 6 By mercy and truth iniquity is purged: and by the fear of the LORD men depart from evil. 7 When a man's ways please the LORD, he maketh even his enemies to be at peace with him (KJV).

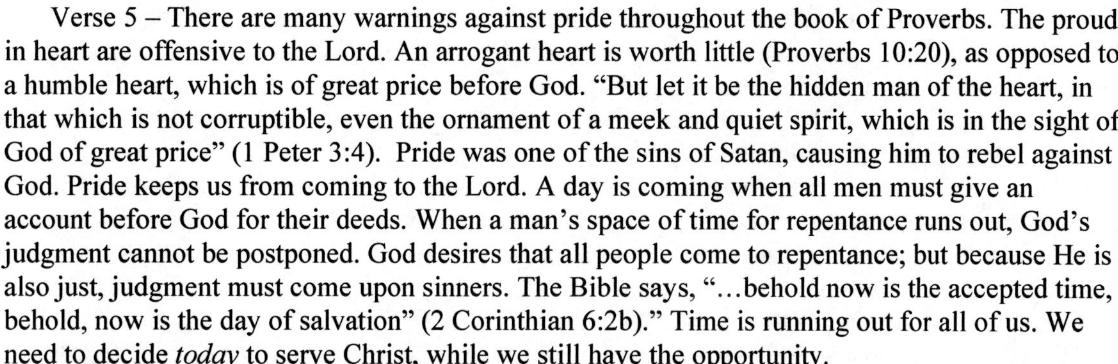

Verse 5 – There are many warnings against pride throughout the book of Proverbs. The proud in heart are offensive to the Lord. An arrogant heart is worth little (Proverbs 10:20), as opposed to a humble heart, which is of great price before God. "But let it be the hidden man of the heart, in that which is not corruptible, even the ornament of a meek and quiet spirit, which is in the sight of God of great price" (1 Peter 3:4). Pride was one of the sins of Satan, causing him to rebel against God. Pride keeps us from coming to the Lord. A day is coming when all men must give an account before God for their deeds. When a man's space of time for repentance runs out, God's judgment cannot be postponed. God desires that all people come to repentance; but because He is also just, judgment must come upon sinners. The Bible says, "...behold now is the accepted time, behold, now is the day of salvation" (2 Corinthian 6:2b)." Time is running out for all of us. We need to decide *today* to serve Christ, while we still have the opportunity.

Verse 6 – The Lord can free us from our sin and iniquity. Our part is to line up with His truth and receive His mercy; He will purge our hearts. By the fear of the Lord men depart from evil. This fear is a holy respect for God and His Word. It causes us to take seriously what the Bible says. If we really believe His Word that says "sinners will go to hell," a holy respect for the Truth will drive us to Him and we will depart from evil.

Verse 7 – When our ways please God, He will make even our enemies to be at peace with us. What a wonderful promise! God does not want us to be in strife. Our enemies are not other people, but rather the devil and his demons who use people for their evil work (Ephesians 6:12). If we take authority over the real enemy and pray for those who are pawns in his hands, we can experience deliverance for ourselves and others. When we obey the Lord's commandment to overcome evil with good, He strips our enemies of the means to attack us, forcing them to be at peace with us.

"If it be possible, as much as lieth in you, live peaceably with all men. Dearly beloved, avenge not yourselves, but rather give place unto wrath: for it is written, Vengeance is mine; I will repay, saith the Lord. Therefore if thine enemy hunger, feed him; if he thirst, give him drink: for in so doing thou shalt heap coals of fire on his head. Be not overcome of evil, but overcome evil with good" (Romans 12:18-21).

Dear Father in heaven, I want to please You. Help me to walk in Your ways and obey Your Words. I know if You ask anything of me, it is for my good, even if I do not understand some things at the moment. I cannot love my enemies in my own strength; I need Your supernatural love. Thank You for fighting my battles for me. Help me to trust You more every day. Lord, I bless my enemies right now with this prayer. Forgive those who would judge me wrongly and say unkind things. Please deliver them and change their hearts so that they might know Your kindness. Also, help me not to judge others, but pray for them and really love them the way You love them. I ask this in the name of Jesus Christ. Amen.

Proverbs 16:8-10 8 Better is a little with righteousness than great revenues without right. 9 A man's heart deviseth his way: but the LORD directeth his steps. 10 A divine sentence is in the lips of the king: his mouth transgresseth not in judgment.

Verse 8 – Having righteousness with little money is better than having great wealth with injustice. "A little that a righteous man hath is better than the riches of many wicked" (Psalm 37:16). This truth is repeated in other scriptures: Proverbs 15:16; 1 Timothy 6:6-11. We need a revelation of God's greatness. When we call upon Him, we have access to all He has. If we need money, He can supply it. If chasing after money consumes our energy so that He is not the most important thing in our lives, then money has become our god.

Verse 9 – Everyone makes plans, but if we are committed to God, He directs our steps. In seeking the LORD, we must be willing to do whatever He tells us to do. When we come to the point that it does not matter to us what we do as long as it is what God wants us to do, it frees the Lord to intervene in our lives to overcome any threatening circumstances, we may face. He is waiting for us to say: "Thy will be done."

Verse 10 – The position of a king equates to any ruler, so anyone in a position of authority must be careful not to sin by making unrighteous judgments. Authority should be used to govern a nation righteously, thereby helping people. When God places a man in authority, He desires to give him guidance and instruction. Decisions made by wicked world leaders throughout history have had adverse (and even horrific) affects upon people. A good leader, rather than exploiting those under his authority, is desirous of their welfare. Any leader who calls upon God will find Him available to guide him in important decisions. We should pray for the leaders of our nations, as instructed by the Scriptures. "I exhort therefore, that, first of all, supplications, prayers, intercessions, and giving of thanks, be made for all men; For kings, and for all that are in authority; that we may lead a quiet and peaceable life in all godliness and honesty. For this is good and acceptable in the sight of God our Saviour; Who will have all men to be saved, and to come unto the knowledge of the truth. For there is one God, and one mediator between God and men, the man Christ Jesus" (1 Timothy 2:1-5).

Many people today are wrongly trying to bring change to their nations through anarchy and rebellion. God would not have us change the world through destructive means, but through prayer and obedience to His Word. Of course, we can voice our concerns through the proper and legal channels such as voting and peaceful demonstrations and by speaking out when we have the opportunity. When we obey God, He will then fight our battles and grant us victory His way.

Dear heavenly Father, thank You for the many blessings that You send my way each day, and especially for the friends that You have given me. They are priceless treasures. Bless them all today. I want my life to be what You would have it to be. I want You to be satisfied with me. So remove those things that are not pleasing to You. Thank You for Your daily provision. I know that when I have You, it is enough. You will take care of all my concerns and needs. May this truth be in the hearts of all of Your children. Thank You for Your mercy and amazing grace. I pray in the name of Jesus. Amen.

Proverbs 16:11 A just balance or scales are the LORD's; all the weights of the bag are His work (established on His eternal principles) (AMP).

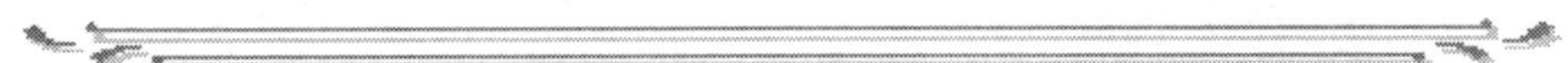

A pair of scales is a symbol for justice and equity. Scales were used in Biblical times to determine quantity and price of certain goods (see Day 67). Dishonest men used stones weighing less than they were supposed to, thus cheating their customers out of what they paid for. People could not see the deception, but God could and declared it an abomination (Proverbs 11:1). God is the Author of all that is balanced and just.

Many Biblical teachings are also out of balance. Some take extreme views of God's Word; using a "false weight" by pulling out portions of Scripture and building them into false doctrines. Scripture must be considered in context and compared with other verses to give them true "weight" and bring teaching into balance. Using portions of Scripture out of context is like creating a false balance, resulting in error. Unbalanced teaching has caused a great deal of division in the body of Christ. Those on the outside are affected, since they see extremes that should not exist, and therefore want no part of Christianity.

We have all been out of balance at times. Walking in perfect balance with the Lord is not easy. However, the Holy Spirit desires that we learn this balanced walk. It is the only way we will come into maturity. When we learn a new truth, we are often like a pendulum. Sometimes we swing too far in one direction because we are so eager to hear and practice new things. However, after these are learned, it is important that we swing back into balance, incorporating what is newly learned with the whole of what has already been learned. If we "camp" on just one new aspect of truth, and forget everything else, we end up in advocating extremes that bring discord and possible deception into our lives.

Jesus is the Rock. He is solid and stable; He does not change. For this reason, we can trust the word He has spoken to us. If He said it, it is truth because He cannot lie. If we believe what He has said, faith in His Word will produce those things promised to us. Knowing only portions of the Word can cause us to become unbalanced. We must seek to know the whole truth and completely surrender to the will of God for us to be victorious Christians. Stressing only *one* portion of God's Word invariably results in error. This is the reason for many "faith" failures today. It is not so much lack of faith that fails to produce the answers that people seek, but faith in something that God has not said. This is the result of failing to "rightly divide the Word of truth" (2 Timothy 2:15).

Father God, we come to You in Jesus' precious name, thanking You for Your love. Lord, You see those areas in our lives that are not in balance. We ask that You reveal them to us and help us to walk in the path of righteousness and Your holy balance. Deliver us from error and all that is an abomination to You. Heal us today, spirit, soul, and body, so that we might serve You by walking in a victorious Christian life. Let our light shine so that others truly might see Your love in us. In the name of Jesus we pray. Amen.

Proverbs 16:12-15 12 It is an abomination to kings to commit wickedness: for the throne is established by righteousness. 13 Righteous lips are the delight of kings; and they love him that speaketh right. 14 The wrath of a king is as messengers of death: but a wise man will pacify it. 15 In the light of the king's countenance is life; and his favour is as a cloud of the latter rain.

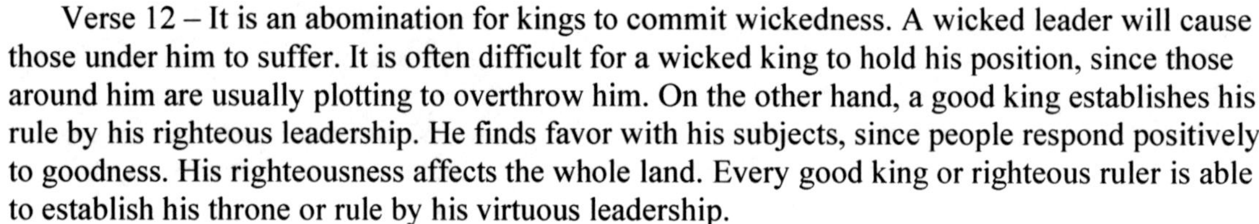

Verse 12 – It is an abomination for kings to commit wickedness. A wicked leader will cause those under him to suffer. It is often difficult for a wicked king to hold his position, since those around him are usually plotting to overthrow him. On the other hand, a good king establishes his rule by his righteous leadership. He finds favor with his subjects, since people respond positively to goodness. His righteousness affects the whole land. Every good king or righteous ruler is able to establish his throne or rule by his virtuous leadership.

Verse 13 – Good leaders appreciate having righteous people around them. A good king delights in kind and righteous words from his subjects. He loves those who speak what is just. Leaders favor those who speak with sound wisdom. These are the kind of people who will be chosen to help rule. Those who rebel against the king's authority will bring his wrath upon themselves.

Verse 14 – Rebels against a king's authority bring his wrath upon themselves. A man unwise enough to stir up a king's wrath could even endanger his life. It would be wise for this man to humble himself and try to pacify the king's anger.

Verse 15 – A wise man should seek to please his king. When he does, he will find the king's countenance reflecting his pleasure in a smile. The king's favor will prosper him, just as a cloud, full of spring rain, waters the earth and causes it to flourish with plant life.

We can also apply a spiritual application in today's verses. Since Jesus is the righteous King of all people, we should strive to please Him. In doing so, we will find favor with God. Sin cuts us off from the King's favor. We may pacify His anger by approaching Him with a humble and repentant heart. When we do this, He will forgive us and show us His favor. His favor is more beneficial to us than that of any earthly ruler.

Dear heavenly Father, I honor You as my King and Lord, and I submit myself to Your will. Thank You for Your love. I am grateful that You are a forgiving God. Thank You also for the abundant blessings that You have given me. One of those blessings is that I can lay my head down at night and enjoy sweet sleep. At times, You even speak to me in my dreams. It is such a blessing to have Your peace and joy. No amount of money can buy these gifts, and I want to give a special thanks for them. Bless my brothers and sisters with Your love and guidance. Lead us all into more truth. I ask this in Jesus' name. Amen.

Proverbs 16:16-17 16 How much better it is to get wisdom than gold! and to get understanding rather to be chosen than silver! 17 The highway of the upright is to depart from evil: he that keepeth his way preserveth his soul.

Verse 16 – Those who are struggling financially might wonder if this statement is true, but money alone helps no one. The ability to use money wisely is more valuable than money itself. Wisdom keeps money growing, when properly invested. Without wisdom, even a large sum of money will disappear. Better than money is the wisdom to seek God and walk in His ways. This brings greater reward and fulfillment, both now and for eternity.

Verse 17 – The highway of the upright turns aside from evil. This not only means refusing to join in evil with others, but repenting of a sin that the Holy Spirit reveals, and guarding the way we walk in this life. Obeying the Lord brings health to all our being, spirit, soul, and body. Money cannot buy us the promises of God. For example:

- We are promised peace. Knowing God brings peace to our minds, despite what may be going on around us.
- We are promised the ability to love others. We gain wholeness in our souls by experiencing God's love. When we ask Christ into our hearts, He begins to free us from our selfishness and enable us to love others.
- We are promised wisdom. With His wisdom, we are spared from making mistakes that can harm us in the future.
- We are promised guidance. When we are in need, He will show us the way to go.
- We are promised sweet sleep and rest. Millions of people suffer from insomnia because they do not have access to God's rest when they lie down. "When thou liest down, thou shalt not be afraid: yea, thou shalt lie down, and thy sleep shall be sweet" (Proverbs 3:24).
- We are promised protection when we look to Him in faith. No amount of money can buy this kind of protection. I call Psalm 91 my "life insurance policy."
- We are promised long life. When we understand what things cause death, we can depart from them.
- We are promised provision. God will provide for us because we are His children, and He takes care of His own.

Let us seek the Lord and His righteousness before anything else, and He will provide all that we need. "But seek ye first the kingdom of God, and his righteousness; and all these things shall be added unto you. Take therefore no thought for the morrow: for the morrow shall take thought for the things of itself. Sufficient unto the day is the evil thereof" (Matthew 6:33-34).

Dear heavenly Father, thank You for always being faithful. Many times I have not known how my needs would be supplied, but when I sought You for the answers, You always came through and provided for me. Lord, please give all of Your children the wisdom and understanding that they need at this hour, since we live in uncertain times and are in need of Your guidance. Protect us from the plans of the evil one. Thank You for watching over us and keeping us and our families and friends from harm. Give us strength to live each day that we might delight Your heart. I ask this in the name of Jesus. Amen.

God's Wisdom for Daily Living — ***Betty Miller***

May 15 — ***Day 135***

Proverbs 16:18-20 18 Pride goeth before destruction, and an haughty spirit before a fall. 19 Better it is to be of an humble spirit with the lowly, than to divide the spoil with the proud. 20 He that handleth a matter wisely shall find good: and whoso trusteth in the LORD, happy is he.

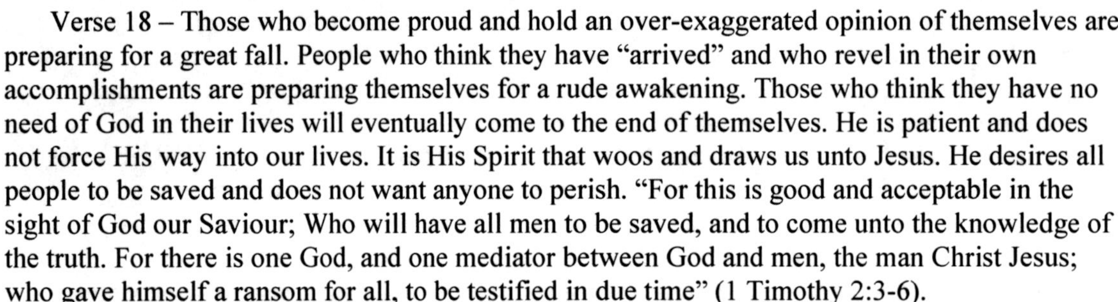

Verse 18 – Those who become proud and hold an over-exaggerated opinion of themselves are preparing for a great fall. People who think they have "arrived" and who revel in their own accomplishments are preparing themselves for a rude awakening. Those who think they have no need of God in their lives will eventually come to the end of themselves. He is patient and does not force His way into our lives. It is His Spirit that woos and draws us unto Jesus. He desires all people to be saved and does not want anyone to perish. "For this is good and acceptable in the sight of God our Saviour; Who will have all men to be saved, and to come unto the knowledge of the truth. For there is one God, and one mediator between God and men, the man Christ Jesus; who gave himself a ransom for all, to be testified in due time" (1 Timothy 2:3-6).

Pride is man's biggest hindrance from coming to God. All have sinned and come short of the glory of God, and therefore all are in need of a Savior. God provided a Savior by sending Jesus, His only begotten Son, to take our sins upon Himself. Through His death, burial, and resurrection, we can receive eternal life. People can only be saved by humbling their hearts before God and acknowledging these things.

Verse 19 – It is better to be humbly associated with the lowly, than to have the riches of plunder divided with the proud. We must ask the Lord to help us remain humble. Society encourages the spirit of pride. True humility reveals strength of character. The humble person is secure in God and does not need to prove himself to others. The Christian who is dependant on God has found the way to victory in his life.

Verse 20 – All who lean on God, placing their trust in Him, are happy and blessed. We have access to all the resources of heaven when we humble our hearts before God and ask Him to supply all that we need. "A man's pride shall bring him low: but honour shall uphold the humble in spirit" (Proverbs 29:23). "But my God shall supply all your need according to his riches in glory by Christ Jesus" (Philippians 4:19).

Dearest Father, thank You for the many blessings that are mine because I am Yours. I am most blessed. Please use me to bless others with the overflow of what You have given me. Encourage Your people today that need hope and faith. Please remove all the vestiges of pride from my heart, since I desire to be truly humble before You and others. Father, I trust You to fight my battles for me as I look to You. Thank You for meeting my needs. I know You will never leave me nor forsake me. Bless my brothers and sisters in the Lord. Amen.

**Proverbs 16:21-24 21 The wise in heart shall be called prudent, understanding and knowing; and winsom speech increases learning (in both speaker and listener).
22 Understanding is a wellspring of life to him who has it, but to give instruction to fools is folly. 23 The mind of the wise instructs his mouth, and adds learning and persuasiveness to his lips. 24 Pleasant words are as a honeycomb, sweet to the mind and healing to the body (AMP).**

Verse 21 – The wise in heart are called "prudent." This kind of wisdom comes from the Lord, who places it in our hearts when we seek Him. There is another kind of wisdom that the Bible calls earthly, sensual, and devilish. It produces strife, confusion, and every evil work. "Who is a wise man and endued with knowledge among you? let him shew out of a good conversation his works with meekness of wisdom. But if ye have bitter envying and strife in your hearts, glory not, and lie not against the truth. This wisdom descendeth not from above, but is earthly, sensual, devilish. For where envying and strife is, there is confusion and every evil work. But the wisdom that is from above is first pure, then peaceable, gentle, and easy to be intreated, full of mercy and good fruits, without partiality, and without hypocrisy. And the fruit of righteousness is sown in peace of them that make peace" (James 3:13-18).

Learning to control what we say is the first step in gaining godly wisdom. God's wisdom is pure, peaceable, gentle, easy to be entreated, and merciful. It bears good fruit. It is impartial and has no hypocrisy. A wise person is a good learner and listener. Proverbs has much to say about wisdom and understanding; both are increased by the words we hear and speak.

Verse 22 – A fool is rebellious and unteachable. It is a waste of time to try to instruct him. If we take the time to attentively study God's Word, then understanding will rise within us, becoming a wellspring from which we may draw upon in life's situations.

Verse 23 – If we are wise, we will stop and think before we say something. People who just blurt out what comes into their head when they are upset invariably cause damage with their mouths. The wise are able to persuade others to their way of thinking by presenting things in a winsome way.

Verse 24 – Like honey, wholesome words are sweet to the mind and bring healing to the body. Harboring resentment and bitterness leads to harsh words. Cruel words, repeated over and over, can produce physical illness or bring other curses, both to the recipient and the speaker. No one likes to associate with those who have ugly dispositions and who continually voice destructive or even unpleasant things. Two ways to guard our hearts are by being careful to quickly forgive others and by watching what we say. "Keep thy heart with all diligence; for out of it are the issues of life. Put away from thee a froward mouth, and perverse lips put far from thee" (Proverbs 4:23-24).

Dear Father, I am thankful for all of Your many blessings this day. Lord, I desire to have Your wisdom. You see the future, so help me to make the best decisions, so that I do not have greater problems tomorrow. Help me to guard my mouth and restrain my lips from any evil. Help me to be a loving witness of Your goodness and give me the boldness to proclaim the gospel. Bless all of those who touch my life and keep them from harm. I am grateful to be Your child. I ask this in the name of the Lord Jesus Christ. Amen.

Proverbs 16:25 There is a way that seemeth right unto a man, but the end thereof are the ways of death.

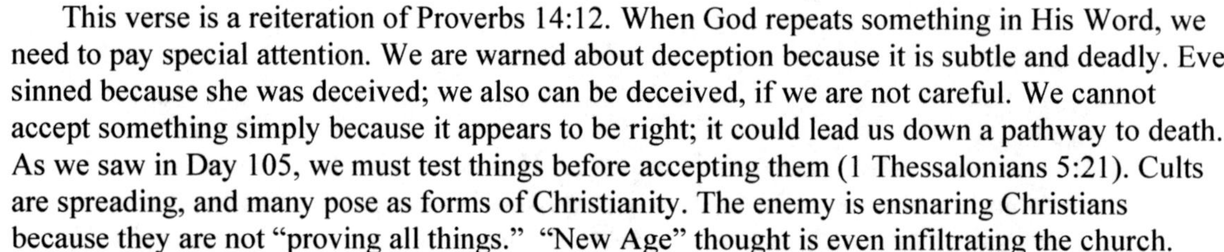

This verse is a reiteration of Proverbs 14:12. When God repeats something in His Word, we need to pay special attention. We are warned about deception because it is subtle and deadly. Eve sinned because she was deceived; we also can be deceived, if we are not careful. We cannot accept something simply because it appears to be right; it could lead us down a pathway to death. As we saw in Day 105, we must test things before accepting them (1 Thessalonians 5:21). Cults are spreading, and many pose as forms of Christianity. The enemy is ensnaring Christians because they are not "proving all things." "New Age" thought is even infiltrating the church.

How do we test something? We must look to God and His Word to prove all things. If it does not agree with the Bible, we should not believe it. People spread many ideas as truth. However, truth can only be found in the Word of God. The truth will set us free when we adhere to it (John 8:31-32). "Let no man deceive you with vain words: for because of these things cometh the wrath of God upon the children of disobedience. Be not ye therefore partakers with them. For ye were sometimes darkness, but now are ye light in the Lord: walk as children of light: (For the fruit of the Spirit is in all goodness and righteousness and truth;) Proving what is acceptable unto the Lord" (Ephesians 5:6-10).

Lack of discernment is a serious problem in the church today because of people's lust for things of this world. If we have uncommitted hearts, containing a mixture of love for this world and love for the Lord, we will be in deception, which will ultimately bring destruction into our lives.

The Lord Jesus warned of a day when deception would be rampant. (Matthew 24:4-5,11). Only by coming before God with a teachable spirit can we learn the truth and recognize error. Satan has a counterfeit for every truth of God. As we become acquainted with God, we will be able to better discern Satan's counterfeits. We need not fear being deceived if we are in fellowship with the Lord, for He will deliver us from every evil as we continue to follow Him. The way to keep from being deceived is to depart from sin, study the Word of God, and obey what we find in its pages. Just hearing the Word will not save us; we must practice it or we will deceive ourselves. "Wherefore lay apart all filthiness and superfluity of naughtiness, and receive with meekness the engrafted word, which is able to save your souls. But be ye doers of the word, and not hearers only, deceiving your own selves" (James 1:21-22).

Dear heavenly Father, please cleanse me from all error and renew my mind. I desire to know the truth even if it means correction and embarrassment for me. Change my heart and thoughts to be Your thoughts and heart. Give me a teachable spirit. Take my desires and dreams and give me Yours. Cleanse me from all that offends You. Create within me a clean heart, O Lord. Give me eyes to see things the way You see them and keep me from deception. Thank You for the gift of discernment so that I do not fall into the devil's traps. May You also do this for all of my brothers and sisters in Christ. Amen.

Proverbs 16:26-30 26 The appetite of the laborer works for him, for the need of his mouth urges him on. 27 A worthless man devices and digs up mischief, and in his lips there is as a scorching fire. 28 A perverse man sows strife, and a whisperer separates close friends. 29 The exceedingly grasping, covetous and violent man entices his neighbor, leading him into the way that is not good. 30 He who shuts his eyes to devise perverse things, and who compresses his lips (as if in concealment) will bring evil to pass (AMP).

Verse 26 – One of the principles of life that God established, is the principle that man must work for his food (Genesis 3:19). After the fall of man, all of mankind is subject to laboring to eat. Because some men are lazy and idle, it takes hunger to drive them to work so they can eat. In the New Testament, we find this admonition. "For even when we were with you, this we commanded you, that if any would not work, neither should he eat. For we hear that there are some which walk among you disorderly, working not at all, but are busybodies. Now them that are such we command and exhort by our Lord Jesus Christ, that with quietness they work, and eat their own bread" (2 Thessalonians 3:10-12).

Verse 27 – Those who dig up evil about others are like a wildfire scorching everything it touches. Our culture is guilty of this sin. Some actually make a living by finding out dirt on people and broadcasting it through all the gossip channels in the media. As Christians, we should not be a part of writing exposés and spreading gossip. Only God knows the real truth. Love does not expose, but covers sin (1 Peter 4:8).

Verse 28 – Through gossip, a perverse man can separate close friends. As Christians, we should not listen to gossip, since that makes us a party to it. If the one that is being talked about is not there to defend himself, it is not a fair conversation. If there is cause for a true accusation, the issue should be taken up with the offender. If he does not repent, two or three witnesses should be brought along and the offender addressed on the issue again. If he will still not repent, it should be brought before the church, but at no time should a person discuss someone's fault with anyone besides the person at fault (Matthew 18:15-17). To do so is to participate in gossip and slander.

Verses 29-30 – Evil men are not content to sin by themselves; they try to influence others to join them. We need to avoid people like this. We must also resist evil, giving no place to the wicked one. We can do this by keeping our minds on wholesome things (Philippians 4:8) and casting down every imagination that would exalt itself against the knowledge of God (2 Corinthians 10:5).

Dear Father God, I thank You that I am strong and able to work. I appreciate the work You have called me to do. Sometimes I get weary, but help me not to complain. I am blessed to be Your child and I thank You for Your abundant blessings. Many lack the blessings I have. I am grateful that I am not hungry and I do not have bombs going off above my house. I pray for my brothers and sisters in the world that are experiencing those trials. Protect and provide for them. I will not complain of my light afflictions when I think of many in the world who do not even have the essentials of a secure home. Lord, use me to reach out to those who do not have the blessings that I have. I ask this in Jesus' name. Amen.

Proverbs 16:31 The hoary head is a crown of glory, if it be found in the way of righteousness.

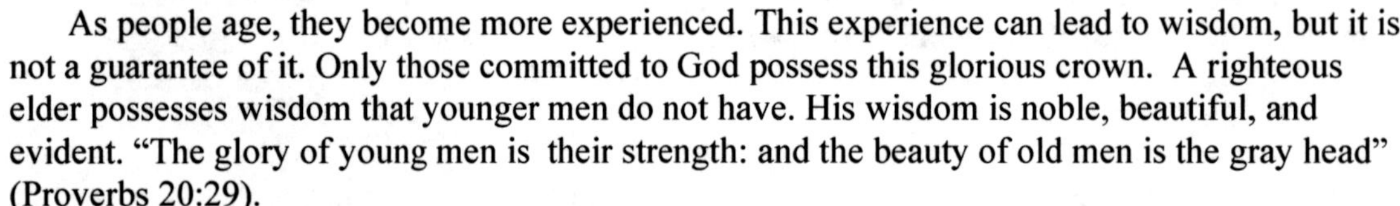

As people age, they become more experienced. This experience can lead to wisdom, but it is not a guarantee of it. Only those committed to God possess this glorious crown. A righteous elder possesses wisdom that younger men do not have. His wisdom is noble, beautiful, and evident. "The glory of young men is their strength: and the beauty of old men is the gray head" (Proverbs 20:29).

Older men and women who know Christ do not have to face the sunset of their lives with dread, since God's Word contains great promises for them. One of those promises is that their lives shall be fruitful. It is not God's will that they should waste away in their latter years. "The righteous shall flourish like the palm tree: he shall grow like a cedar in Lebanon. Those that be planted in the house of the LORD shall flourish in the courts of our God. They shall still bring forth fruit in old age; they shall be fat and flourishing" (Psalm 92:12-14).

Another wonderful promise for older people who may feel weak is found in Isaiah: "He giveth power to the faint; and to them that have no might he increaseth strength. Even the youths shall faint and be weary, and the young men shall utterly fall: But they that wait upon the LORD shall renew their strength; they shall mount up with wings as eagles; they shall run, and not be weary; and they shall walk, and not faint" (Isaiah 40:29-31).

What a wonderful promise: to run without weariness and walk without fainting! Moses' life was an example of how God fulfills this promise; his latter years were blessed with good health and vitality. "And Moses was an hundred and twenty years old when he died: his eye was not dim, nor his natural force abated" (Deuteronomy 34:7).

God desires that we live long and productive lives, leaving a godly inheritance to those who follow us. Our latter years should be "golden." We should be healthy and strong, able to do the will of God until we have completed His purpose for us. When our assignment is complete, it will be time for us to leave this earth. The devil is the one who wants to cut our lives short. There are many promises in the Word of God concerning long life: "He shall call upon me, and I will answer him: I will be with him in trouble; I will deliver him, and honour him. With long life will I satisfy him, and show him my salvation" (Psalm 91:15-16). "So teach us to number our days, that we may apply our hearts unto wisdom" (Psalm 90:12).

Dear Father in heaven, thank You for Your many wonderful promises. Thank You for the promise of long life, not only for me, but for all of my family. I claim Psalm 91 over our lives. Thank You for watching over us. Now that I am older and have had many experiences, help me to be gracious in sharing the things that I have learned over the years. Help me to keep my mouth shut when I should, and allow others to learn directly from You. Thank You for helping me to grow old graciously. Bless all of Your older saints who are still serving You around the world. Strengthen and protect them. I ask this in the name of Jesus. Amen.

Proverbs 16:32 He that is slow to anger is better than the mighty; and he that ruleth his spirit than he that taketh a city.

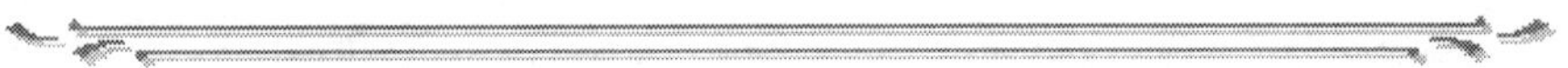

In Proverbs, we find many profound truths, which when applied to our lives, will bring great victories. To experience anger is not a sin, since the Bible says that God Himself is angry about certain things. Anger is an emotion that we all experience. In fact, we *should* be angry when we see an injustice or the ill treatment of others.

The sin is not in experiencing anger, but in how we deal with it. We can turn our anger into prayer, which will change things. If we allow our anger to turn into vindictiveness, we become just as guilty as the one with whom we are angry. We are told in Scripture to overcome evil with good. "If it be possible, as much as lieth in you, live peaceably with all men. Dearly beloved, avenge not yourselves, but rather give place unto wrath: for it is written, Vengeance is mine; I will repay, saith the Lord. Therefore if thine enemy hunger, feed him; if he thirst, give him drink: for in so doing thou shalt heap coals of fire on his head. Be not overcome of evil, but overcome evil with good" (Romans 12:18-21).

So, what should we do when we become angry? "Be ye angry, and sin not: let not the sun go down upon your wrath: Neither give place to the devil" (Ephesians 4:26-27). First, we should be willing to prayerfully examine our own hearts: Why we are reacting with such anger? Is our anger justified, or are we merely suffering wounded pride? Are we partially to blame? If God brings conviction, we must repent. We must also forgive the other person, even if they will not change. We must be just as willing for the Lord to change us, as the one we are angry at. Unforgiveness is a deadly sin which hardens the heart, cuts us off from God, and brings torment (Matthew 18:34-35). Anger must be dealt with quickly so that it does not turn into a bitter root of unforgiveness. "Follow peace with all men, and holiness, without which no man shall see the Lord: Looking diligently lest any man fail of the grace of God; lest any root of bitterness springing up trouble you, and thereby many be defiled" Hebrews 12:14-15).

God commands us to love our enemies and to forgive those who have hurt us. This is impossible without God's grace. I cannot love my enemies and neither can you. We must call on God to do this impossible thing; He will enable us to do it. If we refuse, and harbor unforgiveness, we block God from forgiving us (Matthew 6:14-15).

Self-control is a fruit of the Spirit that we must cultivate, if we are to do any mighty works for God. Handling anger properly is part of "ruling our spirits;" and it is better to have this ability than to conquer a city. When a man can rule his own life through the power of the Holy Spirit, he is fit to rule a city.

Dear Father, thank You for being patient with me in the past when my sin caused You grief. Help me to have the same kind of patience toward those who cause me to be angry. I choose to love them. Thank You for the power to demonstrate that love. I forgive all who would sin against me and I bless them with the knowledge of Your love and truth. I pray especially for my brothers and sisters in the Lord. May we all walk in Your love and forgiveness toward each other so that the world may see Your love in us. As they witness this love, may they desire to know You, the God of love. I ask this in Jesus' name. Amen.

Proverbs 16:33 Into the centre is the lot cast, And from Jehovah is all its judgment! (Young's Literal Translation).

Proverbs continually stresses the fact that when we seek God and leave the outcome of all circumstances to Him, He will bring about the results that are right.

In ancient times, important matters were often decided by "lot." Lots (i.e. various sizes of sticks and stones) were used as objects to decide matters such as distribution of tasks or land, etc. They were placed in a container and cast out at random to determine the choice in question. This method of deciding portentous issues was widely used in Old Testament times. A modern equivalent is that of "drawing straws." Let us say that an important task must be done, but no one wants to do it. They agree to draw straws. All parties decide that whoever draws the shortest straw will be the one chosen for the task. Their leader gathers the straws and cuts them in different lengths. He holds them in his hand. Only the tops, arranged evenly, can be seen. The uneven ends are hidden in his hand. Each person draws a straw and the one who draws the shortest straw must do the pre-assigned task. Drawing straws or casting lots is an impartial way to make a difficult decision. Those participating cannot complain, since the selection was not done by a vote. "The lot causeth contentions to cease, and parteth between the mighty" (Proverbs 18:18).

God commanded the Israelites to use the lot to divide the Promised Land among the tribes (Numbers 26:55-56). This was fair. Otherwise, some of the tribes could have complained if they felt that the distribution was done in favor of one tribe over another. Since the land consisted of hills, mountains, fertile plains, and coastlands, this was an impartial way to distribute it. No one would have trusted man's decision; however, because they trusted God in this kind of selection, they felt that the one selected was God's choice. Unseen by man, God is working behind the scenes. Those chosen by lot were ultimately God's choice. He is the One who removes a person from a position and puts another into it. "But God is the judge: he putteth down one, and setteth up another" (Psalm 75:7).

The Lord is the righteous Judge of all the earth. "....Shall not the Judge of all the earth do right?" (Genesis 18:25b).

Dear Father, thank You for being in charge of my life. Because I belong to You, I know that I am not just a lost boat drifting in a storm. Thank You for guiding and directing me in all of my ways. Lord, when You choose me to do anything for You, please empower me and give me the grace to accomplish it. I know that my life is planned by You and that when I am committed to You, each person who comes into it is sent by You. May I grow from those encounters and be a blessing to everyone You bring into my life. I ask this in the name of Jesus. Amen.

God's Wisdom for Daily Living **_Betty Miller_**
May 22 **_Day 142_**

Proverbs 17:1 Better is a dry morsel, and quietness therewith, than an house full of sacrifices with strife.

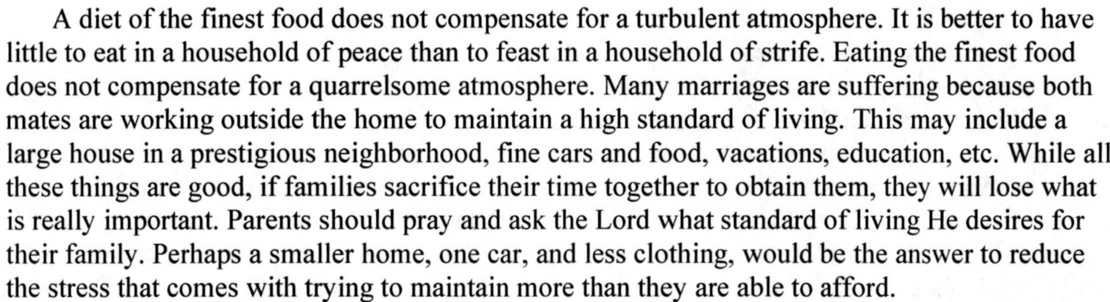

A diet of the finest food does not compensate for a turbulent atmosphere. It is better to have little to eat in a household of peace than to feast in a household of strife. Eating the finest food does not compensate for a quarrelsome atmosphere. Many marriages are suffering because both mates are working outside the home to maintain a high standard of living. This may include a large house in a prestigious neighborhood, fine cars and food, vacations, education, etc. While all these things are good, if families sacrifice their time together to obtain them, they will lose what is really important. Parents should pray and ask the Lord what standard of living He desires for their family. Perhaps a smaller home, one car, and less clothing, would be the answer to reduce the stress that comes with trying to maintain more than they are able to afford.

The Bible tells us how to have a happy home. Many families today are hurting because they have not learned how to love and serve each other. When mates are selfish, they bicker. The Bible instructs us to love one another and avoid this kind of railing at each other (1 Peter 3:8-12). Christian husbands and wives should love and honor each other as brothers and sisters in Christ.

"Beloved, let us love one another: for love is of God; and every one that loveth is born of God, and knoweth God. He that loveth not knoweth not God; for God is love...God is love; and he that dwelleth in love dwelleth in God, and God in him" (1 John 4:7-8,16).

The kind of love that is mentioned here is not the kind of love that is in the world. The original language of the New Testament was Greek. In Greek there are three words that are all translated as *"love."* In the above verse, the word for *"love"* is *agape.* It is a love that is divine. It is selfless and gives sacrificially. In Greek there are three words for love: (1) Love that is divine, called "agape"; (2) Love of high ideals, called "phileo" (our city of Philadelphia is named for this brotherly love); and (3) Love of physical passion, called "eros" (our word erotic stems from this word). Since the original text of the New Testament was written in Greek we know the verse above was referring to "agape" love and not the other two.

Yes, it is far better to have less of this world's goods, with God's love in our lives, than to have much worldly wealth but not know God. Our Father promises that He will always take care of His children, and He will supply our daily needs. "Let your conversation be without covetousness; and be content with such things as ye have: for he hath said, I will never leave thee, nor forsake thee" (Hebrews 13:5).

Dear heavenly Father, I am thankful for all that You have provided for me. When I need certain things and I do not see how they will be supplied, help me not to be stressful. My trust is in You and I know that You will never leave me nor forsake me. Lord, I am grateful for a peaceful home. Fill all who visit our home with Your peace. Let us serve those whom You send to our house. I pray for marriages that are hurting because of stress. Show them the changes that they need to make, and give them the grace to make them. May Your peace permeate the whole body of Christ as You have intended. I ask this in Your name. Amen.

Proverbs 17:2 A wise servant shall have rule over a son that causeth shame, and shall have part of the inheritance among the brethren.

A good businessman would rather entrust his business to a capable, diligent employee, rather than to a prodigal son who cares nothing for his father's company. Many an irresponsible natural-born son has lost his inheritance, while many a faithful employee has been promoted in business and eventually "inherited" the company in place of a son.

Some have even sold their inheritance for a passing pleasure. Genesis 25:20-34 recounts such a story of two brothers: Esau, a hunter and Jacob, a farmer. Esau was the firstborn, which gave him a birthright of inheritance. On one occasion, he was famished and faint from hunting. Jacob had prepared a pot of lentil stew and Esau came in and asked Jacob for some of it. Jacob told him that he would feed him the stew in exchange for his birthright. Esau despised and cared so little about his birthright, that he sold it to his brother in a moment of hunger and weakness. "Then Jacob gave Esau bread and pottage of lentils; and he did eat and drink, and rose up, and went his way: thus Esau despised his birthright" (Genesis 25:34).

Many Christians despise their eternal inheritance in a similar way. When a child of God "sells out" for temporary pleasure, he may miss a great calling that God had for him. Opportunities can be lost forever, if we fail to obey when God calls and prompts us to do something. "Looking diligently lest any man fail of the grace of God; lest any root of bitterness springing up trouble you, and thereby many be defiled; Lest there be any fornicator, or profane person, as Esau, who for one morsel of meat sold his birthright. For ye know how that afterward, when he would have inherited the blessing, he was rejected: for he found no place of repentance, though he sought it carefully with tears" (Hebrews 12:15-17). What Esau had done could *not* be undone. He sold his birthright to Jacob under an oath and God would not permit the reversal of that oath. God can, and does, forgive any sin that we may commit, but we are still left with their consequences. For instance, a woman with an illegitimate child can ask God to forgive her of her fornication, and she will be clean in God's sight as far as her sin is concerned, but she will still have the child to raise. Another example is of those who find the Lord in prison. They can receive forgiveness from God, but they must still live with the consequences of their sin and pay their debt to society. The good news is that they now can live above their circumstances, and in many cases, their sentences are cut short because of His grace and mercy.

Every day, God brings us opportunities to serve Him, to witness, or to serve others. Some people "sell out" just to get some quick relief from their burdens of the moment. Lost opportunities cannot be restored to us. Like Esau, we may seek for them with tears, but they are lost forever, and who knows but that the fate of other souls depended on them?

Dear heavenly Father, I thank You for calling me to be Your servant. Lord, give me the grace to serve You well. I do thank You for Your wisdom also. Guide me daily in the things that I must do and show me my priorities. Help me to be sensitive to the needs of those around me. Lord, I am looking to You to meet all of my needs. Give me peace and confidence when I must deal with situations that are difficult for me. May I speak the truth in love and be open myself for correction when You see something in my life that needs changing. I ask this in the name of Jesus. Amen.

Proverbs 17:3 The fining pot is for silver, and the furnace for gold: but the LORD trieth the hearts.

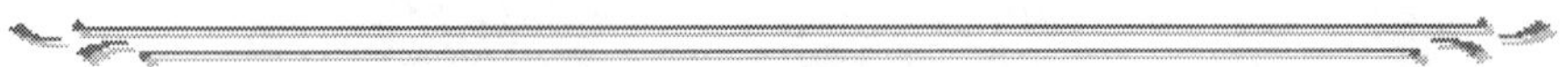

In this verse, we see the analogy between the refining of silver and gold and the refining of God's people. God tries the hearts of all people in order to find out what is in them. He does this by giving us a choice when we are faced with temptation. We can yield to the pressure that Satan brings against us, or we can resist it and stand in faith to receive God's promises. No matter what Satan does, we have been given a way to overcome him through the Holy Spirit (1 Corinthians 10:13). We can praise God in our trials, believing that He will bring us through victoriously, or we can turn on God and blame Him for all our troubles.

Just as the refining pot is heated to bring out the impurities in silver and gold, the devil "heats up" our circumstances. In moments of temptation, we are faced with what is in our hearts. Sometimes fear, doubt, and unbelief will come to the surface. These will conquer us, if we do not turn to God. Only by calling upon Him to deliver us from the evil in our hearts can we have victory. "The heart is deceitful above all things, and it is exceedingly perverse and corrupt and severely, mortally sick! Who can know it (perceive, understand, be acquainted with his own heart and mind)? I the LORD, search the mind, I try the heart, even to give every man according to his ways, according to the fruit of his doings" (Jeremiah 17:9-10 AMP).

Evil does not proceed from God; it is present in our hearts and the world because of our sin. He has instructed us on how to overcome it, and He made a way through the Holy Spirit for us to do so. We must choose to resist sin; God will not do it for us. When we do what is right and obey His Word, the Spirit empowers us to overcome every sin and Satanic attack. Each time we pass a test, we grow in His righteousness. "And he shall sit as a refiner and purifier of silver: and he shall purify the sons of Levi, and purge them as gold and silver, that they may offer unto the LORD an offering in righteousness" (Malachi 3:3).

In the refining process, gold is reduced to a liquid by very high temperatures. Its impurities come to the surface and the dross is skimmed off. This process is repeated many times, at higher temperatures. When there is no more dross that surfaces and the refiner can see his own image in the gold, he knows that it is completely pure. This is a picture of the refining process we go through as God's children. Like gold, we are not destroyed by this process, however uncomfortable it may be. We simply become pure and pliable, reflecting the beauty of Christ Himself.

Dearest Father, thank You for being patient with me in my trials. I have failed many of my tests the first time around, but because of Your love and mercy, I have been given other chances to overcome. Each time You have strengthened me until I have been able to overcome the devil with his temptations. I do want to be conformed into Your image. It seems so impossible, but You said that with You all things are possible, so I am believing You to do the work in my life that is necessary so that I might overcome and please You. Lord, be merciful and help all of us, Your children. I ask this in the name of Jesus. Amen.

Proverbs 17:4-5 4 An evildoer gives heed to wicked lips, and a liar listens to a mischievous tongue. 5 Whoever mocks the poor reproaches his Maker, and he who is glad at calamity shall not be held innocent or go unpunished (AMP).

Verse 4 – God hates all sin, but we saw in Proverbs 6:16-19 that there are seven sins which God particularly hates, and lying is one of them. Giving an ear to a known liar is just as bad as telling a lie. At times, we are all exposed to lies without knowing it, but most people's attitudes reveal if their words should be trusted or not. Haughty, critical, and demeaning people cannot be trusted to speak without bias. Those with the habit of spreading gossip and trying to get people to side with them against others must also be avoided. Such people are not content to do mischief themselves, but they try to enlist others to join them. We certainly must not encourage such people by listening to them.

Verse 5 – God hates pride, which leads us to despise anyone who (in comparison to ourselves) is "poor" in talent, intelligence, looks, spirituality, or skills–in addition to those who are economically poor. He is interested in every soul. He loves the poor and desires that we love them, too. We are all poor before Him! Expressing His love to others in practical ways opens a door through which we might lead them to salvation.

As Christians, we have been commissioned not only to preach the gospel to the poor, but teach them laws that govern the affairs of life. People are destroyed through lack of knowledge. "My people are destroyed for lack of knowledge: because thou hast rejected knowledge, I will also reject thee, that thou shalt be no priest to me: seeing thou hast forgotten the law of thy God, I will also forget thy children" (Hosea 4:6). Only the knowledge and application of God's Word can overcome our problems. The poor need this knowledge. The Bible is not only filled with the spiritual principles of life, but also wisdom in the area of physical laws. Some of the subjects that are covered in the Bible are: nutrition, sanitation, land conservation, animal husbandry, ecology, social etiquette, government administration, and family structure. This is just a partial list, since the Bible has much to say on many subjects. When we seek God's answers to any problem, we can find something that the Bible has to say about it.

We should never be glad when calamity occurs, not even the destruction of the wicked. We can be glad when justice is done, but if we have God's heart, we will be saddened that the wicked did not repent. "Say unto them, As I live, saith the LORD GOD, I have no pleasure in the death of the wicked; but that the wicked turn from his way and live: turn ye, turn ye from your evil ways; for why will ye die, O house of Israel?" (Ezekiel 33:11).

Dear Father, thank You for Your love for me. I ask You to place in me the same kind of love that You have for the lost and the poor. I pray for them and ask You to work in the hearts of those who are seeking You, yet they are looking in the wrong places. Father, I need a tender and understanding heart toward the poor. May I be sensitive to Your leading so that I know how to help in the right way. Thank You for blessing me so that I can bless others. I ask this in the precious name of Jesus. Amen.

Proverbs 17:6-7 6 Children's children are the crown of old men, and the glory of children is their fathers. 7 Fine or arrogant speech does not become (an empty–headed) fool; much less do lying lips become a prince (AMP).

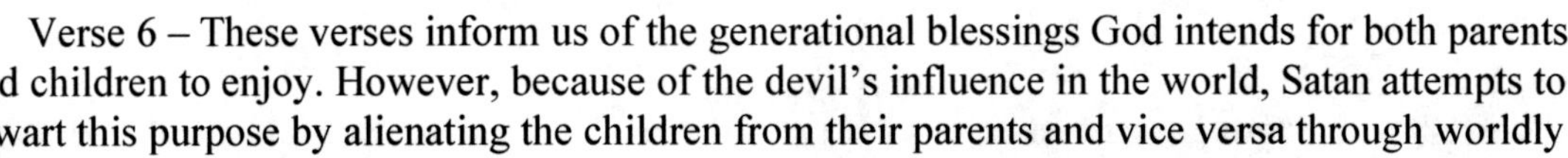

Verse 6 – These verses inform us of the generational blessings God intends for both parents and children to enjoy. However, because of the devil's influence in the world, Satan attempts to thwart this purpose by alienating the children from their parents and vice versa through worldly influences. Wickedness used to be confined to specific geographical areas, like cities or individual countries, but now–due to the internet, films, and television–humanistic ideas have exerted a uniformly evil influence not only across America, but also across the entire world.

"Lo, children are an heritage of the LORD: and the fruit of the womb is his reward. As arrows are in the hand of a mighty man; so are children of the youth. Happy is the man that hath his quiver full of them: they shall not be ashamed, but they shall speak with the enemies in the gate" (Psalm 127:3-5). A father's children were meant to bless him by being a defense to him if any enemy should speak against him. Godly children will not only defend their father and mother, but will honor them, as the Bible admonishes them to do. They will glory in having good parents and be thankful to God for their heritage. Many families today lack this generational blessing, as both parents and children have broken God's laws and do not have a godly relationship with each other. One of the Ten Commandments states the importance of children honoring their parents. "Honour thy father and thy mother: that thy days may be long upon the land which the LORD they God giveth thee" (Exodus 20:12).

One of the purposes of the righteous is to declare the glory of God to the next generation (Psalm 145:4; Psalm 127:3-5; Psalm 71:18 NIV). From these and other scriptures, we can see that each generation is called to build upon the foundation left by the previous one. All generations need each other in order to complete the work that God has called His body to fulfill. Fathers and mothers need to be godly examples to their children so that the torch will be passed down to them, and they in turn will pass it on to their children.

Verse 7 – A man is judged by how he speaks. It is a foolish Christian who does not align his words with God's. It is unseemly for a fool to frame his thoughts in persuasive or elegant words. There are many people who speak well, but their words are humanistic rubbish. This is as inappropriate as a gold ring in a pig's snout (Psalm 14:1). Those in positions of leadership need integrity to rule well. A liar can never be a good leader, since dishonesty will eventually undermine the trust of all his followers. A godly leader should carry himself as a prince would. We even use the expression, "he is a prince of a fellow," to describe one who has integrity and honesty.

Dear heavenly Father, I am thankful for all that You have given me. Lord, forgive this generation of families that have failed one another. Restore the breaches in families and homes. Give the children a submissive spirit toward their parents and speak to them to honor their mothers and fathers. Give the fathers and mothers the love and wisdom that they need to minister to their children. Heal those relationships and restore the broken homes. Heal our land, O Lord. I ask this in the name of Jesus. Amen.

Proverbs 17:8-9 8 A gift is as a precious stone in the eyes of him that hath it: whithersoever it turneth, it prospereth. 9 He that covereth a transgression seeketh love; but he that repeateth a matter separateth very friends.

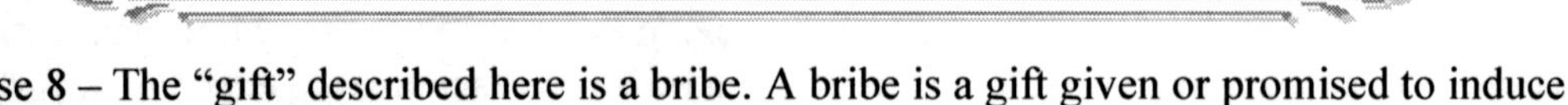

Verse 8 – The "gift" described here is a bribe. A bribe is a gift given or promised to induce a person to do something illegal, wrong, or against his wishes. Like a jewel, it dazzles both the one who offers it, as well as the one who receives it.

If people do not have strong convictions, their opinions can be bought with a bribe. As Christians, we not only should refuse any kind of bribe, but also any involvement in anything that we know the Lord disapproves of. A bribe blinds our eyes to truth. "And thou shalt take no gift: for the gift blindeth the wise, and perverteth the words of the righteous" (Exodus 23:8). The Word of God forbids judges and officers from taking bribes. Judges and police officers must be honorable if our judicial system is to work properly. They must hold their offices without being a respecter of persons. They are to rule righteously, according to the law and not personal preference. In the Biblical judicial system, all people were treated fairly regardless of color, religious belief, or economic status (Deuteronomy 16:18-20).

God is the ultimate righteous Judge, and He will judge all people according to their deeds. He will be completely fair, since He has access to all hidden evidence and He knows who is guilty and who is innocent. Human beings will not be able to lie when they come before God; He knows what is in every man's heart and nothing is hidden from Him. God, the Judge of all the earth, will do what is right (Genesis 18:25).

Verse 9 – This verse gives us a means of testing ourselves to see if we are walking in God's love. If we really seek to love, we will not only forgive an offense, but we will also cover it. We will not go about recounting the incident, especially to the offender's friends. It is evil to try to break up a friendship. We only strengthen a bad situation when we continue to bring it up. We must ask God to deliver us from gossip and harboring unforgiveness.

We should never take up another's offense, but encourage people to settle their differences between themselves; not siding with either party. Certainly, we can side with what is right, but we should not take part in a dispute unless it directly involves us. Those in disagreement should work out their differences according to the Word of God. We should pray and seek peace with all people (Romans 12:16-19).

Dear heavenly Father, thank You for teaching me Your Word. Help me to always obey it as I know that You bless all who adhere to Your commandments. Forgive me when I fail You, and give me the grace to forgive those who have offended and sinned against me. Lord, help me guard my mouth and not to repeat things that are not edifying to others. Help me to be a peacemaker. May I never be guilty of taking a bribe. May all the gifts I give to others be totally given in love, with no strings attached. I do not want to be guilty of expecting someone to return a favor to me just because I gave to them. Help us all to live as godly examples before our friends and family. I ask this in the name of Jesus. Amen.

Proverbs 17:10-12 10 A reproof entereth more into a wise man than an hundred stripes into a fool. 11 An evil man seeketh only rebellion: therefore a cruel messenger shall be sent against him. 12 Let a bear robbed of her whelps meet a man, rather than a fool in his folly.

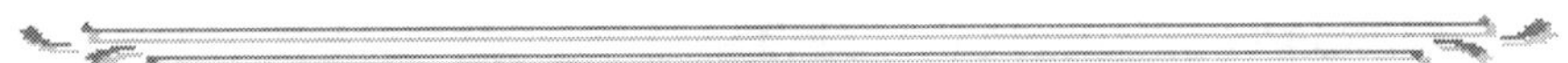

Verse 10 – When corrected, our natural inclination is to defend ourselves. Reproof may come as a painful "lash," but if we desire wisdom, we will receive it with thanksgiving (Proverbs 9:8-9). One distinct quality that sets the wise person apart from the fool is humility. We tend to think of wisdom as the ability to understand difficult concepts. While this is a characteristic of wisdom, there is more to being wise than understanding something. True wisdom, like all the great things of God, is something that any of us can attain, if we are willing to humble ourselves. This is comforting to me. I may not be the smartest person in the world, but I know that, if I am willing to humble myself when I am reproved, it will make me wiser. No one has to remain a fool. It is possible to grow in wisdom, just as it is possible to grow in foolishness. This is a sobering thought! A wise man will benefit from reproof, while a fool might be lashed all day long and still never change his ways.

Verse 11 – As illustrated by the story of the prodigal son, if we are bent on rebellion, a "stern and pitiless messenger" will be sent against us in the hopes of bringing us to our senses so that we will repent. Satan was the "stern and pitiless messenger" into whose hands the prodigal son fell. He was reduced to squalor and starvation, and he had to learn obedience the hard way. Eventually, he was able to make the wisest decision of his life–to turn back to the loving arms of his father.

Verse 12 – A bear may injure our bodies, but a raging fool is even more deadly; he can wound our soul. "A wise man feareth, and departeth from evil: but the fool rageth, and is confident" (Proverbs 14:16). Self-confidence in these verses could be translated as self-righteousness. It does not refer to the confidence or righteousness of God, but a "devil-may-care" attitude that does not tolerate correction by anyone, especially by one perceived as inferior. We may learn by observing self-righteous people with whom we may have no choice in associating with, but we are foolish ourselves if we become close to them. Nothing blinds us more quickly to wisdom than thinking that we are already wise. It is easier to get free of an angry bear than a proud spirit that has no fear of God. One who is gripped by this kind of foolishness cannot even perceive God's correction through his circumstances, Instead, he persists in rebellion to the end.

If we have been proud of our intellect or abilities; if we have been haughty toward those who have tried to correct us; if we have led others astray through our own foolishness, it is not too late to humble ourselves and change our ways. Let us humbly receive the Word of God, which is able to save our very souls!

Dear Father, I thank You for Your mercy on me when I have made wrong and rebellious choices in my life. Thank You for giving me the eyes to see my folly and turn to You. I ask for the grace to continue to walk in wisdom. Help me to be humble when I am corrected, and not to think of myself more highly than I ought to. Let me hear You when You speak to me, through whatever means You may use. Bless all of those who are struggling right now in their lives. Strengthen the weak and give them a song in their heart which will be their strength. Thank You for Your forgiveness and mercy! In Jesus' mighty Name, Amen.

Proverbs 17:13-15 13 Whoever rewards evil for good, evil shall not depart from his house. 14 The beginning of strife is as when water first trickles (from a crack in a dam); therefore stop contention before it becomes worse and quarreling breaks out. 15 He who justifies the wicked and he who condemns the righteous are both an abomination–exceedingly disgusting and hateful–to the LORD (AMP).

Verse 13 – Those who have been helped by someone and then return an evil act toward them will find they are cursed with evil in their own house. A man helps a homeless person and is mugged. A supervisor helps a friend become a manager and that same friend fires him in order to secure his own position. Parents invest their money and time in nursing a sickly child who grows up only to ignore them when they are elderly. These are but a few examples of how good can be rewarded by evil. Those who selfishly return evil for good will only bring evil upon themselves. "Be not deceived; God is not mocked: for whatsoever a man soweth, that shall he also reap" (Galatians 6:7).

Verse 14 – Strife can begin with a few unkind words and end in a bitter quarrel, just as a small crack in a dam quickly widens until the whole dam bursts. We must stop contention before it becomes a quarrel. One way to do this is to learn what triggers a quarrel and to refrain from saying such things. Another way is to walk in humility. Proverbs 13:10 says contention comes by pride. It is not wise to approach others with a proud, demeaning attitude. We should remain humble when others arrogantly challenge us wrongly. It does not mean that we compromise our position, but that we maintain a basic respect for all people, because they are made in God's image and He loves them.

Verse 15 – It is easy to see that it is an abomination to justify a criminal or condemn a righteous person, but we ought also to be careful not to oppose those doing a good work for God simply because we do not agree with them in some area. We should repent if we have been guilty of doing this. Likewise, we should be careful about what we support. Many companies, for instance, produce popular products but support abortion and other evil things. Some people are now attacking the Bible and calling it "hate literature," because it calls their sins "sin." Isaiah has some strong words for those who do these things: "Woe unto them that call evil good, and good evil; that put darkness for light, and light for darkness; that put bitter for sweet, and sweet for bitter! Woe unto them that are wise in their own eyes, and prudent in their own sight! Woe unto them that are mighty to drink wine, and men of strength to mingle strong drink: Which justify the wicked for reward, and take away the righteousness of the righteous from him! Therefore as the fire devoureth the stubble, and the flame consumeth the chaff, so their root shall be as rottenness, and their blossom shall go up as dust: because they have cast away the law of the LORD of hosts, and despised the word of the Holy One of Israel" (Isaiah 5:20-24).

Dear heavenly Father, I am thankful for the wonderful ways in which You take care of me. I appreciate Your care over my family and friends. I desire to remain humble in my dealings with others who oppose me. Give me grace and wisdom when I must handle controversy. May I be humble when I am tested in this way and trust You to defend me instead of getting into a fight with others. Lord, bless those who are reading this today and strengthen them to do Your will. I ask this in the name of Jesus. Amen.

Proverbs 17:16-17 16 Wherefore is there a price in the hand of a fool to get wisdom, seeing he hath no heart to it? 17 A friend loveth at all times, and a brother is born for adversity. 18 A man void of understanding striketh hands, and becometh surety in the presence of his friend.

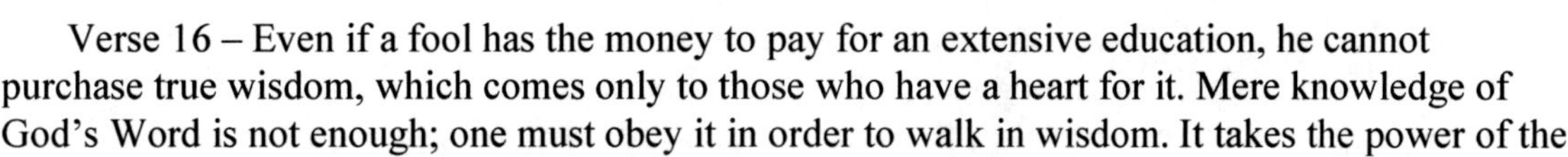

Verse 16 – Even if a fool has the money to pay for an extensive education, he cannot purchase true wisdom, which comes only to those who have a heart for it. Mere knowledge of God's Word is not enough; one must obey it in order to walk in wisdom. It takes the power of the Holy Spirit to obey the Bible and walk according to its commands.

Verse 17 – Like a brother who cannot change the fact that he is our brother and cares about us no matter what we do, a true friend will always love us, whether in times of plenty or times of adversity. Even if we fail him, and no longer deserve his friendship, he remains our friend. No matter how good our brothers or friends may be, they may fail us because they *are* human. They may be unable to come when we need them. Jesus, however, is *not* restricted by anything. He is both our elder brother (Romans 8:29) and the faithful friend who sticks closer than a brother. "A man that hath friends must shew himself friendly: and there is a friend that sticketh closer than a brother" (Proverbs 18:24). He will never leave us nor forsake us. "Let your conversation be without covetousness; and be content with such things as ye have: for he hath said, I will never leave thee, nor forsake thee" (Hebrews 13:5). We can always depend upon Him, even when we fail Him. He is a mighty Lord, abundantly available for help in time of need, and His love never changes.

Verse 18 – We are told that it is not wise to become a guarantee for another's debt and seal it by a witness who is a friend or neighbor. This financial advice is given so that we can avoid having problems in our relationships. As we saw in Day 36, we are advised not to become security (surety) for another's debts. Many friendships have been destroyed because this advice was not taken. Though the borrower may have the best intentions, sometimes he is unable to pay his note. When this happens, it leads to complications. These complications, at best, greatly strain the relationship between the guarantor, borrower, and the neighbor who was witness to the pledge. If problems arise when the borrower is unable to pay his note, it forces the witness to side with one party or the other, thus endangering their friendship also.

Dear Father God, thank You for the many gifts You have given me. I appreciate the gifts of wisdom and discernment. I am grateful that You have spared me from many a heartache. Thank You also for the sound advice in the Word of God. Give me the grace and strength to always obey Your Word, as I know You know what is best for me. Bless my family and friends today and keep them from the wicked one. Thank You for Your provision for this day. Help me not to fret about tomorrow. I trust that You have all things under Your control and I believe You will take care of me and my problems. Give this same faith to others who need to hear from You. I ask this in the name of the Lord Jesus Christ. Amen.

Proverbs 17:19-21 19 He loveth transgression that loveth strife: and he that exalteth his gate seeketh destruction. 20 He that hath a froward heart findeth no good: and he that hath a perverse tongue falleth into mischief. 21 He that begetteth a fool doeth it to his sorrow: and the father of a fool hath no joy.

Verse 19 – Those who love to sin and enjoy strife are seeking destruction. This is not talking about those who occasionally fall into sin and repent, since the Lord will help those people overcome their weaknesses. However, those who run toward evil will find it and eventually be destroyed.

This verse also states that those who "raise their gate high" are inviting destruction. What does this mean? It can be referring to those who leave the gate to their houses open all the time, thus inviting the wrong kind of people into their homes. We must shut our homes at night and be discreet about who we invite into them. We do not want to tempt others to come in, by boasting and not being discreet about what we have. It can also be referring to the "gate" of our lips. When we open wide the gate of our mouths, we invite destruction into our lives. We must be wise and speak those things that will turn the enemy away. One example would be if we speak softly to someone who is railing at us, we will not stir up his wrath against us. "A soft answer turneth away wrath: but grievous words stir up anger" (Proverbs 15:1).

Verse 20 – Guarding what we say and think is important. Those who allow their thoughts to turn to evil will eventually also do what is wrong. A perverse mind and a foul mouth pave the way for mischief and difficulty. We need the Lord's help to guard our minds and our mouths in order to say what edifies and blesses others. Then we, in turn, may be blessed.

Verse 21 – Fool is used to translate the Hebrew words *kesel* and *nabal. Kesel* might be said to mean "self-confident fool" and *nabal,* "wicked fool.[20]" The self-confident fool is wise in his own eyes. The wicked fool despises God and pursues evil. Both are rebellious.

A fool causes his parents grief and shame. His attitude and speech embarrass them even when he is not in trouble with an authority (such as a teacher or a policeman). Parents truly can have no joy in a son or daughter who is a wicked fool. The parents of a self-confident fool may not have grief, but neither can they have joy. Their child is neither getting into major trouble nor is he reaching his potential by seeking God. It breaks the heart of a Christian parent to see a child walk after the world and not after Christ. Sons and daughters of any age who honor their parents can avoid many of the traps of the devil, and they will live long, blessed lives (Ephesians 6:1-3).

Dear Father, thank You for our parents. It is a blessing to have parents who care about You. May we always honor them as You told us to do. I pray for our young people; may they have respect and obedience toward their parents. Lord, help us, as parents, to guard our mouths and speak the things that are good and edifying. Let us all seek peace and be peacemakers. Deliver us from any rebellion, and may we walk in love with our families and our friends and co-workers. I ask this in the name of our Lord Jesus Christ. Amen.

[20] Strong's Exhaustive Concordance of the Bible, Hebrew and Chaldee Dictionary

Proverbs 17:22 A merry heart doeth good like a medicine: but a broken spirit drieth the bones.

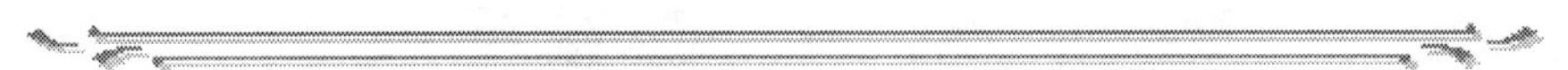

Maintaining a joyful spirit is like taking a dose of healing medicine. Scientists are beginning to see the Biblical truth that one's mental state affects one's physical state. A negative outlook causes people to succumb to sickness more readily than a positive one. According to many studies, a happy outlook may actually help cardiac patients avoid heart attacks and other health problems, because a hearty laugh causes a small, but fleeting decrease in blood pressure and releases endorphins, which have a pain-relieving and soothing effect upon the body. Some doctors recommend that patients suffering serious illness add laughter to their treatment regimen, advising that they regularly watch comedy shows.

We must not allow Satan to break our spirits; for a broken spirit "dries up the bones." Our bones contain marrow which is vital for a healthy body; it consists largely of blood cells in all stages of development. Red blood corpuscles contain the iron compound, hemoglobin, that gives us strength and energy; white blood cells protect the body from infections and disease; and blood platelets are essential for blood clot formation. New blood cells are released into the bloodstream from the bones every second. Thus, we can see how important our bone marrow is.

If we succumb to the devil's lies and attacks, he can rob us of our joy which can cause the "drying of our bones." In essence, this means it can weaken our immune system, thus affecting all areas of our body, soul (the mind, the emotions, the will), and spirit. We are triune beings, designed to function as a unit. The regenerated spirit should be in control of the soul, with the body in subordination to them. If bodily appetites or emotions control us instead of our quickened spirit, God's order is violated. We function abnormally; that is below our God-given potential. Jesus came as the Great Physician to minister wholeness to His people (Matthew 4:24).

To function properly, we must become "born again" by receiving the Spirit of Life. We will never be whole without this first step. Next, we must ask God to cleanse us, that we might truly love Him with all our hearts. This is the first and greatest commandment (Matthew 22:36-38). Finally, we need to appropriate the healing Jesus purchased for us.

Before dying on the cross, Jesus was lashed with Roman whips which literally tore pieces of flesh from His back. These are the stripes by which we were healed. "Who his own self bare our sins in his own body on the tree, that we, being dead to sins, should live unto righteousness: by whose stripes ye were healed" (1 Peter 2:24; see also Isaiah 53). God wants us to be whole: spirit, soul, and body. We can maintain wholeness by keeping a joyful heart; praising God and enjoying His blessings. Truly, it is like a dose of good medicine that brings healing.

Dear heavenly Father, thank You for saving my soul, and also for the promise of healing. I appreciate the many times over the years that You have healed me personally. I also thank You for the gift of healing, as when I prayed, You have touched others with Your healing virtue. Lord, heal those who are in need of Your touch right now. You truly are the Great Physician. I appreciate that about You. Lord, I want to always remain in a joyful attitude, no matter what might come my way. Fill me with Your love, joy, and peace daily, so that I might be an example of Your goodness. I ask this in the name of the Lord Jesus. Amen.

Proverbs 17:23-25 23 A wicked man taketh a gift out of the bosom to pervert the ways of judgment. 24 Wisdom is before him that hath understanding; but the eyes of a fool are in the ends of the earth. 25 A foolish son is a grief to his father, and bitterness to her that bare him.

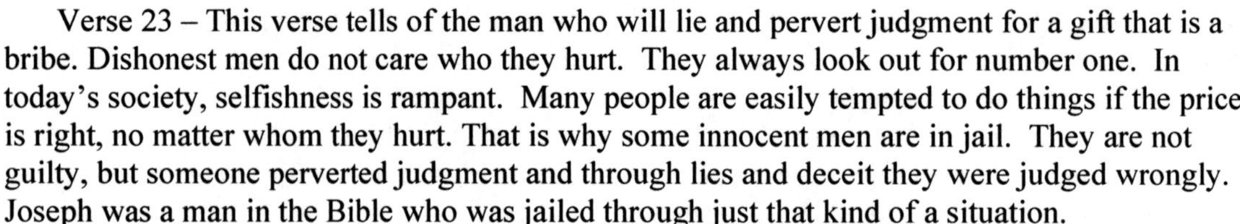

Verse 23 – This verse tells of the man who will lie and pervert judgment for a gift that is a bribe. Dishonest men do not care who they hurt. They always look out for number one. In today's society, selfishness is rampant. Many people are easily tempted to do things if the price is right, no matter whom they hurt. That is why some innocent men are in jail. They are not guilty, but someone perverted judgment and through lies and deceit they were judged wrongly. Joseph was a man in the Bible who was jailed through just that kind of a situation.

Genesis 39 tells how Joseph was jailed through a false accusation. He was a steward over Potiphar's house. Potiphar's had a wife who was a flirt and she tempted Joseph to have an affair with her while her husband was gone, but he refused. This angered her and when her husband came home, she accused Joseph of trying to seduce her because she was spurned by him. This led to Joseph's imprisonment because of her false accusations. However, he refused to become bitter, even as he suffered in prison. He used that time to get closer to God; and in time, the Lord made a way for his release and promotion to the second highest position in Egypt as Pharaoh's right-hand man (Genesis 39:7-21).God blessed Joseph because of his attitude. His experiences trained him to be trusted with the leadership of an entire country. This was in accordance with God's plan to save many lives through him (Genesis 45:4-8). This should be an encouragement to all who are in prisons of any kind, physical, mental, emotional, financial, etc. God can make any evil in our lives work for our own good and the good of others when He brings us out of our prisons. He is able to honor us in bad, as well as good circumstances, and use what Satan meant for evil to bring good to us and unto the lives of others. "But as for you, ye thought evil against me; but God meant it unto good, to bring to pass, as it is this day, to save much people alive" (Genesis 5:20).

Verses 24-25 – Unlike Joseph, self-confident fools do not keep their eyes on the Lord. They do not honor Him in their attitudes or their habits. Instead, they are always "looking to the ends of the earth" to see how much they can get from the world. Many have a wanderlust spirit and would like to roam the world with no responsibilities. Because they do not take their responsibilities seriously, they are rarely promoted in this life. If they are, they will be misled by their pride and unable to retain their position. At any age, they cause their parents much grief because they never truly succeed or prosper in anything they do.

Dear heavenly Father, I come to You with a thankful heart for everything that You have done in my life. Thank You for the many answers to my prayers. I appreciate You always being there when I call. Lord, I pray for all of those who do not know You. Use Your children to tell them about the good news of salvation. Give each of us holy boldness to witness to those around us who need to hear about the love of Jesus. May our lives be a testimony of Your love. Forgive us when we fail You and help us to overcome all the things that would hinder us from being like You. I ask this in the name of the Lord Jesus. Amen.

Proverbs 17:26-28 26 Also to punish the just is not good, nor to strike princes for equity. 27 He that hath knowledge spareth his words: and a man of understanding is of an excellent spirit. 28 Even a fool, when he holdeth his peace, is counted wise: and he that shutteth his lips is esteemed a man of understanding.

Verse 26 – Those who have punished the righteous in order to deter others from following their faith have found that that it backfires. Smiting those who are just, noble, and upright is not a good thing. Throughout history, those who have punished the righteous to make an example of them in some way, made them martyrs instead, and in the eyes of the people, they became heroes. Their followers were inspired to fight even stronger for their faith and goals. Those who die for their beliefs are honored by others, even their enemies. It has been said that the church is built on the blood of the martyrs. Many unbelievers, who witnessed Christians die for their faith were convicted and believed in Christ. This still happens. We can be a witness for Jesus by how we conduct ourselves under persecution, as well as by how we live our lives daily.

Verses 27-28 – Many problems can be traced to speaking foolishly. Disrespectful and loud words only stir up trouble. A foul mouth paves the way for many troubles, but even a fool is thought to be wise if he keeps quiet. Those who use words wisely are known as people of understanding and an excellent spirit.

Because sin easily entangles us, we need to be reminded of the truth. "Wherefore seeing we also are compassed about with so great a cloud of witnesses, let us lay aside every weight, and the sin which doth so easily beset us, and let us run with patience the race that is set before us" (Hebrews 12:1). This is why God instructs us to read His Word every day (Proverbs 8:34), and why the Bible repeats many things. Repetition is an excellent means of learning. It is not out of place here to review some principles regarding wise and foolish speaking habits: The mouth cannot utter what is not in the heart. "A good man out of the good treasure of his heart bringeth forth that which is good; and an evil man out of the evil treasure of his heart bringeth forth that which is evil: for of the abundance of the heart his mouth speaketh" (Luke 6:45). Proud, boastful words reveal foolishness in the heart (Jude 16). The wise speak constructively because they guard their hearts. They ask God to search them and bring to light whatever does not line up with His ways. They quickly resolve their anger and forgive others. They fill their minds with God's Word and whatever is wholesome. They refuse to harbor bitterness. It is foolish to believe Satan's lies instead of God's Word. Unbelief leads us to utter negative things which can bring curses upon us. We need the Holy Spirit to help us guard our mouths so that we speak edifying things. When we line up our speech with God's word, we shall be blessed.

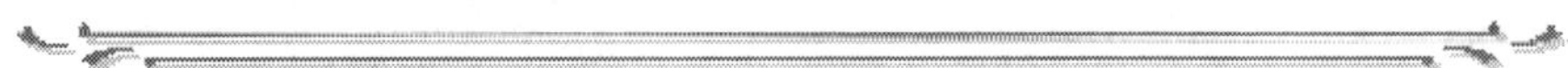

Dear Father, thank You for Your many blessings. As I face each new day, Lord, may I do so with an expectation that You will prevail in my life and help me to do Your will. Help me to guard my lips and speak things that are good and right. Let me refrain my lips from all evil. I want my tongue to be an instrument of righteousness in Your ears. Help me to keep my mouth shut when I need to do so, and help me to open it and speak when You are prompting me to do so. Give me the holy boldness to witness to others about Your love and grace, and to hold my peace when I should. I ask this in the holy name of Jesus. Amen.

Proverbs 18:1-3 1 He who willfully separates and estranges himself (from God and man) seeks his own desire and pretext to break out against all wise and sound judgment. 2 A (self-confident) fool has no delight in understanding, but only in revealing his personal opinions and himself. 3 When the wicked comes in (to the depth of evil), he becomes a contemptuous despiser (of all that is pure and good), and with inner baseness comes outer shame and reproach (AMP).

These verses tell us that those who seek to live without God and without other people are not only selfish, but they also seek their own way and refuse all wisdom and good judgment.

Verse 1 – This verse gives us a description of one who has abandoned society to pursue his own way and do his own thing. This is sinful, since God created man for two purposes. One, He desires a personal relationship with us; and two, He desires us to live together in harmony so we will be a help and blessing to each other. After God created Adam, He said it was not good that man should live alone. So He made him a companion and helper. "And the LORD God said, It is not good that the man should be alone; I will make him an help meet for him" (Genesis 2:18).

The Lord is the inventor of marriage and families. In today's society, the devil is trying to destroy families in many different ways. Homosexuals are trying to redefine the family unit by sanctioning men to live with men in a sexual relationship (as well as women with women). The Biblical definition of a family is a husband and a wife who procreate by having children. This is the core family. Certainly when a member of this family dies or leaves, the others are still considered family. Some families also include others in their circle by inviting them to live with them. This may include an extended family member, or those who are adopted.

The devil also seeks to separate families by divorce. It is sad that most divorces are caused by selfishness. Each party wants his own way and is not serving the other. As Christians, we must love each other and lay our lives down for one another. If this is not done at the basic level in a marriage, then our Christianity is hollow. In our society, doing our own thing is glamorized. We have all heard statements like: "I should be fulfilled." "I should not waste my life in a bad marriage." "I should not put up with the things in my mate that I do not like." "I have my rights and they should come first." These are just a few arguments that the enemy uses to make his case for divorce.

As Christians, our goal should not be to please ourselves, but to please Him who gave His life for us. If we are truly committed to God, we will seek to obey and serve Him in all of our ways. The first place that our Christian love gets tested is in our homes. If we cannot love one another there, how then, can we love others outside our homes? 1 Corinthians 13 gives us a definition of what true Christian love is. The word "love" is used loosely in the world. It usually means an emotional feeling, a desire to be with someone, and can even be mere physical lust for someone. This is not the definition of God's love. He loves even when He is not loved. He laid His life down so that we might have life. God is a giver not a taker. As His children, we are challenged to be like Him. We can only do this as we allow Him to live in and through us.

Verses 2-3 – These verses describe many a person in today's society. They have no delight in understanding God's ways or even listening to another's opinion. They are prideful and revel in their personal opinions. A self-absorbed person who serves only himself will go deeper into evil, as selfishness leads to many other sins. The baseness of his own heart will cause him to commit overt sins that will eventually be seen by all. Many of our public figures have had to endure shame when their secret sins were exposed. We can avoid this kind of life, if we seek God and seek to do His will. When we serve and obey God, we will serve those around us in love.

Dear heavenly Father, thank You for loving us. Lord, You loved us even when we were unloveable. I am ever grateful for Your love. Fill me today with Your love so that I can be like You; loving the unlovely and showing kindness to everyone, including the wicked. You love everyone, as You send Your rain upon the unjust, as well as upon the just. Help me to love those who touch my life who are not always kind to me. Fill me with Your Holy Spirit so that my character does not change when people come against me. I truly want to be able to bless my enemies and do good to them. I know I can only do this through allowing Your love to come through me. I ask this in the name of the Lord Jesus Christ. Amen.

Quotes About Gossip

It is emotional violence to speak ugly things about others. Scripture warns us to guard our mouths and speak only what is edifying, for we reap the effects of our words. --Day 60

As we grow in Him, we will not want to expose people's sins but rather to cover them. Digging up and exposing the sins of others has always been a popular pastime of the ungodly. --Day 61

As Christians we should not listen to gossip, since that makes us party to it. If the one that is being talked about is not there to defend himself, it is not a fair conversation. --Day 138

Just as ingested food becomes part of one's body, ingested gossip becomes part of one's thoughts and opinions. --Day 157

People who talk in a degrading fashion about others cannot be trusted, especially with private issues. --Day 194

When we lie or gossip, our negative words go out into the spiritual dimension to unleash destructive power. We must learn to speak what is good and pray for everyone, even our enemies, so that our words release a blessing. --Day 274

God's Wisdom for Daily Living **_Betty Miller_**
June 5 **_Day 156_**

Proverbs 18:4 The words of a man's mouth are as deep waters, and the wellspring of wisdom as a flowing brook.

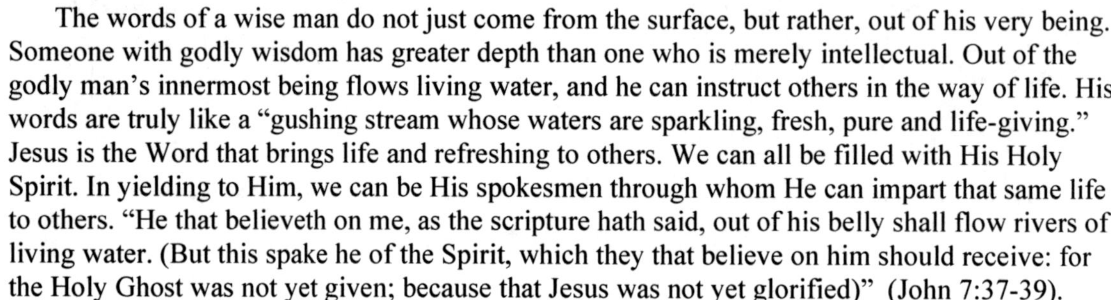

The words of a wise man do not just come from the surface, but rather, out of his very being. Someone with godly wisdom has greater depth than one who is merely intellectual. Out of the godly man's innermost being flows living water, and he can instruct others in the way of life. His words are truly like a "gushing stream whose waters are sparkling, fresh, pure and life-giving." Jesus is the Word that brings life and refreshing to others. We can all be filled with His Holy Spirit. In yielding to Him, we can be His spokesmen through whom He can impart that same life to others. "He that believeth on me, as the scripture hath said, out of his belly shall flow rivers of living water. (But this spake he of the Spirit, which they that believe on him should receive: for the Holy Ghost was not yet given; because that Jesus was not yet glorified)" (John 7:37-39).

Before the charismatic renewal, there were only a few people in denominational churches who knew about the gifts of the Holy Spirit. God saw the need for this truth to be restored to His church, so He began pouring out His Spirit upon all of His people regardless of their church affiliation. Many received the baptism of the Holy Spirit (Matthew 3:11; Acts 1:4-8; 2:1-4; 38, 39; 10:44-46) and began "speaking in tongues and praising the Lord."

Peter, addressing the crowd that gathered the first time when the Holy Spirit was poured out, quoted the prophecy of Joel 2:18-32, which foretold that the baptism in the Holy Spirit would be available to all believers in the last days (Acts 2:16-18). The term "last days" refers to the time between Christ's First Advent (His birth) and Second Advent (His return to earth to establish His kingdom). The First Advent has already occurred and He is coming soon to establish His reign. It is obvious that we live in the last days and that the baptism in the Spirit is being poured out today upon all who will receive Him to give them the power to live the overcoming life.

The Lord desires us to enjoy *all* of His blessings. The baptism of the Spirit should not be a point of contention. Those who have received spiritual gifts must not think less of those who do not know the blessings of Pentecost. Those who have not experienced the baptism in the Spirit must not view those who "speak in tongues" with distaste, especially if they have not sought the Lord regarding this experience. We should not reject something we do not understand. We would have never been saved with this attitude because none of us really understood how salvation worked at the time we received it. We simply repented and received and we were saved. We need to bring new things before God in prayer and prove them against Scripture (1 Thessalonians 5:21). If we bring our questions before God with an open heart, asking Him to show us the truth, He will certainly do so. He will not give us a stone if we ask for bread. If we ask Him for the gift of the Holy Spirit, He will not give us something else (Luke 11:11-13).

Dear Father, thank You for the wonderful gift of the Holy Spirit. When You baptized me in the Spirit, You gave me a gift of boldness to witness and a desire to pray, as well as a new power that enabled me to resist temptation. Without the Holy Spirit, I would be overcome by the enemy. With Your Spirit, I can resist the devil and cause him to flee. I appreciate the freedom to worship You by praying in the Spirit. Through this gift, You have revealed more of the Bible to me. Lord, fill us all daily with Your love and Spirit. Thank You for Your grace and mercy in my life, and in the lives of those I pray for. We need You, Lord. Help us to be open to receive all that You have for us. I ask this in Jesus' name. Amen.

Proverbs 18:5-8 5 To respect the person of the wicked and be partial, so as to deprive the (consistently) righteous of justice, is not good. 6 A (self confident) fool's lips bring contention, and his mouth invites a beating. 7 A (self-confident) fool's mouth is his ruin, and his lips are a snare to himself. 8 The words of a whisperer or talebearer are as dainty morsels; they go down into the innermost parts of the body (AMP).

Verse 5 – It is wrong to show partiality to the wicked for any reason, but especially if it deprives the innocent from receiving justice. As God's children, we are not to allow money or position to influence us when making judgments. Our heavenly Father treats everyone fairly and expects us to do likewise. Kind-hearted people are just as apt to show partiality for the underprivileged as others are apt to be impressed by a person's wealth, fame, or profession. Though often exploited, the poor are not always innocent. A rich man is not always wrong and a poor man is not always right. A person should be esteemed according to his character, which is revealed by his words and actions; not by his income, profession, education, race, creed, etc. "You shall do no injustice in judging a case; you shall not be partial to the poor or show a preference for the mighty, but in righteousness and according to the merits of the case judge your neighbor" (Leviticus 19:15, AMP). "My brethren, have not the faith of our Lord Jesus Christ, the Lord of glory, with respect of persons. For if there come unto your assembly a man with a gold ring, in goodly apparel, and there come in also a poor man in vile raiment; And ye have respect to him that weareth the gay clothing, and say unto him, Sit thou here in a good place; and say to the poor, Stand thou there, or sit here under my footstool: Are ye not then partial in yourselves, and are become judges of evil thoughts?" (James 2:1-4).

God, Himself, is not a respecter of persons. He loves everyone equally. Non one person is loved more than another. However, there is one thing that God is a respecter of – that is His Word. If we practice and keep His Word, He will honor us because of it. Therefore, anyone who keeps the Word of God will be respected by God.

Verses 6-7 – Self-confident fools are often unaware and uncaring of how their words affect others. They perceive themselves as right and air their opinions freely, with no respect to anyone's feelings but their own. Because they do not restrain themselves from saying arrogant or hurtful things, their own words bring them to ruin. Their own lips are a trap set to catch them, always ready to get them into trouble with other people. For more on this subject, see Day 27.

Verse 8 – A talebearer's words are like "dainty goodies" to those who enjoy gossip. The listener gobbles them up. Just as ingested food becomes part of one's body, ingested gossip becomes part of one's thoughts and opinions. Words which are dainty morsels to gossipers are blows to the soul of their victim. Gossip can destroy a person's reputation, career, or business. Without the Lord's help, such injuries are hard to overcome. We all need to guard our mouths. Unkind, sinful words can truly damage and wound others.

Dear Father in heaven, I thank You for Your love today. I am grateful that You are no respecter of persons. Help me to be like You and not show partiality to anyone. Let me be loving and kind to all. Help me to guard my mouth so that I do not speak unadvisedly. I want to be a peacemaker. Father, I yield to You and ask that You help me not to fall into the trap of gossiping about others. May I bring healing to others and not wounding. Forgive my sins and fill me with Your love. I ask this in the name of Jesus. Amen.

Proverbs 18:9 He also that is slothful in his work is brother to him that is a great waster.

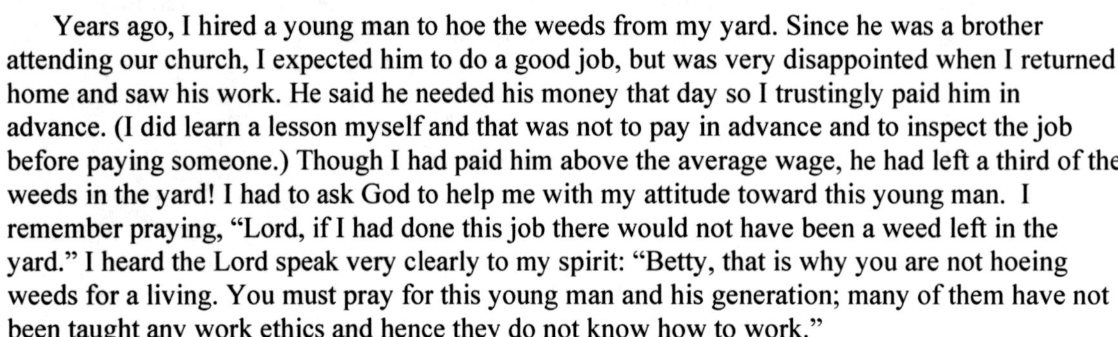

Years ago, I hired a young man to hoe the weeds from my yard. Since he was a brother attending our church, I expected him to do a good job, but was very disappointed when I returned home and saw his work. He said he needed his money that day so I trustingly paid him in advance. (I did learn a lesson myself and that was not to pay in advance and to inspect the job before paying someone.) Though I had paid him above the average wage, he had left a third of the weeds in the yard! I had to ask God to help me with my attitude toward this young man. I remember praying, "Lord, if I had done this job there would not have been a weed left in the yard." I heard the Lord speak very clearly to my spirit: "Betty, that is why you are not hoeing weeds for a living. You must pray for this young man and his generation; many of them have not been taught any work ethics and hence they do not know how to work."

Please do not misunderstand; hoeing weeds is an honorable job. If one does a good job in yard work, he will prosper. His work will be in demand and he will have to hire additional workers to help him. He will be able to ask top wages for his services. Whatever our job may be, if we do it well, we will prosper. Genesis 39-40 recounts the story of Joseph, who was an excellent worker. Everything he did prospered; even his work in jail brought a promotion.

The pace of today's world is a hindrance to good workmanship. Sloth and disorganization reflect a lack of care and values. Many people take shortcuts that lower the quality of their work. They end up wasting time and money because their job must be redone. God is not wasteful. Jesus, after feeding the five thousand, commanded His disciples to gather up the leftovers so that nothing would be lost (John 6:12).

Though many of the younger generation are to be commended for their work, others have not been taught proper work habits and they have difficulty holding jobs. Children's messy rooms are symptoms of the neglect of an entire generation of parents to teach their children work ethics. Many parents joke about the condition of their children's rooms when they should be training them to keep them tidy. Proverbs 22:6 instructs us to "train up a child in the way he should go." The key word here is *train.* Training is more than simply teaching a child how to be proficient at something. It also includes instilling in them a set of values through discipline. We need to train our children to do their best. Training others requires us to work patiently with them until the job is done correctly. Remember, most people do not do what we "expect" but rather what we "inspect." Good teachers implant moral values along with proper instruction. If we have been negligent in any area pertaining to our work, we could be guilty of hurting our children or our witness for the Lord. "Whatsoever thy hand findeth to do, do it with thy might" (Ecclesiastes 9:10a). "With good will doing service, as to the Lord, and not to men" (Ephesians 6:7).

Dear heavenly Father, thank You for giving us a job and a task to do. Lord, let us not view work as a drudgery; rather, let us be grateful that we are able to work. Let us work with joy, and not complain about our lot in life. Let us realize that we are working for You and You shall promote and reward us, even as You did Joseph in the Bible. You use men as instruments of blessing in our lives, and let us also be instruments of blessing to others. In our work places let us be a blessing to those around us, and thank You for blessing us, too. Strengthen us for each day's tasks. Lord, use each of us to contribute our portion to making this world a better place. I ask this in the name of Jesus. Amen.

Proverbs 18:10 The name of the LORD is a strong tower; the (consistently) righteous man–upright and in right standing with God–runs into it and is safe, high (above evil) and strong (AMP).

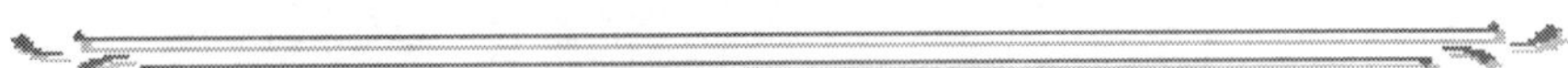

This verse reveals the safety that is in the name of the Lord. All through the Bible, whenever anyone called on His name, we see that God responded in power to help them. Why is the name of the Lord so powerful? What is in a name? Behind every name there is a person or object. A name represents the person or describes the object. Behind the name of the Lord, is the name of Jesus, the name of God and the power of the Holy Spirit. The name of the Lord Jesus is backed up by all the power and resources of Heaven itself! Therefore, when a believer calls on the name of Jesus, he has access to all the resources of Heaven as well.

God revealed Himself through many names in the Old Testament, but their English translations do not reveal what is expressed in Hebrew. *Yahweh,* translated as Lord, means the Eternal, Unchanging Covenant-maker[21], and is combined with other names; for example: *Yahweh Yireh,* the Lord my Provider; *Yahweh Shalom,* the Lord my Peace, etc. There are a number of others. These names provided aspects of God's nature, which has been fully revealed in Jesus. In the New Testament we find that Jesus Christ is the name above all names. "Wherefore God also hath highly exalted him, and given him a name which is above every name" (Philippians 2:9). We can find comfort through God's Old Testament names, as all that He is, is available to us through Jesus. His name is indeed like a strong tower!

When we call on the name of Jesus, we have access to all the resources of heaven. By way of illustration, when a woman marries a man, she takes his name as her own. Legally, she has the right to all he owns and all he is. If he is honorable, she is also held in honor and esteem. She could withdraw all the money from their joint bank account if she wanted to, because she has the legal right to do so. If her husband were to die, everything he owned which he did not allocate to someone else in a will would be hers. When we give our lives to the Lord, we take His name. We then have access to all that belongs to Jesus. We can ask anything in His name and receive it. When we have this kind of relationship, we will not ask for the wrong things, but only for those things that are according to His will. "And whatsoever ye shall ask in my name, that will I do, that the Father may be glorified in the Son. If ye shall ask any thing in my name, I will do it. If ye love me, keep my commandments" (John 14:13-15). His name is like a high tower that we can run into for safety, because Jesus came to save us and deliver us from our sins and Satan's power.

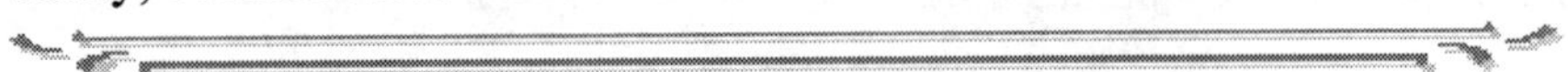

Father God, I am so thankful that we can run to You and find safety. There are so many things we face in this world that are dangerous; it is good to know that You are a high tower of safety. Thank You, for watching over me and my loved ones. I pray for the whole family of God and ask that You watch over each of Your own. Guide Your people in the right ways. Keep us from harm and temptation. Thank You for the privilege of using the mighty name of Jesus, at which the enemy flees. May we realize the power that we can have through the Holy Spirit, and grant us the faith to use it. I ask this in the precious name of Jesus. Amen.

[21] Strong's Exhaustive Concordance of the Bible, Hebrew and Chaldee Dictionary

Proverbs 18:11-12 11 The rich man's wealth is his strong city, and as an high wall in his own conceit. 12 Before destruction the heart of man is haughty, and before honour is humility.

Verse 11 – In ancient times, those who lived within the strong walls of a fortified city were secure from enemies. Archaeology reveals that some walls were wide enough that two lanes of cars could drive upon them! In the rich man's conceit, he believes his wealth surrounds him with as much security as the huge walls of an ancient city. He tends to think money will save him from any threatening circumstances. He does not look to God for anything. Wealth, however, can easily slip away through bad business deals and stock market failures. Inclement weather and fires can destroy businesses and homes. Insurance may cover some losses, but often the rich cannot recuperate. Many a wealthy man has seen the "high protecting walls" of his strong city tumble down. In his pride, he attributed his success to his own abilities, intelligence, and hard work. Personal commitment and hard work do bring rewards, but when one leaves God out of the picture, one is headed for a great fall.

Verse 12 – Haughtiness leads to destruction. Many fail to recognize that if it were not for God's grace and mercy, they could not have achieved anything. Men and women who trust in material possessions instead of God will be in great misery one day if they should lose them.

Money cannot buy health. Yet, many take good health for granted and never thank God for their blessing of freedom from sickness. They also fail to realize that good mental health is a blessing too. When we are able to walk free of depression and lie down at night and enjoy a peaceable night's sleep, this is a blessing from God. Rich people without God are some of the most miserable people on the planet. "Go to now, ye rich men, weep and howl for your miseries that shall come upon you. Your riches are corrupted, and your garments are moth-eaten. Your gold and silver is cankered; and the rust of them shall be a witness against you, and shall eat your flesh as it were fire. Ye have heaped treasure together for the last days" (James 5:1-3).

Men who take pride in their possessions and accomplishments will find that "pride goeth before a fall." Honor, however, will be bestowed upon the humble; those who acknowledge God in all their ways, and recognize that all that they have and are (all of their abilities and successes) come from Him. "But he giveth more grace. Wherefore he saith, God resisteth the proud, but giveth grace unto the humble" (James 4:6).

Dear heavenly Father, thank You for teaching me that true wealth is found in You. Truly, Lord, You are all that we need. Having a relationship with You will bring the answer to any problems that I may face. I can trust You to supply all of my needs because You promised to take care of me. There is such freedom in this knowledge. I know that every day my needs shall be met in You. Lord, help all my friends and family to rest in Your promises too. Strengthen us to trust You daily. I know when I am weak, You are strong. May we all look to You for our answers. I ask this in the name of Jesus. Amen.

June 10 ***Day 161***

Proverbs 18:13-15 13 He that answereth a matter before he heareth it, it is folly and shame unto him. 14 The spirit of a man will sustain his infirmity; but a wounded spirit who can bear? 15 The heart of the prudent getteth knowledge; and the ear of the wise seeketh knowledge.

Before making a statement about any matter, we should be sure we have heard all the facts. It is foolish to make premature judgments. It can be costly, as well as embarrassing, if our suppositions should turn out to be wrong.

Everyone in America seems to want to be heard on all kinds of issues, even if they know nothing about them. Talk shows and members of the media encourage people to voice their opinions for airing on television. This is not bad in some circumstances, but when a person is unaware of the facts about an issue, it is better that he or she not voice an opinion. Many people repeat something they heard someone else say, without having thought the matter through or researched it themselves. This is how rumors spread.

There is an old saying: God gave us two ears and one mouth, so we should listen twice as much as we speak. God's Word does instruct us repeatedly to be careful about what we say. "Let the words of my mouth, and the meditation of my heart, be acceptable in thy sight, O LORD, my strength, and my redeemer" (Psalm 19:14). "Wherefore, my beloved brethren, let every man be swift to hear, slow to speak, slow to wrath. (James 1:19).

Verse 14 – A broken spirit can destroy someone. Cruel words spoken repeatedly against a person can wear him down until he is unable to recover. It is very important that we build up our "spiritual man" by reading the Bible daily. This does the same thing for our spirits that eating good food does for our bodies; it builds us up, making us strong in God. When attacked by the devil through sickness, pain, the words of others, or any kind of trouble, we will be able to overcome by applying God's Word to our situation. The Lord has provided the answer to every problem we face, so that we may be overcomers.

Verse 15 – The wise are continually learning. They truly seek God and ask Him to guide them into the knowledge and wisdom that they need in every day life, as well as for the bigger problems they encounter. We all face trials and tribulations in life, but the Bible tells us not to worry. Jesus has made it possible for us to overcome. Furnishing us with His wisdom is one of the ways by which He has made this possible. Proverbs, like all Scripture, truly contains a wealth of wisdom for all who seek God diligently. "These things I have spoken unto you, that in me ye might have peace. In the world ye shall have tribulation: but be of good cheer; I have overcome the world" (John 16:33).

Dearest Father, we love and worship You today. Thank You for giving us the revelation of Your Word so that we may have the knowledge and wisdom we need as we walk in this world. Help me not to be one who thinks that I must speak about every situation that arises, but rather to guard my mouth and speak only when I can edify others. I do not want to speak just to be heard. Lord, I ask You also to forgive me when I have spoken inadvisably and brought pain to someone because my words were not kind. Fill my mouth daily and let me be a blessing in this world. Also, let me be a good listener as well. When I do give advice, let it be Your Word. I ask this in the name of the Lord Jesus Christ. Amen

Proverbs 18:16 A man's gift maketh room for him, and bringeth him before great men.

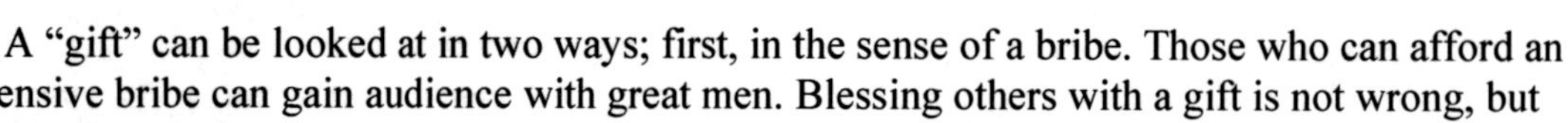

A "gift" can be looked at in two ways; first, in the sense of a bribe. Those who can afford an expensive bribe can gain audience with great men. Blessing others with a gift is not wrong, but using it to manipulate them for favor is wrong. We must trust the Lord to give us favor with others when we need it and not resort to methods of manipulation.

Years ago, Bud and I made a missionary journey to Africa, traveling from Kenya to Uganda and then back to Kenya before returning home. We were required to have certain immunizations in order to enter these countries, and we thought we had all things in order. However, when we came back to Kenya from Uganda we discovered that somehow I had failed to have a yellow fever shot. We were not required to have these shots to go into Kenya or Uganda from the USA, but when we came back through customs, they informed us that they would allow Bud to enter Kenya, but that I could not.

We had been staying in mud huts in the bush country for ten days, and were very tired when we got to the airport. We were ready for a bath and a good night's sleep in a hotel! I did not want to sit at the airport overnight until our flight left for the USA the next day, so I began to testify to the man at customs. I told him that I could not possibly have yellow fever, since the Lord had healed me seventeen years earlier of all my infirmities and I hadn't had any illness since then. Furthermore, we had just prayed for many sick people in Uganda, including a lame man and a leper, and the Lord had healed them.

The customs official looked at me rather strangely, but he told me that there was no way he could allow me to enter the country. I continued telling him of the other miracles the Lord had done during our trip. He finally sighed, and waved me through. A local man told us later that the customs official was waiting for a bribe, which is common practice. Twenty dollars would have been enough to have gotten my passage into the country. However, the Lord's favor is more valuable than what we could buy with money. Because it was God's will for us to be in Africa, He gave us favor with the man by touching his heart to allow me back into Kenya without us having to resort to bribery.

Secondly, this "gift" can be looked at in the sense of God's giftings to men. The spiritual gift that God gives us will "make room for us" to gain an audience or favor with great men. The Bible relates that the apostle Paul gained the right to preach before King Agrippa (Acts 25) and other men of authority. We do not have to use gifts or money to buy our way into a situation. When we have God's gift of favor, He will make room for us.

Dear Father in heaven, I bless You today. Thank You for the favor You give me when I serve You. You have made a way many times for me when there was no way in the natural. I am grateful for Your gifts. May I always use them to bless those whom You send me to. Lord, keep me from the temptation to use money as a means of manipulation, but rather let me use my money to bless and help others. May I never be guilty of using the spiritual gifts You give me to manipulate others or for self gain. Forgive Your ministers who have succumbed to this and deliver them. Purify our heart and motives Lord, that we might bring glory to You and never any reproach. I ask this in the name of Jesus. Amen.

Proverbs 18:17-18 17 He who states his case first seems right, until his rival comes and cross-examines him. 18 To cast lots puts an end to disputes, and decides between powerful contenders (AMP).

Verse 17 – The first person to present his case is convincing until he is cross-examined. My husband and I have been in ministry for many years and we have done a lot of counseling and listened to many married couples who were considering divorce. We have always insisted on hearing the viewpoint of *both* parties. Most of the time, we were shocked to hear the other side of the story. Neither party sounded like they could possibly be the one that the other described. Each one described an entirely different person than the one with whom we sat and spoke.

After patiently listening to both sides separately, we would proceed to bring the couple together to share the Word of God with them, and spend the remainder of the time praying with them. We would have each ask forgiveness of the other for his or her wrongs, and then pray for each other. From that point on, we would not allow either one to bring up old grievances in our sessions. The key to healing in any relationship is not to dwell on the past, but to forgive and go forward, building one another up in love (1 Peter 3).

Verse 18 – In the past, when two contenders had equal claim to something, disputes were often settled by drawing lots (see Day 141). In the Old Testament world, this method was used widely. Drawing lots peacefully ends disputes, since neither contender can complain that a biased judge had made the decision. Even very powerful and influential men have no grounds upon which to argue the outcome when lots are drawn, since it is determined entirely by chance.

We are commanded as God's children to live in harmony with our mates, families, and friends. This is only possible whenever we allow the Holy Spirit to dwell in our hearts. We are to avoid disputes and wrangling and display the love of God in our affairs. "Do all things without murmurings and disputings: That ye may be blameless and harmless, the sons of God, without rebuke, in the midst of a crooked and perverse nation, among whom ye shine as lights in the world" (Philippians 2:14-15).

Dear heavenly Father, we do appreciate Your patience and love toward us. May we show this same love to those around us; especially to those with whom we might have a disagreement. Grant us grace to be gracious and not get into contention with others. Please remove murmuring and disputing from our hearts and let us be peacemakers and full of joy. Father, guard our tongues, so we do not say things that we will later regret. Forgive us when we fail You and give us Your grace to forgive others who have hurt us. We ask this in your Son, Jesus' name. Amen.

Proverbs 18:19 A brother offended is harder to be won than a strong city: and their contentions are like the bars of a castle.

This verse deals with two things that we should always try to avoid: *contention* and *offense.* As Christians, we should not allow offense to separate us from our brothers and sisters, since this reveals pride in our hearts (Proverbs 13:10). If we have a problem with someone, we are to humbly try to work it out. If we will lovingly consider the other person, the Lord will give us the grace and wisdom to work out our problems. Contention comes when we refuse to humbly deal with the conflicting issues in our flesh.

We are not only told to avoid offences between us, but we are also warned not to become offended with God about anything. We read this account regarding John the Baptist in Matthew 11:2-6: "Now when John had heard in the prison the works of Christ, he sent two of his disciples, And said unto him, Art thou he that should come, or do we look for another? Jesus answered and said unto them, Go and show John again those things which ye do hear and see: The blind receive their sight, and the lame walk, the lepers are cleansed, and the deaf hear, the dead are raised up, and the poor have the gospel preached to them. And blessed is he, whosoever shall not be offended in me."

Jesus knew that because John was in prison, he began to doubt the promises of God. Even so, the Lord has no criticism toward John and He commended him as a great prophet. I'm sure that John began to think thoughts such as this: "If Jesus was really the Christ, why has He not done a miracle to get me out of this prison? I was preaching repentance and paving the way for His ministry, so why has he abandoned me?" Jesus told John's disciples to tell him that he would be blessed if he did not become offended with Him. Did John receive this message, or did he allow offense to come into his heart?

We have another story about two of Jesus' disciples who were also thrown into prison for preaching the gospel, but their story turned out differently than John's (John had his head chopped off). When Paul and Silas were chained in prison, they took a different approach. Instead of allowing fear or doubt to overcome them, they began to sing and praise God. The prison could not hold them; because an earthquake came and loosed them (Acts 16:20-26). They did not allow their "chains" and "pains" to cause them to be offended with God.

When we are tempted to become offended with God, we block the way out of our prison. John had his head cut off, but Paul and Silas were released. The secret to being released from our prisons (financial, mental, emotional, physical, etc.) is to stay in a place of rejoicing in Him instead of blaming Him. We are not to praise Him *for* the problems, but praise Him *in the midst* of them. He will bring us through, and we will come out victorious!

Heavenly Father, I thank You for the many blessings You have given me. I never want to become offended with You. Help me to realize that it is the devil who is bringing me the problems in my life and it is You Who will make a way for me to overcome him. Help me to remain joyful even in my trials and tribulations, knowing that You will bring me through them victoriously! I also ask that I will be able to resist all contention with any brother or sister in the Lord. Let me love them with Your love. Lord, I humble myself to You, knowing that You will take care of all my troubles when I honestly give them to You, and yield to Your ways. I ask this in the name of Jesus. Amen.

Proverbs 18:20-21 20 A man's belly shall be satisfied with the fruit of his mouth; and with the increase of his lips shall he be filled. 21 Death and life are in the power of the tongue: and they that love it shall eat the fruit thereof.

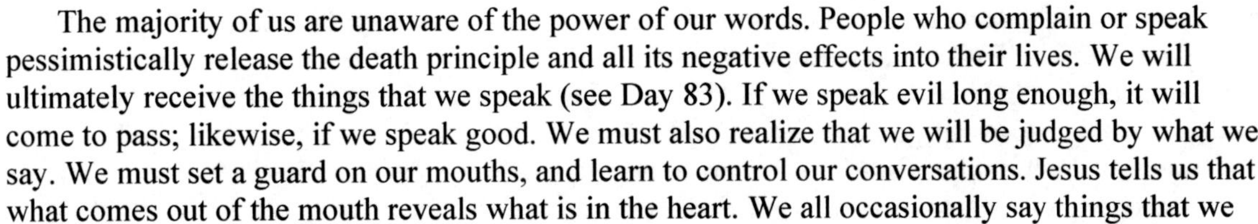

The majority of us are unaware of the power of our words. People who complain or speak pessimistically release the death principle and all its negative effects into their lives. We will ultimately receive the things that we speak (see Day 83). If we speak evil long enough, it will come to pass; likewise, if we speak good. We must also realize that we will be judged by what we say. We must set a guard on our mouths, and learn to control our conversations. Jesus tells us that what comes out of the mouth reveals what is in the heart. We all occasionally say things that we should not; however, the things that we speak "in abundance" reveal what is in our hearts in abundance.

"Either make the tree good, and his fruit good; or else make the tree corrupt, and his fruit corrupt: for the tree is known by his fruit. O generation of vipers, how can ye, being evil, speak good things? For out of the abundance of the heart the mouth speaketh. A good man out of the good treasure of the heart bringeth forth good things: and an evil man out of the evil treasure bringeth forth evil things. But I say unto you, That every idle word that men shall speak, they shall give account thereof in the day of judgment. For by thy words thou shalt be justified, and by thy words thou shalt be condemned" (Matthew 12:33-37). "And the burden of the LORD shall ye mention no more: for every man's word shall be his burden; for ye have perverted the words of the living God, of the LORD of hosts our God" (Jeremiah 23:36).

If we do not properly care for our bodies, illness will eventually set in. On the other hand, healthy food and exercise, brings life to our bodies. Likewise, the words that we speak release life or death (Proverbs 17:22). When I feel weak or tired, I remember Ephesians 6:10: "Finally, my brethren, be strong in the Lord and in the power of his might." I voice it as a prayer, thanking God that I can depend upon His strength rather than my own. When I do this, I feel stronger. My fatigue may be real, but the Word of God is greater than my feelings. However, if I start complaining about how weak I feel, it has the opposite affect upon me. Truly, life and death are in the power of the tongue. "Let the words of my mouth, and the meditation of my heart, be acceptable in thy sight, O LORD, my strength, and my redeemer" (Psalm 19:14).

Dear heavenly Father, I thank You for Your goodness to me. Help me to guard my mouth so that those things that are edifying and good will come out. May I bless others with my tongue and never be guilty of cursing anyone. Let my words be gracious and may they bring healing to others. Let my words be kind and gentle and loving. May I reflect Your goodness in all that I do. Forgive me when I say the wrong things. Let me speak and pray the Word of God over my life and others. Give all of us grace to say things that bring life into this world. I ask this in Jesus' holy name. Amen.

Proverbs 18:22 Whoso findeth a wife findeth a good thing, and obtaineth favour of the LORD.

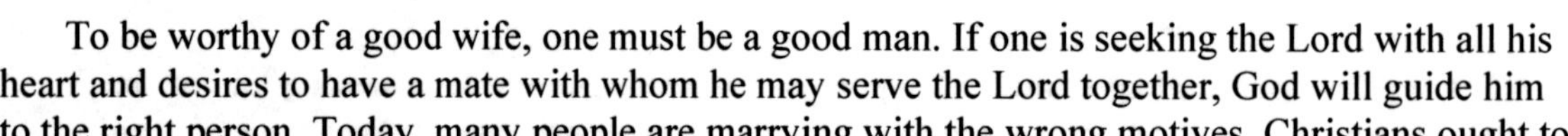

To be worthy of a good wife, one must be a good man. If one is seeking the Lord with all his heart and desires to have a mate with whom he may serve the Lord together, God will guide him to the right person. Today, many people are marrying with the wrong motives. Christians ought to have three criteria in considering a mate. They should make sure that the person is: (1) committed to Christ (2) demonstrates good character, and (3) shares the same vision for serving God.

The most important decision that we make in life is whether to follow Jesus. The second is whether to marry. If you desire to be married, then you need not be anxious or lonely if you commit to follow Christ daily. God will direct your path and prepare you for marriage. While men or women are single it is a wonderful time for them to prepare for marriage. As they seek to know God better and allow Him to help them become the kind of husband or wife who would bless someone, they will soon find they are not lonely.

Satan will try to mislead us regarding this second-most important decision. One of the easiest ways for him to deceive us is by playing on our emotions. At times, we can all be susceptible to developing "feelings" for the wrong person. We can guard against this by committing ourselves to God and His will for every part of our lives, including marriage. God knows what is best for us and there are worse things than being alone. One of these is being married to the wrong person. We can be out of God's will by compromising and marrying someone who does not feel the same way we do toward the Lord. We find Satan misleading God's men throughout the Bible. Solomon's heathen wives led him into idolatry; Samson's eyes were put out because of the woman Delilah; and David committed murder because of passion for Bathsheba.

Though emotion and passion are a wonderful part of love, they cannot be the foundation for a good marriage. Good character and commitment to God strengthen a marriage, while selfishness, jealousy, laziness, and so forth, affect it adversely. A good woman's worth is far above rubies! If you want to marry, seek God diligently that you may find a good wife or husband–and ask God to prepare you to be a good mate.

Dear Father God, thank You for my good husband. I am most blessed, Lord. I pray for those who are seeking a good mate, that they will be guided by Your Holy Spirit and find just the right person with whom they will share their lives. I also pray for those who are already married, that You would strengthen the good marriages and heal those who have suffered wounds. May each mate seek more of Your love and be willing to lay down his or her life for the other. Let us all be filled with more of Your love. May love pour from me today no matter what I face. I ask this in the name of the Lord Jesus. Amen.

Proverbs 18:23-24 23 The poor useth entreaties; but the rich answereth roughly (KJV). 24 The man of many friends (a friend to all the world) will prove himself a bad friend, but there is a friend who sticks closer than a brother (AMP).

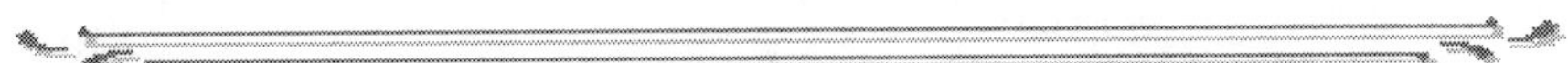

Verse 23 – Proverbs addresses many relationship issues, among these: how most poor people approach things, as opposed to how some rich people would respond in those circumstances. If a poor man needs something from a rich man, he does so in a nice way, pleading earnestly. If he were to demand or raise his voice he would stand a chance of being denied. A man whose only recourse is to appeal to the compassion of others is desperate. He has nothing to offer, nothing to give him dignity. His situation has robbed him of confidence and shattered his pride. Most rich people are at ease, and they do not know what it is like to be humbled by desperation. Since they have money and power, they feel that they can get away with answering roughly or unkindly. They believe that their position entitles them to have an unpleasant attitude whenever they feel like it.

Christians are in the world, but not of the world. "I have given them thy word; and the world hath hated them, because they are not of the world, even as I am not of the world. I pray not that thou shouldest take them out of the world, but that thou shouldest keep them from the evil. They are not of the world, even as I am not of the world (John 17:14-17). We are called to a higher way; to love all men (1 Corinthians 12:31–13:4-8). Love is courteous, no matter what our position or another's position is. If God has promoted us to positions of influence or given us wealth, we must not think more highly of ourselves than we ought. Impolite answers are demeaning. We must retain a basic respect for all people because they are made in God's image and Christ loves and died for each one of them.

Verse 24 – A man who is friendly with the whole world does not make a good friend. He can only be everyone's friend by either having no convictions or by having only superficial friendships. The Bible warns us to choose our friends carefully because they will influence us. We should not choose as a friend, someone who is "everyone's friend," a wicked person, or someone who worships other gods (Deuteronomy 13:6-8). Those who are close to us; whether family or friends are in a position to influence us, often without saying anything. Consciously or unconsciously, we all want to imitate those we love and admire. This is why we must choose our friends carefully.

There is a friend that "sticks closer than a brother." That friend is Jesus. If we commit ourselves to God, He can lead us to Christian brothers and sisters who will be true friends to us. Best of all, we can rest in the assurance that He will never leave us nor forsake us. Jesus is the Friend and Brother who never fails. He is always with us to help and guide us. (Hebrews 13:5b).

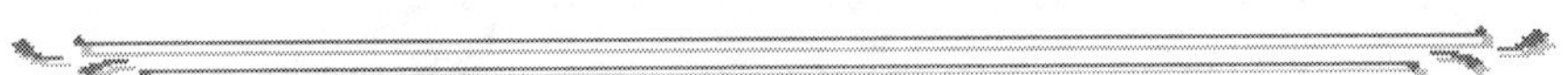

Dear heavenly Father, I am thankful for Your love and friendship. Truly, You are a Friend who sticks closer than a brother. You are always there for me. Father, help me to be a good friend to those whom You have joined with me in friendship. I always want to be a loving, kind, and faithful friend. I need Your kind of love to do this. Fill me with Your Spirit today so that I will be a blessing to all that I meet. Lord, help me not answer people in a rough manner. May I always be kind and patient in my dealings with people everywhere as a witness of Your love. Thank You also for all the wonderful friends You have given to me. Bless each of them today. I ask this in the name of Jesus. Amen.

God's Wisdom for Daily Living **_Betty Miller_**
June 17 **_Day 168_**

Proverbs 19:1-2 1 Better is the poor who walks in his integrity, than the rich who is perverse in his speech and is a (self-confident) fool. 2 Desire without knowledge is not good, and to be over-hasty is to sin and miss the mark (AMP).

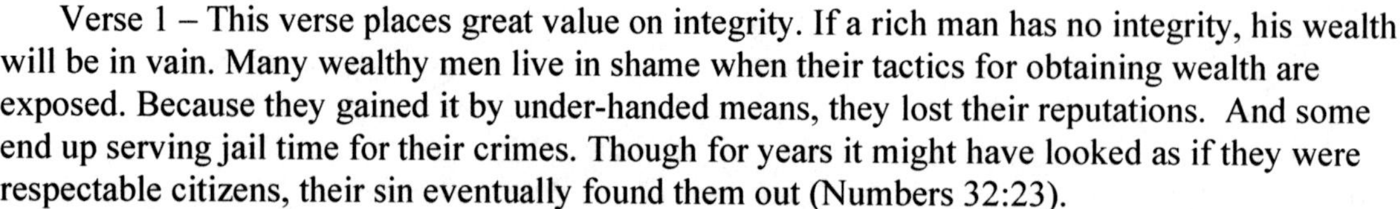

Verse 1 – This verse places great value on integrity. If a rich man has no integrity, his wealth will be in vain. Many wealthy men live in shame when their tactics for obtaining wealth are exposed. Because they gained it by under-handed means, they lost their reputations. And some end up serving jail time for their crimes. Though for years it might have looked as if they were respectable citizens, their sin eventually found them out (Numbers 32:23).

It is better to be poor and store up riches for eternity, than to be a rich fool. The poor man who walks in godly integrity and follows the Bible's principles for prosperity will, in time, be blessed with an abundance that he can use to bless others and pass on to his children's children. We shall all reap what we have sown; good things if we are honest and follow God's ways; evil things if we are dishonest (Galatians 6:7-9).

Verse 2 – The simple fact that we want something does not mean that it would be good for us to have it. If we do not have proper knowledge about what we desire, it may hurt us. Being over-hasty to obtain something may cause regret once we receive it. Years ago, I knew a woman and her husband who were traveling evangelists. She told me that she was tired of staying in people's homes and motels, so she had started praying for an RV. When she did not receive one right away, she became more insistent in her prayers. Rather than considering that God might be answering with a "no," she assumed the devil was robbing her of her desire. Finally, they bought an RV on monthly payments. What she thought would be a blessing, however, turned out to be a curse for them both. Since travel takes longer in an RV, they were more exhausted than before. It was also harder to find parking places. Since the money that they would have used to eat in restaurants was spent on monthly payments, she had to shop, prepare meals, and wash dishes, in addition to ministering at each place they went. The RV led to more work for her, instead of less work.

This is an example of desire without knowledge. "And he gave them their request; but sent leanness into their soul" (Psalm 106:15). Major decisions should not be made quickly. It is easier to avoid getting into a bad situation, than to get out of one. It can take years to a correct a mistake that we made in haste. Taking the time to ask God for wisdom, gathering information, and prayerfully thinking things through can save much suffering. It is better to go too slow than to go too fast. If we are moving slow, at the least the Lord is still ahead of us; however, if we go too fast we can get ahead of God.

Dear heavenly Father, I thank You for Your love and patience toward me. Lord, help me to trust You when I do not see an answer to my prayers right away. I do want to take the time to come before You and find out if there is a reason for my delayed answer. Perhaps it is a "God delay" instead of the enemy delaying it. Give me Your wisdom as to what You want me to do in the matters I face in this life. Lord, help me not to make hasty decisions that would not only wrongly affect my life, but others as well. Help me to be more faithful in prayer. I ask this in the name of the Lord Jesus Christ. Amen.

Proverbs 19:3 The foolishness of man perverteth his way: and his heart fretteth against the LORD.

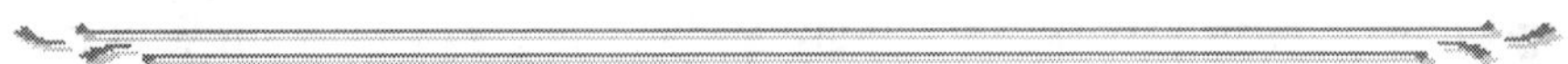

Because man does not understand God's ways or know His Word, he does many things that are foolish and sinful. When he begins to suffer the natural consequences of his own actions, his tendency is to blame God. As we have seen, the Bible teaches that a man reaps what he sows. "Be not deceived; God is not mocked: for whatsoever a man soweth, that shall he also reap. For he that soweth to his flesh shall of the flesh reap corruption; but he that soweth to the Spirit shall of the Spirit reap life everlasting"(Galatians 6:7). When we break God's commandments, we suffer the consequences of our sins.

Not all people break the laws of God willfully; some people break them ignorantly. God's laws are given to us for our good, so that we might live a good life. If we break them, we are the ones who are hurt. This applies not only to people who do not know God, but to God's own children as well. One of the tactics of the devil is to feed us the lie that God is so angry with us when we sin that He punishes us with evil things. If Satan can get us to believe this, we will blame things on God that are not His fault. Most of our troubles are the result of our own sins or the sins of others. This is the reason Jesus died for us–to save us from our sins. When we receive Him into our hearts, He can repair the damage done by sin, whoever's it is, and enable us to overcome evil with good. Jesus came to redeem us and to help us become overcomers in this life.

"Thine own wickedness shall correct thee, and thy backslidings shall reprove thee: know therefore and see that it is an evil thing and bitter, that thou hast forsaken the LORD thy God, and that my fear is not in thee, saith the LORD GOD of hosts" (Jeremiah 2:19 and Job 37:23). Also Hosea 7:2 says, "And they consider not in their hearts that I remember all their wickedness: now their own doings have beset them about; they are before my face."

God is for us, not against us. Romans 8:31-32 says, "What shall we then say to these things? If God be for us, who can be against us? He that spared not his own Son, but delivered him up for us all, how shall he not with him also freely give us all things?" Certainly, we can learn things by going through adverse circumstances, but many such circumstances could be avoided, if we took the time to learn God's Word. If we are committed totally to God, we will want to study His Word to know His ways. If we are good students, we can escape many snares of the devil designed to destroy us. We are responsible to learn God's ways. Bibles are available in most countries, especially America. Where they are available, we should be ashamed if we are not reading God's Word and learning His ways. "My people are destroyed for lack of knowledge: because thou hast rejected knowledge, I will also reject thee" (Hosea 4:6).

Father God, I am most grateful for Your abundant love for me. When I am going through trials, help me never to blame You for what the devil is trying to do. Give me discernment not only to see what the devil is doing, but also the power and courage to rise up against him and overcome him. Lord, I want to always submit unto You and resist the devil as You tell us in Your Word to do in James 4:7. You said if we would do this, the devil would flee from us. Help me to overcome evil with good and not to resort to my own ways in dealing with difficult situations. I ask this in the name of the Lord Jesus Christ. Amen.

Proverbs 19:4-9 4 Wealth brings many friends, but a poor man's friend deserts him. 5 A false witness will not go unpunished, and he who pours out lies will not go free. 6 Many curry favor with a ruler, and everyone is the friend to a man who gives gifts. 7 A poor man is shunned by all his relatives–how much more do his friends avoid him! Though he pursues them with pleading, they are nowhere to be found. 8 He who gets wisdom loves his own soul; he who cherishes understanding prospers. 9 A false witness will not go unpunished, and he who pours out lies will perish (NIV).

Verse 4 – People with wealth or high status will always be sought for their favors; therefore, they have many "friends." On the other hand, the poor are avoided since they have nothing to give. Many worldly friendships are superficial and based on selfishness. If a man suddenly becomes poor, and he can no longer afford to do the things he previously did with his friends, they desert him. A true friend loves and values you for who you are, and he remains your friend even when adversity strikes. Jesus is like that. He is always there for us no matter what we are going through. "A friend loveth at all times, and a brother is born for adversity" (Proverbs 17:17).

Verse 5-6 – Many seek favors from a prince. Those who fawn upon a ruler for his favor are not people of conviction, but of greed. They will support his agenda, good or bad, so long as the ruler prospers. Some rulers (or leaders) readily give valuable gifts, such as positions of authority in government, in order to buy the support of powerful people and to strengthen their rule. This is true of people and leaders in all types of government.

Verse 7 – The slothful poor man is shunned because he constantly needs money and help, but never works for it. The poor man who is not slothful is avoided for different reasons. Even if he does not ask for help, those who are close to him know that he needs it. Some may be unable to help; others may not want to help, but all avoid him so they will not feel an obligation to help. If he is out of sight, he is out of mind; and they do not feel guilty for not helping him. We are not to avoid a relative who becomes poor, but we ought to give as the Lord directs us to give. If He does not direct us to help with money, we can help in other ways, such as simply being a friend who listens and prays.

Verse 8 – The secret for overcoming poverty is by walking in God's wisdom. The poor people need Biblical teaching, or they will remain poor and unproductive. Since all the treasures of wisdom are in Jesus (Colossians 2:2-3), we must first point people to Him. The Lord will give them understanding of His principles that will help them overcome poverty.

Verses 9 – Our judicial systems set stern punishments for those who lie under oath. A false witness will not escape punishment. "Thou shalt not raise a false report: put not thine hand with the wicked to be an unrighteous witness" (Exodus 23:1).

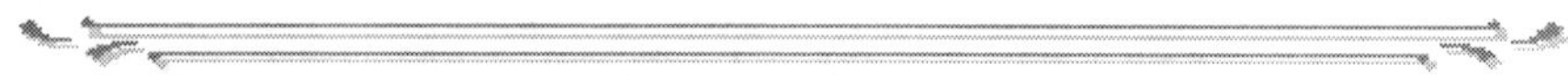

Dear Father, thank You for leading me in Your paths of righteousness. I know that as I seek You, You will give me the answers I need so that I might prosper and be in good health. Lord, I need these things to serve You and to help others. Thank You for my prosperity so that I am able to help those who are needy. Show me the people I need to help. Give me prayers for the lost and the hurting. Prayers just cost me my time. Let me be willing to take the time to pray, and to reach out to others. I ask this in Jesus' name. Amen.

June 20 *Day 171*

Proverbs 19:10-12 10 It is not fitting for a fool to live in luxury–how much worse for a slave to rule over princes! 11 A man's wisdom gives him patience; it is to his glory to overlook an offense. 12 A king's rage is like the roar of a lion, but his favor is like dew on the grass (NIV).

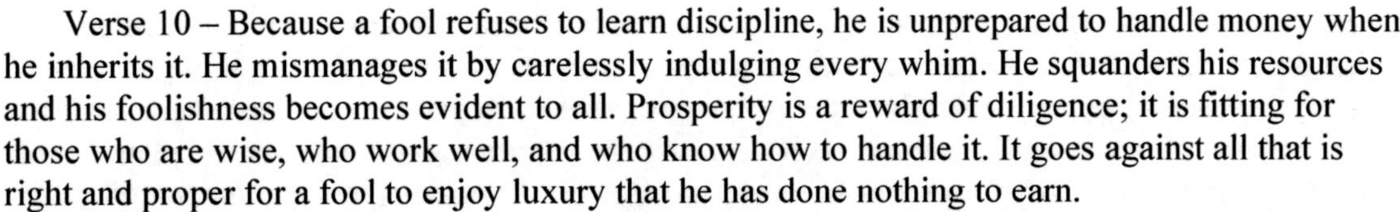

Verse 10 – Because a fool refuses to learn discipline, he is unprepared to handle money when he inherits it. He mismanages it by carelessly indulging every whim. He squanders his resources and his foolishness becomes evident to all. Prosperity is a reward of diligence; it is fitting for those who are wise, who work well, and who know how to handle it. It goes against all that is right and proper for a fool to enjoy luxury that he has done nothing to earn.

In the same way that luxury is not fitting for a fool, so it is not fitting for a servant to rule over princes. When a person with a servile mentality is put in a position of authority, he usually becomes arrogant and abusive of those under him. It is repugnant to see such a person belittle and overrule those with the princely qualities of true leadership.

Verse 11 – A wise man is patient and not easily offended. He graciously overlooks people's faults rather than letting them irritate him. It is a man's glory to reflect God's character. Patiently bearing with the weaknesses and faults of others reflects God's forgiving nature. Patience and love are part of the fruit of the Spirit. We can ask God for wisdom and to be filled with the Holy Spirit, who produces that fruit within us. When we are filled with God's love, we do not allow offences to disturb us. "Love (God's love in us) does not insist on its own rights *or* its own way, *for* it is not self-seeking; it is not touchy *or* fretful *or* resentful; it takes no account of the evil done to it [it pays no attention to a suffered wrong]" (1 Corinthians 13:5b AMP).

Verse 12 – This verse is simply saying that the king's wrath is as terrifying as the roaring of a lion, but his favor is as refreshing as dew upon the grass. The "king" can be anyone who is in a position of authority. Those who are in positions of authority can cause fear in the hearts of those beneath them if they are unhappy, and begin "roaring" about something. However, if the same people in authority are gracious to those beneath them, it is refreshing like the dew on grass. If God has blessed us by allowing us to be in a position of authority, we should show "kingly" kindness to those we manage. This brings glory to our Lord. However, if we are like a roaring lion to those under our authority, we are not pleasing to the Lord. We should show His nature in all of our affairs.

Dear heavenly Father, I appreciate all that You have done for me. Thank You for the favor and kindness You show me through others. May I show love and kindness to all who know me. Lord, You tell me in Your Word that I am to love others; and when I do that, I bring glory to Your name. You tell me that when I truly love others, men will see it and know that I am Your disciple. May I demonstrate Your love to all who know me. Forgive me when I have failed to show love and have yielded to my own selfishness. I know that if I proclaim my love for You, that I must also demonstrate it by loving others. My prayer is that You would change me and fill me with Your love. I ask this in the name our Lord, Jesus Christ. Amen.

Proverbs 19:13-14 13 A foolish son is his father's ruin, and a quarrelsome wife is like a constant dripping. 14 Houses and wealth are inherited from parents, but a prudent wife is from the LORD (NIV).

Verse 13 – Wilson's Old Testament Word Studies gives a very insightful definition for "fool." It means to act stupidly, absurdly, or inconsistently. It can also mean being infatuated or acting out of emotion. It indicates any kind of straying from what is true, right, and prudent. A fool uses no caution in practical affairs and does not have the foresight to provide for the future. He is aimless, refuses counsel, and has no concern for the proper use of money or the planning of a career. He is always ready to form rash hopes, and carelessly commits to uncertain ventures. He is ungodly and easily provoked. His only reason for doing anything is merely because he wants to do it. He takes no pleasure in understanding, but trusts in his own heart or mind. It is easy to see how any son fitting any part of this description would bring heartache and loss to his father.

If the father also has a contentious and nagging wife, he is doubly cursed! A woman who complains all the time is as annoying as dripping water. Strife is damaging, costly, unhealthy, and as irritating as the sound of constant dripping. Christians ought not to be quarrelsome. 1 Peter 3:8-12 says, "Finally, be ye all of one mind, having compassion one of another, love as brethren, be pitiful, be courteous: Not rendering evil for evil, or railing for railing: but contrariwise blessing; knowing that ye are thereunto called, that ye should inherit a blessing. For he that will love life, and see good days, let him refrain his tongue from evil, and his lips that they speak no guile: Let him eschew evil, and do good; let him seek peace, and ensue it. For the eyes of the Lord are over the righteous, and his ears are open unto their prayers: but the face of the Lord is against them that do evil."

Strife is a product of the old nature and activates the death principle (Galatians 5:19-21). It is especially unseemly for a wife to be quarrelsome (Ephesians 5:21-33). If we are guilty of this kind of behavior, we need to ask the Lord to forgive us and to give us a sweet spirit that produces blessing and joy for those around us.

Verse 14 – A man can inherit riches from his father, but a prudent wife is a gift from the Lord. The value of a godly woman is spoken of in Proverbs 31:10-11: "Who can find a virtuous woman? for her price is far above rubies. The heart of her husband doth safely trust in her, so that he shall have no need of spoil. She will do him good and not evil all the days of her life."

What husband would not love such a wife? Money cannot buy such a woman. She is truly a gift from God.

Dear Father God, thank You for Your kindness in giving me a good husband. Help me to be a good wife to my husband in every way. Let our marriage bring glory to You. I pray for those who are having problems in their marriages. Heal them and give them Your love and patience for each other. Father, as Christians, may our families reflect Your love and goodness to all around us. Restore the broken families that are seeking You. Touch their children and heal them also. I ask this in the name our Lord, Jesus Christ. Amen.

Proverbs 19:15-16 15 Slothfulness casteth into a deep sleep; and an idle soul shall suffer hunger. 16 He that keepeth the commandment keepeth his own soul; but he that despiseth his ways shall die.

Verse 15 – The Bible speaks of the fate of those who are lazy and idle. They can end up with no money to buy food and will go hungry. These scriptures also state that those who break the commandments and refuse instruction will die prematurely. As parents, we must instill good work habits in our children while they are young so they do not become lazy and slothful. Many of the younger generation were not taught proper work habits and now have difficulty in holding a job. Slothfulness, shoddy workmanship and disorganization reflect a lack of caring. Many people take short cuts that hamper the quality of the job, just to finish the task so they can eliminate any problems of the moment. Later the job must be repeated which wastes time because the job was not done right the first time. Children's messy rooms are a symptom of how a generation of parents has neglected to teach their children this truth while they were growing up. Many of today's children are taught to "play" instead of taught to work. The older generation has failed them by giving them an overabundance of toys, games, play times, and entertainment. Well-meaning parents have created a generation of extreme party and super vacation lovers. Certainly times of resting and relaxation are in order but they must be balanced with work.

Verse 16 -- We take action upon whatever is important to us. Being slow to obey God's Word means our ways are more important to us than His. Choosing God's way or our way is a matter of fulfillment or frustration; blessing or cursing; life or death. Embracing deception makes us spiritually sleepy. When our spirits slumber, our lives become dreamlike; distorted shadows instead of clear reflections of reality. Just as we are unaware of what happens around us when we are physically sleeping, we become increasingly insensible to the enemy's tactics and lies when spiritually sleepy. If we do not get up and get active (repent and apply God's Word to our lives), we will soon be slumbering spiritually. We will be out of God's will and our hearts will grow cold toward Him. Either the spiritual or physical condition is dangerous, especially in such days as ours, when deception is multiplied. We must not be slothful, but diligent to respond to the Holy Spirit's promptings (1 Thessalonians 5:4-6, Mark 13:33-37). Just as those who are lazy and refuse to work will not have money to buy food, we will suffer spiritual malnutrition and frustration if we are slow to obey God's Word. As God's children, we need to be careful to avoid an undisciplined lifestyle. If we do not learn to obey the Word of God early, it will lead to some form of death, possibly even a premature physical death.

Dear heavenly Father, thank You for giving me work to do. A good occupation brings satisfaction to my life when I am faithful to do a good days work. Lord, help me to be a diligent worker and deliver me from sloth; especially spiritual sloth. Deliver me from spiritual laziness. Energize me by Your grace to seek You and bring about Your kingdom on this earth. Also, Lord, keep me from the opposite sin – the sin of being a workaholic, or striving to achieve what You have given me freely! May I be balanced in my work and rest. I ask this in the name of the Lord Jesus Christ. Amen.

Proverbs 19:17 He that hath pity upon the poor lendeth unto the LORD; and that which he hath given will he pay him again.

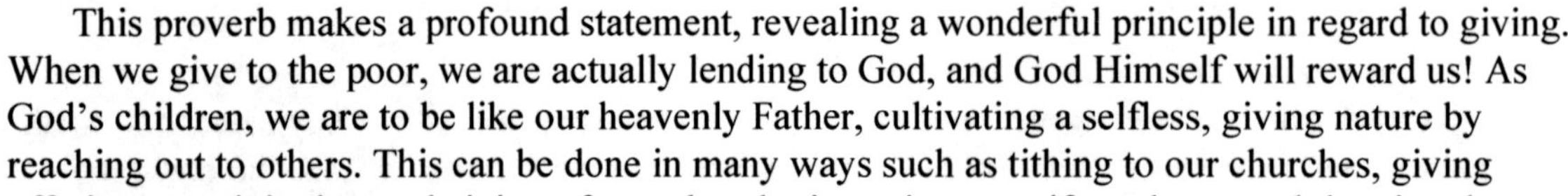

This proverb makes a profound statement, revealing a wonderful principle in regard to giving. When we give to the poor, we are actually lending to God, and God Himself will reward us! As God's children, we are to be like our heavenly Father, cultivating a selfless, giving nature by reaching out to others. This can be done in many ways such as tithing to our churches, giving offerings to ministries, and giving of ourselves by investing our gifts, talents, and time in others. Giving to the poor, however, is so near to God's heart that when we do it, it is as if we are actually giving to God Himself!

God is holy, just and righteous. He is faithful to render to each of us according to what we do. If we lend to Him, we will never have to worry about Him paying us back. God is never indebted to anyone. If we give to the poor, our Lord will never fail to reward us. His rewards come back in many forms, such as money, if that is what we need. However, they can also come as healing, strength, protection, peace, love, etc. These rewards are greater than monetary compensation.

Another Scripture, Psalm 41:1-3, also promises reward when we give to the poor: "Blessed is he that considereth the poor: the LORD will deliver him in time of trouble. The LORD will preserve him, and keep him alive; and he shall be blessed upon the earth: and thou wilt not deliver him unto the will of his enemies. The LORD will strengthen him upon the bed of languishing: thou wilt make all his bed in his sickness."

The Lord promises that if we are considerate of the poor, He will deliver us in our time of trouble; He will protect us and keep us alive. He also promises us that we will not be given over to the desire of our enemies or those who hate us. If we are languishing with any kind of disease, He will heal us so we can get up and make our bed. What wonderful promises for the simple act of giving to the poor! As the saying goes, we cannot out-give God! He always rewards us with more than we gave!

Dear heavenly Father, thank You for giving us the opportunity to give to the poor. Give us Your heart for those who are less fortunate than we are. We want to keep a compassionate attitude for those who are suffering in poverty. Lord, use us to share the gospel with the poor, as when they find You, they are able to rise above their circumstances. Thank You for blessing me financially so that I am able to give generously to the poor and also to Your works that are spreading the gospel. I ask this in the name of Jesus. Amen.

Proverbs 19:18 Chasten thy son while there is hope, and let not thy soul spare for his crying.

The sooner one begins to discipline a child, the better. The longer a child is left to himself, the harder it is to bring him under control. A point can be reached when hope is lost of a child's ever yielding to correction. That is why it is important to start training and disciplining a child at an early age, whenever a child begins to defy the parent.

We are warned not to allow a child's crying and pleading to keep us from disciplining him. Most children try to play on a parent's sympathy to escape punishment; however, if we really love them we will not allow this to happen. For small children, punishment should be a whack on the buttocks with a small reed-like rod. (This rod could be a switch from a fruit or willow tree or a small wooden spoon. It is not to be a heavy rod or anything that would cause physical damage.) The purpose of a spanking is not to cause any lasting physical harm, but to cause spiritual correction. It should be swift and cause short-lived pain that makes a point. That point is that the small pain they feel now will prevent them from feeling great pain by failing to learn obedience, which could cause them loss of their lives in some cases.

Some parents have a mistaken idea of what love is. Some are compassionate and do not wish to "hurt" their children physically or emotionally. In reality, however, such sentiments are selfish and do not express true love for a child. The parents refrain from fulfilling their duty to properly teach the child right from wrong, in order to spare their own feelings. To fail to discipline a child is actually cruel. It is like failing to clean a child's cut finger simply because cleaning the cut hurts the child. Allowing infection to set in, however, brings the child worse pain. The momentary pain of discipline is far better than the devastating pain that rebellion brings for disobeying God's ways. Rebellion unchecked in a child can even lead to his eternal damnation.

Children can be very manipulative. If a child senses an adult's sensitivity or compassion, he may pretend or exaggerate fright or pain. Many children are experts at manufacturing "crocodile tears." A child unchecked or undetected in the art of manipulation is deceived by his own sin. Every one of us is born with a sinful heart. Jeremiah 17:9 describes the heart as "...deceitful above all things, and desperately wicked...." (NIV). Sin is very deceptive and will destroy us. Every child needs to be taught right from wrong, and not to follow the inclinations of his heart, which is full of the deceitfulness of sin. The discipline that a parent gives his child today will determine that child's well-being as an adult tomorrow. "For the waywardness of the simple will kill them, and the complacency of fools will destroy them" (Proverbs 2:32).

Dear Father God, thank You for allowing me to have children, grandchildren, and great-grandchildren. Help me to be the kind of parent who loves her children enough to discipline them. Forgive me when I have failed my children. Help me to be patient, loving, and kind in all disciplinary acts. I pray for the parents and grandparents of this generation. Give them wisdom, love, and guidance in their relationships with their children and grandchildren. Give our children a submissive heart and an obedient spirit toward authority so that our society can function in peace and order. May we all have the fear of the Lord in our lives which causes us to respect the authority that God has ordained. I ask this in the name of the Lord Jesus. Amen.

Proverbs 19:19-20 A man of great wrath shall suffer punishment: for if thou deliver him, yet thou must do it again. 20 Hear counsel, and receive instruction, that thou mayest be wise in thy latter end.

Verse 19 – Habitually angry people repeat their offenses. Trying to help a person with a bad temper is futile; it will not change him. He will just get into another scrape and expect you to get him out of it. Parents can fall into this trap very easily, especially if they have a rebellious child who ends up in jail, and they pay their fines over and over again. Until a person truly repents of his anger and learns to forgive, he will never be free from an ingrained bad temper. Only the Lord can help a person do this.

I can think of a good example of this that occurred when my husband I were co-pastors. A young girl who went to our church called us in desperation. She wanted us to help her boyfriend who had been jailed for not paying his traffic fines. It would only cost $75.00 to get him out of jail, and since we cared for her, we went down to the jail to facilitate his release by paying his fine. Since he would not be able to drive for a season, we waited for the jailer to bring him out, so that we could give him a ride home. We were absolutely shocked when, as the jailer brought him out to meet us, he began cursing the policemen, the jailer, and the system. He did not even bother to slow down his speech long enough to thank us for helping him. We immediately took him by the arm, told him to be quiet, and dragged him out of there quickly before he was arrested again!

When anger and rebellion fill a person's heart, the mere fact that you are kind and try to help him does not mean that he will change his behavior. He must be willing to change before you can help him, just as this verse says: "If you deliver an angry man, you will have to do it again." It was not long before this same young man was back in jail, this time for violating his driving restrictions. The only way we helped him the next time was to pray for him to come to the end of his rebellion so that he could truly be helped.

Verse 20 – This verse tells us that the way to change is to listen to counsel and receive instruction. If we do that, we will be wise in the time to come. Biblical instruction will keep us from destruction and error if we heed it. The keeping of God's Word will bring great reward. God's laws are given so that we might live a good life in this earth. (Psalm 19:7-11).

Dear Father, I thank You that You have given me the Bible so that I might receive godly wisdom and learn how to live by it. Lord, I know that by following Your advice, I will be saved from much heartache in this world. Help me to walk in the Spirit so that I will have Your discernment as to the things I should and should not do. Guide me in all of my affairs. Help me to overcome any tendencies toward anger, since I do not want to become an angry person. Let me be gentle and forgiving in my dealings with others. I ask this in the name of the Lord Jesus Christ. Amen.

God's Wisdom for Daily Living — ***Betty Miller***
June 26 — ***Day 177***

Proverbs 19:21 There are many devices in a man's heart; nevertheless the counsel of the LORD, that shall stand.

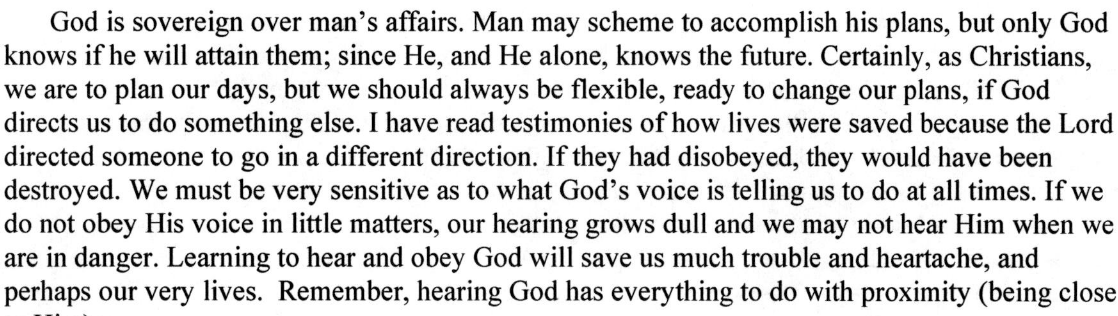

God is sovereign over man's affairs. Man may scheme to accomplish his plans, but only God knows if he will attain them; since He, and He alone, knows the future. Certainly, as Christians, we are to plan our days, but we should always be flexible, ready to change our plans, if God directs us to do something else. I have read testimonies of how lives were saved because the Lord directed someone to go in a different direction. If they had disobeyed, they would have been destroyed. We must be very sensitive as to what God's voice is telling us to do at all times. If we do not obey His voice in little matters, our hearing grows dull and we may not hear Him when we are in danger. Learning to hear and obey God will save us much trouble and heartache, and perhaps our very lives. Remember, hearing God has everything to do with proximity (being close to Him).

Many Christians confidently pursue their plans to make money without submitting them to God. James 4:13-15 admonishes those who make gain their life's goal: "Go to now, ye that say, To day or to morrow we will go into such a city, and continue there a year, and buy and sell, and get gain: Whereas ye know not what shall be on the morrow. For what is your life? It is even a vapour, that appeareth for a little time, and then vanisheth away. For that ye ought to say, If the Lord will, we shall live, and do this, or that."

The only safe place for anyone is in the will of God. If we remain in His will, we can rest assured that His promises will not fail us. By setting our plans above God's, we can open ourselves up for Satan to attack us. If God is speaking to us to do certain things, it is so that we might be spared pain tomorrow. He loves us and has the best plan for our lives. It is vital that we learn to live according to Proverbs 3:5-7: "Trust in the LORD with all thine heart; and lean not unto thine own understanding. In all thy ways acknowledge him, and he shall direct thy paths. Be not wise in thine own eyes: fear the LORD, and depart from evil."

God promises to direct our way when we ask Him and are ready to obey. He will never fail us, but will give strength and wisdom for every situation. The Lord desires to give us every righteous desire of our hearts, since He is a good God who desires to bless His children with good things. If He refrains from granting a request, it is always for a good reason. He knows what is best. Perhaps we are not ready or able to receive what we ask. Also, if it involves the wills of other people, He must work with them until they are willing for what we are praying to happen. This can create long delays. However, if we commit our way unto the LORD and obey Him, He will bring it to pass. "Delight thyself also in the LORD; and he shall give thee the desires of thine heart. Commit thy way unto the LORD; trust also in him; and he shall bring it to pass" (Psalm 37:4-5).

Dear heavenly Father, thank You for Your care for me. Forgive me when I fail to trust You and try to take matters into my own hands. I know that You have the best plan for my life. Please give me the grace to accept it and to do the things that you are speaking to me each day. Help me to be patient as You work in other people's lives that affect mine. May I extend to them the same grace and mercy that You have extended to me. Lord, grant me the grace to change the things in my life that are not pleasing to You. I delight in You, knowing that Your plan for my life is being worked out according to Your will and not mine. I ask this in the name of Jesus, my Lord. Amen.

Proverbs 19:22 That which is desired in man is loyalty and kindness, and his glory and delight are his giving, but a poor man is better than a liar (AMP).

This verse tells us what people expect of each other; and that God considers our character more important than our circumstances. It tells us that we, as human beings, desire that other people would be kind and loyal to us. No one wants to be treated in a wrongful manner by others. We all like to be treated kindly and fairly. The way that we can attain this kind of treatment is for us to give others that kind of treatment, since the Bible tells us that we shall reap what we sow. If we are receiving harsh treatment from anyone, the way to overcome this kind of treatment is to sow good things back to that person, no matter what wrongs they have done to us. If we cannot sow actual deeds to them, we can sow kind prayers and thoughts toward them. It is not possible for us to do this in our own selves; we must have the power of the Holy Spirit to help us. However, when we choose to pursue this path, the Lord will move on the hearts of others to respond to us differently. Romans 12:21 says, "Be not overcome of evil, but overcome evil with good."

We are also commanded by Jesus, our Lord, to love one another and to treat others as we would like to be treated. "And as ye would that men should do to you, do ye also to them likewise" (Luke 6:31). If we are children of the Lord, we must act like Him and reflect His nature in our dealings with others. He then will deal with our enemies. We do not have to. God is interested in changing our natures and character to reflect His. The circumstances we go through give Him the opportunity to do this. When we choose to act like our Lord, He empowers and changes us in each negative circumstance that we face, so that we can overcome in it and become more like Him.

The last half of this scripture states that "a poor man is better than a liar." It is better to endure trying circumstances than to have a bad character, for the Lord is more interested in changing our characters than our circumstances. He can change our circumstances in a moment, but it takes longer for our character to change. We are eternal beings, being prepared for an unimaginably glorious future. God's purpose for our lives is to change us to reflect the nature and ability of Christ (Romans 8:29; 2 Corinthians 3:18). Every circumstance we go through gives Him the opportunity to do this when we choose to obey Him.

In every circumstance we make a choice: to do things God's way or ours. The Holy Spirit is our Helper, empowering us to choose to die to self and enabling us to obey God as Jesus did (Philippians 2:13). He forms the character of Christ in us as we do this, producing the fruit of the Spirit. We must all ask God for the grace to take up our crosses daily and put to death everything that is not like Him.

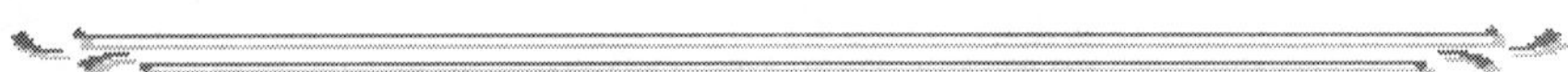

Dear heavenly Father, I am thankful for Your love and patience. Help me to extend that same love and patience to others. Help me to be kind and loyal in all circumstances. Open my eyes to see my own faults so that I might present them to You for the needed changes. Forgive me for my wrong attitudes. Change my heart to be like Yours. I release to Your care all those who have caused me pain and trouble. Be merciful to them and help them to change also. Lord, give us all Your grace and mercy in this hour when there is so much evil in the world. I ask this in the name of Jesus. Amen.

Proverbs 19:23 The fear of the LORD tendeth to life: and he that hath it shall abide satisfied; he shall not be visited with evil.

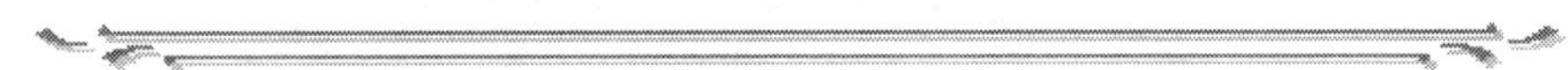

When one honors the Lord, he can live in a place of provision far above other men. However, we need to define both the "fear of the Lord" and "visited with evil" before we can understand what this verse means.

As we saw in Day 4, the "fear of the Lord" is not a tormenting fear, but rather a respect and honor for God and His Word. To reverence God by obeying His Word will lead to abundant life and satisfied rest: "The fear of the LORD is the beginning of wisdom: a good understanding have all they that do his commandments: his praise endureth for ever" (Psalm 111:10).

"Come, ye children, hearken unto me: I will teach you the fear of the LORD. What man is he that desireth life, and loveth many days, that he may see good? Keep thy tongue from evil, and thy lips from speaking guile. Depart from evil, and do good; seek peace, and pursue it" (Psalm 34:11-14).

What does it mean that we shall not be "visited with evil?" If we honor God, we do not release the death principle in our lives; therefore, we will not be visited by the consequences of what we have sown. It does not mean that the devil will never attack us, but rather that God will give us the way to overcome him. Therefore, evil will not actually hurt us. We can rest in God, unafraid of evil. When we are "born again," we have access to God and all the good He desires for us. Jesus came to destroy the works of the devil (1 John 3:8). Because Jesus overcame the devil through His death on the cross, no weapon formed against us shall prosper (Isaiah 54:17).

There are many promises of deliverance in the Bible that we can stand upon, such as Psalm 91:3-7 and Job 5:19-22 which says, "He shall deliver thee in six troubles: yea, in seven there shall no evil touch thee. In famine he shall redeem thee from death: and in war from the power of the sword. Thou shalt be hid from the scourge of the tongue: neither shalt thou be afraid of destruction when it cometh. At destruction and famine thou shalt laugh: neither shalt thou be afraid of the beasts of the earth." We can also look at the lives of many Bible saints and see how these scriptures protected them in their time of trial. For example, God fulfilled the promise of Job 5:22, for the Israelites and Daniel. In Exodus, the Jews were protected from the plagues sent upon the Egyptians. He shut the mouths of lions for Daniel. God has not changed; His power has not diminished. He is the same yesterday, today and forever (Hebrews 13:8). He is no respecter of persons! If we respect His Word, He will keep His promises and do the same things for us today that He did long ago for those whose narratives are recorded throughout the Bible. He is simply looking for those who dare to believe Him!

Dear heavenly Father, I praise You today for Your greatness! Create in me a heart that will always believe You and trust in Your Word. I want to always have the "fear of the Lord" in my heart. Then, I will not have to fear man for what they would do unto me, since You are greater than all people. Thank You for Your many promises of provision and protection throughout Your Word. I claim them for my life and for those in my family. Deliver me from any doubt and unbelief that would keep me from receiving all that You have promised me in the Bible. I ask this in the name of the Lord Jesus Christ. Amen.

Proverbs 19:24-25 24 A slothful man hideth his hand in his bosom, and will not so much as bring it to his mouth again. 25 Smite a scorner, and the simple will beware: and reprove one that hath understanding, and he will understand knowledge.

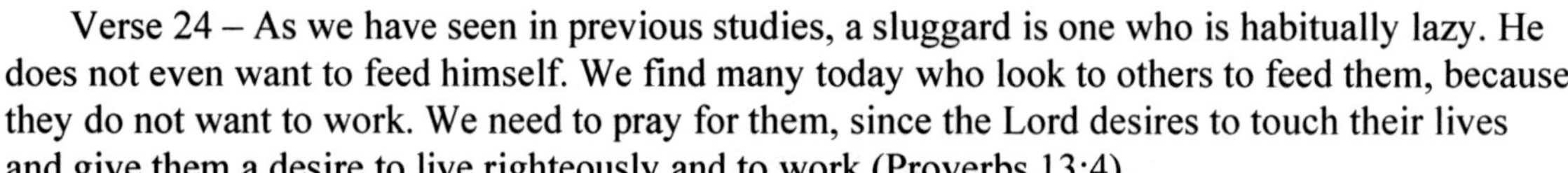

Verse 24 – As we have seen in previous studies, a sluggard is one who is habitually lazy. He does not even want to feed himself. We find many today who look to others to feed them, because they do not want to work. We need to pray for them, since the Lord desires to touch their lives and give them a desire to live righteously and to work (Proverbs 13:4).

Verse 25 – Anyone who scorns authority by disturbing a public meeting should not be allowed to take the platform, but should be admonished and removed from the assembly. While pastoring the church, my husband and I had to deal with some difficult situations. Once, a woman got up during the service and began to admonish us and our congregation with some very strong words. We asked the Lord what to do. He spoke to our hearts that we should walk over to her, lay hands on her, and pray for her. We prayed along these lines: "Lord, we know our sister is concerned about some things in this church. We ask You to work in all of our lives so that we remain a church that is loving and kind. Help our sister to be loving also; to respect the others in this service and refrain from speaking out while another is speaking. Lord, let everything be done decently and in order." She immediately sat down and we finished the service without further disturbance.

On another occasion, a stranger entered our service. When we acknowledged him as a visitor, he began chastising our congregation for things that we were not guilty of; and he prophesied that the whole church would be destroyed. This time, we told the man before all the people, "Sir, we do not receive the words that you just spoke over this church. Our people are loving and kind and your words do not come from our Lord." He immediately left, stomping out the back door. When he was gone, we all prayed for him to be set free from an accusing spirit, and that he would come to know the true love of God.

We only had a few situations like these, because we learned that we could take authority in prayer ahead of time and bind any disturbing spirits from our meetings.

When a man of understanding is reproved, he gains more knowledge. If anyone admonishes us about something, we should take it to the Lord and ask Him if it is the truth, even if they tell us something in a wrong manner, we should still ask the Lord about it because there may be a grain of truth in it.

Dear heavenly Father, thank You for helping me in my relationships. I desire to be kind and gentle in situations that require me to take corrective measures. Help me to hear Your voice as to how to deal with unpleasant situations; whether it be with my children or those who work with me. May I treat others as kindly as possible. Lord, I do not want to use my position of authority wrongly, but in a way that will be an example to others of Your Spirit in my life. Thank You for teaching me things I need to know, and may I always have a teachable spirit. I ask this in the name of the Lord Jesus Christ. Amen.

Proverbs 19:26-27 26 He that wasteth his father, and chaseth away his mother, is a son that causeth shame, and bringeth reproach. 27 Cease, my son, to hear the instruction that causeth to err from the words of knowledge.

The Hebrew word used for *waste* means "to practice violence; to destroy.[22]" It is shocking to hear of the violent crimes committed by children today. Children have even murdered their own parents. This kind of evil is demonic and shows the extent to which morals have been eroded by humanistic teaching. When man rejects God's ways, lawlessness and violence result. Such evil in a nation that once followed the Lord is shameful. Our condition is worse than many nations who have never heard the Gospel because we have been exposed to the light.

It is very important that parents teach children not only to respect authority, but also to handle anger. Children, particularly unruly and violent children who do not learn to properly handle anger by forgiving others and controlling their actions, can be very destructive. Not all will commit acts of violence, but many will continue to have angry outbursts as adults. They may not lose their tempers often, but when they do, they ruin relationships, reputations, and often property. Parents of unruly children should honestly evaluate themselves to see if they have learned to control their own anger. To exchange angry shouts with one's children is childish. Angry outbursts show lack of self-control, and uncontrolled anger begets uncontrolled anger. Parents need God's help to learn self-control themselves and to teach it to their children.

The Bible admonishes fathers not to provoke their children to wrath but to raise them in the nurture and admonition of the Lord (Ephesians 6:1-4). Parents must use wisdom and love in dealing with their children, but love does not mean letting a child have his own way. A child may feel anger when disciplined; however, their anger will be short-lived when the discipline is fair and done in love.

Friends and adult acquaintances influence young people by their actions and words. If young people admire someone of bad character, they can be influenced to stray from their parents' instructions and be lead into dangerous situations. Even if there is no immediate danger, bad friends can implant lies in their minds which will lead them to make destructive choices later in life.

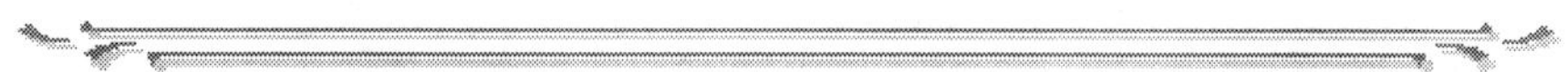

Dear heavenly Father, thank You for giving us instructions in the Bible as to how we are to help our children. Help us to be good parents. When we need to discipline them, help us to do so in Your love. We do not want to yield to becoming so upset that we lose our temper and hurt them more than help them. Lord, help us not to shrink from disciplining our children when they need it, knowing that it will cause them to cease from rebellion and evil. May our children understand Your ways and desire to follow You and have a spirit of obedience. Please heal any breaches between parents and their children and cause our families to walk in Your love. I ask this in the name of Jesus. Amen.

---

[22] Wilson's Old Testament Word Studies

Proverbs 19:28-29 28 A worthless witness scoffs at justice, and the mouth of the wicked swallows iniquity. 29 Judgments are prepared for scoffers, and stripes for the back of (self–confident) fools (AMP).

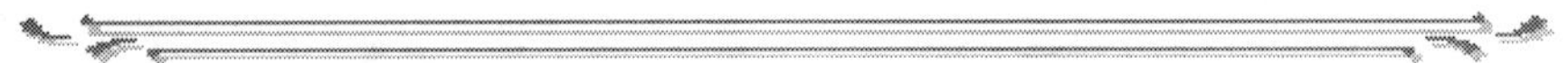

The Bible speaks much about judgment. In these verses, we are told that ungodly witnesses care only for their own gain. They will send the innocent to jail if it profits them. Such people feed upon sinful and iniquitous ideas. They are deluded to believe that they will not face the results of their sins, scoffing at justice and judgment.

Judgments are prepared for scoffers, not believers. Disobeying God brings sorrow and death. The Lord knew that all people would fall into sin; however He sent Jesus Christ into this world to make a way of escape for us from hell and death. Jesus, who committed no sin or crime went to the cross to die in our place. He paid the penalty of our sins so that we would not have to. Death and hell have no power over any who repent and turn to Christ. When we make Jesus Lord of our lives, we are promised eternal life. Christ has freed us to live for Him and to tell others about His wonderful plan of redemption.

In ancient times, scoffers were publicly beaten and received stripes. Proud fools will suffer painful punishments in life, as well as hell in eternity. If we will humble ourselves, ask for God's forgiveness, and turn our lives over to Him, we can have peace and joy. We can walk in the Spirit of life daily. We can experience heaven now in this earth, where there is so much hell around us. When we have the Creator of heaven and earth living in our hearts, our eyes are opened to truth, and we can experience the depths of His love. God loves each of us and has a mighty plan for all who allow Him to rule their lives.

Someone once asked me what I had given up to serve Christ. I replied, "I did not give up anything that was not already killing me! In Christ, I am promised heaven for hell, health for sickness, joy for sorrow, peace for torment, faith for fear, love for hate, release from addictions, and all blessings instead of evil curses." What a wonderful exchange! After I made a total commitment to God, I never looked back to my old life. The old man is dead and I am a new creature in Christ, praise God! My old way of life cannot compare to my life in Christ. If you do not know Jesus as your Savior, it is my prayer that you will allow Him to write your name in His Book of Life.

Dear heavenly Father, I am so thankful that my name is written in the Book of Life. I pray that all who read these words will allow You to write their name in that same book, if it is not already recorded there. Lord, I thank You for Your sacrifice on the cross. I did not deserve it, but I am eternally grateful for Your love for me. Lord, help me to be obedient to You daily and follow in Your will for my life. Help me to overcome the desires of my flesh and to always choose the way of life in You. May I always have the courage to share with others what You have done for me. I ask this in the name of Jesus. Amen.

Proverbs 20:1 Wine is a mocker, strong drink is raging: and whosoever is deceived thereby is not wise.

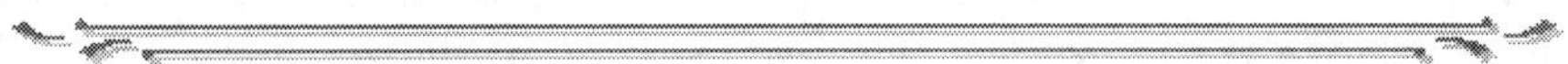

Some religious circles like to debate whether or not "wine" in the Bible refers to non-intoxicating grape juice or fermented, alcoholic grape juice. To answer this question, we must study the original language in which the Bible was written. The first scripture in which wine is mentioned is found in the book of Genesis, the Hebrew word, *yayin.* It always means fermented wine; primarily from grapes.[23] This is also obvious from the text: "And Noah began to be a husbandman, and he planted a vineyard: And he drank of the wine, and was drunken" (Genesis 9:20–21). Only alcohol could make one drunk!

In the New Testament, the Greek word *oinos* is usually used for wine.[24] Jesus' first miracle was turning water into wine (John 2:1-11). "When the ruler of the feast had tasted the water that was made wine, and knew not whence it was: (but the servants which drew the water knew;) the governor of the feast called the bridegroom, And saith unto him, Every man at the beginning doth set forth good wine; and when men have well drunk, then that which is worse: but thou hast kept the good wine until now." This verse indicates that the wine was fermented, since good wine was usually served first, with the inferior wine served later. After their senses were dulled from drinking wine, no one would notice or care that the wine served later was not as good. Many other Biblical references to wine show that it is an alcoholic drink.

Some Christians might ask if it is a sin for us to drink wine today. I believe that because sin is in the heart of man and not in any object, wine itself is not sinful. However, becoming drunk can cause us to sin (Galatians 5:18-21). The Bible teaches moderation; even eating too much food is a sin (gluttony). Alcohol can cause people to go out of their heads. Alcoholism is responsible for broken homes, health problems, and many deaths (through disease or drunk drivers). Unborn babies can be damaged by it. The Bible says that drunkards will not inherit the kingdom of God (1 Corinthians 6:9-10).

In the Old Testament, there was a group of people known as Nazarites. Each one took a vow to dedicate himself to the Lord and did not drink alcohol at all (Numbers 6:2-3). Would it not please God if we love Him and our brethren enough to give up a passing pleasure that might cause someone to stumble? If a new Christian with an alcoholic past sees you drinking, he or she may fall prey to addiction all over again. Paul taught that we should not use our liberty in Christ in ways that would cause others to stumble (Romans 14). Galatians 5:13 says, "For, brethren, ye have been called unto liberty; only use not liberty for an occasion to the flesh, but by love serve one another." 1 Corinthians 8:9: "But take heed lest by any means this liberty of yours become a stumblingblock to them that are weak."

Would it not be a more powerful witness to others in our age to stand out as one who did not drink alcoholic beverages because we had no need to do so? When we are filled with the Spirit of God, His spirit gives us the joy and release that many are seeking by drinking. May we instead desire to be filled with the Holy Spirit and have no need for "spirits."

"And be not drunk with wine, wherein is excess; but be filled with the Spirit; Speaking to yourselves in psalms and hymns and spiritual songs, singing and making melody in your heart to the LORD; Giving thanks always for all things unto God and the Father in the name of our Lord Jesus Christ" (Ephesians 5:18-20).

---

[23] Strong's Exhaustive Concordance of the Bible, Hebrew and Chaldee Dictionary
[24] Strong's Exhaustive Concordance of the Bible, Greek Dictionary of the New Testament

Dear Father, thank You for the liberty that we have in Christ. Help us not to judge one another in regard to drinking a little wine, but rather to be honest before You as to the issue in our own hearts in this regard. May we be a good witness to those around us. When we make choices in this life, may they be pleasing to You and show love to those around us. You told us the highest law is the law of love. We are to love You first, and then to love one another. May we do this in word and deed. Keep us from temptation and let our actions prove to the world that we are true Christians. Deliver those who are addicted to alcohol and are caught in this snare of the devil. I ask this in the name of the Lord Jesus Christ. Amen.

Quotes About Conviction and Repentance

We must not allow the enemy to discourage us from coming to God when we have fallen, but immediately repent, receive God's forgiveness, and go on with the Lord. The devil seeks to keep us out of fellowship with our Father by making us feel unworthy of forgiveness. --Day 126

It is important to discern when the Holy Spirit is convicting of sin versus when the enemy is accusing us. True conviction leads to seeking God and repentance. It results in joy, freedom and growth. --Day 234

As Christians, there is no room to side with people. We are to side with the Word of God. When my actions do not line up with His, I must even side against myself and agree with Him. --Day 266

Fear and shame is the fruit of sin. If we fellowship with God on a daily basis, we find that there is simply no guilt that troubles us. However,

Proverbs 20:2-3 2 The fear of a king is as the roaring of a lion: whoso provoketh him to anger sinneth against his own soul. 3 It is an honour for a man to cease from strife: but every fool will be meddling.

Verse 2 – By angering those in authority, we make things difficult for ourselves. The Bible tells us that we are to respect those in authority; whether presidents, governors, or policemen. Granted, not all who fill these offices are godly people; however, the Lord instructs us to be respectful of their position of authority. Daniel, who was deported to Babylon, served several pagan kings during his life. He did not refuse to serve them because they were unbelievers, but honored their authority. He was a witness of God to them by his life and work.

It is prudent to respect those in authority. However, like Daniel, we must choose to honor God above those in positions of human authority, if they desire us to do what dishonors the Lord (Acts 5:21). God is the King of all kings; it is more foolish to risk eternal death by rejecting salvation through Jesus Christ than to rouse the anger of human authorities who pressure us to deny Him. Not to honor (fear) God is indeed to sin against one's own soul. "And fear not them which kill the body, but are not able to kill the soul: but rather fear him which is able to destroy both soul and body in hell" (Matthew 10:28).

In the New Testament, John the Baptist was one who angered the queen (Mark 6:17-28). Perhaps his lack of wisdom in attacking her cost him his life. In spite of his plight, the Lord honored him, calling him a great man of God. We can be sure that even if we do unwise things, the Lord is pleased that we would speak up and serve Him in spite of the persecution that comes when we do. Notice in the scripture below, that the kingdom of heaven suffers violence. We are not to be cowardly when this happens, but should stand in the spirit of prayer, violently attacking the forces of darkness that are arrayed against us. "Verily I say unto you, Among them that are born of women there hath not risen a greater than John the Baptist: notwithstanding he that is least in the kingdom of heaven is greater than he. And from the days of John the Baptist until now the kingdom of heaven suffereth violence, and the violent take it by force (Matthew 11:11-12). This does not mean we are to attack people, but rather we are to attack the spirits of darkness that are influencing the people who are bringing evil against us. The Lord gave us the authority to overcome these spirits through prayer and obedience to Him.

Verse 3 – The Bible admonishes us to honor God by avoiding anger and strife. Strife causes breaches in our relationships which can be difficult to mend. Prayer and love will do more to remedy a situation than quarreling. It is a man's honor to avoid strife, for this displays wisdom and strength of character. Any fool can take offense and argue with others. When others attack us, we should not contend with them. Our battle is not against people, but against the spirits of darkness that influence them to bring evil against us. The Lord has given us authority to overcome these spirits through prayer and obedience to Him. We should respond in the manner that God would have us to respond. In the Old Testament, when King David was attacked by enemies, it was recorded that he "inquired of the Lord." We must always inquire of the Lord as to how we are to fight our battles.

Dear heavenly Father, thank You for Your Words of wisdom. Please help us to avoid anger and strife toward each other. Give us a spirit of love and a burden to pray for those who try to stir up trouble with us. Lord, please be the Umpire in matters where we disagree with others. Help us to have a humble attitude toward You and the people around us, and yet maintain a vigilant and forceful prayer life against the powers of darkness. Help us to fight our battles in the spirit and not in the flesh. May You bring us the victories that we need. I ask this in the name of the Lord Jesus Christ. Amen.

Quotes About Giving

If we are truly committed to God and walking in the Spirit, we will always desire to give; it will not be a burden, but a joy. --Day 19

Some people are waiting until they have more money to give their tithes and offerings. These people will never have more money to give until they are faithful to give out of what they have. --Day 218

When we give, we not only help those who are needy, but we also help ourselves, because God always repays a kindness. Continuous giving creates a wonderful cycle that blesses everybody. --Day 219

Some businessmen think that giving tithes and offerings fulfills their calling. This is commendable, but every disciple of the Lord has a higher calling–to live their lives totally dedicated to Jesus in everything they do. Giving is only one of those things. --Day 229

The Old Testament and New Testament instruct us to help the poor and to deal fairly with all people–poor or rich. Doing so honors God. Failing to do this was part of the iniquity of Sodom and Gomorrah, whose people spent their wealth and free time on self-indulgence. --Day 355

Quotes About Making Judgments

The Lord will judge all men fairly, as He knows what happened in every situation. He sees the motives of men's hearts, and is the final judge of all. --Day 188

Some Christians mistakenly believe that we should not judge others at all; but that is not what scripture teaches. Jesus did not say we should never judge, but rather, told us *how* to judge. --Day 258

Proverbs 20:4-5 4 The sluggard will not plow by reason of the cold; therefore shall he beg in harvest, and have nothing. 5 Counsel in the heart of man is like deep water; but a man of understanding will draw it out.

Verse 4 – The observation made here is that when it gets uncomfortable or difficult, a person who is lazy will cease to work. A good farmer knows that he must take care of his soil in the winter, as well as summer. We know that certain crops will not grow in the winter; however, the soil must still be plowed and laid to rest after the fall harvest so that a spring crop can be planted early. This entails working in the fall as winter is setting in, as well as working the ground in late winter and early spring for a summer crop.

Anyone unwilling to work in uncomfortable weather, or when the job calls for major exertion, is a sluggard. When harvest comes, he has no crops to gather for food for the coming year. He is reduced to begging from others or becoming dependent on a person or institution to feed him. He will remain poor. Work is part of God's plan for man. The Bible declares that those who do not work should not eat. 2 Thessalonians 3:10-12 says, "For even when we were with you, this we commanded you, that if any would not work, neither should he eat. For we hear that there are some which walk among you disorderly, working not at all, but are busybodies."

"He that observeth the wind shall not sow; and he that regardeth the clouds shall not reap" (Ecclesiastes 11:4). In the natural, hardships and difficulties must be overcome in order to sow. Perseverance is necessary if we are to be successful in any endeavor. This principal can also be applied to spiritual things. We must be persistent in order to reap a blessing. The Lord encourages us not to give up if we do not receive an answer to our prayers right away. We must keep on asking, seeking, and knocking. And eventually, the way will be opened unto us. "Ask, and it shall be given you; seek, and ye shall find; knock, and it shall be opened unto you: For every one that asketh receiveth; and he that seeketh findeth; and to him that knocketh it shall be opened" (Matthew 7:7-8).

Verse 5 – The Hebrew word for counsel includes deliberation and purpose. Only God knows what thoughts and purposes are in a person's innermost being; the "deep wells" of his heart. God will let us see the soul of another if we pray and seek Him. The purpose being, He wants us to be aware of people whose motives are evil, so that we will avoid being entrapped in bad situations. The Lord also wants us to know who has godly counsel so that we may pay attention to it. He wants us to have discernment or understanding of the purposes of other people.

Dear heavenly Father, thank You for allowing us to work. It is a blessing to labor, and to receive the fruit of our labor. Help us to overcome any laziness and procrastination that would keep us from receiving the things You want us to have. Lord, we also ask You to give us a spirit of discernment so that we might not be fooled or manipulated by others. Also, help us to recognize Your voice in Your servants who have godly counsel and wisdom that we should heed. I ask this in the precious name of Jesus. Amen

Proverbs 20:6-7 6 Most men will proclaim every one his own goodness: but a faithful man who can find? 7 The just man walketh in his integrity: his children are blessed after him.

Verse 6 – Since we all want others to respect and like us, we generally present ourselves in the best light, letting our good deeds be known. No one likes to mention their failures. Even so, God knows everything about us. When we come to Him, the first thing we must do is to confess our sins and failures to Him so that He can forgive us and help us to overcome them. This is humbling, but it allows the Holy Spirit to lift us from the state we are in. "Humble yourselves in the sight of the Lord, and he shall lift you up" (James 4:10). "If we confess our sins, he is faithful and just to forgive us our sins, and to cleanse us from all unrighteousness" (1 John 1:9).

We will never be truly faithful until we first come to the One who is always faithful. By faith in the Lord Jesus, we are made righteous and enabled to do what is right and good. As God's children, we should not broadcast our good deeds but make known the One enabling us to do them. "Let another man praise thee, and not thine own mouth; a stranger, and not thine own lips" (Proverbs 27:2).

Jesus Himself said there was no good thing in Him, but His goodness came from the Father who sent Him. Matthew 19:16-17 says, "And, behold, one came and said unto him, Good Master, what good thing shall I do, that I may have eternal life? And he said unto him, Why callest thou me good? there is none good but one, that is, God: but if thou wilt enter into life, keep the commandments." John 5:19 also says, "Then answered Jesus and said unto them, Verily, verily, I say unto you, The Son can do nothing of himself, but what he seeth the Father do: for what things soever he doeth, these also doeth the Son likewise."

If Jesus, who was without sin, had to rely on the Father and the Holy Spirit to do good, how much more must we? Paul wrote to the Romans, "For I know that in me (that is, in my flesh,) dwelleth no good thing: for to will is present with me; but how to perform that which is good I find not" (Romans 7:18). God promises to enable us to desire and accomplish His will in Philippians 2:13: "For it is God which worketh in you both to will and to do of his good pleasure."

Verse 7 – To walk in righteousness, we must walk in the Spirit, allowing Christ to live His life in us and letting the world see that we are guided by His Word. Matthew 5:16 says, "Let your light so shine before men, that they may see your good works, and glorify your Father which is in heaven."

God will enable us to keep His commandments and do the things that Jesus did. We will thus be an example to our children and leave them a spiritual inheritance. We may also be the only "Bible" that unbelievers will read. Our deeds should inspire others to know God better. The greatest thing we can do for our children, or anyone else, is to bring them to the knowledge of God.

Dear heavenly Father, help me to be the kind of witness that I should be to the world. May others see Christ in me and in the deeds I do. Forgive me when I get in the flesh and do things that I should not do. Help me to overcome my flesh and truly bring glory to You by the way I live. Fill me with the Spirit so that I can express Your love to all I come in contact with. Help me to be faithful and obedient to Your Words. Thank You for Your mercy and grace. I ask this in the name of Jesus Christ. Amen.

Proverbs 20:8-9 8 A king that sitteth in the throne of judgment scattereth away all evil with his eyes. 9 Who can say, I have made my heart clean, I am pure from my sin?

Verse 8 – One of the goals of every good leader is to preserve order and protect the inhabitants of his country. He is continually looking for ways to preserve his kingdom by removing the evil from it; and he deters wickedness by punishing evildoers. Although this verse is speaking about a natural king, God is also the King over all the earth. He watches the deeds of men and nations, and at some point they are all judged. When the heart and soul of a nation turns from righteousness to become more wicked than good, an automatic spiritual law of sowing and reaping begins not only to expose evil, but to judge it as well. This is evidenced even today by the destructive things happening in the earth. Although God is very merciful to the wicked, there is a point where their sins must be judged or everyone would be destroyed by them, including the good and the righteous. So, for the sake of preserving the good, the evil must be dealt with.

God cannot do evil. He is not the one who initiates destruction; but rather merely removes His hand of protection and allows people to reap the consequences of their sin. God desires to intervene and save those who will repent and call upon Him. "Behold therefore the goodness and severity of God: on them which fell, severity; but toward thee, goodness, if thou continue in his goodness: otherwise thou also shalt be cut off" (Romans 11:22). "Thine own wickedness shall correct thee, and thy backslidings shall reprove thee: know therefore and see that it is an evil thing and bitter, that thou hast forsaken the LORD thy God, and that my fear is not in thee, saith the LORD GOD of hosts" (Jeremiah 2:19).

Verse 9 – Since the fall of man, everyone has been born with a sinful nature. God knew that there was only one way to bring His creation back to Himself. That is why He sent Jesus to lay down His life for all people. Jesus, the sinless One was crucified, buried, and rose from the dead. He is alive forevermore, to bring people back to God. No man is pure in himself, and no one can make himself pure. Jesus alone can purify man from sin. When we accept by faith what Jesus did for us, we are cleansed by His blood. Romans 3:23 says, "For all have sinned, and come short of the glory of God; Being justified freely by his grace through the redemption that is in Christ Jesus: Whom God hath set forth to be a propitiation through faith in his blood, to declare his righteousness for the remission of sins that are past, through the forbearance of God; To declare, I say, at this time his righteousness: that he might be just, and the justifier of him which believeth in Jesus." Our salvation comes by Christ's atonement alone, apart from any good work that a man does. Our good works only reveal what Christ has done in us.

Dear heavenly Father, thank You for sending Your Son, Jesus, to die for our sins so that we might have eternal life. I am grateful to be Your child. I thank You for purifying me from the things that are not like You. Lord, I cannot cleanse myself, but I know when I ask You to remove the things in my life that are wicked, You will come and do it. Keep me this day from temptation and fill me with Your love and help me to become more and more like You. I ask this in the name of Your precious Son, Jesus. Amen.

Proverbs 20:10 Diverse weights (one for buying and another for selling) and diverse measures, both of them are exceedingly offensive and abhorrent to the LORD (AMP).

As we saw in Day 67, a scale was used in Israel to balance the weight of an item against stones of specified weight. Dishonest weights were stones that were heavier or lighter than they were supposed to be. For example, if a customer wanted a pound of food, a dishonest merchant would use stones weighing a little less than a pound so that the customer would pay for a pound, but not quite receive it. When a foreign trader came to sell to that same merchant, he would use stones that were heavier than a pound. The merchant would pay for a pound, but he would get a little more than that. When a high-ranking official or one who would not be deceived came, he used yet other stones that were true weights so he would not be caught cheating.

We have all cheated and been cheated at some time. We may not have cheated on our taxes or spouses, but we have probably cheated in other ways. We can cheat others of respect, or our families of time. We can cheat employers by wasting time rather than honestly working. We can cheat God of honor by obeying Him only when it is easy for us to do so. We can cheat unbelievers by not witnessing to them, or by not backing up our witness with a righteous life. We cheat our brethren if we do not walk in love, but selfishly insist on our liberty in Christ, not caring if we cause others to stumble. We all take more and give less than we ought at different times.

The Lord will forgive and deliver us, if we come to Him and confess our sin. We need to ask Him to reveal any ways in which we have cheated, and repent for being dishonest. "If we say that we have no sin, we deceive ourselves, and the truth is not in us. If we confess our sins, he is faithful and just to forgive us our sins, and to cleanse us from all unrighteousness" (1 John 1:8-9).

After we receive forgiveness, we should also forgive those who have cheated us. We are told to pray for those who despitefully use us. If we do not, we can become very bitter, and that attitude could destroy us. We must learn to give our hurt to Jesus and ask Him to forgive those who have wronged us. "But I say unto you, Love your enemies, bless them that curse you, do good to them that hate you, and pray for them which despitefully use you, and persecute you; That ye may be the children of your Father which is in heaven: for he maketh his sun to rise on the evil and on the good, and sendeth rain on the just and on the unjust" (Matthew 5:44-45). "For if ye forgive men their trespasses, your heavenly Father will also forgive you: But if ye forgive not men their trespasses, neither will your Father forgive your trespasses" (Matthew 6:14).

In time, the Lord will judge all people fairly. He knows what really happened in every situation. He sees the motives of our hearts, and is the final Judge of all. He will do what is right.

Dear Father, thank You for the love and forgiveness that You show me daily. Help me to overcome any sin that the enemy may try to tempt me in. Please forgive me for the times I fail You. I also forgive those who hurt and sin against me. May they come to repentance so that they might know Your forgiving love too. We all need Your love and mercy. Lord, be merciful to my family and my friends. Watch over my children and my grandchildren and keep them from harm. Guide me daily in the right path so that I do not stray from the straight and narrow. I ask this in the name of Jesus Christ. Amen.

Proverbs 20:11-12 11 Even a child is known by his doings, whether his work be pure, and whether it be right. 12 The hearing ear, and the seeing eye, the LORD hath made even both of them.

Verse 11 – Children, like adults, are known by their actions; whether good or bad. Outward deeds reveal inward sin and need to be taken seriously. When certain types of words or actions are continually repeated, they establish a child's character. We all have known people who are habitually tardy or lie; they have bad reputations. It is important that parents not be lazy, but work with their children to develop their character. Teaching is not enough; we must also train them by patiently reinforcing good habits and helping them overcome bad ones. Proverbs 22:6 tells us to "Train up a child in the way he should go, and when he is old, he will not depart from it." Notice this says "train" not "teach" a child in the way he should go. Knowledge that is learned from hearing teaching is not enough. We must reinforce what we teach by training.

It is unkind for a parent to tell their children that they will take certain actions if they are disobedient, and continually fail to follow through on their word. Children stop listening to their parents' advice if they know they will not really be disciplined. Parents who do this actually train their children to disrespect them. Many times, undisciplined children simply reflect undisciplined parents. Raising children of good character requires real love and dedication, hard work, patience, and prayer. The Bible instructs that children be brought up in the nurture and admonition of the Lord (Ephesians 6:4).

Verse 12 – Notice that this verse follows the one about how a child acts. There is a definite correlation between what a child hears and sees, and how he will act. Children imitate the role models presented in movies and television. Movies depicting strong morals inspire children to do what is right. Children who are allowed to view violence or immorality will often attempt to do the things they see. It is very important that we do not allow our children to view any media that portrays violence, occult themes and illicit sex as normal, nor should we watch them ourselves.

Pornography also deteriorates our society, by creating unhealthy relationships on all levels. Marriages are damaged, and preoccupation with lustful thoughts prevents many people from enjoying life. We must protect both our thoughts, and our children's thoughts by guarding what we allow to pass before our eyes and enter our ears. If a child views violent, pornographic images, it can have a life-long negative effect upon them. Our homes should be places where our children are protected from such evil; not where they might accidentally stumble across something that could wound and defile them. Like David of old, we must determine that we will "...set no wicked thing before our eyes" (Psalm 101:2-4).

Heavenly Father, please help me keep my thoughts pure, resisting any temptation to view anything that is corrupt and vile. Please also keep my children and grandchildren safe from being exposed to pornographic material, since I know that evil men and women are peddling these things. Lord, deliver the people who are bound up in this snare. Forgive them and set them free. Dry up the resources behind the production of these magazines and videos, etc. Move on the hearts of those in our government to pass laws that will prevent pornography from spreading. Cause Your people to desire things that are pure and to put away from their homes the things that are evil. In Jesus' name I pray. Amen.

Proverbs 20:13 Love not sleep, lest thou come to poverty; open thine eyes, and thou shalt be satisfied with bread.

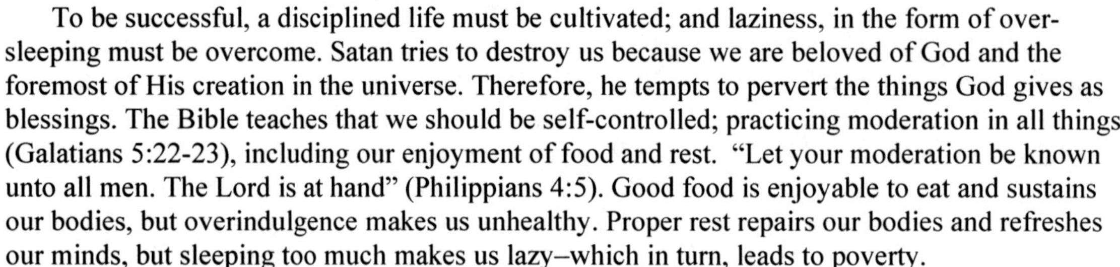

To be successful, a disciplined life must be cultivated; and laziness, in the form of over-sleeping must be overcome. Satan tries to destroy us because we are beloved of God and the foremost of His creation in the universe. Therefore, he tempts to pervert the things God gives as blessings. The Bible teaches that we should be self-controlled; practicing moderation in all things (Galatians 5:22-23), including our enjoyment of food and rest. "Let your moderation be known unto all men. The Lord is at hand" (Philippians 4:5). Good food is enjoyable to eat and sustains our bodies, but overindulgence makes us unhealthy. Proper rest repairs our bodies and refreshes our minds, but sleeping too much makes us lazy–which in turn, leads to poverty.

A disciplined Christian life is difficult to establish, and we all need the Holy Spirit's help to accomplish this. Getting up early to pray and to seek God about the day and meditate upon His Word is not easy, but it brings great reward. It honors God, and He then honors us by setting the tone for the day and guiding us from its beginning. When I neglect to seek God at the start of the day, it not only begins wrong, but inevitably some problem arises that I am unprepared to face. I am then forced to stop in the middle of the workday to pray in order to get back on track. "Preventative prayers" require less time than "corrective prayers." When I seek God first in the day, He prepares me for what lies ahead and guides me so that mistakes are avoided.

Physicians say that we need seven to ten hours of sleep each night. Part of the discipline of rising early is learning to go to bed earlier. As a young Christian, I struggled with getting up early enough to carve a time for God into my morning schedule. When I asked my pastor for prayer about this problem, he did not immediately pray; instead he asked me what time was I going to bed. When I told him 1:00 or 2:00 a.m. every night, he simply told me that if I wanted to get up earlier, I should go to bed earlier. Since I could not break the habit at that time, I began praying at night before I went to sleep. I would pray about the next day, and the Lord honored this arrangement until I could let Him deal with my habit of staying up late. I am still awake more in the evenings than in the mornings, as the Lord knows about the internal clock in me that still needs some adjusting. However, what He really cares about is that we set a time to pray consistently. As long as we do that, He will meet us. We just need to form a habit that allows nothing to prevent us from seeking God at the time we decide upon–whether morning, noon, or night–and preferably all three like Daniel in Daniel 6:10. That is my goal.

Dear heavenly Father, I thank You for Your kindness toward me in working with me to overcome the areas of my life that need more discipline. I want a prayer life that is pleasing to You. Help me in this endeavor. Correct those areas in my life that would hinder me from spending more time with You. Grant me the grace to overcome any laziness that tempts me. Fill me with Your Spirit this day and let me be a blessing to all I come in contact with. I ask this in the name of the Lord Jesus Christ. Amen.

Proverbs 20:14-15 14 It is naught, it is naught, saith the buyer: but when he is gone his way, then he boasteth. 15 There is gold, and a multitude of rubies: but the lips of knowledge are a precious jewel.

Verse 14 – Haggling over a price is normal in the Middle East and bargaining is an art, but some use their skills to cheat others. A buyer can make a transaction to his benefit by convincing a seller that his goods are worth less than what the seller asks for. If the seller is desperate and without bargaining skills, they can be swindled. This sort of dealing is just as much a form of cheating as a false balance. I am ashamed to say that I have heard Christians boasting about how they took advantage of people to get great bargains–and worse, attributing their success to God's favor! God, however, instructs us to make fair, and not one-sided deals. Before my husband and I sell something we always pray that it will bring a fair market value so that both we and the buyer may be blessed in the transaction. Negotiations should be honest. It is good if someone wants to reduce the price as a kindness, but bargaining should begin from a fair starting price. There is nothing wrong with offering bargain prices due to overstocks, seconds, closeouts, etc. as long as the merchandise is honestly presented. If items are damaged or irregular, they should be noted as such. The Lord hates deception.

Some businessmen use two financial statements: one, when they want their company to look prosperous (such as when borrowing money) and the other when they want their company to appear less prosperous (such as when paying taxes). It is not wrong to take every tax break that one is entitled to, but juggling the books for dishonest gain is another matter. God is calling businessmen to serve Him, and He is looking for those with integrity.

Verse 15 – The worth of precious gold, pearls, or rubies are not as valuable as one who has the priceless ability to speak with godly knowledge. When we know God's Word and line our words up with its truth, the gracious things that we speak will bring untold blessing to others. The Bible contains pure wisdom, we need to study it so that we will speak truth and become overcomers. "The words of the LORD are pure words: as silver tried in a furnace of earth, purified seven times" (Psalm 12:6).

Dear heavenly Father, we desire to be like You! Please help us to be honest in all of our dealings with others. May we be concerned about the other party when we purchase something and not just look for what is always advantageous to us. Help us to overcome selfishness. Lord, help us to control the things that we speak. Let our words be kind and edifying. Deliver us from anger and resentment and help us to keep a forgiving attitude when others wrong us. Help us to always be fair and honest in our dealings. I ask this in the name of the Lord Jesus Christ. Amen.

Proverbs 20:16-17 16 Take his garment that is surety for a stranger: and take a pledge of him for a strange woman. 17 Bread of deceit is sweet to a man; but afterwards his mouth shall be filled with gravel.

These Proverbs, in essence, tell us to avoid a man who has a bad character. We have a description of that character in these scriptures.

Verse 16 – In the Amplified version, this verse begins like this: "The judge tells the creditor..." In other words, this is a declaration of how a man who is deceitful should be treated by the court. The judge says he is not to be trusted; therefore his garment must be kept for security until he settles with the court.

Proverbs advises us not to take surety for a stranger. What is surety? It means that a person will secure another's payment with something, or will pledge to pay his debt if he fails to pay it. We are told that if we do this for someone whom we do not know that well, we will end up hurting for it, since we can lose all that we have put up for them. Strangers, who have the audacity to ask someone they do not even know to be surety for them, usually do not possess the character to repay the debt. It is better to avoid this kind of dealing, so that we will not be stuck with the penalty of paying someone else's debt.

There are many scams going around and most of them could be avoided if we heeded the principal of not trusting a stranger when they ask for money for an investment. Many times the person who is gullible and falls for these scams will end up not only losing their money, but they can also end up being arrested as part of the scam too, if they get deeply involved with the wrong kind of people.

Verse 17 – This verse sends a warning to those who would be tempted to use deceit and fraud. At first, a stolen thing tastes good, but after a while it will turn to gravel in one's mouth. Anything that we do in a deceitful manner will come back to haunt us because it triggers the law of sowing and reaping: "Be not deceived; God is not mocked: for whatsoever a man soweth, that shall he also reap. For he that soweth to his flesh shall of the flesh reap corruption; but he that soweth to the Spirit shall of the Spirit reap life everlasting" (Galatians 6:7-8).

Proverbs is full of good advice and, as we apply it to our lives, we will dwell in peace in this earth. We will not fall into the traps of the devil that will cause us trouble and pain, if we heed the advice in this book of wisdom.

Dear heavenly Father, I come to You today and I thank You for all of the wonderful advice You have recorded in the Bible. Help me to heed it and live by it, for I know that when I do, I will experience blessings in this life. Lord, help me not to get caught up in anything that is deceptive or that plays on the fleshly desires in my life. Give me discernment and wisdom in my monetary affairs. Help me to put You first in my finances by giving tithes and offerings. I know then You will protect me from the snares of the devil who comes to rob, steal and kill. Thank You for Your provision today and help me to be sensitive as to how I can help others and the work of the gospel. I ask this in the name of Jesus. Amen.

Proverbs 20:18 Every purpose is established by counsel: and with good advice make war.

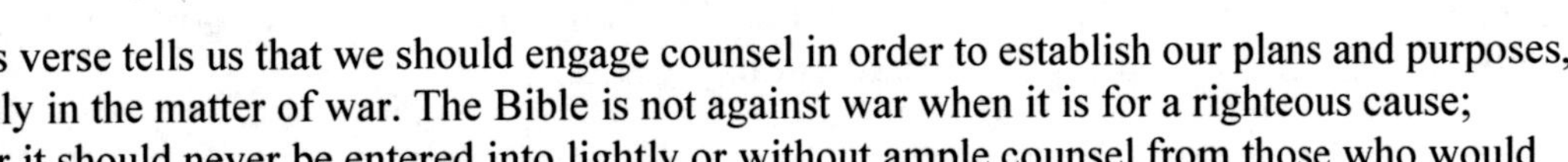

This verse tells us that we should engage counsel in order to establish our plans and purposes, especially in the matter of war. The Bible is not against war when it is for a righteous cause; however it should never be entered into lightly or without ample counsel from those who would be allies. When called to face any kind of battle it is especially important to have the counsel of fellow Christians. "Without counsel purposes are disappointed: but in the multitude of counsellors they are established" (Proverbs 15:22).

Team work is vital for any large vision to be accomplished. A good counselor is one who weighs out the pros and cons of a situation and suggests the best way to accomplish or correct something. With a multitude of counselors, the goals and purposes will not be frustrated, but will be completed. Each department will have good suggestions to get the thing established. This is especially important in any kind of warfare.

Some Christians struggle to reconcile Christ's command to love their enemies with their government's decision to go to war. Capital punishment also raises similar questions, especially if the criminal is reformed. How do we reconcile these questions? We must understand that the Bible defines different responsibilities for individuals and governments. While individuals are commanded to love their enemies and forgive those who do them wrong, the main role of a government is to protect its people from invaders and maintain law and order within its borders. Governments fulfill these responsibilities by maintaining military and police forces. Those who would dispute their country's military position, must also ask themselves what their nation would be like without laws, policemen, or prisons.

Before sin, Adam lived in fellowship with God with no need of laws. When he rejected the authority of his Father, sin entered the world. We are Adam's seed, and sin has been passed down to all of us. Jesus laid down His life that we might be forgiven and restored to God. He will one day reign on earth as King of Kings. Until then, God has established governments to restrain the wickedness of man. Unregenerate society, without any restraints, would destroy the righteous along with itself. God's laws rule men's hearts, and governments enforce laws (Romans 13:1-5).

As individuals, we are required to forgive those who sin against us; and as citizens of earthly governments, to support our government's enforcement of the law. Although war is a terrible course to take, the alternative is far worse: allowing evil to overtake one's country. Sometimes wars must be fought to bring justice to bear. Wars will remain until Christ returns and sets up His kingdom of peace in the earth. At that time, war shall be no more. "And he shall judge among the nations, and shall rebuke many people: and they shall beat their swords into plowshares, and their spears into pruninghooks: nation shall not lift up sword against nation, neither shall they learn war any more" (Isaiah 2:4).

Father, we know that You hate war, but You also hate what evil men do to innocent men, women, and children; therefore, wars come when good men take a stand against evil. May You grant all who fight in righteous causes Your grace, wisdom, strength, and ability to overcome evil. Give righteous rulers and leaders Your wisdom as they direct the course of war. Protect those who are on the battlefields. Bless their families and give them comfort and faith in Your ability to keep those who call upon You! May we prevail in every righteous cause and stand united behind all those who must pursue the course of war to overcome evil. I ask this in Jesus' name. Amen.

July 13 — *Day 194*

Proverbs 20:19-21 19 He that goeth about as a talebearer revealeth secrets: therefore meddle not with him that flattereth with his lips. 20 Whoso curseth his father or his mother, his lamp shall be put out in obscure darkness. 21 An inheritance may be gotten hastily at the beginning; but the end thereof shall not be blessed.

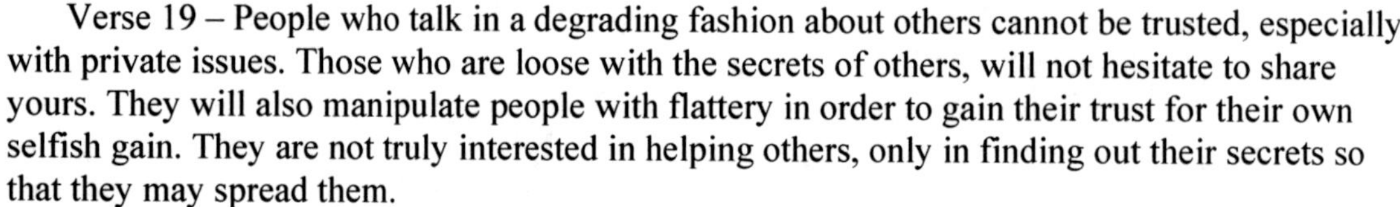

Verse 19 – People who talk in a degrading fashion about others cannot be trusted, especially with private issues. Those who are loose with the secrets of others, will not hesitate to share yours. They will also manipulate people with flattery in order to gain their trust for their own selfish gain. They are not truly interested in helping others, only in finding out their secrets so that they may spread them.

Verse 20 – Although the basic meaning of the word used for *"curse"* can include "to wish or to speak evil," the basic meaning here is "to esteem lightly."[25] Many people say they are not guilty of cursing their parents, but they may not consider that they are esteeming them lightly. According to the Hebrew meaning of this verse, to disrespect or disobey one's parents is actually to curse them. One of the Ten Commandments tells us to honor our father and mother, so that our days may be long upon the earth (Exodus 20:12).

"Children, obey your parents in the Lord: for this is right. Honour thy father and mother; which is the first commandment with promise; That it may be well with thee, and thou mayest live long on the earth" (Ephesians 6:1-2). According to verse 20, the penalty for cursing one's parents is that the children will lose their guidance in this dark world (their lamp will be put out). If we cannot see the proper path to walk down, we will end up on the wrong path which leads to destruction.

Verse 21 – Greed can lead people to obtain their inheritances underhandedly. An inheritance obtained unjustly will not give the benefit expected of it. Genesis tells how Jacob gained his brother Esau's inheritance by deceiving their father. It cost him the loss of a relationship with his brother and many years of living in fear that Esau would kill him for his act of treachery. The whole incident caused years of heartache for the entire family. Jacob also later reaped treachery from his own sons and suffered bitterly when they sold their youngest brother into slavery. The Bible teaches us to value relationships more than riches or material things.

Dear Father, thank You for my wonderful friends and family. May I always value these gifts of love and never violate them. I want to be the kind of friend that is trustworthy, one who can keep a secret. Guard my mouth and let me only speak things that are edifying and needful. May I always respect my parents and elders and give them honor. Lord, may I treasure my relationships and value them above material things. If I lose things, they can be restored; but if I lose a relationship because I cause a brother to be offended, I may never win their trust again. Help me to remember that my relationships are the most valuable thing I have. I ask this in the name of the Lord Jesus Christ. Amen.

[25] Strong's Exhaustive Concordance of the Bible, Hebrew and Chaldee Dictionary

Proverbs 20:22-23 23 Say not thou, I will recompense evil; but wait on the LORD, and he shall save thee. 23 Divers weights are an abomination unto the LORD; and a false balance is not good.

Verse 22 – Vengeance belongs to God, not man. God knows how to deal with all injustice. A number of scriptures instruct us not to repay evil for evil, but to wait on God to deal with our enemies and any injustice done to us (Romans 12:17-21).

Our natural reaction to injustice is to retaliate with vengeance. It is impossible for us, in our own strength, to repay evil with good. Yet, the Lord teaches that we are to rise above evil and not return wickedness to anyone. We are to show the world that God's children are different from the devil's. When we are lied about, we are to tell the truth and trust God to defend us, even if by telling the truth we become vulnerable. If a spouse, neighbor, co-worker, or anyone else should lose their temper against us, we are not to respond in the same way, but with "a soft answer" that "turns away wrath." We can do these things only through the power of the Holy Spirit.

"But and if ye suffer for righteousness' sake, happy are ye: and be not afraid of their terror, neither be troubled; But sanctify the Lord God in your hearts: and be ready always to give an answer to every man that asketh you a reason of the hope that is in you with meekness and fear: Having a good conscience; that, whereas they speak evil of you, as of evildoers, they may be ashamed that falsely accuse your good conversation in Christ" (1 Peter 3:14-16).

If vengeance or resentment arises in our hearts, we must call out to God to cleanse us from those evil traits and to give us His love and solution to the problem. He has the power to change other people's attitudes toward us if we keep our hearts right. He sees all that is happening, and He will rescue us if we cry out to Him in faith. He can change any heart designing evil against us or change the circumstances surrounding any problem in our favor if we trust Him and ask Him to forgive and bless those who are persecuting us.

Verse 23 – We have looked at this subject of a false balance in two previous proverbs (Day 67 and Day 168). When Scripture repeats something it is not by accident. The Lord is emphasizing a subject and wants us to pay close attention. Cheating others of what is rightfully theirs by using false standards is a vile thing to the Lord. God loves honest dealings and truth, and He hates robbery and deception. We ought to be careful not to cheat in any matter, no matter how seemingly insignificant. Everything we say and do affects our character and relationships. God desires us to be faithful in little matters so that we will be trustworthy in great ones. "He that is faithful in that which is least is faithful also in much: and he that is unjust in the least is unjust also in much" (Luke 16:10).

Dear heavenly Father, I want to be like You, so help me to react with Your love when someone does something evil toward me. I confess that I cannot do this in myself, but I ask that You give me the love, understanding, and patience that I need to overcome evil with good. Jesus forgave those who crucified Him, even in the midst of His agony; let me remember what You did on the cross, when I need to forgive trespasses done against me. Lord, empower and sustain all of Your children through their trials. We all need Your grace to overcome and be like You. I ask this in the name of Jesus, my Lord. Amen.

Proverbs 20:24-25 24 Man's goings are of the LORD; how can a man then understand his own way? 25 It is a snare to the man who devoureth that which is holy, and after vows to make inquiry.

Verse 24 – Why was I born and what is my purpose in life? This question is one of the oldest asked by mankind. Man was created by God and his "goings" are laid out by Him. He created us to be like Him. Without God, we cannot understand life; why we were born, or where we are going. God created us to know Him personally. "Now this is eternal life: that they may know you, the only true God, and Jesus Christ, whom you have sent" (John 17:3).

Sin separates every human being from God. With Jesus' blood, He purchased our salvation. By His death, burial, and resurrection, He broke the power of sin and death over us, making it possible for us to have everlasting life. "For God so loved the world that He gave His only begotten Son, that whosoever believeth in Him should not perish, but have everlasting life" (John 3:16). To have eternal life, we must repent of our sins and ask Jesus to come into our hearts. When we do this by faith, we are "born again" into the family of God and given His nature; we become a child of God. He will then show each of us our part in the scheme of His world.

In the Bible, we receive revelation about how God wants us to act and what we are to do. He shows us how we are to help others know His love and goodness. He gives us understanding, and shows us what steps in our walk with Him we are to take daily. When we make mistakes and fall, He helps us to get up and walk on with Him. "The steps of a good man are ordered by the LORD: and he delighteth in his way. Though he fall, he shall not be utterly cast down: for the LORD upholdeth him with his hand" (Psalm 37:23-24). As we follow Him, He will show each of us our part in His plan for creation. We each have a unique gifts and God has a plan and purpose to use us and our gifts.

Verse 25 – This verse warns us to be careful about what we tell God we will do. The Lord desires that we be like Him, and this includes keeping our word. Many people promise God that they will do something, but then fail to do it. It is bad enough when we treat other people this way, but when we do this in regard to holy things, it is a serious matter. We are to reverence God, and not treat Him lightly. The Lord is merciful when we fail, but we should not tempt Him by making promises to Him that we can not keep. We should be very serious about any vows we make to God. "When thou vowest a vow unto God, defer not to pay it; for he hath no pleasure in fools: pay that which thou hast vowed. Better is it that thou shouldest not vow, than that thou shouldest vow and not pay. Suffer not thy mouth to cause thy flesh to sin; neither say thou before the angel, that it was an error: wherefore should God be angry at thy voice, and destroy the work of thine hands?" (Ecclesiastes 5:4-6).

Dear Father, thank You for saving my soul. I am so glad that You are my Father and I can come to You, no matter what kind of problem I have. You are always so kind and merciful to me when I fail, and I do appreciate it. Help me to walk in the straight and narrow and not take steps that are out of the way. I want to please You and have my steps ordered by You. Show me what You would have me to do and then strengthen me to do it. Also, help me to guard my mouth and not to promise things to others what I am not able to perform. I ask this in the name of Jesus. Amen.

Proverbs 20:26-28 26 A wise king scattereth the wicked, and bringeth the wheel over them. 27 The spirit of man is the candle of the LORD, searching all the inward parts of the belly. 28 Mercy and truth preserve the king: and his throne is upholden by mercy.

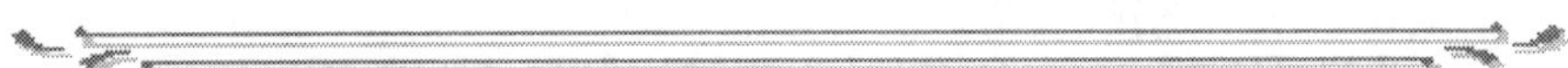

Verse 26 – This verse uses illustrations from ancient agriculture. Threshing with a sledge was a method of separating chaff from grain. The sledge consisted of three or four heavy rollers or "wheels" of wood, iron, or stone joined together in a square frame formed into a sledge. The driver sat on a seat affixed to its top, his weight helping to keep the heavy wheels close to the ground. As oxen dragged the sledge over harvested grain, the husks (chaff) cracked and separated from it.

A good ruler "winnows out" corrupt members of his government and "brings the wheel" over them. He applies pressure to separate the double-minded from the righteous, so that justice prevails. John the Baptist described Jesus as the ultimate King: "Whose fan is in his hand, and he will thoroughly purge his floor, and gather his wheat into the garner; but he will burn up the chaff with unquenchable fire" (Matthew 3:12). The Lord Jesus also told a parable about the separation of wheat from tares–the removal of the wicked from His kingdom when He returns to reign over all the earth (Matthew 13:24-40).

Verse 28 – A ruler's government can be upheld only by his people's loyalty. When good men rule in our governments, supporting what fosters truth, integrity, and mercy, we should gratefully support them. Those of us that are blessed to have a part in electing our leaders should pray for guidance to make the right choices and to see which candidates support what the Bible upholds. We are accountable before God for how we vote, or if we do not vote.

Verse 27 – God created us as spiritual beings (Genesis 2:7), and our spirit is like a lamp by which He searches us. Every thought and intent of our heart is clearly visible to God. Until we see that we are made in God's image, we cannot begin to understand ourselves. Man is a trichotomy: spirit, soul, and body. God is a trinity: Father, Son, and Holy Spirit. We cannot fully understand this mystery, but perhaps through some analogies we can gain an understanding both of Him and ourselves. A man might be a father, a husband, and a son; one man with three different roles. He relates to his children, wife, and parents in different ways. In the same way, God relates to us in three different roles. In another example, we see that water can be a solid, liquid, or vapor, and yet it is still one compound. God is seen as Jesus, who was in a physical body; He can be felt like rivers of living water as the Holy Spirit, and He is known as our Father. Jesus is the Word of God, through whom the Father is revealed. Man is a spirit who has a soul (mind, will, and emotions), and lives in a body. Though separable; man's body, soul, and spirit are interconnected and comprise one being. Thus, man reflects the triune God.

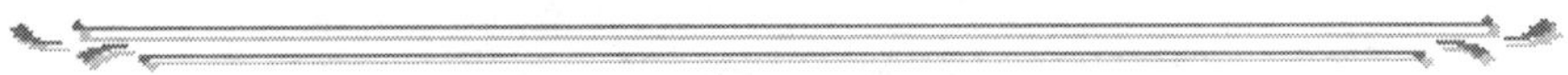

Dear Father, thank You for the wisdom revealed in the wonderful book of Proverbs. Help us to heed it in all of our business affairs, being especially careful not to neglect our civil duties, such as voting. Give us Your wisdom and guidance as we go to the polls. Let us see the candidates with Your eyes and hear them with Your ears. May we not be so traditionally tied to a political party that we would be blinded and not see the things You would have us see in the men and women running for the various offices. Let us look at issues and people with Biblical principles in mind, so that we vote for the things that You approve of. I ask this in the name of Jesus. Amen.

Proverbs 20:29-30 29 The glory of young men is their strength, and the beauty of old men is their gray head (suggesting wisdom and experience.) 30 Blows that wound cleanse away evil, and strokes (for correction) reach to the innermost part (AMP).

Verse 29 – All societies need the strength of younger men and the experience of older men to thrive. Cultures that reject this truth, waste priceless resources locked within older citizens. Some people in America are waking up to this and tapping into a wealth of knowledge to everyone's benefit. The knowledge, insight, and experience of older men can expand, release, improve, and turn into workable possibilities the ideas of younger men. Younger men can implement and bring into working reality the ideas of older men, often physically constrained. This proverb points out the complementary strengths of the generations. The old and the young need each other.

Many societies are suffering the consequences of young men being raised without a father figure. These young men are dysfunctional and others are aimless. Proverbs 22:28 says, "Remove not the ancient landmark, which thy fathers have set." This means that children should not tear down the parameters that their fathers have set. Fathers know from experience many things that are harmful, as well as what will and will not work. This can also apply to mothers as well. Titus 2:1-5: "But speak thou the things which become sound doctrine: That the aged men be sober, grave, temperate, sound in faith, in charity, in patience. The aged women likewise, that they be in behaviour as becometh holiness, not false accusers, not given to much wine, teachers of good things; That they may teach the young women to be sober, to love their husbands, to love their children, To be discreet, chaste, keepers at home, good, obedient to their own husbands, that the word of God be not blasphemed."

The church is to be built on the foundation of the apostles and prophets (Ephesians 2:19-20). Many people are being deceived and embracing false doctrines because they have failed to build on the doctrine of Christ which He established through His apostles and prophets of old, as recorded in the Bible, and taught through today's ministers. "...Build yourselves up [founded] on your most holy faith..." [Jude 1:20 (AMP)]. "Obey them that have the rule over you, and submit yourselves: for they watch for your souls, as they that must give account..." (Hebrews 13:17). "Likewise, ye younger, submit yourselves unto the elder. ---- and be clothed with humility: for God resisteth the proud, and giveth grace to the humble" (1 Peter 5:5).

Verse 30 – Correction, in the form of blows aimed at rebellious actions has a cleansing effect on the soul. Some strong-willed children need a spanking to get the message across. In no way do I advocate beating a child. This is not scriptural. To give a good swat on the buttocks, however, is not beating a child. Such discipline has helped many a child to listen to his parents, saving him from danger. "He that spareth his rod hateth his son: but he that loveth him chasteneth him betimes" (Proverbs 13:24).

Dearest Father, I pray today for the gap between the generations to be healed. May fathers have Your wisdom in dealing with their children, and young men honor their elders. Lord, convict fathers to be good role models for their children and love them with Your love. Your discipline is never to destroy us, but to turn us away from things that are harming us. May fathers look to You to learn how to deal with their rebellious children. Give the children and young men submissive spirits so that they heed their father's good advice and offer their strength to help their fathers. I ask this in the name of Jesus. Amen.

God's Wisdom for Daily Living *Betty Miller*
July 18 *Day 199*

Proverbs 21:1-2 1 The king's heart is in the hand of the LORD, as the rivers of water: he turneth it whithersoever he will. 2 Every way of a man is right in his own eyes: but the LORD pondereth the hearts.

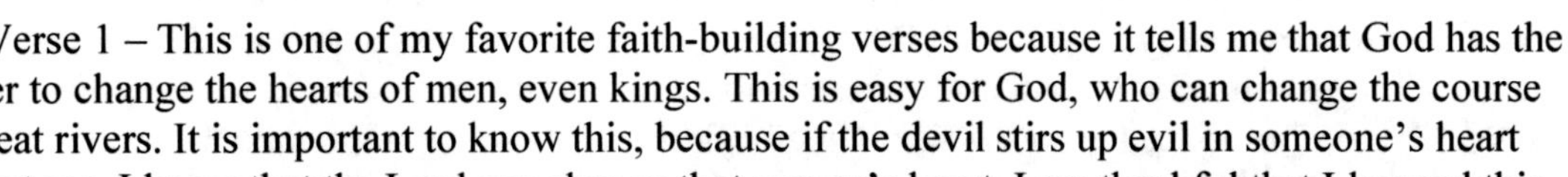

Verse 1 – This is one of my favorite faith-building verses because it tells me that God has the power to change the hearts of men, even kings. This is easy for God, who can change the course of great rivers. It is important to know this, because if the devil stirs up evil in someone's heart against me, I know that the Lord can change that person's heart. I am thankful that I learned this truth early in my walk with God! I have watched God turn nasty situations around many times in my life. Frequently, the very people the enemy used to come against me later apologized for their behavior.

One of the greatest lessons that the Lord taught me is to immediately turn to Him in prayer whenever a problem comes up in my relationships with people and ask why it is happening. First, I examine my own heart. I ask God if any of my actions or attitudes caused the problem, and if I need to ask forgiveness or change anything. I have learned to humble myself first before God and then before the angry party. If I am not at fault in a situation, I am careful to maintain an attitude of love and respect toward them, and trust God to defend me. I've seen hearts softened toward me when I practice overcoming evil with good (Romans 12:19-21) and took the position of trusting Him to defend me, even as Jesus did (1 Peter 2:21-23). Contention comes from pride (Proverbs 13:10). If we humble ourselves and refuse to be contentious, God will defend us. He will take bad situations and turn them into something good for us, which brings glory to Him!

Verse 2 – People do what is right in their own eyes, but God looks into our hearts to see what *motivates* us. Good deeds may be done out of the desire for man's approval or attention rather than out of love and the true desire to serve. Sometimes our deeds may not appear worthwhile to others, but if we are obediently serving God, He is pleased–and that is all that really matters. A mother who stays home to raise her children in the nurture and admonition of the Lord may be derided by other women set on pursuing their careers. However, God looks at the commitment of the stay-at-home mom as she ministers to her children and is well pleased, seeing the heart of a mother who puts her children before herself. It is not wrong for women to work outside the home; some women have no choice, being the sole providers for their families. However, the point is that God sees our hearts and judges us by what He finds there. We can rely on God absolutely, for He is omniscient (knows all things), omnipresent (everywhere present at the same time), and sovereign over all things.

Dear Father in heaven, thank You for always being there. I want to keep my heart right before You and the people whom You have placed in my life. Please forgive me when I fail to do the right thing. Help me to be kind toward others–especially my own family, and to overcome the fear of what people think. I want to be more concerned about what You think. I know that You look at my heart and see things that are not pleasing to You. I submit to You the right to deal with those things and remove them from my life. Help me to be meek and lowly like You, and not to allow pride to keep me from communicating with those with whom I would rather not have to deal. Fill me with Your love and wisdom in all my relationships. I humbly ask this in Jesus' name. Amen.

God's Wisdom for Daily Living ***Betty Miller***
July 19 ***Day 200***

Proverbs 21:3-4 3 To do justice and judgment is more acceptable to the LORD than sacrifice. 4 An high look, and a proud heart, and the plowing of the wicked, is sin.

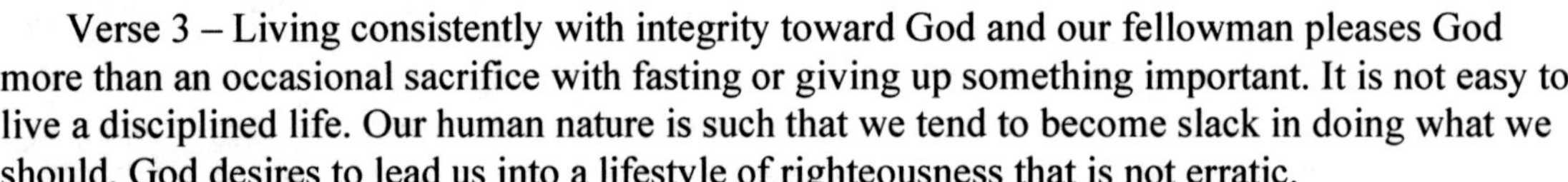

Verse 3 – Living consistently with integrity toward God and our fellowman pleases God more than an occasional sacrifice with fasting or giving up something important. It is not easy to live a disciplined life. Our human nature is such that we tend to become slack in doing what we should. God desires to lead us into a lifestyle of righteousness that is not erratic.

Sometimes we think outward actions, such as good works, giving tithes and offerings, etc, are sufficient to please God. God, however, desires a relationship with us. Sacrifices may help us live unselfishly and uprightly before God, but they should not be motivated by a desire to pacify Him or to earn His love. They should be the natural results of loving Him and walking in faith and obedience with Him. "Woe unto you, scribes and Pharisees, hypocrites! For ye pay tithe of mint and anise and cummin, and have omitted the weightier matters of the law, judgment, mercy, and faith: these ought ye to have done, and not to leave the other undone" (Matthew 23:23).

Verse 4 – Pride causes a man to feel that he is above others, thus looking down on them, revealing that he considers himself superior to them. Earlier in Proverbs, we found a list of seven things that are an abomination to God. A proud look heads the list: "These six things doth the LORD hate: yea, seven are an abomination unto him: A proud look, a lying tongue, and hands that shed innocent blood. An heart that deviseth wicked imaginations, feet that be swift in running to mischief, A false witness that speaketh lies, and he that soweth discord among brethren" (Proverbs 6:16-19). God resists the proud and exhorts us to humble ourselves before Him. "...God resisteth the proud, but giveth grace unto the humble. Submit yourselves therefore to God. Resist the devil, and he will flee from you. Draw nigh to God, and he will draw nigh to you ...Humble yourselves in the sight of the Lord, and he shall lift you up" (James 4:6-7).

Where the King James reads "plowing" in verse 4, the Amplified Bibles reads "tillage or lamp of joy." The good things in this world, like food (tillage) and entertainment (lamp of joy), can become stumbling blocks for us, if we do not honor God in them. God made these things for us to enjoy. However, if we pursue them with our time and money so that we have little time to spend with God or to do His will, they become sin to us. Jesus said that if we seek first His kingdom and righteousness, that all those things would be added unto us (Matthew 6:31-33). Pride in any form will cause us to sin and set us up for a fall. "For all that is in the world, the lust of the flesh, and the lust of the eyes, and the pride of life, is not of the Father, but is of the world. And the world passeth away, and the lust thereof: but he that doeth the will of God abideth for ever" (1 John 2:16-17).

Dear heavenly Father, thank You for supplying all of my needs. Help me to always trust You. I don't want to worry about having a supply of food and clothes and the other things that I need in this world, but to just seek You and Your will in my life daily. I want to be more concerned about having a pure heart in Your sight than any material thing. Lord, I humble myself in Your sight and ask You to remove all pride and critical attitudes from my heart. Give me a heart of mercy and love for others and most of all, I want to always love You and follow You in all things. I ask this in the name of Jesus. Amen.

Proverbs 21:5-6 5 The thoughts of the diligent tend only to plenteousness; but of every one that is hasty only to want. 6 The getting of treasures by a lying tongue is a vanity tossed to and fro of them that seek death.

Verse 5 – Prosperity begins with our thought life. Negative thinking stunts us and our circumstances, while positive thoughts and a good outlook cause us to flourish. The Bible tells us that whatever is manifested in our lives has a deeper origin, that is our hearts (Proverbs 23:7a). Man is a spirit; he has a soul, and he lives in a body. Thoughts occur in the mind, but it is the spirit-man that influences the mind. The spirit within the diligent person fuels his thoughts and brings forth creativity. He learns all that he can to better himself and his life. He considers how to work more efficiently and considers practical and serious matters. His thoughts lead to prosperity.

Many non-Christians are extremely diligent, while many Christians are not diligent at all. This should not be. Christians should be diligent to seek God and to walk in His ways, becoming diligent also in practical matters. When "born again," we are given a new nature, by which we have access to the Holy Spirit, and the mind of Christ. The devil will try to tempt us by putting evil ideas in our minds and tempting us through our old natures. But in Him, we have the power to cast down imaginations and bring our thoughts captive to Christ. Thereby we put the devil to flight (2 Corinthians 10:3-5).

The Lord told Solomon that He would bless him so that he would have an inheritance for his children, if he would serve God with a perfect heart and a willing mind (1 Chronicles 28:9). Since we are diligent to follow God, He will guide our thoughts so that we will prosper in all our ways. Those who are impatient to gain wealth only bring themselves to poverty. This principle is illustrated by gambling. Gamblers waste their money on attempts to become rich quickly. Instead of pondering how to better themselves, they constantly speculate on new strategies or invest in "get-rich-quick" schemes. They squander money that could have been invested wisely, and thus they only end up robbing from themselves.

Verse 6 – Unscrupulous methods of trying to get wealth by lying will lead a person down a path to death. The Bible tells us that we will reap what we sow. A modern expression is "what goes around, comes around." If a person lies, others will lie to him. Thieves tend to run with thieves, and liars with liars. There is no honor among thieves; since they are ultimately looking out for their own advantage; and some will not even stop at murder to get their desires.

Dear Father in heaven, thank You for giving me Your guidelines for every area of my life. I know that when I follow Your ways I will enjoy blessings in this life. Help me to be honest in all of my dealings with money so that I will be blessed. Forgive me when I have put money into the wrong things. Lord, forgive those who have stolen from me and taken advantage of me. I look to You to restore what was lost. Help me to be wise and not be tricked into using my money in the wrong ways. May I use my money and resources to not only take care of my responsibilities; but to also give, to help others and to help get the gospel out to the world. I ask this in Jesus' name. Amen.

Proverbs 21:7-8 7 The robbery of the wicked shall destroy them; because they refuse to do judgment. 8 The way of man is froward and strange: but as for the pure, his work is right.

Verse 7 – Because the wicked know what is right but refuse to do it, their own violence will sweep them away. Those who live by violence perish by it. Everyone reaps what he sows (Galatians 6:7-9). Whatever we "plant" will grow to produce a crop. When we choose to follow our old nature (sow to our flesh), our words and actions produce no lasting benefits and lead to death. If we choose to walk (or sow) to the Spirit, our words and actions will produce life and eternal reward. If we invest in God's work, one of our rewards will be that we will get to meet people in heaven whom we helped to know the Lord. This passage also tells us not to be weary in well doing, for we will reap in time, if we faint not.

Satan tries to discourage us when we see the wicked prosper and it seems that our prayers are unanswered. But we must keep our eyes on Jesus and His promises, not our circumstances. That is what faith is: believing God's truth and not allowing Satan to rob our confidence in Him. "I have seen the wicked in great power, and spreading himself like a green bay tree. Yet he passed away, and, lo, he was not: yea, I sought him, but he could not be found. Mark the perfect man, and behold the upright: for the end of that man is peace" (Psalm 37:35-37).

Verse 8 – Those who are crafty are always looking for ways to cover up their wrongs. Their ways are convoluted and shifty. Honest people are straightforward, without pretense. Their work is exactly what it is supposed to be; there is no trickery. Man is crooked by nature. We all try to hide our sins and mistakes. We cannot change until we receive God's forgiveness. Upon receiving Jesus into our hearts, we become pure in God's sight. All the privileges of God's children become available to us. The Holy Spirit purifies our thinking. We no longer desire our old life. The evil we once loved, we now hate. It is a wonderful miracle that God can make us pure and good like Himself!

Psalm 32:10 tells us that the wicked will have many sorrows, but those who trust in God will be surrounded by mercy. The last verse of Psalm 23 also speaks of mercy, and has always blessed me: "Surely goodness and mercy shall follow me all the days of my life …" I used to wonder why this scripture spoke of goodness and mercy as following, rather than as leading us. The Lord showed me that goodness and mercy are always behind us to catch us and pick us up when we fall. When do we need God's goodness and mercy? After we have made a mistake and fallen down. When we trust God, He is right there to help us up so that we can continue to walk with Him. God goes before us and is behind us and on every side. How great is His love for us!

Dear Father, I love You so much. You have been so good to me. Thank You for Your goodness to me over the years. I have not deserved Your great patience, but I am thankful that You were there for me every time I fell down and every time I failed You. Thank You for picking me up, forgiving me and washing me clean so I could start again on that narrow path where my careless feet went astray. Help me to be merciful like You, to those in my life who need Your mercy through me. Give me grace not only to forgive others but to love them as You have loved me. I ask this in the precious name of Jesus. Amen.

Proverbs 21:9-10 It is better to dwell in a corner of the housetop (on the flat oriental roof, exposed to all kinds of weather) than in a house shared with a nagging, quarrelsome and faultfinding woman. 10 The soul or life of the wicked craves and seeks evil; his neighbor finds no favor in his eyes (AMP).

Verse 9 – In ancient Israel, houses were built with flat roofs surrounded by a low protective wall to prevent falls. The roof was considered the best part of the house because it was spacious and cool. It was used as a special room. It was on the roofs of their houses that the people of ancient Israel transacted business, met with friends, housed special guests, prayed, kept watch, made announcements, erected booths, slept in summer, and laid their dead before burial. This proverb says that dwelling in a corner of the housetop exposed to bad winter weather would be preferable to sharing a house with a nagging and quarrelsome person! Choosing a spouse is one of the biggest decisions we will make in life and one that can result in much joy or much grief. As a man or woman of God, we need to carefully seek God when choosing a marriage partner, as we saw in Day 122 and Day166. This is why it is so important to seek God diligently in regard to this decision. We should never enter into it without much prayer. To rush into a marriage can be disastrous. This happens sometimes when people allow just their emotions to rule them. "Feeling in love" is not the gauge for entering into a lifelong relationship. If our emotions and mind (our soul) have not been cleansed, we can be led astray by them. Our feelings of love can really be lust. The definition of love is, "God is love."

What this world calls love is really lust, since it is built on what the other person does for me, and not what I can do for him or her. If one person fails to keep up their end of the bargain, a divorce occurs because the offended mate is no longer pleased. This is the attitude of the world's so-called "love." God, however, loves without receiving back. His love is forgiving and patient. His love is gentle and kind. His love waits, and makes sacrifices for the other. This is the character needed in both mates to make a marriage work. None of us really know how to love until we experience and practice God's love. 1 Corinthians 13 gives us a good definition for real, Christ-like love. The word "charity" is the King James Version's term for love. If we put our name in the place of "charity" in this chapter we can see if we pass the test of possessing true love.

Verse 10 – Wicked people seek the opposite of God's will. They actually enjoy doing what is evil. They are completely selfish and without regard for anyone but themselves. If you have ever lived next door to a covetous or greedy person, or next to a haughty or prejudiced person, you know that wicked people are difficult neighbors. You can never please them. While there simply is no fellowship between darkness and light, good and evil; we are, however, called to pray for those around us who are evil so that they might come to know Jesus as their Savior.

Dear heavenly Father, I am grateful for all the guidelines You have given us in this wonderful book of Proverbs. Help me to heed the warnings and apply the wisdom that I find in these pages. I pray that I will walk as a godly woman; a blessing to all those around me. Forgive me when I fail to be gracious and become impatient with people. May I apply Your love, wisdom, and goodness to all of my daily affairs. Lord, draw the lost souls in my neighborhood to Your saving grace. Use me to be a witness to them. I am claiming their souls for Your kingdom I ask these things in the name of Jesus Christ. Amen.

God's Wisdom for Daily Living ***Betty Miller***
July 23 ***Day 204***

Proverbs 21:11-12 11 When the scorner is punished, the simple is made wise: and when the wise is instructed, he receiveth knowledge. 12 The righteous man wisely considereth the house of the wicked: but God overthroweth the wicked for their wickedness.

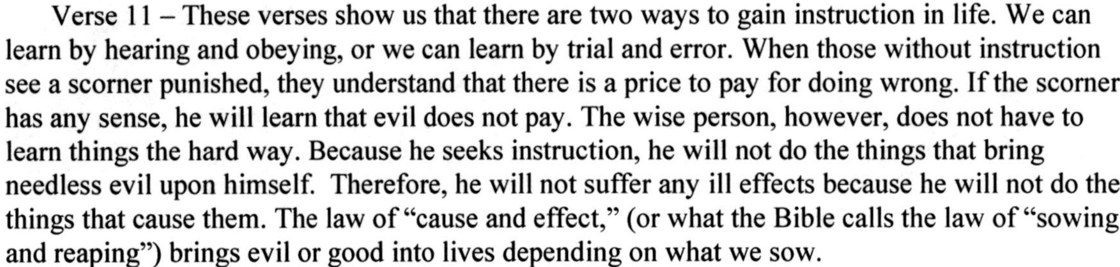

Verse 11 – These verses show us that there are two ways to gain instruction in life. We can learn by hearing and obeying, or we can learn by trial and error. When those without instruction see a scorner punished, they understand that there is a price to pay for doing wrong. If the scorner has any sense, he will learn that evil does not pay. The wise person, however, does not have to learn things the hard way. Because he seeks instruction, he will not do the things that bring needless evil upon himself. Therefore, he will not suffer any ill effects because he will not do the things that cause them. The law of "cause and effect," (or what the Bible calls the law of "sowing and reaping") brings evil or good into lives depending on what we sow.

God is often blamed for things that He did not cause. He has set limits and boundaries; and when we violate them, we cause problems for ourselves. God does not bring those problems upon us. We bring them upon ourselves. For instance, if we are speeding down the road in our car, and we get pulled over by a policeman, it would be stupid to blame the car or the policeman for our ticket. It is our own fault. We can avoid much of the pain we suffer in this world by simply obeying Him.

Some people declare they learned a lot through their tragic experiences. In many cases, however, the same lessons could have been learned by studying and obeying God's Word. For example, I do not have to learn the truth that "the way of transgressors is hard" (Proverb 13:15) by committing some evil and suffering for it. I can simply believe that what the Bible says is the truth, and commit no transgression. The Lord loves us and His commandments were given for our protection.

Verse 12 – The wicked are destroyed by reaping what they have sown (Psalm 9:16a). They may live many years before they are brought to ruin, and many foolish observers may be tempted to think it pays to follow in their ways. The righteous, however, wisely observe the wicked man's actions, and know that eventually God will judge him. His ruin, when it comes, will not be worth all his years of ease and luxury. The Lord advises us to follow Him in willing obedience; not like a mule that must have a bit and bridle in its mouths to guide it. "I will instruct thee and teach thee in the way which thou shalt go: I will guide thee with mine eye. Be ye not as the horse, or as the mule, which have no understanding: whose mouth must be held in with bit and bridle, lest they come near unto thee. Many sorrows shall be to the wicked: but he that trusteth in the LORD, mercy shall compass him about" (Psalm 32:8-10).

Dear heavenly Father, I praise and thank You for hearing and answering my prayers. Lord, help me stay on the straight and narrow path so that I do not go down the wrong roads and have to learn the hard way. Lord, I know that when I diligently seek You, that You will answer me and save me from many pitfalls. Help me to avoid the things that will cause me pain and trouble in the future. I want to hear Your voice so that I can make wise decisions and avert many of the traps and tribulations that the enemy wants to use to destroy me. Keep me from evil, and help me to trust You. Please give me the strength to obey You in all things. I ask this in Jesus' name. Amen.

Proverbs 21:13-14 13 Whoso stoppeth his ears at the cry of the poor, he also shall cry himself, but shall not be heard. 14 A gift in secret pacifieth anger: and a reward in the bosom strong wrath.

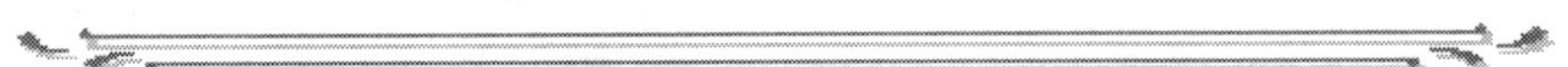

Verse 13 –We can ignore the plight of those less fortunate than we, but if we do, our cries for help will likewise be ignored when we have a need. To ignore something is to refuse to look at it. We may pass by needy people as if they do not exist, but remember, we reap what we sow. We don't know what kind of trials we may face in the future. Someday, we may greatly need someone to be merciful to us. In a sense, we can "store up" mercy so that the Lord will be merciful to us when we need it. "Blessed are the merciful: for they shall obtain mercy" (Matthew 5:7). If we show mercy to the poor and weak, the Lord will move people to help us in our time of need. "Therefore to him that knoweth to do good, and doeth it not, to him it is sin" (James 4:17). Failing to help the poor is to commit a sin of omission. True faith in God causes us to reach out to the poor and helpless. "If a brother or sister is poorly clad and lacks food for each day, And one of you says to him, Goodbye! Keep (yourself) warm and well fed, without giving him the necessities for the body, what good does that do? So also faith if it does not have works (deeds and actions of obedience to back it up), by itself is destitute of power–inoperative, dead" (James 2:15-17 AMP).

Verse 14 – The dictionary defines "bribe," as "something, such as money or a favor, that is offered or given to a person in a position of trust in order to influence that person's views or conduct.[26]" The wording of this verse suggests underhanded dealing between the parties involved. The silence (or cooperation) of people without morals can be easily bought. Money was not as widely used in ancient times as today; and items of value, or "gifts" were often used as bribes. Today, the wicked use monetary bribes as gifts or pay-offs to deal with people's anger. We think of a bribe as something only wicked people such as mobsters might employ, but the principle of bribery can be subtle. Giving a child a treat or a toy to stop a tantrum is really a form of bribery. The adult uses a treat to bribe the child into good behavior, and the child learns to use his bad behavior to get what he wants. The adult is twice guilty in such a case: first, guilty of not loving the child enough to teach him to obey out of respect, and secondly guilty of teaching the child to disrespect his parent and bring a curse upon himself. We need the Holy Spirit's help to diligently follow God's ways.

Dear Father God, I appreciate all that You have given me. Lord, please help me to overcome any selfishness or insecurity that would keep me from giving to the poor and needy. Help me to be sensitive to the needs of others and not just concerned about my own needs. Also, let me not neglect to pray for those who may not have anyone praying for them. I do pray for my family and friends, but Lord, enlarge my heart to reach out beyond my circle of relationships, that I may pray for and give to those needs that You show me. Let me always be merciful to those who need mercy and I thank You for the many times that You have shown mercy to me. I ask this in the name of Jesus. Amen.

[26] The American Heritage Dictionary of the English Language, Fourth Edition

Proverbs 21:15-16 15 It is joy to the just to do judgment: but destruction shall be to the workers of iniquity. 16 The man that wandereth out of the way of understanding shall remain in the congregation of the dead.

Verse 15 – When the word "judgment" is mentioned, it usually brings to mind the execution of the penalty for sin. However, there is another side to judgment. We can see from Galatians 6:7-9 and Revelation 20:12-13 that sowing evil reaps a judgment of destruction, while sowing good reaps a judgment of reward. This is true for both individuals and nations.

In America, we have sown both good and evil. I believe God has been merciful to us because we have helped other nations. The American Church has sent many missionaries around the world. Our nation has supported humanitarian works in every nation. The U.S. government has poured billions of dollars into foreign aid and forgiven other countries of billions of dollars of debt. We are usually among the first on the scene with assistance when natural disasters strike other countries. We have helped rebuild the infrastructures of nations ravaged by war. Many more things could be named that America has done for others throughout the world.

America has also sown much evil. We have exported ungodly music, movies, and pornography among other things. We have hypocritically called ourselves a "Christian nation," yet we allow abortion and other evils to be legalized. Many Americans are drug addicts and others are consumed with pornography. Many commit adultery without blushing and are sex-crazed. I have noticed that the most prevalent types of e-mail ads are marketing something pertaining to sex, or becoming a millionaire, or some form of gambling. Sharing Christ with other nations is difficult when they see our rampant lust and materialism. Our culture has been shot through with every type of sin and temptation designed by Satan to keep us weak and powerless. God desires to bless us with good, but our sins prevent God from blessing us. Judgment comes upon us as we reap what we have sown. "Your iniquities have turned away these things, and your sins have withholden good things from you" (Jeremiah 5:25).

Verse 16 – Destruction awaits those who fail to understand that we are all being judged by God's Word. When we fail to keep His commandments, we are judged in that respect. When we honor His word we are judged as faithful. There is one way to avert destructive judgment: by walking in relationship with Jesus and allowing the Holy Spirit to convict us of sin. When we repent, we no longer come under judgment, because Jesus received the penalty of our sins on the cross. We must pray that the church comes to true repentance that will produce genuine revival in our nations and the world: "And if any man hear my words, and believe not, I judge him not: for I came not to judge the world, but to save the world. He that rejecteth me, and receiveth not my words, hath one that judgeth him: the word that I have spoken, the same shall judge him in the last day" (John 12:47-48).

Dear Father in heaven, thank You for Your great mercy to us individually, and to our nations. Father, move on the hearts of Your people to repent and turn back to You, so that we can avert any evil judgments on our land. Forgive us for our apathy and sin. Lord, help us to study Your Word, pray Your Word, speak Your Word and walk in Your Word. Use us, Your children, to bring light into this dark world by showing others the way to Christ. I ask this in the name of Jesus Christ. Amen.

Proverbs 21:17-18 17 He that loveth pleasure shall be a poor man: he that loveth wine and oil shall not be rich. 18 The wicked shall be a ransom for the righteous, and the transgressor for the upright.

Verse 17 – Pleasure-seekers will not become rich. Thousands waste money by making entertainment, partying, gambling, or illicit sexual encounters a lifestyle. Those who make pleasure their god, become addicts to pleasure. They become enslaved to the thing that initially gave them happiness. Virtues such as unselfishness, serving others, and saving, quickly disappear when a person's world revolves around pleasure. This verse does not refer to occasional celebrations, but warns against living for continual pleasure.

Verse 18 – The schemes of the wicked against the righteous often end up turning against them. The story of Esther exemplifies this as recorded in the book of Esther in the Bible. Beautiful Esther, keeping her Jewish identity a secret, was made Queen to King Ahasuerus, king of the Persian empire. Because of his commitment to God, Esther's uncle, Mordecai, refused to bow to Haman, the king's chief official. In revenge, Haman plotted to kill not only Mordecai, but also all of the Jews. The king gave Haman authority to create the edict and Haman sent orders throughout the empire that all the Jews were to be destroyed on a certain date.

Mordecai informed Esther of Haman's actions, asking her to plead with the king for her people. Esther agreed to try, even though the king might have her put to death. She instructed Mordecai to have all the Jews in Susa pray and fast for her for three days before she went to the king. Because of their prayer and fasting, Ahasuerus was favorable to Esther. Esther requested that he and Haman come to a banquet she had prepared. At the banquet, Esther asked that he and Haman return the next day to another banquet, saying she would present her petition then. As he went home, Haman, proud that only he had been invited to accompany the king to the queen's banquet, took offense again at Mordecai. That night he had a gallows built on which to have Mordecai hanged.

That night, Ahasuerus had the records of memorable deeds read to him and discovered that Mordecai had once saved his life, but never been rewarded. The king asked Haman what should be done for a man that the king wanted to honor. Thinking that the King meant to honor him, Haman told the King that the he should be dressed in the king's royal apparel, a crown placed on his head, and led through the city by one of the King's princes, on the king's own horse. Ahasuerus then told Haman to do all this for Mordecai. Haman went home in bitter humiliation. After this, he was summoned to Esther's second banquet, where Esther revealed Haman's plot against the Jews, and petitioned for her people. In the end, Haman was hanged on the very gallows that he had prepared for Mordecai; thus illustrating the Biblical principle that the wicked will fall into the pit that they dig for the righteous. God will always have the last word.

Dear heavenly Father, I do thank You for all the wonderful things You have given me to enjoy in this life; however, I never want to be guilty of allowing those things that bring pleasure to become more important to me than the things that are important to You. May I always put You and Your will first in my life. Lord, even as Esther went before the King, to petition for her people at the very threat of her life, may I be as courageous as she was. If the occasion should ever arise that I would need to stand up for others in the face of danger, let me do so with strength and honor. I ask this in the name of Jesus. Amen.

Proverbs 21:19-20 19 It is better to dwell in the wilderness, than with a contentious and an angry woman. 20 There is treasure to be desired and oil in the dwelling of the wise; but a foolish man spendeth it up.

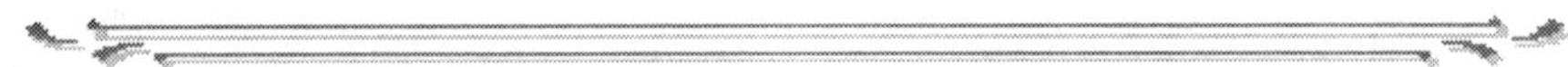

Verse 19 – Usually, a wilderness or desert is a harsh environment, and there are not many people dwelling there. In essence, this verse is saying that there are many things worse than living alone, and one of them is living with the wrong person such as an angry woman. King Solomon usually wrote from a man's perspective, addressing his proverbs to his sons and other men. Of course, the same warning applies to women also. A woman should not marry a man with a bad temper, who is also without character.

Verse 20 – When Scripture speaks of oil, it is usually referring to olive oil, which was a very valuable commodity in Biblical times. It was used as a medium of exchange, and was the evidence of prosperity. Having oil meant a person had the necessities to make his home comfortable. Olive oil was used for cooking, lamps, as an ingredient in cosmetics and medicinal compounds, to anoint the body after bathing, and to anoint the dead for burial. In the temple, it was offered with certain sacrifices. It was also used to keep the lamp of the tabernacle, and later, the lamps of the temple, burning at all times. The priests also used it to prepare a holy oil for anointing purposes.

The wise man stores up supplies and precious treasure. His "precious treasure" consists of more than material things; it includes intangibles such as peace and joy. A wise man does what it takes to create a godly and joyful environment for his family. He considers his family a precious treasure and treats them that way. The foolish man, on the other hand, is lustful and wasteful. Being self-indulgent, he consumes his resources with no thought of saving. The Bible calls this lasciviousness. "For from within, out of the heart of men, proceed evil thoughts, adulteries, fornications, murders, thefts, covetousness, wickedness, deceit, lasciviousness, an evil eye, blasphemy, pride, foolishness: all these evil things come from within, and defile the man" (Mark 7:21-23). When we come to the Lord Jesus, He will deliver us from these things if we ask Him to do so.

Wastefulness is a sin which abounds especially in affluent societies. Those with many possessions often think nothing of throwing away what is perfectly good, without considering that it might be useful to the less fortunate. They may feel that it is too much trouble to fix something or find another use for it. Resourceful people, for example, might tear up old clothes that can not be worn, and use them for cleaning rags. Jesus Himself practiced frugality. On two occasions of multiplying food, He ordered His disciples to gather up the remains (Matthew 14:20; and 15:37). A wise man will have plenty, but a foolish, wasteful man who wastes resources, will have nothing.

Dearest Father in heaven, I am grateful that You have given me a good mate who is gentle and kind. I am very blessed. I do pray for my brothers and sisters in Christ who are going through marital problems of all kinds. Give them Your love and grace to overcome their relationship problems. May they discover that the secret to a happy marriage is laying down one's life for the other, praying for the other, preferring the other–honoring and loving them. Lord, we cannot change people, but You can. May each of us ask for the changes needed in our own lives first. In doing that, we trust You to give us the love and patience to deal with any problems in our

relationships. Give us Your wisdom and help us to overcome any waste in our lives. I ask this in Jesus' name. Amen.

Quotes About Gossip

It is emotional violence to speak ugly things about others. Scripture warns us to guard our mouths and speak only what is edifying, for we reap the effects of our words. --Day 60

As we grow in Him, we will not want to expose people's sins but rather to cover them. Digging up and exposing the sins of others has always been a popular pastime of the ungodly. --Day 61

As Christians, we should not listen to gossip, since that makes us party to it. If the one that is being talked about is not there to defend himself, it is not a fair conversation. --Day 138

Just as ingested food becomes part of one's body, ingested gossip becomes part of one's thoughts and opinions. --Day 157

People who talk in a degrading fashion about others cannot be trusted, especially with private issues. --Day 194

When we lie or gossip, our negative words go out into the spiritual dimension to unleash destructive power. We must learn to speak what is good and pray for everyone, even our enemies, so that our words release blessing. --Day 274

Proverbs 21:21 He that followeth after righteousness and mercy findeth life, righteousness, and honour.

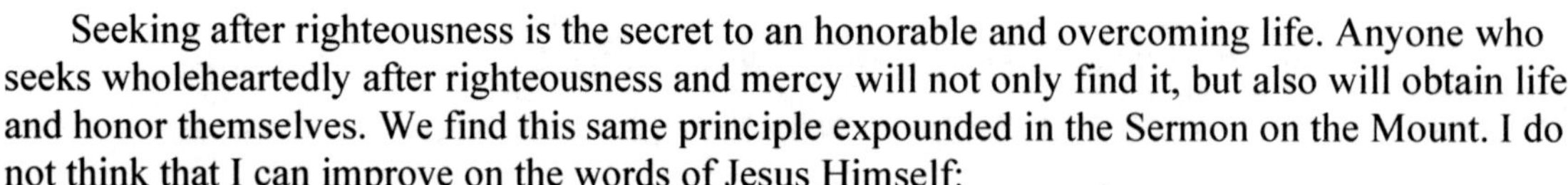

Seeking after righteousness is the secret to an honorable and overcoming life. Anyone who seeks wholeheartedly after righteousness and mercy will not only find it, but also will obtain life and honor themselves. We find this same principle expounded in the Sermon on the Mount. I do not think that I can improve on the words of Jesus Himself:

"And he opened his mouth, and taught them, saying, Blessed are the poor in spirit: for theirs is the kingdom of heaven. Blessed are they that mourn: for they shall be comforted. Blessed are the meek: for they shall inherit the earth. Blessed are they which do hunger and thirst after righteousness: for they shall be filled. Blessed are the merciful: for they shall obtain mercy" (Matthew 5:2-7).

"Therefore take no thought, saying, What shall we eat? or, What shall we drink? or, Wherewithal shall we be clothed? (For after all these things do the Gentiles seek:) for your heavenly Father knoweth that ye have need of all these things. But seek ye first the kingdom of God, and his righteousness; and all these things shall be added unto you" (Mathew 6:31-33).

The Biblical definition of righteousness means to be in right standing with God. If we are in right standing with God, we will then be in right standing with people, since the Lord will always lead us to do the right thing in relation to others. The Bible is very clear that we cannot love God whom we have not seen, if we do not love our brother that we can see. If we love God, we will love others also.

"If any one says, I love God, and (detests, abominates) hates his brother (in Christ), he is a liar: for he who does not love his brother whom he has seen, cannot love God whom he has not seen. And this command (charge, order, injunction) we have from Him, that he who loves God shall love his brother (believer) also" (1 John 4:20 AMP).

Righteousness and mercy are so important in God's economy that when we seek His kingdom and His righteousness first, it will bring us life and honor. We can also rest assured that the Lord will provide for our material needs since that is His promise to us.

Dear Father in heaven, I am grateful for all of Your promises in the Bible. Since You are not a man that You would lie, I know that I can confidently trust You to keep Your Word. Help me to obey You, for I know that in doing so, I shall receive Your promises. I desire to be righteous and holy. I know that I cannot attain this without You, but with the Holy Spirit I am able to do all things through Christ Jesus. I am asking in faith that You help me to follow You in everything so that I bring honor to You. In Jesus' name I pray. Amen.

God's Wisdom for Daily Living ***Betty Miller***
July 29 ***Day 210***

Proverbs 21:22 A wise man scales the city walls of the mighty and brings down the stronghold they trust (AMP).

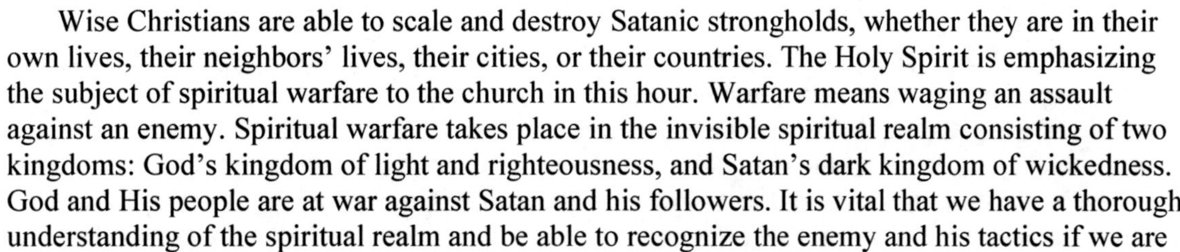

Wise Christians are able to scale and destroy Satanic strongholds, whether they are in their own lives, their neighbors' lives, their cities, or their countries. The Holy Spirit is emphasizing the subject of spiritual warfare to the church in this hour. Warfare means waging an assault against an enemy. Spiritual warfare takes place in the invisible spiritual realm consisting of two kingdoms: God's kingdom of light and righteousness, and Satan's dark kingdom of wickedness. God and His people are at war against Satan and his followers. It is vital that we have a thorough understanding of the spiritual realm and be able to recognize the enemy and his tactics if we are to obtain victory.

Do ye look on things after the outward appearance?" (1 Corinthians 2:9-14). If so, it will never suffice. We cannot rely on the appearance of things in the natural; the spiritual realm influences everything in it. We are not to walk after the flesh but the Spirit (Romans 8:4). If we walk close to Him, He will give us discernment in the spiritual realm and we will understand what is really happening in the natural. We will begin to see things correctly. At church, for example, we will properly perceive one another as brothers and sisters in Christ. Instead of focusing on other's faults and shortcomings, we will be set to help each other overcome any weaknesses, supporting each other with prayer and lovingkindness.

Warfare begins on a personal level as we learn to reign in our own lives, crucifying our old natures and yielding to Christ. Unless we are victorious in our personal lives, we will never be able to help others gain their victories, much less be able to battle spiritually for our cities and nation. To win our spiritual battles, we must learn to use God's armor and sword (Ephesians 6: 10-18) and be aggressive against our enemy, Satan. We cannot be passive. We must take the offensive, casting down Satan's strongholds in our thinking and perceptions (lining up our thinking and speaking with God's Word instead of agreeing with Satan's lies) and overcoming evil with good.

"For though we walk in the flesh, we do not war after the flesh: (for the weapons of our warfare are not carnal, but mighty through God to the pulling down of strongholds;) casting down imaginations, and every high thing that exalteth itself against the knowledge of God, and bringing into captivity every thought to the obedience of Christ" (2 Corinthians 10:3-5). We can do mighty things for God as we take the enemy's strongholds and bring them down through prayer and fasting. Truly, God is calling His people to rise up in this hour!

Father, help me to be a strong warrior and not shrink back from spiritual warfare. In James 4, You told us to submit to You, and to resist the devil and he would flee. Lord, I voice my submission to You, to do Your will. Now, I know the devil flees at Your Word, so I say to the enemy: "Satan, I resist you in the name of Jesus and command you to leave me, my family and my ministry. You are defeated and have no authority in my life; therefore, you must flee with your temptation, division, sickness, and every evil thing you would try to bring against me and those whom I am praying for. No weapon formed against me shall prosper! Be gone in the name of Jesus!" Thank You, Lord, that You gave us victory over the devil and all of his plans. Amen.

Proverbs 21:23-24 23 He who guards his mouth and his tongue keeps himself from troubles. 24 The proud and haughty man–scoffer is his name–deals and acts with overbearing pride (AMP).

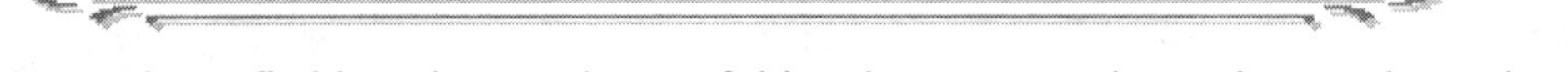

Verse 23 – It is profitable to learn to be careful in what we say, since wise words can keep us from trouble. There is another scripture in the New Testament that elaborates on this:

"… If any one does not offend in speech–never says the wrong things–he is a fully developed character and a perfect man, able to control his whole body and to curb his entire nature. If we set bits in the horses' mouths to make them obey us, we can turn their whole bodies about. Likewise, look at the ships: though they are so great and are driven by rough winds, they are steered by a very small rudder wherever the impulse of the helmsman determines. Even so the tongue is a little member, and it can boast of great things. See how much wood or how great a forest a tiny spark can set ablaze! And the tongue is a fire. [The tongue is a] world of wickedness set among our members, contaminating and depraving the whole body and setting on fire the wheel of birth (the cycle of man's nature), being itself ignited by hell (Gehenna). For every kind of beast and bird, of reptile and sea animal, can be tamed and has been tamed by human genius (nature). But the human tongue can be tamed by no man. It is a restless (undisciplined, irreconcilable) evil, full of deadly poison. With it we bless the Lord and Father, and with it we curse men who were made in God's likeness! Out of the same mouth come forth blessing and cursing. These things, my brethren, ought not to be so. Does a fountain send forth [simultaneously] from the same opening fresh water and bitter? Can a fig tree, my brethren, bear olives, or a grapevine figs? Neither can a salt spring furnish fresh water" (James 3:2-12 AMP).

We all say things that we regret later. When we do, the only way to correct the situation that we created is to admit that what we said was wrong and apologize for it. This is difficult to do, but it will win us more respect than allowing pride to rule us and refusing to admit that we were wrong.

Verse 24 – Man's pride is delicate and he will become defensive and easily offended if provoked (unless he yields to the Holy Spirit). This is why proud people become angry easily and are overbearing. No one likes an arrogant, domineering person. We must ask God to forgive and change us if we tend to demean and control others. God resists the proud but gives grace to the humble. May we all learn, therefore, to humble ourselves before Him! "Likewise, ye younger, submit yourselves unto the elder. Yea, all of you be subject one to another, and be clothed with humility: for God resisteth the proud, and giveth grace to the humble. Humble yourselves therefore under the mighty hand of God, that he may exalt you in due time" (1 Peter 5:5-6).

Dear heavenly Father, I am thankful for Your grace and mercy toward me. I need help in the area of guarding my lips. Give me the grace to keep my mouth shut when I should not speak, and give me the holy boldness to speak up when I need to do so, without fearing what others will think about me. May I be a person who blesses others and not one who curses others with a negative confession. Cleanse my heart, O Lord, so that I will not even want to speak evil or bad things. I humble myself before You, Lord, and ask for a meek and lowly spirit like Jesus, our Savior. In His name I pray. Amen.

Proverbs 21:25-27 25 The desire of the slothful killeth him; for his hands refuse to labour. 26 He coveteth greedily all the day long: but the righteous giveth and spareth not. 27 The sacrifice of the wicked is abomination: how much more, when he bringeth it with a wicked mind?

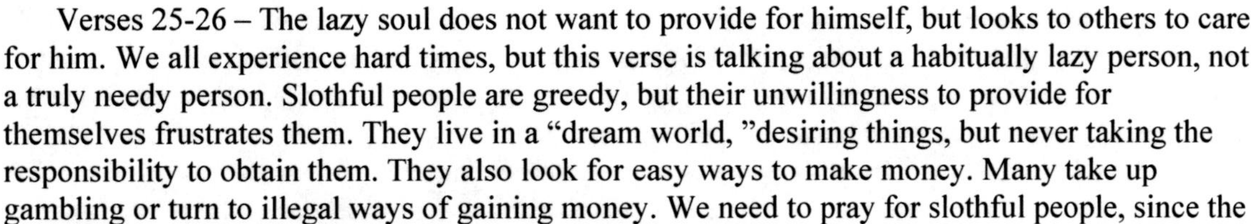

Verses 25-26 – The lazy soul does not want to provide for himself, but looks to others to care for him. We all experience hard times, but this verse is talking about a habitually lazy person, not a truly needy person. Slothful people are greedy, but their unwillingness to provide for themselves frustrates them. They live in a "dream world, "desiring things, but never taking the responsibility to obtain them. They also look for easy ways to make money. Many take up gambling or turn to illegal ways of gaining money. We need to pray for slothful people, since the Lord desires to change their lives and give them a desire to work.

The righteous man is entirely different; he reaches out and gives. He does not try to withhold those things that he is able to help others with. He does not have to be told to help others because his new nature in Christ desires to give. Jesus demonstrated God's own selfless nature. God did not withhold His most precious possession (His own Son), but sacrificed Him, so that all who turn to Him could be saved: "For God so loved the world, that he gave his only begotten Son, that whosoever believeth in him should not perish, but have everlasting life" (John 3:16).

Verse 27 – When the wicked make a sacrifice to appease God without truly surrendering to Him, it is an abomination in the eyes of God. People often use gifts to win approval. It may work with man, but not with God. God cannot be "bought." There is only one thing that will move the hand of God, and that is our faith and obedience. When a person gives up something in order to manipulate God; it constitutes a form of "tempting God." When the Pharisees tried this, God did not respond favorably to them. "And the Pharisees came forth, and began to question him, seeking of him a sign from heaven, tempting him. And he sighed deeply in his spirit, and saith, Why doth this generation seek after a sign? verily I say unto you, There shall no sign be given unto this generation" (Mark 8:11-12).

The Pharisees had no intention of accepting Jesus. They tempted Him to act on His own to prove Himself, and not in submission to the Father's will. They echoed their father, the devil, who had tempted Jesus to throw Himself from the temple, inferring that when the people saw the angels rescue Him, they would believe that He was the Messiah.

Because God knows what is in the heart of every person, we cannot fool Him about our intentions. As Jesus showed us, the only way to come to God is in total surrender to His will. He then will answer our questions and also answer our prayers. In fact, He will answer any prayer prayed in faith (1 John 3:22) that is in line with the Word of God.

Dear Father, I am thankful that You hear us when we pray, and I know that You will answer those prayers that are according to Your will. I know that what You have stated in Your Word is Your will; therefore, I can confidently ask You for those things and You will not turn me down. Help me not to waver in faith when I pray, but believe in Your goodness and willingness to answer all that I ask in Jesus' name. Deliver me from all unrighteousness, and grant me grace to keep Your commandments. Give me the desire to study Your Word more, so that I know how to pray. I ask this in the name of Jesus. Amen.

Proverbs 21:28-29 28 A false witness shall perish: but the man that heareth speaketh constantly. 29 A wicked man hardeneth his face: but as for the upright, he directeth his way.

Verse 28 – A man that listens to the wisdom of God attentively will endure, since God's Word is the final authority. False witnesses lie under oath and are punished when found out. A man who listens attentively to God's Word understands and obeys it and will not lie. An honest man respects others enough to pay attention to what they say and so can accurately relate what he hears. His testimony is dependable and stands up in court.

Since the book of Proverbs is about wisdom, one of the main things it stresses is to give thought to what we speak and what we listen to. Most of us have probably seen the portrayal of three monkeys, each with its hands over a different part of its head. One has his hands over his ears, another covers his eyes, while the last one covers his mouth. The caption beneath the picture says, "Hear No Evil, See No Evil, and Speak No Evil." This little analogy is actually proclaiming Biblical advice. If we practiced this admonishment, it would keep us out of a lot of trouble. Honesty is a virtue that we all should walk in. "Take heed therefore how ye hear: for whosoever hath, to him shall be given; and whosoever hath not, from him shall be taken even that which he seemeth to have" (Luke 8:18).

Verse 29 – The wicked man has hardened himself against his conscience and trained himself to remain expressionless when doing evil. His frozen face betrays no twinge of guilt. A righteous man, on the other hand, directs his way by heeding God's Word. He has nothing to hide and his face reflects that. Years ago, I heard an interview with an old-time political figure. The reporter commented on his good memory and asked him how he was able to remember the promises he had made, and to whom he had made them, without contradicting himself concerning what he had told different people. He replied, "That's easy! When you tell the truth, you never have to remember any lies you told, that would require additional lies to cover them." Walking in truth, and maintaining integrity, should be the goal of every Christian.

Dear Father, thank You for giving us Your Word in the Bible. Help me to read and study it more. Lord, I not only want to hear what You have to say, but I also want to do the things You have instructed us to do in the Word of God. Give me Your grace to be obedient to Your Word. Lord, I also ask You to help me not to listen to things that I should not hear. Give me grace to turn my eyes away from those things that hinder my growth in You. I know if I see and listen to Your Words, then I will be able to speak the things I need to say. I ask this is the name of Jesus. Amen.

God's Wisdom for Daily Living — ***Betty Miller***
August 2 — ***Day 214***

Proverbs 21:30-31 30 There is no wisdom or understanding or counsel (that can prevail) against the LORD. 31 The horse is prepared for the day of battle, but deliverance and victory are of the LORD (AMP).

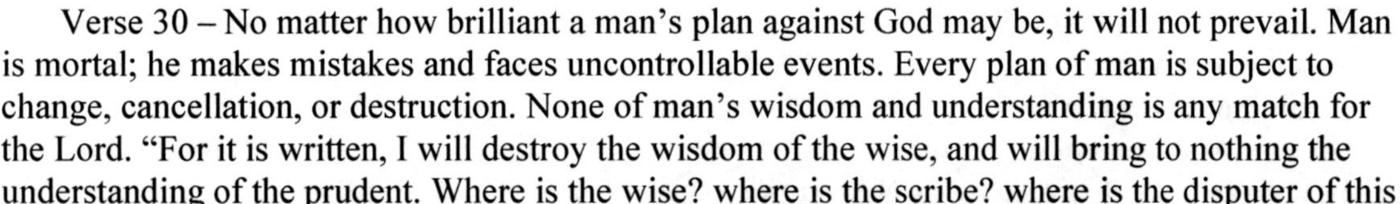

Verse 30 – No matter how brilliant a man's plan against God may be, it will not prevail. Man is mortal; he makes mistakes and faces uncontrollable events. Every plan of man is subject to change, cancellation, or destruction. None of man's wisdom and understanding is any match for the Lord. "For it is written, I will destroy the wisdom of the wise, and will bring to nothing the understanding of the prudent. Where is the wise? where is the scribe? where is the disputer of this world? Hath not God made foolish the wisdom of this world?" (1 Corinthians 1:19-20). All plans of God are guaranteed success, as Romans 8:31b says: "If God be for us, who can be against us?"

"But if ye have bitter envying and strife in your hearts, glory not, and lie not against the truth. This wisdom descendeth not from above, but is earthly, sensual, devilish. For where envying and strife is, there is confusion and every evil work. But the wisdom that is from above is first pure, then peaceable, gentle, and easy to be entreated, full of mercy and good fruits, without partiality, and without hypocrisy" (James 3:15-17). Man's wisdom is based on selfishness, while God's wisdom is pure and impartial. God calls each of us to die to our own desires and ways and live according to His. How wonderful it would be if we would all trust God and obey His Word!

Verse 31 – The horse symbolizes a country's strength in warfare. It is not wrong to prepare an army for the defense of a nation, because we live in a world of evil men and we must be prepared to protect ourselves. This is true for all emergency situations. We should be prepared in case something happens. Because of man's propensity to error, and because we live in a fallen world, we make mistakes that can create the need to instigate emergency measures. However, we should remember that our real protection comes from God. Ultimately, no matter how formidable a battle looks, and no matter how well prepared we might be, the outcome and victory of that battle rests in our faith in the Lord and His capabilities.

"Blessed is the nation whose God is the LORD; and the people whom he hath chosen for his own inheritance...There is no king saved by the multitude of an host: a mighty man is not delivered by much strength. An horse is a vain thing for safety: neither shall he deliver any by his great strength" (Psalm 33:12,16-17).

Dear heavenly Father, thank You for Your protection and blessing upon us in this land. Forgive us for the many ways in which we have failed and sinned against You. I am reminded of Psalm 20:7 which says, "Some trust in chariots, and some in horses: but we will remember the name of the Lord our God." Dear Lord, bring revival to our land and heal us. Work in my own heart, and give me a more sacrificial spirit that will give up things I want to do and do only Your will. Let revival begin in me. I ask this in the name of the Lord, Jesus Christ. Amen.

Proverbs 22:1-2 1 A good name is rather to be chosen than great riches, and loving favour rather than silver and gold. 2 The rich and poor meet together: the LORD is the maker of them all.

Verse 1 – It is wise to choose a good name and God's favor over money. Solomon, who wrote this proverb from experience, could testify to this, since he was given a similar choice. At the beginning of his reign, God appeared to him in a dream, permitting him to ask for whatever he wanted. Solomon requested an understanding heart to serve his people. Because this request honored God, God also gave him riches, power, and honor (1 Kings 3:11-14).

Solomon had the loving favor of God upon him. The favor of God comes in many forms such as protection, health, blessing, and favor with people. In the New Testament, we find that Jesus had that favor on his life as He increased in wisdom (Luke 2:52). Situations often arise in which we must choose between obtaining better-paying positions or other advantages, versus honoring God. For example: Some jobs might offer large salaries, but require that we compromise our integrity, or God may call us to leave a lucrative business to preach His Word. God may not bless us with wealth such as Solomon's, but if we honor Him above worldly gain and prestige, and walk in fellowship with Him, He will bless us in this life with His favor and daily provision, and in the next life, with imperishable riches.

Verse 2 – In this world, the rich and poor have little in common and rarely meet. One day, however, all men will stand together before the judgment seat of God (Romans 14:11-12). There will be neither rich nor poor, only people giving accounts of their deeds to an impartial Judge. At that time, money will not do the rich any good, as they will not be able to "pay off" God for a favorable report about their lives. "For we must all appear before the judgment seat of Christ; that every one may receive the things done in his body, according to that he hath done, whether it be good or bad …" (2 Corinthians 5:10-11a).

Jesus is a righteous Judge, because He came to earth as a Man to save people, giving His life on the cross. He didn't come to judge people, but to save them. In eternity, we will be judged by our adherence (or lack thereof) to the Word of God and Jesus' commandments. If we confess our sins, He will forgive and cleanse us from all unrighteousness (1 John 1:8-9). We can look forward to seeing the Savior who loves us instead of dreading to face Christ on the Day of Judgment as a sinner to be condemned. "I am come a light into the world, that whosoever believeth on me should not abide in darkness. And if any man hear my words, and believe not, I judge him not: for I came not to judge the world, but to save the world. He that rejecteth me, and receiveth not my words, hath one that judgeth him: the word that I have spoken, the same shall judge him in the last day" (John 12:46-48).

Dear Father God, I am so grateful that You sent Your Son to die for my sins. Thank You for saving my soul, and writing my name in the Book of Life. Please use me to tell others that their names can be written in that same Book. If I forget to pray for the lost, please remind me to do so. I do not want to stand before You ashamed because I have failed in my witness on this earth. I want to hear those words, "Well done, thou good and faithful servant." Open my eyes and give me eternal vision so that the things of heaven are more important to me than just the things of the earth. I ask this in the name of Jesus Christ. Amen.

Proverbs 22:3-4 3 A prudent man foreseeth the evil, and hideth himself: but the simple pass on, and are punished. 4 By humility and the fear of the LORD are riches, and honour, and life.

Verse 3 – Prudence (the ability to make sound judgments), enables us to avoid Satanic entrapments. It develops as we grow in the knowledge of good and evil by daily walking with God and obeying the principles in His Word. Developing a sensitivity and instant obedience to God's voice is prudent, because God will warn us of evils that we have no way of knowing about apart from Him. Many Christians testify of having been saved from life-threatening situations because they heard a warning in their hearts from the Lord. The Bible is full of accounts of how the Lord preserved the lives of His children by warning them of danger. Even the life of Jesus, as a child, was saved when an angel of the Lord warned Joseph in a dream to flee Bethlehem (Matthew 2:13-14).

God warned Noah of the coming catastrophic flood, and told him how to build an ark and make provision for survival. God warned Lot and his family of the coming destruction of Sodom and Gomorrah and told them to flee. God warned a Pharaoh in Egypt, through a dream, to prepare for seven years of abundance that would be followed by seven years of famine in the days of Joseph. He warned the Israelites in Egypt that "the angel of death" would kill the first-born of every family and told them to place the blood of a lamb on the lintels and doorposts of their houses so that the destroyer would pass over them. God warned Nineveh of impending judgment through Jonah.

The Lord still warns individuals and nations today (through the Bible and His servants) to repent so that they will not be destroyed. When any nation's sins reach a certain level, judgment is inevitable if that nation does not repent. God does not desire to see any individual or nation destroyed by the fruit of their own sins. He even spared a heathen nation (the Amorites) for a while longer, until their cup of iniquity was full and He could no longer tolerate their sin. "But in the fourth generation they shall come hither again: for the iniquity of the Amorites is not yet full" (Genesis 15:16).

Verse 4 – We can escape destruction and find riches, and honor by humbling ourselves before the Lord. He wants to bless us. The curses coming upon our nations are not from Him, but are the result of rejecting Him and idolizing such things as materialism, lust, and perversion (Jeremiah 2:19). It is never too late to seek the Lord. He is loving and forgiving, and yearns to bring us into a "Promised Land" of safety and blessing. He Himself paid the penalty of our sins for us.

"Humble yourselves therefore under the mighty hand of God, that he may exalt you in due time: Casting all your care upon him; for he careth for you. Be sober, be vigilant; because your adversary the devil, as a roaring lion, walketh about, seeking whom he may devour: Whom resist stedfast in the faith, knowing that the same afflictions are accomplished in your brethren that are in the world. But the God of all grace, who hath called us unto his eternal glory by Christ Jesus, after that ye have suffered a while, make you perfect, stablish, strengthen, settle you" (1 Peter 5:6-10).

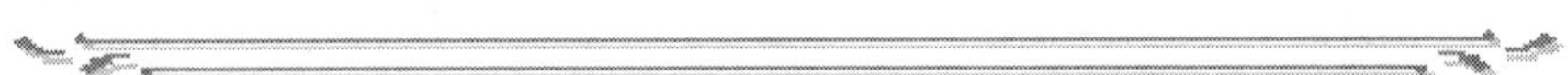

Dear heavenly Father, thank You for Your divine protection over me and my family. I am sure that You have kept me from harm more times than I know. Lord, help me to be prudent and wise in all of my actions, as I know that when I fail to hear You and proceed in an unwise path, I bring

suffering on myself. Lord, help me resist evil and overcome the temptations in my life through faith in the Lord Jesus Christ. Thank You for continued safety in these perilous times. May I hear Your warnings when I need to take action to avoid trouble and destruction. I ask this in the name of Jesus. Amen.

Quotes About Growing in God

Remember, hearing God has everything to do with proximity. --Day 177

To walk in truth, we must daily seek to know and obey Jesus better. The more we know Him, the more truth we know, and the more brightly shines the spiritual light in which we walk. --Day 224

To grow spiritually, we need the company of those who are at least as spiritually mature as we are. We should not befriend people simply because they are intelligent or even because they attend many church meetings. We should look for those who know and practice God's Word. --Day 226

One of the best habits we can develop is the habit of daily prayer and Bible reading, which enables us to draw spiritual strength from the Lord. --Day 358

We must take the responsibility of choosing to think about what is edifying and reject what is compromising. --Day 359

Quotes About Unity in Christ

God created us to need Him first of all, and then to need each other. --Day 81

All societies need the strength of younger men and the experience of older men to thrive. Cultures that reject this truth, waste priceless resources locked within older citizens. --Day 198

The Bible instructs us to lift one another up in encouragement and praise. We should esteem our fellow believers more highly than ourselves. --Day 299

God's Wisdom for Daily Living — *Betty Miller*

August 5 — ***Day 217***

Proverbs 22:5-6 5 Thorns and snares are in the way of the froward: he that doth keep his soul shall be far from them. 6 Train up a child in the way he should go: and when he is old, he will not depart from it.

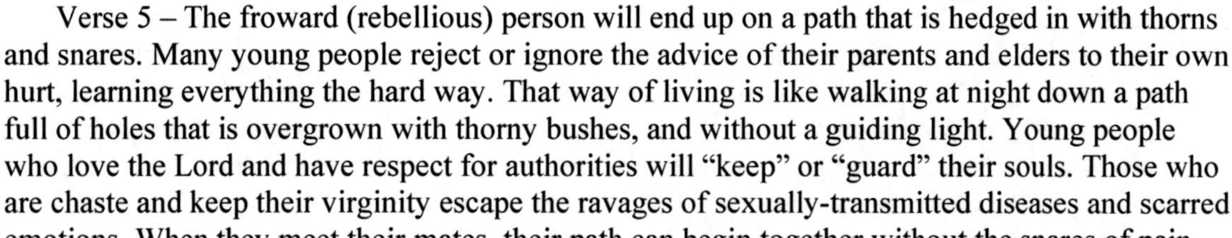

Verse 5 – The froward (rebellious) person will end up on a path that is hedged in with thorns and snares. Many young people reject or ignore the advice of their parents and elders to their own hurt, learning everything the hard way. That way of living is like walking at night down a path full of holes that is overgrown with thorny bushes, and without a guiding light. Young people who love the Lord and have respect for authorities will "keep" or "guard" their souls. Those who are chaste and keep their virginity escape the ravages of sexually-transmitted diseases and scarred emotions. When they meet their mates, their path can begin together without the snares of pain and guilt because they have no past sexual sins to mar their relationship.

Verse 6 – We are told in this verse to *"train"* up our children in the Lord. Many parents grieve over children who have gone astray from Christian teachings. They wonder why they do not walk in what they were taught. One possible reason is that they were not trained to walk in God's ways, but only *"told"* about the things of God. There is a big difference between teaching and training. The duty of parents is to help their children find the right path through teaching (giving information); and then to help them stay on the right path through training (integrating the teaching into the lifestyle); third, to pray and ask the Lord to help them recognize their children's God-given gifts and direct them into the callings He has for them. Training involves enforcing and reinforcing what is taught, and requires discipline, diligence, and commitment from parents. When parents abdicate the position of a mentor, their children derive their values from the world; from humanistic teachers in public schools, from baby-sitters, secular movies, videos, CDs, games, books, magazines, and last but not least, their own peers.

The Bible commands children to obey their parents in all things if they want to please the Lord. (Of course, this means in all moral and right things. There are corrupt parents who would ask their children to do evil things, and a child should not obey in those things.) Parents are also told not to provoke their children to anger, and thereby discourage them. Parents are to be kind and good to their children, since the Lord is kind and good to us, His spiritual children. "Children, obey your parents in all things: for this is well pleasing unto the Lord. Fathers, provoke not your children to anger, lest they be discouraged" (Colossians 3:20-21). If we call on Him, He will give us the wisdom, love, and patience to raise our children properly even in a wicked world, so that when they are grown, they will not depart from God's ways.

Dear heavenly Father, thank You for all You have done for my children and grandchildren. I am grateful that they all know You. It was Your love and grace that made it possible. I pray that You keep each of them in Your Hand and protect them from the evil influences in this world. Help me to continue to be a mentor and model for all of them; and most of all, help me to always show love to them. Lord, lead each of them into the ministry that You have ordained for them. May they find the right mate, so they can walk together in their life's calling. Protect them all. I ask this in the name of Jesus. Amen.

Proverbs 22:7-8 7 The rich ruleth over the poor, and the borrower is servant to the lender. 8 He that soweth iniquity shall reap vanity: and the rod of his anger shall fail.

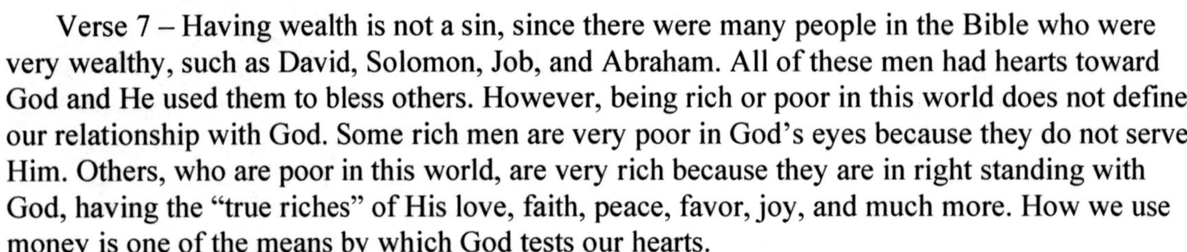

Verse 7 – Having wealth is not a sin, since there were many people in the Bible who were very wealthy, such as David, Solomon, Job, and Abraham. All of these men had hearts toward God and He used them to bless others. However, being rich or poor in this world does not define our relationship with God. Some rich men are very poor in God's eyes because they do not serve Him. Others, who are poor in this world, are very rich because they are in right standing with God, having the "true riches" of His love, faith, peace, favor, joy, and much more. How we use money is one of the means by which God tests our hearts.

Jesus said, "He that is faithful in that which is least is faithful also in much: and he that is unjust in the least is unjust also in much. If therefore ye have not been faithful in the unrighteous mammon, who will commit to your trust the true riches?" (Luke 16:10-11). I have observed over and over again that when a person fails in the small issues, he also fails in larger issues. People who say they will call right back and fail to do so will also fail to send the check they said they would send. (I am not referring to occasional oversights, since we all forget things occasionally, but of habitual failings.) When I was young, I had a neighbor who always blamed the untidiness of her apartment on the fact that it was too small to keep in order. She would complain to her husband that if he would just get her a bigger house, she would be able to keep it tidy. They finally did get a bigger house, but rather than keeping it nice, she just kept a bigger mess instead! I never give someone an important job, until I first see how they will handle a less important one, because I have found this scripture to be absolutely true.

Some people are waiting until they have more money to give their tithes and offerings. These persons will never have more money to give until they are faithful to give out of what they have. The Bible speaks of giving a tithe (ten-percent) to the Lord. We can give this much to the Lord's work, whether we have little or much. If I earn a dollar, I can give a dime to the Lord. Giving is one way in which we can get out of debt because it releases the favor of God toward us. Getting out of debt is always wise. As long as we are in debt, we are "servants" to those who have lent us the money. Because we must work to pay them back, we are, in a sense, working for them. Just as servants are not free to do as they would like to do, debt limits our ability to be free to go where the Lord calls us.

Verse 8 – Bad things are bound to happen to people who continually threaten others with angry words to get them to do things. These people are manipulators; however, in time, their angry words will fail to get them what they want, and people will finally leave them to their own devices.

Dear heavenly Father, thank You for Your abundant blessings! I am grateful to be rich with Your many spiritual blessings; and I also appreciate the material blessings that You have given me. You take good care of me, and I am grateful. Lord, I ask that You help all of Your people to get out of debt and stay out of debt. I pray this personally as well. I want to do what Your Scriptures say; in that I do not want to owe anyone anything except the debt of love–and I will gladly pay that debt. Help me to show integrity in all my dealings in regard to money and finances. May I be generous and always give to the work of the Lord and help others as well. I ask this in the name of Jesus. Amen.

Proverbs 22:9-10 9 He that hath a bountiful eye shall be blessed; for he giveth of his bread to the poor. 10 Cast out the scorner, and contention shall go out; yea, strife and reproach shall cease.

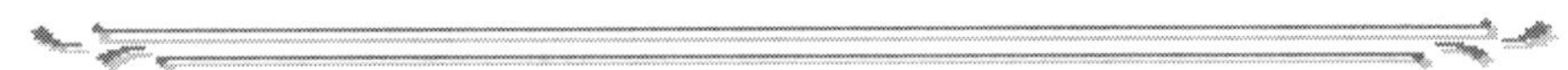

Verse 9 – One of the things Paul the Apostle said to the leaders of the church of Ephesus when he saw them for the last time, was that they should support the weak and poor. Paul reminded the leaders that he himself had given to others while ministering in Ephesus for three years and that Jesus had said that it is more blessed to give than to receive (Acts 20:33-35). Later, while in prison, he encouraged the Corinthian church to give cheerfully and not grudgingly, because God loves a cheerful giver. "But this I say, He which soweth sparingly shall reap also sparingly; and he which soweth bountifully shall reap also bountifully. Every man according as he purposeth in his heart, so let him give; not grudgingly, or of necessity: for God loveth a cheerful giver" (2 Corinthians 9:6-7).

God gives to us in the same way that we give to others. If we give generously, we will reap bountifully. If we give sparingly, that is the way we will reap. Someone who has a "bountiful eye" gives generously and graciously. People who give like that will always be blessed. When we give, we not only help those who are needy, but we also help ourselves, because God always repays a kindness. Continuous giving creates a wonderful cycle that blesses everybody. Sometimes we may be the giver, and sometimes we are the receiver. At times, we all need help. God did not make us to be totally independent. We need each other.

Verse 10 – Strife and contention break out when a scorner is among people. Scorners reject authority, thinking themselves more knowledgeable or capable than the person in authority. They incite others to murmur and complain, question and reproach those in authority, and contend about issues and take sides. To eliminate strife and contention the instigators of discontent must be dealt with. There are two ways to do this. One is to actually "drive out," or dismiss, the one who is the cause of the strife. The other is take that person aside, confront them about their behavior, and warn them that if they do not cease causing strife, corrective measures will be taken. Troublemakers, whether in the church, the office, or even the home, must be dealt with; not only to re-establish order, but to help the troublemaker. Since our goal is peace, not more strife, we must handle these situations with wisdom. Whether dealing with an adult or child, we must do so in love, with redemptive purposes in mind. We must also prepare ourselves first, praying for wisdom and insight, and then against any spirits of strife. We must remember that our real enemy is the devil, not people. If we will pray for the people involved and resist the devil, he will flee. "Submit yourselves therefore to God. Resist the devil, and he will flee from you" (James 4:7).

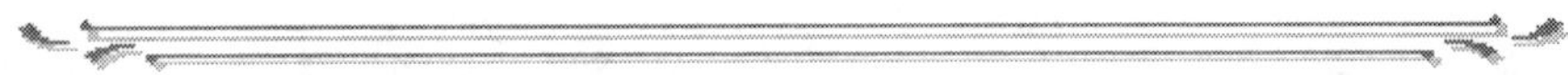

Dearest Father, I thank You for Your generosity to me. Help me to be sensitive to the needs of the poor and those around me. I want to be a bountiful giver and remember those who do not have the things that I have. Lord, may I always be generous to Your works and not take things for granted. Guide me as to where and how much I should give, so that I can bless others. I also ask You to help me avoid contention. Help me never to be one who would instigate strife. Give me the grace to deal with problem-people in a loving way. Father, help me to be generous and kind in every aspect of my life. In Jesus' name I pray. Amen.

God's Wisdom for Daily Living ***Betty Miller***
August 8 ***Day 220***

Proverbs 22:11-12 11 He that loveth pureness of heart, for the grace of his lips the king shall be his friend. 12 The eyes of the LORD preserve knowledge, and he overthroweth the words of the transgressor.

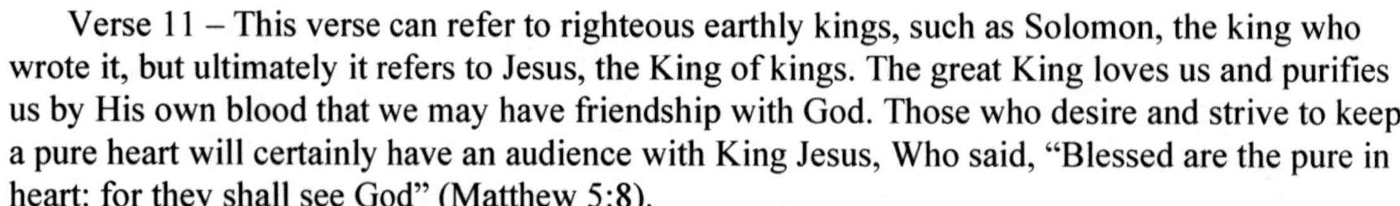

Verse 11 – This verse can refer to righteous earthly kings, such as Solomon, the king who wrote it, but ultimately it refers to Jesus, the King of kings. The great King loves us and purifies us by His own blood that we may have friendship with God. Those who desire and strive to keep a pure heart will certainly have an audience with King Jesus, Who said, "Blessed are the pure in heart: for they shall see God" (Matthew 5:8).

How do we keep our hearts pure? One must begin by acknowledging that one is a sinner, accepting Jesus as Savior, and asking for forgiveness. Even after we do this, there will still be sins, and sometimes strongholds, from which we must be delivered. We must ask God daily to cleanse our minds from things we embraced before we were born again. "For from within, out of the heart of men, proceed evil thoughts, adulteries, fornications, murders, thefts, covetousness, wickedness, deceit, lasciviousness, an evil eye, blasphemy, pride, foolishness: All these evil things come from within, and defile the man" (Mark 7:21-23). Our hearts are changed and we grow more like Jesus each time we overcome temptation. The more pure our hearts become, the more pure our speech will become.

"Let us draw near with a true heart in full assurance of faith, having our hearts sprinkled from an evil conscience, and our bodies washed with pure water. Let us hold fast the profession of our faith without wavering; (for he is faithful that promised;) And let us consider one another to provoke unto love and to good works: Not forsaking the assembling of ourselves together, as the manner of some is; but exhorting one another: and so much the more, as ye see the day approaching" (Hebrews 10:22-25).

Should we fail to resist a temptation, God will forgive us. However, if we keep yielding to sin and do not strive to resist it, our hearts can become a little more hardened against the things of God each time we sin. If this continues, we can harden our hearts to the point that God will withdraw His grace and allow us to suffer the fruit of our own sins.

Verse 12 – God not only preserves knowledge, but also those who have His knowledge. The Bible contains the knowledge that we most need. One reason why many Christians are overcome by the devil's tactics is their ignorance of God's Word. "My people are destroyed for lack of knowledge: because thou hast rejected knowledge, I will also reject thee, that thou shalt be no priest to me: seeing thou hast forgotten the law of thy God, I will also forget thy children" (Hosea 4:6). "Study to show thyself approved unto God, a workman that needeth not to be ashamed, rightly dividing the word of truth" (2 Timothy 2:15).

Dear heavenly Father, thank You for cleansing me from the impurities in my life. Lord, give me a desire to study Your Word and also give me revelation as I read it, so that I can be changed by Your Words. I know that Your words contain life, so help me to live by them. I ask You to cleanse my heart from everything that is against Your Word. Set me free from those things that are evil. Keep me from temptation. Thank You for purifying my heart so that I may see God. I ask this in the name of Jesus, Your Son. Amen.

Proverbs 22:13-14 13 The slothful man saith, There is a lion without, I shall be slain in the streets. 14 The mouth of strange women is a deep pit: he that is abhorred of the LORD shall fall therein.

Verse 13 – This verse demonstrates another characteristic of the slothful; they convince themselves to avoid responsibility with any kind of excuse. The slightest inconvenience or difficulty will keep a sluggard from going outside to get to work, just as the imagined fears of the idle person will also do. Solomon lived in a country where lions lived, but it was as unlikely then as now that a lion would have gotten within the gates of Jerusalem. Wild animals avoid large cities. Idle people easily become prey to wild imaginations and fears as well as physical disorders. A slothful man will use excuses to keep from doing his duty or going to work, just as this man used the excuse that he was afraid of a lion killing him.

Whatever goals or call of God that we may have, there will always be obstacles to overcome in order to fulfill them. As Christians, we can rely on God's grace and strength to help us in all things and to develop an overcoming spirit. One cannot escape from a lazy mindset without the desire to change. When a person repents of slothfulness and cries out to God for help to overcome it, God begins to deliver him from his old nature and enables him to find satisfaction in working. "He that observeth the wind shall not sow; and he that regardeth the clouds shall not reap" (Ecclesiastes 11:4).

Verse 14 – The Bible warns people to avoid speaking with loose and immoral women who may trap and seduce them with flattery and convincing words. An adulteress' tempting words are like flimsy branches and leaves, covering a deep pit that is dug to trap a wild beast. The unsuspecting animal walks right over it and falls in. Of course, the reverse is true also, as lustful men can lure unsuspecting females too, but since King Solomon wrote these Proverbs, he addresses this from a male standpoint.

Ultimately, the men who become ensnared by loose women are those who ignore God's Word. They are full of pride and think they can escape the consequences of resisting God's principles and ignoring His advice. They allow their lust and pride to rule them. Scripture states that God resists the proud. "But he giveth more grace. Wherefore he saith, God resisteth the proud, but giveth grace unto the humble" (James 4:6). God cannot help people who consistently refuse His ways.

Dear heavenly Father, thank You for Your Words to us in the Book of Proverbs, the wonderful book of wisdom. Lord, help us to learn from this book. Help us to avoid the things that are not good which You have shown us through these verses. Please deliver me from any laziness and slothful habits that keep me from doing and enjoying my work. Give me strength to do all that You would call me to do. Keep me pure and deliver me from evil. I submit to You and Your will. I will resist the devil and his temptations with Your Word and I expect him to flee from me. I pray in the name of Jesus. Amen.

Proverbs 22:15-16 15 Foolishness is bound in the heart of a child; but the rod of correction shall drive it far from him. 16 He that oppresseth the poor to increase his riches, and he that giveth to the rich, shall surely come to want.

Verse 15 – The Bible says that foolishness is in the hearts of all children. This is expressed by several words in Hebrew. One definition of foolishness is *silliness*. Children are notorious for doing silly things that could endanger their lives. Another Biblical definition of foolishness is *rebellion,* which can reside in a child even at a very young age. Both silliness and rebellion are dangerous attributes. When rebellion surfaces in a child, it is the parent's duty to drive it out. In Day 97 we looked at the fact that if we love our children, we will consistently discipline them. In Day 175 we saw that it is important to begin disciplining our children at an early age, and that we must not allow their crying to deter us from disciplining them. In Day 235 we will look at how to discipline a child according to Biblical guidelines.

Children who are not properly disciplined are among the most miserable of children. Unruly and spoiled children are not the blessings that they should be to parents. When a child is given no boundaries, he or she feels lost. Children must have boundaries that are consistently maintained. If they are not maintained, it causes great harm to a child, since he will not only be in dangerous territory, but will also lose respect for authority. This is where we find so many of the youth of today. They are rebels who not only disrespect, but they openly defy all authority figures, such as teachers, policemen, clergy, and their own parents. The blame rests upon the parents of these children for not consistently disciplining them, as Proverbs teaches: "Withold not discipline from the child, for if you strike and punish him with the (reed-like) rod, he will not die. Thou shalt beat him with the rod, and shalt deliver his soul from hell." (Proverbs 23:13-14).

Verse 16 – If we take advantage of the poor and use them for our own advantage to make money, we ourselves will become poor. The Bible also tells us that if we give gifts to the rich to gain an advantage or favor from them, that will also bring us to want. There is nothing wrong with giving a wealthy friend a gift if it is given with the proper motives, and not with a manipulative reason. God looks at our hearts and motives and if they are impure, we will reap what we sow toward others. According to this scripture, when we take advantage of the poor and pander to the rich, we will come to poverty.

Dear Father God, I am thankful for my children and grandchildren. They are a blessing. I know that I have failed many times over the years in the department of parenting, but I thank You that You are merciful and have been there to help me as a parent. Grant me wisdom and love in my ongoing relationships with my children and grandchildren. May I be the kind of mother and grandmother that the generations after me will remember as good and godly. Purify my heart so that I never would take advantage of the poor or pander to the rich. May I always have the assurance that You are my source and You will always take care of me and my offspring. In the blessed name of Jesus I pray. Amen.

Proverbs 22:17-18 17 Listen (consent and submit) to the words of the wise, and apply your mind to my knowledge; For it will be pleasant if you keep them in your mind (believing them); your lips will be accustomed to (confessing) them (AMP).

Learning to claim God's Word is important. Confessing it aloud helps us to remember it. It also builds our faith and helps us to hold on to God's promises when it is a real battle to do so. We must confess what God's Word says about our circumstances and ourselves, not what the world or our fears may tell us. Speaking God's Word causes the rest of our words to begin to line up with it. We should confess the Word over our problems, instead of confessing only our problems. When feeling discouraged or doubtful, we must continue to confess in faith what the Bible says about us or our situations.

We must, however, be careful to have a *Biblical* (and not merely a *positive*) confession.[27] A Biblical confession speaks God's Word back to Him, while a positive confession is simply speaking what one wants to hear and is directed primarily toward self-interest. We honor God by lining up what we think and say with His truth and trusting Him to provide our needs because we know He is good. Our aim must never be to try to manipulate God into doing what we want. Some so-called "confession teachers" say we should never speak anything negative; we should never say that we have an illness or a problem. This is not what the Bible teaches. We can certainly state the facts, but we should always resolve to speak the greater facts of God's Word over them. Faith-filled words invite the Holy Spirit into the problem. For example, in telling people that you are under an attack of illness, it would be wise to phrase it like this: "My doctor says I have (name the disease or condition), but I believe that God is my Healer and therefore I am claiming the Scripture that says, '...by the stripes of Jesus I am healed' (1 Peter 2:24b). Would you agree with me in prayer for healing?" The Bible contains many promises that we may claim. If we do not know what God says about a problem, we need only open the Bible and research the subject to learn what God has promised to do for us in each particular circumstance.

Abraham is a wonderful example of believing God's promises and acting in faith. God promised Abraham that his descendents would be exceedingly numerous. Although Abraham knew he was too old to father children, he "...staggered not at the promise of God through unbelief; but was strong in faith, giving glory to God; and being fully persuaded that, what he had promised, he was able also to perform" (Romans 4:20-21).

Dear heavenly Father, thank You for Your many promises of blessing to us, Your children. I want to receive everything that Jesus died for when He went to the cross to save me. Salvation and healing are just the beginning of why He died on that cross for me, and I do not want His death to be in vain. I want to receive all the covenant promises that He suffered for on my behalf. Lord, deliver me from doubt and unbelief and help me to guard the things I say. May I always confess what Your Word says, and not allow the devil to rob me of the blessings that are mine. I ask this in the name of Jesus, my Lord and Saviour. Amen.

---

[27] Please review Day 83 for the difference between these types of confession and details on what to confess and not to confess.

Proverbs 22:19-21 19 That thy trust may be in the LORD, I have made known to thee this day, even to thee. 20 Have not I written to thee excellent things in counsels and knowledge, 21 That I might make thee know the certainty of the words of truth; that thou mightest answer the words of truth to them that send unto thee?

As Solomon often addressed his sons in his proverbs, God, who inspired the Proverbs, also addresses His children through them. Proverbs reveals truth to us, so that we may put our trust in the Lord (verse 19). The entire Bible contains the words of truth to which verse 21 refers. God is the truth, the certainty, behind the Scripture. What is truth? Actually, the question should be, *Who* is truth? We find that answer in the Bible, in both the Old Testament and New Testament. Solomon prophetically says in verse 20, "Have I not written to you (long ago) excellent things in counsels and knowledge" (AMP).

"Ascribe ye greatness unto our God. He is the Rock, his work is perfect: for all his ways are judgment: a God of truth and without iniquity, just and right is he" (Deuteronomy 32:3b and 4).

God is a *God of truth.* Jesus said that He Himself is the truth. "Jesus saith unto him, I am the way, the truth, and the life: no man cometh unto the Father, but by me" (John 14:6). He also said that we could receive the Holy Spirit who is the Spirit of Truth. "And I will pray the Father, and he shall give you another Comforter, that he may abide with you for ever; Even the Spirit of truth; whom the world cannot receive, because it seeth him not, neither knoweth him: but ye know him; for he dwelleth with you, and shall be in you" (John 14:16-17). Therefore, if we desire to know the truth, we must seek to know our Father God through His Son Jesus Christ. After we receive Jesus in our hearts, we must read and obey His Word if we want to walk in truth. The Bible tells us we have an enemy who is opposed to the truth and tries to keep us from knowing it. The devil is a liar and the father of lies. Everyone is fathered either by God or the devil, and each life reflects God's or Satan's character.

"Ye are of your father the devil, and the lusts of your father ye will do. He was a murderer from the beginning, and abode not in the truth, because there is no truth in him. When he speaketh a lie, he speaketh of his own: for he is a liar, and the father of it. And because I tell you the truth, ye believe me not. Which of you convinceth me of sin? And if I say the truth, why do ye not believe me? He that is of God heareth God's words: ye therefore hear them not, because ye are not of God" (John 8:44-47).

To walk in truth, we must daily seek to know and obey Jesus better. The more we know Him, the more truth we know, and the more brightly shines the spiritual light in which we walk. "In him was life; and the life was the light of men. And the light shineth in darkness; and the darkness comprehended it not...That was the true Light, which lighteth every man that cometh into the world" (John 1:4,9).

Dear Father in heaven, I am so thankful to know the truth of Your word. It has not only brought me light, but Your love as well. Thank You for loving and forgiving me, giving me the precious Holy Spirit. May I always share this marvelous light through allowing You to live in me, and through me. May others desire to know You through my witness. Lord, forgive me when I fail You and am not a good representative of Your nature. Fill me with Your Holy Spirit daily and guide me in the way that will bring glory to You. I ask this in the name of Jesus Christ. Amen.

Proverbs 22:22-23 22 Rob not the poor, because he is poor: neither oppress the afflicted in the gate: 23 For the LORD will plead their cause, and spoil the soul of those that spoiled them.

Unlike the rich, the poor are vulnerable, having no means of protecting themselves; therefore, those who exploit them are detestable in the eyes of God. No person is less important to God than another. God loves the poor and instructs His followers to help them. Psalm 41:1-3 records special promises that God makes to those who consider and help the poor. "Blessed is he that considereth the poor: the LORD will deliver him in time of trouble. The LORD will preserve him, and keep him alive; and he shall be blessed upon the earth: and thou wilt not deliver him unto the will of his enemies. The LORD will strengthen him upon the bed of languishing: thou wilt make all his bed in his sickness." Here God says He will bless them and deliver them in their time of trouble. He will preserve them and keep them alive. Then, to top it off, He promises to heal them when they languish on a sick bed. What wonderful promises for simply helping others!

Helping the poor does not mean helping the lazy. The Bible clearly teaches that those who do not work should not eat. Lazy busybodies and those who engage in disorderly conduct need instruction on changing their ways, not material help. "For even when we were with you, this we commanded you, that if any would not work, neither should he eat. For we hear that there are some which walk among you disorderly, working not at all, but are busybodies" (2 Thessalonians 3:10-12). However, to neglect those who are truly needy and helpless, is sin. Ungodly societies that destroy their weak and "burdensome" members are eventually destroyed.

The last part of verse 22 warns against using the law to oppress the poor. Our present-day judicial system has drifted away from its original intent to convict lawbreakers and protect the innocent. Swift punishment of the guilty has been abandoned. Court appeals and delays stretch into costly trials lasting for years at public expense. Criminals are often not even sentenced. Many lawyers misuse the law for personal gain, obtaining settlements for clients in amounts far above rightful compensation, as well as people who want to use the legal system beyond what would be a fair settlement. Outlandish court rulings, so lucrative for lawyers, have a domino effect on the American economy. Doctors, professionals, companies, etc., must insure themselves heavily against lawsuits. Higher insurance rates result for everyone, increasing costs for medical services and everything else. If justice is to be seen in America again, we must return to Biblical principles and shape our laws by them. The Lord requires justice for all people, rich and poor. We should pray for godly judges in our courts, and vote for men of character who will make good judges. "The God of Israel said, the Rock of Israel spake to me, He that ruleth over men must be just, ruling in the fear of God" (2 Samuel 23:3).

Dear Father God, I do appreciate all that You have done for me. You have taken care of all my needs. We Americans have so much abundance; we are rich by the world's standards. Lord, help me to be more sensitive to the needs of the poor. Help me to reach out and to help them, and also to give to those ministries that support them. Strengthen and meet the needs of those who are working in orphanages, and in some of the poorest areas of the world. Let me not turn my eyes away from suffering, but may I alleviate the pain of those whom You want me to help. I ask this in the name of Jesus. Amen.

Proverbs 22:24-25 24 Make no friendship with an angry man; and with a furious man thou shalt not go: 25 Lest thou learn his ways, and get a snare to thy soul.

Angry people are always stirring up trouble. Today's verses warn that if we associate with an angry man, we will learn to think and act as he does. An angry mob starts by someone getting mad about an issue, and then inciting others to take up their offences. A man given to anger vents his feelings through angry words (from swearing to verbal abuse) and violent actions (from breaking things to hurting people), or both. His ways are foolish, for he speaks and acts rashly. He is unstable; no one knows when his anger will be kindled next. His ways encourage selfishness, pride, impatience, irritability, and lack of self-control. Once established, these patterns are hard to break. Many evil consequences are reaped from them, including bringing curses on himself from things he says in anger; gaining a bad reputation; and damaged relationships with his loved ones.

For this reason, friendship or even casual association with a person given to anger (or any other sin), is harmful. This does not mean that when we come in contact with sinners we should become cold and aloof or isolate ourselves from them. It simply means that we should not form relationships with them. Children are especially prone to the influence of others. Parents should warn their children to choose their friends very carefully, and be aware of who they "hang out" with. We all ought to choose friends, and especially spouses, carefully, and pay attention to whom they associate with. "He that walketh with wise men shall be wise: but a companion of fools shall be destroyed" (Proverbs 13:20).

To grow spiritually, we need the company of those who are walking in the spirit. We should not befriend people simply because they are intelligent or even because they attend many church meetings. We should look for those who know and practice God's Word. These are industrious, godly Christians walking with the Lord and growing in the fruit of the Spirit (Galatians 5:22-23), not carnal, smug, or pleasure-seeking people who only profess to be Christians.

Scripture instructs us not to be yoked in marriage, friendship, or business with unbelievers. We must choose our relationships wisely. "Be ye not unequally yoked together with unbelievers: for what fellowship hath righteousness with unrighteousness? and what communion hath light with darkness? And what concord hath Christ with Belial? or what part hath he that believeth with an infidel? And what agreement hath the temple of God with idols? for ye are the temple of the living God; as God hath said, I will dwell in them, and walk in them; and I will be their God, and they shall be my people. Wherefore come out from among them, and be ye separate, saith the Lord, and touch not the unclean thing; and I will receive you" (2 Corinthians 6:14-17).

Dear Father in heaven, I thank You for the good friends You have given me. Help Your people in all walks of life who are struggling with unrighteous relationships. Help them to live a life that is pleasing to You. Deliver them from the fear of man and give them the grace to cut all ties with those who would lead them into wickedness. Fill them with Your Spirit so that they will have the holy boldness to take a stand for truth and righteousness. As we encounter wicked people in our lives, help us to treat them with compassion and kindness; yet be able to speak the truth in love. I ask this in the name of Jesus. Amen.

Proverbs 22:26-27 26 Be not thou one of them that strike hands, or of them that are sureties for debts. 27 If thou hast nothing to pay, why should he take away thy bed from under thee?

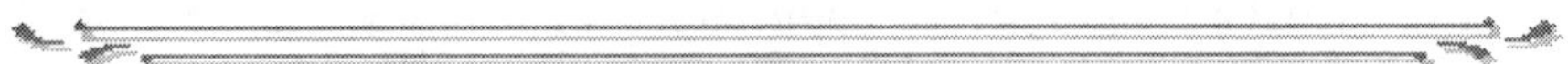

Verse 26 – As we saw in Day 36, it is unwise to become surety for someone else's debt, or to co-sign someone else's loan. This verse speaks of "striking hands." Years ago in America, many people entered formal agreements merely by shaking hands. A handshake sealed a bargain, signifying that a person was giving his word to uphold his end of an agreement. Because most people were honorable, they carried out their part of the agreement; when they gave their word, they kept it. Today we still shake hands on an agreement, but only after we have signed papers that legally bind us to fulfill the conditions of the contracts that we have signed. We should take every agreement that we sign very seriously. Giving our word to do something is a serious thing before God and people. Even if we are not legally bound to do something, as God's children we must keep our word when we give it, though it may be inconvenient or damaging financially, socially, or in any other way. In Psalm 15:4 David, describing the characteristics of a godly man, said that he "...sweareth to his own hurt, and changeth not." Often after telling someone that I would do something I have wished that I had not done so, for it became very difficult for me to keep my word. At times, we have all "sworn to our own hurt," but God expects us to keep our word, just as He keeps His Word, even if it hurts to do so.

Verse 27 – Many people request loans in order to maintain an unaffordable lifestyle, rather than for emergency help. Often, it becomes too difficult for them to keep up the loan payments and the co-signer is held accountable. This not only creates a financial burden for the co-signer, but jeopardizes his own financial position if he is unable to assume the requirements of the loan. Depending on the laws involved, it might even lead to the loss of his house and furniture–his bed being literally taken from him. At the very least, it could damage his credit. Co-signing loans for those who have not learned Biblical financial principles is actually unkind. Ultimately, loans do not help them, and many later feel animosity toward those who helped them incur the debt by co-signing the loan.

Do these verses imply that we should never help those who ask us for financial help? Certainly not; but rather that we be wise in giving help. We must be careful to help those with genuine needs, but not necessarily by co-signing a loan for them. Perhaps the Lord would want us just to give–instead of loan–to them.

Dear Father, thank You for the wisdom in the Book of Proverbs. Help us to apply it in every area of our lives, and to be wise in our spending and in our financial affairs. Help us also to keep our word in both the greater matters of life, and the small things. When I tell someone I will do something, help me to follow through. Remind me, should I forget. May I be known as a person who keeps her word. Help us all, as Your people, to be honest and operate with integrity in all of our financial affairs. Teach us Your financial principles. Help us resist going the way of the world that leads to more and more debt. We need Your wisdom in all areas of life. I ask in the name of Jesus. Amen.

God's Wisdom for Daily Living — ***Betty Miller***
August 16 — ***Day 228***

Proverbs 22:28 Remove not the ancient landmark, which thy fathers have set.

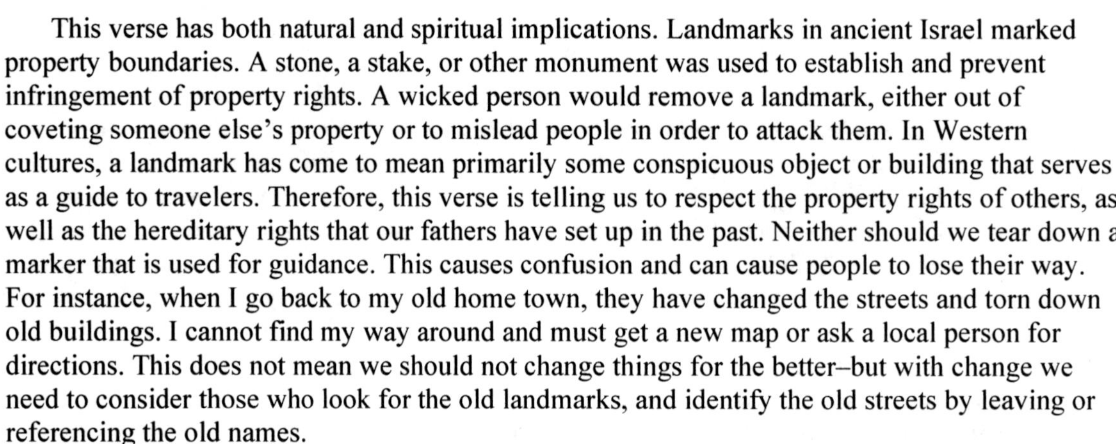

This verse has both natural and spiritual implications. Landmarks in ancient Israel marked property boundaries. A stone, a stake, or other monument was used to establish and prevent infringement of property rights. A wicked person would remove a landmark, either out of coveting someone else's property or to mislead people in order to attack them. In Western cultures, a landmark has come to mean primarily some conspicuous object or building that serves as a guide to travelers. Therefore, this verse is telling us to respect the property rights of others, as well as the hereditary rights that our fathers have set up in the past. Neither should we tear down a marker that is used for guidance. This causes confusion and can cause people to lose their way. For instance, when I go back to my old home town, they have changed the streets and torn down old buildings. I cannot find my way around and must get a new map or ask a local person for directions. This does not mean we should not change things for the better–but with change we need to consider those who look for the old landmarks, and identify the old streets by leaving or referencing the old names.

Young Christians should respect their elders' boundaries. There are reasons for the boundaries, and the younger generation would be wise to honor them. This is actually part of obeying the commandment to honor our parents (Exodus 20:12). Young people, in their desire for independence, will often disregard their elders' advice, sometimes to their own detriment. Satan is trying to rid our nation of the ancient moral landmarks that our founding forefathers set in place, especially the Ten Commandments. He knows that without these standards in the earth, he will be able to destroy society. Without respect for authority, our world will be reduced to chaos.

The same can also apply to teachings. Some of the so-called "new" teachings in the Church are really not new at all, but old erroneous ones. They are "winds of doctrine" that toss people to and fro. The Lord gave the church apostles, prophets, evangelists, pastors, and teachers to help us walk in the right way, that we may mature in Christ. It is wisdom to listen to our godly church elders. "And he gave some, apostles; and some, prophets; and some, evangelists; and some, pastors and teachers; For the perfecting of the saints, for the work of the ministry, for the edifying of the body of Christ: Till we all come in the unity of the faith, and of the knowledge of the Son of God, unto a perfect man, unto the measure of the stature of the fullness of Christ: That we henceforth be no more children, tossed to and fro, and carried about with every wind of doctrine, by the sleight of men, and cunning craftiness, whereby they lie in wait to deceive; But speaking the truth in love, may grow up into him in all things, which is the head, even Christ" (Ephesians 4:11-14).

Dear heavenly Father, I thank You for both the elders in my family and the church elders before me, who have paved the way for my life to be blessed. Even though I am an older person myself, may I always be child-like and humble in realizing that without my elders, I would not be one today. May I always honor and appreciate them. Help me to respect the young people in my life and not discard their ideas, but be able to embrace those ideas that come from You, not allowing pride to prevent me from recognizing the things that You are giving them. Lord, may You restore the hearts of the fathers to the children in our day. I ask this in the name of Jesus. Amen.

God's Wisdom for Daily Living — ***Betty Miller***
August 17 — ***Day 229***

Proverbs 22:29 Do you see a man diligent and skillful in his business? He will stand before kings; he will not stand before obscure men (AMP).

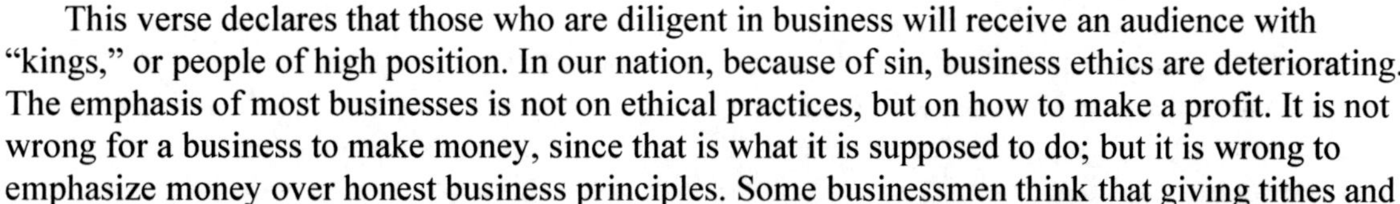

This verse declares that those who are diligent in business will receive an audience with "kings," or people of high position. In our nation, because of sin, business ethics are deteriorating. The emphasis of most businesses is not on ethical practices, but on how to make a profit. It is not wrong for a business to make money, since that is what it is supposed to do; but it is wrong to emphasize money over honest business principles. Some businessmen think that giving tithes and offerings fulfills their calling. This is commendable, but every disciple of the Lord has a higher calling: to be totally dedicated to Jesus in everything they do. Giving is only one of those things.

Every Christian has the primary call to share the Gospel, as Jesus commanded in the Great Commission (Matthew 28:19-20). This is our true vocation. It is fulfilled through our avocation, which is our means of livelihood. Wherever we are in life, we are to share the gospel. A stay-at-home mother's field would be her home and neighborhood. She raises her children in the nurture of the Lord, and shares the Gospel with her neighbors. An employee's field is his workplace. He tries to be the best employee possible to demonstrate the nature of Jesus to his employer and those around him. A minister's field is his congregation, as he helps equip them to minister the Gospel wherever they go. "Whatsoever thy hand findeth to do, do it with thy might …" (Ecclesiastes 9:10a).

A businessman or businesswoman should run their businesses in such a way that all may see Jesus through it. They can offer prayer meetings after work hours, or many other things as the Lord leads them. Does this mean that they should neglect their business or turn it into what resembles a church service? No, it means basing their business operations on Biblical principles. Practicing diligence, honesty, and justice with other businessmen and their employees, will make them successful. Their main objective however, is to witness to their employees not only by what they say, but by demonstrating kindness through their actions: by investing in providing a safe work environment; being as generous with salaries and bonuses as possible; being kind in correcting mistakes; being understanding when employees have problems, and serving their customers from the heart.

Diligence in business will bring recognition from people in positions of power, enabling a man to stand before them in confidence. Many businessmen who have practiced evil in their corporations are paying the price for it. However, good businessmen stand out by providing shining examples of what a business should look like. These will not go unnoticed, but will be recognized in their communities. Most importantly, they will receive the approval of the King of kings. That is true success!

Dear Father, thank You for showing me how to live in the business world. May I be an example of integrity and honesty in all that I do. As a boss, help me to be the best one possible; showing my employees and customers Your nature in all of my affairs. When I am working for someone else, let my work habits be exemplary as a witness to Your grace in my life. Let me be considerate of my workmates, that they see Jesus in all that I do. Lord, return our nation to godly business practices so that we can be proud of our work as Americans and find satisfaction in the job that we do. Most of all, let us all remember that ultimately we are working for You. May our lives be pleasing in Your sight. I ask in Jesus' name. Amen

Proverbs 23:1-3 1 When thou sittest to eat with a ruler, consider diligently what is before thee: 2 And put a knife to thy throat, if thou be a man given to appetite. 3 Be not desirous of his dainties: for they are deceitful meat.

Whatever dinner function we attend, our conduct should never bring reproach to Christ. We should always abstain from excessive drink or food that leads to drunkenness and gluttony. The phrase "put a knife to your throat" is a Jewish idiom which expresses the meaning that we can "kill an opportunity" if we care more about indulging at the dinner than finding out why we were invited and enjoying the fellowship. People who are gluttons and excessive drinkers lose respect in the eyes of others. Those given to fleshly or carnal appetites can make regrettable agreements while intoxicated, or be led into wicked partnerships by greed. The Bible teaches discipline and moderation in all things pertaining to appetite. "Let your moderation be known unto all men. The Lord is at hand" (Philippians 4:5).

Dinner invitations are perceived as expressions of friendship or approval. Dining encourages a pliable frame of mind. As one saying has it: "the way to a man's heart is through his stomach." The honor of dining with a powerful person can generate pride and an imprudent eagerness to please. His excellent foods can be deceiving. They may be offered with strings attached. A banquet can be given with the motive to win people over to the wrong side of issues. A charming host can be very persuasive. Some shrewd marketers use the "free meal" invitation to persuade people to invest in their schemes or buy their products, while others present legitimate offers. (Some people just like to entertain and be gracious, so this verse does not apply to all invitations, but only those given with wrong motives.) As Christians, we must not yield to manipulation just because someone has furnished a nice meal. Rich food and surroundings can easily arouse the desire for money and what it can buy, tempting one to become involved in something foolish. This is why it is important that we exercise moderation and self-control in all things.

We should also consider not overindulging in the overly-rich and unhealthy foods offered at these banquets. Although rich foods are now abundantly available to the average person in many countries, we would be wise to seek God about what we eat as well. Modern societies choose fast foods, and highly processed foods that contain multitudes of unhealthy additives, instead of foods in their natural forms as God created them. Doctors attribute many ailments to the Western diet, which is high in unhealthy fats and sugars. The overly sweet, salty, greasy, rich and processed foods to which we can become addicted truly qualify as "deceitful foods;" pleasing to the taste and appetite, but robbing the body of nutrients and filling it with toxins.

Daniel, a captive from Israel in Babylon, was given the extremely rich diet of the Gentile king, but requested for himself and his friends a simple diet of *pulse* (legumes such as beans and lentils, as well as fruits and vegetables). Not only were Daniel and his friends healthier than those who ate rich foods, but God blessed them because they abstained from food that was not good for them. God will also bless us, as we seek to honor Him with our eating habits (Daniel 1:8-17).

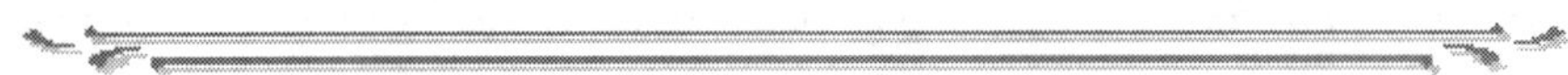

Dear heavenly Father, I am thankful for the variety of foods You created for me to enjoy. I do appreciate all the wonderful things that You made for us to eat. Lord, give me wisdom in the area of eating. Forgive me for partaking in any form of gluttony. Help me to eat in moderation, and deliver me from any lust and addiction to food. Help all of Your people who are struggling with being overweight, to overcome in this area. Correct our appetites so that we do not desire those

things that are bad for us, and help us not to over-indulge in food and drink. Give us strength to resist the temptation to continue eating more than we need. May You be "Lord of the Fork" in my life. I ask in the name of Jesus. Amen.

Quotes About the Family

According to Malachi 4:5 and Luke 1:17, healing must begin with the fathers. Being more mature, parents must reach out to rebellious children with forgiveness, prayer and love. --Day 57

A wise man does what it takes to create a godly and joyful environment for his family. He considers his family a precious treasure and treats them that way. --Day 208

Many Christians show the love of Jesus to everyone outside their homes while their own families are starved for it, and often crying out through rebellion. We should certainly demonstrate Christ's love to others, but should show it first in our homes. --Day 364

Quotes About Trusting in the Lord

If we are in God's will, He will protect us regardless of geographic location or circumstances. We could be in a war zone and still be safe. --Day 16

The Lord delights in answering our prayers, even if a miracle is needed to do so. Remember: miracles are God's specialty! --Day 11

Proverbs continually stresses the fact that when we seek God first and leave the outcome of all circumstances to Him He will bring about the results that are right. --Day 141

Fear is the opposite of faith. There is only one way we can live without fear in a world of turmoil, war, and uncertainty: to trust the One who told us not to be troubled or fearful. --Day 289

Proverbs 23:4-5 4 Labour not to be rich: cease from thine own wisdom. 5 Wilt thou set thine eyes upon that which is not? for riches certainly make themselves wings; they fly away as an eagle toward heaven.

Verse 4 – There is nothing wrong with having material wealth, but it should not be our primary focus. Our goal should be to know God personally; becoming like Jesus and growing in His wisdom. God promises to liberally give us wisdom when we ask for it in faith (James 1:5-8). Man's wisdom says to obtain wealth for ourselves; God's wisdom instructs us to rely on Him for our needs. We are never told to seek wealth or the "American dream."

When we serve God, He promises to meet our every need. "Therefore take no thought, saying, What shall we eat? or, What shall we drink? or, Wherewithal shall we be clothed? (For after all these things do the Gentiles seek:) for your heavenly Father knoweth that ye have need of all these things. But seek ye first the kingdom of God, and his righteousness; and all these things shall be added unto you" (Matthew 6:31-33). God loves to bless us but He is not pleased with greed. "Ye ask, and receive not, because ye ask amiss, that ye may consume it upon your lusts" (James 4:3). Jesus taught us to make our needs known to the Father. "And in that day ye shall ask me nothing. Verily, verily, I say unto you, Whatsoever ye shall ask the Father in my name, he will give it you. Hitherto have ye asked nothing in my name: ask, and ye shall receive, that your joy may be full" (John 16:23-24). Should our need be money or material things, He will provide for us if we humbly seek Him in faith.

Verse 5 – Financial wealth is uncertain and temporal. We can have it one day and the next day lose it all. However sizable the bank account, funds shrink as rapidly as a flying eagle shrinks from view. Men who look to money for security will find that it will fail them. Riches are deceitful (Mark 4:19), giving a false sense of security and importance that can cause us to miss eternal life (Luke 12:15-16). Many are robbed when their companies go bankrupt, and their long-term jobs and pensions disappear. Some lose everything in natural disasters for which there is no insurance coverage. Others face failed business ventures, down-sizing, stock market losses, or costly treatments for long-term health problems that devour their savings. Some people have everything stolen from them. People everywhere are facing financial challenges.

The Bible has the answer to these and all problems facing mankind, which is putting our trust in Christ and following God's plan for our individual lives. God does not promise that we will not face difficulties, but rather that we can be more than conquerors in all of them, through Christ. "These things I have spoken unto you, that in me ye might have peace. In the world ye shall have tribulation: but be of good cheer; I have overcome the world" (John 16:33). The only sure investments in life are spiritual. Those investing in God's kingdom are accumulating treasures for eternity (Matthew 6:19-21).

Dear heavenly Father, first of all, I want to thank You for Your provision for all of my needs. You have never failed to take care of me. I am grateful. Please deliver me from all fear and insecurity about the future. I know You will never fail me and will continue to meet all of my needs. Lord, I want to be like You. Do the work in my heart to set me free from looking to the provision that comes from this world. I know my true source of supply comes through You. Give me grace to not look to men for security. You are my security and I set my eyes upon You, Lord. I ask this in the name of Jesus, my Provider. Amen.

God's Wisdom for Daily Living ***Betty Miller***
August 20 ***Day 232***

Proverbs 23:6-8 6 Eat thou not the bread of him that hath an evil eye, neither desire thou his dainty meats: 7 For as he thinketh in his heart, so is he: Eat and drink, saith he to thee; but his heart is not with thee. 8 The morsel which thou hast eaten shalt thou vomit up, and lose thy sweet words.

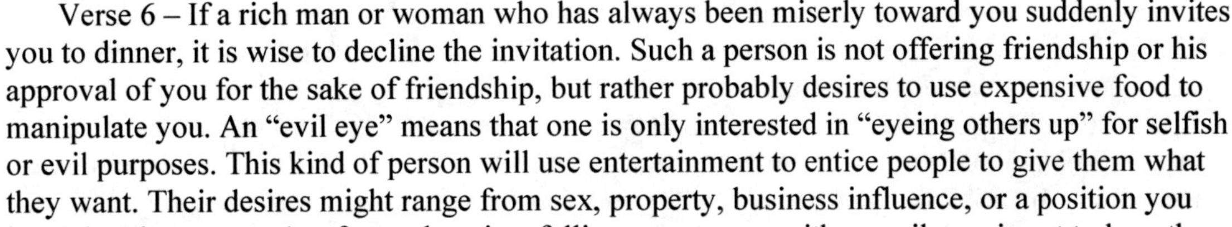

Verse 6 – If a rich man or woman who has always been miserly toward you suddenly invites you to dinner, it is wise to decline the invitation. Such a person is not offering friendship or his approval of you for the sake of friendship, but rather probably desires to use expensive food to manipulate you. An "evil eye" means that one is only interested in "eyeing others up" for selfish or evil purposes. This kind of person will use entertainment to entice people to give them what they want. Their desires might range from sex, property, business influence, or a position you have that they covet. A safeguard against falling prey to one with an evil eye, is not to love the things in this world and not to follow after those given to the lusts of the flesh (appetite), or eyes (desire), or the pride of life. Then we will not be susceptible to their manipulations.

"Love not the world, neither the things that are in the world. If any man love the world, the love of the Father is not in him. For all that is in the world, the lust of the flesh, and the lust of the eyes, and the pride of life, is not of the Father, but is of the world. And the world passeth away, and the lust thereof: but he that doeth the will of God abideth for ever" (1 John 2:15).

Verse 7 – Jesus verified that "as a man thinks in his heart, so is he." Thieves, slanderers, and lovers of money express in words and deeds the evil in their hearts. "And Jesus said, Are ye also yet without understanding? Do not ye yet understand, that whatsoever entereth in at the mouth goeth into the belly, and is cast out into the draught? But those things which proceed out of the mouth come forth from the heart; and they defile the man. For out of the heart proceed evil thoughts, murders, adulteries, fornications, thefts, false witness, blasphemies: These are the things which defile a man: but to eat with unwashen hands defileth not a man" (Matthew 15:16-20). An "evil eye" describes the attitude of a man who cares more about his money than his friends. He may invite you to dine with him, serving gourmet food and urging you to enjoy yourself only for the sake of appearances. If, in his heart, he begrudges the cost of entertaining you, he is no true friend. Your time with such a person is wasted. Friendship does not flourish where the host calculates with misgivings the expense of what his guest consumes.

Verse 8 – This kind of meal will end up making you sick, and all the seemingly "good time" and "sweet words" will have been in vain. We are warned not to get trapped into circumstances like this. We will end up regretting it if we do.

Dear heavenly Father, I am grateful that You have given us so much wise advice in this amazing Book of Proverbs. Thank You for pointing out things that would cause problems in our lives. Give me discernment when someone comes into my life who has an "evil eye," so that I will not fall into a trap set by a manipulator. Lord, I will pray for them to be set free, but I do not want to keep company with this kind of person. Please remove lust from my heart, as well as anything else that is evil. Help me to resist the temptation of the lust of the eyes, and the lust of the flesh and the pride of life. Put Your holy and righteous desires in my heart so that I might please You. I ask this in the name of Jesus. Amen.

God's Wisdom for Daily Living — ***Betty Miller***
August 21 — ***Day 233***

Proverbs 23:9-11 9 Speak not in the ears of a fool: for he will despise the wisdom of thy words.10 Remove not the old landmark; and enter not into the fields of the fatherless: 11 For their redeemer is mighty; he shall plead their cause with thee.

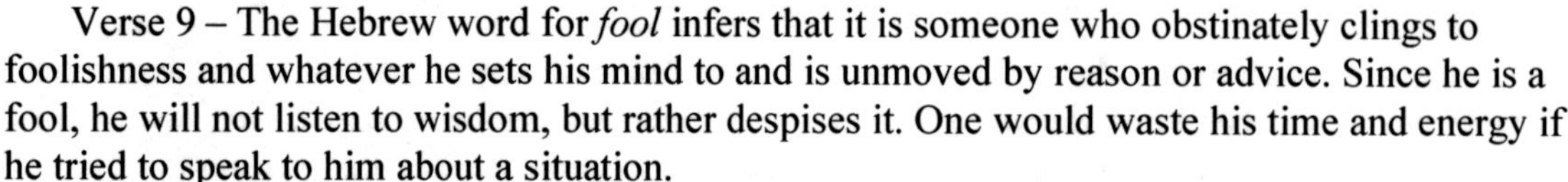

Verse 9 – The Hebrew word for *fool* infers that it is someone who obstinately clings to foolishness and whatever he sets his mind to and is unmoved by reason or advice. Since he is a fool, he will not listen to wisdom, but rather despises it. One would waste his time and energy if he tried to speak to him about a situation.

It is wise to listen to others and weigh what they say against God's Word. After I have heard someone's input, either positive or negative, I make a practice of what I call "running it through the Holy Ghost filter." I always try to allow the Holy Spirit to filter things before acting on them. By doing that, my husband and I have been saved from many problems in our ministry and personal lives. The Lord will grant wisdom when we ask for it in faith and "filter out," or make us aware of anything that is not of Him or not His will for us. We can trust that whatever "gets through the filter" is of God and proceed with it. When we have failed to do this, and just acted on men's well-intentioned advice it has caused us to suffer greatly.

Verses 10-11 – As we saw in Day 228, landmarks in Biblical times were boundary markers. They were extremely important in ancient cultures because the vast majority of people survived on the produce of their land. Wicked people coveted their neighbors' lands and sometimes demolished a boundary marker in order to claim the land for themselves. A strong man could defend his land, but not a poor widow. A widow with no relative to act on her behalf and redeem her land would have been helpless indeed. The Bible tells us that God will be a husband to the widow and will also be the orphan's mighty Redeemer. Corrupt earthly judges might deny a widow's rights; but God, who sees all, promises to defend and maintain her cause.

When we accept Christ as Savior, we receive help that is not visible to the natural eye. Our heavenly Father sends angels to watch over us (Matthew 18:10). God especially watches over the fatherless, the weak, and the helpless belonging to Him. Millions today are fascinated by the subject of angels, but a lot of unscriptural notions have been circulated. There are three kinds of holy angels: messenger, warrior, and worshiper angels. They are ministering spirits whom God sends to help us. "Are they not all ministering spirits, sent forth to minister for them who shall be heirs of salvation?" (Hebrews 1:13-14). They also maintain the cause of the fatherless. Angels can position people to help the fatherless and influence their hearts to do so. Help may come through people, but it is activated by angels. It is God's nature to continually reach out to the poor and helpless. He is the mighty God who defends their cause. May we, also, be used to help the weak and the fatherless.

Dear heavenly Father, thank You for Your wisdom and discernment in the daily affairs of my life. Lord, help me to use wisdom when I must deal with foolish and obstinate people. Help me keep my mouth closed and not speak, when You know that the person I am trying to reason with cannot receive what I have to say. Also, give me grace and boldness to speak when I need to share with others about the wisdom that is in Your Word. Lord, use me to help the weak and fatherless and plead their causes. May I be used as one of Your messengers in the natural, like one of Your angels, to bring a blessing to someone who needs to hear from You. I ask this in the name of our Lord Jesus Christ. Amen.

Proverbs 23:12 Apply thine heart unto instruction, and thine ears to the words of knowledge.

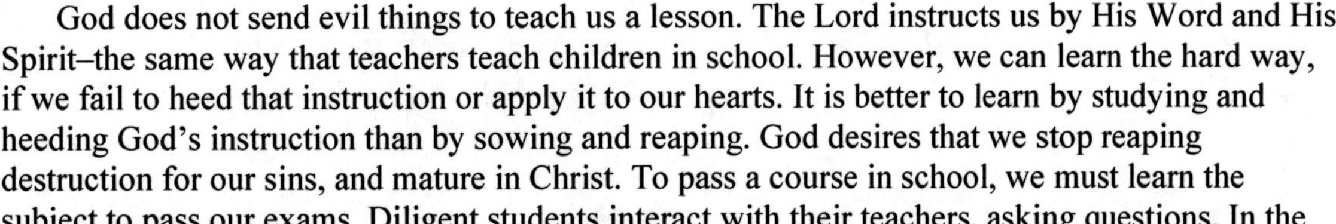

God does not send evil things to teach us a lesson. The Lord instructs us by His Word and His Spirit–the same way that teachers teach children in school. However, we can learn the hard way, if we fail to heed that instruction or apply it to our hearts. It is better to learn by studying and heeding God's instruction than by sowing and reaping. God desires that we stop reaping destruction for our sins, and mature in Christ. To pass a course in school, we must learn the subject to pass our exams. Diligent students interact with their teachers, asking questions. In the same way, Christians must know God in a living relationship, for Him to be able to share His wisdom with them. The Holy Spirit is our teacher; the Bible is our textbook; becoming like Jesus is the course; and the classroom is our life on earth. If we pay attention when the Holy Spirit speaks to our hearts and study His textbook, we are enabled to pass life's tests. We find few overcomers because many may know God's Word, but they do not apply it to their lives.

Ignorance of God's Word invites Satan to destroy us (Hosea 4:6a). Can "doing our homework" by praying and studying the Bible prevent negative things in our life? Yes, it can. We may know that prayer changes things, but how much time do we spend in prayer and Bible study, versus watching television or other time-wasters? God made a way for us to overcome through Jesus Christ and instructs us in His Word. If life's trials overwhelm us and we are living in defeat as Christians, it is not God's fault.

The Holy Spirit teaches us God's ways, both correcting and reproving us for sin (John 16:8). We need both! He convicts us that we may turn from the sins that destroy us. The Greek word for "chastise" means primarily "to train children."[28] Used in the New Testament, it brings to mind the fact that classical education brought correction through both admonition and corporal punishment. The Holy Spirit admonishes us through both Scripture and conscience. Realizing how wrong we are is painful. If we ignore Him, He may allow the sharper pain of reproof through people or embarrassing circumstances. If we still ignore Him, He may chastise us by allowing us to reap what we sow. In grasping this, we will understand that God is not the author of evil, but it is our own sinful choices that produce destructive consequences in our lives.

It is important to discern when the Holy Spirit is convicting of sin versus when the enemy is accusing us. True conviction leads to seeking God and repentance. It results in joy, freedom and growth. When the Holy Spirit convicts us, He shows us specifically both the sin and the way out of it. Sometimes Satan accuses vehemently, but is vague about the sin. He uses condemnation in an attempt to cause us to avoid God, which results in torment and stunted growth. Satan's lies bring condemnation and fear, while God's truth lifts us up, and shows us the way out of defeat. He will enable us to overcome, if we will choose His ways instead of our own. If we turn to God and forsake evil, we will never be condemned.

Father, I am grateful that You sent Your Word to guide me in the way that I should go. I do appreciate You keeping me on the straight and narrow path, as You know my flesh wants to wander at times. Thank You for correcting me when that happens. I love Your Word. It is filled with life and faith. Give me the desire to study it more diligently. Open my understanding so that I

[28] Strong's Exhaustive Concordance of the Bible, Hebrew and Chaldee Dictionary

will be able to apply the truths found in it to my life. I know the answer to every problem I face can be solved by seeking You with my whole heart and applying Your Word to my life. I ask this in the name of Jesus. Amen.

Quotes About Work and Personal Responsibility

If we desire to be used of God, we must learn how to work well for people. God commissions faithful people who do not shirk responsibility. --Day 64

A fool avoids hard work; his aim is immediate gratification. For this reason he never improves his status. --Day 78

Persevering when we do not feel like doing something is a godly trait we must develop to become overcomers in Christ. --Day 95

The Bible tells us that whatever we are working at, we should give it our best effort and work as unto Him, and not men. If we do this, God Himself will reward us. --Day 100

Dissatisfied people expect their leaders to create change, but all needed change begins with individuals. Every person is responsible for contributing to the betterment of our world. --Day 316

Quotes About the Words We Speak

Much of what we reap in life can be traced directly to things we have spoken. --Day 72

Sound words create a wholesome atmosphere; evil words create an offensive one. When we agree with God's Word and speak the things the Bible declares to be true, we create an atmosphere in our hearts in which faith can flourish. --Day 90

If you prayed about your problems as much as you talk about your problems you would not even have the problems. --Day 108

Proverbs 23:13-14 13 Withhold not correction from the child: for if thou beatest him with the rod, he shall not die. 14 Thou shalt beat him with the rod, and shalt deliver his soul from hell.

There has been much debate on the subject of corporal punishment. Depending on how it is administered, it can either be either abusive or constructive. Webster's Dictionary defines *spank* as: "(1) To strike with something flat, as the open hand, especially on the buttocks, as in punishment." We are never to spank our children with uncontrolled anger, or from resentment, and thus, hand out unjust punishment. "Discipline your son while there is hope, but do not (indulge your angry resentments by undue chastisements and) set yourself to his ruin" (Proverbs 19:18 AMP). "And, ye fathers, provoke not your children to wrath: but bring them up in the nurture and admonition of the Lord" (Ephesians 6:4).

Some believe that spanking is child abuse, but the Bible reveals that this is not true. Child abuse is committed by parents who are out of control. These parents need help and correction themselves. Some beat their children in angry rages or hurt them in other ways; some do not take care of their children; some let their children go hungry. These parents need the love of Christ so that the whole family can be healed.

Parents should not fear that spanking will damage a child, although some scream loud enough that it sounds that way. On the contrary, if done properly and for the right reason, it is a kindness, because it teaches a child to respect authority. Really, it is a form of abuse *not* to spank children when they need correction.

Children should be disciplined by a whack on the buttocks with a small, reed-like rod. This can be a switch from a small tree, or a small wooden spoon. It is not to be a heavy object that could cause physical damage. The purpose of spanking is to bring spiritual correction, not bodily harm. Spanking should be swift, followed by a calm explanation of the wrong that was done. The short-lived pain of discipline prevents the devastating pains–and even death–that rebellion brings. Administering godly discipline keeps a child from becoming a dysfunctional adult, for Proverbs 22:6 says, "Train up a child in the way he should go: and when he is old, he will not depart from it." Notice it says *train*, not teach. Many parents teach their children right from wrong, but fail to train them to obey. They threaten, but because they never follow through with punishment, their children have their own way. Spanking is part of training a child. A disciplined child is a delight to parents, but an undisciplined child brings shame (Proverbs 29:15,17 AMP).

Dear Father, thank You for wisdom in raising my family. Give me Your grace when I must correct my children and grand-children. May I never deal with them in anger or when I am out-of-control. Deliver all of us from anger, and teach us how to discipline our children with love. Lord, give my children and grand-children submissive and obedient spirits; and most of all, I claim that all my offspring will know and serve You. Please keep them safe in this dangerous world. May they honor You first; as well as their parents and grand-parents, as You have instructed in Your Word. I ask this in the name of Jesus. Amen.

Proverbs 23:15-16 15 My son, if your heart is wise, my heart will be glad, even mine; 16 Yes, my heart will rejoice when your lips speak right things (AMP).

Parents who neglect to train their children will be robbed of the joy they could have in them. A well-mannered child gladdens a parent's heart. Grown children that display godly wisdom bring their parents joy. Modern society has mostly rejected good manners. In my generation, children were taught to address their elders politely, with "Sir" and "Ma'am" and "Please" and "Thank you." When my husband and I were pastors, our church ran a Christian school. One of the first things we taught the children was to address teachers and elders by their titles, such as "Pastor Miller" and "Mrs. Miller." The philosophy that parents should be "buddies" with their children is not Biblical. It promotes insecurity and disrespect for authority. This does not mean we cannot play on the floor with them, and we should certainly not demean them. It means that we need to act like adults and take responsibility for ourselves, fulfilling our duties before God. This will give our children a sense of security, and when we take on a playful role with them they will know that is a demonstration of our love.

"And thou shalt love the LORD thy God with all thine heart, and with all thy soul, and with all thy might. And these words, which I command thee this day, shall be in thine heart: And thou shalt teach them diligently unto thy children, and shalt talk of them when thou sittest in thine house, and when thou walkest by the way, and when thou liest down, and when thou risest up" (Deuteronomy 6:5-7).

Children reflect their upbringing. They learn from the life that we live before them, not merely from what we tell them. We cannot guide them in God's ways if we do not walk in them ourselves. Parents that smoke or live with someone in adultery, and yet do not want their children to do so, are deluded and irresponsible. If we expect our children to embrace our beliefs, we must live our beliefs. We must develop our ability to discern good from evil, without which we cannot guide our children. Some aspects of our cultures are not just worldly, but Satanic. Many young people are being led into a culture of death and witchcraft, but their parents ignore their evil dress, music, and friends or treat it as a mere fad. In doing ungodly things, however, these young people are sinning. Unless repented of, that sin will eventually bring destruction into their lives. We cannot turn our children away from evil things if we ourselves are unable to discern which things are evil and the only way we can do this is to exercise ourselves in the meat of God's Word. "But strong meat belongeth to them that are of full age, even those who by reason of use have their senses exercised to discern both good and evil" (Hebrews 5:14).

Dear Father in heaven, I am grateful that You are there to help us in the upbringing of our children. Forgive me when I have failed, and give me Your wisdom in dealing with the things that my children embrace that are not of You. Help me to share the dangers of evil things in such a way that they will turn from them. Give me Your love and grace as I live my life before them. Give my children wisdom so that they will be good examples in the world. Please deliver me and my family from the things that would turn our hearts from You. Give us a love for Your Word, and may we walk in it. I ask in the name of Jesus. Amen.

Proverbs 23:17-18 17 Let not thine heart envy sinners: but be thou in the fear of the LORD all the day long. 18 For surely there is an end; and thine expectation shall not be cut off.

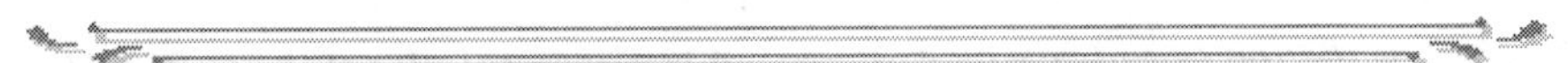

Some Christians are troubled by the fact that they struggle financially from day to day, while many sinners have an abundance of possessions and are seemingly trouble-free. Today's verses instruct us not to envy them, since the Lord will abundantly reward those who revere Him in due time: "Fret not thyself because of evildoers, neither be thou envious against the workers of iniquity. For they shall soon be cut down like the grass, and wither as the green herb. Trust in the LORD, and do good; so shalt thou dwell in the land, and verily thou shalt be fed. Delight thyself also in the LORD; and he shall give thee the desires of thine heart. Commit thy way unto the LORD; trust also in him; and he shall bring it to pass. And he shall bring forth thy righteousness as the light, and thy judgment as the noonday. Rest in the LORD, and wait patiently for him: fret not thyself because of him who prospereth in his way, because of the man who bringeth wicked devices to pass" (Psalm 37:1-7).

We are called to wait for blessings, so that the character of the Lord may be formed in us. We all appreciate God's patience toward us when He is dealing with our weaknesses. To be like Him, we must also be patient in dealing with others (Galatians 5:22-23). Fruit takes time to develop. The Bible calls patience "*long*-suffering;" not "*short*-suffering." (The Greek word for suffering means to "bear" or "endure."[29]) There are two kinds of suffering: (1) suffering that comes as a result of our sins or the sins of others, and (2) suffering by choice for the cause of Christ. When we first come to the Lord, most of our suffering is because we have broken spiritual and physical laws. This form of suffering comes upon the Christian and the non-Christian alike. However, if we walk with the Lord He will lead us out of this kind of suffering as it is the result of sin. Jesus suffered on the cross to relieve us of this. Types of this suffering would be sickness, depression, fear, poverty, filth, torment, emotional pain stemming from divorce or broken relationships, anxiety, loneliness, grief, stress, disorder, confusion, etc.

Suffering for the Lord is different. It involves laying down our lives for others. Jesus' suffering and death on the cross is the greatest example of suffering for others. We learn patience and suffer for the cause of Christ by obeying His leading when it is inconvenient; by choosing to fast; to pay someone else's bill; to "go the second mile;" to pray in the middle of the night; to minister to others. We can suffer by being falsely accused because we live godly lives. Our flesh can ache as we resist temptation. Our souls can grieve over a loved one who is unsaved. "But let none of you suffer as a murderer, or as a thief, or as an evildoer, or as a busybody in other men's matters. Yet if any man suffer as a Christian, let him not be ashamed; but let him glorify God on this behalf...Wherefore let them that suffer according to the will of God commit the keeping of their souls to him in well doing, as unto a faithful Creator" (I Peter 4:15-16;19).

In undergoing trials, we may be tempted to envy those who are not being tested at the time. Today's verses assure us that our sufferings will end, and we will be rewarded for obedience and faithfulness to God. "Blessed are ye, when men shall revile you, and persecute you, and shall say all manner of evil against you falsely, for my sake. Rejoice, and be exceeding glad: for great is your reward in heaven: for so persecuted they the prophets which were before you" (Matthew 5:11-12).

[29] Strong's Exhaustive Concordance of the Bible, Greek Dictionary of the New Testament

Dear Father, I come to You in Jesus' name. I willingly submit to all that You ask of me, and will endure and bear all that You place before me. However, Lord, I know there are some things that the devil wants me to suffer that are not of You, and I will not receive those things that he would try to put upon me. I yield to You, Lord; and if You want me to continue to bear long in any circumstance, I am willing, for I know You will give me abundant grace to do so. Even so, I resist the devil and the abuses he would put upon me, and I know that he must flee according to Your Word. Lord, develop the fruit of faith and patience in my life, so that I may be like You in this earth. Amen.

Quotes About Love

A mark of maturity in Christ is respecting the rights of others while being willing to lay down our own rights. --Day 2

Those who choose to love and forgive others will not be mastered by sin. --Day 61

The key to healing in any relationship is not to dwell on the past, but to forgive and go forward, building one another up in love. --Day 163

As God's children, love should motivate us to abstain from anything that might cause someone else to stumble. --Day 354

It is good to do things out of love, without expecting anything in return. --Day 364

Quotes About Self-Control

Many find themselves on the wrong path simply because they do not stay away from places that lead them into temptation. --Day 31

Learning to control what we say is the first step in gaining godly wisdom. --Day 136

Because a fool refuses to learn discipline, he is unprepared to handle money when he inherits it. He mismanages it by carelessly indulging every whim. --Day 171

The Bible teaches self–control in all things, the lack of which can cost one's health or life. --Day 238

Proverbs 23:19-21 19 Hear thou, my son, and be wise, and guide thine heart in the way. 20 Be not among winebibbers; among riotous eaters of flesh: 21 For the drunkard and the glutton shall come to poverty: and drowsiness shall clothe a man with rags.

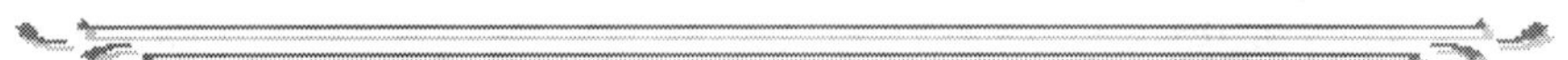

When we find a subject mentioned multiple times in the Bible, it is because it has very serious implications. Through Solomon, our heavenly Father again warns us to shun pleasure-seeking drunkards and gluttons whose sins lead to poverty. Hell is another subject that has strong warnings attached to it; and drunkenness, gluttony, and other lusts can lead a person there. "Know ye not that the unrighteous shall not inherit the kingdom of God? Be not deceived: neither fornicators, nor idolaters, nor adulterers, nor effeminate, nor abusers of themselves with mankind, Nor thieves, nor covetous, nor drunkards, nor revilers, nor extortioners, shall inherit the kingdom of God" (1 Corinthians 6:9-10).

Jesus warned people that one could go to hell for continuing in their sin. For emphasis, He repeated three times that hell is a terrible place of continual torment: "And if thy hand offend thee, cut it off: it is better for thee to enter into life maimed, than having two hands to go into hell, into the fire that never shall be quenched: Where their worm dieth not, and the fire is not quenched. And if thy foot offend thee, cut it off: it is better for thee to enter halt into life, than having two feet to be cast into hell, into the fire that never shall be quenched: Where their worm dieth not, and the fire is not quenched. And if thine eye offend thee, pluck it out: it is better for thee to enter into the kingdom of God with one eye, than having two eyes to be cast into hell fire: Where their worm dieth not, and the fire is not quenched" (Mark 9:43-48).

Whether as part of a wild life of pleasure or to dull emotional pain, the drunkard wastes his time and money on alcohol instead of improving himself and working hard to prosper. Drunkenness makes him unreliable and impairs his performance at work. Hangovers make him sick and cause him to miss work. Alcoholism can destroy his life. Gluttony is also a major sin of affluent societies. Americans currently suffer from many obesity-related diseases. Many Christians die prematurely because they over-indulge with food. The Bible teaches self-control in all things (Galatians 5:22-23), the lack of which could cost one's health or life.

The antidote to over-eating and drinking is to take positive action and direct our minds toward the Lord (Proverbs 23:19). It is not enough to turn away from sinful actions; we must also pursue God, in whom we perform the good works God prepared for us to walk in (Ephesians 2:10).

Dear heavenly Father, I thank You for all of the good things You have given me to eat and drink. Lord, help me not to over-indulge in those things. Help me to be a good witness by a moderate lifestyle. In a world with so many choices and temptations, empower me to choose the right things, and resist those things that are bad for me. May my physical body bring glory to You, as well as my spiritual life. Strengthen me, so that I might serve You better. I ask this in the name of Jesus Christ. Amen

Proverbs 23:22-23 22 Hearken unto thy father that begat thee, and despise not thy mother when she is old. 23 Buy the truth, and sell it not; also wisdom, and instruction, and understanding.

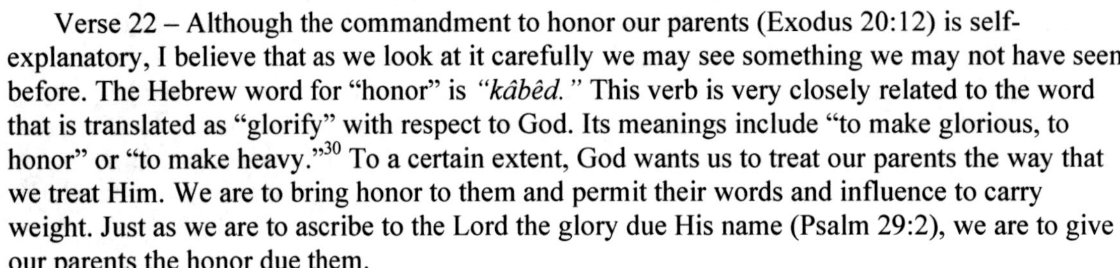

Verse 22 – Although the commandment to honor our parents (Exodus 20:12) is self-explanatory, I believe that as we look at it carefully we may see something we may not have seen before. The Hebrew word for "honor" is *"kâbêd."* This verb is very closely related to the word that is translated as "glorify" with respect to God. Its meanings include "to make glorious, to honor" or "to make heavy."[30] To a certain extent, God wants us to treat our parents the way that we treat Him. We are to bring honor to them and permit their words and influence to carry weight. Just as we are to ascribe to the Lord the glory due His name (Psalm 29:2), we are to give our parents the honor due them.

"Children, obey your parents in the Lord: for this is right. Honor thy father and mother; which is the first commandment with promise; That it may be well with thee, and thou mayest live long on the earth" (Ephesians 6:1-3). All parents present a picture of our heavenly Father as the Creator of life. Good parents also present the picture of God as a loving Father. The blessing upon our natural lives for honoring our parents is a picture of the blessing upon our eternal lives for honoring our heavenly Father. I believe we may also include spiritual parents; those who disciple and teach us. If children do not learn to respect their parents whom they see, they will not know how to respect God, whom they do not see. Part of training a child involves honoring one's own parents. In watching his parents treat his grandparents respectfully, a child learns how to respect his elders.

Ultimately, the root of every sin is rebellion: choosing our ways instead of God's. We cannot love God with all of our hearts if we embrace rebellion. God thinks, wills, and does only what is good, right and true. Submitting to what is good, right and true (God's will) results in abundant and eternal life. It is for this reason that God desires that we should submit to Him. Parents and elders represent the heavenly Father's authority and love. That is why it is so important that we learn to honor and submit to them.

Verse 23 – How does one "buy" truth? It will certainly cost something to obtain it. Time is valuable; once spent, it can never be recovered. When we spend it studying God's Word and learning from others, we are, in a sense, "buying" the truth. We are also told to seek understanding by coming to the Lord, Who feeds us with spiritual bread, milk and wine. "Ho, every one that thirsteth, come ye to the waters, and he that hath no money; come ye, buy, and eat; yea, come, buy wine and milk without money and without price" (Isaiah 55:1).

Dear heavenly Father, thank You for our families. May we especially be mindful to honor our parents and elders. Lord, give me a teachable spirit so that I might learn from those who are wiser than I am. Set me free from a prideful attitude and help me to listen to the voice of my elders. In my quest for truth, may I keep an open heart to receive those things that are of You, and give me discernment to recognize those things that are not of You. Open my understanding and instruct me in Your ways in all of the affairs of my life. I ask this in the name of my Lord and Saviour, Jesus Christ. Amen.

---

[30] Strong's Exhaustive Concordance of the Bible, Hebrew and Chaldee Dictionary

Proverbs 23:24-25 24 The father of the righteous shall greatly rejoice: and he that begetteth a wise child shall have joy of him. 25 Thy father and thy mother shall be glad, and she that bare thee shall rejoice.

We have already seen several verses showing us that a wise son gladdens his parents' hearts. A grown child's academic ability or business acumen will not bring a godly parent much joy if he lacks godly wisdom and righteousness. Young or old, when children honor their parents, they bring happiness to all. However, if they are rebellious, their sin can cause their parents great heartache. The Bible speaks of a generation that will cause godly parents much grief; it is the generation before the Second Coming of Christ. This generation is described as being lawless and wicked, even betraying its own parents (Mark 13:12). It is unthinkable that children could commit such evil; however, we are already reading in the newspapers of increasing numbers of such crimes being committed by even young children. These perilous times are spoken of in 2 Timothy 3:1-5: "This know also, that in the last days perilous times shall come. For men shall be lovers of their own selves, covetous, boasters, proud, blasphemers, disobedient to parents, unthankful, unholy, Without natural affection, trucebreakers, false accusers, incontinent, fierce, despisers of those that are good, Traitors, heady, highminded, lovers of pleasures more than lovers of God; Having a form of godliness, but denying the power thereof: from such turn away."

In the last days, men are described as being without natural affection. God created the family unit, and instills a natural affection in the hearts of each member for the others. It causes fathers to protect and provide for their families; mothers to nurture and care for the children; and children to naturally respect and love their parents. Families that love God and walk in His commandments will grow in love and respect for one another as they overcome selfishness and the sin that would separate them.

The devil wants to change how God structured the family. As natural affection declines, it gives way to unnatural affection, such as homosexuality. Satanic attacks on the family now extend to attempts to legally approve same-sex marriage. These perverted unions destroy what God intended for families. In attempting to re-define marriage, men presume to be wiser than God. He certainly loves homosexuals, but He hates their sin. He will set anyone free who cries out to Him to be delivered from unnatural affection, just as He sets people free from any other sin. Let us bring joy to the heart of our heavenly Father, as well as our earthly parents, by wisely walking in righteousness.

Dear Father God, I want not only to make my parents glad, but also to make Your heart glad. Cause me to be more like You in all that I do. May my life be a good witness, so that others may see my good works, and give glory to You. Deliver those who have strayed from the Bible's commandments and are living a perverted lifestyle. Minister mercy and grace to them, and restore the natural love and affection that You want them to walk in. Lord, I pray against the devil's plans for changing the law in our nation that would redefine marriage. Spare us, so that this unholy action will not become law, thus bringing our nation under a greater judgment. I ask this in the name of Jesus Christ. Amen.

Proverbs 23:26 My son, give me your heart, and let your eyes observe and delight in my ways (AMP).

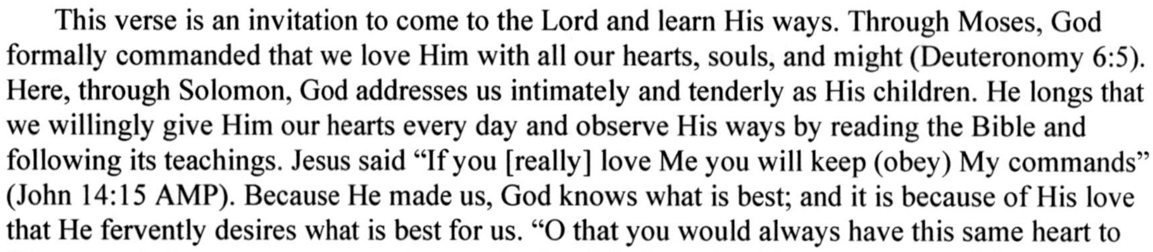

This verse is an invitation to come to the Lord and learn His ways. Through Moses, God formally commanded that we love Him with all our hearts, souls, and might (Deuteronomy 6:5). Here, through Solomon, God addresses us intimately and tenderly as His children. He longs that we willingly give Him our hearts every day and observe His ways by reading the Bible and following its teachings. Jesus said "If you [really] love Me you will keep (obey) My commands" (John 14:15 AMP). Because He made us, God knows what is best; and it is because of His love that He fervently desires what is best for us. "O that you would always have this same heart to fear me and observe my commandments that it might be well with you and your children always" (Deuteronomy 5:29).

The Hebrew word for *heart* refers to the seat of our affections, intellect, understanding and insight[31]. The Lord is asking us to give Him the love of our hearts and the full attention of our minds. We can know God if we turn to Him with all our hearts. Jeremiah 24:7 says, "And I will give them an heart to know me, that I am the LORD: and they shall be my people, and I will be their God: for they shall return unto me with their whole heart."

Once we are born again, we must walk in the Spirit to grow in Christ. The "new birth" is not a religion, not living up to a creed, not a set of rituals, nor joining a church or denomination. It is a *transformation*. Our old nature is changed and we receive a new one. Old things pass away and all things become new in Christ. We receive a new heart, new desires, new ideas, and a new direction because of this new nature. A birth is the coming into being of a new life which has the nature of its parents. When you were born the first time, you were made a partaker of the nature of natural man. When you are "born again," you become a partaker of the divine nature (2 Peter 1:4). God can then become our heavenly Father. One of the best ways to grow in God is to "Set [our] affections on things above, not on things on the earth" (Colossians 3:2) and to be careful about what we look at. We tend to imitate what we love and admire. We need to turn our eyes away from evil things and keep the Word of God in front of us. This is very important because the things we see influence us.

"I will behave myself wisely in a perfect way. O when wilt thou come unto me? I will walk within my house with a perfect heart. I will set no wicked thing before mine eyes: I hate the work of them that turn aside; it shall not cleave to me. A froward heart shall depart from me: I will not know a wicked person" (Psalm 101:2-4).

Dear Father God, I come in Jesus' name, thanking You for Your love toward me. Give me a revelation of Your true nature and character, so that I might be able to trust You and follow You at all costs. Let me share this revelation with those who do not know You as a loving God. Let me never blame You for the sin and evil in the world, but rather look to my own heart and allow You to cleanse me of those things that offend You. May I daily walk in more knowledge of You and Your ways. You are a mighty God who desires to do good to me. Make me whole; spirit, soul and body. In Your name, I pray, Amen.

---

[31] Strong's Exhaustive Concordance of the Bible, Hebrew and Chaldee Dictionary

Proverbs 23:27-28 27 For a whore is a deep ditch; and a strange woman is a narrow pit. 28 She also lieth in wait as for a prey, and increaseth the transgressors among men.

The first verse compares sexual involvement with a whore to a deep ditch. A car stuck in a deep ditch needs a truck to pull it out. Likewise, one cannot climb out of a narrow pit, but must be pulled out. Adultery, fornication, and all sexual sins, are like deep ditches leading to demonic oppression and spiritual bondage that create the need to get help in order to be delivered. This kind of sin usually requires exorcism by "casting out demons." Pornography is a spiritual ditch that often becomes a devastating addiction. Many good men wish they had never sampled it.

The Bible teaches that a man becomes one with a prostitute through sexual intercourse. "Now the body is not for fornication, but for the Lord...Know ye not that your bodies are the members of Christ? Shall I then take the members of Christ, and make them the members of an harlot? God forbid. What? Know ye not that he which is joined to an harlot is one body? for two, saith he, shall be one flesh. But he that is joined unto the Lord is one spirit. Flee fornication. Every sin that a man doeth is without the body; but he that committeth fornication sinneth against his own body" (1 Corinthians 6:13-18).

Many men, thinking sex with a prostitute is a harmless pleasure, wake up from this lie to a living nightmare. Some contract incurable venereal diseases; some lose wives and families; some lose reputations and careers; some undergo all of these. God's loving power can pull a man out of these spiritual pits, if he will repent and cry out to Him for help. Some may also need others to pray deliverance over them, to free them from the hold of demons that encourage and feed on lust. Satan uses sexual sin to entangle a man in a web of bondage and leech him of inner life. However, there is hope for both the licentious man and the prostitute. Some may think of those caught in sexual sin as "trash." This is a lie. They are precious souls so loved by God that Christ died for them.

The Bible includes stories of adulteresses who became women of faith. A Samaritan woman was living in fornication when she met Jesus. Without condemning her, He revealed Himself to her. She became a great witness for Him (John 4). Another woman, caught in adultery, was brought to Jesus by some religious leaders. He said, "He that is without sin among you, let him first cast a stone at her" (John 8:7). He did not condemn her, but told her not to sin any more. Rahab, a harlot, hid two spies in Jericho. Because she helped the people of God, she and her family were spared when they captured Jericho. She married an Israelite, and became an ancestress of Jesus Himself (Joshua 2 and 6; Matthew 1:5).

Many women and children are forced or tricked into prostitution. They need God's power to be delivered. He is kind and loving; desiring to free all those enslaved by sexual sin, whether because they were forced into it, or entered into it willingly.

Dear Father, please help young men and women not to yield to the temptation of living a lustful life. There are so many sexual temptations everywhere; keep those who desire to walk with You from falling into these traps. Lord, please deliver those who are already in bondage to sexual sin and perversion. I especially pray for those who have fallen into the deep pit of pornography. God have mercy on them, and grant them the power of the Holy Spirit to overcome the bondage of this addictive evil. Deliver our world from the sexual sins that are destroying our societies. I ask this in Jesus' name. Amen.

God's Wisdom for Daily Living — *Betty Miller*

August 31 — ***Day 243***

Proverbs 23:29-35 29 Who hath woe? Who hath sorrow? Who hath contentions? Who hath babbling? Who hath wounds without cause? Who hath redness of eyes? 30 They that tarry long at the wine; they that go to seek mixed wine. 31 Look not thou upon the wine when it is red, when it giveth his colour in the cup, when it moveth itself aright. 32 At the last it biteth like a serpent, and stingeth like an adder. 33 Thine eyes shall behold strange women, and thine heart shall utter perverse things. 34 Yea, thou shalt be as he that lieth down in the midst of the sea, or as he that lieth upon the top of a mast. 35 They have stricken me, shalt thou say, and I was not sick; they have beaten me, and I felt it not: when shall I awake? I will seek it yet again.

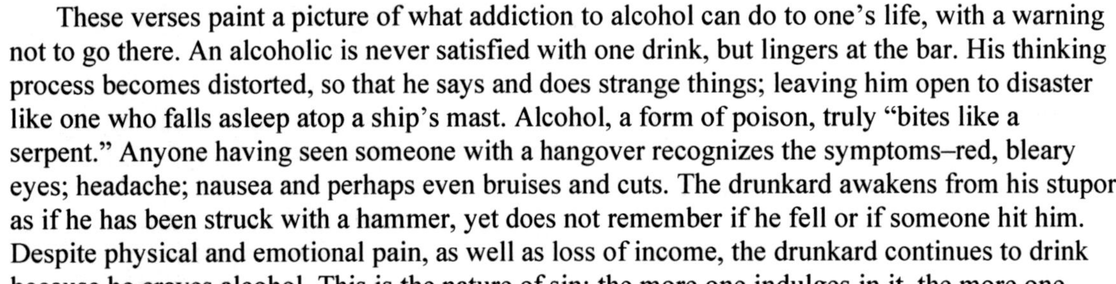

These verses paint a picture of what addiction to alcohol can do to one's life, with a warning not to go there. An alcoholic is never satisfied with one drink, but lingers at the bar. His thinking process becomes distorted, so that he says and does strange things; leaving him open to disaster like one who falls asleep atop a ship's mast. Alcohol, a form of poison, truly "bites like a serpent." Anyone having seen someone with a hangover recognizes the symptoms–red, bleary eyes; headache; nausea and perhaps even bruises and cuts. The drunkard awakens from his stupor as if he has been struck with a hammer, yet does not remember if he fell or if someone hit him. Despite physical and emotional pain, as well as loss of income, the drunkard continues to drink because he craves alcohol. This is the nature of sin; the more one indulges in it, the more one wants it, until he is finally destroyed.

Christians need to extend God's compassion and mercy to alcoholics, who through Him, can be permanently freed from their addiction. Mere human sympathy cannot bring deliverance. Calling alcoholism an illness is an injustice to those seeking deliverance from it. It is not an illness, but a sin that *produces* illness, as do other sins. Like drug abuse, it has its roots in rebellion, irresponsibility, escapism, lust, and over-indulgence. To be free from alcoholism, one must recognize it as a sin, and deal with it Biblically. Submitting to Christ as Lord, taking up one's cross daily and overcoming lust breaks sin's power.

Rehabilitation programs available to addicts are helpful, but some programs tell addicts that they will always be addicts. Permanent freedom from addiction can be found through the power of God. When God makes us free, we are free indeed. When we are born again, we become new creatures (2 Corinthians 5:17). Christians caught in alcoholism can also find deliverance. There is a way out through the Lord Jesus Christ. When we cry out to Him with all of our heart, He hears and delivers us (Romans 7:15-25).

Dear heavenly Father, so many people are caught up in the evil of alcoholism today. I want to pray for them. Please deliver those who are in bondage to alcohol and drugs. Forgive them, and touch them with Your Hand of mercy and grace. Lord, go deep in their souls and heal the wounds and remove the desire for this addiction. Let them feel Your love and set them free from the dependency on substances. May they depend on You to overcome the things that have brought them to this place. Cause their family and friends to be merciful to them and help them in the right way. May they experience Your touch this very moment. I ask this in the powerful name of Jesus! Amen.

Proverbs 24:1-2 1 Be not thou envious against evil men, neither desire to be with them. 2 For their heart studieth destruction, and their lips talk of mischief.

We must not envy anyone for their possessions; particularly not the wicked. We are not even to desire the company of those who do wrong for profit. We must choose to keep away from evil men and seek God, for His ways are the ways of blessing. The dictionary defines envy as "...a feeling of discontent and ill-will because of another's advantages, possessions, etc.; resentful dislike of another who has something that one desires.[32]"

Envying is the twin sister to coveting, which is forbidden in the Ten Commandments. "Thou shalt not covet thy neighbour's house, thou shalt not covet thy neighbour's wife, nor his manservant, nor his maidservant, nor his ox, nor his ass, nor any thing that is thy neighbour's" (Exodus 20:17).

One may wonder why covetousness is listed in the Ten Commandments; surely there are worse sins! Actually, it is a root for many other sins; leading to idolatry, hatred, adultery, thievery, and even murder. The commandment, for example, mentions coveting servants. Servants did the menial work done nowadays by machine. We can be guilty of coveting someone's kitchen appliances, gardening equipment, or computers. We can covet someone else's job or position. It is covetous to look at somebody and say, "Why was he chosen for that job? I am better qualified and I work harder than that person." The sins of covetousness and envy can lie hidden deep in the heart. We all need to ask God to examine our hearts and show us if any trace of them lies within us.

Though envy is a sin, it isn't necessarily wrong to desire something that God would do for others, because God wants to bless us all. If God does not supply something we ask for, we must trust His wisdom and set our hearts on following Him. God knows what is best for us and His provision and gifts never disappoint. He is not a respecter of persons and does not love one person more than another. The only thing that God is a respecter of is His Word. If we get into the Word of God and obey it, we will be blessed. He will begin to use us in ministry, and His gifts will flow through us, blessing us and those around us.

Dear Heavenly Father, I thank You for all You are doing in my life. Lord, I purpose not to envy or covet anything that belongs to another. I am looking to You for my provision. I believe You will supply all my needs. You are the God of everything, so You have an abundant supply of all that I might ever need or want. Please help me to just be content with the things I have today, knowing that You will send additional things as I ask for them, have need of them and walk in faith to receive them. Thank You for always taking care of me. Deliver me from any insecurity or fear and give me the faith to always trust in Your provision. I ask this in the name of Jesus. Amen.

[32] Webster's New World Dictionary of the American Language, Second college edition

Proverbs 24:3-4 3 Through wisdom is an house builded; and by understanding it is established: 4 And by knowledge shall the chambers be filled with all precious and pleasant riches.

These verses in Proverbs tell us that through wisdom, knowledge and understanding, we can lay a proper foundation for our lives. God said in Hosea 4:6a: "My people are destroyed for lack of knowledge…" Many of God's people are destroyed because they are ignorant of His ways. Proverbs mentions "wisdom" over 50 times. The Bible tells us why we are here, and what our purpose in life is. Life does not make sense until we find God and begin to understand His ways. Trusting Jesus Christ as your Savior gives our lives the only sure foundation there is. As we follow Him daily, we build solidly on that foundation.

To illustrate this truth, we can liken it to a manufacturer who includes an instruction book with his product. For best results, we must follow the operation instructions. God is the manufacturer who gave us the Bible as an instruction book. The operation of a steam iron can illustrate this principle. If we buy a steam iron, we must read the instruction book for it to work properly, or we could scorch or burn the item we intended to press. First, the iron must be plugged in. That is the foundational principle. It will not work until that is done. Then, water must be poured into the iron in the proper amount. After that, the gauge on the iron must be set for the proper temperature for the proper fabric. Only then can the iron be used properly to achieve the proper results.

God is our "manufacturer." He gave us life, but life without Him is like having an iron without the proper instructions to use it. Upon accepting Christ, we are given a new life that comes with a new instruction manual: the Bible. To live wisely, we must study and practice the truths of this new manual. An iron is useless unless plugged in and turned on. We must nourish and cultivate a living relationship with God, without whom we can do nothing. A steam iron must constantly be filled with water, and we must constantly be filled with the Holy Spirit who instructs and empowers us. An iron has a temperature gauge to handle both the toughest and most delicate fabrics, and in the same way the Holy Spirit gives us wisdom for every situation in life.

Accepting Christ as Savior and knowing what the Bible says is not enough to make us overcomers in life. Every day we must spend time with God, and live according to what we learn. As we do this, we gain wisdom to build sound lives and families. As a mansion is filled with fine furnishings and art, knowledge of God and His Word fills every part of our lives with riches such as love, joy, peace, righteousness, physical healing, soundness of mind, and material provision as needed. It enriches every area of life: marriage, business, and all endeavors.

Dear heavenly Father, thank You for showing us how to live in this life through Your Word. Lord, help me to give more attention to the Bible instead of the things that the world is saying. Help me to hide Your Word in my heart so that I do not sin against You. I desire to have Your wisdom in every area of my life. Please open my understanding to Your Word so that I might do the right things and avoid the things that create problems. May Your wisdom prevail in my life, my home, and my business, so that You will be glorified in all that I do. I ask this in the name of the Lord Jesus Christ. Amen.

Proverbs 24:5 A wise man is strong; yea, a man of knowledge increaseth strength.

So many people today talk about being tired or "burned out." One of the major reasons for this is that man tries to live without God's strength. We may be endued with natural strength and ability, but there is always a limit to it. Wisdom gives additional strength over mere physical power; it enables us to escape evil and to prosper in our soul. The Bible teaches that we are to be strong in the Lord and not rely on human strength or wisdom which easily fail us. When we have the wisdom to obey God, we can walk in the power of His might (Ephesians 6:10). Sometimes we need mental or emotional strength; other times we need physical strength. All of these are available to us through the Holy Spirit. Men in the natural grow old and lose their strength; however, the Bible records old men who served Him who were not weak but strong. "Moses was a hundred and twenty years old when he died, yet his eyes were not weak nor his strength gone" (Deuteronomy 34:7 NIV). At 85 years old, Caleb was still a strong warrior, that was ready to battle for his inheritance (Joshua 14:10-13).

My husband and I are in our "golden years," but we are not planning to retire. Rather, we are asking God to "re-fire" us; trusting that by His grace we will not go to be with Him until we complete the work He has for us on earth. Strength and long life are promised to God's people, but we must live for God and not for self. If we yield to sin, we can lose our strength as Samson did. The Bible records his deeds in Judges 13-16. When Samson served God, he triumphed in every battle; but when he yielded to lust and had an affair with Delilah, a Philistine woman, God's supernatural empowering left him. He was captured by his enemies, who blinded him and threw him in prison. In his agony, he cried out to God and was given one last burst of strength by which he brought down his enemies (Judges 16:28-30).

A commitment to God brings strength for any task. Even in old age, when our strength is waning, the Lord will give us His strength to witness to the generation in which we live. Psalm 71 records that King David asked the Lord for, and received, that strength. "Cast me not off in the time of old age; forsake me not when my strength faileth…Now also when I am old and greyheaded, O God, forsake me not; until I have showed thy strength unto this generation, and thy power to every one that is to come" (Psalm 71:9,18).

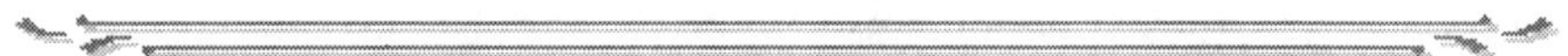

Dear heavenly Father, I thank You for Your promise of strength. I know that it is through Your wisdom and knowledge that we gain patient endurance. I am grateful that I can call on You when I feel weak and unable to go on. I want to use my strength to do Your will. I want to love You with all my heart, and with all my soul, and with all my mind, and with all my strength. I know then, that I will be able to love my neighbour as myself. You said that there is no greater commandment than this. May I always be faithful in loving You first, and then in loving others. I ask this in the name of the Lord Jesus. Amen.

Proverbs 24:6 For by wise counsel thou shalt make thy war: and in multitude of counsellors there is safety.

The Bible records many wars throughout its pages. Many of them document the accuracy of Scripture, since archeology has uncovered artifacts that verify their records as recorded in the Bible. Why does God allow wars? What is the role of soldiers, and how can one reconcile taking the lives of other humans? When God created the earth and put man upon it, He said that it was all good–until man sinned and fell from that estate. Because we were given a free will and can choose to do good or evil, we now live in an environment where evil men and good men are at war. God hates war, but it is necessary to maintain order in the earth and overcome those who would like to destroy good. In fact, the first war ever recorded was the war in heaven where Satan and his angels fought against God and his angels. We know this war was won by God. "And there was war in heaven: Michael and his angels fought against the dragon; and the dragon fought and his angels, And prevailed not; neither was their place found any more in heaven. And the great dragon was cast out, that old serpent, called the Devil, and Satan, which deceiveth the whole world: he was cast out into the earth, and his angels were cast out with him" (Revelation 12:7-9).

All forms of killing, terror, and death will be ended only when God's kingdom is established and men yield to God and His laws. For those who refuse to allow His reign in their lives, God has set governmental authorities in the earth to restrain evil by enforcing the laws of the land. Granted, the ruling authorities are imperfect and some are even evil, but without them evil would overcome the just and innocent. The time is soon coming when Jesus will return to this earth. At His second coming, the devil's followers will be destroyed, Satan will be chained in the abyss, and Christ will rule the nations with a rod of iron. Imprisoned, Satan will no longer deceive the nations, so there will be no wars in the earth. We shall enter the Millennial Reign of Christ, when the earth shall rest from its tribulations. "And he shall judge among the nations, and shall rebuke many people: and they shall beat their swords into plowshares, and their spears into pruninghooks: nation shall not lift up sword against nation, neither shall they learn war any more" (Isaiah 2:4).

May the King come quickly! Until He comes, God has instructed us to pray that His kingdom be manifested in our lives and communities. His kingdom is established when we allow Christ to reign in our everyday lives, thus affecting those around us with His love and grace. We can change corrupt leadership and bad laws by allowing God to use us in our spheres of influence, to make those changes. We must pray and become involved in the world to change it for the better.

Dear heavenly Father, give us good leaders in government who will employ wise men and women as their advisors. May our leaders be those who have a heart for You and live principled lives of integrity. You told us to pray for kings and those who are in positions of authority so that we may live quiet and peaceable lives that demonstrate godliness in all we do. Please help us to minister to others by serving in our communities. Give us wisdom and discernment to see the hearts of those who seek our vote. May we see the truth as we examine their lives and records to see if they stand for Biblical principles. May we not be critical; but discerning, as we make our choices. In the precious name of Jesus. Amen.

God's Wisdom for Daily Living ***Betty Miller***
September 5 ***Day 248***

Proverbs 24:7-8 7 Wisdom is too high for a fool: he openeth not his mouth in the gate. 8 He that deviseth to do evil shall be called a mischievous person.

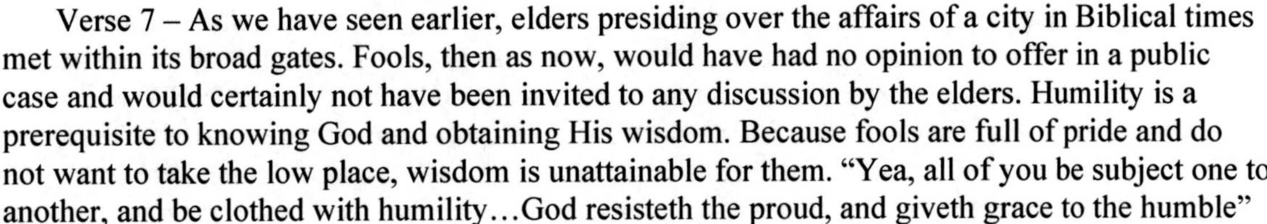

Verse 7 – As we have seen earlier, elders presiding over the affairs of a city in Biblical times met within its broad gates. Fools, then as now, would have had no opinion to offer in a public case and would certainly not have been invited to any discussion by the elders. Humility is a prerequisite to knowing God and obtaining His wisdom. Because fools are full of pride and do not want to take the low place, wisdom is unattainable for them. "Yea, all of you be subject one to another, and be clothed with humility...God resisteth the proud, and giveth grace to the humble" (1 Peter 5:5).

In Christ, we are promised His wisdom. The man who rejects Christ is the greatest fool of all, since we receive not only redemption and righteousness in Him, but also access to His wisdom and knowledge. In Christ, old things pass away and all things become new. We now have redemption, righteousness, love, peace, joy, health, provision, and victory over sin and the devil. It is an awesome thing that the Lord has done for us. When we walk in the spirit and demonstrate His love and power, we could be tempted to glory in how God is using us, but we are admonished not to glory in what we are doing, but rather glory in our God who made it all possible. "But of him are ye in Christ Jesus, who of God is made unto us wisdom, and righteousness, and sanctification, and redemption: That, according as it is written, He that glorieth, let him glory in the LORD" (1 Corinthians 1:30-31).

Verse 8 – Good or bad, nothing is accomplished without a plan, and devising one takes time and effort. What we plan in our hearts, we usually act upon. It is bad enough to unintentionally cause harm, but to spend time in planning it in order to deliberately perform it is much worse. Satan, the master planner of mischief, never ceases to devise evil against us as well. We can offset his schemes and weapons by praying and standing against him with God's Word. I daily declare in faith that "No weapon formed against me shall prosper" based on Isaiah 54:17. Notice the word *"formed"* used in this scripture. Before a builder lays concrete, he first builds "forms" into which to pour the concrete into. When it hardens, it takes the shape of those forms. Satan continuously "forms" plans against us, but we can destroy those "forms" before he has a chance to build a stronghold against us. "But no weapon that is formed against you shall prosper, and every tongue that shall rise against you in judgment you shall show to be in the wrong. This [peace, righteousness, security, triumph over opposition] is the heritage of the servants of the Lord [those in whom the ideal Servant of the Lord is reproduced]; this is the righteousness or the vindication which they obtain from Me [this is that which I impart to them as their justification], says the Lord" (Isaiah 54:17 AMP).

Dear Lord, thank You for all of the wonderful things that You have done for me. I do appreciate Your wisdom, Your love, Your provision and Your watch care over my life and my family. I am grateful that no weapon formed against me will prosper. Lord, I humble myself before You and ask You to help me to walk in Your ways and not yield to the temptations that the devil would whisper to me. Lord, I especially resist any of his remarks that would attempt to lift me up in pride. May You always receive the glory for those things that You are doing in my life and this ministry. May You be glorified in all that I do. I ask this in the name of Jesus Christ. Amen.

Proverbs 24:9 The plans of the foolish and the thought of foolishness are sin, and the scoffer is an abomination to men (AMP).

The word *foolishness* carries the meaning of trusting in one's own heart and mind. Planning our own way and leaving God out of those plans, is foolish indeed. The Bible tells us to trust in the Lord and not to rely on our own understanding: "Trust in the LORD with all thine heart; and lean not unto thine own understanding. In all thy ways acknowledge him, and he shall direct thy paths. Be not wise in thine own eyes: fear the LORD, and depart from evil" (Proverbs 3:5-7).

Because only God is "all-knowing," He alone can lead us in the right pathway. "For my thoughts are not your thoughts, neither are your ways my ways, saith the Lord. For as the heavens are higher than the earth, so are my ways higher than your ways, and my thoughts than your thoughts" (Isaiah 55:8-9). The Lord tells us that His thoughts are higher than ours. That is why we need to allow the Holy Spirit to renew our minds from conformity to the world and allow the mind of Christ to dwell in us. "And be not conformed to this world: but be ye transformed by the renewing of your mind, that ye may prove what is that good, and acceptable, and perfect, will of God" (Romans 12:2). "Let this mind be in you, which was also in Christ Jesus" (Philippians 2:5). As our thoughts become holy and righteous, we will be able to reject carnal thinking, to cast down imaginations and any high thing that exalts itself against God and bring every thought captive to the obedience of Christ. "For though we walk in the flesh, we do not war after the flesh: (For the weapons of our warfare are not carnal, but mighty through God to the pulling down of strong holds;) Casting down imaginations, and every high thing that exalteth itself against the knowledge of God, and bringing into captivity every thought to the obedience of Christ" (2 Corinthians 10:3-5). We must ask God to cleanse our thought-lives to root out sin.

When the devil attempts to get us to believe a lie, we must, in faith, quote scripture that will offset and overcome that lie. "Submit yourselves therefore to God. Resist the devil, and he will flee from you" (James 4:7). Submission to God is a heart-attitude, and it is revealed by obedience to His Word. To "resist the devil" means to refuse to cooperate with him. "Walking in the Spirit" means that we live in a state of prayer and obedience to the Holy Spirit. This really is not much different from walking with a friend. We become friends with God through His Son, Jesus Christ. We come to know Him through reading the Word and praying. God provided a way for us to be victorious, even when we fail and yield to temptation. We simply need to repent, confess our sin, and get back on the right track with Jesus; not allowing Satan to keep us away from God.

We must also guard against becoming a scoffer. This attitude will alienate us from other people. Nobody wants to be around someone who is continually railing against and mocking others. People who mock at sacred principles and responsibilities are an abomination to God and insulting to others.

Dear Father, thank You for Your patience and love toward me. I have failed You many times, but You have never failed me. Purify my thoughts so that they will be pleasing to You. May Your Words dwell in my heart so that I will not sin against You. Lord, may I think loving and kind thoughts toward others and may I never be a scoffer who demeans others. Deliver me from all foolish thoughts and give me the mind of Christ, so that I am a good witness for You in this world. I ask this in the name of Jesus. Amen.

Proverbs 24:10 If thou faint in the day of adversity, thy strength is small.

No one likes to face adversity, but it is part of life. Accepting Christ as Savior does not exempt us from the trials of life. Jesus said that we will have tribulation in the world (John 16:33), but we must not lose heart, because He has overcome the world. God has enabled us to stand through adversity victoriously by the power of the Holy Spirit.

"Therefore whosoever heareth these sayings of mine, and doeth them, I will liken him unto a wise man, which built his house upon a rock: And the rain descended, and the floods came, and the winds blew, and beat upon that house; and it fell not: for it was founded upon a rock. And every one that heareth these sayings of mine, and doeth them not, shall be likened unto a foolish man, which built his house upon the sand: And the rain descended, and the floods came, and the winds blew, and beat upon that house; and it fell: and great was the fall of it" (Matthew 7:24-27).

Strength to endure adversity comes from acting upon Christ's words. James 1:22 tells us that if we are only hearers, but not *doers* of the Word, we deceive ourselves. Through obedience to Him, we can become overcomers. We cannot expect to walk in victory if we continue to sin. Once we come to God, we must study the Bible to find out what is required of us. Ignorance is no excuse for disobeying God's commands, as Hosea 4:6a tells us that we can be destroyed for lack of knowledge. We cannot claim ignorance if we have the Holy Spirit within us, because He promises to guide us. He would never lead us to sin. God writes His laws on our heart, and leads us in His ways as we yield to Him. We are accountable to obey God's Word once we hear it. Obedience brings victory! "For this is the covenant that I will make with the house of Israel after those days, saith the Lord; I will put my laws into their mind, and write them in their hearts: and I will be to them a God, and they shall be to me a people" (Hebrews 8:10). "For if ye live after the flesh, ye shall die: but if ye through the Spirit do mortify the deeds of the body, ye shall live. For as many as are led by the Spirit of God, they are the sons of God" (Romans 8:13-14).

Affliction, adversity, and tribulation may come against us, but we need not be overcome by them. We have been given God's Word and the power of the Holy Spirit to overcome anything with which Satan may attack us. God in us is greater than Satan. "Ye are of God, little children, and have overcome them: because greater is he that is in you, than he that is in the world" (1 John 4:4). In Christ, we are more than conquerors.

"Who shall separate us from the love of Christ? shall tribulation, or distress, or persecution, or famine, or nakedness, or peril, or sword? As it is written, For thy sake we are killed all the day long; we are accounted as sheep for the slaughter. Nay, in all these things we are more than conquerors through him that loved us" (Romans 8:35-37). Our natural strength may be small, but in Christ we can overcome every adversity. "I can do all things through Christ which strengtheneth me" (Philippians 4:13).

Father, thank You for sustaining me in my afflictions. I appreciate the strength to overcome those things that the enemy has tried to use to destroy me. When You open doors for me to testify to Your saving and sustaining grace, give me the boldness to share with others what You have done. Fill me with Your Spirit, that I might overcome anything that I face–both today and in the future. Give me grace not to look at the adverse circumstances around me, but rather look at the greatness of Your power! May I be reminded of the things You have done for me in the past, knowing that You will continue to help me today in my need. I ask this in Jesus' name. Amen.

God's Wisdom for Daily Living — ***Betty Miller***

September 8 — ***Day 251***

Proverbs 24:11-12 11 Deliver those who are drawn away to death, and those who totter to the slaughter hold back (from their doom). 12 If you (profess ignorance and) say, Behold, we did not know this, does not He Who weighs and ponders the hearts perceive and consider it? And He Who guards your life, does not He know it? And shall not He render to (you and) every man according to his works? (AMP).

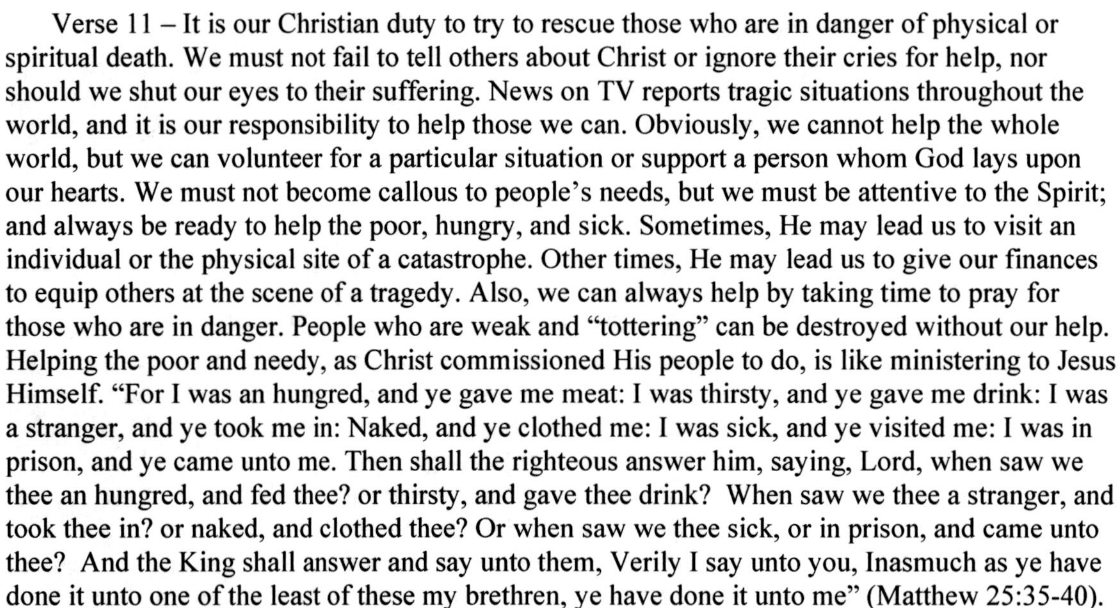

Verse 11 – It is our Christian duty to try to rescue those who are in danger of physical or spiritual death. We must not fail to tell others about Christ or ignore their cries for help, nor should we shut our eyes to their suffering. News on TV reports tragic situations throughout the world, and it is our responsibility to help those we can. Obviously, we cannot help the whole world, but we can volunteer for a particular situation or support a person whom God lays upon our hearts. We must not become callous to people's needs, but we must be attentive to the Spirit; and always be ready to help the poor, hungry, and sick. Sometimes, He may lead us to visit an individual or the physical site of a catastrophe. Other times, He may lead us to give our finances to equip others at the scene of a tragedy. Also, we can always help by taking time to pray for those who are in danger. People who are weak and "tottering" can be destroyed without our help. Helping the poor and needy, as Christ commissioned His people to do, is like ministering to Jesus Himself. "For I was an hungred, and ye gave me meat: I was thirsty, and ye gave me drink: I was a stranger, and ye took me in: Naked, and ye clothed me: I was sick, and ye visited me: I was in prison, and ye came unto me. Then shall the righteous answer him, saying, Lord, when saw we thee an hungred, and fed thee? or thirsty, and gave thee drink? When saw we thee a stranger, and took thee in? or naked, and clothed thee? Or when saw we thee sick, or in prison, and came unto thee? And the King shall answer and say unto them, Verily I say unto you, Inasmuch as ye have done it unto one of the least of these my brethren, ye have done it unto me" (Matthew 25:35-40).

Verse 12 – God knows our hearts. If we do not sow kindness, but make excuses for not helping others when they have a need, we will reap what we sow, and no one will help us when we need it. God desires His children to have a heart like His. He is merciful, kind, loving, and giving, and we should strive to be like Him. He promises to heal us and deliver us from trouble because we have given to the poor. What wonderful "insurance!"

"Blessed is he that considereth the poor: the LORD will deliver him in time of trouble. The LORD will preserve him, and keep him alive; and he shall be blessed upon the earth: and thou wilt not deliver him unto the will of his enemies. The LORD will strengthen him upon the bed of languishing: thou wilt make all his bed in his sickness" (Psalm 41:1-3). To sum up our Christian duty to the needy, I am reminded from the words of an old hymn to *"Rescue the Perishing; Care for the Dying."*

Dear heavenly Father, thank You for blessing me. Give me a greater heart to reach out and bless others. Please keep me from selfishness, insecurity, lust, indifference, and any other thing that would keep me from sharing the things You have given me. May I always be reminded that all I own belongs to You; I am only a steward over it. Lord, I want to hear Your voice as to where and how much I should give. I always want to be generous and kind; one who reaches out to the poor and the needy. Help me to be sensitive to those who are hurting, and deliver me from any hardness of heart that would cause me to turn a deaf ear to the needs of others. I ask this in the name of Jesus Christ. Amen.

Proverbs 24:13-14 13 My son, eat thou honey, because it is good; and the honeycomb, which is sweet to thy taste: 14 So shall the knowledge of wisdom be unto thy soul: when thou hast found it, then there shall be a reward, and thy expectation shall not be cut off.

Verse 13 – As honey is sweet to the taste, godly wisdom is sweet to the soul. Since Jesus is Wisdom, this verse is telling us to taste of His life and discover how sweet He is. All the treasures of wisdom are hidden in Him. When we taste of God's character as revealed through Christ, we find Him sweet and good. Jesus is also called *"the Word."* Reading and absorbing God's Word is satisfying to our souls, as noted by the Psalmist David: "How sweet are thy words unto my taste! yea, sweeter than honey to my mouth" (Psalm 119:103).

The wisdom found in Jesus will produce a future with fulfillment and reward in this life. It gives us an expectation for eternal life and salvation that will not be cut off. God has recorded His commandments and statutes, giving us examples through the lives that are recorded in the Bible. He knows all things and shows no partiality. He is completely good, upright and wise. His judgments are true and righteous and we do not need to fear them, if we have reverential fear for our Lord. It is little wonder that David praised God's judgments in this way: "The statutes of the LORD are right, rejoicing the heart: the commandment of the LORD is pure, enlightening the eyes. The fear of the LORD is clean, enduring for ever: the judgments of the LORD are true and righteous altogether. More to be desired are they than gold, yea, than much fine gold: sweeter also than honey and the honeycomb. Moreover by them is thy servant warned: and in keeping of them there is great reward" (Psalm 19:8-11).

Verse 14 – Canaan, the land promised to the Israelites, was exceptionally fruitful. The cattle had lush grass upon which they could graze, making them superior milk producers. From the pollen of innumerable flowering trees and plants, bees produced an abundance of honey. Hence, the land was described as "flowing with milk and honey" (Leviticus 20:22-24). Spiritually our "land of milk and honey" is when we receive the promises of God. We have been given great and precious promises. When we walk in obedience, we meet the conditions and God fulfills the promises. The Lord desires that we taste of His ways by obeying Him; when we do, we will find they are sweeter than honey! He promises us many wonderful things; including health, provision, protection, guidance, and victory over Satanic attacks! Knowing God personally, however, is the most wondrous, satisfying, "sweet" experience of all. Jesus is our Rock, and there is honey in this Rock!

Dear heavenly Father, thank You for saving my soul. I am grateful to be Your child and to have sweet fellowship with You. Lord, it is a privilege to be a part of the family of God! I am so happy to know that my name is written in the Book of Life. May I always have a joyful spirit so that those who do not know You might be drawn to You through my life of happiness. Thank You Lord, for the many delights I have known because of my wonderful Savior, Jesus. I ask that I might know You even deeper and more intimately. Let Your Word become as honey when I read it. I ask this in the name of Jesus. Amen.

Proverbs 24:15-16 15 Lay not wait, O wicked man, against the dwelling of the righteous; spoil not his resting place: 16 For a just man falleth seven times, and riseth up again: but the wicked shall fall into mischief.

Verse 15 – God sustains the righteous through difficulties, but the wicked will be overthrown by their own evil. God's children are the apple of His eye (Deuteronomy 32:9-10; Zechariah 2:8), and He is very protective of them. Whoever harms them will be punished.

God does not want the wicked to perish, but He desires all to come to repentance. Because God is merciful and slow to anger, the wicked are often given many years to repent. Because of this, they may think they have escaped God's wrath, but there is a day of reckoning for all people. Woe to the wicked person who dies unrepentant! "The LORD is known by the judgment which he executeth: the wicked is snared in the work of his own hands. Higgaion. (Pause for meditation). Selah. The wicked shall be turned into hell, and all the nations that forget God. For the needy shall not alway be forgotten: the expectation of the poor shall not perish for ever. Arise, O LORD; let not man prevail: let the heathen be judged in thy sight" (Psalm 9:16-19).

God spares the righteous from the judgment that they bring upon themselves when they sin if they will repent. He will also spare the wicked for the sake of the righteous. We see an example of this when God visited Abraham before destroying Sodom and Gomorrah. Genesis 18:22-33 records that Abraham interceded for the cities. God agreed to spare them if fifty righteous men were found in them. Abraham asked God five more times to spare the cities, each time for the sake of a smaller number of righteous men. God would have spared them had there been only ten righteous men in Sodom, but apparently there were not. Only Lot and his family escaped. God is easily entreated. He may spare the wicked, granting them more time to repent, if we intercede for them. God is concerned and kind toward evil people even though they fail to recognize and acknowledge Him. "That ye may be the children of your Father which is in heaven: for he maketh his sun to rise on the evil and on the good, and sendeth rain on the just and on the unjust" (Matthew 5:45).

Verse 16 – Even if a righteous man falls down in sin seven times, he will rise again to get the victory if he repents. Numbers are often symbolic in the Scriptures, with the number seven standing for "perfection" or "completion." For example, when Jesus told Peter to forgive seventy times seven, He was not saying to forgive 490 times. He was telling Peter to forgive completely and perfectly. To the Jew, numbers were descriptions, rather than mathematics, as each number represented something. With this in mind, when a righteous man falls completely down, He can still rise again, because of what Jesus did for him on the cross. In Christ, there is "complete" forgiveness, even in spite of our "complete" failure. Praise God!

Dear Father, thank You for Your great mercy and goodness toward me. I am thankful that You are kind even to the wicked; since You desire that no one perish. Lord, may I be patient with the wicked, as You are, and pray for them to come to the saving knowledge of Christ. I do know that we must all face You in judgment one day, and I want to come to You now so that I may deal with any sin and failures. Then, when I face You on that Day, I will not have anything hidden or left undone that I should have taken care of today. Cleanse me from all unrighteousness. I pray this in the name of Jesus, my Lord. Amen.

God's Wisdom for Daily Living **Betty Miller**
September 11 ***Day 254***

Proverbs 24:17-18 17 Rejoice not when your enemy falls, and let not your heart be glad when he stumbles or is overthrown; 18 Lest the LORD see it, and it be evil in His eyes and displease Him, and He turn away His wrath from him (to expend it upon you, the worse offender).

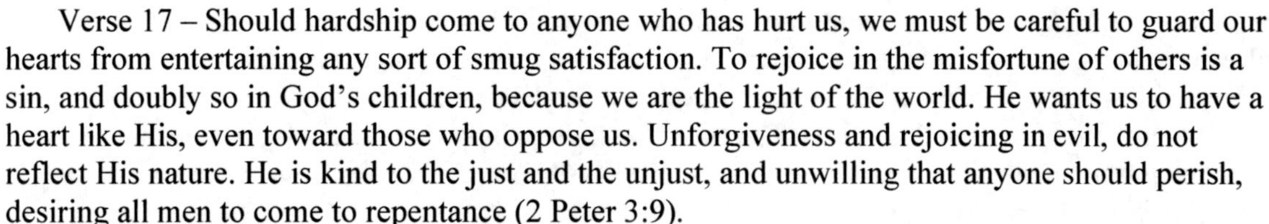

Verse 17 – Should hardship come to anyone who has hurt us, we must be careful to guard our hearts from entertaining any sort of smug satisfaction. To rejoice in the misfortune of others is a sin, and doubly so in God's children, because we are the light of the world. He wants us to have a heart like His, even toward those who oppose us. Unforgiveness and rejoicing in evil, do not reflect His nature. He is kind to the just and the unjust, and unwilling that anyone should perish, desiring all men to come to repentance (2 Peter 3:9).

"But I say unto you, Love your enemies, bless them that curse you, do good to them that hate you, and pray for them which despitefully use you, and persecute you; That ye may be the children of your Father which is in heaven: for he maketh his sun to rise on the evil and on the good, and sendeth rain on the just and on the unjust" (Matthew 5:44-45).

It would be impossible to truly love our enemies, if God were not living in our hearts. However, if we yield to Him, His grace causes us to do what is impossible. Many wicked people have turned to Christ because those whom they hurt forgave them and demonstrated Jesus' love to them. "Dearly beloved, avenge not yourselves, but rather give place unto wrath: for it is written, Vengeance is mine; I will repay, saith the Lord. Therefore if thine enemy hunger, feed him; if he thirst, give him drink: for in so doing thou shalt heap coals of fire on his head. Be not overcome of evil, but overcome evil with good" (Romans 12:19-21).

Evil things happen to people who commit evil, for they reap what they sow, but it is not God's desire for this to happen. There are spiritual laws which govern the wrath of God. Just as there are laws of physics, there are spiritual laws in operation in the universe. If I were to defy the law of gravity and step off the top of a cliff, I would suffer the consequences of a fall that might kill me. Likewise, when I defy God's spiritual laws, I activate the death principle, bringing harm to my spirit, soul, and body. The heart of God is ever wooing and drawing people away from sin, so that they may avert its consequences. He is always ready to forgive us of our sins and restore us.

Dear heavenly Father, I am grateful that You loved me and kept me before I ever gave my heart to You. I ask for Your grace to love and reach out to those who persecute me and do all manner of evil against me. Fill me with the Holy Spirit so that I can love others the way You love them. Lord, I choose to forgive all who have something against me. I do want to be perfect in You, so I ask for Your mercy and grace to lead me in the path that will produce Your likeness in me. May I extend that same mercy and grace to all, especially my enemies. I ask this in the name of the Lord Jesus. Amen.

God's Wisdom for Daily Living ***Betty Miller***
September 12 ***Day 255***

Proverbs 24:19-20 19 Fret not thyself because of evil men, neither be thou envious at the wicked; 20 For there shall be no reward to the evil man; the candle of the wicked shall be put out.

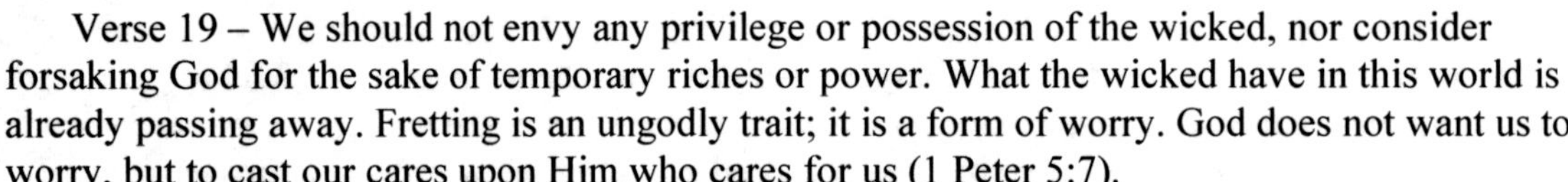

Verse 19 – We should not envy any privilege or possession of the wicked, nor consider forsaking God for the sake of temporary riches or power. What the wicked have in this world is already passing away. Fretting is an ungodly trait; it is a form of worry. God does not want us to worry, but to cast our cares upon Him who cares for us (1 Peter 5:7).

We are told to remain thankful, no matter what kind of situation we find ourselves in, and look to God in prayer for the needed answers to the problems of that situation. When we do this, God furnishes His peace to us, even in a storm or fearful circumstances. God's peace is one of the most wonderful gifts that He gives to us because it is not dependent upon our circumstances. Every child of God can testify to this, since we all face problems in life, and many times we should be worried or upset. However, because we pray, we are given His peace that passes all human understanding. "Do not fret or have any anxiety about anything, but in every circumstance and in everything by prayer and petition (definite requests) with thanksgiving continue to make your wants known to God. And God's peace (be yours, that tranquil state of a soul assured of its salvation through Christ, and so fearing nothing from God and content with its earthly lot of whatever sort that is, that peace) which transcends all understanding, shall garrison and mount guard over your hearts and minds in Christ Jesus" (Philippians 4:6-7 AMP).

Verse 20 – Wicked men will not be rewarded by God. They do reap what they sow, but they will never be given a reward from God, as the righteous man receives. Jesus tells us that when he returns, He will be bringing a reward with Him to give to every person according to what he has done. We are not saved by works; salvation is God's free gift to all who repent of their sin and give their lives to Jesus Christ. However, after we are saved, God records our works in a book. We will be rewarded for everything we have done for Him at Christ's coming (Revelation 22:12).

This verse also states that the lamp of the wicked shall be extinguished. Light is God's blessing to us. Without light, no one can walk safely, either physically or spiritually. The first thing we do when the power fails is to search for a flashlight or a candle. Living in permanent darkness would be an awful thing. Natural darkness is only a picture of the true darkness which is spiritual. Jesus is described as the light of the world: "... I am the light of the world: he that followeth me shall not walk in darkness, but shall have the light of life" (John 8:12b). Following Jesus, causes us to walk in the light, so that we can see the proper path, do our tasks, know when things are dirty so that we can clean them, enjoy seeing beauty and the people we love, and so much more. "But ye are a chosen generation, a royal priesthood, an holy nation, a peculiar people; that ye should show forth the praises of him who hath called you out of darkness into his marvelous light" (1 Peter 2:9-10).

Dear heavenly Father, I am grateful for the peace that You have given me. Thank You for delivering me from worry and fear, so that I will not fret about the evil in the world. I am also thankful for the daily guidance You give me, so that I can walk in the light of Your ways. I appreciate Your goodness. Teach me more about Your ways, so that I do not stumble on the path of life. May I shine with Your light, so that others may see my good works and glorify my Father in heaven. I ask this in the name of the Lord Jesus. Amen.

Proverbs 24:21-22 21 My son, reverently fear the LORD and the king, and do not associate with those who are given to change (of allegiance, and are revolutionary); 22 For their calamity shall rise suddenly, and who knows the punishment and ruin which both (the LORD and the king) will bring upon the rebellious? (AMP).

Verse 21 – This verse makes it clear that we are to give reverential fear to God. God is the one who set the authority structures in the earth; therefore we should honor those positions. He set government authority over cities and countries, ministry order over the church, and parental order over families. It was God who created the home and put the husband as head of it. He put the offices of the five-fold ministry over the church with the apostles, prophets, evangelists, pastors, and teachers as the leaders. He also wanted for Old Testament Israel, as the first nation led by God, to be an example of His leadership over a group of people. God's plan in the earth is one of order, and therefore He expects us to honor the offices and positions of earthly leaders who rule in authoritative roles. Anarchy and rebellion are acts that are motivated by the devil. (There is a Biblical and proper way to deal with those in authority who abuse their positions; however, it is not revolt and anger that has a mob mentality behind it.) "Let every soul be subject unto the higher powers. For there is no power but of God: the powers that be are ordained of God. Whosoever therefore resisteth the power, resisteth the ordinance of God: and they that resist shall receive to themselves damnation. For rulers are not a terror to good works, but to the evil. Wilt thou then not be afraid of the power? do that which is good, and thou shalt have praise of the same: For he is the minister of God to thee for good. But if thou do that which is evil, be afraid; for he beareth not the sword in vain: for he is the minister of God, a revenger to execute wrath upon him that doeth evil" (Romans 13:1-4).

God set the five-fold ministry of the offices of apostles, prophets, evangelists, pastors, and teachers over the church for leadership. "And he gave some, apostles; and some, prophets; and some, evangelists; and some, pastors and teachers; For the perfecting of the saints, for the work of the ministry, for the edifying of the body of Christ" (Ephesians 4:11-12). It was God who established the family unit and set the husband as the head of it. "Wives, submit yourselves unto your own husbands, as unto the Lord. For the husband is the head of the wife, even as Christ is the head of the church: and he is the saviour of the body. Therefore, as the church is subject unto Christ, so let the wives be to their own husbands in every thing. Husbands, love your wives, even as Christ also loved the church, and gave himself for it" (Ephesians 5:22-25).

Verse 22 – Today's verses also entreat us to avoid rebellious and double-minded people who are unstable and keep changing their loyalties, taking first one side then another of an issue. These are unstable in all of their ways (James 1:5-8). Those who are given to changing loyalties will suddenly come to ruin. Punishment could come as a judgment for breaking God's laws, or it could come as a penalty from a ruler for breaking the law of the land, or it might be both.

Father, I am grateful that You are a God of order. I ask You to help me to always obey Your laws and the laws in our land which are for our good. I ask You to remove any rebellion from my heart and give me a submissive spirit. Lord, may I always honor and respect those whom You have placed over me. I also pray that we will be given good men and women to rule over us in all government offices of the land. Lord, may they take advice from godly counsel and heed the Bible so that we all may lead quiet and peaceable lives. I ask this in the name of Jesus. Amen.

Proverbs 24:23 These things also belong to the wise. It is not good to have respect of persons in judgment.

This verse is addressed to the wise, who are told not to discriminate or show partiality when sitting in a position of judgment. In order to make a fair judgment about anything, there first must be laws that are considered the standard in a situation. The standard for Christians consists of God's laws that are recorded in the Bible. These rules and commandments were given so that people could live blessed and peaceable lives. God's laws preserve order on earth and also show man his sin and need of a Savior. Those who walk in the Spirit, fulfill the law by loving others. They reap the blessings that come from walking in God's ways.

The Bible outlines various penalties for breaking God's laws. The ultimate penalty for sinners is that they will go to hell. I want to repeat what has been included in previous verses, because of its utmost importance. The good news is that Jesus, the son of God, came to the earth and died on a cross, giving Himself as the only sacrifice that could make atonement for our sin. He was raised from the dead and is now seated at the right hand of God. As the ultimate Judge, He is not a respecter of persons. What He will do for one, He will do for another. All who come to God through Jesus will be pardoned, no matter what sin they have committed. "But God commendeth his love toward us, in that, while we were yet sinners, Christ died for us. Much more then, being now justified by his blood, we shall be saved from wrath through him. For if, when we were enemies, we were reconciled to God by the death of his Son, much more, being reconciled, we shall be saved by his life" (Romans 5:8-10).

America's founding fathers were Christians and based much of her legal structure on the Bible's moral laws. Many laws in the U.S. are based directly on laws found in Deuteronomy. To our detriment, many sound laws have been altered or abandoned. Scripture describes times such as ours: "And he shall speak great words against the most High, and shall wear out the saints of the most High, and think to change times and laws: and they shall be given into his hand until a time and times and the dividing of time" (Daniel 7:25).

Our present-day judicial system has drifted from its original intent of protecting the innocent and convicting the wicked. Today, the law is being exploited by some people who want to use it for gain. Many are seeking outlandish settlements, that in the end all people will pay for. Through unfair settlements such as these, lawyers are the ones most rewarded. Of course, not all lawyers are greedy. Many good lawyers seek to help and serve their clients. However, due to a faulty legal system, protection of the innocent has often been over-ruled, while criminals are not justly dealt with. We need to return to Biblical principles and shape our laws accordingly, if we desire to see justice in our land. "The God of Israel said...He that ruleth over men must be just, ruling in the fear of God" (2 Samuel 23:3). "Shall not the Judge of all the earth do right?" (Genesis 18:25b).

Dear heavenly Father, I am eternally grateful that You have forgiven me of my sins and that You paid the price for them on the cross. I now want to serve You faithfully every day. I am also thankful that You are a righteous judge. I can always commit my case to You, and You will treat me fairly in everything. Since You are no respecter of persons, You will do this for all who look to You. Lord, I pray that as a nation, we will be given righteous judges so that all people will receive justice in the courts of our land. I ask this in the name of the Lord Jesus Christ. Amen.

Proverbs 24:24-26 24 He who says to the wicked, You are righteous and innocent–peoples will curse him, nations will defy and abhor him. 25 But to those (upright judges) who rebuke the wicked, it will go well with them and they will find delight, and a good blessing will be upon them. 26 He kisses the lips (and wins the hearts of men) who give a right answer (AMP).

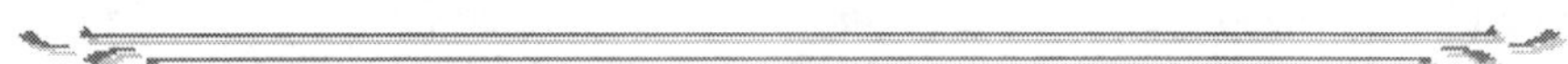

People approve of righteous judges, but hold authorities in contempt who favor the wicked. Judges who reward evildoers with a light sentence will be cursed by the people and be judged severely themselves. The Bible tells us that there is a very strong penalty for perverting justice (Isaiah 5:20-24 and Proverbs 17:13).

Judges need discernment from God in order to serve the people in a fair manner. Those who are motivated by self-interest are not in a position to receive wisdom from God, but are prone to deception. People of good character possess the most important qualification for sitting as a judge. They will bring forth justice when they rule in difficult cases.

We all must make judgments in life. Some Christians mistakenly believe that we should not judge others at all; but that is not what scripture teaches. Most of us are familiar with Matthew 7:1: "Judge not, that ye be not judged." If we look only at this one verse, we will feel guilty about making an evaluation of a situation. However, we need to look at the verse in its proper context: "… For with what judgment ye judge, ye shall be judged: and with what measure ye mete, it shall be measured to you again. And why beholdest thou the mote that is in thy brother's eye, but considerest not the beam that is in thine own eye? Or how wilt thou say to thy brother, Let me pull out the mote out of thine eye; and, behold, a beam is in thine own eye? Thou hypocrite, first cast out the beam out of thine own eye; and then shalt thou see clearly to cast out the mote out of thy brother's eye" (Matthew 7:2-5).

Jesus did not say we should never judge, but rather told us *how* to judge. This passage was part of the Sermon on the Mount, which began with the Beatitudes. "Blessed are the merciful: for they shall obtain mercy" (Matthew 5:7). If we want others to be merciful to us when we make mistakes, we must extend mercy to others. We should not judge by our feelings or impressions, but according to God's Word. "Stop judging by mere appearances, and make a right judgment" (John 7:24 NIV). If we see sin in our own lives, or the lives of others, we must not gloss over it or excuse it (and thus call evil good), but call it sin. Then, we are to repent of our sins and pray for others who are in sin, asking the Lord to forgive and deliver them. As we make these kinds of honest judgments, we bring help–and not condemnation–to those who are in sin. This will point them to the One who both loves and forgives them.

Dear heavenly Father, thank You for Your Word. I do appreciate You teaching me to be kind and merciful. Help me to judge fairly and correctly when I am called to evaluate a situation. May I have a heart to reach out and help people deal with their sin and help them find their answers in You. Lord, give me wisdom and discernment in dealing with others. Give us righteous judges in our land so that people will receive fair judgments. Be merciful to all of us and deliver us from evil. I ask this in the name of Jesus. Amen.

God's Wisdom for Daily Living — ***Betty Miller***
September 16 — ***Day 259***

Proverbs 24:27 Prepare thy work without, and make it fit for thyself in the field; and afterwards build thine house.

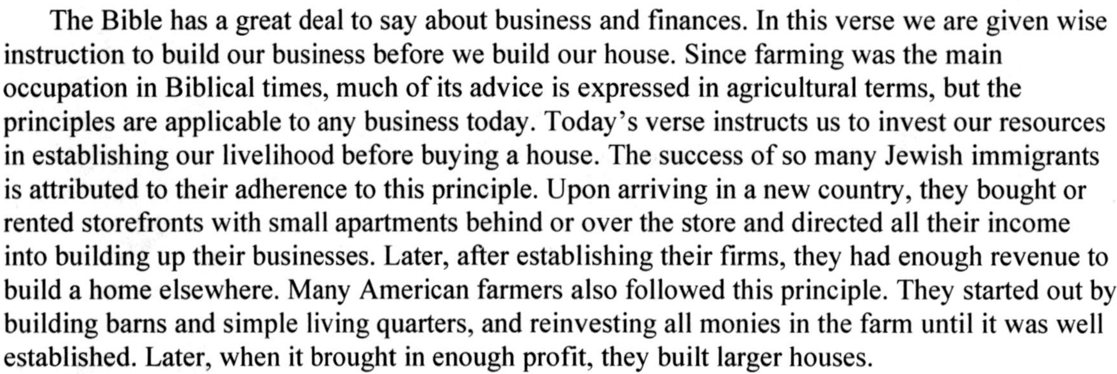

The Bible has a great deal to say about business and finances. In this verse we are given wise instruction to build our business before we build our house. Since farming was the main occupation in Biblical times, much of its advice is expressed in agricultural terms, but the principles are applicable to any business today. Today's verse instructs us to invest our resources in establishing our livelihood before buying a house. The success of so many Jewish immigrants is attributed to their adherence to this principle. Upon arriving in a new country, they bought or rented storefronts with small apartments behind or over the store and directed all their income into building up their businesses. Later, after establishing their firms, they had enough revenue to build a home elsewhere. Many American farmers also followed this principle. They started out by building barns and simple living quarters, and reinvesting all monies in the farm until it was well established. Later, when it brought in enough profit, they built larger houses.

Ignorant of good business principles, many young couples today go bankrupt. They start out by buying big homes and creating such high monthly overhead that they are unable to support the companies they begin. If they would start by renting a small place until the business did well, they would be able to buy the big house later. The American Dream usually slips through the grasp of those who pursue it without establishing a foundation of hard work and sacrifice. God desires to bless us with material things, but He does not want us to be so consumed with life's cares that we do not make time for Him. Not having time to pray with our families, read our Bibles, or fellowship with believers gives Satan an opening to destroy our homes and finances.

"And it shall be, when the LORD thy God shall have brought thee into the land which he sware unto thy fathers, to Abraham, to Isaac, and to Jacob, to give thee great and goodly cities, which thou buildedst not, And houses full of all good things, which thou filledst not, and wells digged, which thou diggedst not, vineyards and olive trees, which thou plantedst not; when thou shalt have eaten and be full; Then beware lest thou forget the LORD, which brought thee forth out of the land of Egypt, from the house of bondage. Thou shalt fear the LORD thy God, and serve him, and shalt swear by his name. Ye shall not go after other gods, of the gods of the people which are round about you; (For the LORD thy God is a jealous God among you) lest the anger of the LORD thy God be kindled against thee, and destroy thee from off the face of the earth" (Deuteronomy 6:10-15).

Dear Father in heaven, thank You so much for Your provision for me. I appreciate Your faithfulness to furnish my needs each and every day. I am looking to You to guide me in the financial affairs of my life. I resist greed, and ask for contentment with the things that I own today. I know that You will bless me more as I learn Your ways and follow You. Help me to be a good steward over my finances, my home and all the things that You have given me. I appreciate the material blessings You have given me; but most of all, I appreciate the spiritual blessings that are mine, which money cannot buy. In Jesus' name I pray. Amen

God's Wisdom for Daily Living ***Betty Miller***
September 17 ***Day 260***

Proverbs 24:28-29 28 Be not a witness against thy neighbour without cause; and deceive not with thy lips. 29 Say not, I will do so to him as he hath done to me: I will render to the man according to his work.

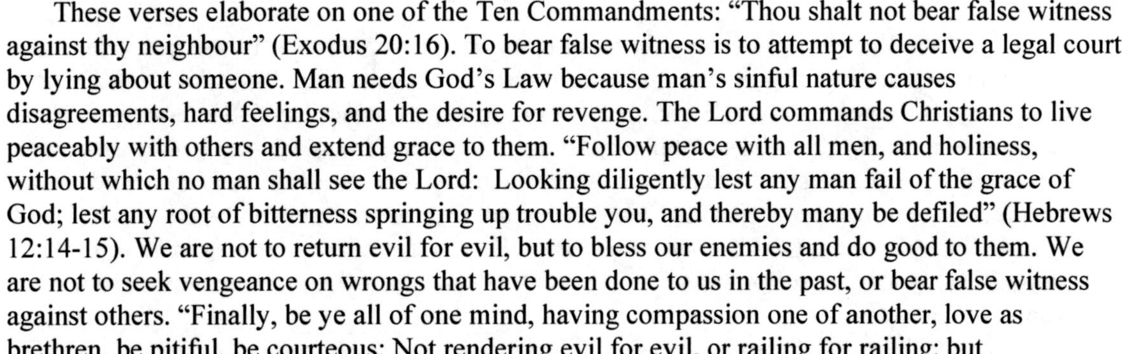

These verses elaborate on one of the Ten Commandments: "Thou shalt not bear false witness against thy neighbour" (Exodus 20:16). To bear false witness is to attempt to deceive a legal court by lying about someone. Man needs God's Law because man's sinful nature causes disagreements, hard feelings, and the desire for revenge. The Lord commands Christians to live peaceably with others and extend grace to them. "Follow peace with all men, and holiness, without which no man shall see the Lord: Looking diligently lest any man fail of the grace of God; lest any root of bitterness springing up trouble you, and thereby many be defiled" (Hebrews 12:14-15). We are not to return evil for evil, but to bless our enemies and do good to them. We are not to seek vengeance on wrongs that have been done to us in the past, or bear false witness against others. "Finally, be ye all of one mind, having compassion one of another, love as brethren, be pitiful, be courteous: Not rendering evil for evil, or railing for railing: but contrariwise blessing; knowing that ye are thereunto called, that ye should inherit a blessing. For he that will love life, and see good days, let him refrain his tongue from evil, and his lips that they speak no guile: Let him eschew evil, and do good; let him seek peace, and ensue it" (1 Peter 3:8-12).

God will bless us when we obey His Word, whether or not our opponents acknowledge or appreciate our right actions. Vengeance alienates people, whether neighbors, fellow-Christians, or enemies, and an offended brother is harder to win back than a strong city (Proverbs 18:19). We cannot win the lost to Christ nor help a Christian in error if we exact vengeance upon them for hurting us. "Dearly beloved, avenge not yourselves, but rather give place unto wrath: for it is written, Vengeance is mine; I will repay, saith the Lord. Therefore if thine enemy hunger, feed him; if he thirst, give him drink: for in so doing thou shalt heap coals of fire on his head. Be not overcome of evil, but overcome evil with good" (Romans 12:19-21). God knows how to deal justly with every person.

If we are wise, we will learn to guard our mouths and not say things we will later regret. It is possible to be wrong, even when we are right, by having a wrong attitude. If we want to be leaders in the church, we must not enter into strife with others, but deal gently with everyone. If we ask, God will help us to do this and cause His goodness to flow through us. "And the servant of the Lord must not strive; but be gentle unto all men, apt to teach, patient, in meekness instructing those that oppose themselves; if God peradventure will give them repentance to the acknowledging of the truth" (2 Timothy 2:24-25).

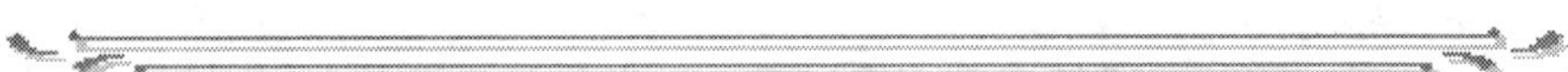

Dear heavenly Father, I want to be a person who is not easily offended, one who trusts You to deal with those who would seek to do evil against me. I know that I cannot do this within myself, so I am asking You to fill me with the Spirit so that I can honestly love my enemies and do good to them. I know this kind of love only comes from You. Lord, forgive those who plot evil against me and say evil things about me. Open their eyes to the truth. Give me the grace and patience to allow You to deal with them, since I truly want to overcome evil with good. I ask this in the name of Jesus Christ. Amen.

Proverbs 24:30-32 30 I went by the field of the slothful, and by the vineyard of the man void of understanding; 31 And, lo, it was all grown over with thorns, and nettles had covered the face thereof, and the stone wall thereof was broken down. 32 Then I saw, and considered it well: I looked upon it, and received instruction.

These verses in Proverbs tell us that the slothful or lazy person's property will be evidenced by the obvious neglect and lack of care that it shows. What does the word "slothful mean?" The dictionary[33] tells us that it means "Disinclined to work or use exertion; lazy." Someone who is lazy will not take care of the things that belong to them. They are irresponsible. That is the reason they never will acquire an estate. Laziness is one of the things that produces poverty. (Of course, some people are born into poverty and it is not their fault they are in it; however, they do not have to stay in it. If they come to God, He will show them the way out of it by helping them to find a good job.) There is another scripture in Proverbs that tells us that a slothful person is a brother to one who is a great waster.

Solomon noted the evidence of laziness; fields overgrown with thorns and vineyards and stone walls in disrepair. Thorns and nettles choke whatever crop one plants, and overtake it (Matthew 13:7), making them very difficult to dislodge. Broken walls allow foxes (or enemies) to enter and spoil one's vineyard (Song of Solomon 2:15). Since agriculture was the main occupation in Biblical times, most Israelites owned fields and vineyards. Those who were poor workers reaped poor harvests. Though we have different "fields" of work today, the Biblical observations on slothfulness remain applicable. If we do a poor job, the results will be the same: both our performance record and income will be poor.

"He also that is slothful in his work is brother to him that is a great waster" (Proverbs 18:9). Because slothful people are self-serving, they neglect their responsibilities at work and perform poorly, wasting their employers' time and money. To the employer, this is like sustaining a loss because someone destroyed equipment. A godly person has a servant's heart and works well, as unto the Lord. "Servants, be obedient to them that are your masters according to the flesh, with fear and trembling, in singleness of your heart, as unto Christ; Not with eyeservice, as menpleasers; but as the servants of Christ, doing the will of God from the heart; With good will doing service, as to the Lord, and not to men" (Ephesians 6:5-7). Organized, efficient workers stand out and receive promotions. We can learn what not to do by observing how the laziness of others wastes time and resources.

Dear heavenly Father, thank You for giving me talents and gifts to contribute my portion to making this world a better place. Lord, I do appreciate the strength and grace to be able to do my job daily. May I always be a good and cheerful worker. Help me not to complain in the work place, but to do my job with a joyful attitude. Give me a servant's heart to serve, not only those in charge, but also to be mindful of all of my co-laborers. May my labor be a tribute to Your touch on my life, and let everything I do be of excellent quality and workmanship. I ask this in the name of the Lord Jesus Christ. Amen.

---

[33] The American Heritage® Dictionary of the English Language, Fourth Edition
Copyright © 2006 by Houghton Mifflin Company.
Published by Houghton Mifflin Company. All rights reserved.

Proverbs 24:33-34 33 Yet a little sleep, a little slumber, a little folding of the hands to sleep: 34 So shall thy poverty come as one that travelleth; and thy want as an armed man.

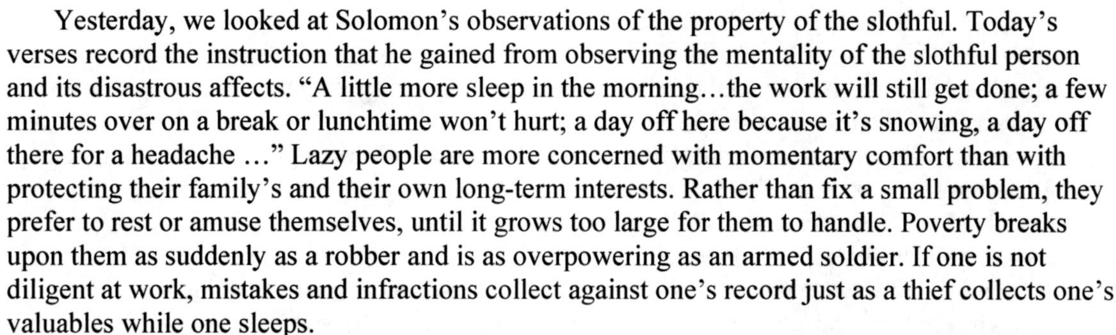

Yesterday, we looked at Solomon's observations of the property of the slothful. Today's verses record the instruction that he gained from observing the mentality of the slothful person and its disastrous affects. "A little more sleep in the morning...the work will still get done; a few minutes over on a break or lunchtime won't hurt; a day off here because it's snowing, a day off there for a headache ..." Lazy people are more concerned with momentary comfort than with protecting their family's and their own long-term interests. Rather than fix a small problem, they prefer to rest or amuse themselves, until it grows too large for them to handle. Poverty breaks upon them as suddenly as a robber and is as overpowering as an armed soldier. If one is not diligent at work, mistakes and infractions collect against one's record just as a thief collects one's valuables while one sleeps.

God allots everyone the same number of hours in a day. We choose to wisely use or waste them. Some people waste their precious time by over-indulging in sleep. We are admonished as "children of light" to be spiritually alert and watchful. We must ask God to help us balance our time between work, sleep, rest, play, prayer, study, and ministry to others. Time and sleep are both God's gifts. When we are careful to balance our lives properly, and give our worries to God, our sleep will be refreshing. "When thou liest down, thou shalt not be afraid: yea, thou shalt lie down, and thy sleep shall be sweet" (Proverbs 3:24). With His guidance and enabling, we will not neglect the important things that must be accomplished in our allotted 24-hour day.

The Bible says that a man who labors will have sweet sleep, while those who are gluttons will not rest well. Sometimes, they will even have bad dreams. As Christians, we are to remember whether we are sleeping or awake, we belong to God. "Ye are all the children of light, and the children of the day: we are not of the night, nor of darkness. Therefore let us not sleep, as do others; but let us watch and be sober. For they that sleep in the night; and they that be drunken are drunken in the night. But let us, who are of the day, be sober, putting on the breastplate of faith and love; and for an helmet, the hope of salvation. For God hath not appointed us to wrath, but to obtain salvation by our Lord Jesus Christ, Who died for us, that, whether we wake or sleep, we should live together with him" (1 Thessalonians 5:5-10).

Dear heavenly Father, thank You for the gift of sweet sleep. I am grateful to be able to lie down at night and be able to find rest. Help me to be disciplined in all areas of my life and not to over-sleep, nor over-eat. I want to be a good example, walking in moderation in all things. Lord, may I never neglect my spiritual duties of prayer and devotion, so that I can be guided in Your ways and avoid the snares of the devil. May my light always shine for You in this dark world. I ask this in the name of the Lord Jesus Christ. Amen.

Proverbs 25:1-3 1 These are also proverbs of Solomon, which the men of Hezekiah king of Judah copied out. 2 It is the glory of God to conceal a thing: but the honour of kings is to search out a matter. 3 The heaven for height, and the earth for depth, and the heart of kings is unsearchable.

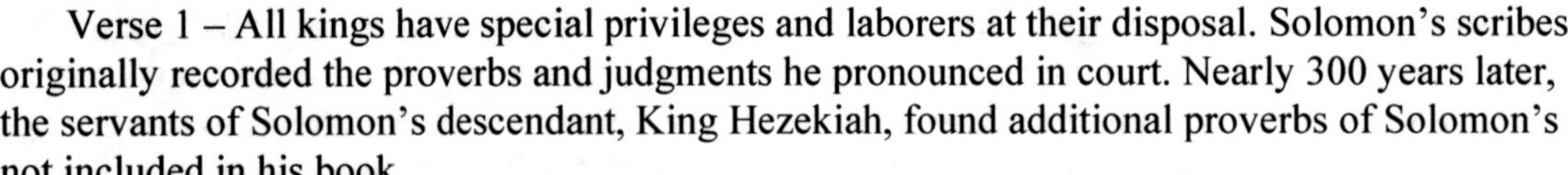

Verse 1 – All kings have special privileges and laborers at their disposal. Solomon's scribes originally recorded the proverbs and judgments he pronounced in court. Nearly 300 years later, the servants of Solomon's descendant, King Hezekiah, found additional proverbs of Solomon's not included in his book.

Verse 2 – This verse begins the collection of Solomon's proverbs found by Hezekiah's men. God's wisdom is concealed from men, but we can search it out, even as Solomon did. However, we must commit our lives to God and study the Bible to avail ourselves of this wisdom. God hides His wisdom from those who will not apply it to their lives, but reveals it to those who search it out. "The secret things belong unto the LORD our God: but those things which are revealed belong unto us and to our children for ever, that we may do all the words of this law" (Deuteronomy 29:29).

"O the depth of the riches both of the wisdom and knowledge of God! How unsearchable are his judgments, and his ways past finding out! For who hath known the mind of the Lord? Or who hath been his counsellor? Or who hath first given to him, and it shall be recompensed unto him again? For of him, and through him, and to him, are all things: to whom be glory for ever. Amen" (Romans 11:33-36).

Verse 3 – Solomon was a diligent ruler who had a heart toward God. Because of his unsearchable wealth within, he accomplished many monumental projects and made his kingdom the richest in the world. He was intelligent, observant, and thoughtful. Many of his proverbs show that his father, David, instructed him as a boy and brought him up to serve God and know His ways. This gave Solomon the ability to recognize his limitations and ask God for wisdom to rule Israel. Many hidden treasures are stored within the Bible's pages for us to seek out, even as Solomon did. Studying the Bible and searching out God's wisdom will sharpen our minds. Men mine for gold and precious stones, but wisdom, mined from God's Word, is far more precious. We can glimpse God's glory by seeking Him and learning of His ways. King Solomon's proverbs were inspired by the Holy Spirit. They are God's words, part of our heavenly Father's instructions to us. "The Proverbs (truths obscurely expressed, maxims, and parables) of Solomon son of David, king of Israel: That people may know skillful and godly Wisdom and instruction, discern and comprehend the words of understanding and insight..." (Proverbs 1:1-2 AMP).

Dear Father in heaven, thank You for making the Bible accessible to us today in a way that generations before us did not have. I appreciate the many study books that make our search so much easier. Now, using computers, we can search for any word in the Bible with ease and find it quickly. I appreciate these tools; but, most of all, I appreciate the Holy Spirit, who reveals the truths of the Bible to us. Lord, open my understanding to more of Your Word and give me the grace to apply those truths in my life. I do not want to be a hearer only, but a doer of the Word. I ask this in the name of Jesus Christ. Amen.

Proverbs 25:4-5 4 Take away the dross from the silver, and there shall come forth a vessel for the finer. 5 Take away the wicked from before the king, and his throne shall be established in righteousness.

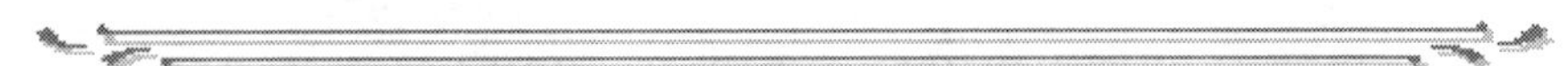

Removing dross from silver in order to form it into a precious vessel, is comparable to removing wicked administrators from positions of authority. Before silver can be fashioned into a beautiful vessel, it must be refined. When melted, the "impurities" surface and can be removed. A righteous king's administrators represent him throughout his kingdom. His rule will not be righteous until the wicked are removed. This is what will happen when Jesus returns to rule as the King of kings: the wicked will be removed from the earth and the righteous will remain: "The way of the Lord is strength to the upright: but destruction shall be to the workers of iniquity. The righteous shall never be removed: but the wicked shall not inhabit the earth" (Proverbs 10:29-30).

"...Let every one that nameth the name of Christ depart from iniquity. But in a great house there are not only vessels of gold and of silver, but also of wood and of earth; and some to honour, and some to dishonour" (2 Timothy 2:19a, 20). God's people are likened to two kinds of vessels: gold and silver "vessels of honour" and wood and clay "vessels of dishonour." Gold and silver vessels are durable and beautiful. Clay vessels chip and shatter; wooden vessels warp in water and burn in fire; neither have the strength of gold and silver. God desires that we have a place among His vessels of honor. "If a man therefore purge himself from these, he shall be a vessel unto honour, sanctified, and meet for the master's use, and prepared unto every good work" (2 Timothy 2:21).

How we respond to life's trials determines what kind of vessel we become. Trials "heat up our circumstances" and bring hidden sins to the surface. "For thou, O God, hast proved us: thou hast tried us, as silver is tried" (Psalm 66:10). Each time we choose to obey God and put to death our old nature or resist the devil, a little more of the "dross" is removed, until we come forth as pure as silver or gold.

Following is a portion of Psalm 119. Its author, knowing that God will remove the wicked like dross, cried out to God to help him keep His commandments. He knew that he could not respect God without respecting His Word. May we be as wise: "Hold thou me up, and I shall be safe: and I will have respect unto thy statutes continually. Thou hast trodden down all them that err from thy statutes: for their deceit is falsehood. Thou puttest away all the wicked of the earth like dross: therefore I love thy testimonies" (Psalm 119:117-119)

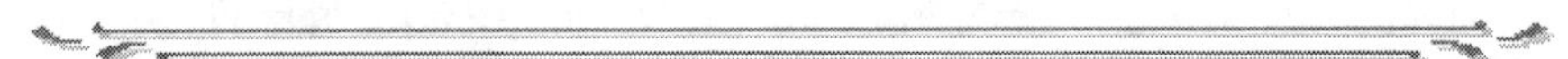

Dear heavenly Father, thank You for the ongoing work that You are doing in my life. I want to cry out as David did for grace and strength to keep Your commandments. May I always love and respect You and Your Word above all else. I know that when I choose to do this, that You will protect me from the enemy and keep me in a place of safety. Lord, cleanse me from every evil thing so that I will become a vessel of honor for Your glory. Purge the "dross" from my life so that I will shine for You as silver and gold. I ask this in the name of the Lord Jesus. Amen.

God's Wisdom for Daily Living **Betty Miller**
September 22 ***Day 265***

Proverbs 25:6-7 6 Put not forth thyself in the presence of the king, and stand not in the place of great men: 7 For better it is that it be said unto thee, Come up hither; than that thou shouldest be put lower in the presence of the prince whom thine eyes have seen.

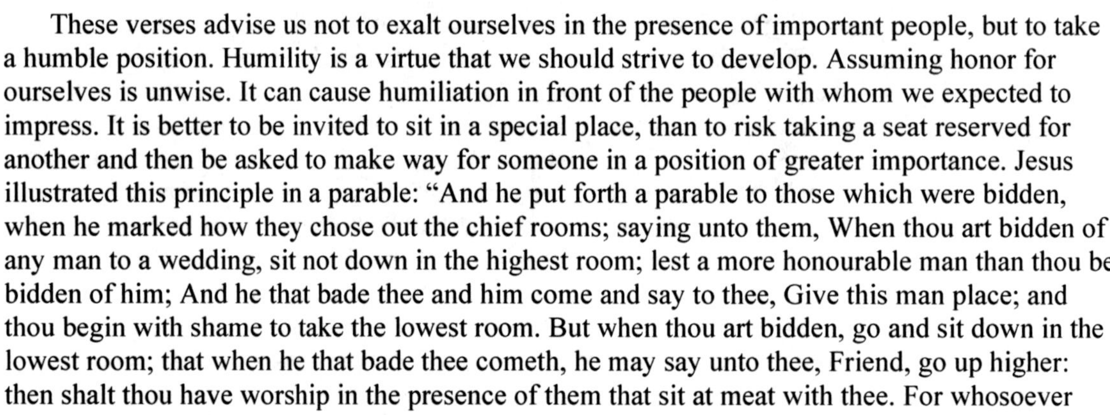

These verses advise us not to exalt ourselves in the presence of important people, but to take a humble position. Humility is a virtue that we should strive to develop. Assuming honor for ourselves is unwise. It can cause humiliation in front of the people with whom we expected to impress. It is better to be invited to sit in a special place, than to risk taking a seat reserved for another and then be asked to make way for someone in a position of greater importance. Jesus illustrated this principle in a parable: "And he put forth a parable to those which were bidden, when he marked how they chose out the chief rooms; saying unto them, When thou art bidden of any man to a wedding, sit not down in the highest room; lest a more honourable man than thou be bidden of him; And he that bade thee and him come and say to thee, Give this man place; and thou begin with shame to take the lowest room. But when thou art bidden, go and sit down in the lowest room; that when he that bade thee cometh, he may say unto thee, Friend, go up higher: then shalt thou have worship in the presence of them that sit at meat with thee. For whosoever exalteth himself shall be abased; and he that humbleth himself shall be exalted" (Luke 14:7-11).

Anyone who attempts to exalt himself in front of others will eventually be humbled. Allowing ourselves to become prideful, sets us up for a fall, according to the Word of God. "Pride goeth before destruction, and an haughty spirit before a fall. Better it is to be of an humble spirit with the lowly, than to divide the spoil with the proud" (Proverbs 16:18-19). Those who think they do not need God are the proudest of all. At some point, all people will come to the end of themselves and face the fact that they are not in control of all of their circumstances. We all need God, since without Him, we face an eternity in hell.

The same scriptures that warn against exalting ourselves, tell us that if we humble ourselves we shall be honored in due season, and recognized by others. "Humble yourselves in the sight of the Lord, and he shall lift you up" (James 4:10). If we boast of anything, it should be our boast of what the Lord has done for us! Without Him we can do nothing. "My soul shall make her boast in the Lord: the humble shall hear thereof, and be glad" (Psalm 34:2).

Dear heavenly Father, thank You for all of the wonderful things You have done for me! I appreciate each and every one of them. Lord, I want to always remain humble, not only in Your sight, but in the sight of men as well. May I have the grace to be a servant to others and not think of myself more highly than anyone else, as every child of God is important in Your sight. Not one of Your children is more important than another. We are all important, because we belong to You. Help us to be humbled by that fact. I ask this in the name of Jesus, who humbled Himself to endure the cross for each of us. Amen.

Proverbs 25:8-10 8 Go not forth hastily to strive, lest thou know not what to do in the end thereof, when thy neighbour hath put thee to shame. 9 Debate thy cause with thy neighbour himself; and discover not a secret to another: 10 Lest he that heareth it put thee to shame, and thine infamy turn not away.

These verses warn us not to get into a public quarrel, but rather, to try to settle the problem with our neighbor first privately, since he could testify against us and take us to court. The Bible counsels us to avoid strife and lawsuits, if at all possible, since the Lord wants us to walk in peace with all people. It is much better to take a humble position and try to work out our differences with a neighbor. We are not to gossip about the matter, telling secrets to others, as this will only rile the neighbor more and he could cause more trouble. We have no guarantee as to the judge ruling in our favor and we may even be in the wrong to some degree. If we are proven wrong, the Bible tells us to agree with our adversary quickly, because he can deliver us to the judge and the judge can rule that we are to be given over to the officer to lock us in prison. If that should happen, we will not be released until we have paid our penalty in full. God especially desires that we maintain good relationships with our brothers and sisters in Christ. 1 Corinthians 6:1-8 urges us to lay down our rights rather than become involved in a court case with another believer before unbelievers. However, these scriptures do not preclude a person or company from defending themselves against false charges. As Christians, there is no room to side with people. We are to side with the Word of God. When my actions do not line up with His, I must side against myself and agree with Him. I must acknowledge my sin to God and my brother in Christ.

If a brother sins against me, I am to go to him privately, without involving others, since people often take up the offense of the first person they hear instead of listening impartially. If he acknowledges his sin and repents, I have gained a brother. This is only likely to happen if I go to him in love and humility. If he does not repent of an obvious sin, I am then to take two or three more people with me and talk with him again. The goal is to show him his error by speaking the truth in love, so that our fellowship may be restored. If he fails to respond in the presence of witnesses, the matter is to be taken before the entire church. If he fails to take advantage of this last opportunity to repent, he is to be excommunicated from the church without any privileges of fellowship.

"Moreover if thy brother shall trespass against thee, go and tell him his fault between thee and him alone: if he shall hear thee, thou hast gained thy brother. But if he will not hear thee, then take with thee one or two more, that in the mouth of two or three witnesses every word may be established. And if he shall neglect to hear them, tell it unto the church: but if he neglect to hear the church, let him be unto thee as a heathen man and a publican" (Matthew 18:15-17).

Dearest Father, we are grateful that we can call on You for the grace we need when others trespass against us. Help us to maintain a loving attitude when we are faced with ill will. You said, "Blessed are the peacemakers." Help me to be one who maintains peace among my acquaintances. Help me to deal with trouble-makers in the proper Biblical manner, so they may be delivered. I ask You to help me refrain from anger, resentment, and rejection and to deal with them in love and wisdom. In Jesus' name I pray. Amen.

Proverbs 25:11 A word fitly spoken is like apples of gold in pictures of silver.

The ability to speak the right thing in a situation is a precious gift, and here it says this kind of word is like golden apples displayed in settings of silver. Solomon compared it to the artistic achievements of the metalworkers who decorated his palace. The beauty of saying what is good and fitting is more difficult to portray than that of art or music, but it is far more valuable. It can change the course of a life or history. How many times have the words of generals inspired armies to conquer nations. How many times have leaders such as Churchill or Lincoln spoken to the hearts of their people to lead them through the darkness of grave national crises. How beautiful it is to aptly speak words of salvation to the lost! How much more beautiful in heaven's sight than a mansion full of the finest works of art it is to speak words of comfort and hope and faith to the ill, the weary, the discouraged, or the weak at the right time.

We must always be mindful that "death and life are in the power of the tongue" (Proverbs 18:21). Because our words are powerful, whether we think we can influence others or not, the Bible instructs us to guard our mouths and to be careful about everything we say. Jesus warned that "...every idle word that men shall speak, they shall give account thereof in the day of judgment. For by thy words thou shalt be justified, and by thy words thou shalt be condemned" (Matthew 12:36-37). If we want to speak words that edify others, we must make every effort to line up our words and thinking with God's Word and to speak the truth in love. In this way, we will be able to bless and edify others.

One of the most important things we can learn is to speak praises and thanks to God for who He is and all that He has done. "Whoso offereth praise glorifieth me: and to him that ordereth his conversation aright will I shew the salvation of God" (Psalm 50:23). We offer praise to the Lord by telling about what He has done for us, as well as singing or speaking praises to Him. As we do this, God frees us from the old habits of sin and brings forth the fruit of the Spirit in our lives. The more we thank and praise Him, the more our hearts will rejoice in Him and love Him; the more we will be centered on what is good and right; the more our conversations will bless people; and the more our words will become acceptable to God. "Let the words of my mouth, and the meditation of my heart, be acceptable in thy sight, O LORD, my strength, and my redeemer" (Psalm 19:14).

Dear heavenly Father, I first want to thank You for the wonderful promises You have given us in the Bible. I want to be a person who not only speaks the Word of God, but also who puts that Word into actions. Lord, help me to guard my mouth and speak only those things that are edifying which will bless others. May You be glorified by all that I speak. May I never doubt Your Word and may I rely on it in everything I do. I ask this in the name of Jesus Christ. Amen.

Proverbs 25:12 Like an earring of gold or an ornament of fine gold is a wise man's rebuke to a listening ear (NIV).

A wise man's reproof to one who heeds it is likened to a costly earring, and he will regard it as precious gold. If a young scientist were to begin a line of experimentation to prove a theory, he would consider any correction to his work from an established scientist invaluable. The wise among God's children value the corrections of other saints, knowing that heeding their reproofs will make their character more Christ-like. Most precious of all are the Holy Spirit's corrections, Who alone brings to light hidden sin. God's reproof frees us from death and leads us to abundant life and fellowship with Him.

Obedience is a necessary element of wisdom and faith. Faith, without works produced by obedience, is dead (James 2:17-18). The works spoken of here are inspired and empowered by God; the result of walking with Him in faith and obedience. When we obey God, we do the works of the Spirit, which alone are acceptable to Him. We can do many good works that do not please God. Teaching a children's Sunday school class is a good work, but not if God is telling us to teach the adult class instead. We must beware of expecting God to accept our way of doing things, as Cain and Abel's story in Genesis 4 shows. When each brought an offering to God, God accepted Abel's but rejected Cain's. Abel came to God God's way, offering a blood sacrifice in faith and obedience (Hebrews 11:4). Rebellion was in Cain's heart. He did not do what God required but came to God in his own way, bringing an offering he thought should be accepted.

Many see no answers to their prayers because they refuse to obey when the Lord speaks to them. The Lord does not always require it of us, but we must be willing to be used by God to answer every prayer we pray. If we ask God to meet someone's financial needs, we must be willing to be the one through whom He does so. If we ask God to provide someone with a place to stay, we must be ready to open our house. Whatever our request, if God can provide it through us, we must be willing to let Him do so. We must determine to follow God regardless of the cost, and obey even if our flesh resists His ways.

Our own efforts produce only the futile works of the flesh. Praying long hours, fasting, and sacrificing in many ways is vain if we do not obey. "And Samuel said, Hath the LORD as great delight in burnt offerings and sacrifices, as in obeying the voice of the LORD? Behold, to obey is better than sacrifice, and to hearken than the fat of rams. For rebellion is as the sin of witchcraft, and stubbornness is as iniquity and idolatry" (I Samuel 15:22--23). Disobedience is rebellion and rebellion is the same as witchcraft so that is why we must obey. God's ways are higher than our ways. Our precious Lord would never ask us to do anything that would not bless us, though the blessing may not immediately be seen. If we hold fast and continue to obey Him, we will discover that His plans for us are more fulfilling, exciting, and beautiful than anything we could imagine.

Dear heavenly Father, thank You for all of the things You are doing in my life. Lord, I want to have a listening and obedient ear to all You are speaking to me. Help me to obey quickly when You speak to me to do something. I want to overcome my flesh and walk in the spirit and always have trust in You. I choose to do it Your way and not mine, no matter what the cost. I want to go all the way with You. Remove anything from my heart that would hinder my walk in You. I ask this in the name of Your Son, Jesus Christ. Amen.

God's Wisdom for Daily Living — *Betty Miller*
September 26 — *Day 269*

Proverbs 25:13 As the cold of snow in the time of harvest, so is a faithful messenger to them that send him: for he refresheth the soul of his masters.

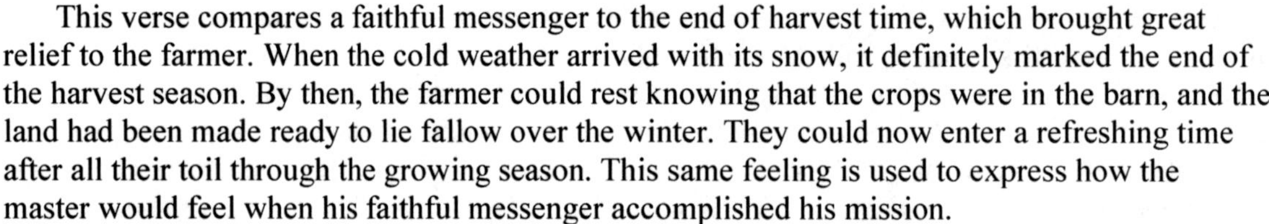

This verse compares a faithful messenger to the end of harvest time, which brought great relief to the farmer. When the cold weather arrived with its snow, it definitely marked the end of the harvest season. By then, the farmer could rest knowing that the crops were in the barn, and the land had been made ready to lie fallow over the winter. They could now enter a refreshing time after all their toil through the growing season. This same feeling is used to express how the master would feel when his faithful messenger accomplished his mission.

In Biblical times, messages had to be sent by servants; and a faithful servant was of great value. His master could rest with the assurance that the message would never be poorly given or fall into the wrong hands. He would not only deliver the message, but convey it correctly and faithfully bring the response. He could not be bribed, and he would not be slack in his duty. If he had to travel a long distance, he would not be deterred by inclement weather, danger from bandits, darkness of night, sickness in body, or weariness of the journey.

As the moral climate of society has deteriorated, lying has become a major problem. The character trait of faithfulness is rare. Married people are unfaithful to their partners; employees and employers cheat one another; family members undermine each other; and people in general seldom keep their word. Businesses are particularly plagued with the problem of faithless employees, company thefts and broken contracts. Lying is now so commonplace that even Christians have become unfaithful in their dealings with others.

One of the biggest faults of many Christians is that we over-commit. Over-commitment undermines integrity by making it impossible to faithfully keep one's word. Company owners, motivated by greed, generate more business than they can handle. Rather than risk losing customers, they commit to jobs that they know they cannot meet the deadline for. Many companies consider it normal to have a continual backlog of past-due jobs. Business people must now factor in lengthy delays just to compensate for the general lack of business ethics. People tend to over-commit themselves out of pride or the desire to please, not knowing how to say no when asked for favors.

We are called to be like Jesus. God is faithful in all His ways. He is faithful, and keeps His word: every promise in the Bible. Through the empowering of the Holy Spirit, we can also maintain a high level of integrity. We can be good witnesses for Christ to all who know us; keeping our word and refreshing the soul of everyone who depends upon us.

Dear heavenly Father, thank You for allowing me to know many faithful people. It is certainly refreshing to be acquainted with those who are trustworthy and honest. Help me to be an example of one who is faithful and steadfast in God. I want to walk in integrity, so please remind me when I forget anything that I have promised to someone. Help me not to over-commit, Lord. Not only do I not want to be a liar, but I also do not want to fail in keeping my word. I want people to know that I am honest, faithful and trustworthy. Empower me to do this. I ask this in the name of the Lord Jesus Christ. Amen.

Proverbs 25:14 Whoso boasteth himself of a false gift is like clouds and wind without rain.

During Israel's six-month dry season, the ground sometimes becomes so arid that it cracks. Rain is expected when clouds appear. In a drought, clouds without rain are a bitter disappointment. In the same way, people who make empty boasts are likened to clouds without rain. Some mean well, but they forget to keep their word. Some attempt to manipulate others with empty promises. Others seek admiration by pretending to be something they are not. Feigning benevolence or generosity is hypocrisy. Jesus sternly rebuked the Pharisees for their hypocrisy. Prideful and legalistic, they were very concerned about their outward appearance, and desired praise for their righteousness. However, Jesus looked into their hearts and saw that they were impure and wicked; full of greed and selfishness.

"And the Lord said unto him, Now do ye Pharisees make clean the outside of the cup and the platter; but your inward part is full of ravening and wickedness. Ye fools, did not he that made that which is without make that which is within also? But rather give alms of such things as ye have; and, behold, all things are clean unto you. But woe unto you, Pharisees! for ye tithe mint and rue and all manner of herbs, and pass over judgment and the love of God: these ought ye to have done, and not to leave the other undone. Woe unto you, Pharisees! for ye love the uppermost seats in the synagogues, and greetings in the markets" (Luke 11:39-43).

These Pharisees carefully gave a tithe of every source of income, including their herb crops, and made a big display of doing so. Christ sternly upbraided them for ignoring the greater responsibilities of loving God and practicing righteous and merciful judgment. He directed them to help the poor from their substance, in addition to tithing. He also admonished them for the pride they displayed in taking places of honour and making sure that their deeds were noticed. Although Jesus dealt strongly with hypocrites, He was always kind to those who recognized their sin, no matter how great it was. God listens to honest hearts. He will not deny salvation to even the most wicked and vile person who comes to Him in sincere repentance (Luke 18:9-14).

As Christians, we must beware of making empty boasts and promises. As seen in yesterday's study, it is very important to be faithful to keep our word. Whether making business appointments, promising our families a vacation, or agreeing to do something for someone, we should not promise what we cannot perform.

Dear heavenly Father, thank You for Your great mercy to me personally and to all people who call upon You. Father, I desire to have a good and honest heart, so please convict me of all deception and pride so that I may repent of it and be free from these two evils. Help me to always be honest and never try to pretend about anything I have done. Forgive me for yielding to pride, and deliver me from trying to please other human beings, instead of pleasing You. I ask this in the name of Jesus. Amen.

Proverbs 25:15 By long forbearing is a prince persuaded, and a soft tongue breaketh the bone.

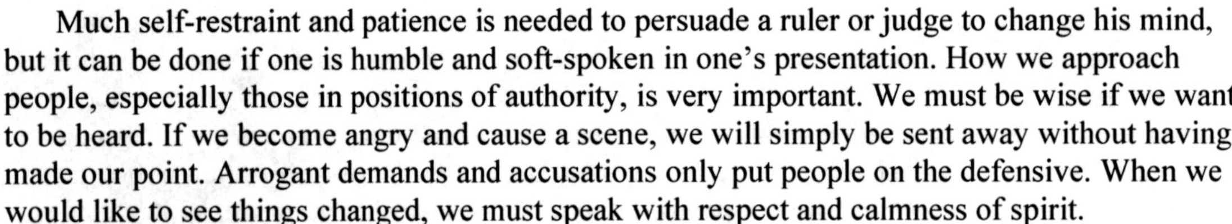

Much self-restraint and patience is needed to persuade a ruler or judge to change his mind, but it can be done if one is humble and soft-spoken in one's presentation. How we approach people, especially those in positions of authority, is very important. We must be wise if we want to be heard. If we become angry and cause a scene, we will simply be sent away without having made our point. Arrogant demands and accusations only put people on the defensive. When we would like to see things changed, we must speak with respect and calmness of spirit.

Proper preparation fosters calmness. The first step is to pray for wisdom in regard to the situation and person with whom we will be speaking. The next step is to think through how to logically present our case and support it with evidence rather than hearsay. Third, we should remember that speaking calmly with a pleasant manner, and using words that are not accusatory can gain us both an audience and a listening ear. Fourth, we should be prepared to practice forbearance: exercising self-control when provoked. We must hold back from expressing irritation when confronting those in authority on issues we would like to see changed. Even if they are incorrect or abusive towards us, God desires that we respect their office. Losing our tempers does not help others to see our viewpoint. It usually causes them to become angry and argumentative and to cling to their opinions more stubbornly. Finally, we should recognize that some issues simply will not be settled overnight. We must be prepared to present our case patiently and respectfully.

"A soft answer turneth away wrath: but grievous words stir up anger. The tongue of the wise useth knowledge aright: but the mouth of fools poureth out foolishness" (Proverbs 15:1-2).

Dear heavenly Father, I thank You for Your Word and Your faithfulness to keep it. Lord, may I be one who also keeps my word. I also ask You to help me guard what comes out of my mouth. May my words be gracious to others and also words of faith and kindness. Father, when I am trying to convince someone about You or Your Word, may I be gracious, trusting You to break down any defensiveness that they may have. Give me love and patience while I am witnessing and sharing with others who do not know You. I ask this in the name of the Lord, Jesus Christ. Amen.

Quotes by Betty Miller

We have taught our children and youngsters to play, instead of work, by giving them an overabundance of toys.

Money has a way of disappearing, but God is always there.

Let us exchange solutions with one another, instead of criticisms.

God's Wisdom for Daily Living **_Betty Miller_**
September 29 **_Day 272_**

Proverbs 25:16 Hast thou found honey? eat so much as is sufficient for thee, lest thou be filled therewith, and vomit it.

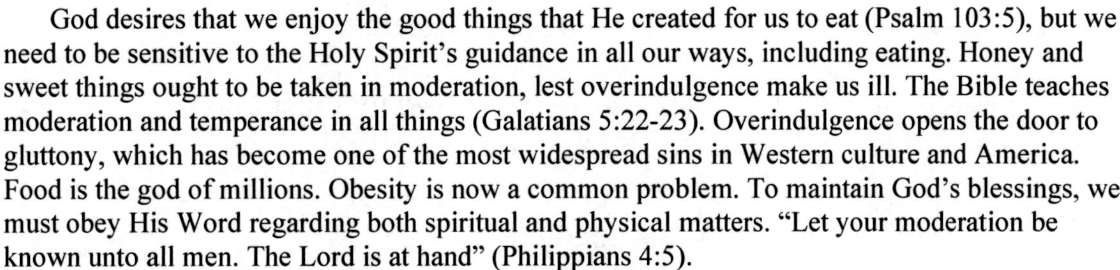

God desires that we enjoy the good things that He created for us to eat (Psalm 103:5), but we need to be sensitive to the Holy Spirit's guidance in all our ways, including eating. Honey and sweet things ought to be taken in moderation, lest overindulgence make us ill. The Bible teaches moderation and temperance in all things (Galatians 5:22-23). Overindulgence opens the door to gluttony, which has become one of the most widespread sins in Western culture and America. Food is the god of millions. Obesity is now a common problem. To maintain God's blessings, we must obey His Word regarding both spiritual and physical matters. "Let your moderation be known unto all men. The Lord is at hand" (Philippians 4:5).

The world has set the standard when it comes to eating, rather than the Word of God. Here is another area where we need to be sensitive to the Holy Spirit's guidance. First, we need to make sure that we are receiving proper spiritual food; however, the Lord is also emphasizing to His people that they need to make changes in their physical diets and receive the proper natural foods. Most of God's people have experienced His healing in their bodies, but one problem that seems to be prevalent is that after receiving healing, the devil comes back to rob them of God's gift of healing. However, if we exercise our faith and rebuke the enemy in the name of Jesus, he will flee. If you have done this and are still experiencing illness, perhaps the problem is one of maintaining the gift God has given you. By this I mean we must not only obey and keep spiritual laws, but also we must keep physical laws if we expect to walk in God's blessings.

Our body is the temple of the Holy Spirit. We are each a caretaker of our body, but many of us do not honor the God of glory who lives within us. Rather than keep His temple in good shape, we neglect it and fill it with garbage foods. We ought to assess our eating habits to bring them in line with Biblical guidelines. Many are tired and sick because a large part of their diet consists of highly-refined, nutritionally-dead foods. A good rule is to eat the "living foods" God created: fresh vegetables, fruits, grains, nuts, legumes and dairy. God's guidelines for meats are given in Leviticus 11. In ourselves, we may not be able to overcome old eating habits, but through prayer and with His help, we can (Philippians 4:13). If we seek God on this important subject, He will direct us to a solution. Ultimately, it is faith and obedience to God that gives us victory.

While it is good to emphasize proper eating and physical exercise, we must beware of extremes. Our spiritual health should always be given top priority, since it determines the quality of our lives on earth and in eternity (1 Timothy 4:8). Many people have become unbalanced by putting too much emphasis on the physical man, while neglecting the spiritual man. We must not neglect our physical health, but we should avoid becoming overly concerned about it and allowing it to absorb too much of our time. God desires that we learn self-discipline and temperance in all things. I appreciate a book that I read years ago on dieting: *More of Jesus, Less of Me.* Submitting to Christ's Lordship is the key to a proper balance between the care of our spiritual man and physical bodies. We should make Jesus "Lord of the Fork."

Dear heavenly Father, I am thankful for all of the good foods that You created for our pleasure. They are a blessing and I have enjoyed them. Lord, help me not to over-indulge and put too much emphasis on food. Give me a desire to eat things that are good for me and deliver me from those things that are not healthy for me. Since You created our bodies, I trust Your wisdom to know what things are best for me to eat. Forgive me for any lust for food, and may I eat those things that will cause me to have a healthy body so that I can serve You with health and energy. I ask this in the name of Jesus. Amen.

Quotes About Obedience

Whenever God grants me understanding, I find that just knowing His Word is not enough; I must also obey it. --Day 9

The highest form of worship is obedience. --Day 109

Obedience is the evidence that we are true disciples of Christ. --Day 116

Mere knowledge of God's Word is not enough; one must obey it in order to walk in wisdom. --Day 150

Sometimes our deeds may not appear worthwhile to others; but if we are obediently serving God, He is pleased—and that is all that really matters. --Day 199

God does not desire forced obedience. He does not want us to be driven to Him by a rod of correction, but rather that we obey Him from our hearts because we love and trust Him. --Day 284

Obedience is doing all of what we are told to do. We are not to change instructions because we think we know better. --Day 352

September 30 — *Day 273*

Proverbs 25:17 Withdraw thy foot from thy neighbour's house; lest he be weary of thee, and so hate thee.

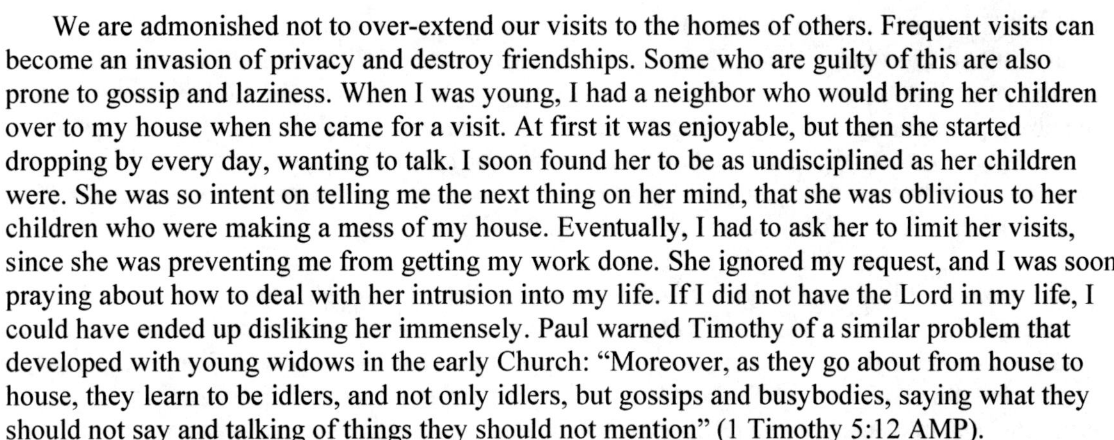

We are admonished not to over-extend our visits to the homes of others. Frequent visits can become an invasion of privacy and destroy friendships. Some who are guilty of this are also prone to gossip and laziness. When I was young, I had a neighbor who would bring her children over to my house when she came for a visit. At first it was enjoyable, but then she started dropping by every day, wanting to talk. I soon found her to be as undisciplined as her children were. She was so intent on telling me the next thing on her mind, that she was oblivious to her children who were making a mess of my house. Eventually, I had to ask her to limit her visits, since she was preventing me from getting my work done. She ignored my request, and I was soon praying about how to deal with her intrusion into my life. If I did not have the Lord in my life, I could have ended up disliking her immensely. Paul warned Timothy of a similar problem that developed with young widows in the early Church: "Moreover, as they go about from house to house, they learn to be idlers, and not only idlers, but gossips and busybodies, saying what they should not say and talking of things they should not mention" (1 Timothy 5:12 AMP).

A busybody is someone who is always interfering in other people's affairs. My neighbor fell into that category. When she could no longer come to my house every day, she found other women who would entertain her, and she made the rounds with her gossip. Her own house was never clean because she was never home to do any work. I invited her to attend church with me, but she found it too difficult to get up on Sundays and dress her children. Eventually, she not only lost many friends, but also her husband. He grew tired of a dirty house, a wandering wife, neglected children, and not having his meals cooked on time. The Bible admonishes against being idle busybodies: "For even when we were with you, this we commanded you, that if any would not work, neither should he eat. For we hear that there are some which walk among you disorderly, working not at all, but are busybodies. Now them that are such we command and exhort by our Lord Jesus Christ, that with quietness they work, and eat their own bread" (2 Thessalonians 3:10-12).

If we take care of our own homes and businesses, it shuts the door for the devil having opportunity to lead us astray. I have known many women who destroyed their marriages because they would not heed this advice. Because they would not work quietly at home, they fell into sin with some seemingly godly man who was full of deceit. The Bible says to turn away from such people. "Having a form of godliness, but denying the power thereof: from such turn away. For of this sort are they which creep into houses, and lead captive silly women laden with sins, led away with divers lusts" (1 Timothy 3:5-6).

Dear heavenly Father, I pray that You would deliver Your people from the sin of gossip and being busy-bodies. May we help those who are engaged in this activity by speaking the truth in love to them. May we also have the courage to refuse to give a listening ear to gossip. Father, give me strength to take care of my duties and not be negligent in anything that is my responsibility. Help me to speak edifying things that uplift and help people and deliver me from any form of gossip. I ask this in the name of Jesus. Amen.

Proverbs 25:18 A man that beareth false witness against his neighbour is a maul, and a sword, and a sharp arrow.

Today's proverb emphasizes how hurtful a false testimony can be. This form of lying under formal witness is forbidden in the Ten Commandments (Exodus 20:16). A false witness damages you and your reputation or career. One can do as much damage to your intangible possessions by lying about you as he can do to your car with a sledgehammer. He also wounds your soul with a gash as real as a stab to the body. To hear a neighbor bear false witness, you feel just as much attacked as if he had come at you with a drawn sword. If you are not present when he speaks, its affect is like an arrow fired without your knowing. Suddenly, without warning, it strikes and injures you deeply.

We all know it is a crime to give false testimony in court, but we should be aware that in a sense we give a positive or negative "witness" every time we say something about a person. Repeating damaging rumors or negative gossip is akin to bearing false witness. People are always judging each other. When we talk about someone, it is like testifying in an informal, social courtroom. The informal judgments that society makes, whether that society is the populace of a large city, small town, or a circle of friends, can be just as damaging to someone as the formal judgments of a court of law. God will not hold us guiltless for this. David's cry to God regarding his enemies is very insightful: "My soul is among lions: and I lie even among them that are set on fire, even the sons of men, whose teeth are spears and arrows, and their tongue a sharp sword" (Psalm 57:4).

When the Holy Spirit comes in our heart, He begins to cleanse us from unrighteousness and remove those things in us that do not look like Jesus. Years ago, when I made a total commitment and surrender to God, the first thing He dealt within my life was the sin of gossip. He revealed that my critical words were bringing destruction to my life, as well as others. Scripture makes many references to the tongue. Because the power of life and death is in the tongue, we are to guard them very carefully. Our words will make or break us; give us victory or destroy us according to Proverbs 18:20-21: "A man's belly shall be satisfied with the fruit of his mouth; and with the increase of his lips shall he be filled. Death and life are in the power of the tongue: and they that love it shall eat the fruit thereof." When we lie or gossip, our negative words go out into the spiritual dimension to unleash destructive power. We must learn to speak what is good and pray for everyone, even our enemies, so that our words release blessing.

Dear heavenly Father, I thank You for forgiving me of all the things that I have said that have not agreed with Your Word. Father, please cancel all of the negative words that I have spoken against anyone. Lord, I truly want to use my tongue in a godly manner by speaking those things that will bless and edify others. Teach me how to pray correctly and may my lips now speak Your Word. May the words of my mouth and the meditation of my heart be acceptable in Your sight. I ask this in the name of Jesus. Amen.

Proverbs 25:19 Confidence in an unfaithful man in time of trouble is like a broken tooth, and a foot out of joint.

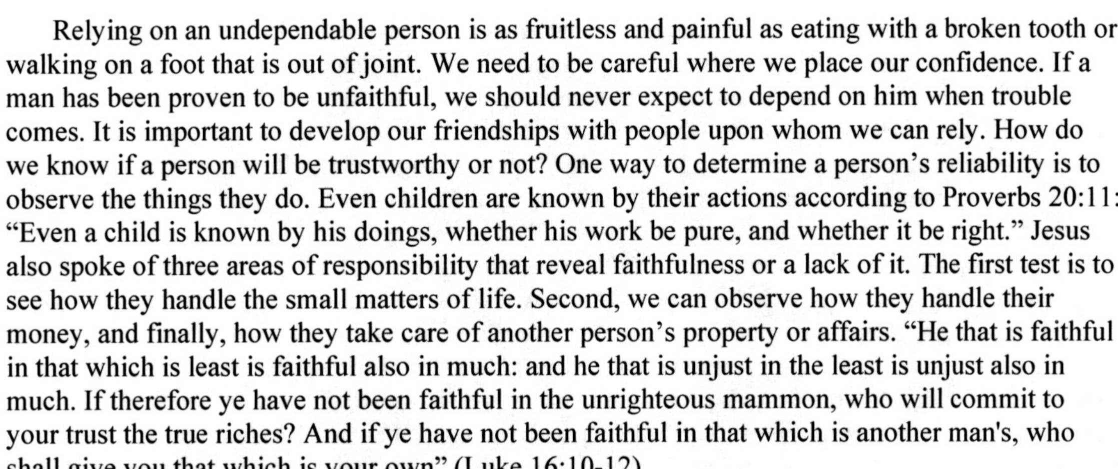

Relying on an undependable person is as fruitless and painful as eating with a broken tooth or walking on a foot that is out of joint. We need to be careful where we place our confidence. If a man has been proven to be unfaithful, we should never expect to depend on him when trouble comes. It is important to develop our friendships with people upon whom we can rely. How do we know if a person will be trustworthy or not? One way to determine a person's reliability is to observe the things they do. Even children are known by their actions according to Proverbs 20:11: "Even a child is known by his doings, whether his work be pure, and whether it be right." Jesus also spoke of three areas of responsibility that reveal faithfulness or a lack of it. The first test is to see how they handle the small matters of life. Second, we can observe how they handle their money, and finally, how they take care of another person's property or affairs. "He that is faithful in that which is least is faithful also in much: and he that is unjust in the least is unjust also in much. If therefore ye have not been faithful in the unrighteous mammon, who will commit to your trust the true riches? And if ye have not been faithful in that which is another man's, who shall give you that which is your own" (Luke 16:10-12).

Tithing may seem a small matter, but it reveals a great deal about a person's reliability. During our many years of pastoring our church, my husband and I noticed that people who never tithed because they did not have enough money; didn't give when they had more. They never gave when they got a raise, sold something, came into an inheritance, or the like. Conversely, those who gave out of small incomes always gave more when God blessed them with more. How people handle their money in other ways also reveals responsibility–if they are a faithful person or not; such as paying bills on time and living within their means. The Bible says if we are not faithful with unrighteous mammon (deceitful riches, money and possessions), we will not be faithful with the things of God.

According to today's verse, it would be wise not to trust in those who are unfaithful, and especially not to call on them when you are in trouble. Choose a faithful friend instead. Dependable friends are invaluable, but even they are limited and can fail us. God, however, never fails or forsakes us. He is always able to help us through natural or supernatural means. He is the most faithful friend anyone can have and He will stand with us even if all others forsake us. As His children, we also need to be good and faithful people, helping others in need and glorifying our Father. "And the very God of peace sanctify you wholly; and I pray God your whole spirit and soul and body be preserved blameless unto the coming of our Lord Jesus Christ. Faithful is he that calleth you, who also will do it" (1 Thessalonians 5:23-24).

Dear heavenly Father, thank You for Your faithfulness to me. Lord, I have failed You many times in my life; however, You have never failed me. I am grateful for Your love and mercy to me when I have fallen down. I appreciate all the times You have picked me up and helped me to continue on the straight and narrow path of Your will. Strengthen me to be a faithful witness for You. Help me not to put my confidence in people, but rather to lean on You and trust You to help me. I am thankful You have used many people over the years to help me, but I know it was You who gave me favor with them. Thank You. I ask this in the name of Jesus. Amen.

God's Wisdom for Daily Living — *Betty Miller*
October 3 — *Day 276*

Proverbs 25:20 He who sings songs to a heavy heart is like him who lays off a garment in cold weather and like vinegar upon soda (AMP).

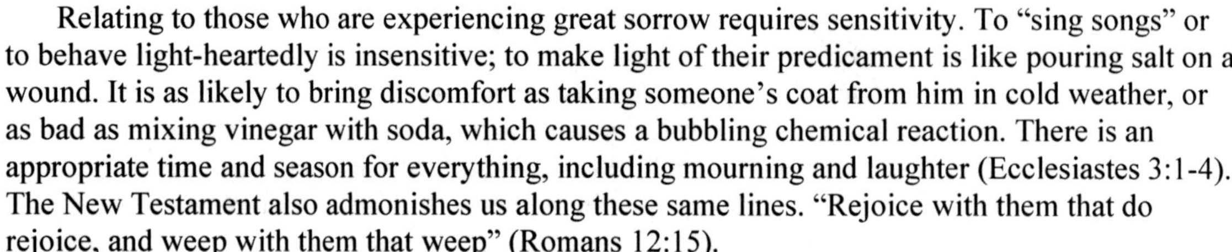

Relating to those who are experiencing great sorrow requires sensitivity. To "sing songs" or to behave light-heartedly is insensitive; to make light of their predicament is like pouring salt on a wound. It is as likely to bring discomfort as taking someone's coat from him in cold weather, or as bad as mixing vinegar with soda, which causes a bubbling chemical reaction. There is an appropriate time and season for everything, including mourning and laughter (Ecclesiastes 3:1-4). The New Testament also admonishes us along these same lines. "Rejoice with them that do rejoice, and weep with them that weep" (Romans 12:15).

Even unbelievers understand this concept; no one needs to be told to celebrate at weddings or mourn at funerals. As Christians, however, we are to share as deeply in the sorrows as well as joys of our brethren. When they rejoice over their blessings, we should rejoice with them. When they are hurting, we should do all that we can to bring them comfort and hope. We ought also to remember our Christian brethren throughout our country and abroad. We should be the first to help in practical ways when people suffer in the wake of natural disasters. We ought daily to remember those suffering persecution for their faith in Christ in other countries, supporting them in prayer as if we were in prison with them (Hebrews 13:3). And we should give generously to Christian organizations, through which we can support their needs and those of their families. We are to be known for our love for one another (John 13:34-35).

The Bible tells us that there is a time and season for everything; weeping, as well as laughing. "To every thing there is a season, and a time to every purpose under the heaven: A time to be born, and a time to die; a time to plant, and a time to pluck up that which is planted; A time to kill, and a time to heal; a time to break down, and a time to build up; A time to weep, and a time to laugh; a time to mourn, and a time to dance" (Ecclesiastes 3:1-4).

In suffering, as in all things, Christians have many advantages unknown to those who do not trust in Christ. Our weeping will be turned into joy. Jesus will remove all grief from our souls if we ask Him to do it for us. In exchange for our sorrow, He gives us a peace that is beyond our understanding (Philippians 4:6-7; John 16:33). Unlike those who are lost, our sorrow is only temporal. When we enter heaven, our bodies will be changed, and there will be no more pain or death; this is God's promise to all that make Jesus Christ the Lord of their lives (Revelation 21:3-4). Another advantage is that we do not grieve as those who are without Christ and without hope (1 Thessalonians 4:13). We shall be reunited with our loved ones who knew Christ. We shall see them again and together rejoice in Him forever. Until then, we must be alert and sensitive to those who are hurting.

Dear heavenly Father, thank You for Your wonderful promise of peace and comfort when I need it. You have lifted sorrow from me many times in my life. I am truly grateful, as I would not have been able to bear it without the strength and comfort of Your Spirit. May I be sensitive to those who are hurting, and reach out and bring that same comfort to them. I am thankful that we shall see all of our loved ones in Christ once again, when we all get to heaven. How wonderful it is to have the hope that is ours as Your children. Blessed be Your name! I pray in Jesus' name, Amen.

Proverbs 25:21-22 21 If thine enemy be hungry, give him bread to eat; and if he be thirsty, give him water to drink: 22 For thou shalt heap coals of fire upon his head, and the LORD shall reward thee.

We can overcome evil from an enemy by helping him, but we can do this only with God's enabling power, through the impartation of His love for others to our hearts. This is the kind of love that Jesus demonstrated by coming to earth in order to die on the cross in our place for our sins. He was raised from the dead by Father God. "And when they were come to the place, which is called Calvary, there they crucified him...Then said Jesus, Father, forgive them; for they know not what they do" (Luke 23:33-34a). We are called to follow in His steps and demonstrate that same kind of love to those who persecute us.

"For even hereunto were ye called: because Christ also suffered for us, leaving us an example, that ye should follow his steps: Who did no sin, neither was guile found in his mouth: Who, when he was reviled, reviled not again; when he suffered, he threatened not; but committed himself to him that judgeth righteously..." (1 Peter 2:21-23).

I have often wondered what the expression, "heaping coals of fire upon his head" meant, since it sounded like a hostile action. However, I discovered that it was referring to the way fires were started in Biblical times. The general populace used small clay ovens for cooking and heating their homes, and they used wood or grass in them. Most of the ovens were easily portable and women would carry them on their heads. The ovens were stoked at night so that there would be live coals left in the morning by which to start a fire for breakfast. If the coals died out in the night, the practice was to find a neighbor who had some live coals, and borrow from them. A woman would go to her neighbor, carrying her clay oven on her head. Therefore, the reference about "heaping coals of fire on their head," would be an act of kindness.

As children of God, we are called to overcome evil with good, to go the second mile, to bless those who persecute us and to do good to our enemies (Romans 12:17-21). By doing these things, we will not only demonstrate God's love but also conquer evil. When we help our enemies, it pleases God our Father, who treats His enemies in the same way. "But I say unto you, Love your enemies, bless them that curse you, do good to them that hate you, and pray for them which despitefully use you, and persecute you; That ye may be the children of your Father which is in heaven: for he maketh his sun to rise on the evil and on the good, and sendeth rain on the just and on the unjust. For if ye love them which love you, what reward have ye? do not even the publicans the same? Be ye therefore perfect, even as your Father which is in heaven is perfect" (Matthew 5:44-48).

Dear Father God, thank You for forgiving me of my sins. I need Your love for the sinners that touch my life. Fill me with the Holy Spirit so that I might love them the way You do. Jesus, show me how to reach out in love to those who are coming against me in an evil way. May I demonstrate Your love in such a way that they will want to know You, the One who gives us love for our enemies. Fill me daily with Your love and grace so that I am a good example of what it means to be a Christian. I ask this in the name of Jesus. Amen.

Proverbs 25:23-24 23 The north wind driveth away rain: so doth an angry countenance a backbiting tongue. 24 It is better to dwell in the corner of the housetop, than with a brawling woman and in a wide house.

Verse 23 – As surely as the north wind brings rain after the long dry season, speaking evil of someone in their absence produces anger; if not in those listening, in the slandered person when he hears it. Backbiters expect others to agree with them. In mixed company, they can address the friends, as well as the enemies of the person they attack, bringing trouble upon themselves.

No one wants to be around a backbiter except other backbiters. Their talk is spiteful and unpleasant. Common sense tells you that anyone who will talk to you about others will also talk about you. There is a danger of being drawn into their sin, if you listen to them and happen not to like the person of whom they complain. That is one reason we should not give an ear to people like that. However, the main reason that we should avoid gossip and backbiting is because it will drive us from God's presence. Hearing someone slander others behind their backs should be as unpleasant to God's children as being caught in a heavy rain driven by a cold, blasting wind. We should let it be known, by our expressions if nothing else, that we disapprove of such talk. Notice in Psalm 15:1-3, the qualities of those who abide in God's presence: "LORD, who shall abide in thy tabernacle? Who shall dwell in thy holy hill? He that walketh uprightly, and worketh righteousness, and speaketh the truth in his heart. He that backbiteth not with his tongue, nor doeth evil to his neighbour, nor taketh up a reproach against his neighbour."

Verse 24 – This is a repeat of Proverbs 21:9, which we looked at on Day 203. We noted earlier that when Scripture repeats something, it is like a red flag; it should draw our attention. God intends marriage to be a life-long commitment. We must choose the one with whom we will spend our lives with great care. Any character flaws that we notice in someone (including ourselves) before marriage will be amplified afterward. Contentious people make life miserable for those around them. Continual nagging can, in time, destroy friendships and even marriages. We must guard what we say, as well as what we give an ear to. "What man is he that desireth life, and loveth many days, that he may see good? Keep thy tongue from evil, and thy lips from speaking guile. Depart from evil, and do good; seek peace, and pursue it" (Psalm 34:12-14).

Dear Father, thank You for the wisdom that is found in Your Word. I desire to take heed to the things that You have written in the Bible. Give me the grace to speak good and righteous things and to avoid listening to those who would "bad mouth" others. Lord, help me not to be one who would yield to nagging or belittling others. Guide me in my choice of friends and let me be a faithful and loyal friend at all times. I give You my heart and mouth–may they both agree with Your Word and be pleasing to You. I ask this in the name of Jesus. Amen.

Proverbs 25:25 As cold waters to a thirsty soul, so is good news from a far country.

When we are far from home and hear good news, it is like a drink of cold water when one is crossing the desert. Every living thing needs water for health and survival. Even slight dehydration causes impaired function and drowsiness. What water is to our bodies, God is to our spirit and soul. Without God, our spirits are dead and our souls parched. The good news of Jesus Christ from that "distant land of heaven," truly refreshes the soul parched by separation from God.

The Bible contains many allegories in which water symbolizes spiritual truths. Jesus Himself described the Holy Spirit as the living water which He gives to men. John 4:7-15 recounts Jesus giving this "living water" to a Samaritan woman whom he met at the well: "...whosoever drinketh of the water that I shall give him shall never thirst; but the water that I shall give him shall be in him a well of water springing up into everlasting life." When the Holy Spirit dwells in us, we have access to the Source of life; to all that we will ever need. His presence is a well that never runs dry. Many of our Christian songs have expressions about coming to Jesus when we are spiritually thirsty and receiving that wonderful drink of "living water" that quenches our thirst.

We are commanded to be baptized in water once we have received Christ. However, John spoke of another baptism that Jesus Himself would perform, the baptism in the Holy Spirit. In this baptism, rivers of living water flow out of us, as Jesus declared (John 7:37-39). Many Christians know the reality of the Holy Spirit, but have never received the baptism in the Holy Spirit which gives us the power needed to overcome in Christ. This gift of God is available to whoever asks for it. "If ye then, being evil, know how to give good gifts unto your children: how much more shall your heavenly Father give the Holy Spirit to them that ask him?" (Luke 11:13, also Acts 1:8).

There were Christians in Paul's day who did not know that the Holy Spirit was available to them. "Paul...said unto them, Have ye received the Holy Ghost since ye believed? And they said unto him, We have not so much as heard whether there be any Holy Ghost...And when Paul had laid his hands upon them, the Holy Ghost came on them; and they spake with tongues, and prophesied" (Acts 19:2,6).

Many people have been "born again" and have the Holy Spirit working in their lives, but they have never received the "Baptism in the Holy Ghost" which equips them for service and gives them the power needed to overcome in Christ. This gift of God is available to us, if we ask for it.

If, as a Christian, you know that the Holy Spirit dwells within you but you have not known God's power to overcome sin, to witness, or to know God in His fullness, you can ask Him to baptize you in the Holy Spirit.

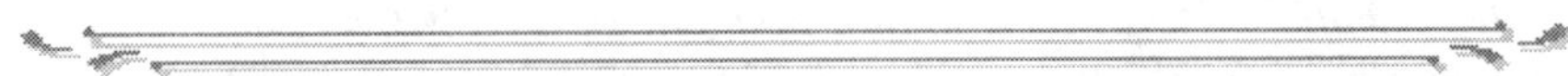

Dear heavenly Father, thank You for the wonderful gift of the Holy Spirit. Truly, Your spiritual water has quenched my thirsty soul. May I be like one who brings good news from a far land, as I testify and witness to those around me who do not know about the living water found in Christ. Lord, fill me daily with the Holy Spirit so that I may overflow with those living waters and minister life to others. Speak to Your children who do not have this gift, and reveal to them their need to receive the baptism in the Holy Spirit. I ask this in the name of Jesus Christ. Amen.

Proverbs 25:26 Like a muddied fountain and a polluted spring is a righteous man who yields, falls down, and compromises his integrity before the wicked (AMP).

We should be as springs of living water to people who are thirsting for God. A spring polluted by bacteria brings disease instead of life. It is unfit to drink from. If we yield to compromise, our Christian witness becomes muddied, thus allowing unbelievers to mock us.

The Old Testament relates that the people of Judah became like polluted springs and were led away to exile in Babylon because of their sins. Jerusalem lay in ruins for many years and became a picture of a Christian whose life is wasted by the enemy. Nehemiah was a Jewish exile in Persia who became the king's cupbearer. This position enabled him to obtain permission to return to Jerusalem and rebuild it. Because of his uncompromised integrity, God chose him to lead in the rebuilding of the walls of Jerusalem. When he met with ridicule and threats of attack, he resorted to prayer. When he was confronted with discouragement, he leaned on God and overcame it. When he discovered corruption and greed in Jerusalem's rulers, he confronted them in a godly manner. Through his example of unselfishness, during his 12-year term as governor, he rebuilt the moral, civil, and physical walls of Jerusalem.

To rebuild the church's reputation and morality of our nations, we must be people of integrity. Too many Christians have become polluted springs. How does this happen? Many fall into sin because they accept leadership too soon. Integrity takes time to establish. Early promotion leads to pride, which precedes a fall. One who has not learned to withstand Satan's common attacks that come upon all believers cannot bear his crushing attacks that are aimed at leaders. Look carefully at the qualifications for leaders listed in 1 Timothy 3:2-7: "An overseer, then, must be above reproach, the husband of one wife, temperate, prudent, respectable, hospitable, able to teach, not addicted to wine, or pugnacious, but gentle, peaceable, free from the love of money. He must be one who manages his own household well, keeping his children under control with all dignity (but if a man does not know how to manage his own household, how will he take care of the church of God?), and not a new convert, so that he will not become conceited and fall into the condemnation incurred by the devil. And he must have a good reputation with those outside the church, so that he will not fall into reproach and the snare of the devil" (NASB).

Whether or not we become church leaders, we all must walk in integrity. A good place to begin that walk is by watching what we say (James 3:9-13). By allowing the Holy Spirit to convict us of any sin, we can keep our words and heart attitudes pure. By guarding our hearts, we can keep from becoming a polluted spring.

Dear Father, fill me with the Holy Spirit so that I am one through whom sweet water can always flow. Help me to guard my mouth and speak good things from Your Word. Deliver me from all compromise and give me the grace to always stand in integrity before men. Help Your people to be good witnesses in this world so that we do not bring any reproach on the Kingdom of God. Lord, forgive us when we fall down. Please lift us back up and rebuild our walls, so that the enemy is defeated in our lives. I ask in the name of Jesus Christ. Amen.

God's Wisdom for Daily Living — *Betty Miller*
October 8 — *Day 281*

Proverbs 25:27-28 27 It is not good to eat much honey: so for men to search their own glory is not glory. 28 He that hath no rule over his own spirit is like a city that is broken down, and without walls (AMP).

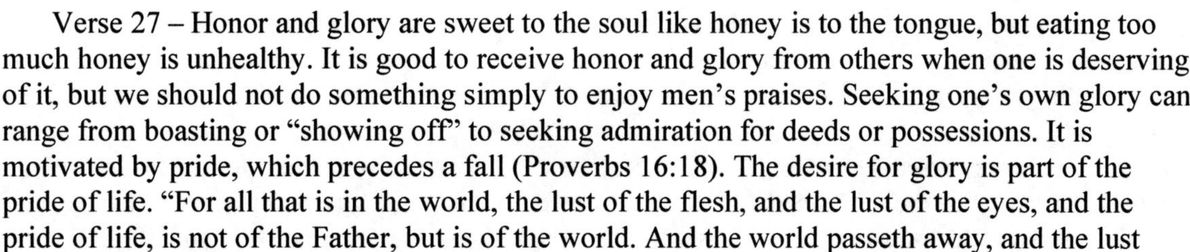

Verse 27 – Honor and glory are sweet to the soul like honey is to the tongue, but eating too much honey is unhealthy. It is good to receive honor and glory from others when one is deserving of it, but we should not do something simply to enjoy men's praises. Seeking one's own glory can range from boasting or "showing off" to seeking admiration for deeds or possessions. It is motivated by pride, which precedes a fall (Proverbs 16:18). The desire for glory is part of the pride of life. "For all that is in the world, the lust of the flesh, and the lust of the eyes, and the pride of life, is not of the Father, but is of the world. And the world passeth away, and the lust thereof: but he that doeth the will of God abideth for ever" (1 John 2:16-17).

At times it is fitting to honor people for their accomplishments. However, if we are the recipient of those honors, they should be received with a humble heart. We should also remember to give praise to the others who helped us in the accomplishments. We need to acknowledge that if we are able to accomplish anything, it is because God has gifted us with the ability, strength, and desire to achieve those things. The best and brightest of us are prone to weakness and error. Confidence in one's own abilities is a poor foundation upon which to build one's life. It is like the sand upon which the foolish man built his house (Matthew 7:24-27). If we rely on self instead of building upon a foundation of faith in God, we will at some point in life face a situation we cannot handle by ourselves. If our own confidence does not crumble under the attack of the devil in this life, it will crumble in the day of judgment. Only God can defeat the devil's attacks.

Verse 28 – In Biblical times, cities were protected by thick walls. Huge gates were open in the day, allowing for tradesmen to come and go, and shut at night against intruders. Spiritually, each Christian is like a city and our faith in Christ like a strong wall. Our faith will protect us if we practice God's Word. Scripture instructs us to "rule our spirits;" to exercise self-control. Being undisciplined makes us as vulnerable to temptation as a broken city wall is to an army. We need to strengthen our walls so that our "cities" (our inner beings) can grow in Christ. Self-control includes guarding our gates and not permitting ungodliness to enter. If we allow sin to enter, the enemy can torment us.

Jesus Christ is an impenetrable fortress and high tower of safety to which we can run (2 Samuel 22:1-4). He is the one who keeps our hearts sound and steady so that we are able to resist the enemies' attacks. "In that day shall this song be sung in the land of Judah; We have a strong city; salvation will God appoint for walls and bulwarks. Open ye the gates, that the righteous nation which keepeth the truth may enter in. Thou wilt keep him in perfect peace, whose mind is stayed on thee: because he trusteth in thee. Trust ye in the LORD for ever: for in the LORD JEHOVAH is everlasting strength" (Isaiah 26:1-4).

Father, I am glad that You are a High Tower that we can run to when we need defense from the enemy of our souls. Keep me from pride and deliver me from all that would offend You. I appreciate being able to read the Bible and find strength and comfort within its pages. Lord, I acknowledge You as my God and King. I rely on You alone and do not put my confidence in my own self, nor any other man. Thank You for protecting me from the attacks of the devil. I pray in the name of Jesus Christ. Amen.

Proverbs 26:1 As snow in summer, and as rain in harvest, so honour is not seemly for a fool.

Honor bestowed upon a self-confident fool is not fitting, because when attention and honor are given to one who is already prideful, it only causes them to be more prideful and haughty. Just as snow in summer will damage the plants, so praise and honor cause a prideful person to cause damage to others. Rain in harvest-time is also unfitting, as it prevents the farmer from being able to harvest his crops. Honor is fitting only for those who prove themselves worthy of it. What a travesty for an ungodly fool to be put on a par with heroes and leaders, simply because he has wealth or influence with people in power. In the book of Isaiah we find a scripture that describes how a fool acts: "For the fool speaks folly and his mind plans iniquity: practicing profane ungodliness and speaking error concerning the LORD, leaving the craving of the hungry unsatisfied and causing the drink of the thirsty to fail" (Isaiah 32:6 AMP).

"The wicked in his pride doth persecute the poor: let them be taken in the devices that they have imagined. For the wicked boasteth of his heart's desire, and blesseth the covetous, whom the LORD abhorreth. The wicked, through the pride of his countenance, will not seek after God: God is not in all his thoughts" (Psalm 10:2-4). Proud, self-confident people are consumed with accomplishing their own desires. We saw in Proverbs 19:29 and 21:11 that fools should be punished, that the simple may be warned not to do evil. Even if a fool is too stubborn to let his punishment turn him from wickedness, some of those who see him punished will turn away from doing evil.

As frost coming in summer would destroy crops, praise and honor coming on a fool hurts people. Honoring a fool increases his stubbornness and pride because it implies that we approve of his godlessness. Rather than help him to find the Lord, we help him harden his heart and thus share in his guilt. By praising a fool, we may also cause others to stumble. Sometimes it is costly not to do as the crowd does. Not giving honor to an ungodly fool may cost us a great deal in this world, but we need to choose the eternal riches of good character over earthly gain. We ought to be careful not to share in the guilt of a fool's sin or sow compromise in ourselves and cause others to stumble, for we all shall reap what we sow (Galatians 6:7-8).

If we sow evil things, we shall also reap those things; however, we have a choice, and can sow good things. If we reach out to the poor and help others, God will send people to help us in our hour of need. If we are merciful to those who sin against us, God will be merciful to us when we fail Him. If we give to others and the work of the Lord, the Lord will cause our finances to be blessed. If we encourage others, others will encourage us when we need encouragement. If we humble ourselves, the Lord will lift us up, but if we brag and exalt our own selves, then we shall fall. We should ask God to help us remain humble and pray for those who walk in pride.

Dear Father, I love You! Thank You for the many blessings You have bestowed upon me. I humble myself before You and ask You to forgive me for demonstrating any pride before men. I know that I could do nothing without You. You are the One who gives both life and breath; health and well-being. Without Your touch on my life, I could not do the things that I do every day. Lord, I bless Your name and worship You! You are a mighty God. Reach out to all of Your children and help us, as we follow in the straight and narrow path of holiness. I pray in Jesus' name. Amen.

Proverbs 26:2 As the bird by wandering, as the swallow by flying, so the curse causeless shall not come.

This verse tells us that the curses that come to someone's life are not by accident; there is a reason behind them. What is a curse? Today, we think of *"cursing"* as using foul language, profanity, or perhaps, even blasphemous words against God. Our definition usually is synonymous with "swearing." This is a form of cursing, but it is only a small portion of what "curses" mean in the Bible. Cursing in the Bible is not only speaking evil of someone, but evil coming upon someone. If a person is under a curse, according to the Bible, evil has come upon them in some way. Sickness, tragedy, or bad circumstances are occurring in their lives.

There is a reason behind every evil that comes against us, just as there is a reason that birds migrate south in winter and north in the summer. It has long been a mystery as to why the swallows return to certain places each year, like the migration of the swallows to San Juan Capistrano, California. The incredible flight of the swallows happens every spring around the 19th of March to the old Spanish mission located there. Most scientists cannot explain the migration of birds other than to say that it is just a fulfillment of some inner biological destiny. The Bible tells us that God is the one who created the birds and has made them like they are. Therefore, it is God who set up the spiritual laws of cause and effect. When we break them, we reap what we sow. Curses come because of broken spiritual laws. We may not be aware of why some curse or evil has come upon us, but there is a reason. As we seek God for the answer, He will give us the revelation as to not only why, but also the remedy for it.

In today's culture, some Christians have curses operating against them. That is because various occult practices are openly practiced in our societies. Christians need to be freed from curses spoken against them before they were saved, or from curses that have come upon them through involvement in idolatry and witchcraft (Deuteronomy 29:24-28).

Curses can work against Christians if they are in rebellion, out of the will of God, or not walking in faith and love. However, if we are walking where God wants us to walk, a hundred curses against us would just bounce off and would do us no harm. If we have been affected by a curse, the good news is that by accepting Jesus, we can be free from demonic oppression and actually have authority over the devil and his curses, instead of his spirits having power over us and our family. "Behold, I give unto you power to tread on serpents and scorpions, and over all the power of the enemy: and nothing shall by any means hurt you" (Luke 10:19).

The story of Balaam and Israel gives us a good example of this principle (Numbers 22). Although Balaam was not an Israelite, he was a prophet of God. The kings of Moab and Midian wanted him to curse the Israelites during the journey from Egypt to Canaan. Elders of those nations offered him what apparently was a lot of money, and he tried to do what their king wanted, but he could not curse them. He tried three times but was unable to do anything, but bless Israel. "How shall I curse, whom God hath not cursed? or how shall I defy, whom the LORD hath not defied?" (Numbers 23:8).

Before we are born again, we walk under the law of sin and death; but, after we are regenerated, we are under the law of life in Christ Jesus, who took the curse for us. "For the law of the Spirit of life in Christ Jesus hath made me free from the law of sin and death" (Romans 8:2). "Christ hath redeemed us from the curse of the law, being made a curse for us: for it is written, Cursed is every one that hangeth on a tree: That the blessing of Abraham might come on the Gentiles through Jesus Christ; that we might receive the promise of the Spirit through faith" (Galatians 3:13-14).

How wonderful is our inheritance as Christians! We do not get the evil that should be ours. We all deserve hell, but when we come to Jesus, we get Heaven. We are not under the curse of sickness and death any longer. We now have power over sin through Jesus. The way to break a curse is to repent for whatever involvement has occurred on the enemy's territory and rebuke him from our life.

Dear heavenly Father, I ask You first to forgive my sins and cleanse me from any area where I have allowed the devil to enter my life. I renounce any involvement with the works of darkness. In the name of Jesus, I cancel every curse, and Father, I ask You to forgive the people who have spoken them against me. I thank You that those curses will no longer operate against me. In Jesus' name, they are broken right now, by the power of Almighty God. I ask You to cover me and my family with Your protection according to Your Word in Psalm 91. Thank You for cancelling every curse by the blood of Jesus. I ask this is the name of Jesus. Amen.

Quotes About Patience and Mercy

We must not be legalistic about God's Word, but always have mercy in our hearts toward those that break the laws of God. The Lord tells us that if we desire to obtain mercy in our time of need, we must be merciful to those who fall short of the truth and hurt us. --Day 17

Those who are merciful to the poor are happy and blessed, for they follow in the steps of Jesus Himself. --Day 107

A wise man is patient and not easily offended. He graciously overlooks people's faults rather than let them irritate him. --Day 171

We all appreciate God's patience toward us when He is dealing with our weaknesses. To be like Him, we also must be patient in dealing with others. --Day 237

Proverbs 26:3 A whip for the horse, a bridle for the ass, and a rod for the fool's back.

Some people will only be persuaded to obey by receiving their instruction through punishment, like a horse or a donkey. Some animals are more sensitive or intelligent than others and train more quickly. Others are very stubborn and will only obey if a bridle or whip is used, which is what today's proverb refers to. The "fool" in this verse is likened to an unreasonable animal that stubbornly refuses to obey despite its training. It will take a rod on his back to get him to respond.

Many of us act like stubborn fools at times, going our own way instead of obeying the Word of God. We would not have to receive the "rod to the back" for correction if we would simply obey in the first place. God comes to bring life and blessing, but to receive it we must learn to obey His Word. We choose hardship when we disobey. There are two ways to learn obedience: One is to learn from instruction. God instructs us by speaking to us through His Word, directly by His Holy Spirit to our hearts, and also through other people. Another way we can learn is by suffering the results of our own rebellion, which will cause us to change. When we refuse to seek God's instruction, or to obey what we know, we invite the enemy to do us harm. The Bible also reveals that when we leave God out of our homes, businesses, schools, and governments, it allows the enemy to wreak havoc in our entire societies.

God does not desire forced obedience. He does not want us to be driven to Him by a rod of correction, but rather that we obey Him from our hearts because we love and trust Him. All of His commandments are for our good. He freed us from the tyranny of sin so that we could obey Him; and He is worthy of our love and trust as no one else is. Our precious Lord would never ask us to do anything that would not ultimately be a blessing to us. Sometimes that blessing is not immediately seen; yet, if we hold fast and continue to follow in Him, we will discover His beautiful plan. We must let Him work His patience into our lives and not always expect instant answers. This is difficult, as we are living in an age in which everything is instant: coffee, tea, mashed potatoes, etc. Our Father longs for us to respond as mature sons, instead of as unreasoning animals. "I will instruct you and teach you in the way you should go; I will guide you with My eye. Do not be like the horse or like the mule, which have no understanding, which must be harnessed with bit and bridle, else they will not come near you" (Psalm 32:8-9).

Dear Father, I am grateful that You have given us the Bible so that we may know and understand Your ways. I ask You to forgive me for the times that I have rebelled against Your Word and have experienced the pain caused by my own disobedience. Father, give me the grace to obey Your Word. I know that You have given us Your commandments so that we can be blessed in the earth. Deliver me from rebellion and all pride that would cause me to do it my own way. I do trust You and I know that by obeying You, I will not suffer the consequences that sin causes. I ask this in the precious name of Jesus. Amen.

God's Wisdom for Daily Living **_Betty Miller_**
October 12 **_Day 285_**

Proverbs 26:4-5 4 Answer not a fool according to his folly, lest thou also be like unto him. 5 Answer a fool according to his folly, lest he be wise in his own conceit.

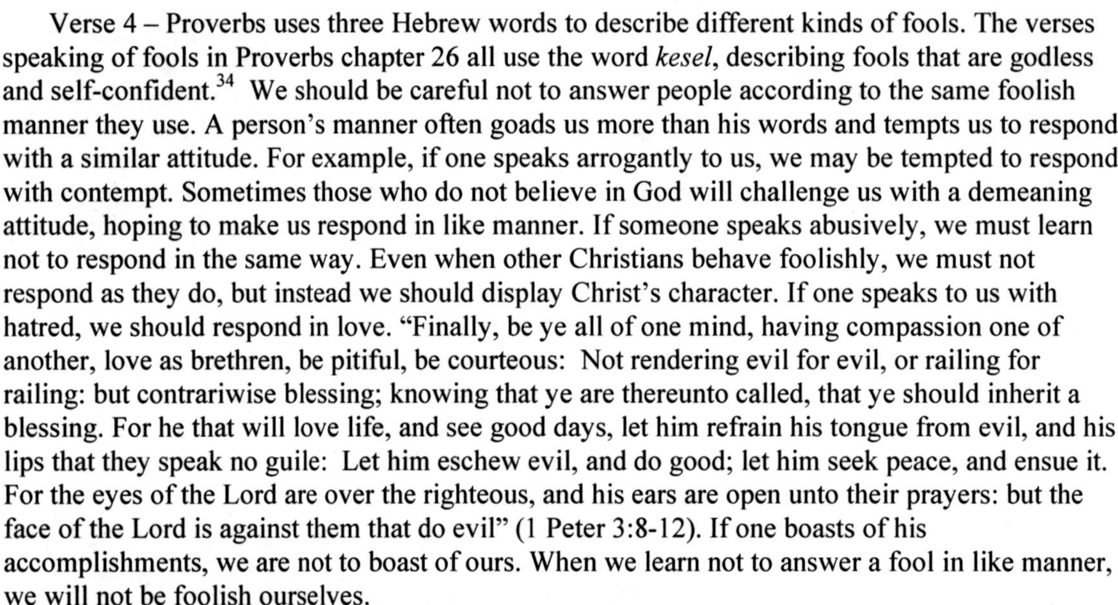

Verse 4 – Proverbs uses three Hebrew words to describe different kinds of fools. The verses speaking of fools in Proverbs chapter 26 all use the word *kesel*, describing fools that are godless and self-confident.[34] We should be careful not to answer people according to the same foolish manner they use. A person's manner often goads us more than his words and tempts us to respond with a similar attitude. For example, if one speaks arrogantly to us, we may be tempted to respond with contempt. Sometimes those who do not believe in God will challenge us with a demeaning attitude, hoping to make us respond in like manner. If someone speaks abusively, we must learn not to respond in the same way. Even when other Christians behave foolishly, we must not respond as they do, but instead we should display Christ's character. If one speaks to us with hatred, we should respond in love. "Finally, be ye all of one mind, having compassion one of another, love as brethren, be pitiful, be courteous: Not rendering evil for evil, or railing for railing: but contrariwise blessing; knowing that ye are thereunto called, that ye should inherit a blessing. For he that will love life, and see good days, let him refrain his tongue from evil, and his lips that they speak no guile: Let him eschew evil, and do good; let him seek peace, and ensue it. For the eyes of the Lord are over the righteous, and his ears are open unto their prayers: but the face of the Lord is against them that do evil" (1 Peter 3:8-12). If one boasts of his accomplishments, we are not to boast of ours. When we learn not to answer a fool in like manner, we will not be foolish ourselves.

Verse 5 - So how do we answer a fool? According to verse 5, while we should not answer a fool according to his attitude, we should answer a fool according to the folly of his words or actions. If someone says or does something foolish, he needs correction. To ignore an error is to give it silent approval. This causes a person to think himself to be wise and to advise others to do as he does. If others are present, it encourages them in their own foolishness. We are to speak the truth in love, and not to ignore the error. The proper way to answer a fool is to address his folly without stooping to his ungodly attitude. Our motive should be to help the person see their own folly or wrong actions so that they may be spared its consequences.

"That we henceforth be no more children, tossed to and fro, and carried about with every wind of doctrine, by the sleight of men, and cunning craftiness, whereby they lie in wait to deceive; But speaking the truth in love, may grow up into him in all things, which is the head, even Christ" (Ephesians 4:14-15).

Dear heavenly Father, thank You for giving us Your wisdom as to how to deal with so many issues in life situations. The wonderful Book of Proverbs addresses so many relationship problems. I am grateful that You are not silent about how we are to relate with one another. Help me to take Your advice to heart and apply it to my relationships with others. May I respond in love and with Your wisdom when I am challenged by those who would want to argue. Fill me with Your Holy Spirit so that I may be an example of how You deal with difficult people. I ask this in the name of Jesus. Amen.

[34] Strong's Exhaustive Concordance of the Bible, the Hebrew and Chaldee Dictionary

October 13 *Day 286*

Proverbs 26:6-9 6 He who sends a message by the hand of a fool cuts off the feet (of satisfactory delivery) and drinks the damage. 7 Like the legs of a lame man which hang loose, so is a parable in the mouth of a fool. 8 Like he who binds a stone in a sling, so is he who gives honor to a (self-confident) fool. 9 Like a thorn that goes (without being felt) into the hand of a drunken man, so is a proverb in the mouth of a (self-confident) fool (AMP).

These verses tell us the damage a fool can do if given the opportunity. Fools, (those who are obstinate, rebellious, or self-confident) cannot receive godly wisdom.

Verse 6 – Sending a message by a fool "cuts off the feet" of satisfactory delivery. The message will probably not get there, or it will arrive late. A foolish messenger will probably perform his task poorly and leave a bad impression of the person who sent him. Instead of being useful, he creates more work for his employer. I have experienced this when I gave a duty to one whom I thought would surely take care of delivering my bills to the post office for me. They got sidetracked, and so did my mail. Although I would not call this person a "fool" they had done a foolish thing. We all do foolish things at times. This does not make us fools, but we should strive not to allow the enemy to cause us to be foolish in our ways.

Verse 7 – A parable in the mouth of a fool will not be of any use. This verse makes the comparison to one who has lame legs and cannot walk. A person who is lame must be carried about by others; they have to have help. So it is when a fool tries to put forth a parable. Someone else has to explain it or it cannot be understood. Foolish talk never makes sense. In the mouth of a fool, a parable becomes as useless as paralyzed legs.

Verse 8 – Only a moron would tie a stone into a sling, and only a moron gives honor to a fool. Our modern equivalent of this term would be "giving someone ammunition" that is faulty. It would fire in the gun or go the wrong direction. Honor given to a fool is like ammunition backfiring.

Verse 9 – A fool misapplies a proverb so that its point is no more felt than a thorn cutting into a drunkard's hand. He puts a "spin" on a thorny issue so that one does not feel the point that is made. He is self-confident, trusting more in his own judgment than in God's. He waters down the truth. Sometimes God's Word causes us pain when we hear it, as it pierces our hearts. However, in the mouth of a fool, even God's Word can be distorted, so that one does not feel the pain of conviction and thus continues in the path of sin.

Dear Father, thank You for Your words of wisdom in the Bible. I do want to adhere to them and avoid doing foolish things. Forgive me for the foolish things I have done in the past. Give me discernment to recognize the voice of fools, so that I am not taken in by their deceptive talk. I want to hear the truth, even if it is painful, because the truth of God's Word is what sets us free. Give me ears to hear what the Spirit of God is saying, and then give me the grace to obey Your Words. I ask this in the name of Jesus. Amen.

Proverbs 26:10-11 10 The great God that formed all things both rewardeth the fool, and rewardeth transgressors. 11 As a dog returneth to his vomit, so a fool returneth to his folly.

Verse 10 – This verse tells us that since God has formed all things, He will justly reward both the transgressors and the fools. Sometimes people are concerned about sinners who seemingly are not suffering for the wicked things they have done to others. This verse assures us that God will deal with them; and because He is a just God, it will be a just and fair punishment. Since He created the entire universe, and all mankind, He certainly is capable of dealing with the ones who rebel against Him. In fact, the Bible states that God is the Judge of the whole earth and He will deal with the righteous and the wicked in a just manner (Genesis 18:25; 2 Peter 3:10-11). Those who rebel against Him, shall not escape when He calls them to account. "Therefore the ungodly shall not stand in the judgment, nor sinners in the congregation of the righteous. For the LORD knoweth the way of the righteous: but the way of the ungodly shall perish" (Psalm 1:5-6).

God earnestly desires all people to turn to Him and be saved. He expects His children to pray for the lost and reach out to them in love. As we do, we may be persecuted for His name's sake. After much long-suffering toward the wicked, God will finally allow the unrepentant to reap what they have sown and His judgment will come upon them. As Christians, we are not to try to take vengeance upon anyone who hurts us. We are to trust God, who will deal with all people. It is for God to administer vengeance, not us. "For we know him that hath said, Vengeance belongeth unto me, I will recompense, saith the Lord. And again, The Lord shall judge his people. It is a fearful thing to fall into the hands of the living God" (Hebrews 10:30-31).

Verse 11 – Rebellious fools will repeat the same sins over and over again, just like a dog returning to its own vomit. 2 Peter 2:20-22 tells us the same thing, only this is a warning to those who have been cleansed by the Holy Spirit: "For if after they have escaped the pollutions of the world through the knowledge of the Lord and Saviour Jesus Christ, they are again entangled therein, and overcome, the latter end is worse with them than the beginning. For it had been better for them not to have known the way of righteousness, than, after they have known it, to turn from the holy commandment delivered unto them. But it is happened unto them according to the true proverb, The dog is turned to his own vomit again; and the sow that was washed to her wallowing in the mire."

The only way anyone who keeps returning to a filthy addiction can be completely redeemed is by turning to God and receiving deliverance. God will never turn away those with penitent hearts. He will deliver them from the addictions that keep them wallowing in filth. "All that the Father giveth me shall come to me; and him that cometh to me I will in no wise cast out" (John 6:37).

Dear Father in heaven, I am thankful that You are a just and fair Judge of all of us. Help me not to judge others, but to pray for those who would sin against me or others. Lord, I trust You to take care of those who persecute me and come against me. I ask You to forgive them, and bring them into the knowledge of Your dear Son. I especially pray for those who are bound in addictions and ask that You set them free so that they may serve You and find peace in their souls. I ask this in the name of Jesus, my Lord. Amen.

Proverbs 26:12 Do you see a man wise in his own eyes and conceit? There is more hope for a (self–confident) fool than for him (AMP).

We all are prone to trust our own understanding rather than the Lord. Proverbs 3:5-6 tells us to "Trust in the LORD with all thine heart; and lean not unto thine own understanding. In all thy ways acknowledge him, and he shall direct thy paths." A fool rejects good counsel and stubbornly trusts his own inclinations. He is wise in his own estimation. Intelligent people consider themselves to be wise, and usually are–but with mere worldly wisdom. Godless, intellectual people are knowledgeable about many things, but knowledge "puffs up." 1 Corinthians 8:1 says, "Now as touching things offered unto idols, we know that we all have knowledge. Knowledge puffeth up, but charity edifieth." Pride makes it difficult for people to turn to God and learn true wisdom. Many intellectuals see no need to believe in God or for a nation to follow His laws. They measure everything by their own understanding, reflecting Lucifer's pride. The arrogant person who trusts his intellect and rejects the Bible as untrue, is a greater fool. "The fool hath said in his heart, There is no God. (Psalm 14:1a). This is because he simply relies on his own opinions and instincts and neglects God's Word. Man's wisdom alone, without God, will eventually fail him.

Pride is a deadly sin. David cried out to be delivered from the sins in his life which were hidden from his personal knowledge. "Who can understand his errors? cleanse thou me from secret faults. Keep back thy servant also from presumptuous sins; let them not have dominion over me: then shall I be upright, and I shall be innocent from the great transgression" (Psalm 19:12-13). He especially asked to be held back from sins of presumption that would lead to the sin of the "great transgression." I believe that great transgression is pride. Exalting oneself in one's own thinking is the opposite of God's character. It is especially wicked if it leads one to exalt oneself above God. As we saw in Day 129, Satan, originally named Lucifer, committed this great transgression. Though he was the anointed cherub, his heart was lifted up because of his beauty. He corrupted his wisdom for the sake of his splendor. In his pride, he desired God's throne and set his will against God's (Ezekiel 28:12-19). Because he chose to rebel, he lost his position in heaven and will be banished to hell (Isaiah 14:12-15).

"Where is the wise? Where is the scribe? Where is the disputer of this world? Hath not God made foolish the wisdom of this world? For after that in the wisdom of God the world by wisdom knew not God, it pleased God by the foolishness of preaching to save them that believe. For the Jews require a sign, and the Greeks seek after wisdom: But we preach Christ crucified, unto the Jews a stumblingblock, and unto the Greeks foolishness; But unto them which are called, both Jews and Greeks, Christ the power of God, and the wisdom of God. Because the foolishness of God is wiser than men; and the weakness of God is stronger than men" (1 Corinthians 1:20-25).

Dear heavenly Father, we want to pray as David did, for deliverance from the great transgression of pride. Lord, show us any sin in our lives that we are blinded to, so that we may repent. Set us free from those things that would keep us from becoming like You. I desire to have a humble heart before You and others. Help me not to be condescending, but to prefer others and esteem them. May we all give honor to whom honor is due, and especially may we bring honor to You. I ask this in the name of Jesus. Amen.

God's Wisdom for Daily Living ***Betty Miller***
October 16 ***Day 289***

Proverbs 26:13-14 13 The slothful man saith, There is a lion in the way; a lion is in the streets. 14 As the door turneth upon his hinges, so doth the slothful upon his bed.

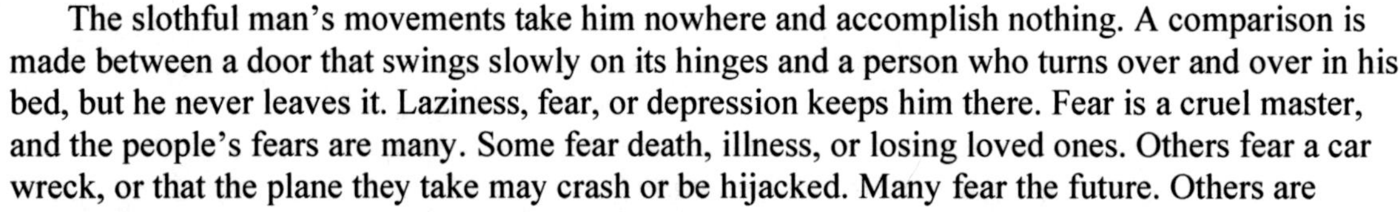

The slothful man's movements take him nowhere and accomplish nothing. A comparison is made between a door that swings slowly on its hinges and a person who turns over and over in his bed, but he never leaves it. Laziness, fear, or depression keeps him there. Fear is a cruel master, and the people's fears are many. Some fear death, illness, or losing loved ones. Others fear a car wreck, or that the plane they take may crash or be hijacked. Many fear the future. Others are tormented by a fear of the dark or of being alone. Some fear being molested or raped. Fear is tormenting whatever form it takes, driving some people to act foolishly and even incapacitate them because they are ruled by their fears.

Fear is the opposite of faith. There is only one way we can live without fear in a world of turmoil, war, and uncertainty: that is, to trust the One who told us not to be troubled or fearful. The Lord calls us to trust Him and walk in faith. The devil continually tries to make us do the opposite; to be afraid and doubt God. Only through His power can we walk in peace and safety. We must give our lives completely to Him and yield to His will. Making a total commitment to God means giving Him first place in every area of our lives: our time, our money, our careers, our families, and our futures. Those who entrust themselves to Him in this way will never be shaken in the day of trouble. "He shall not be afraid of evil tidings: his heart is fixed, trusting in the LORD" (Psalm 112:7).

The Bible speaks of our times as the "last days," during which there will be great trouble. "This know also, that in the last days perilous times shall come" (2 Timothy 3:1). Instead of overcoming fear, many will be overcome by fear. "And there shall be signs in the sun, and in the moon, and in the stars; and upon the earth distress of nations, with perplexity; the sea and the waves roaring; men's hearts failing them for fear, and for looking after those things which are coming on the earth: for the powers of heaven shall be shaken…" (Luke 21:25-26).

Fear is a horrible monster no matter what form it takes. We can ask God to deliver us and give us the courage to overcome whatever frightens us. Fear and weakness should have no power over a Christian, for "God hath not given us the spirit of fear; but of power, and of love, and of a sound mind" (2 Timothy 1:7). "Strengthen ye the weak hands, and confirm the feeble knees. Say to them that are of a fearful heart, Be strong, fear not: behold, your God will come with vengeance, even God with a recompense; he will come and save you" (Isaiah 35:3-4).

Dear heavenly Father, thank You that we can overcome fear through our faith in You. It is so wonderful to walk in peace and faith when trouble surrounds us. Lord, You have never failed me in the past and I know You will not fail me now. You are so faithful and I am grateful for Your mercy and love over and over again. Help me to overcome the lies of the devil that would try to get me to doubt Your love and provision when I am facing a need that seems overwhelming. I voice my trust in You and thank You, even before I receive the answers to my prayers. I pray in the name of Jesus. Amen.

Proverbs 26:15-16 15 The slothful and self-indulgent buries his hand in his bosom; it distresses and wearies him to bring it again to his mouth. 16 The sluggard is wiser in his own eyes and conceit than seven men who can render a reason and answer discreetly (AMP).

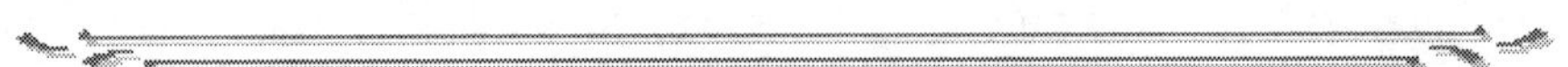

Even more sinful than laziness is the sluggard's prideful attitude of being wise in his own eyes. My husband and I pastored for many years, and during that time, many beggars would come to our church asking for money for food or gas. Since we had trusting, compassionate hearts, it was difficult for us to believe that people would lie to us about their conditions. However, we learned early not to give these people money, since some of them would later be seen down the road with a bottle of liquor which they had purchased with the money we'd given them. After that, we made it a practice to send them to a restaurant or service station and have the owners serve them and bill us. By doing that, we truly helped the needy and avoided giving them money that would support a harmful habit.

Although most of those people lied to us, what shocked me most about many of them was their pride. On more than one occasion, when we would try to share some wisdom to help them out of their poverty, they would become quite indignant. I came to realize that most did not want real help, but just a hand-out in order to continue a lifestyle that they were accustomed to; which included answering to no one and doing as they pleased. When we offered them a job or opportunity to help out in our church, they refused and went on their way; thinking they were smart enough to avoid work and still get by.

Of course, people who were simply in bad circumstances also came to us. These were grateful for our help and willing to listen to advice. They were unlike the irresponsible sluggards who took advantage of others and never made an attempt to change. Though cautious, we always prayed for the sluggards and reached out to them in love, since God cares for them and desires to help them overcome their bad habits. Our prayer was that our witness to them would plant a seed in their hearts, so that they might come to the Lord when they became weary of wasting their lives.

Through these experiences, I realized that people can be prideful when they have absolutely nothing to be proud about. Appearances can be deceiving. Pride and humility are attitudes of the heart. A poor person can be arrogant, just as a wealthy person can be humble. "...the LORD seeth not as man seeth; for man looketh on the outward appearance, but the LORD looketh on the heart" (1 Samuel 16:7b).

Dear Father in heaven, thank You for being a God of compassion. May we, as Your children, have Your compassionate heart also. Lord, give us wisdom as to how we should deal with those who are sluggards. Let us help them by sharing Your love with them; but may we also be strong enough to say no to people who are manipulating us in order to use us for the wrong purposes. Give us Your discernment, and the wisdom and love to respond in the proper way. I ask this in the name of the Lord Jesus Christ. Amen.

God's Wisdom for Daily Living ***Betty Miller***
October 18 ***Day 291***

Proverbs 26:17 He that passeth by, and meddleth with strife belonging not to him, is like one that taketh a dog by the ears.

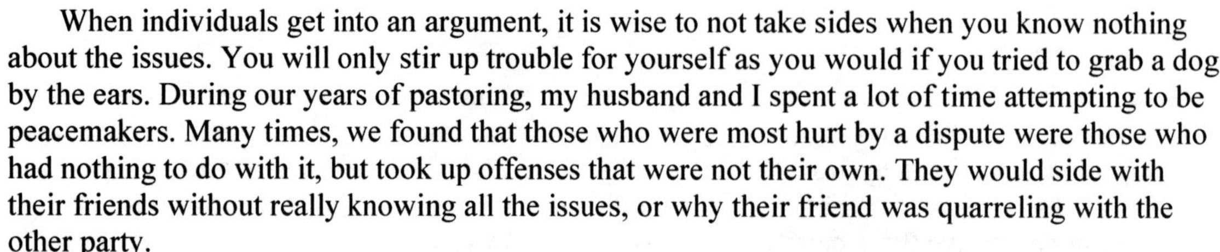

When individuals get into an argument, it is wise to not take sides when you know nothing about the issues. You will only stir up trouble for yourself as you would if you tried to grab a dog by the ears. During our years of pastoring, my husband and I spent a lot of time attempting to be peacemakers. Many times, we found that those who were most hurt by a dispute were those who had nothing to do with it, but took up offenses that were not their own. They would side with their friends without really knowing all the issues, or why their friend was quarreling with the other party.

Romans 12:17-18 tells us to avoid strife and to seek peace with all men insofar as it depends upon us. In the Sermon on the Mount, Jesus spoke these words: "Blessed are the peacemakers: for they shall be called the children of God" (Matthew 5:9). The way to achieve this is by maintaining a humble attitude, for contention only comes by pride (Proverbs 13:10). Being dogmatic about one's position engenders strife. This does not mean we become a "door mat" and allow others to walk upon us, but rather it means that we should learn to listen to other's complaints, and work toward finding a beneficial solution for all. We are not to approach situations from a self-centered perspective, but ask God to give us love and wisdom when dealing with a difference of opinion. Those of us that are married should allow the Holy Spirit to be the referee in differences that arise with our spouses, and be willing to change when we are in the wrong.

"What man is he that desireth life, and loveth many days, that he may see good? Keep thy tongue from evil, and thy lips from speaking guile. Depart from evil, and do good; seek peace, and pursue it" (Psalm 34:12-14). Pursuing peace on a personal basis means forgiving those who hurt or offend us. It is vital to our relationship with God. We fail to appropriate God's grace when we don't forgive. Refusing to forgive those who have hurt us will cause roots of bitterness to spring up in our hearts, which defile us and others. Unforgiveness and bitterness are sins that separate us from God. We must seek God with our whole hearts in order to walk in love toward those who come against us. Remember, we hear Him only when we maintain a close relationship with Him. Hearing and seeing God has to do with proximity. When at a great distance from someone, we cannot see or hear him. How close are we to the Lord? One minister commented, "We are as close to God as we want to be."

"Follow peace with all men, and holiness, without which no man shall see the Lord: Looking diligently lest any man fail of the grace of God; lest any root of bitterness springing up trouble you, and thereby many be defiled" (Hebrews 12:14-15).

Dear heavenly Father, I want to be close to You, so help me to spend the time in prayer and reading Your Word in order to make that a reality. And Lord, when You speak something to my heart, help me to obey and not resist the things that You are asking me to do. I want to be a peacemaker, so fill my mouth with Your wisdom when I encounter an opportunity to minister to those who are opposed to each other. Also, help me to remain in peace with those in my circle of acquaintances. I ask this in the name of Jesus. Amen.

October 19 — *Day 292*

Proverbs 26:18-19 18 As a mad man who casteth firebrands, arrows, and death, 19 So is the man that deceiveth his neighbour, and saith, Am not I in sport?

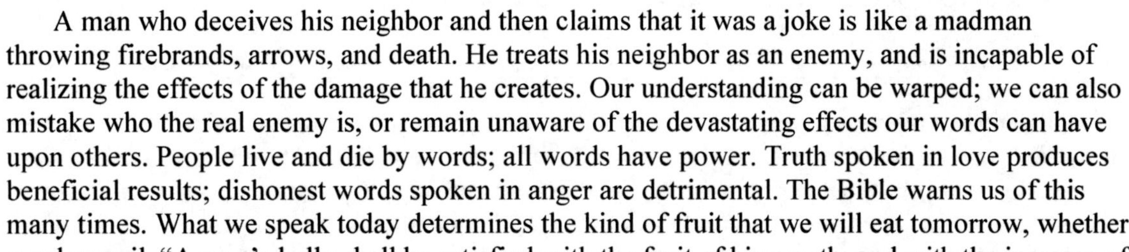

A man who deceives his neighbor and then claims that it was a joke is like a madman throwing firebrands, arrows, and death. He treats his neighbor as an enemy, and is incapable of realizing the effects of the damage that he creates. Our understanding can be warped; we can also mistake who the real enemy is, or remain unaware of the devastating effects our words can have upon others. People live and die by words; all words have power. Truth spoken in love produces beneficial results; dishonest words spoken in anger are detrimental. The Bible warns us of this many times. What we speak today determines the kind of fruit that we will eat tomorrow, whether good or evil. "A man's belly shall be satisfied with the fruit of his mouth; and with the increase of his lips shall he be filled. Death and life are in the power of the tongue: and they that love it shall eat the fruit thereof" (Proverbs 18:20-21).

It is a serious thing to accuse someone wrongly or to describe a person detrimentally. Trying to pass it off as a joke is inappropriate. It is best not to say negative things about others in the first place. There are many "madmen" today spewing deadly words. We must ask God for discernment, so that we may recognize when others are untruthful, lest we embrace a lie. "But fornication, and all uncleanness, or covetousness, let it not be once named among you, as becometh saints; Neither filthiness, nor foolish talking, nor jesting, which are not convenient: but rather giving of thanks...Let no man deceive you with vain words: for because of these things cometh the wrath of God upon the children of disobedience. Be not ye therefore partakers with them" (Ephesians 5:3-4, 6-7).

Since words have power, we should choose ours carefully. What we say should agree with God's Word and His thoughts. We are commanded to refrain from speaking evil, and to speak truth and counteract the evil that many in this world are speaking.

"If my people, which are called by my name, shall humble themselves, and pray, and seek my face, and turn from their wicked ways; then will I hear from heaven, and will forgive their sin, and will heal their land" (2 Chronicles 7:14). Notice God addressed *His* people in this verse, not the sinners! If we want to see our land healed, we must follow His instructions to humbly seek Him with our whole hearts, confess our sins and those of our nation, and ask Him to forgive us. Only then will we see our land healed.

Dearest Father, we are grateful that You are trustworthy. We want to be like You. May our words on earth line up with Your Words in the heavens. We want to act with integrity in all of our ways. May we always be honest with people. Give us discernment when others are lying, so that we do not get trapped into any unholy alliances. Lord, let us be good and loving neighbors so that our neighbors will desire to know You by the demonstration of our lives in this world. I ask this in the precious name of Jesus. Amen.

Proverbs 26:20-22 20 For lack of wood the fire goes out, and where there is no whisperer, contention ceases. 21 As coals are to hot embers and as wood to fire, so is a quarrelsome man to inflame strife. 22 The words of a whisperer or slanderer are like dainty morsels or words of sport [to some, but to others are like deadly wounds]; and they go down into the innermost parts of the body [or of the victim's nature] (AMP).

Slanderers or talebearers spread lies, and then gossipers treat their words as "dainty morsels." However, their victims can be severely wounded from these verbal assaults. Their words are like wood added to a fire. When a fire lacks fuel, it dies out; and when this sort of talk is rebuked or dismissed, contention ceases. "Cast out the scorner, and contention shall go out; yea, strife and reproach shall cease" (Proverbs 22:10). Businesses and churches could avoid many problems by heeding this advice. Of course, before the parties are dismissed, they should first be approached by their superiors and warned to repent, if they have been caught lying or gossiping. If they continue to do so, a supervisor should follow through with disciplinary action. Such action should always be administered with just cause and never based on personality differences.

Some Christians are deceived into believing that in the name of love, we should continue to put up with people who are troublemakers. The Lord gave instructions about dealing with those who sin against others in the church in Matthew 18:15-17. His thoughts are also echoed by Paul in 1 Corinthians 5:11 which says, "But now I have written unto you not to keep company, if any man that is called a brother be a fornicator, or covetous, or an idolator, or a railer, or a drunkard, or an extortioner; with such an one no not to eat." The first action is to try to win them by going to them alone and lovingly speak the truth to them. If they refuse to hear, we are to take two or three witnesses and confront them again. If they still refuse to listen, then their sin is to be made known to the whole church (the pastor should be involved at this point of the process). If they still refuse to repent, the church should no longer offer them fellowship. Slander and gossip are among the sins that should be dealt with in this manner.

Although God is very merciful and patient, at some point, if we continue to disobey Him in our personal walk, He must deal with us in a stronger manner to prevent a greater evil from coming upon us. He will deal with the one who is a bad influence on of the rest of His children, and may cut off that individual from the congregation for the purpose of sparing the whole. He does this for the good of the entire church. "For if God spared not the natural branches, take heed lest he also spare not thee. Behold therefore the goodness and severity of God: on them which fell, severity; but toward thee, goodness, if thou continue in his goodness: otherwise thou also shalt be cut off" (Romans 11:21-22).

Dear heavenly Father, thank You for Your words of wisdom in dealing with tale bearers. May we have the courage to go to a brother or sister who has sinned against us and confront them in love, that we may win them. Lord, deliver me from any spirit of gossip. Give me the grace not only to refrain from speaking amiss, but also to refuse to listen to it. By walking away, I will not be adding fuel to the fire. May I speak graciously and kindly of others and defend those who are targets of gossip. I ask this in the name of Jesus. Amen.

Proverbs 26:23 Burning lips [uttering insincere words of love] and a wicked heart are like an earthen vessel covered with the scum thrown off from molten silver [making it appear to be solid silver] (AMP).

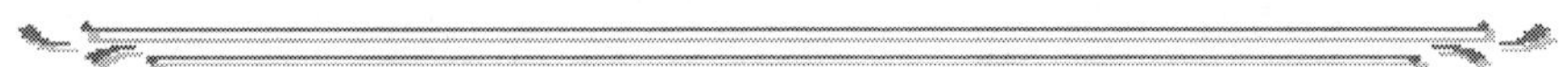

Professions of love from the wicked are comparable to a silver veneer on earthenware vessels. They look good on the surface; but upon thorough examination, they are not what they appear to be. We should assess people by their *actions*, not their words or appearance (Proverbs 20:11). Otherwise, they will deceive us, like a merchant selling a cheap vessel coated with silver.

The Bible has much to say about people who profess to love God but whose actions prove otherwise. Jesus called those who observe their religious traditions without loving God or their fellow-men, hypocrites: "...Well hath Esaias prophesied of you hypocrites, as it is written, This people honoureth me with their lips, but their heart is far from me. Howbeit in vain do they worship me, teaching for doctrines the commandments of men. For laying aside the commandment of God, ye hold the tradition of men, as the washing of pots and cups: and many other such like things ye do...Full well ye reject the commandment of God, that ye may keep your own tradition" (Mark 7:6-9).

Bondage to man-made religious traditions is one of the things that keep people from a true relationship with God. Tradition in itself is not a bad thing, if it is not followed blindly. However, Christianity for many people is merely a cultural tradition. They follow certain religious practices only because they were raised to do so. Many trust religious tradition to save them, but salvation is found only in a personal relationship with Jesus Christ. The only way to heaven is through faith in Him.

Cultural traditions can also lead us astray. We should ask God to show us the truth about them and cleanse us from all deception and unrighteousness. The fact that a tradition has been practiced for centuries, or that all society now behaves a certain way, does not make it right. These traditions can be cheap imitations of abundant life. No matter how popular or accepted certain things may be, if they do not line up with God's Word, we must renounce them. The Bible, not society, is our standard.

Jesus was always kind and extended mercy to the sinners who came to Him with honest hearts. To hypocrites, however, He was very harsh. Though they appeared to the world to be pure as silver, they could not hide their hidden, inward sins from Him: "Woe unto you, scribes and Pharisees, hypocrites! for ye are like unto whited sepulchres, which indeed appear beautiful outward, but are within full of dead men's bones, and of all uncleanness. Even so ye also outwardly appear righteous unto men, but within ye are full of hypocrisy and iniquity" (Matthew 23:27-28)

Dear Lord, I am asking that You be merciful to our nation and deliver us from evil. Father, You said in Your Word that judgment begins at the house of God, so convict Your people of their sins so that they may repent of them and return to You with their whole hearts. Lord, if You see anything in me that I am blind to, or that I have clung to because of tradition, please show me my need to repent and change my thinking. May I always choose Your Word over all traditions of men. Create in me a clean heart. I ask this in the name of Jesus. Amen.

Proverbs 26:24-26 24 He who hates pretends with his lips, but stores up deceit within himself. 25 When he speaks kindly, do not trust him, for seven abominations are in his heart. 26 Though his hatred covers itself with guile, his wickedness shall be shown openly before the assembly (AMP).

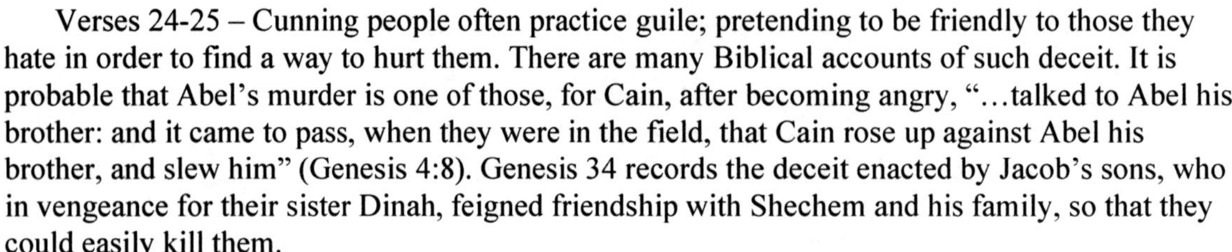

Verses 24-25 – Cunning people often practice guile; pretending to be friendly to those they hate in order to find a way to hurt them. There are many Biblical accounts of such deceit. It is probable that Abel's murder is one of those, for Cain, after becoming angry, "...talked to Abel his brother: and it came to pass, when they were in the field, that Cain rose up against Abel his brother, and slew him" (Genesis 4:8). Genesis 34 records the deceit enacted by Jacob's sons, who in vengeance for their sister Dinah, feigned friendship with Shechem and his family, so that they could easily kill them.

We ought to be cautious in making new friends and should certainly beware if anyone who has previously hated us suddenly becomes friendly. Verse 25 says that there are seven abominations in the heart of one who poses as a friend. These abominations may be the ones listed in Proverbs 6:16-19: "These six things doth the LORD hate: yea, seven are an abomination unto him: A proud look, a lying tongue, and hands that shed innocent blood, An heart that deviseth wicked imaginations, feet that be swift in running to mischief, A false witness that speaketh lies, and he that soweth discord among brethren."

We will recall that Jesus said that he who hates anyone commits murder in his heart, and that he who looks at a woman with lust commits adultery in his heart. In the same way, these seven sins can be present in the hearts of those who pretend friendship. We should be careful to befriend only those of proven good character. This does not mean we are to shun people in the world, as we should witness to them through our godly actions, but we should not make friends with sinners.

Verse 26 – A cunning person may successfully conceal his hatred, but regardless of how many people he deceives, his wickedness will eventually be exposed. There may be a public exposure on earth or exposure before the church on Judgment Day, when Christ separates those who think themselves to be Christians from those who really are (Matthew 7:21-23). Sooner or later, sins concealed by guile will be revealed. "...Ye have sinned against the LORD: and be sure your sin will find you out" (Numbers 32:23b).

Dear heavenly Father, we are grateful that You are a merciful God. We appreciate Your love toward us when we fail You. Set us free from any trace of guile, and forgive those who have used treacherous words against us. Lord, warn us when people are trying to deceive us with smooth words, so that we are not tricked into any agreements that are not of You. Have mercy on those whose sins are exposed and cause their shame to turn them back to You in repentance. In Jesus' name I pray. Amen.

God's Wisdom for Daily Living ***Betty Miller***
October 23 ***Day 296***

Proverbs 26:27 Whoever digs a pit (for another man's feet) shall fall into it himself, and he who rolls a stone (up a height to do mischief), it will return upon him (AMP).

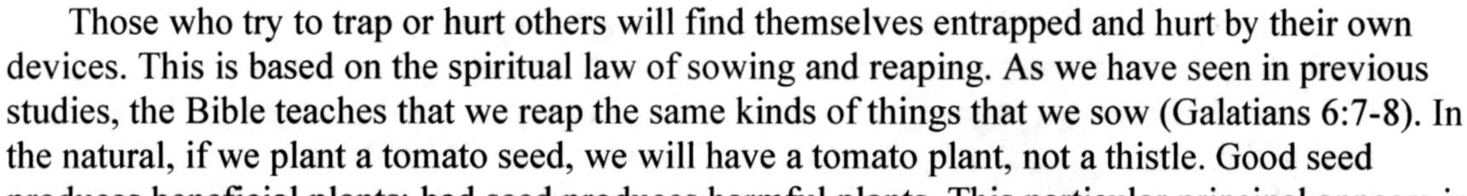

Those who try to trap or hurt others will find themselves entrapped and hurt by their own devices. This is based on the spiritual law of sowing and reaping. As we have seen in previous studies, the Bible teaches that we reap the same kinds of things that we sow (Galatians 6:7-8). In the natural, if we plant a tomato seed, we will have a tomato plant, not a thistle. Good seed produces beneficial plants; bad seed produces harmful plants. This particular principal appears in different forms throughout the Bible, starting in Genesis, where we find the law that everything produces fruit after its kind (Genesis 1:11&29).

In the beginning, everything God created for man was blessed and good. However, when Adam and Eve sinned, the earth came under a curse, and now the ground would also produce things that brought pain to mankind. "And unto Adam he said, Because thou hast hearkened unto the voice of thy wife, and hast eaten of the tree, of which I commanded thee, saying, Thou shalt not eat of it: cursed is the ground for thy sake; in sorrow shalt thou eat of it all the days of thy life; Thorns also and thistles shall it bring forth to thee; and thou shalt eat the herb of the field" (Genesis 3:17-18).

After God evicted Adam and Eve from the Garden of Eden, man was given the responsibility to choose good or evil. He still holds this responsibility in the natural and spiritual realm. As Adam was given the choice between life through obedience and death through disobedience, so are we. We now choose which law we submit to: the law of life in Christ, or the law of sin and death. We are freed from the law of sin and death when we accept Jesus as our Savior (Romans 8:1-2). When we submit to Him and resist the devil, he must flee. He can no longer enforce his case against us; nor has he any authority over us, as Jesus stripped him of his power. However, we must by faith stand in this position of authority.

"Submit yourselves therefore to God. Resist the devil, and he will flee from you. Draw nigh to God, and he will draw nigh to you. Cleanse your hands, ye sinners; and purify your hearts, ye double minded. Be afflicted, and mourn, and weep: let your laughter be turned to mourning, and your joy to heaviness. Humble yourselves in the sight of the Lord, and he shall lift you up" (James 4:7-10). We humble ourselves by confessing our sin with godly sorrow; by turning from it in our actions; by honoring the Lord in obeying His Word. If we sow His Word in prayer, we will in time rejoice, for our prayers will produce a harvest of blessings. "They that sow in tears shall reap in joy. He that goeth forth and weepeth, bearing precious seed, shall doubtless come again with rejoicing, bringing his sheaves with him (Psalm 126:5-6).

Dear Father God, thank You for the opportunity to sow good things in the kingdom. Deliver me from any fear that would keep me from turning loose of things I need to sow into Your work. Grant me grace to give freely of all You have given me, knowing that I will reap in kind. If I need finances, may I obediently give to Your works. If I need encouragement, may I take the time to sow it into those around me. May I be known as You were known, as One who went about doing good. Cleanse my thoughts, so that I will not even sow a bad thought in my mind toward others. I ask this in the name of Jesus. Amen.

God's Wisdom for Daily Living ***Betty Miller***
October 24 ***Day 297***

Proverbs 26:28 A lying tongue hateth those that are afflicted by it; and a flattering mouth worketh ruin.

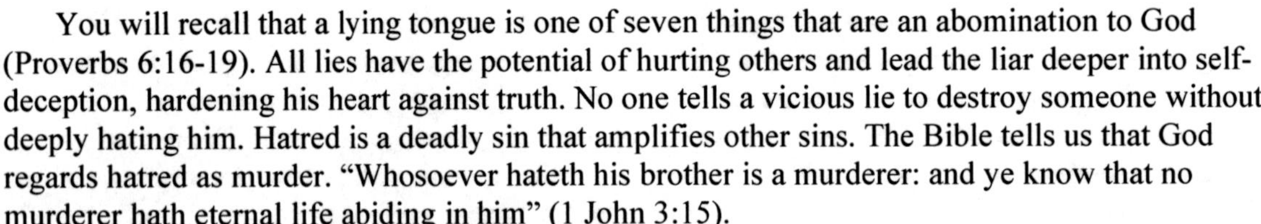

You will recall that a lying tongue is one of seven things that are an abomination to God (Proverbs 6:16-19). All lies have the potential of hurting others and lead the liar deeper into self-deception, hardening his heart against truth. No one tells a vicious lie to destroy someone without deeply hating him. Hatred is a deadly sin that amplifies other sins. The Bible tells us that God regards hatred as murder. "Whosoever hateth his brother is a murderer: and ye know that no murderer hath eternal life abiding in him" (1 John 3:15).

A vicious liar is an obvious enemy. A flatterer is an even deadlier one. He hides his hatred with pretended friendship while working ruin in a subtle fashion. "Flattery" in Hebrew means smooth flattering, with deceit implied. Hatred in the heart lures and manipulates one into saying or doing things that will destroy him.

Telling a lie without hatred may not be vicious, but it is still sin–and so is flattery. A sincere compliment, expressing deserved praise or admiration is different from flattery, since it is the truth. Flattery is always used with an ulterior motive. Those who flatter wish to please a person for selfish reasons. If we truly love as Christ commanded, we will not flatter one another. Flattery does not build others up, for it promotes vanity and deception; not godliness.

Jesus Himself and His Word are truth. "Jesus saith unto him, I am the way, the truth, and the life: no man cometh unto the Father, but by me" (John 14:6). Jesus prayed, "Sanctify them through thy truth: thy word is truth" (John 17:17). When we give our lives to Christ and practice His Word, we will walk in the truth and in love and speak the truth in love. This will guard our hearts against the dangerous sins of lying and hatred.

"We know that we have passed from death unto life, because we love the brethren. He that loveth not his brother abideth in death. Whosoever hateth his brother is a murderer: and ye know that no murderer hath eternal life abiding in him. Hereby perceive we the love of God, because he laid down his life for us: and we ought to lay down our lives for the brethren" (1 John 3:14-16).

Dear heavenly Father, I am grateful that You are a God of truth. Establish my lips to always speak the truth and deliver me from any deceitfulness. Fill me daily with the Holy Spirit so that I am empowered to walk in love toward all my sisters and brothers in the Lord. May I always be gracious toward others, but deliver me from any false flattery. I never want to be manipulative, but to always be honest and sincere in all my dealings with others. You are the God of truth, so may I always embrace truth and resist every lie. I ask this in the name of Jesus. Amen.

Proverbs 27:1 Boast not thyself of to morrow; for thou knowest not what a day may bring forth.

It is not good to boast about anything that we might do, since we do not know what a day may bring. Jesus spoke to his disciples about this very thing in a parable in the New Testament. "And he said unto them, Take heed, and beware of covetousness: for a man's life consisteth not in the abundance of the things which he possesseth. And he spake a parable unto them, saying, The ground of a certain rich man brought forth plentifully: And he thought within himself, saying, What shall I do, because I have no room where to bestow my fruits? And he said, This will I do: I will pull down my barns, and build greater; and there will I bestow all my fruits and my goods. And I will say to my soul, Soul, thou hast much goods laid up for many years; take thine ease, eat, drink, and be merry. But God said unto him, Thou fool, this night thy soul shall be required of thee: then whose shall those things be, which thou hast provided? So is he that layeth up treasure for himself, and is not rich toward God" (Luke 12:15-21).

Many of those who strive to protect their fortunes for themselves, without any thought of others or God, could lose it all in one moment. Jesus warns against covetousness, since God does not measure wealth by worldly possessions. What God desires of us is that we become rich toward God. It is not wrong to have riches in this world, but it is wrong if we do not to use them as the Bible commands us to. True riches are spiritual possessions that are not dependent upon anything in the world, but upon God alone. They are the riches of glory: God's character, favor, protection, vision, revelation, and wisdom (Romans 11:33).

"He that trusteth in his riches shall fall; but the righteous shall flourish as a branch" (Proverbs 11:28). We need to trust God with each day because only He knows what it holds, and He is there to help us deal with any evil that we may encounter. "But seek ye first the kingdom of God, and his righteousness; and all these things shall be added unto you. Take therefore no thought for the morrow: for the morrow shall take thought for the things of itself. Sufficient unto the day is the evil thereof" (Matthew 6:33-34).

May we never be like the man who boasts about his plans, but rather let us boast in the Lord, knowing that He knows the future and will never leave us nor forsake us, no matter what a day may bring. Let our boasting be in Him. "My soul shall make her boast in the LORD: the humble shall hear thereof, and be glad" (Psalm 34:2). As we trust Him, He will meet every need of our lives according to His the riches in glory by Christ Jesus! (Philippians 4:19 and Romans 9:23).

Dear Father in heaven, I am thankful that I am Your child, and that You are always there to meet my every need. My faith and trust are in You; I know that whatever a day brings, You will be there with me. Give me the grace to deal with the problems that I must face. May I remain humble when You reward and bless me in special ways. May I always be mindful to give You thanks and praise for everything that You have done for me and my family. I do not want to take Your blessings for granted. All praise belongs to You! I pray this prayer in Jesus' name. Amen.

Proverbs 27:2 Let another man praise thee, and not thine own mouth; a stranger, and not thine own lips.

Everyone reacts negatively to a braggart. It is bad manners to speak about nothing but one's own accomplishments. It is especially inappropriate for God's people, as it is evidence of pride and self-centeredness. These do not reflect God's nature, but Satan's. Pride and selfishness blind us to the needs of others and keep us from loving God and others. The Bible instructs us to lift one another up in encouragement and praise. We should esteem our fellow believers more highly than ourselves. "Be kindly affectioned one to another with brotherly love; in honour preferring one another" (Romans 12:10). We should rejoice to see fellow believers honored even when we are not acknowledged, and not allow ourselves to feel slighted.

"Clothe yourselves therefore, as God's own chosen ones (His own picked representatives), [who are] purified and holy and well-beloved [by God Himself, by putting on behavior marked by] tenderhearted pity and mercy, kind feeling, a lowly opinion of yourselves, gentle ways, [and] patience [which is tireless and long-suffering, and has the power to endure whatever comes, with good temper]. Be gentle and forbearing with one another and, if one has a difference (a grievance or complaint) against another, readily pardoning each other; even as the Lord has [freely] forgiven you, so must you also [forgive]. And above all these [put on] love and enfold yourselves with the bond of perfection [which binds everything together completely in ideal harmony]. And let the peace (soul harmony which comes) from Christ rule (act as umpire continually) in your hearts [deciding and settling with finality all questions that arise in your minds, in that peaceful state] to which as [members of Christ's] one body you were also called [to live]. And be thankful (appreciative), [giving praise to God always]" (Colossians 3:12-15 AMP).

The Lord instructs us to be humble and kind to each other. We ought not to be so wrapped up in ourselves that we are unaware of what others are doing. We should acknowledge others when they do a good job, no matter how menial that job may be. Every task done with excellence and unto the Lord, is worthy of praise. Ephesians 5:18 instructs us to give thanks to God in everything. If we live in an attitude of giving thanks and praise to God, we will have a heart to appreciate those around us. People enjoy the company of those having a joyful nature and a grateful heart. Their attitude spills over to all who know them. A smile costs nothing, and a word of praise to those with whom we live and work is a wonderful testimony to the Spirit of Christ dwelling within us.

Dear Father, please remind me to be thoughtful and sensitive to those around me. May I be mindful to share my thankfulness and offer praise to others. Help me to overcome selfishness and pride. May I never boast in the things I do, but rather in the things You do. I praise You for Your kindness that You daily show me. May I also be good and kind to others by noticing them and voicing my appreciation for their accomplishments. Lord, many in the world are rude, and I do not want to be like them. I desire to be like You, and demonstrate Your kindness to others. I ask this in the name of Jesus. Amen.

Proverbs 27:3-4: 3 A stone is heavy, and the sand weighty; but a fool's wrath is heavier than them both. 4 Wrath is cruel, and anger is outrageous; but who is able to stand before envy?

Verses 3-4 – These verses tell us that jealousy and envy are greater burdens than the heavy weights of the cruelty of wrath and anger. Wrath and anger are many times vented quickly, whereas envy and jealousy are like a pot that heats slowly to the boiling point. This causes the one who is jealous to seethe within, and the envy they feel will gnaw at them over a long period of time. Jealousy is as cruel as death and a flame of torment to those who embrace it. "Set me as a seal upon thine heart, as a seal upon thine arm: for love is strong as death; jealousy is cruel as the grave: the coals thereof are coals of fire, which hath a most vehement flame" (Song of Solomon 8:6).

We saw in Day 42 that when jealousy erupts in anger it is known as a "jealous rage," and in Day 110 that jealousy and envy can cause physical and mental illnesses. "A sound heart is the life of the flesh: but envy the rottenness of the bones" (Proverbs 14:30). Envy is included in this list of evils: "And even as they did not like to retain God in their knowledge, God gave them over to a reprobate mind, to do those things which are not convenient; Being filled with all unrighteousness, fornication, wickedness, covetousness, maliciousness; full of envy, murder, debate, deceit, malignity; whisperers, Backbiters, haters of God, despiteful, proud, boasters, inventors of evil things, disobedient to parents, Without understanding, covenantbreakers, without natural affection, implacable, unmerciful…" (Romans 1:28-31). These sins will bring judgment upon those who practice them, but through Jesus' sacrifice on our behalf, we can receive forgiveness. We can be saved from hell and receive eternal life, not by any works of righteousness we do, but by God's mercy to us through Jesus Christ. Through the Holy Spirit we can be freed from wrath, anger, envy, and jealousy and filled with God's love.

"For we ourselves also were sometimes foolish, disobedient, deceived serving divers lusts and pleasures, living in malice and envy, hateful, and hating one another. But after that the kindness and love of God our Saviour toward man appeared, Not by works of righteousness which we have done, but according to his mercy he saved us, by the washing of regeneration, and renewing of the Holy Ghost; Which he shed on us abundantly through Jesus Christ our Saviour; That being justified by his grace, we should be made heirs according to the hope of eternal life" (Titus 3:3-7).

Dear heavenly Father, thank You for Your gift of the Holy Spirit so that we have the power to overcome anger, wrath, envy and jealousy. Lord, give us the grace not to yield to these things when we are tempted. May we exhibit Your love in the situations that the devil designs to be used against us, in order to provoke us to anger. Help me not to react in an ungodly way in those kinds of circumstances. May I rejoice in the promotion of others and not yield to a spirit of envy or jealousy. I ask this is the name of Jesus. Amen.

God's Wisdom for Daily Living ***Betty Miller***
October 28 ***Day 301***

Proverbs 27:5-6 5 Open rebuke is better than secret love. 6 Faithful are the wounds of a friend; but the kisses of an enemy are deceitful.

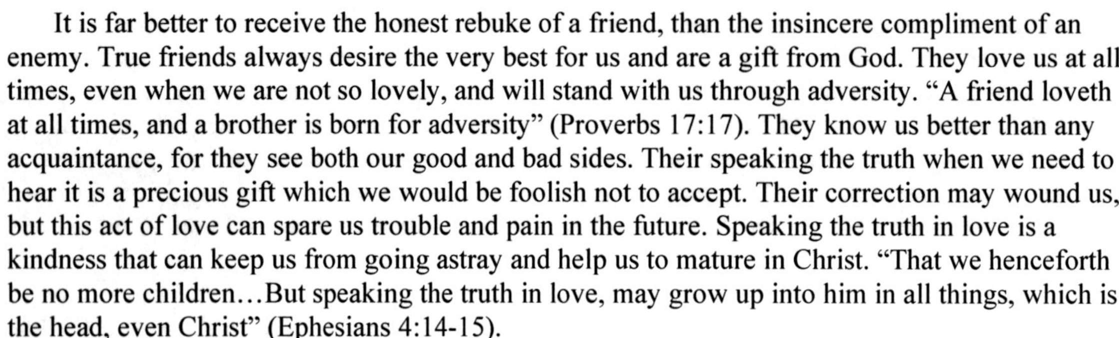

It is far better to receive the honest rebuke of a friend, than the insincere compliment of an enemy. True friends always desire the very best for us and are a gift from God. They love us at all times, even when we are not so lovely, and will stand with us through adversity. "A friend loveth at all times, and a brother is born for adversity" (Proverbs 17:17). They know us better than any acquaintance, for they see both our good and bad sides. Their speaking the truth when we need to hear it is a precious gift which we would be foolish not to accept. Their correction may wound us, but this act of love can spare us trouble and pain in the future. Speaking the truth in love is a kindness that can keep us from going astray and help us to mature in Christ. "That we henceforth be no more children…But speaking the truth in love, may grow up into him in all things, which is the head, even Christ" (Ephesians 4:14-15).

Maintaining friendships requires time. To have friends we must be friendly and nurture our friends with kindness. We see into the souls of our friends by spending time with them. Because the Lord Jesus is in the midst of us, there is a deeper dimension to our Christian friendships than with others. A friend in Christ is among God's greatest blessings. Proverbs 18:24 reveals that there is a Friend that stays even closer to us than a brother, and that friend is Jesus. "A man that hath friends must shew himself friendly: and there is a friend that sticketh closer than a brother." Our friends and family will at times fail or disappoint us, even as we disappoint them, because we all sin and have limitations. The Son of God, however, is limitless in power and love. He will never fail us, no matter how badly we may fail Him. Friendship with Jesus has no constraints. He is always there for us.

Every Christian can cultivate a relationship with Jesus Christ. Friendship, however–even with God–must work both ways. Because of his obedience, Abraham was known as a friend of God. How wonderful it would be to be known as a friend of God as Abraham was! There is only one way to become His friend, and that is by spending quality time with Him. The most important thing that cements our friendship with God is obeying Him. Our obedience demonstrates our faith, love, and commitment to Him. "If ye love me, keep my commandments" (John 14:15).

Dear Father, thank You for being such a good friend to me. I desire to also be a good friend to those You have put in my life. May I be the kind of friend who will not shy away from speaking the truth in love when the occasion calls for it. May I also be mindful to encourage my friends, to speak well of them, and to always be there for them when they need me. Help me to not neglect my friendships. Help me to take the time to nurture them, and may You always be in the middle of them. I pray this in the name of Jesus. Amen.

God's Wisdom for Daily Living ***Betty Miller***
October 29 ***Day 302***

Proverbs 27:7 The full soul loatheth an honeycomb; but to the hungry soul every bitter thing is sweet.

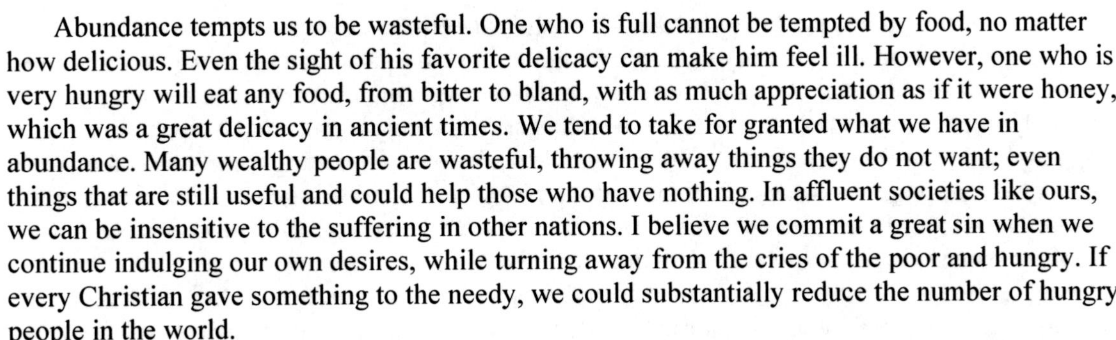

Abundance tempts us to be wasteful. One who is full cannot be tempted by food, no matter how delicious. Even the sight of his favorite delicacy can make him feel ill. However, one who is very hungry will eat any food, from bitter to bland, with as much appreciation as if it were honey, which was a great delicacy in ancient times. We tend to take for granted what we have in abundance. Many wealthy people are wasteful, throwing away things they do not want; even things that are still useful and could help those who have nothing. In affluent societies like ours, we can be insensitive to the suffering in other nations. I believe we commit a great sin when we continue indulging our own desires, while turning away from the cries of the poor and hungry. If every Christian gave something to the needy, we could substantially reduce the number of hungry people in the world.

Jesus went about doing good and ministering to the poor; and we, His followers, should do likewise. He demonstrated both compassion for the poor and also frugality when He provided food for the multitude of over five thousand and later of over four thousand (Matthew 14:14-21; 15:32-38). Both times, Jesus instructed His disciples to gather up the remaining fragments and not waste them.

These two miracles; the feeding of multitudes from what was enough for only a few people at most, demonstrates a Biblical principle: God uses small things to bring about big miracles. People who feel small and inadequate may wonder how God could use them. God, however, delights in confounding the wise of this world by greatly using people and things that seem insignificant. "But God hath chosen the foolish things of the world to confound the wise; and God hath chosen the weak things of the world to confound the things which are mighty; And base things of the world, and things which are despised, hath God chosen, yea, and things which are not, to bring to nought things that are: That no flesh should glory in his presence" (1 Corinthians 1:27-29).

The world may despise many of God's servants, but God uses weak people to show forth His great power. A plaque hanging on my office wall reminds me of this principle. It reads, "God never asks about our ability or our inability, but about our availability." We need to remember to thank God for all that He has given us and share with others less fortunate than ourselves. No matter how little our contribution may be, or how insignificant we may feel, let us remember that our little in God's hands becomes much.

Dear Father, I appreciate the fact that You are a Miracle Worker! It is a great comfort to me to know that if and when I need a miracle, I can call on You. You have blessed me with so much compared to many in the world. May I be sensitive to the needs of the poor. I do not want to be guilty of turning a deaf ear to the cries of those who are hungry. Direct my giving, and create a heart of generosity within me, so that I can be used as an instrument of blessing to the many needy in this world. I ask this in the name of Jesus. Amen.

Proverbs 27:8 As a bird that wandereth from her nest, so is a man that wandereth from his place.

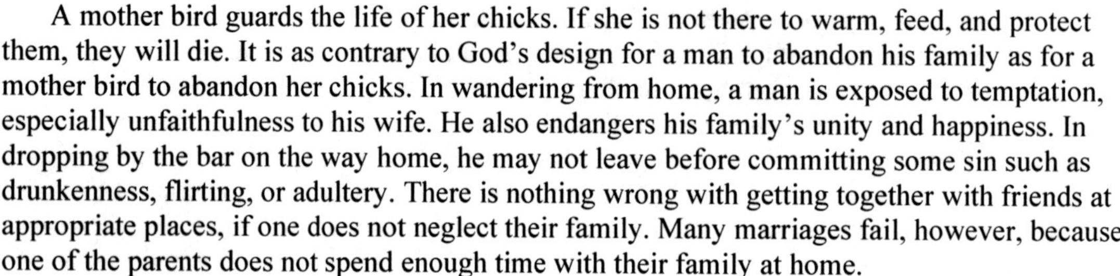

A mother bird guards the life of her chicks. If she is not there to warm, feed, and protect them, they will die. It is as contrary to God's design for a man to abandon his family as for a mother bird to abandon her chicks. In wandering from home, a man is exposed to temptation, especially unfaithfulness to his wife. He also endangers his family's unity and happiness. In dropping by the bar on the way home, he may not leave before committing some sin such as drunkenness, flirting, or adultery. There is nothing wrong with getting together with friends at appropriate places, if one does not neglect their family. Many marriages fail, however, because one of the parents does not spend enough time with their family at home.

God created the family unit and instructs both husbands and wives how to love each other, so the home can be a place of comfort for the whole family: "Wives, submit yourselves unto your own husbands, as unto the Lord. For the husband is the head of the wife, even as Christ is the head of the church: and he is the saviour of the body. Therefore as the church is subject unto Christ, so let the wives be to their own husbands in every thing. Husbands, love your wives, even as Christ also loved the church, and gave himself for it" (Ephesians 5:22-25. See also Colossians 3:18).

If couples would follow these instructions, divorce would not be as rampant in our world. It breaks God's heart when His children cannot live together in harmony. Many Christians do all they can to save their marriages, but to no avail. They divorce at their mates' insistence, according to God's Word: "But if the unbelieving depart, let him depart. A brother or a sister is not under bondage in such cases: but God hath called us to peace" (I Corinthians 7:15). Society, however, uses divorce simply as a way out of a difficult situation. Even many Christians, rather than suffering in behalf of a mate who is out of God's will, take this easy way out. In those instances, divorce is sin. Any minister who seeks the easy way of divorce, cannot expect God to bless his ministry. God will not continue to anoint ministers who have no grief in their hearts for their mates. They actually are destroying their own flesh.

The spirit of division is rampant in the earth today, seeking to destroy not only marriages, but all valid relationships. We must resist this attack of the enemy. A woman may be the heart of the home, but a man is the head that guides and protects it. A man's home should be his castle where everyone in the home is loved and cherished, and he should resist any desire to wander as a bird. "Finally, be ye all of one mind, having compassion one of another, love as brethren, be pitiful, be courteous" (1 Peter 3:8). A man should make his home a refuge where everyone in his family is made secure and given room to grow.

Dear heavenly Father, I pray for all Christians to keep focused on You as the center of their homes. May Your love reign in every home. Lord, deliver Your people from the spirit of division, so that harmony and peace may be in the midst of us. Give us grace to prefer one another above ourselves and not compete with each other. May You be Lord in every home, as wives submit to their husbands, and husbands love and cherish their wives. Heal our land from the sin of divorce so that our children can be raised by both of their parents in the same home. I ask this in the name of the Lord Jesus. Amen.

Proverbs 27:9-10 9 Oil and perfume rejoice the heart; so does the sweetness of a friend's counsel that comes from the heart. 10 Your own friend and your father's friend, forsake them not; neither go to your brother's house in the day of your calamity. Better is a neighbor who is near (in spirit) than a brother who is far off (in heart) (AMP).

These verses tell us the value of true friendship, as a good friend will be there for us in our day of calamity, while sometimes our own family will not support us.

Verse 9 – In the hot weather of ancient Israel, crowded streets would stink of animals, sweating humans, and refuse. The rich anointed themselves with perfumed oil to protect and scent their skin. After the ordeal of traveling such streets, entering a home and being anointed with fragrant oil was pleasurable and refreshing. In the same way, after brushing shoulders with a godless, uncaring world, the sound counsel given by a trusted friend rejoices the heart. There is just nothing like being able to communicate openly and comfortably with a good friend.

Verse 10 – When trouble comes, it is better to go to a neighbor who is a true friend in the Spirit, than to your own brother who is not close to you in his heart. As Christians, we are members of God's family. It is a blessing to have this wonderful relationship with people all over the world! Regardless of race, age, language, or social status, Christ gives us His love for one another. Non-Christians cannot understand our spiritual family ties. It sounds strange to them to hear us speak of one another as "brother" or "sister."

Jesus defined His true family while ministering to a great crowd in someone's house (Matthew 12:46-50). When informed that His mother and brothers desired to speak with Him, He answered that all that came to Him and did His will were His family. As Christians, we have the same access to Jesus that His family had during His earthly ministry. The special privileges given to members of the world's royal families are only a small picture of the privileges granted to us as God's family. We are joint-heirs with Christ and have access to the riches of His glory. We are promised a portion of His love, wisdom and understanding, so that we can become like Him. Through the power of the Spirit He is able to do exceedingly abundantly above all we ask or think! Praise God!

"That he would grant you, according to the riches of his glory, to be strengthened with might by his Spirit in the inner man. That Christ may dwell in your hearts by faith; that ye, being rooted and grounded in love, May be able to comprehend with all saints what is the breadth, and length, and depth, and height; And to know the love of Christ, which passeth knowledge, that ye might be filled with all the fulness of God. Now unto him that is able to do exceeding abundantly above all that we ask or think, according to the power that worketh in us, Unto him be glory in the church by Christ Jesus" (Ephesians 3:16-21).

Dear Father, I praise and thank You for the friends You have given me. What a wonderful blessing! Lord, I also want to thank You for every brother and sister in the greater family of God throughout the whole world. It is such a blessing to get to meet and fellowship with so many of them and to know them by the spirit. I look forward to the day that I will get to meet many others, as I know when we get to heaven, I will get to see them face to face there. It is wonderful to be a member of the family of God and to know that we are all going to be blessed and enjoy one another's company throughout eternity. Thank You, Lord! In Jesus' name I pray. Amen.

God's Wisdom for Daily Living — *Betty Miller*
November 1 — ***Day 305***

Proverbs 27:11 My son, be wise, and make my heart glad, that I may answer him that reproacheth me.

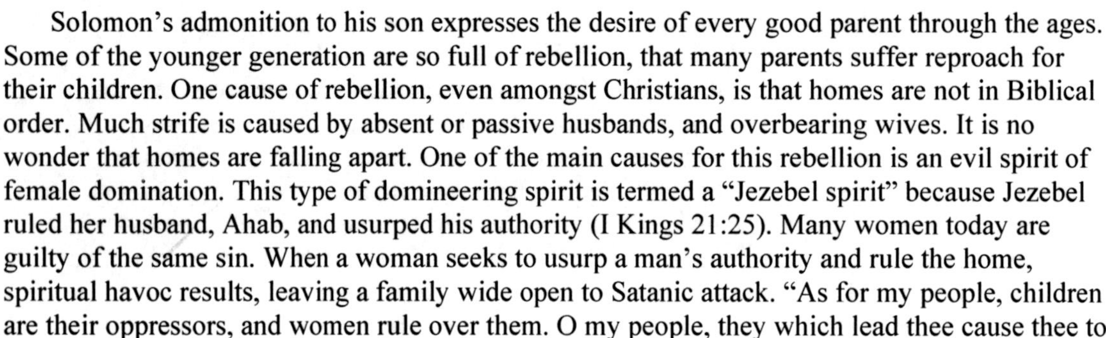

Solomon's admonition to his son expresses the desire of every good parent through the ages. Some of the younger generation are so full of rebellion, that many parents suffer reproach for their children. One cause of rebellion, even amongst Christians, is that homes are not in Biblical order. Much strife is caused by absent or passive husbands, and overbearing wives. It is no wonder that homes are falling apart. One of the main causes for this rebellion is an evil spirit of female domination. This type of domineering spirit is termed a "Jezebel spirit" because Jezebel ruled her husband, Ahab, and usurped his authority (I Kings 21:25). Many women today are guilty of the same sin. When a woman seeks to usurp a man's authority and rule the home, spiritual havoc results, leaving a family wide open to Satanic attack. "As for my people, children are their oppressors, and women rule over them. O my people, they which lead thee cause thee to err, and destroy the way of thy paths" (Isaiah 3:12).

Some of the dilemmas that women reap when not in right relationship with men are, in addition to rebellious children, emotional and sexual problems, as well as divorce. Men that fail to take their godly position in the home are equally at fault for these problems. "But I would have you know, that the head of every man is Christ; and the head of the woman is the man; and the head of Christ is God" (1 Corinthians 11:3).

The husband is to be head of the house, the wife is second-in-command, and the children obedient to both (1 Corinthians 11:3; Ephesians 6:1). The Lord would have our homes to be examples of His love; parental authority should be exercised in love. When one has a "Jezebel spirit," it subtly manipulates the lives of everyone around them. (Men can also operate in this tyrannical spirit towards their family or in undermining those in authority over them.) Let us ask God to deliver us from these evil tendencies if we should find ourselves guilty of being domineering and manipulative. Men should ask God to create within them a proper understanding of the use of authority, and women should ask Him to create in them a submissive spirit, which is pleasing to the Lord. Of course, there are limits to submission, as it should always be "as unto the Lord." No one is to submit to evil. We must first submit to God, and then He will resolve our problems involving submission to others. Submission is a heart attitude and the Bible tells us to submit to one another in the fear of God (Ephesians 5:21).

Dear heavenly Father, thank You for creating me as a woman. May I function in the role that You created me for and give me a submissive spirit, not only toward my mate, but also toward each member in the body of Christ. Let me serve, and not expect to be served. Create within me a lamb-like spirit, even as Christ our Lord had. Give me wisdom in the role of a parent, so that my children might rise up and call me blessed. May I love my mate and my children with Your love. I ask this in the name of the Lord Jesus. Amen.

Proverbs 27:12 A prudent man foreseeth the evil, and hideth himself; but the simple pass on, and are punished.

A watchful man sees the signs of impending trouble, and prepares for it. God gave us warnings in the Bible for the same reason. Many scriptures warn against sin and the devil's schemes. These warnings tell what corresponding action is needed to avert the problem we might encounter. The strongest warning is against refusing God's offer of salvation, telling us a hell awaits those who reject Christ. The law and commandments in the Bible are given for our good, so that we will not suffer in the traps of the devil.

We may mistakenly believe that God is behind all suffering, if we do not understand its different forms. (The many Greek words translated as *suffering* carry either the basic meanings of "to permit" or "to endure"[35]). Most of our suffering is the result of having broken spiritual and physical laws. This includes sickness, depression, fear, poverty, torment, loneliness, disorder, and confusion; all results of sin. Jesus suffered on the cross so we could be free of these things; and if we walk with Him, He leads us out of them. Suffering for Christ, however, is always by choice. It involves laying down our lives for others, because we choose to do so, even as Jesus did (John 10:17-18).

The Apostle Paul chose to suffer many things in obeying God's call to preach the Gospel. Today in some countries, our brethren are imprisoned, tortured, or killed for their faith. There are many forms of suffering for the Lord's sake that are by no means as great as these but are still valid. Some of us suffer when we leave our comfortable homes and go to mission fields across the world. We suffer for Christ by staying in a hard place, rather than finding an easy way out. We suffer for Him when we give up worldly gain for the sake of the kingdom. We suffer by "turning the other cheek." We suffer by giving up what we could have in this present life, for the kingdom of God. Enduring illness, however, is not a form of suffering for Christ, since Jesus took upon Himself our illnesses. The Greek word, *"sozo,"* is used throughout the New Testament to mean both "to save" and "to heal."[36] God does not want us to keep our sickness any more than He wants us to keep our sin. If He paid for it on the cross, we do not have to bear it today (Isaiah 53:5).

When we lack the discernment to know whether our suffering is from Satan or something to be endured for Christ, we can be tricked into accepting things God would not have us bear. Obviously, if it does not agree with God's Word, then God does not want us to embrace it. When in doubt, a good way to deal with problems of this nature is to bring them before the Lord with a submissive attitude, and ask Him to reveal what He would have us do (James 4:7-8). If God calls us to endure suffering, He will give us the grace and strength to pass through it victoriously. When Satan is behind it, it will drain us and destroy our peace. We can hide ourselves in Christ and He will keep us from the destruction planned for us by the devil. "Keep me as the apple of the eye, hide me under the shadow of thy wings, from the wicked that oppress me, from my deadly enemies, who compass me about" (Psalm 17:8-9).

[35] Strong's Exhaustive Concordance of the Bible, Greek Dictionary of the New Testament
[36] Strong's Exhaustive Concordance of the Bible, Greek Dictionary of the New Testament

Dear heavenly Father, I come to You in Jesus' name. I willingly submit to all that You ask of me, and will endure all that You place before me, but I will not receive those things that the devil would put upon me. I yield to You, Lord. If You want me to continue suffering in a difficult situation, I am willing, for I know You will give me abundant grace; but I resist the devil and the abuses he would put upon me. I thank You that Jesus died on the cross and took the punishment for my sin and sicknesses, so I do not have to take them. I pray that others will also know this truth in Jesus' name. Amen.

Quotes About Pride and Humility

Those who allow pride to dominate their heart open the door to many other sins, causing major self-deception. --Day 39

True humility reveals strength of character. The humble person is secure in God and does not need to prove himself to others. --Day 135

Contention comes when we refuse to humbly deal with the conflicting issues in our flesh. --Day 164

We are to reverently fear God. Since all authority stems from Him, He expects us to honor the positions of authority that earthly leaders fill. --Day 256

People who feel small and inadequate may wonder how God could use them. God, however, delights in confounding the wise of this world by greatly using people and things that seem insignificant. --Day 302

Proverbs 27:13-14 13 Take his garment that is surety for a stranger, and take a pledge of him for a strange woman. 14 He that blesseth his friend with a loud voice, rising early in the morning, it shall be counted as a curse to him.

Verse 13 – The Hebrew word translated *stranger* means not only "foreigner," but also "strange woman;" one who is not one's wife. In this sense, it means "adulteress" or "harlot."[37] This verse is identical with Proverbs 20:16. As we saw in Day 192, any man who would guarantee a loan for an unknown foreigner or for a known prostitute, is not to be trusted. Precautions should be taken and the money not loaned unless something of great value is given as surety that the loan will be paid.

Verse 14 – This verse tells us that one who uses flattery to the extreme will be suspected of wrong motives and his flattery will be counted as cursing instead of blessing. It would be like someone who was singing in a loud voice outside your window early in the morning while you were still sleeping. You might appreciate their singing another time. However, if they did this while they were working for you, and they were aware that you were sleeping, you would tend to question their motives, wondering why they were irritating you so early in the morning. Their singing would not be a blessing. We should beware of those who use flattery to gain favor or get something from us.

A bold flatterer might draw public attention to someone in order to manipulate him. People are easily flustered when anyone speaks to them very loudly, especially about themselves. Loud praise could pressure us to give the flatterer what he wants, so as not to look bad in public. We would be doubly humiliated if the flatterer had a bad reputation. His praises would imply that we are his friend, and that we approve, or perhaps even join in his wrongdoing. In order to keep him quiet, we could be pressured into publicly saying or doing something that we do not want to do. Praises loudly given in order to manipulate are certainly a curse. We should always be cautious of those who are prone to flatter.

Dear Father, I appreciate the sound advice and wisdom found in the Book of Proverbs. Help me to apply this advice to situations in my daily life when I am faced with certain issues. Lord, give me Your discernment to know how I should relate to people who irritate or bother me. May I respond to them in love and in wisdom. May I know the difference when I am approached by someone with an honest heart or someone who is manipulating me for the wrong purposes. Fill my mouth with wisdom in these cases. I ask this in the name of the Lord Jesus. Amen.

[37] Strong's Exhaustive Concordance of the Bible, Hebrew and Chaldee Dictionary

Proverbs 27:15-16 15 A continual dripping on a day of violent showers and a contentious woman are alike; 16 Whoever attempts to restrain (a contentious woman) might as well try to stop the wind–his right hand encounters oil (as she slips through his fingers) (AMP).

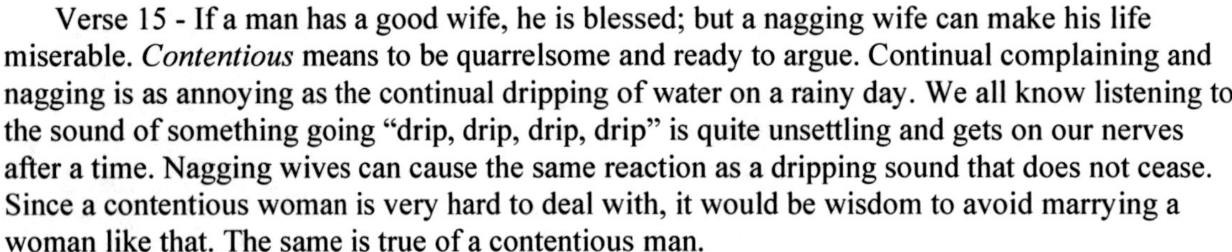

Verse 15 - If a man has a good wife, he is blessed; but a nagging wife can make his life miserable. *Contentious* means to be quarrelsome and ready to argue. Continual complaining and nagging is as annoying as the continual dripping of water on a rainy day. We all know listening to the sound of something going "drip, drip, drip, drip" is quite unsettling and gets on our nerves after a time. Nagging wives can cause the same reaction as a dripping sound that does not cease. Since a contentious woman is very hard to deal with, it would be wisdom to avoid marrying a woman like that. The same is true of a contentious man.

Verse 16 – Trying to restrain a contentious woman is like trying to grasp the wind or hold on to something when your hands are covered with oil. Arguments, complaining and nagging will crop up no matter what you do. A contentious woman is rebellious. Her character and actions are in opposition to the commandment given to wives in Ephesians 5:22-24 to submit to their husbands. The value of a virtuous woman is spoken of in Proverbs 31:10-12. "Who can find a virtuous woman? for her price is far above rubies. The heart of her husband doth safely trust in her, so that he shall have no need of spoil. She will do him good and not evil all the days of her life."

Because contentious people yield to unrighteousness, they will reap indignation and wrath on the Day of Judgment and the eternal tribulation and anguish of hell if they do not repent. Christ died for our sins and can deliver us from a contentious nature. Those who yield to God will do good works, and receive glory, honor, and peace.

"But after thy hardness and impenitent heart treasurest up unto thyself wrath against the day of wrath and revelation of the righteous judgment of God; Who will render to every man according to his deeds: To them who by patient continuance in well doing seek for glory and honour and immortality, eternal life: But unto them that are contentious, and do not obey the truth, but obey unrighteousness, indignation and wrath, Tribulation and anguish, upon every soul of man that doeth evil, of the Jew first, and also of the Gentile; But glory, honour, and peace, to every man that worketh good, to the Jew first, and also to the Gentile: For there is no respect of persons with God" (Romans 2:5-10).

Dear Father, I am thankful that You can set us free of any character traits that are not like You. Lord, fill me with the Holy Spirit so that I do not allow any angry words to come out of my mouth. Help me not to yield to a contentious attitude or have an argumentative spirit. May I be a kind and loving person who is a peacemaker. Help me to speak gracious things and to be a good witness in all that I say and do. May I always love and do good to my husband all the days of my life. I ask this in the name of Jesus. Amen.

Proverbs 27:17-19 17 Iron sharpeneth iron; so a man sharpeneth the countenance of his friend. 18 Whoso keepeth the fig tree shall eat the fruit thereof: so he that waiteth on his master shall be honoured. 19 As in water face answereth to face, so the heart of man to man.

Verse 17 – Good friends bring out the best in one another. This does not mean that they do not see and deal with one another's faults, since this is part of the sharpening of each other's personalities. They will find ways to resolve differences in love. As they do this, each one's character is refined, just as when an iron blade is sharpened by the honing from another piece of iron. Even though sparks may fly, the result is a sharp edge. Anger is an emotion that surfaces in all relationships. It is not a sin to become angry, but it is a sin to vent it *on* others. God Himself experiences anger at injustice, which should anger us too, but it is how we handle our anger that makes us different. Righteous anger motivates us to use our time and influence to overcome evil. Unrighteous anger leads to retaliation, making us no different than the world. We must overcome evil with good.

Verse 18 – The principle of sowing and reaping is taught throughout Scripture. Whoever cares for a fig tree by watering, fertilizing, and pruning it will also eventually receive its fruit. Similarly, the servant that faithfully serves his master will eventually receive honor from him. Since Jesus is our Master, this principle applies to us. If we faithfully serve Him, He will honor us in due season. A day will come when we will hear Him speaking words of praise to us, such as those spoken to the righteous in Matthew 25:21.

Verse 19 – As water reflects a man's image, the heart of man reflects or relates to the heart of another man. If someone speaks from his spirit, those who are spiritually alive and walking in the spirit will hear and receive his words. If someone speaks from his emotions or soul, it moves people's emotions or soul; and what is spoken from the intellect is perceived by the intellect. Spirit communicates with spirit, soul with soul, and mind with mind. These levels of communication are the reason we have feelings of endearment when talking with certain people and sense others to be distant. We reflect the level from which people are coming, sometimes only partially understanding them. Have you ever tried to share wonderful news with a slight acquaintance? You share on an emotional level, but that person can only understand you on an intellectual level. He cannot share your joy.

Christians should not form strong attachments with non-Christians since we can only relate to them through the soul, which can lead us into sin (2 Corinthians 6:14). Only our prayers through the power of the Holy Spirit can change the hearts of those in darkness.

Dear heavenly Father, thank You for the wealth of wisdom from the Book of Proverbs. Help me to apply it to my life in all my daily affairs. May I always be sincere and honest in my relationships with others. Give me a gentle and understanding heart toward those who do not know You, so that my life and prayers will affect them, and bring them to the knowledge of Your dear Son. Fill me with the Holy Spirit today, so that all whom I come in contact with will sense Your presence. I ask this in the name of Jesus. Amen.

Proverbs 27:20 Hell and destruction are never full; so the eyes of man are never satisfied.

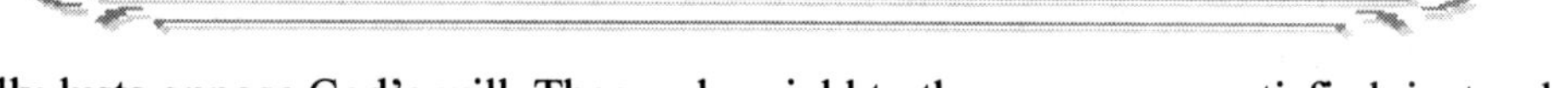

Worldly lusts oppose God's will. Those who yield to them are never satisfied, just as hell is always hungry for more inhabitants. Lust can never be satisfied. "For all that is in the world, the lust of the flesh, and the lust of the eyes, and the pride of life, is not of the Father, but is of the world. And the world passeth away, and the lust thereof: but he that doeth the will of God abideth for ever" (1 John 2:16-17).

Satan tempts us in three areas of lust; by using the same lie he told Adam and Eve. We can benefit from studying how this hostile fallen angel struck at God through the man and woman He had created and loved: "...And the serpent said unto the woman, Ye shall not surely die: For God doth know that in the day ye eat thereof, then your eyes shall be opened, and ye shall be as gods, knowing good and evil. And when the woman saw that the tree was good for food, and that it was pleasant to the eyes, and a tree to be desired to make one wise, she took of the fruit thereof, and did eat, and gave also unto her husband with her; and he did eat" (Genesis 3:4-6).

Notice Satan's method of tempting Adam and Eve. First he challenged God's Word and cast doubt upon His judgment and goodness. Next, he placed three temptations before her through the lust of the flesh (Eve saw that "the tree was good for food"), the lust of the eyes (it was "pleasant to the eyes"), and the pride of life (it was "a tree to be desired to make one wise"). Our desires for the things of the world tempt us today as stated in James 1:14: "But every man is tempted, when he is drawn away of his own lust, and enticed." The "world" consists of the systems of fallen human society without God: education, science, arts, religious systems, politics, etc. This "world" is controlled by Satan. Many of us do not realize that when we touch the things that make up fallen society, we touch the power of Satan. Therefore, we become independent in the way that we use them, if we do not put them under the power and direction of God. God does not want to deny us these things, but if we do not allow Him to rule over us as we partake of them, they become like forbidden fruit to us.

I do not believe that God intended to forever deny man access to the Tree of the Knowledge of Good and Evil, but He had a plan that would have opened his eyes to good and evil in time; when human beings had matured enough to be able to live with that knowledge. By eating prematurely from that tree, it brought death instead of wisdom, just as God warned. Physical death did not come immediately, but spiritual death did, as man could no longer face God. Fear and shame is the fruit of sin. If we fellowship with God on a daily basis, we find that there is simply no guilt that troubles us. However, when we sin and do not repent, we run from the presence of God just as Adam and Eve did.

Dear heavenly Father, I thank You for all the wonderful things You have created in this world for us to enjoy. I know that it is for our good and because You love us that You put restrictions upon us. Help me not to yield to the temptation to go beyond the boundaries that You have set for us in Your Word. Help me to resist the lust of the eyes, lust of the flesh, and the pride of this life. May I set my eyes on eternal things and hold loosely the things of this world, using them for Your glory. I ask this in the name of Jesus. Amen.

Proverbs 27:21 As the refining pot for silver and the furnace for gold [bring forth all the impurities of the metal], so let a man be in his trial of praise [ridding himself of all that is base or insincere; for a man is judged by what he praises and of what he boasts] (AMP).

Just as the refining process brings out impurities in silver and gold, receiving praise will bring out impurities in us, as well. Some of the hardest areas for any of us to handle are fame, success, and the praise of people. Our fallen nature always wants recognition for what we achieve. Certainly, people should be commended for worthy accomplishments, but we must keep in mind that we can do nothing apart from God's grace in our lives. God warns us not to boast about what we have done or plan to do. "Boast not thyself of tomorrow; for thou knowest not what a day may bring forth" (Proverbs 27:1). Everything that we are able to accomplish is due to the fact that the great God gave us the breath of life and He has enabled us to do it.

"So then neither is he that planteth any thing, neither he that watereth; but God that giveth the increase. Now he that planteth and he that watereth are one: and every man shall receive his own reward according to his own labour. For we are labourers together with God: ye are God's husbandry, ye are God's building. According to the grace of God which is given unto me, as a wise masterbuilder, I have laid the foundation, and another buildeth thereon…" (1 Corinthians 3:7-10).

Years ago, the Lord spoke to my heart: "Betty, I desire to free you from man's opinions of you. I want you to grow in Me so that the praises of men will not cause you to feel prideful, nor will their criticisms cause you to be fearful or discouraged. If you will offer the praises to Me, and discuss the criticisms with Me, you will not become lifted up in pride or knocked down by fear. Only by abiding in Me can you know this freedom."

We must remain humble before God, remembering that whatever we do without Him is worthless. One day we will stand before the Judgment Seat of Christ and our works will be tried by fire. Carnal works will not withstand the test. God desires each of us to surrender our will to Him and allow Him to reveal His plan for us. If our works are commissioned by God, He will use life's fiery trials to purify us like gold and bring much glory to Himself. If we abide in Him (John 15:4-7), He will fulfill the amazing promise; to grant whatever we ask! When we truly abide in Him, we will not ask anything amiss! God desires to work in us, with us, and through us so that we will bear much fruit for Him.

Dear heavenly Father, I am humbled that You would use me as an instrument of Your love in this earth. I stand in awe at the amazing plans You have for every one of us who will come to You, and allow You to live Your life through us. I am so happy to be a part of Your family. Lord, I ask that You deliver me from all pride and fear; especially the fear of man. May I always be more concerned what You think about me, than what men may think of me. I ask this in the name of the Lord Jesus Christ. Amen.

Proverbs 27:22 Even though like grain you should pound a fool in a mortar with a pestle, yet will not his foolishness depart from him (AMP).

Bad character traits can become so deeply engrained that it is impossible to correct them even by drastic measures, outside of divine intervention. As we have previously seen, the Biblical definition of a fool is one who is rebellious. Many evil people in jail are incorrigible; they have life-long habits of wickedness embedded throughout their entire personalities. These people have developed criminal natures and their minds are set on evil. Though penal institutions try to rehabilitate them with various programs, most of them return to crime because it is a part of them. Jeremiah 13:23 speaks about the impossibility of those who habitually do evil to turn from it: "Can the Ethiopian change his skin, or the leopard his spots? then may ye also do good, that are accustomed to do evil."

What is impossible for man, however, is not impossible for God; He can change anyone, no matter how wicked! Some of the most hardened criminals have been changed by the Holy Spirit's power. The Bible relates stories of wicked men, even murderers, adulterers and liars, who were changed by God's grace when they surrendered their lives to Him. Saul of Tarsus persecuted and threatened murder against Christians, thinking that he was doing God's will. On his way to arrest more Christians, Jesus Christ supernaturally encountered him and changed his life. God removed the scales from his spiritual eyes, and then he could see the evil he had done (Acts 9:1-22). After his miraculous conversion, he spent the rest of his life in the service of Jesus Christ and wrote a good deal of the New Testament. All of us were sinners until we came to Christ and allowed Him to deliver and cleanse us (Titus 3:3-7).

Throughout history, people have killed Christians, just as Jesus prophesied. More Christians have died for their faith in the 20th century than in all the previous centuries combined. Some religious zealots think that killing Christians is the will of God, even as Saul did before he became Paul. John 16:2-3 says, "They shall put you out of the synagogues: yea, the time cometh, that whosoever killeth you will think that he doeth God service. And these things will they do unto you, because they have not known the Father, nor me," These people need to understand that their religion cannot give them eternal life since it is found only in a personal relationship with Jesus Christ. We must pray that they see the true light of God and experience Christ's saving power. "Then shall they deliver you up to be afflicted, and shall kill you: and ye shall be hated of all nations for my name's sake...But he that shall endure unto the end, the same shall be saved. And this gospel of the kingdom shall be preached in all the world for a witness unto all nations; and then shall the end come"
(Matthew 24:9, 13-14).

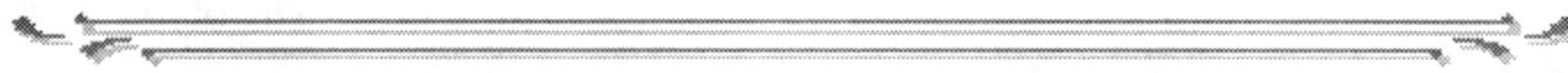

Dear heavenly Father, thank You for Your promise of salvation and eternal life to all who call on You. I am grateful that You, Lord Jesus, came to save me, and that You now live in my heart because I have surrendered to You. I pray for all of those who are trusting in false religions to save them. May they experience true salvation through the love of Christ. Please open their hearts and give them Your light, so that they may know that Jesus is the Son of God. You said that You are the Way, the Truth and the Life. I pray that the lost find their way to You. I ask this in the name of Jesus, my Lord. Amen.

Proverbs 27:23-24 23 Be thou diligent to know the state of thy flocks, and look well to thy herds. 24 For riches are not for ever: and doth the crown endure to every generation?

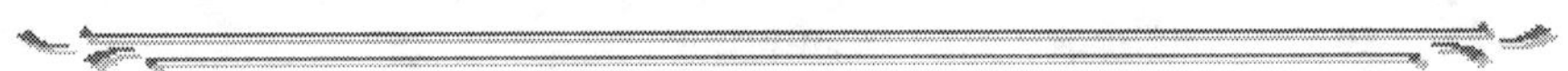

Verse 23 – Although these verses were addressed to farmers, we can relate to them today in regard to our businesses. We are to take responsibility and know the state of our affairs. Large flocks of sheep and goats made a man wealthy in ancient Israel. This proverb advised a wealthy man to personally know the condition of his flocks and ascertain that his overseers fulfilled their responsibilities properly. They were to protect and keep count of them, taking special care of the sick, injured, and pregnant ones; paying special attention to the babies.

Having riches or employment now does not guarantee we will always have them. We need to give diligent care and management to our livelihood. Romans 12:11 says, "Not slothful in business; fervent in spirit; serving the Lord." Negligence creates problems that can lead to severe financial difficulties. Many factors can lead to bankruptcy, such as over-extending oneself (due to greed or lack of sound business principles) or extenuating circumstances beyond one's control. Sometimes it is not people's fault that they are forced into bankruptcy since they are victims of illness, tragedy, or uncontrollable disasters. Despite this, many of the bankruptcies which are filed today could have been avoided if diligence had been practiced. "He becometh poor that dealeth with a slack hand: but the hand of the diligent maketh rich" (Proverbs 10:4).

Verse 24 – Just as a king will not rule throughout every generation, riches do not last forever. There is a good deal of truth to the statement, "money talks: it says 'good-bye." Money says "good-bye" in numerous ways, such as in poor planning for the future. As people age, their work capacity diminishes, which usually decreases their income. Without wise and diligent care of their finances, people may spend all their money when they are young and leave themselves with nothing to live on when they are old. If we heed the Lord and apply good business principles in regard to our finances, we can rest assured that we will have enough when we are in our senior years. Living for God is one of the best insurance policies anyone can have. He can provide what no human agency can, such as good health. He promises that the righteous will still bear fruit in old age (Psalm 92:12-14), meaning that they will remain productive. We must diligently take up our responsibilities if we desire God's blessings, and not forget to help others along the way. If we bless others, God will return those blessings to us when we are in need.

Dear heavenly Father, thank You for Your abundant provision in my life. I am grateful, not only for financial provision, but for the spiritual blessings that You have given me. I appreciate daily strength and health so that I am able to be diligent in my affairs. Give me wisdom so that I might prepare for the future properly. Ultimately, my faith and trust are in You, as You hold the future; however, may I not neglect those things in the natural that need to be done, so that I will be prepared for whatever I have to face. Lord, I do not want to forget to give help to others along the way as well. May I be a good steward over all that You have given me. I ask this in the name of the Lord Jesus Christ. Amen.

God's Wisdom for Daily Living — ***Betty Miller***
November 10 — ***Day 314***

Proverbs 27:25-27 25 The hay appeareth, and the tender grass showeth itself, and herbs of the mountains are gathered. 26 The lambs are for thy clothing, and the goats are the price of the field. 27 And thou shalt have goat's milk enough for thy food, for the food of thy household, and for the maintenance for thy maidens.

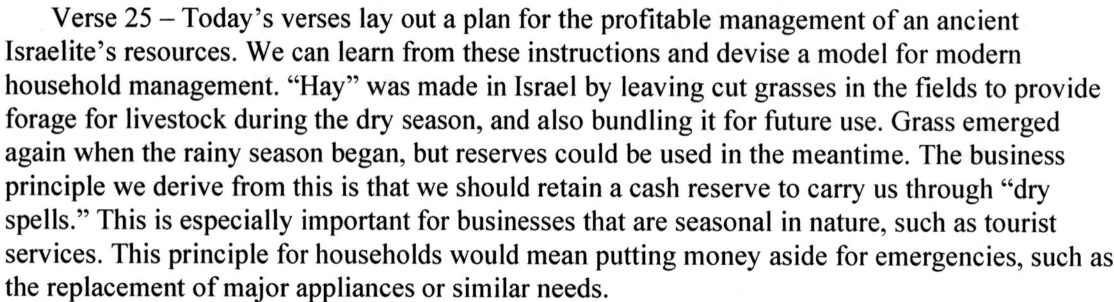

Verse 25 – Today's verses lay out a plan for the profitable management of an ancient Israelite's resources. We can learn from these instructions and devise a model for modern household management. "Hay" was made in Israel by leaving cut grasses in the fields to provide forage for livestock during the dry season, and also bundling it for future use. Grass emerged again when the rainy season began, but reserves could be used in the meantime. The business principle we derive from this is that we should retain a cash reserve to carry us through "dry spells." This is especially important for businesses that are seasonal in nature, such as tourist services. This principle for households would mean putting money aside for emergencies, such as the replacement of major appliances or similar needs.

Verses 26-27 – The farmer's herd would be used as follows: The wool of his lambs was used to make clothing for his family and servants. Some of his goats were used to buy land, and many kept as milk goats. The milk would then be used in several ways. The milk and its by-products fed his household, and the surplus was sold or bartered. From this, we see that to be successful in our homes or businesses we must devise an operating plan and a budget. Many people simply drift along with no plans for anything, lending credence to the saying that people who "fail to plan, plan to fail." To accomplish anything for the Lord, we must have a plan. He will reveal His plans for us and establish them if we ask Him. If we are in trouble financially, it is encouraging to know that He will give us a plan for getting out of debt. Sometimes the first step out of debt is to repent of foolish spending and lack of obedience to God regarding tithing and giving. God has filled the Bible with instructions on handling money because He desires to bless His people. Some rebel at the thought of planning and budgeting, but according to today's verses, it is clear that we all need a plan of action.

Dear heavenly Father, I am amazed at all the good advice that I have discovered in Your Word. Please give me the grace to implement it into my daily living. Help me to lead a disciplined life, so that I will be a good steward over all that You have entrusted to me. Thank You for Your daily provision. Give me Your plans, so that I might order my home and business according to Your Will. Give me divine inspiration to help me conquer the areas in my life that I have not been able to overcome yet. I am thankful that in Christ, all things are possible, and that we are promised victory through the power of the Holy Spirit! I ask this in the name of Jesus Christ. Amen.

Proverbs 28:1 The wicked flee when no man pursueth: but the righteous are bold as a lion.

This verse tells us that those who are righteous and who do not compromise will be as "bold as a lion" in their position, while those who are wicked will back down and flee. Sorrow will come upon those who practice unrighteousness, for they will reap what they sow. The obedient, however, will walk in boldness of faith and courage. "And if ye shall despise my statutes, or if your soul abhor my judgments, so that ye will not do all my commandments, but that ye break my covenant: I also will do this unto you; I will even appoint over you terror, consumption, and the burning ague, that shall consume the eyes, and cause sorrow of heart: and ye shall sow your seed in vain, for your enemies shall eat it. And I will set my face against you, and ye shall be slain before your enemies: they that hate you shall reign over you; and ye shall flee when none pursueth you…And upon them that are left alive of you I will send a faintness into their hearts in the lands of their enemies; and the sound of a shaken leaf shall chase them; and they shall flee, as fleeing from a sword; and they shall fall when none pursueth" (Leviticus 26:15-17,36).

How does God send things upon people? Punishment is simply the penalty for sin or the reaping of the evil that we commit. When this happens, it is called the judgment of God. Although the word *judgment* carries a negative connotation, it also has a positive side since it is linked with sowing and reaping as defined in Galatians 6:7-9: "Be not deceived; God is not mocked: for whatsoever a man soweth, that shall he also reap. For he that soweth to his flesh shall of the flesh reap corruption; but he that soweth to the Spirit shall of the Spirit reap life everlasting. And let us not be weary in well doing: for in due season we shall reap, if we faint not."

From this, we see that on the negative side, evil reaps destruction; while on the positive side, blessings are reaped by the righteous. We are all judged by the Word of God daily and either found faithful to keep His commandments or guilty of breaking them. Although we may fail to keep all of God's laws, Jesus did so perfectly. Therefore, it is only by accepting Him as our Savior that we can avert the ultimate judgment of hell. By daily repenting of our sins and walking with Christ, we can also avoid God's judgments now (1 Corinthians 11:31-32). This is true of nations as well as individuals. "Your iniquities have turned away these things, and your sins have withholden good things from you" (Jeremiah 5:25). We must pray that the church comes to true repentance, which will produce genuine revival in our nation. Otherwise, we will face greater judgments, causing us to be fearful even when we have nothing to be afraid of, as we read in Leviticus 26:17, 36.

When we serve God and keep His commandments, we will not walk in fear, even when it is all around us. The Spirit enables us to walk in faith so that we will be as "bold as a lion" and overcome fearful things in the name of the Lord. This is the reason innumerable missionaries can go into dangerous countries with the Gospel and not fear the evil in those nations, because they know that the greater One is living in them!

Dear heavenly Father, I am grateful that You came to deliver us from fear and terror. Fear produces torment and You said in Your Word that if we served You, we would be far from terror. Lord, please deliver me from those things that produce fear (like fretting, worry, and vain imaginings). Forgive me when I yield to fear. Help me to remember Your promises and to have faith in You. You said that You would never leave me, nor forsake me. Help me to remember I am

not alone when I face any crisis. May I always remember there is victory over every wicked attack against me. In Jesus' name I pray. Amen.

Quotes About Our Relationship With God

Knowing God leads to understanding in everything else. --Day 55

Man is a spiritual being created to worship God. If he does not worship God, he will worship something else; whether demons of false religion, money, relationships, or his own intellect. --Day 103

We must not be led by circumstances, nor by emotions, but by the Holy Spirit's guidance. --Day 128

We may know that prayer changes things, but how much time do we spend in prayer and Bible study, versus watching television or other time–wasters? --Day 234

Life does not make sense until we find God and begin to understand His ways. --Day 245

How wonderful it would be to be known as a friend of God as Abraham was! There is only one way to become His friend, and that is by spending quality time with Him. --Day 301

Many people seek favor from those in positions of authority, but the wise seek favor from God, knowing that all judgment comes from Him. --Day 340

Proverbs 28:2 When a land transgresses, it has many rulers, but when the ruler is a man of discernment, understanding, and knowledge, its stability will long continue (AMP).

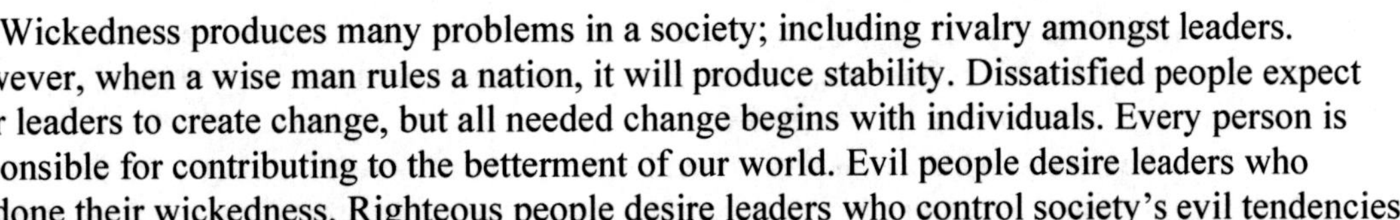

Wickedness produces many problems in a society; including rivalry amongst leaders. However, when a wise man rules a nation, it will produce stability. Dissatisfied people expect their leaders to create change, but all needed change begins with individuals. Every person is responsible for contributing to the betterment of our world. Evil people desire leaders who condone their wickedness. Righteous people desire leaders who control society's evil tendencies by making and enforcing righteous laws. Because the founding fathers of the United States were Christian, our laws were traditionally based on the Bible; and this influence has blessed our national life. We have turned away from this godly foundation, however, and God has begun to lift His blessings and protection from our nation. If we do not repent, we could fall as ancient Judah did:

"For Jerusalem is ruined, and Judah is fallen: because their tongue and their doings are against the LORD, to provoke the eyes of his glory. The show of their countenance doth witness against them; and they declare their sin as Sodom, they hide it not. Woe unto their soul! for they have rewarded evil unto themselves. Say ye to the righteous, that it shall be well with him: for they shall eat the fruit of their doings. Woe unto the wicked! it shall be ill with him: for the reward of his hands shall be given him. As for my people, children are their oppressors, and women rule over them. O my people, they which lead thee cause thee to err, and destroy the way of thy paths" (Isaiah 3:8-12)

Sin, especially the sin of Sodom, brought Judah under a curse. For centuries, God had warned them that judgment would come if they did not repent. In Isaiah's time, the citizens of Judah, like those of Sodom, had grown brazenly open about their sin. About 150 to 200 years after Isaiah prophesied it, Israel reaped a terrible judgment: Jerusalem was destroyed and survivors taken into captivity in Babylon. God rewarded the wicked with the fruit of their sin, while rewarding the righteous with protection amidst national catastrophe. Judah endured many evils as warnings before reaping God's terrible judgment. We notice some of them in verse 12: it was unrighteous leaders who were causing the people to err from the paths of righteousness. Isaiah 3:4-5 lists others: wicked or immature rulers, young people dishonoring their elders, and the foolish behaving arrogantly toward the honorable. Similar evils, along with natural catastrophes, are seen across the world today, and are indications of judgment. Judgment can be averted if our nations will seek Him and forsake their sins. "Blessed is the nation whose God is the LORD" (Psalm 33:12a).

Dear Father in heaven, thank You for giving us godly leadership in our nation at all levels. We ask You to forgive us for our national sins of pride, adultery, lust, materialism, addiction, murder, idolatry and the many other sins that have grieved Your heart. Forgive me on a personal level for my sins. Cleanse our hearts and our nation, so that we might live blessed and godly lives. May we be a people who live and share the truths of the Bible, so that Your kingdom will come on this earth. I pray in the name of Jesus. Amen.

November 13 — *Day 317*

Proverbs 28:3 A poor man that oppresseth the poor is like a sweeping rain which leaveth no food.

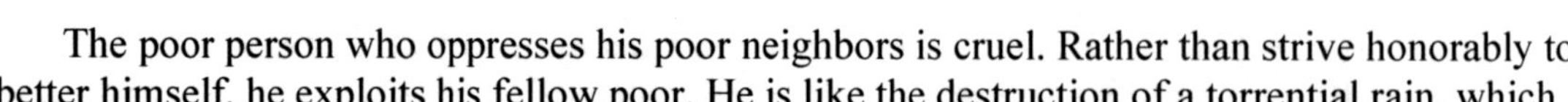

The poor person who oppresses his poor neighbors is cruel. Rather than strive honorably to better himself, he exploits his fellow poor. He is like the destruction of a torrential rain, which washes seed away and destroys what has grown.

Jesus told a parable about a servant who owed his king a huge sum of money (Matthew 18:23-35). The king was going to sell the servant and all he owned in order to get back a portion of the money owed to him. The servant begged for time to repay the debt. The king had pity upon him and completely forgave his enormous debt. That same servant came upon a fellow servant who owed him a small amount of money, but was unable to repay it. However, his attitude toward his fellow servant was not the same as his master's had been toward him. He cruelly had him thrown in prison. The king heard of this treatment, and angrily reminded the wicked servant that he had been forgiven a much greater debt. He chastised him for his lack of compassion and then handed him over to *"the tormentors"* until the debt was fully repaid. That servant's attitude is similar to a poor person who plunders his fellow poor. The fact that he knows how difficult life is, should cause him to recoil from the thought of ever taking anything from his neighbors, but it does not. A person like this is selfish and cruel, like the wicked servant in the parable.

Jesus taught us to ask God to "forgive us our debts, as we forgive our debtors" (Matthew 6:14-15), using parables to emphasize that we must forgive others for their trespasses against us because He has forgiven us of ours. Though it may never cross our minds to take from those who are financially poor, we may be cruel to those who are poor in other ways. Some people trespass against others with their poor manners or attitudes. Others trespass against people because of their ignorance and lack of understanding. We ought to have patience with everyone, knowing that we also have shortcomings and need others to be patient with our weaknesses. No matter what others may do, their debt to us is never as tremendous as our debt to God. Like the wicked servant, we have been forgiven a debt so huge we can never repay it. We cannot afford to be unforgiving. An unwillingness to forgive others hurts us more than anyone else, for it grows into a root of bitterness that hinders our walk with God. If we refuse to forgive others, God will allow us to be tormented by the devil. We will dwell in the prison of our own bitterness and pain.

Because the virtues of compassion and forgiveness are traits of our heavenly Father, they must also become our character traits if we are His children.

Dear Lord, thank You for forgiving me all my sins and trespasses. Father, may I always be quick to forgive others for their trespasses against me. I pray that all of Your children live in harmony with each other, and that we all possess a kind and forgiving disposition. Give us love and understanding for each other in the family of God. Let us lift each other up when any of us fall down and may we have Your virtues of grace and mercy toward each other. I ask this in the name of the Lord Jesus Christ. Amen.

Proverbs 28:4-5: 4 They that forsake the law praise the wicked: but such as keep the law contend with them. 5 Evil men understand not judgment: but they that seek the LORD understand all things.

Those who are rebellious will applaud the wicked, but law-abiding citizens will contend with them. Evil men cannot understand justice, but whoever seeks the Lord has good understanding. We saw in Day 315 that God's judgment is directly connected to the principle of sowing and reaping and comes upon the wicked because of sin. The Bible reveals that all the troubles in the world are due to either my own sin or someone else's. "…For all have sinned and come short of the glory of God" (Romans 3:23). "For the wages of sin is death…" (Romans 5:23). What exactly is sin? It is a heart condition, stemming from pride. Pride is referred to as "original sin." The Hebrew and Greek words for *sin* both convey the meaning *"to miss the mark."*[38] God created us to be like Him, but our pride and rebellion make us fall far short of that glorious purpose.

We cannot deal with our sin by "cleaning ourselves up" on the outside, when our problem is a heart condition. We need to be cleansed from sin; freed from its penalty, which is death; and restored to fellowship with God. We need a new heart and nature. This is what Jesus Christ meant when He said that we "must be born again" (John 3:7), and that "...except a man be born again, he cannot see the kingdom of God" (John 3:3). When we were physically born the first time, we were made a partaker of the nature of natural man. When we are born again spiritually, we become a partaker of the divine nature according to 2 Peter 1:4 which says, "Whereby are given unto us exceeding great and precious promises: that by these ye might be partakers of the divine nature, having escaped the corruption that is in the world through lust." God becomes our spiritual Father. Without the experience of the new birth, we have no hope of enjoying the glories of heaven or escaping the terrors of hell.

Have you been born again? The "new birth" is not a religion, a creed, a set of rituals, or joining a church. It is a transformation, the receiving of a new nature. Old things pass away and all things become new in Christ. "Therefore if any man be in Christ, he is a new creature: old things are passed away; behold, all things are become new" (2 Corinthians 5:17). Whoever receives and obeys Jesus will understand God's judgments. They will understand that all He allows (even punishment for sin) is meant for good. Those who rebelliously reject Christ will not understand. They will praise wicked men for their deeds and resist the righteous.

Dear heavenly Father, thank You for saving me from my sin. I am grateful for what You did on the cross when You took the penalty for my sin. Lord, I pray for the lost who do not understand what You did for them. Draw them by Your love and use me and Your other children to witness to those who do not know You. Reveal Your love for them, so that they understand they do not have to go to hell, but can receive Your life and enjoy a future in heaven with You. Give us understanding of Your ways and grace to live a holy life. I ask in the name of Jesus. Amen.

[38] Strong's Exhaustive Concordance of the Bible

God's Wisdom for Daily Living — ***Betty Miller***
November 15 — ***Day 319***

Proverbs 28:6-7 6 Better is the poor that walketh in his uprightness, than he that is perverse in his ways, though he be rich. 7 Whoso keepeth the law is a wise son: but he that is a companion of riotous men shameth his father.

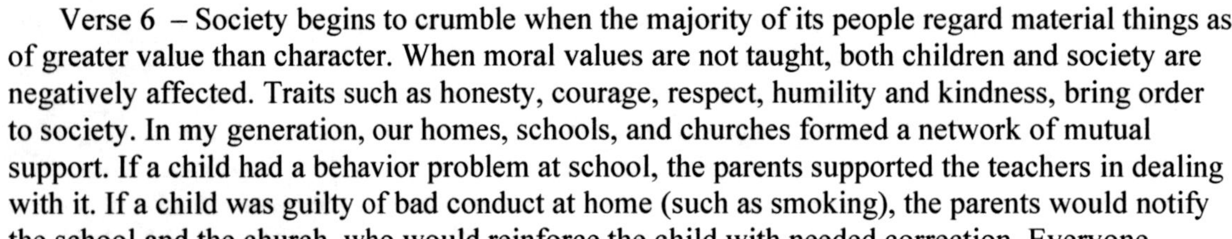

Verse 6 – Society begins to crumble when the majority of its people regard material things as of greater value than character. When moral values are not taught, both children and society are negatively affected. Traits such as honesty, courage, respect, humility and kindness, bring order to society. In my generation, our homes, schools, and churches formed a network of mutual support. If a child had a behavior problem at school, the parents supported the teachers in dealing with it. If a child was guilty of bad conduct at home (such as smoking), the parents would notify the school and the church, who would reinforce the child with needed correction. Everyone worked together to raise good children.

Our present society is so divided that children can now get by with wrong without being corrected for it by anyone. Not only is there no longer communication between these entities, but many have become corrupt. Some schools actually undermine parental authority, teaching humanism and often siding with rebellious children against their parents. So many parents today are child abusers, it is hard to know which ones can be trusted. Wicked men in some of our churches have sexually abused the children in their care. Churches should be a haven from evil, but sexual abuse, greed, false doctrine and other evils have infiltrated them.

What does the Bible say about this? "This know also, that in the last days perilous times shall come. For men shall be lovers of their own selves, covetous, boasters, proud, blasphemers, disobedient to parents, unthankful, unholy, Without natural affection, trucebreakers, false accusers, incontinent, fierce, despisers of those that are good, Traitors, heady, highminded, lovers of pleasures more than lovers of God; Having a form of godliness, but denying the power thereof: from such turn away" (2 Timothy 3:1-5).

Verse 7 – A self-indulgent son will bring shame to his parents. Some children are so wicked that they even curse their own father and mother (Proverbs 30:11-14). It is always a blessing to see Christian young people who honor their parents. These young people stand out as lights in the midst of a today's perverse generation.

The youth of any nation are simply a reflection of that nation's adults. Today, the condition of our society is very similar to Noah's day. This is the time the Bible speaks of, when Jesus Christ will return to this earth to judge the wicked and the righteous (Genesis 6:11-13 and Luke 17: 26-30).

Dear heavenly Father, I am grateful for all of the young people in this generation who have taken a stand for righteousness. Lord, strengthen them to be able to stand strong in their convictions in this perverse and crooked generation. We pray that the leaders in our churches and schools will be righteous, so that our children and our society will be influenced by the standards of the Bible, and we can all dwell in peace and harmony. Forgive our national sins and help us return to the roots that our nation was established upon. "God bless America," is my prayer. I ask this in the name of Jesus. Amen.

Proverbs 28:8-9 8 He that by usury and unjust gain increaseth his substance, he shall gather it for him that will pity the poor. 9 He that turneth away his ear from hearing the law, even his prayer shall be abomination.

Verse 8 – Sinners may heap up riches, but God will see that their wealth is given to the person who will consider and help the poor. "A good man leaveth an inheritance to his children's children: and the wealth of the sinner is laid up for the just" (Proverbs 13:22). "Though he heap up silver as the dust, and prepare raiment as the clay; He may prepare it, but the just shall put it on, and the innocent shall divide the silver" (Job 27:16-17). God will not bless riches gained by unjust means such as usury. Usury is the act of lending money at an excessively high rate of interest. Israel was given instructions about lending to their countrymen. Although they could charge interest on a loan to a stranger, they were not to charge interest on a loan to a fellow Israelite (Deuteronomy 23:19-20). This same principle should apply to loans among Christians.

In the New Testament, Jesus gave us an even higher way, telling us that it is better to give than to lend. We are instructed to give not only to fellow Christians, but also to give mercy and compassion to others as well. At one time in our lives, the Lord instructed my husband and I to cancel all the monetary debts owed to us, telling us that He would repay us. It was very liberating for us to do so, since many of those who owed us money were unable to repay us. When we released them, the Lord released finances to us in a different way that more than compensated for the thousands of dollars we had lost.

"And if ye do good to them which do good to you, what thank have ye? For sinners also do even the same. And if ye lend to them of whom ye hope to receive, what thank have ye? For sinners also lend to sinners, to receive as much again. But love ye your enemies, and do good, and lend, hoping for nothing again; and your reward shall be great, and ye shall be the children of the Highest: for he is kind unto the unthankful and to the evil. Be ye therefore merciful, as your Father also is merciful. Judge not, and ye shall not be judged: condemn not, and ye shall not be condemned: forgive, and ye shall be forgiven: Give, and it shall be given unto you; good measure, pressed down, and shaken together, and running over, shall men give into your bosom. For with the same measure that ye mete withal it shall be measured to you again" (Luke 6:33-38).

Verse 9 – As we have previously noted, a large donation to a church from ill-gotten gain is an abomination to God. "The sacrifice of the wicked is an abomination to the LORD: but the prayer of the upright is his delight" (Proverbs 15:8). God also regards the prayers of those who deliberately turn from His commandments, as an abomination. We must come to God with a submissive attitude and repentance in our heart if we want God to hear and answer our prayers: "If I regard iniquity in my heart, the LORD will not hear me" (Psalm 66:18).

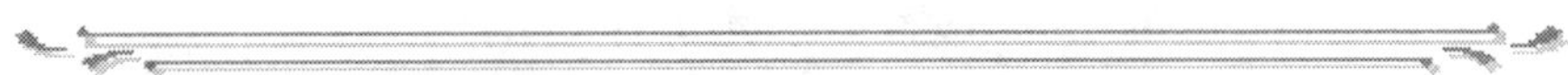

Dear Father God, thank You for Your mercy and kindness to us. May we be like You; showing that same mercy and kindness to others. Please help us to trust You with our financial affairs, should You tell us to forgive a debt that someone owes us. Jesus, You paid a debt You did not owe, and I owed a debt I could not pay. Thank You for releasing me. Lord, I release others today by forgiving them, blessing them and extending mercy to them. May all of Your children have the Father's love and mercy toward one another. I ask this in the name of Jesus Christ. Amen.

God's Wisdom for Daily Living ***Betty Miller***
November 17 ***Day 321***

Proverbs 28:10-12 10 Whoso causeth the righteous to go astray in an evil way, he shall fall himself into his own pit: but the upright shall have good things in possession. 11 The rich man is wise in his own conceit; but the poor that hath understanding searcheth him out. 12 When righteous men do rejoice, there is great glory: but when the wicked rise, a man is hidden.

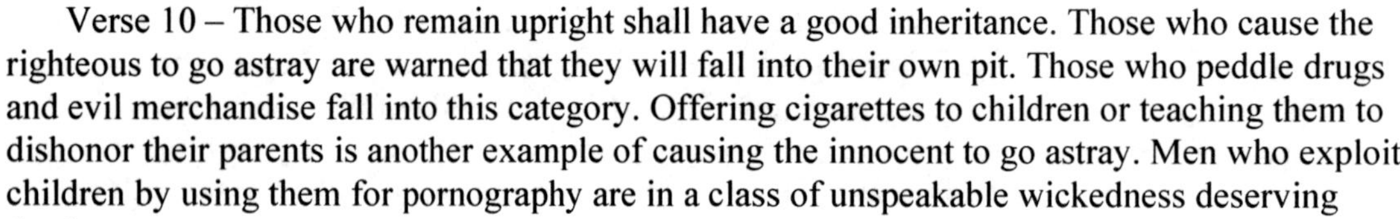

Verse 10 – Those who remain upright shall have a good inheritance. Those who cause the righteous to go astray are warned that they will fall into their own pit. Those who peddle drugs and evil merchandise fall into this category. Offering cigarettes to children or teaching them to dishonor their parents is another example of causing the innocent to go astray. Men who exploit children by using them for pornography are in a class of unspeakable wickedness deserving death.

"And whoso shall receive one such little child in my name receiveth me. But whoso shall offend one of these little ones which believe in me, it were better for him that a millstone were hanged about his neck, and that he were drowned in the depth of the sea. Woe unto the world because of offences! for it must needs be that offences come; but woe to that man by whom the offence cometh!" (Matthew 18:5-7).

Verse 11 – Rich men can easily become conceited. Many think they are invincible, believing their money will buy them out of any situation. However, a poor person who follows God has a greater advantage than the rich man does. The Lord will give poor men who listen to Him the understanding and wisdom that they need to thwart the schemes of the wealthy. Evil men throughout the ages have used their money and power for selfish and wicked agendas. The Lord can strip positions and power from those who abuse them. "For promotion cometh neither from the east, nor from the west, nor from the south. But God is the judge: he putteth down one, and setteth up another" (Psalm 75:6-7).

Verse 12 – People openly rejoice under righteous leaders, knowing they are safe, but the wicked are cruel and vengeful. Any power that they gain will be used to damage, ruin, or even kill people who oppose them. Men hide themselves when wicked rulers are in charge, to protect themselves and their belongings.

Dear Father in heaven, we thank You for good and righteous leaders in our businesses, in our cities and in our nations. Lord, please remove those who are wicked, so that righteousness might reign in the earth. Cleanse our societies of those who prey on the weak, the helpless; and on innocent children. Deliver us from evil. May Your kingdom come in the earth, as it is in heaven. Hallowed be Thy name–and in that name I pray. Amen.

God's Wisdom for Daily Living — ***Betty Miller***
November 18 — ***Day 322***

Proverbs 28:13-14 13 He that covereth his sins shall not prosper: but whoso confesseth and forsaketh them shall have mercy. 14 Happy is the man that feareth always: but he that hardeneth his heart shall fall into mischief.

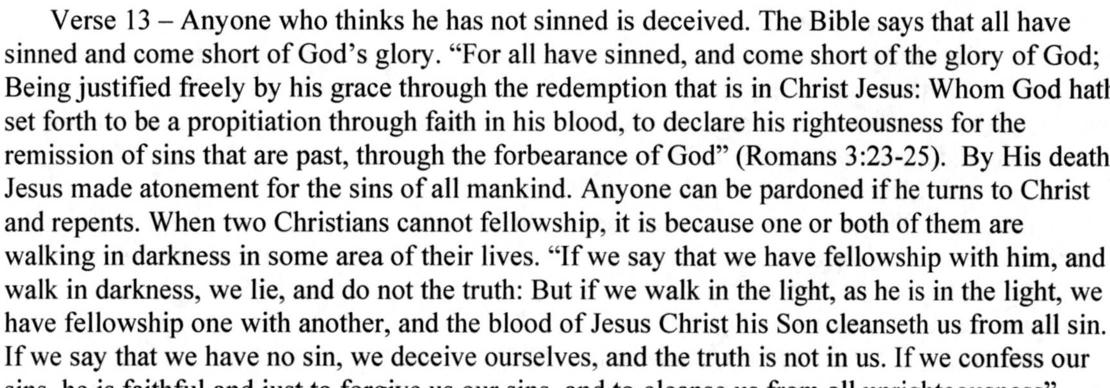

Verse 13 – Anyone who thinks he has not sinned is deceived. The Bible says that all have sinned and come short of God's glory. "For all have sinned, and come short of the glory of God; Being justified freely by his grace through the redemption that is in Christ Jesus: Whom God hath set forth to be a propitiation through faith in his blood, to declare his righteousness for the remission of sins that are past, through the forbearance of God" (Romans 3:23-25). By His death, Jesus made atonement for the sins of all mankind. Anyone can be pardoned if he turns to Christ and repents. When two Christians cannot fellowship, it is because one or both of them are walking in darkness in some area of their lives. "If we say that we have fellowship with him, and walk in darkness, we lie, and do not the truth: But if we walk in the light, as he is in the light, we have fellowship one with another, and the blood of Jesus Christ his Son cleanseth us from all sin. If we say that we have no sin, we deceive ourselves, and the truth is not in us. If we confess our sins, he is faithful and just to forgive us our sins, and to cleanse us from all unrighteousness" (John 1:5-10).

We can have fellowship with Christ only by dealing with our sins. When we sin, we are not to hide, ignore, or excuse it. We are to confess and turn from it. Only then will we be cleansed from our unrighteousness by the blood of Jesus.

Verse 14 – The reverential fear of God brings blessing, but a hard heart brings ruin. If we do not respond to God in obedience when He speaks to us, our hearts will begin to harden. Each time we refuse to obey God, our hearts become a little harder. A person who continues resisting the Holy Spirit will make their hearts insensitive to God, and they will have no rest in their souls.

"Wherefore (as the Holy Ghost saith, To day if ye will hear his voice, Harden not your hearts, as in the provocation, in the day of temptation in the wilderness: When your fathers tempted me, proved me, and saw my works forty years. Wherefore I was grieved with that generation, and said, They do always err in their heart; and they have not known my ways. So I sware in my wrath, They shall not enter into my rest.) Take heed, brethren, lest there be in any of you an evil heart of unbelief, in departing from the living God. But exhort one another daily, while it is called To day; lest any of you be hardened through the deceitfulness of sin. For we are made partakers of Christ, if we hold the beginning of our confidence steadfast unto the end" (Hebrews 3:7-14).

Dear heavenly Father, I am grateful that I can always come to You and confess my sins. Thank You for never turning me away, but always extending mercy and delivering me from evil. Father, may I be sensitive to the Holy Spirit's promptings, and obey You when You tell me to do something. I never want any hardness in my heart toward the things of God. May I always stand before You with a reverential fear, knowing that You are all-powerful and all-wise. Lord, I declare that I will have no fear of what man can do to me, because my faith and trust are in You. I am grateful that I can call on Your name. Amen.

God's Wisdom for Daily Living **_Betty Miller_**
November 19 **_Day 323_**

Proverbs 28:15-16 15 Like a roaring lion or a ravenous and charging bear is a wicked ruler over a poor people. 16 A ruler who lacks understanding is (like a wicked one) a great oppressor, but he who hates covetousness and unjust gain shall prolong his days (AMP).

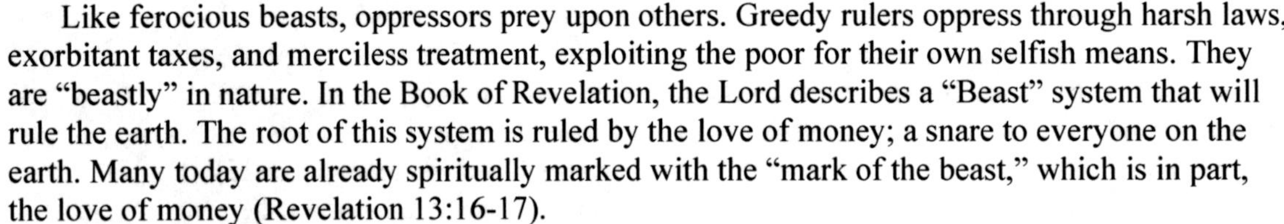

Like ferocious beasts, oppressors prey upon others. Greedy rulers oppress through harsh laws, exorbitant taxes, and merciless treatment, exploiting the poor for their own selfish means. They are "beastly" in nature. In the Book of Revelation, the Lord describes a "Beast" system that will rule the earth. The root of this system is ruled by the love of money; a snare to everyone on the earth. Many today are already spiritually marked with the "mark of the beast," which is in part, the love of money (Revelation 13:16-17).

Buying and selling is the system of the world. Many Christians are seeking after what the Gentiles were seeking in Matthew 6:31-32: the things of this world. There is nothing wrong with Christians buying and selling, but we are not buying and selling our souls. We are in the world, but we are not of it (John. 17:14-16). We handle the things of this world, but it is not in our hearts. Even so, the "beast" system has infiltrated the church through the influence of carnal Christians. These worldly Christians are puzzled by other Christians not seeking after money. They have sold out to the "beast" system by allowing its pleasures to consume their time and money. They have money for the things they desire, but they do not have the money for God. It is sad to see preachers manipulating God's people to give in order to support their own exorbitant lifestyles. There are pastors who will not deal with an elder's sin because he has a lot of money and gives to the church. Such pastors are not wholly serving the Lord but the "beast" system. Many ministries will go where they can receive the largest offering, rather than where God might ask them to go. Despite these abuses, we are not excused to quit giving. If we fail to give to worthy causes where there is a genuine need, we fail our Lord.

Those who are part of the true church; the bride of Christ, will love and honor God in all areas of life. Believers with the mind of Christ, walking in the Spirit and doing the works of God do not compromise with the world system. Its ways and desires are not in their hearts; its mark is not on them. Because they know that true riches are eternal, and their greatest treasure is their relationship with God, they do not commit spiritual adultery by loving the things of this world, or having any friendship with it (1 John 2:15; James 4:4). They are marked with the love of God upon their minds and hearts. They are able to lay everything down, leaving all behind if necessary, in obedience to God. They worship and remain faithful to the true and living Almighty God. They reflect the character of Christ, not that of a ravaging beast that will leave its mark on them.

Dear Father, I am grateful for Your bountiful provision in every area of my life. I do not want to cling to the things of this world and lean upon them for my security. May I always know that my security and blessings come from You alone; no matter what source or channel You have chosen to bless me through. I am grateful for my blessings, but I never want to put them above You. Deliver me from the lust of the eyes, the lust of the flesh and the pride of life and the love of money. May I always desire the true riches of Your kingdom above any earthly treasure. I ask this in the name of Jesus. Amen.

Proverbs 28:17-18 17 If a man willfully sheds the blood of a person [and keeps the guilt of murder upon his conscience], he is fleeing to the pit (the grave) and hastening to his own destruction; let no man stop him! 18 He who walks uprightly shall be safe, but he who willfully goes in double and wrong ways shall fall in one of them. 19 He who cultivates his land will have plenty of bread, but he who follows worthless people and pursuits will have poverty enough (AMP).

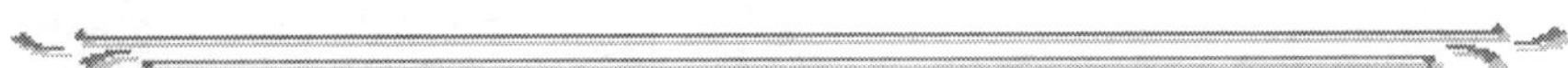

Whoever sheds human blood is on his way to the pit (the grave and hell), for a man will reap what he sows. The Bible tells us that the penalty for murder is death; this verse tells us not to try to stop that process. However, even a murderer can be saved from hell if he accepts what the shed blood of Jesus did for him on the cross and confesses his sin.

Capital punishment is a difficult subject. Some believe that it is just to condemn murderers to death while others think the death penalty is too cruel a punishment for civilized society. Christians are also divided on the issue. Some support the Old Testament law of capital punishment, while others oppose it, basing their stand on the New Testament teaching of forgiveness. Does this mean that the Old Testament and New Testament are in opposition to each other? Since God does not contradict Himself, perhaps a deeper understanding of the Bible as a whole is needed in order to reconcile the truths, since each view contains a measure of truth. Throughout history, various governments have enforced the death penalty for certain crimes such as murder, but it was God Himself who inaugurated capital punishment, before any governments were established. "And surely your blood of your lives will I require; at the hand of every beast will I require it, and at the hand of man; at the hand of every man's brother will I require the life of man. Whoso sheddeth man's blood, by man shall his blood be shed: for in the image of God made he man" (Genesis 9:5-6).

Why did God institute capital punishment? Why would a loving God who is supposed to love all of mankind issue these edicts? To answer this question, we must understand the overall purpose of God. God knew when He created man with a free will that not all people would follow and obey Him. However, He also knew that many would want to love and serve Him. In giving man free will, He also had to establish laws for people to live by. When we look at the Ten Commandments listed in Exodus 20:1-17, we can see that these laws were given for the good of mankind. One of these laws is in verse 13: "Thou shalt not kill." We may wonder if God said "do not kill," why He would then decree that a murderer should be put to death. The reason is that the Hebrew meaning of the word translated as 'kill" actually means "murder" or "to slay someone in a violent manner unjustly." So, God is actually saying, "Thou shalt not murder."

God knew before creating all things, that man would sin and that He would need to establish laws to curb that sinful nature. Knowing that most people would not allow His reign in their lives, God instituted civil authorities to maintain order and restrain evil in our societies. Through Israel, God provided us with a set of laws that apply to both our spiritual and natural life. They apply to the spiritual by showing man that the wages of his sin is death and to the natural by providing merciful laws restricting his lust for vengeance. God's justice demands life for life; but because Christ gave His life in our place, the murderer's debt to justice is paid. God's mercy grants him forgiveness if he accepts Christ's sacrifice. God's pardon for sin, however, is not the same as man's pardon. Even if a murderer should truly repent and is forgiven by God, his country may still inflict the death penalty upon him as stated in Romans 13:1-5.

Dear heavenly Father, the sacrifice of Jesus shedding His blood on the cross so that mankind could be saved is beyond our understanding. It is awesome to think that even a murderer, who comes to You and repents of his sins, can find forgiveness and be made whole. Thank You for forgiving us. Please fill our hearts with love and forgiveness towards those who have hurt and abused us. May we extend mercy towards others, so that when we need mercy, we will have some in our storehouse. I ask this in the name of our merciful Lord Jesus Christ. Amen.

Quotes About Riches and Poverty

Sin is not in things, but in the heart of man. Money is simply a medium of exchange. Used correctly, it can further God's work. --Day 62

The Lord wants to bless us so that we can bless others. How can we give to others if we are poor? We must learn how to receive God's blessings so that we can pass them on to others. --Day 111

Money never solves the root problems of hatred, violence, irresponsibility, or fear; only a change of heart that comes from knowing Christ does. --Day 107

Many today are heard claiming cars and houses, but seldom heard claiming souls. --Day 117

True riches are spiritual possessions that are not dependent upon anything in the world, but upon God alone. They are the riches of glory: God's character, favor, protection, vision, revelation, and wisdom. --Day 298

Proverbs 28:19-20 19 He that tilleth his land shall have plenty of bread: but he that followeth after vain persons shall have poverty enough. 20 A faithful man shall abound with blessings: but he that maketh haste to be rich shall not be innocent.

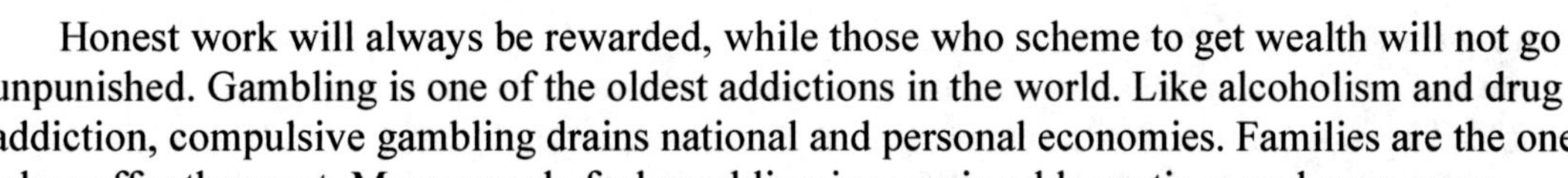

Honest work will always be rewarded, while those who scheme to get wealth will not go unpunished. Gambling is one of the oldest addictions in the world. Like alcoholism and drug addiction, compulsive gambling drains national and personal economies. Families are the ones who suffer the most. Many people feel gambling is an enjoyable pastime, and even some Christians support lotteries, horse racing and casinos. Video poker has become so popular it is referred to as "the crack cocaine" of gambling. However, Scripture is clear that it is a snare that can lead to poverty. It is the ultimate get-rich-quick scheme, and Christians should pay attention to the Biblical instruction regarding it.

Anyone attempting to gain money at someone else's certain loss is definitely not practicing Christian principles. A casino preys on the weakness of people. Gambling is contrary to the principles of working, saving and giving. Gamblers ignore discipline and accountability for their spending. To many, gambling is a scheme to escape work. Some do not realize the gravity of their sin, justifying it because their present income does not meet their needs. God desires these persons to look to Him to meet their needs. He will give a plan for becoming debt-free, if they seek Him and search out His economic principles in the Bible. The Lord can bring deliverance to those caught in the web of compulsive gambling. He will break the bondage of all who call upon Him.

Doing an honest day's work is the way to earn a living. Faithfulness to a job brings its own reward. God's blessing upon honest labor goes beyond any paycheck. No man can buy peace of mind, health, protection, or joy in the Holy Spirit.

"But godliness with contentment is great gain. For we brought nothing into this world, and it is certain we can carry nothing out. And having food and raiment let us be therewith content. But they that will be rich fall into temptation and a snare, and into many foolish and hurtful lusts, which drown men in destruction and perdition. For the love of money is the root of all evil: which while some coveted after, they have erred from the faith, and pierced themselves through with many sorrows. But thou, O man of God, flee these things; and follow after righteousness, godliness, faith, love, patience, meekness" (1 Timothy 6:6-11).

Dear Father God, thank You for Your many blessings. Please help me to be content with Your daily provision in my life. Deliver me from all worry and anxiety. Please help those who have fallen into the snare of gambling. Deliver them so that they will be able to trust You for their needs. May we all be content with Your daily provisions. Thank You for Your wonderful gifts of love, joy and peace, which cannot be purchased with any amount of money. I am most grateful. In the name of Jesus, I pray. Amen.

Proverbs 28:21-22 21 To have respect of persons is not good: for a piece of bread that man will transgress. 22 He that hasteth to be rich hath an evil eye, and considereth not that poverty shall come upon him.

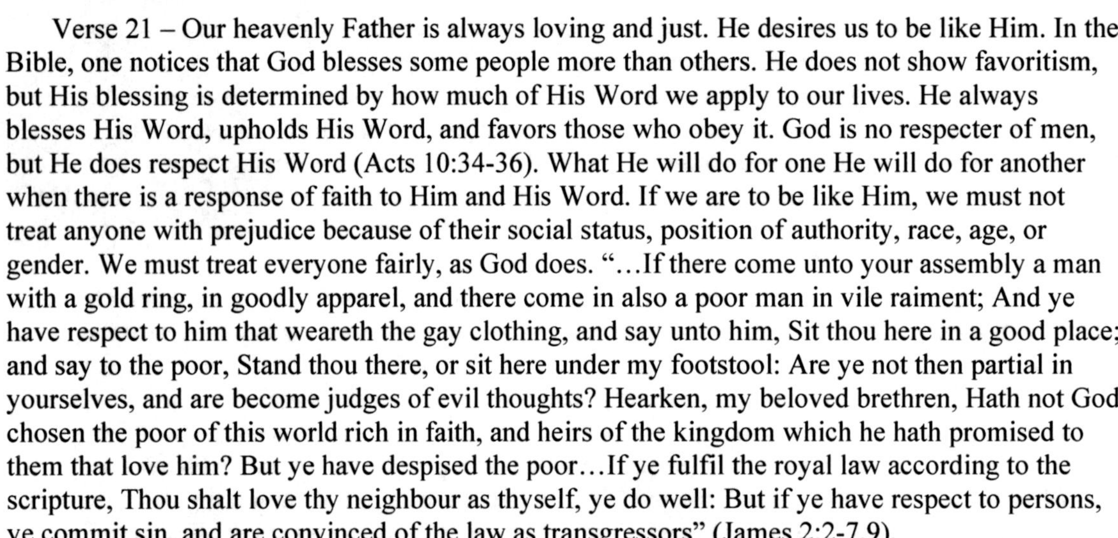

Verse 21 – Our heavenly Father is always loving and just. He desires us to be like Him. In the Bible, one notices that God blesses some people more than others. He does not show favoritism, but His blessing is determined by how much of His Word we apply to our lives. He always blesses His Word, upholds His Word, and favors those who obey it. God is no respecter of men, but He does respect His Word (Acts 10:34-36). What He will do for one He will do for another when there is a response of faith to Him and His Word. If we are to be like Him, we must not treat anyone with prejudice because of their social status, position of authority, race, age, or gender. We must treat everyone fairly, as God does. "…If there come unto your assembly a man with a gold ring, in goodly apparel, and there come in also a poor man in vile raiment; And ye have respect to him that weareth the gay clothing, and say unto him, Sit thou here in a good place; and say to the poor, Stand thou there, or sit here under my footstool: Are ye not then partial in yourselves, and are become judges of evil thoughts? Hearken, my beloved brethren, Hath not God chosen the poor of this world rich in faith, and heirs of the kingdom which he hath promised to them that love him? But ye have despised the poor…If ye fulfil the royal law according to the scripture, Thou shalt love thy neighbour as thyself, ye do well: But if ye have respect to persons, ye commit sin, and are convinced of the law as transgressors" (James 2:2-7,9).

The "royal law" of James 2:8 which says, "If ye fulfil the royal law according to the scripture, Thou shalt love thy neighbour as thyself, ye do well." and the "golden rule" of Luke 6:31 instruct us to love all people as we love ourselves. "And as ye would that men should do to you, do ye also to them likewise."

Neither are we to give the rich special attention nor to despise and ignore the poor. Rich or poor, we are all created in God's image, and every believer is an heir to the promises in His Word. In the Spirit, there are no races, social levels, or gender distinctions; we are all one in Christ (Galatians 3:26-29). Since we have different assignments from God, we fill different roles in life. Some *positions*, such as those of church or state government which affect and influence many lives are more important than others. However, the *people* filling those positions are no more important to God than the poorest men. God highly values the lives of all men and women.

Verse 22 – People who are driven to get rich quickly often use any means of pursuing wealth. This will eventually leave them impoverished. One can be poor in more than finances; for a man who has no peace, who cannot sleep at night and is in a constant state of stress is a poor man indeed.

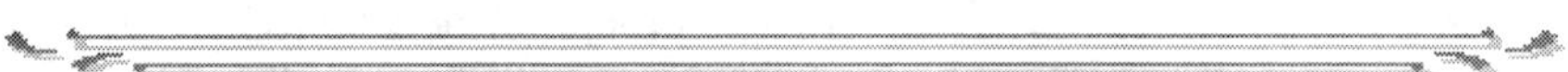

Dear heavenly Father, I am grateful that You are a fair and just God, and that You love all of us equally. I am amazed at Your love for each of us as individuals. You are wonderful! Lord, may we be free from any prejudiced attitudes and actions. May we lift up one another and be kind to one another, even as You are kind to us. Grace us so that we can do unto others as we would have them do unto us. Lord, help us to treat all people with the same love and respect. It is with a grateful heart I voice my thanksgiving to You this day as I count my many blessings. I ask this in the name of Jesus. Amen.

Proverbs 28:23-24 23 He that rebuketh a man afterwards shall find more favour than he that flattereth with the tongue. 24 Whoso robbeth his father or his mother, and saith, It is no transgression; the same is the companion of a destroyer.

Verse 23 – If the body of Christ is to mature, we must conform to Jesus, who is the truth. "That we henceforth be no more children…But speaking the truth in love, may grow up into him in all things, which is the head, even Christ…" (Ephesians 4:14a-15). Giving an honest rebuke is part of speaking the truth in love. This is often difficult to do, since we risk the anger and rejection of the person rebuked. However, we will eventually be appreciated more than a flatterer. A true friend will appreciate our honesty, for it shows genuine concern. Lying flattery leads someone to continue in error. Many portions of Scripture admonish us not to lie to each other, such as Colossians 3:9-10.

A news organization recently did a survey here in America and asked several questions to determine the percentage of people who were dishonest about things. Some of the questions were: "Do you cheat the IRS? "Do you compliment people when you do not mean it? "Do you tell your spouse to tell callers you are not at home? "Do you tell 'little white lies' if it will keep you out of trouble? "Do you tell creditors that the check is in the mail when you have not yet mailed it? "Do you exaggerate when repeating things you have heard?" It was determined that 90% of Americans surveyed are not truthful under certain circumstances.

Lying began with Satan whom Jesus revealed as the father of lies (John 8:43-44,47). We can understand a high percentage of liars in corrupt society, but it is alarming that many Christians are also dishonest. God always keeps His word. He is faithful to every promise recorded in the Bible. That is why we can trust Him. We are called to be like Him, and must prove ourselves honest and trustworthy in order to represent our Father well. Jesus said that a man's words proceed from his heart (Matthew 15:18-20a). If we lie, fib or break our word to others (another form of dishonesty), we need to ask God to cleanse our hearts, and begin studying the Bible so that His Word of truth resides in us.

Verse 24 – Those who steal from their parents are likened to destroyers. Grown children can "steal" from their parents in a number of ways; such as living irresponsibly and relying on their parents to pay their bills. Some parents entrust their businesses or their affairs to their children, only to have the children squander them. Thinking one has the right to steal from their parents in this way and making no effort to repay them, is a terrible evil. To deny this sin makes it even worse. Lying and stealing are evils that we must ask the Lord to deliver us from, if we are to become overcomers.

Dear heavenly Father, I am thankful that You are faithful and that You always keep Your Word. Lord, do a work in the hearts of all Your children and deliver us from lying. May the words that we speak always be the truth. Please help us not to make promises that we are unable to keep. We want our words to be like Your words. You are not a man that You should lie; and every promise that You have made in the Word of God You will keep. Lord, cleanse our hearts so that we will speak the truth in love instead of ignoring confrontations. I ask this in the name of Jesus. Amen.

Proverbs 28:25-26 25 He that is of a proud heart stirreth up strife: but he that putteth his trust in the LORD shall be made fat. 26 He that trusteth in his own heart is a fool: but whoso walketh wisely, he shall be delivered.

Verse 25 – Prideful people, (Christians included) stir up strife by contending for their rights and what they think is due to them. They try to obtain their desires by their own efforts. Those who trust in the Lord do not strive for their rights. They bring a matter of injury or injustice to God and leave it in His hands. They do not give in to the pride of life; the temptation to look good or smart or capable or tough to others by defending themselves or returning insult for insult. They humble themselves by obeying God's commandments, even if it means looking foolish or weak to their enemies and friends. Those who trust God instead of their own ways will be blessed and enriched.

Verse 26 – God has given us gifts and abilities, but relying upon them outside of His guidance is foolish. No one has a sufficient understanding to solve all problems. God alone is the final authority on every subject. We must learn to obey Him even when we do not understand how He is leading. We cannot be guided by His Word, if we do not know what it says. Since keeping God's Word lights the pathway of life and keeps us from stumbling, we should make it a priority to understand God's ways and gain His wisdom.

When we are born again, the Holy Spirit comes to live within us. He gives us "spiritual eyes" to see His ways. When we submit to God, His Spirit begins to lead us. Even when we do not understand His leading, we must follow Him in faith, knowing that He will not lead us astray. Faith is necessary to please God, for whatever is not of faith is sin (Romans 14:23b). The only way to receive faith is by hearing His Word: "So then faith cometh by hearing, and hearing by the word of God" (Romans 10:17). Our faith grows as we study and obey His Word. Jesus Himself is the Word of God Incarnate, and the Bible is the written Word. Therefore, our faith grows when we hear a word from Him. Some refer to Christians as having "blind faith" but our faith is actually in a real person–Jesus Christ–and therefore it is not "blind." Before our eyes were opened to His love, we were blind, but now we see Him, and a new life is ours. If the Holy Spirit leads us, difficult situations are never hopeless, though they might look like that from our perspective. God can take us around any obstacle. Nothing is impossible with him! We are limited, but He is limitless and His specialty is miracles. We only limit Him when we don't trust and obey Him. "Trust in the LORD with all thine heart; and lean not unto thine own understanding. In all thy ways acknowledge him, and he shall direct thy paths" (Proverbs 3:5-6).

Dear Father God, You are such an awesome God! When I am facing difficulty and am tempted to doubt You, help me to remember all that You have done for me in the past. I want to always walk in faith and trust in You, not leaning unto my own understanding. Deliver me from pride and fear, as these twin evils are aimed at destroying my faith. Give me a love for the Bible and open my understanding to things You desire to reveal to me in Your Word. Please give me the grace to obey all that You command. In Jesus' name. Amen.

Proverbs 28:27-28 27 He that giveth unto the poor shall not lack: but he that hideth his eyes shall have many a curse. 28 When the wicked rise, men hide themselves: but when they perish, the righteous increase.

Verse 27 – This verse clearly says that those who minister to the poor will not be in lack. Who are the poor that this scripture is talking about? Certainly, it is not referring to the lazy, as the scripture already talks about how to deal with that problem. The poor are those who are disadvantaged through troubles and circumstances beyond their control. Good examples would be neglected children, helpless people, displaced people, exploited people, victims of tragedies and natural disasters, those who have lost their jobs, the handicapped, those who live in an area of famine, etc. One of the things the Lord desires for His people to possess is a compassionate heart because that is the kind of heart that He has.

"If there be among you a poor man of one of thy brethren within any of thy gates in thy land which the LORD thy God giveth thee, thou shalt not harden thine heart, nor shut thine hand from thy poor brother: But thou shalt open thine hand wide unto him, and shalt surely lend him sufficient for his need, in that which he wanteth...For the poor shall never cease out of the land: therefore I command thee, saying, Thou shalt open thine hand wide unto thy brother, to thy poor, and to thy needy, in thy land" (Deuteronomy15:7-8,11).

One who graciously and generously gives of his own bread (or goods) to the poor, is the kind of person who will always be blessed. Paul encouraged people to support the weak and give to the poor. He both gave and received from others, as he was a minister of God, yet he said it was more blessed to give than to receive. "I have coveted no man's silver, or gold, or apparel. Yea, ye yourselves know, that these hands have ministered unto my necessities, and to them that were with me. I have shewed you all things, how that so labouring ye ought to support the weak, and to remember the words of the Lord Jesus, how he said, It is more blessed to give than to receive" (Acts 20:33-35).

Verse 28 – We saw the negative effects that wicked men coming to leadership have upon a country in Day 321. However, the opposite is true when the wicked perish and righteous men rule. It creates an environment in which righteousness multiplies. Righteous people will stand up and voice their concerns; they generate and support projects that create a healthy society. Righteous leadership has a positive influence on all of society. When there is an increase of good people in the land, the whole land is blessed because of it.

Dear heavenly Father, I am grateful that You have shown me Your compassion many times over the years. May I become like You and show that same attribute to others; especially the poor. Please bless me so that I might bless others who are needy. May I never turn my face away from those who are seeking help. If I am unable to give monetarily, may I remember I can always give of my time and prayers. Deliver me of any fear or insecurity that would keep me from being generous. May I always be a cheerful giver. I ask this in the name of Jesus. Amen.

Proverbs 29:1-2 1 He, that being often reproved hardeneth his neck, shall suddenly be destroyed, and that without remedy. 2 When the righteous are in authority, the people rejoice: but when the wicked beareth rule, the people mourn.

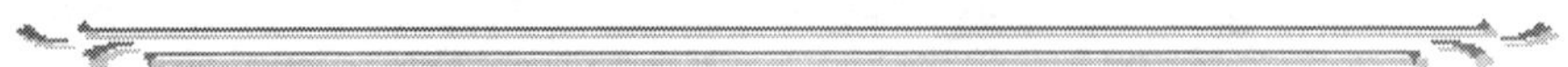

Verse 1 – It is vitally important to heed advice and correction. Stubborn, prideful people refuse to be corrected (Jeremiah 5:3). Sooner or later, those who continue in destructive paths bring upon themselves God's wrath, which is reaping the consequences of one's sinful deeds. Walking in faith and obedience to God keeps us under His protection. By refusing correction, we step out from under God's protection and invite Satan's attacks.

Our choices today will shape our tomorrow; filling them with either blessing or cursing. If we receive God's correction when He convicts us of sin, we will avoid the sorrow that disobedience creates. If we continue in sin, our backsliding will produce difficult circumstances that will correct us. "Thine own wickedness shall correct thee, and thy backslidings shall reprove thee: know therefore and see that it is an evil thing and bitter, that thou hast forsaken the LORD thy God ..." (Jeremiah 2:19a).

God challenges us with this admonition in Deuteronomy 30:19: "I call heaven and earth to record this day against you, that I have set before you life and death, blessing and cursing: therefore choose life, that both thou and thy seed may live." Society stresses our right to choose, but suppresses the truth that our choices have consequences, especially in the areas of lust and selfishness. Movies generally glamorize sin but seldom depict the devastating results of adultery, abortion, and so forth. That these sins have consequences often does not hit home until one suffers a divorce, contracts a sexually-transmitted disease, or suffers the emotional aftermath of getting an abortion. If we become hardened, our wrong choices can destroy us by bringing consequences that will hurt us beyond remedy. Anyone who has continually made bad decisions is on the road to destruction and has only one hope: Jesus. God is able to take the inescapable situations that we have created, and turn them around. God can bring good out of the evil which Satan unleashes against us when we repent.

Verse 2 – In Day 321 and Day 329, we saw that a nation rejoices when ruled by upright leaders and mourns under the oppression of wicked rulers. The same is true in all areas of authority; whether homes, schools, or businesses. Good leaders create an environment that encourages the growth of those under them. A wicked person in a position of authority can wound and destroy many lives. Many people have left good-paying jobs and taken smaller positions simply to work under decent management and employers.

Dear Father, thank You for Your love toward me. I appreciate Your correction when I need it; since I know when I heed Your advice, I am spared a lot of trouble. Deliver me from every trace of rebellion and pride, because I truly desire to walk in humility. I know that Jesus was lowly and humble when He was on this earth and I want to be like Him. Help me to be a good wife, mother, boss, and friend. I also want to remain on the straight and narrow path of obedience. So, guide me daily in Your will. I ask this in the name of Jesus. Amen.

God's Wisdom for Daily Living — *Betty Miller*
November 27 — *Day 331*

Proverbs 29:3-4 3 Whoso loveth wisdom rejoiceth his father: but he that keepeth company with harlots spendeth his substance. 4 The king by judgment establisheth the land: but he that receiveth gifts overthroweth it.

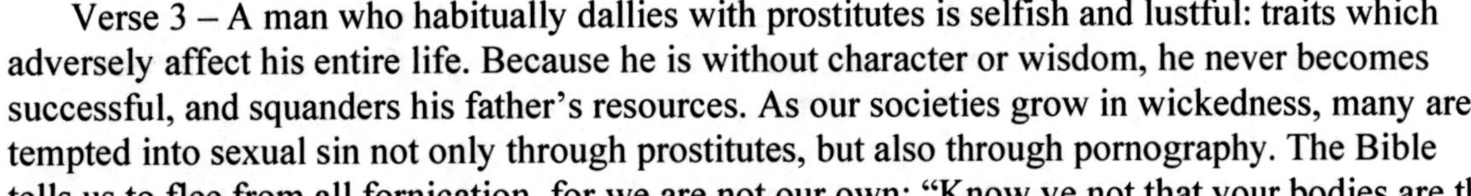

Verse 3 – A man who habitually dallies with prostitutes is selfish and lustful: traits which adversely affect his entire life. Because he is without character or wisdom, he never becomes successful, and squanders his father's resources. As our societies grow in wickedness, many are tempted into sexual sin not only through prostitutes, but also through pornography. The Bible tells us to flee from all fornication, for we are not our own: "Know ye not that your bodies are the members of Christ? shall I then take the members of Christ, and make them the members of an harlot? God forbid. What? know ye not that he which is joined to an harlot is one body? for two, saith he, shall be one flesh. But he that is joined unto the Lord is one spirit. Flee fornication. Every sin that a man doeth is without the body; but he that committeth fornication sinneth against his own body. What? know ye not that your body is the temple of the Holy Ghost which is in you, which ye have of God, and ye are not your own? For ye are bought with a price: therefore glorify God in your body, and in your spirit, which are God's" (1 Corinthians 6:15-20)

Verse 4 – A ruler either establishes the land by good judgment, or overthrows it by the corruption his evil character promotes in others. Evil leaders are more interested in the fulfilling of their own personal desires than the good of the people. Their decisions can be swayed by bribes (gifts) from unscrupulous people. A wicked king or ruler lays heavy burdens on his people, such as high taxes, in order to live luxuriously and glorify himself. There were religious rulers in Jesus' day who did the same kind of things in spiritual matters. He likened them to poisonous snakes and warned them that they were on their way to hell: "For they bind heavy burdens and grievous to be borne, and lay them on men's shoulders; but they themselves will not move them with one of their fingers…Ye serpents, ye generation of vipers, how can ye escape the damnation of hell?" (Matthew 23:4,33).

Dearest Father, thank You for those good and righteous leaders in the world who are concerned about serving the people in a just manner. Bless and protect these men and women. Give them Your wisdom in the decisions they make because they will affect many people. Deliver us from wicked leaders by changing them or removing them from their positions. Have mercy on our land and deliver us from the sexual sins that are destroying our world. Please forgive this nation for the sins of lust, adultery, perversion, fornication, and all the other filthy sexual indulgences that happen in this world on a daily basis. Cleanse us from unrighteousness and make us holy. I ask this in the name of Jesus. Amen.

Proverbs 29:5-7 5 A man that flattereth his neighbour spreadeth a net for his feet. 6 In the transgression of an evil man there is a snare: but the righteous doth sing and rejoice. 7 The righteous considereth the cause of the poor: but the wicked regardeth not to know it.

Verses 5-6 – Hunters in ancient times used nets in several ways to ensnare birds and animals. In the same way, flatterers can spread two sorts of spiritual nets, setting a snare for others. With one net, a flatterer manipulates people to do what he wants. With the other, he entangles them in pride. The one who has these nets set for him can escape them through discernment and God's guidance. Eventually, all flatterers will be tripped by their own nets.

An evil man's sin is like a snare, for it influences and entraps others to sin with him. This is how many people have fallen into a snare of drinking and partying, becoming addicted to alcohol, drugs, or crime. They may not have had an interest in taking drugs, drinking, or stealing, until friends encouraged them to join them. For this reason, it is very important to choose your friends wisely. Bad companions will corrupt good people.

Verse 7 – A wicked person is selfish. His world revolves completely around his own desires. He does not care about the poor, and he has no interest in helping the needy. The Bible tells us that "the poor shall never cease out of any land" (Deuteronomy 15:11). As long as sinful man reigns on earth, he will make decisions and actions that create poverty, and thus there will always be poor people. Only Christ can establish true justice and provide abundantly for all His subjects, thereby eradicating poverty. Only when Christ returns to earth and reigns during the Millennium, will poverty cease because the Lord told us we would always have the poor to minister to. "For ye have the poor with you always, and whensoever ye will ye may do them good: but me ye have not always" (Mark 14:7). We are called to reflect God's heart to the world and the poor, to be compassionate as Jesus was. The strong are to help the weak.

We cannot truly follow Christ and ignore the needy or the helpless. In Israel, "the poor, the orphan, and the widow" described the most destitute and helpless of the people. Today, the most helpless among us are unborn children, murdered by abortion in atrociously painful ways, usually for convenience or out of the ignorance of their parents. The Bible teaches that we are to overcome selfishness, not encourage it. We must do all we can to reverse the laws in our countries that allow abortions so freely. "So ye shall not pollute the land wherein ye are: for blood it defileth the land: and the land cannot be cleansed of the blood that is shed therein, but by the blood of him that shed it" (Numbers 35:33).

Dear Father in heaven, thank You for Your great mercy and compassion toward us. Lord, create in us that same heart of compassion that You possess; not only for Your children, but also for the poor and needy. Use us to reach out and help them both physically and spiritually. Give us heart-felt love for those who are suffering in the world, and anoint us to share the gospel with them so that they might know You. Forgive us for our selfishness, and deliver our land from the curse that abortion and murder bring on a nation. May this evil cease in this country and all others nations in the world. I ask this in the name of Jesus. Amen.

God's Wisdom for Daily Living ***Betty Miller***
November 29 ***Day 333***

Proverbs 29:8-9 8 Scoffers set a city afire (inflaming the minds of the people), but wise men turn away wrath. 9 If a wise man has an argument with a foolish man, the fool only rages or laughs, and there is no rest.

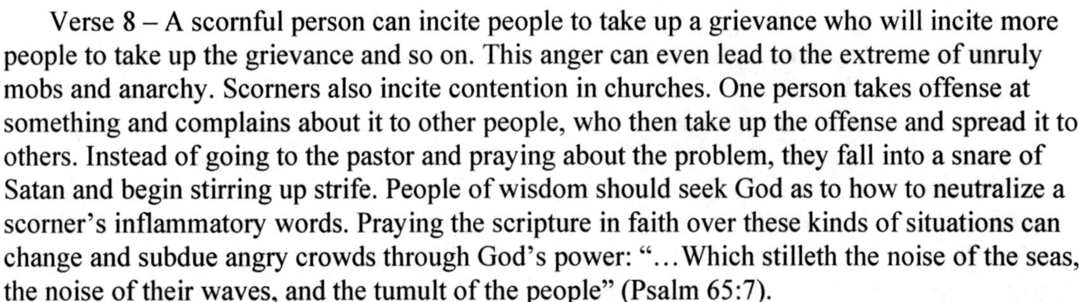

Verse 8 – A scornful person can incite people to take up a grievance who will incite more people to take up the grievance and so on. This anger can even lead to the extreme of unruly mobs and anarchy. Scorners also incite contention in churches. One person takes offense at something and complains about it to other people, who then take up the offense and spread it to others. Instead of going to the pastor and praying about the problem, they fall into a snare of Satan and begin stirring up strife. People of wisdom should seek God as to how to neutralize a scorner's inflammatory words. Praying the scripture in faith over these kinds of situations can change and subdue angry crowds through God's power: "…Which stilleth the noise of the seas, the noise of their waves, and the tumult of the people" (Psalm 65:7).

One of the first things we need to know about God is that He is the source of all good things. He loves us. In fact, the Scripture says He loved us so much He sent His Son, Jesus, to die for us so that we might have life and have it more abundantly. We should not believe in praising God *for* tragedies, for sickness, for bad things; yet we should believe in praising Him in *the midst of* these circumstances. The bad things did not come from God and we don't want to blame the Lord for something the devil sent. Our God is not the author of sickness, sin, tragedies, sorrow and heartache. The devil is the one who sends these things, and then tries to get us to blame them on the Lord. God is on our side, and when we begin blaming God and murmuring against Him, we have fallen into the devil's trap. We invite the "destroyer" into our lives when we yield to the devil's temptation to accuse God for our troubles. This was the source of Job's problems, until he saw the light and repented for uttering things he did not understand. Once Job repented of his own self-righteousness and pride, then the Lord blessed and restored all things to him (Job 42:1-6).

Verse 9 – Because a foolish man's spiritual eyes are blinded, he cannot see the truth nor understand the viewpoint of those who walk in God's wisdom. When a godly man tries to explain the truth to a fool, he cannot be made to see reason, and the foolish man either rants or mocks. It is as 2 Corinthians 4:3-4 says: "But if our gospel be hid, it is hid to them that are lost: In whom the god of this world hath blinded the minds of them which believe not, lest the light of the glorious gospel of Christ, who is the image of God, should shine unto them."

Dear Father, thank You for giving us Your wisdom. May I never blame You when the enemy is attacking me with evil. Please deliver me from any trace of murmuring and complaining when I am faced with trials. May I put on the armor of God instead, and use my faith to put the enemy to flight. May I always trust You to bring me the victory over everything the enemy tries to defeat me with. I declare that he is a defeated foe and that no weapon formed against me shall prosper, and every tongue that rises up against me in judgment You shall prove to be wrong. I thank You for the victory in Jesus' name! Amen.

Proverbs 29:10-11 10 The bloodthirsty hate the blameless man, but the upright care for and seek (to save) his life. 11 A (self-confident) fool utters all his anger, but a wise man holds it back and stills it (AMP).

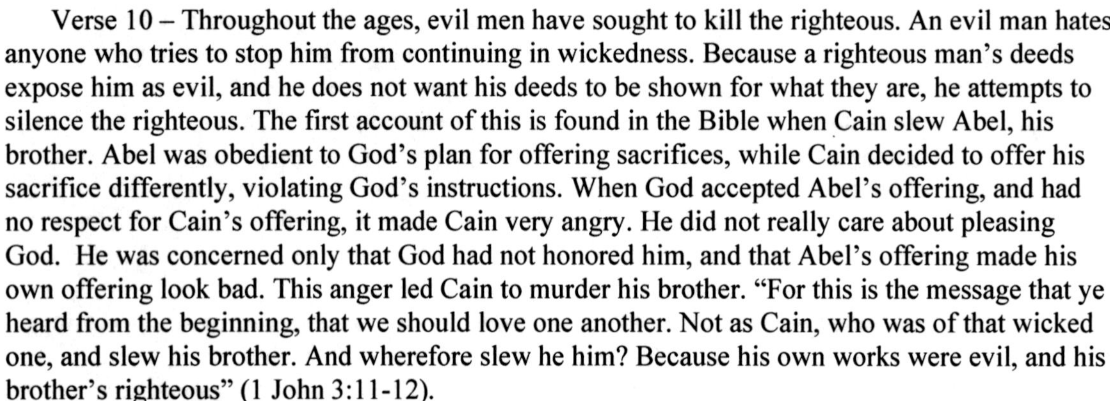

Verse 10 – Throughout the ages, evil men have sought to kill the righteous. An evil man hates anyone who tries to stop him from continuing in wickedness. Because a righteous man's deeds expose him as evil, and he does not want his deeds to be shown for what they are, he attempts to silence the righteous. The first account of this is found in the Bible when Cain slew Abel, his brother. Abel was obedient to God's plan for offering sacrifices, while Cain decided to offer his sacrifice differently, violating God's instructions. When God accepted Abel's offering, and had no respect for Cain's offering, it made Cain very angry. He did not really care about pleasing God. He was concerned only that God had not honored him, and that Abel's offering made his own offering look bad. This anger led Cain to murder his brother. "For this is the message that ye heard from the beginning, that we should love one another. Not as Cain, who was of that wicked one, and slew his brother. And wherefore slew he him? Because his own works were evil, and his brother's righteous" (1 John 3:11-12).

As Christians, we are responsible for more than just our outward actions, for God looks on our hearts as well as our deeds. It is vital that we ask God to deliver us of any hatred, for it is the same as murder in God's eyes. We must overcome evil with good (Romans 12:17-21), learning not only to restrain anger and repent of hatred, but to do what we can to win the souls of those who hate us. We must pray for them and try to find ways to win them to Christ or at least to influence them for good.

Verse 11 – A fool says everything that comes to mind and easily expresses his anger. A wise man rather chooses what he says, restraining his anger until he can deal with his thoughts and feelings properly. Anger can be righteous or unrighteous. Most people experience a righteous anger at injustice when evil men hurt innocent people. It spurs people to action against the wicked. Unrighteous anger, like Cain's, springs from pride and selfishness. It is not to be vented on others by shouting or throwing things. It is to be controlled by confessing it to God, asking Him to remove it from our hearts and grant us His perspective of the situation, and by forgiving whoever angered us.

Dear heavenly Father, I thank You for being a just God who will deal with the wicked in the world. I choose to forgive those who have done evil toward me. Father, deliver them from being used by the devil. Save those who do not know You. Deliver those who are deceived and have embraced anger and hatred in their souls. Lord, show me ways to overcome evil in the world. Please help me to reach out and be an instrument of change when I see injustice and wrongs being committed against others. Give me wisdom and love to overcome evil with good. I ask this in the name of the Lord Jesus Christ. Amen.

Proverbs 29:12-14 12 If a ruler hearken to lies, all his servants are wicked. 13 The poor and the deceitful man meet together: the LORD lighteneth both their eyes. 14 The king that faithfully judgeth the poor, his throne shall be established for ever.

Verse 12 – We know that a ruler who keeps company with liars, is also corrupt himself. Those who are wicked do not want men of integrity around them, so the officials they choose to serve them will also be wicked. It goes back to the old adage: "Birds of a feather, flock together."

Verse 13 – Although the poor and the deceitful may be worlds apart in their manner of living, both receive sight from God. Mankind has been bestowed with life and blessings that come only from God. He created the earth for all people, even those who do not acknowledge that it came from Him. He gives us eyes and sunlight by which to see valleys, mountains, rivers, animals, and all creation. He causes the sun to shine on the good and the evil. He sends rain on the just and the unjust. "...That ye may be the children of your Father which is in heaven: for he maketh his sun to rise on the evil and on the good, and sendeth rain on the just and on the unjust" (Matthew 5:45). He gives men natural gifts, enabling us all to contribute to the good of society. Like snowflakes, each of us are unique. He has a specific purpose for each of us, which we can only fully understand when we give our lives to Him.

In accordance with His plan for mankind, God created the perfect Garden of Eden. There Adam and Eve lived, worked, and enjoyed fellowship with Him. When they disobeyed Him, sin began to defile both them and all the earth; so God then initiated His plan of redemption. At the determined time, He sent His Son, Jesus Christ, into the world to atone for the sins of mankind. According to plan, through Christ, all people can be restored to Him if they accept what Jesus did for them and surrender to God's will. Whoever gives his life to the Lord receives spiritual gifts in addition to his natural gifts. In the natural, God gives us eyes to see the light of the sun and what it illumines. In the spirit, He gives us sight and revelation to perceive His Light and Truth.

Verse 14 – A good ruler faithfully judges the poor. He does not deny them the right to be heard. He does not pervert justice, but judges fairly and upholds the poor man when he is in the right. God establishes the rule of such a man. Jesus will one day return to earth and establish His righteous reign on earth. He is the only completely just and upright King, and His rule shall indeed be established forever.

Dear heavenly Father, I thank You for the many gifts You have given to us, as Your children. I appreciate eyes to see Your beautiful creation. I am grateful that You gave us so many things to see and enjoy in this earth. I also thank You for the gifts You have given to me personally. I know that You have given me the gift of writing and teaching and I am grateful. I am also humbled that You would use me to share the revelations You have given me with Your people. Lord, I dedicate my life and gifts to Your work. Please use them to bring glory to Your Name. I ask this in the name of Jesus. Amen.

Proverbs 29:15-17 15 The rod and reproof give wisdom: but a child left to himself bringeth his mother to shame. 16 When the wicked are multiplied, transgression increaseth: but the righteous shall see their fall. 17 Correct thy son, and he shall give thee rest; yea, he shall give delight unto thy soul.

Verses 15 & 17 – The theme of correcting children is addressed many times in Proverbs. This indicates how important it is to discipline our children. As we have seen in several other studies, it is necessary that we do several things if we desire our children to bring us delight and not shame.

Here is a quick summary of what we have already studied on Day 97, Day 222 and at other times: First, we need to realize that correction is an integral part of raising a child in God's ways. It is not an option if we desire to have joy and not shame from our children. Second, we must administer correction with the rod (spanking). Young children need the discipline of a spanking from time to time, though it must never be administered in anger, which can lead to abuse. Instruction is necessary before and after a spanking, for a child always needs to be told very clearly what he did wrong. Third, we must continue to correct our children by reproof. As a child ages, the rod is used less and reproof is used more. Even as young adults, our children need the correction of reproof from time to time. This prepares them to receive the reproof and correction of the Lord.

Verse 16 – We have looked at several proverbs that speak of the dreadful impact that wicked leaders have upon a nation. This proverb reminds us that regardless of how much wickedness may increase in these last days, Christ will one day return and we, together with all the righteous by faith from all the ages, shall see the fall of the wicked. The Bible tells us in many places that the Lord will remove the wicked from the earth when He establishes His righteous reign. "For the upright shall dwell in the land, and the perfect shall remain in it. But the wicked shall be cut off from the earth, and the transgressors shall be rooted out of it" (Proverbs 2:21-22).

Dear heavenly Father, we thank You for the blessing of children. Lord, help all Christian parents to heed the Bible's instructions for rearing their children. There are many different voices in the world telling us how to do things, but we want to know what the Bible says about child rearing. Father, since You created us, surely Your advice would be the best advice to follow! You know how to do all things in perfection. Give us divine wisdom in the area of child rearing and give us grace to spank our children when they need that discipline. I ask this in the name of Jesus. Amen.

Proverbs 29:18 Where there is no vision (no redemptive revelation of God), the people perish; but he who keeps the law (of God, which includes that of man)–blessed (happy, fortunate, and enviable) is he (AMP).

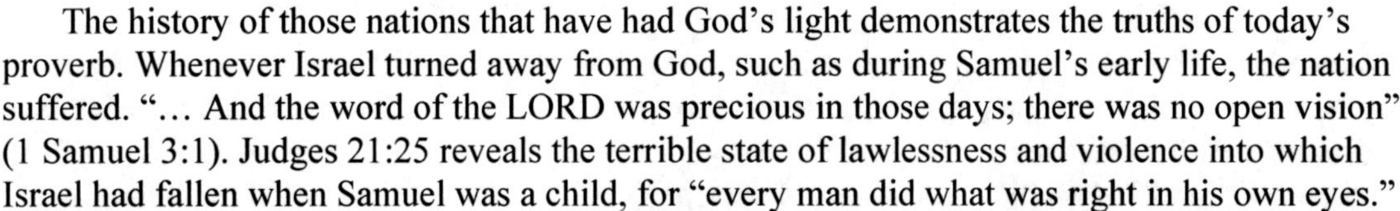

The history of those nations that have had God's light demonstrates the truths of today's proverb. Whenever Israel turned away from God, such as during Samuel's early life, the nation suffered. "… And the word of the LORD was precious in those days; there was no open vision" (1 Samuel 3:1). Judges 21:25 reveals the terrible state of lawlessness and violence into which Israel had fallen when Samuel was a child, for "every man did what was right in his own eyes."

History illustrates that times become very dark when a vision of God's revelation departs. The fall of the Roman Empire in 476 A.D. is generally regarded as ending ancient history and commencing Europe's Dark Ages. The Roman Empire had brought peace, prosperity, culture, and learning to Europe. When it fell, the Romans were followed by illiterate barbarians. Western Europe plunged into political chaos and social disorder. Civilization almost completely disappeared. Illiteracy and ignorance of God's ways governed nobles and peasants alike. Education and literacy were relegated to monasteries. Churchmen preserved the Bible and other books that had been written in Latin before Rome's fall, but records from this period of the "Dark Ages" bear little clarity. The works of the many clerics of this time are inconsistent and show great ignorance because of their acceptance of fanciful stories as truth.

Satan strives to keep people in ignorance, and "in the dark." He has tried many times to destroy Scripture, to prohibit the preaching of the Gospel, and to persecute God's people. When a society turns its back on God and restricts the Gospel, as many nations have done, that nation regresses into violence and immorality. Those opposing the Bible do not realize that they are opposing the very influences that make life pleasant, for God is light and His light brings revelation, which liberates people. The revelation of Biblical truths and the practice of them always produce an orderly and civilized society and affect all aspects of its culture in a positive way.

True Christians strive to obey God's commandments, not as a means of getting to heaven, but because they desire to honor and please God. Heavenly vision and revelation come to those who know Christ. Without this vision, people perish. "Behold, the days come, saith the LORD GOD, that I will send a famine in the land, not a famine of bread, nor a thirst for water, but of hearing the words of the LORD: And they shall wander from sea to sea, and from the north even to the east, they shall run to and fro to seek the word of the LORD, and shall not find it" (Amos 8:11-12).

Dear Father God, thank You for giving us Your revelation and vision. I appreciate the light You give me as I walk through this dark and fallen world. Please fill me with the Holy Spirit so that I will always be overflowing with Your light and love. Draw those in darkness unto that light. Fill my mouth with the right words so that those who do not know You can hear the gospel and come into the knowledge of Your dear Son, Jesus. May I practice good deeds in this life, so that others may see them and thereby bring glory unto You. I ask this in the name of Jesus. Amen.

Proverbs 29:19-21 19 A servant will not be corrected by words: for though he understand he will not answer. 20 Seest thou a man that is hasty in his words? there is more hope of a fool than of him. 21 He that delicately bringeth up his servant from a child shall have him become his son at the length.

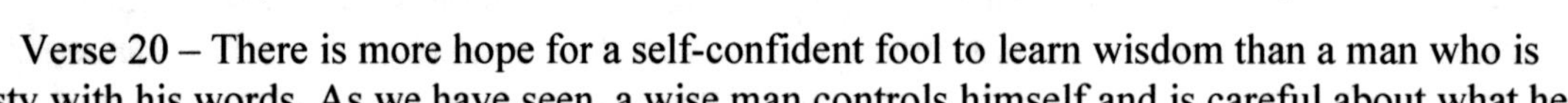

Verse 20 – There is more hope for a self-confident fool to learn wisdom than a man who is hasty with his words. As we have seen, a wise man controls himself and is careful about what he says, because rash words can lead to his ruin.

Verses 19 and 21 – Employees who scorn company rules cannot be corrected by mere words but must be dealt with by disciplinary action. However, before such action, the possibility of a valid grievance should not be ruled out. It is important that employers treat employees fairly. People generally respond to an employer according to their treatment. Negative treatment discourages employees from doing their best. However, just because an employee follows an employer's instructions does not mean that he respects them.

An employee who is treated like part of the employer's family, will eventually expect the privileges of a son. If he is selfish, he will be lazy, expect long vacations, consider himself exempt from company regulations, keep his own hours, and be indignant at a reprimand. On the other hand, if he is a person of good character, he could end up running the company, if the owner has no heir. Ephesians 6:5-9 gives instructions to both employees and employers. Employees are to remember that they are God's servants and work as unto Him. We can determine what kind of employee we are in God's eyes by asking ourselves these questions: "Do I take shortcuts on the job? "Do I cost others time or money by hiding my mistakes? "Do I gossip about my employer when I have a problem with him instead of communicating properly? "Do I steal? "Am I disciplined? "Do I avoid slothful habits such as tardiness? "Do I lie about my qualifications? "Do I quit a job without giving proper notification?"

Employers are instructed to treat their employees in the way that they themselves wish to be treated. They can determine what kind of servants they are in God's eyes by asking themselves these questions: "Do I compensate each of my employees with fair and just wages and benefits? "Do I unfairly terminate employees to save money? "Do I observe and give a Sabbath rest for all employees? "Do I treat all workers fairly? "Am I furnishing good, safe working conditions for my employees? "When correction is necessary, do I correct with kindness and grace?"

These lists are by no means complete, but they will help us examine ourselves to see if we are living a Christian life on the job. Unless people allow Jesus to change their nature, the conditions and morals of workplaces will continue to deteriorate. Christians should be examples in demonstrating good work ethics. It is sad that many behave no better than the world.

Dear Father, thank You so much for instructing us in our business relationships. Lord, may we serve one another in love, regardless of our position. If we are serving our employer, may we be the best employee we can be; realizing that our service to them is also our service to You. If we serve in the capacity of a manager, then may we be one who is just, fair and honest in all of our ways; treating our employees with kindness and respect. Lord, we invite You into our workplaces and businesses. May our work be holy work because You are there. I ask this Jesus' name. Amen.

God's Wisdom for Daily Living ***Betty Miller***
December 5 ***Day 339***

Proverbs 29:22-24 22 An angry man stirreth up strife, and a furious man aboundeth in transgression. 23 A man's pride shall bring him low: but honour shall uphold the humble in spirit. 24 Whoso is partner with a thief hateth his own soul: he heareth cursing, and bewrayeth it not.

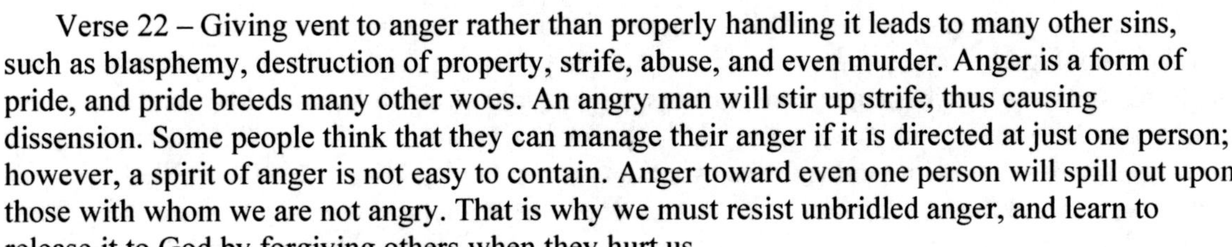

Verse 22 – Giving vent to anger rather than properly handling it leads to many other sins, such as blasphemy, destruction of property, strife, abuse, and even murder. Anger is a form of pride, and pride breeds many other woes. An angry man will stir up strife, thus causing dissension. Some people think that they can manage their anger if it is directed at just one person; however, a spirit of anger is not easy to contain. Anger toward even one person will spill out upon those with whom we are not angry. That is why we must resist unbridled anger, and learn to release it to God by forgiving others when they hurt us.

Verse 23 – Pride is another deadly sin. If we exalt ourselves, we will be brought down from our lofty place. "Pride goeth before destruction, and an haughty spirit before a fall" (Proverbs 16:18). Pride is always denounced in Scripture, while humility is prized. The Lord looks for those having a humble, contrite attitude and who respect His Word. They will receive His blessings and be brought to honor: "...but to this man will I look, even to him that is poor and of a contrite spirit, and trembleth at my word" (Isaiah 66:2b). "The fear of the LORD is the instruction of wisdom; and before honour is humility" (Proverbs 15:33).

Jesus told us the same things: that the way "up" in the kingdom of God is "down." "But he that is greatest among you shall be your servant. And whosoever shall exalt himself shall be abased; and he that shall humble himself shall be exalted" (Matthew 23:11-12). "God resisteth the proud, but giveth grace unto the humble...Humble yourselves in the sight of the Lord, and he shall lift you up" (James 4:6,10).

Verse 24 – A man who partners with a thief is his own worst enemy. He risks his life in every way, for not only may the thief turn on him and kill him, but he is twice cursed: first for participating in a crime, secondly for withholding evidence and (if brought to trial) for lying under oath.

Dear heavenly Father, I come to You, asking that You deliver me from all pride and anger. I truly want to be like Jesus, who was meek and lowly. Father, help me to remain humble and always be willing to assume the place of a servant. May I be sensitive to the needs of others and look for ways to help them. I am reminded in Your Word that we are told to serve one another in love. Fill me with Your love, so that I might love those around me and serve them as You would. I ask this in the name of Jesus. Amen.

Proverbs 29:25-27 25 The fear of man bringeth a snare: but whoso putteth his trust in the LORD shall be safe. 26 Many seek the ruler's favour; but every man's judgment cometh from the LORD. 27 An unjust man is an abomination to the just: and he that is upright in the way is abomination to the wicked.

Verse 25 – The fear of man, and allowing people to intimidate us, brings a snare upon us. Fear is as confining as a trap, preventing us from doing what we ought. We must put our trust in the Lord, and not fear what man might do to us. We must learn to cry out to Him when we are in trouble, for He will keep us safe (Psalm 56:9-11). Those who are *"born again"* will find that the Lord is on their side, and if God is for us, what man can stand against us? God is the final authority, and nothing can separate us from His love. "What shall we then say to these things? If God be for us, who can be against us? He that spared not his own Son, but delivered him up for us all, how shall he not with him also freely give us all things? Who shall lay any thing to the charge of God's elect? It is God that justifieth. Who is he that condemneth? It is Christ that died, yea rather, that is risen again, who is even at the right hand of God, who also maketh intercession for us. Who shall separate us from the love of Christ? shall tribulation, or distress, or persecution, or famine, or nakedness, or peril, or sword? As it is written, For thy sake we are killed all the day long; we are accounted as sheep for the slaughter. Nay, in all these things we are more than conquerors through him that loved us. For I am persuaded, that neither death, nor life, nor angels, nor principalities, nor powers, nor things present, nor things to come, Nor height, nor depth, nor any other creature, shall be able to separate us from the love of God, which is in Christ Jesus our Lord" (Romans 8:31-39).

Verse 26 – Many people seek favor from those in positions of authority, but the wise seek favor from God, knowing that all true judgment comes from Him. God is the Almighty, the highest authority. The hearts of earthly authorities are in His Hand, and He is able to turn them to favor us. "The king's heart is in the hand of the LORD, as the rivers of water: he turneth it whithersoever he will" (Proverbs 21:1). If we trust and wait upon Him, He will not fail us.

Verse 27 –The righteous and wicked are not merely opposed to each other, they are an abomination to each other. The wicked perceive the righteous as abominable, but unrighteous deeds are an abomination to God and the wicked will reap destruction. We must choose to follow God, if we desire life and blessing, as we clearly see from Deuteronomy 30:16-19.

Today's verses conclude the collection of proverbs attributed to Solomon. Solomon's wisdom paled next to that of Jesus. His life shows that even at his wisest, man is still sinful and needs a Savior, and that the fear of the Lord is the beginning of wisdom. Solomon lost that fear, and, in his old, age turned away from God. True wisdom dictates that we must maintain our relationship with God throughout our entire life. Any Christian who reveres God and depends upon Christ in faith, is wiser than Solomon.

Dear heavenly Father, I thank You for the wonderful truth that You are on my side. Lord, deliver me from any trace of the fear of man. Rather, may I always have the fear and respect of God in my heart, above any man. I know You will defend me and take care of me, no matter what I face; therefore, I will not fear what man can do unto me. Thank You that nothing can separate me from Your love. Lord, I choose to walk in Your ways and keep Your commandments. I choose life and blessing for myself and for my children. I declare this in the name of Jesus. Amen.

Proverbs 30:1-4 1 The words of Agur the son of Jakeh, even the prophecy: the man spake unto Ithiel, even unto Ithiel and Ucal, 2 Surely I am more brutish than any man, and have not the understanding of a man. 3 I neither learned wisdom, nor have the knowledge of the holy. 4 Who hath ascended up into heaven, or descended? who hath gathered the wind in his fists? who hath bound the waters in a garment? who hath established all the ends of the earth? what is his name, and what is his son's name, if thou canst tell?

Chapter 30 was not written by Solomon, but by Agur. Solomon, respecting Agur's observations, may have included them in his book, or Hezekiah's scribes might have done so two centuries later. However the words of Agur came to be added to Solomon's proverbs, and we know that they were written and included by the Holy Spirit's inspiration.

Verses 1-3 – Little is known of Agur. This chapter records his words to Ithiel and Ucal, who had evidently come to him to learn wisdom. In response, Agur humbled himself. Rather than boast of being a great man of learning, he confessed his ignorance; knowing that all he had learned of God was nothing compared to what there was to know. His confession brings to mind Elihu's words in the Book of Job. Like Agur, Elihu, was able to correctly assess his own knowledge. These men humbly regarded their own understanding and secular education as nothing, and acknowledged the incomparable greatness of God's wisdom. Elihu knew that neither having great authority nor old age guarantees that a man has good judgment or wisdom, because truth and understanding come from God (Job 32:8-9).

Verse 4 – Agur asks five rhetorical questions that reveal his faith. He describes God as having gathered the wind in His fists, having bound the waters in His garments and having established the ends of the earth. This reveals the wisdom and power of God, the Ruler of all! In Agur's day, the answer to his first and fifth questions was still hidden. The answer to them both, "...What is His Son's name, if you know?" and "Who hath ascended up into heaven, or descended?" is Jesus Christ (1 John 3:13-15). "...When he ascended up on high, he led captivity captive, and gave gifts unto men. (Now that he ascended, what is it but that he also descended first into the lower parts of the earth? He that descended is the same also that ascended up far above all heavens, that he might fill all things)...And no man hath ascended up to heaven, but he that came down from heaven, even the Son of man which is in heaven" (Ephesians 4:8-10,13).

When Jesus died on the cross for the sins of all mankind, He then was in the grave and hell (or *Sheol;* the place of the dead), for three days and three nights, before he ascended to heaven. He took all those who were held captive in paradise with Him to heaven above. (Those Old Testament saints who walked in faith were kept in paradise until Jesus paid the price for their sins on the cross. Paradise was a compartment in the lower regions of hell. "He seeing this before spake of the resurrection of Christ, that his soul was not left in hell, neither his flesh did see corruption. This Jesus hath God raised up, whereof we all are witnesses. Therefore being by the right hand of God exalted, and having received of the Father the promise of the Holy Ghost, he hath shed forth this, which ye now see and hear" (Acts 2:31-33). Jesus "led captivity captive," which was to lead them out of that place into heaven with Him, after He rose from the dead.) Jesus' death, burial and resurrection made a way for all since then who repent and believe in Christ to follow Him to heaven also.

Agur's questions, written hundreds of years before Christ, foreshadowed this fuller revelation of God. They were indeed prophetic questions!

Dear Father, we worship You as the Almighty God, Maker of heaven and earth! May we, as Your children, always keep an attitude of being meek and lowly before Your throne. If we have any wisdom and understanding, it is because You have enlightened us. Thank You for Your gift of Jesus, so that we do not have to go to hell and can have our home in heaven with You. I am eternally grateful for Your love and sacrifice. It makes me ask, as David did, "What is man, that thou art mindful of him? and the son of man, that thou visitest him?" I thank You for crowning us with glory and honor because of Jesus. Amen.

Quotes About Sin

One person's sin will not remain an island to himself, but will eventually infect others–even the innocent. --Day 14

Sin–like righteousness–is progressive. Daily, we become either more wicked by serving sin, or more like the Lord by serving Him. --Day 34

The tiniest trace of sin is more deadly than a single cancer cell, which multiplies and devours a person's life. --Day 97

Those who make pleasure their god, become addicts to pleasure. They become enslaved to the thing that initially gave them happiness. --Day 207

This is the nature of sin; the more one indulges in it, the more one wants it, until he is finally destroyed. --Day 243

Quotes About the Character of God

God is a generous and loving Father who desires to bless His people. He wants us to have the same generous heart that He does. --Day 50

God does not bring evil upon us; we bring it upon ourselves through our own sin and waywardness. By moving out of God's will, we move into the enemy's territory and make ourselves vulnerable to him. --Day 68

Throughout the Gospel accounts, we find that Jesus never called for illness or evil to come upon anyone. He always freed people from the devil's oppressions and healed the sick, refusing no one who came to Him for healing or deliverance. --Day 78

Proverbs 30:5-6 5 Every word of God is pure: he is a shield unto them that put their trust in him. 6 Add thou not unto his words, lest he reprove thee, and thou be found a liar.

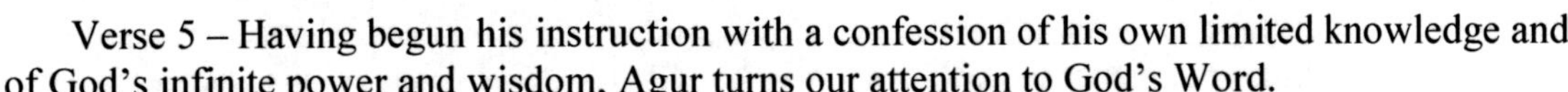

Verse 5 – Having begun his instruction with a confession of his own limited knowledge and of God's infinite power and wisdom, Agur turns our attention to God's Word.

The Bible tells us that all Scripture came by the inspiration of God and it is the guide by which we are to live. His Word is pure, and we can confidently trust it. Many Christians quote famous men's sayings, but could gain more by quoting the Word of God. If we do not study the Bible (2 Timothy 2:15), we will end up learning God's ways the hard way, through the pain of trial and error. However, if we apply God's Word to our lives, He will be a shield for us. We can always trust God: "God is not a man, that he should lie; neither the son of man, that he should repent: hath he said, and shall he not do it? or hath he spoken, and shall he not make it good?" (Numbers 23:19).

Verse 6 – Having made his pupils aware of the value of knowing God's Word, Agur warned them not to add anything to it. The Holy Spirit also spoke a similar warning through Moses: "What thing soever I command you, observe to do it: thou shalt not add thereto, nor diminish from it" (Deuteronomy 12:32). God's Word is extremely important to Him, and He gives a stern warning not to tamper with it. Through the Apostle John, the Holy Spirit warned us again: "For I testify unto every man that heareth the words of the prophecy of this book, If any man shall add unto these things, God shall add unto him the plagues that are written in this book: And if any man shall take away from the words of the book of this prophecy, God shall take away his part out of the book of life, and out of the holy city, and from the things which are written in this book" (Revelation 22:18-19).

We must be careful neither to add to God's Word, nor to seek wisdom beyond what He has revealed. We also should not focus just on certain parts of Scripture and ignore other parts, but read and study the entire Bible.

Dear heavenly Father, thank You for giving us the Holy Bible. Please give me a desire to study Your Word. Cleanse me from all error and renew my mind. I desire to know the truth, even if it means correction and admitting that I have been wrong. Change my thoughts and heart to be like Your thoughts and heart. Father, give me a teachable spirit. Take my desires, dreams and visions and give me Yours. Cleanse me from all that offends You. Create within me a clean heart, O Lord. I ask this in the name of Jesus. Amen.

Proverbs 30:7-9 7 Two things have I asked of You (O LORD): deny them not to me before I die: 8 Remove far from me falsehood and lies; give me neither poverty nor riches; feed me with the food that is needful for me. 9 Lest I be full and deny You and say, Who is the LORD? Or lest I be poor and steal, and so profane the name of my God (AMP).

We have already seen that Agur began teaching Ithiel and Ucal by confessing his own limitations, by rhetorical questions, and by statements of faith. He next instructed them by praying. The cry of Agur's heart demonstrates the kind of prayer that pleases God. Desiring a pure heart, he asked God to remove from him all falsehood and lies. Falsehood includes conformity to anything that is not true, such as false beliefs, ideas, or suppositions. "Behold, thou desirest truth in the inward parts: and in the hidden part thou shalt make me to know wisdom" (Psalm 51:6). His prayer revealed the importance of desiring to know and conform to the truth that one might not sin against God.

Next, Agur asked God to supply his needs in such a way as would make him neither rich nor poor. His prayer taught his disciples to ask for their needful bread, much as Jesus taught His disciples to ask for their daily bread. It taught them that certain temptations come with both wealth and poverty, and to ask not to be led into those temptations that they might avoid sin and honor God. Being full, whether of food or pleasures, can easily cause one to forget God, and become distracted with pleasure and things. It also causes men to trust and find their security in money instead of God. The greatest danger in poverty is desperation. Poverty hangs over people like a black cloud, causing fear, self-pity, discouragement, hopelessness, and depression. The desperate are tempted to resort to such things as stealing, gambling, lying, peddling drugs, or prostitution to survive.

Agur saw the ways in which both poverty and riches tempt one to turn from God. The Apostle Paul found that through the Spirit he could overcome those temptations; that he could do all things through Christ and be content, whether enduring need for the sake of the Gospel, or enjoying abundance. "Not that I speak in respect of want: for I have learned, in whatsoever state I am, therewith to be content. I know both how to be abased, and I know how to abound: every where and in all things I am instructed both to be full and to be hungry, both to abound and to suffer need. I can do all things through Christ which strengtheneth me (Philippians 4:11-13). He learned to rely on God to meet his every need. God desires that we also learn to trust Him in all things. "Therefore take no thought, saying, What shall we eat? or, What shall we drink? or, Wherewithal shall we be clothed? (For after all these things do the Gentiles seek:) for your heavenly Father knoweth that ye have need of all these things. But seek ye first the kingdom of God, and his righteousness; and all these things shall be added unto you" (Matthew 6:31-33).

Dear heavenly Father, thank You for Your promise of provision for our needs. Deliver me from any worry about what I shall eat or wear, for I know You will take care of me. Please give me the grace and faith I need, so that I can better trust You to meet all of my needs. Forgive me when I have been wasteful or careless, and help me to be a good steward over all that You have entrusted to me. Lord, may I be as the Apostle Paul who was content with a little or a lot. I lean on Your strength to overcome all situations I face, and I am confident that I shall have the victory in Christ's name. Amen.

Proverbs 30:10 Accuse not a servant unto his master, lest he curse thee, and thou be found guilty.

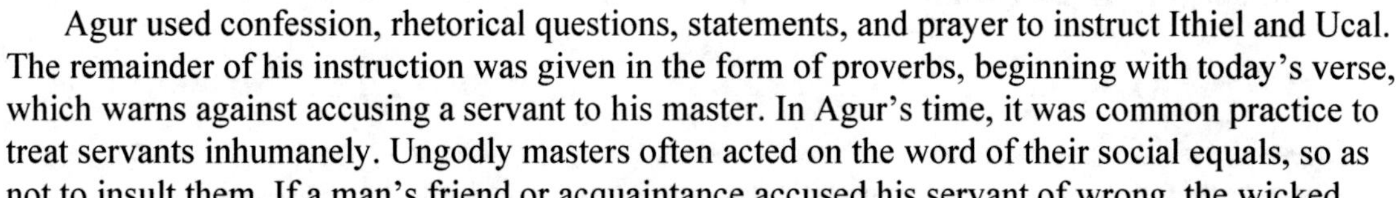

Agur used confession, rhetorical questions, statements, and prayer to instruct Ithiel and Ucal. The remainder of his instruction was given in the form of proverbs, beginning with today's verse, which warns against accusing a servant to his master. In Agur's time, it was common practice to treat servants inhumanely. Ungodly masters often acted on the word of their social equals, so as not to insult them. If a man's friend or acquaintance accused his servant of wrong, the wicked master often had his servant beaten or even executed. Servants had no rights, even when innocent. Even light punishment brought great hardship.

Agur understood that God upholds justice for all of His people, whatever their position, and holds all accountable that needlessly stir up trouble, especially out of pride or spite. It is never good to speak ill of those in lowly positions to their employers or supervisors. Many such people are struggling to make a living. Undue criticism might deprive them of desperately needed jobs or raises. It is wicked to cause others needless suffering because of our own our pride, or because we are impatient or in a bad mood.

Christian employers should protect trusted workers from abuse and never accept unproven accusations against them. Customers often become unnecessarily impatient regarding service or disgruntled about merchandise. Instead of discussing a problem civilly, some customers berate the employee who is trying to help them, then demand to speak to a supervisor to accuse the employee of wrongdoing. In many cases, the supervisor finds his employee is not at fault, but that the customer is guilty of a bad attitude.

God is the creator of all mankind: each life is important to Him, and He is no respecter of men. He looks on peoples' hearts, not their outward appearance or accomplishments. All who are born into God's family through Christ become brothers and sisters in Him. We are to honor each other, as well as all others; regardless of their class, race, position, age, or sex. "Be kindly affectioned one to another with brotherly love; in honour preferring one another" (Romans 12:10). We are to especially honor elders at church and widows (1 Timothy 5:1-3,17); our employers and supervisors (or masters: 1 Timothy 6:1-2); our parents (Matthew 19:19), and people in authority (Romans 13:1-7). Above all, we must honor God Himself. One way in which we honor Him is by obeying His Word. "Now unto the King eternal, immortal, invisible, the only wise God, be honour and glory for ever and ever. Amen" (1 Timothy 1:17).

Dear Father God, I thank You for all the things You have done for me; but I honor You for Who You are–my Lord and King. May I always show respect for the whole family of God, as I know that is one way I can honor You. Help me to be sensitive and respectful to all people, no matter what position they hold. Lord, deliver Your people from all prejudice and disrespect for one another. May we obey Your Word that tells us to prefer and honor one another as brothers and sisters in the Lord. May we also be especially kind toward those who are in occupations in the service sector, and may we all serve one another in love. I ask this in the name of Jesus. Amen.

Proverbs 30:11-14 11 There is a generation that curseth their father, and doth not bless their mother. 12 There is a generation that are pure in their own eyes, and yet is not washed from their filthiness. 13 There is a generation, O how lofty are their eyes! and their eyelids are lifted up. 14 There is a generation, whose teeth are as swords, and their jaw teeth as knives, to devour the poor from off the earth, and the needy from among men.

These verses describe a generation so wicked that they curse their own parents; and so prideful that they do not see their own wickedness.

Verses 11-14 – Verse 1 describes Agur's words as prophecy. I believe it may not only have spoken of an evil generation in Agur's time, but also point to the generation that will exist before the second coming of the Lord Jesus. The Apostle Paul also describes this generation in 2 Timothy 3:1-5: "This know also, that in the last days perilous times shall come. For men shall be lovers of their own selves, covetous, boasters, proud, blasphemers, disobedient to parents, unthankful, unholy, Without natural affection, trucebreakers, false accusers, incontinent, fierce, despisers of those that are good, Traitors, heady, highminded, lovers of pleasures more than lovers of God; Having a form of godliness, but denying the power thereof: from such turn away."

Agur's words describe a generation that curses their parents; Paul states that in the last days people will be disobedient to their parents. Agur describes a generation that is prideful and sinless in their own eyes; Paul speaks of a people being haughty and having only a form of godliness. Agur speaks about a generation that takes advantage of the poor, while James 5:1-5 speaks of men who heap up riches for the last days at the expense of those who labor for them, by paying them inadequate wages.

"Wherefore as the Holy Ghost saith, To day if ye will hear his voice, Harden not your hearts, as in the provocation, in the day of temptation in the wilderness: When your fathers tempted me, proved me, and saw my works forty years. Wherefore I was grieved with that generation, and said, They do alway err in their heart; and they have not known my ways. So I sware in my wrath, They shall not enter into my rest" (Hebrews 3:7-11).

Dear heavenly Father, thank You for Your many blessings. May all of Your people be mindful of honoring and blessing their parents. I pray that You will use me to reach out to the poor and needy. Scatter this wicked generation of people who are exploiting the poor and needy. Send Your servants out to minister to the poor, the hungry, the needy, the hurting, the sick, and the lost. As You use each of us to do our part, we can be the answer to the cries of the needy, helping to meet their needs. I ask in Jesus' name. Amen.

Proverbs 30:15-16 15 The horse leach hath two daughters, crying, Give, give. There are three things that are never satisfied, yea, four things say not, It is enough: 16 The grave; and the barren womb; the earth that is not filled with water; and the fire that saith not, It is enough.

To introduce four things that are never satisfied, Agur described the leech; a blood-sucking worm. It feeds through two suckers, one at each end of its body, thus the depiction of "two daughters" clamoring for blood. Horse leeches live in well water and spring water. As animals and humans drink, tiny leeches enter their mouths and attach themselves inside the throat or similar places. Feeding on their host's blood, they grow rapidly and can cause bleeding, obstruction, and even death. The leech presents a vivid picture of human parasites. They enrich themselves by draining others, and giving nothing but trouble in return. Like the leech, the following four things are never satisfied:

The Grave or Sheol: It takes countless souls every day but is never full. "Therefore hell hath enlarged herself, and opened her mouth without measure: and their glory, and their multitude, and their pomp, and he that rejoiceth, shall descend into it" (Isaiah 5:14).

The Barren Womb: The affects of sin upon humanity rob some women of the ability to conceive. It is heartbreaking for a woman yearning to have a child to be unable to conceive. She is never satisfied and tries every method possible to become pregnant. God's promise and power can break the curse of a barren womb (Deuteronomy 7:13). Whoever follows Christ has God's blessing, including the ability to conceive. My husband and I have seen many women able to become pregnant after being prayed for.

The Earth: It is never satisfied with water. No matter how much rain falls, the earth will become dry and need more. Drought is a curse. Israel was warned that if they turned from the living God to idols, the earth would suffer for it. (Deuteronomy 11:13-17).

Fire: Its very life depends upon consuming everything that it touches. It is devastating to view the aftermath of a fire. At the time of this writing, Arizona has endured its worst drought in over a hundred years, and many fires have ravaged the land. When driving by these areas it is sad to see mile after mile of charred timber that had once been a green forest. It is far sadder, however, to see people's lives ravaged and destroyed by sin. Like fire, sin is never satisfied, but consumes more and more of a person's soul and life.

God has promised to provide for all our needs. He entreats us to trust in Him. "Let your character or moral disposition be free from love of money [including greed, avarice, lust, and craving for earthly possessions] and be satisfied with your present circumstances and with what you have; for He [God] Himself has said, I will not in any way fail you nor give you up nor leave you without support. [I will] not, [I will] not, [I will] not in any degree leave you helpless nor forsake nor let [you] down (relax My hold on you)! [Assuredly not!]" (Hebrews 13:5 AMP).

Dear heavenly Father, praise be to Your Name for delivering us from the curses of the enemy! Thank You for Your many blessings. Lord, set us free from all discontent. Today, may I find my peace and contentment in You. Thank You for protecting our property from fire and sending us rain in due season. I am grateful for the refreshing rains that You send and I know the animals, trees, grasses and the earth are happy, too. We thank You for Your many blessings and pray in the name of Jesus. Amen.

God's Wisdom for Daily Living — *Betty Miller*
December 13 — *Day 347*

Proverbs 30:17 The eye that mocks a father and scorns to obey a mother, the ravens of the valley will pick it out, and the young vultures will devour it (AMP).

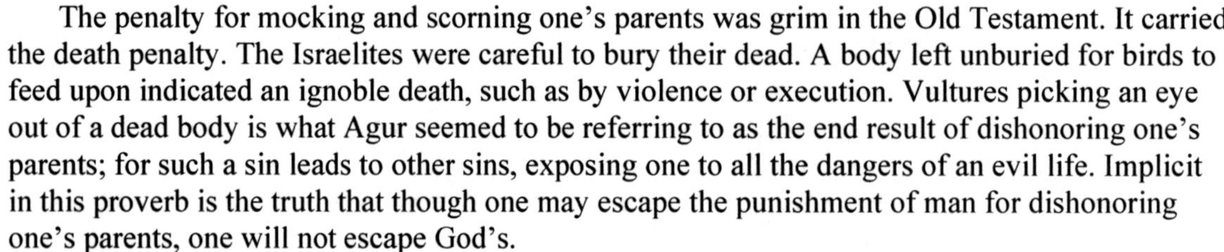

The penalty for mocking and scorning one's parents was grim in the Old Testament. It carried the death penalty. The Israelites were careful to bury their dead. A body left unburied for birds to feed upon indicated an ignoble death, such as by violence or execution. Vultures picking an eye out of a dead body is what Agur seemed to be referring to as the end result of dishonoring one's parents; for such a sin leads to other sins, exposing one to all the dangers of an evil life. Implicit in this proverb is the truth that though one may escape the punishment of man for dishonoring one's parents, one will not escape God's.

The Bible stresses that children are to respect their parents. It is so important to God, that He made it one of the Ten Commandments: "Honour thy father and thy mother: that thy days may be long upon the land which the LORD thy God giveth thee" (Exodus 20:12).

God gave other laws that charged Israel to deal very strongly with rebellious children in the Old Testament. The penalty for striking or cursing one's parents had the same penalty as for adultery or murder; the guilty party was to be stoned to death. "And he that smiteth his father, or his mother, shall be surely put to death. ……And he that curseth his father, or his mother, shall surely be put to death" (Exodus 21:15,17). It was a serious offense before God. The word for "curseth" in Hebrew is *"qâlal,"* meaning "to bring into contempt, curse, despise." [39] Belittling or mocking one's parents is a serious offence to God. Even if there is nothing about them that commands respect, we must refrain from speaking reviling words against them. Children with unholy parents should pray for them and ask God to change them. This is especially important for young people to understand. We are to bless our parents and speak respectfully to them and of them. Praise God, that under the New Testament law, children can find mercy and forgiveness if they have been rebellious to their parents. Spiritually dishonoring parents can result in spiritual blindness and even spiritual death unless rebellious children repent.

The Old Testament law often sounds extreme to our modern ears because our culture is so lenient about rebellion and even glamorizes it. It would help society to better enforce punishment for crimes that are directed against those in positions of authority. These punishments would be an example to cause those bent on evil to fear and respect the laws. It would work for everyone's good, especially the young. Those who honor their parents and elders seldom come to the evil end that Agur depicted.

Dear Lord, I honor You as my heavenly Father and gladly submit unto You, trusting You in all things. Please remove any trace of rebellion from my heart. I also honor my natural parents and my spiritual parents. I desire to always be respectful to the church elders and authorities that You have designated in the earth. Deliver me from any anger against those in authority; if I have been wronged by any of them, I am trusting that You will deal with them in the proper fashion. I want to have a heart that is submissive and trusting and free from all rebellion. I humbly ask this in the name of Jesus. Amen.

---

[39] Strong's Exhaustive Concordance of the Bible, Hebrew and Chaldee Dictionary

Proverbs 30:18-20 18 There be three things which are too wonderful for me, yea, four which I know not: 19 The way of an eagle in the air; the way of a serpent upon a rock; the way of a ship in the midst of the sea; and the way of a man with a maid.

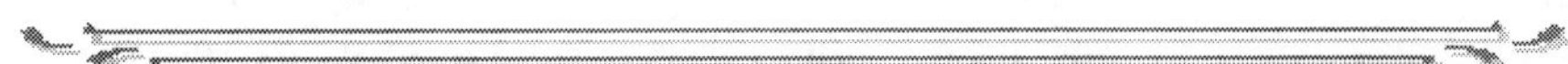

Verses 18-20 – These verses state that there are four things which are very wonderful, and yet mysterious: how an eagle flies; how a serpent slithers; how a ship sails; and how a man and woman are attracted to one another. Solomon respected these observations by Agur and included them in his own book. We all wonder at times why things are the way they are. The only and final answer is that God created them to act this way. God's creation is truly amazing and we can learn many things by observing it.

Verse 19 - *The Eagle*: This bird mounts up on thermal air currents to soar at amazing heights. It must have puzzled the ancients to watch them ascend, barely flapping their wings. They are not afraid of storms, which create the best wind currents–they fly high above them. The eagle is a symbol of overcoming Christians who rise above life's storms by waiting upon the Lord. "But they that wait upon the LORD shall renew their strength; they shall mount up with wings as eagles..." (Isaiah 40:31a). This is one of my favorite verses. I have claimed it many times, when I have been so weary that I did not think I could not go on. The Lord has never failed to give me the strength that I have needed, when I ask Him in faith to help me. This scripture states that those who "wait upon the Lord" shall renew their strength. What does it mean to "wait upon the Lord?" Certainly, the first application of this would be to wait upon the Lord's timing, and to wait for Him to show us what to do; however, there is also another application to the meaning. When we dine in a restaurant, a "waiter" comes to our table to serve us or "wait on us." When we are committed to serving God, then we are "waiting on Him;" therefore, we will be given the strength for the task He has given us to do. Even young men who do not know the Lord, will not have the strength that we are given, when we obey Christ's commands.

The Serpent: A snake's bones, muscles, and plates on the skin of its belly enable it to move on land without limbs. From Genesis 3 we find that the serpent did not always slither, but was originally created to walk as a beast. After its part in tempting Adam and Eve to sin, God reduced it to crawling on its belly, eating dust (Genesis 3:14-15). The devil, called "the serpent," preys on men who were made of dust and crawl in the dirt of sin until they are "born again" and then the Lord causes them to rise up spiritually and fly like eagles.

A Sailing Ship: The third thing that Agur mentions that amazed him is how a ship can sail in the ocean. There are physical laws that God set in motion in the earth that govern all things. These are verifiable scientific laws. In the case of a ship floating in the ocean, the laws that affect it are: the law of gravity; the law of motion; the laws of nature; and the laws of the universe. Just looking at the size and weight of a boat (especially when we see warships constructed from mega tons of steel) floating in a liquid like water, it looks impossible. However, when one understands the invisible laws that govern such a feat, then it becomes possible. In the Bible, we are asked to believe in spiritual things and things we cannot see; yet, we know they are real, because we understand the law of faith and the law of life in Christ Jesus (Matthew 19:26).

A Man With A Maid: The fourth thing that was "too wonderful" for Agur was "the way of a man with a maid." The way a man and woman are attracted to one another and "fall in love" is a very wonderful gift that God gave to men and women. Erotic and sexual love was designed by God, but it has limits and boundaries attached to it. It is to only be entered into within the bonds of matrimony. The devil has come against this husband and wife relationship by perverting it and causing men to indulge in it illegally. We find adulterers, fornicators, and homosexuals, (where men are sexually attracted to men, and women to women.) God is the one who set the standard for a marriage relationship and when men start trying to redefine marriage, they are setting themselves up to take the place of God, which is idolatry. The beautiful relationship, of love and marriage, between a man and a woman, is a type of our relationship with Christ; and that is a very holy thing (Ephesians 5:23-27).

Dear heavenly Father, You are amazing and wonderful! I stand in awe of Your creation. Your plans for mankind were good and perfect, and we have messed it up because of our sins. Forgive us, Lord, and help us to restore and correct those things the devil has used to destroy Your beautiful creation. Give us grace to pray and reach out to those around us with the gospel of Jesus Christ. Change us to be like You, and use us to change this world and bring about the kingdom of God in the earth. I ask in the name of Jesus. Amen.

Quotes About Disciplining Children

Many parents think that taking their children to Sunday school is sufficient for their Christian training, but Sunday school should be only a supplement to teaching them at home. --Day 28

To fail to discipline a child is actually cruel. It is like failing to clean a child's cut finger simply because cleaning the cut hurts the child. --Day 175

Many times, undisciplined children simply reflect undisciplined parents. --Day 189

A child without discipline feels insecure. Failing to maintain boundaries greatly harms children, exposing them to physical danger and causing them to lose respect for authority. --Day 222

Many parents teach their children right from wrong, but fail to train them to obey. They threaten, but because they never follow through with punishment, their children have their own way. --Day 235

Children reflect their upbringing. They learn from how we live, not merely from what we tell them. We cannot guide them in God's ways, if we do not walk in them ourselves. --Day 236

Proverbs 30:20-23 20 Such is the way of an adulterous woman; she eateth, and wipeth her mouth, and saith, I have done no wickedness.21 For three things the earth is disquieted, and for four which it cannot bear: 22 For a servant when he reigneth; and a fool when he is filled with meat; 23 For an odious woman when she is married; and an handmaid that is heir to her mistress.

Verses 20-23 – These verses describe an array of people who are types of rebellious sinners that cause trouble for others.

An Adulterous Woman: This woman simply does what she does, in the same way a person would eat a meal and wipe his mouth after they finish. She is so hardened, she feels no guilt and claims she has done no wrong. The Bible tells us that we are all sinners in need of a Savior, and that we must confess our sins and ask God to forgive us; only then can we be cleansed (1 John 1:8-10).

A Servant When He Reigns: People suffer when a servant who is not trained for the office of a king obtains that position.

A Rebellious Fool When He Is Prosperous: The Hebrew word for "fool" in this verse indicates a vile, ungodly person who rejects God's Word. Only the rich in ancient times had an abundance of food; thus "filled with meat" indicates prosperity. An ungodly person uses position and money selfishly and often for evil purposes. Nabal, (1 Samuel 25:2-38) and modern-day mobsters are examples of this kind of fool.

An Odious Woman who Marries: A bitter woman of hateful characteristics can cause much trouble and make life unpleasant for her family and others. Marriage tends to give a woman a degree of authority and respectability, increasing the pride of a woman with bad character. The Bible instructs women not to become busybodies. "And withal they learn to be idle, wandering about from house to house; and not only idle, but tattlers also and busybodies, speaking things which they ought not. I will therefore that the younger women marry, bear children, guide the house, give none occasion to the adversary to speak reproachfully. For some are already turned aside after Satan" (1 Timothy 5:13-15).

A Servant who Is Heir To Her Mistress: There have been instances throughout history of maids persuading mistresses to make them heirs of their possessions, or servant girls who displace mistresses in the affections of their husbands. When servile, mean-spirited people come into a position of power, however slight, they are prone to become proud and use whatever advantage they can to promote themselves.

Each situation is bad enough in itself, but if all of these were true in the life of one person, it would be unbearable. If the servant who reigned was a bitter, adulterous woman, who was also a prosperous rebel and had gained her position by displacing her mistress, this would be an unbearable combination. God calls us to be holy, whatever our position or status (1 Peter 3:3-5).

Dear Father, thank You for liberating women to be what You have called them to be. May we, as women, please You first, and then please our husbands. May we have a submissive spirit toward our mates and seek to serve and minister to them as You would. Purify my heart and create a right spirit in me. May Christian marriages be an example of Your love in this earth. Deliver us from all quarrelling, bitterness and anger and give us a meek and quiet spirit, which is of great price in Your sight. I ask in Jesus' name. Amen.

Proverbs 30:24-28 24 There be four things which are little upon the earth, but they are exceeding wise: 25 The ants are a people not strong, yet they prepare their meat in the summer; 26 The conies are but a feeble folk, yet make they their houses in the rocks; 27 The locusts have no king, yet go they forth all of them by bands; 28 The spider taketh hold with her hands, and is in kings' palaces.

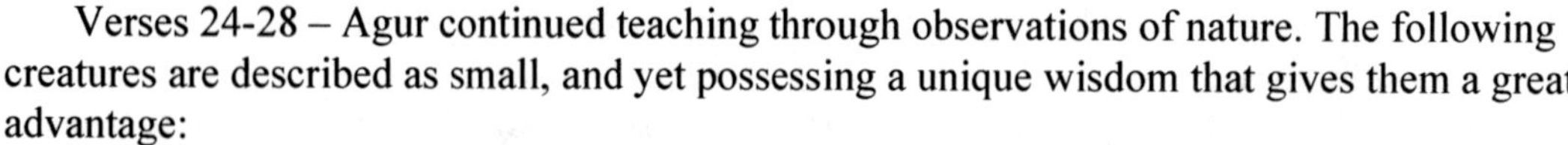

Verses 24-28 – Agur continued teaching through observations of nature. The following creatures are described as small, and yet possessing a unique wisdom that gives them a great advantage:

The Ant: This tiny creature is applauded for its industry. During summer, it stores food for the long winter months. We all face difficult times when we need a reserve of money to fall back on. Today we call it "saving for a rainy day." Saving prudently is not the same as hoarding. Hoarding has a fear and greed element, while preparing for the future is wise. By God's direction, Joseph stored up grain in Egypt during seven years of bounty in order to feed Egypt and other nations during seven years of famine (Genesis 41).

The Coney: Although scholars are uncertain which animal is meant by the Hebrew for *coney*, we may assume that it was a small rabbit-like and vulnerable animal. However, it achieved safety because it made its home in rocky fortresses. Larger animals could not navigate in the rocks as well as open ground; nor could they uncover its rocky home. We can learn from this animal by making our homes secure before we purchase other things. Many people take secondary loans against their houses instead of paying off the mortgage. This is unwise, as a mortgage–free house provides security in difficult times.

The Locust: Locusts are considered to be wise also. Although they have no king or ruler, they join together in organized ranks when they attack an area. They can fly for miles, often all day, landing in the evening to form "camps." As they advance, they strip the land of every growing thing. Christians could well learn from this. If we banded together on major issues that are coming against our Christian principles and rights, we could ravage the enemy, even as the locusts ravage a field when they attack. Each one devours the foliage directly around them, and as they all go forward, soon there is nothing left in the field. If every Christian attacked the field of evil in their area, we could win the entire battle that the devil has assailed against us.

The Spider: Not even a king can keep spiders out of his palace. It is able to climb quickly to high places or find hidden low places, wisely avoiding open areas. Like the spider, we would be wise to be discreet in our affairs. Careless boasting and parading ourselves, invites a fall. King Hezekiah was rebuked by the prophet Isaiah for displaying his treasures to the envoys of Babylon. Those same treasures were carried off 250 years later by the very nation to whom he displayed them (2 Kings 20:12-17).

Wisdom compensates for the smallest creatures, giving them protection and great power. I believe this list of creatures is included in Proverbs so that we can learn to be as resourceful as they are in many practical areas of life.

Dear Father in heaven, thank You for the wonderful teachings You have given us in the Bible. Help us to apply these analogies to our personal lives. We can learn a lot just by observing Your magnificent creation. Thank You for pointing out the examples of wisdom found in Your tiny creatures. Teach us Your wisdom in our daily affairs, so that we learn how to prevent problems in our lives. Lord, may we walk in love in all of our affairs, as that is one of the wisest things we can do. We ask in the name of the Lord Jesus. Amen.

Quotes About Spiritual Warfare

Warfare begins on a personal level as we learn to reign in our own lives; crucifying our old natures and yielding to Christ. Unless we're victorious in our personal lives, we'll never be able to help others gain their victories, much less be able to battle spiritually for our cities and nation. --Day 210

We must remember that our real enemy is the devil, not people. If we will pray for the people involved and resist the devil, he will flee. --Day 219

To "resist the devil" means to refuse to cooperate with him. --Day 249

Quotes About Self-Control

Many find themselves on the wrong path simply because they do not stay away from places that lead them into temptation. --Day 31

Learning to control what we say is the first step in gaining godly wisdom. --Day 136

Because a fool refuses to learn discipline, he is unprepared to handle money when he inherits it. He mismanages it by carelessly indulging every whim. --Day 171

Many Christians die prematurely because they over–indulge with food. The Bible teaches self–control in all things, the lack of which can cost one's health or life. --Day 238

Proverbs 30:29-31 29 There be three things which go well, yea, four are comely in going: 30 A lion which is strongest among beasts, and turneth not away for any; 31 A greyhound; an he goat also; and a king, against whom there is no rising up.

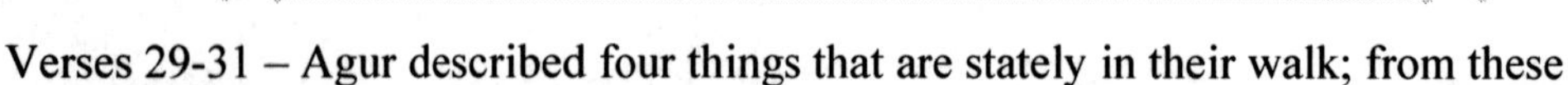

Verses 29-31 – Agur described four things that are stately in their walk; from these observations we can gain spiritual truths.

The Lion: The lion is called the "king of the beasts," but it is not strength alone that causes it to stride in majestic confidence. He is fearless, turning away from no beast. We too, can be strong and unafraid if we walk with God, and claim His strength and His confidence. "Finally, my brethren, be strong in the Lord, and in the power of his might. Put on the whole armour of God, that ye may be able to stand against the wiles of the devil" (Ephesians 6:10-11). We are to be strong in the Lord and the power of *His* might, not our own. When we put on our spiritual armor, the enemy's fiery darts cannot harm us. We must not fear what man can do, for God is greater than any man (Psalm 56:11). If we pray for the people the devil is using against us, and take authority over those powers in the name of Jesus, then the devil will have to cease his attacks against them and us. We are not to fear what man can do to us, as God is greater than any man.

The Greyhound: Graceful in its walk, the greyhound can out-run pursuer or prey. It is needful to be swift about some things in life, while slow about others. We ought to be swift to repent, swift to forgive, swift to obey God's voice, swift to do good. Scripture tells us to be swift to hear, but slow to speak and slow to become angry (James 1:19-20). Someone has said that God gave us two ears and only one mouth, so we should listen twice as much as we speak.

The He-Goat: The mountain goat majestically climbs high into the mountains and leaps upon their steep, rocky slopes. Confident and unafraid of falling, goats are uncannily surefooted. There are many mountains to conquer in life. We can become surefooted and confident in our walk of faith by applying Biblical truths to our lives. Then we will not fear the mountains of difficulties which we must overcome. We can trust the Lord to give us spiritual hinds' feet, for deer are sure-footed like the goats. "He maketh my feet like hinds' feet, and setteth me upon my high places. He teacheth my hands to war, so that a bow of steel is broken by mine arms" (Psalm 18:33-34).

A King: The last example talks about a king who has a kingdom at peace. It is quite a picture to see a military processional parade down a street for review. The king, dressed in his finest, rides on the lead horse who is girded up for the occasion. Backed by his finest men, he rides forth in great confidence, since their are no uprisings against him that he must deal with at the present time. He is stately in appearance, as the other animals mentioned in these verses are. We can also be as this rider, when we allow the Holy Spirit to work His confidence and demeanor in us. We can have confidence in Him when we pray, knowing that if we ask anything of Him that is His will for us, we will receive it (1 John 5:14-15).

Dear heavenly Father, give us the confidence we need in order to overcome the things we face in our daily lives. Deliver us from fear so that we will not allow the pressure of the world to cause us to compromise in any way. May we always trust and have confidence in You, knowing that You will never leave us, nor fail us. Let us walk with our heads high when it comes to being a witness for You. We will gladly bear any reproach that comes because we are a Christian. We are honored to share Your name and ask that we can always walk stately and unafraid in the face of our enemies. In Your name I pray. Amen.

God's Wisdom for Daily Living — ***Betty Miller***
December 18 — ***Day 352***

Proverbs 30:32-33 32 If thou hast done foolishly in lifting up thyself, or if thou hast thought evil, lay thine hand upon thy mouth. 33 Surely the churning of milk bringeth forth butter, and the wringing of the nose bringeth forth blood: so the forcing of wrath bringeth forth strife.

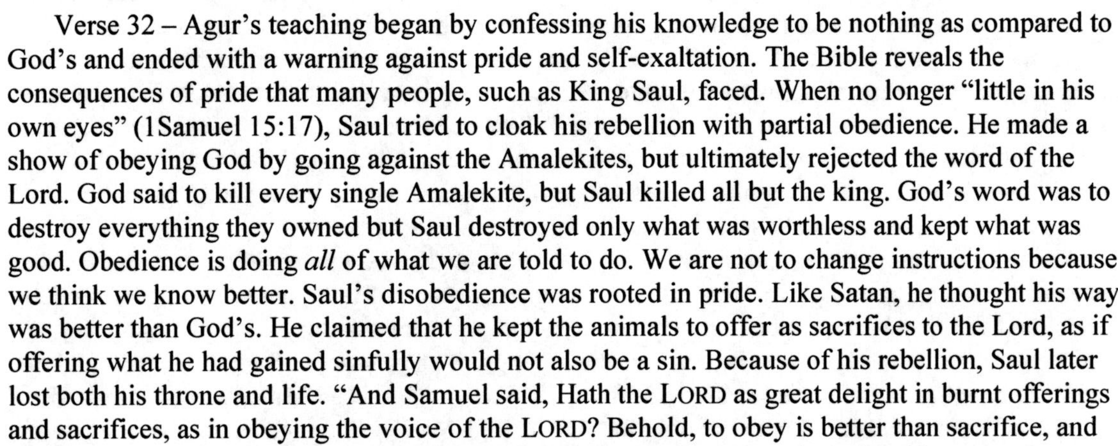

Verse 32 – Agur's teaching began by confessing his knowledge to be nothing as compared to God's and ended with a warning against pride and self-exaltation. The Bible reveals the consequences of pride that many people, such as King Saul, faced. When no longer "little in his own eyes" (1Samuel 15:17), Saul tried to cloak his rebellion with partial obedience. He made a show of obeying God by going against the Amalekites, but ultimately rejected the word of the Lord. God said to kill every single Amalekite, but Saul killed all but the king. God's word was to destroy everything they owned but Saul destroyed only what was worthless and kept what was good. Obedience is doing *all* of what we are told to do. We are not to change instructions because we think we know better. Saul's disobedience was rooted in pride. Like Satan, he thought his way was better than God's. He claimed that he kept the animals to offer as sacrifices to the Lord, as if offering what he had gained sinfully would not also be a sin. Because of his rebellion, Saul later lost both his throne and life. "And Samuel said, Hath the LORD as great delight in burnt offerings and sacrifices, as in obeying the voice of the LORD? Behold, to obey is better than sacrifice, and to hearken than the fat of rams. For rebellion is as the sin of witchcraft, and stubbornness is as iniquity and idolatry. Because thou hast rejected the word of the LORD, he hath also rejected thee from being king" (1 Samuel 15:22-23).

Verse 33 - Agur compared forcing anger to the churning of milk or violently twisting someone's nose. As surely as the one produces butter and the other produces blood; someone who forces an issue will stir up trouble. My husband, Bud, used to run a ranch. He recalls a time when he warned the ranch hands about the way to avoid situations that would cause trouble. He told them, "You cowboys can walk through that cow pen and get to the other side and you won't smell a thing, but if you take a stick and stir up the manure while you walk through the pen, it's gonna stink." This Proverb gives the same advice: just walk on by when there is trouble brewing, or you could cause a "stink." "A soft answer turneth away wrath: but grievous words stir up anger. The tongue of the wise useth knowledge aright: but the mouth of fools poureth out foolishness" (Proverbs 15:1-2).

Agur responded to Ithiel and Ucal (Proverbs 30:1) with different forms of instruction. In a sense, we are all teachers. Others, (especially children, new believers, and unbelievers) learn from how we speak, the questions we ask, what we do, how we use God's Word, and the way we pray, even more than from what we may consciously teach.

Dear heavenly Father, thank You for teaching us wisdom from Your Word. Help me to guard my mouth, and not to think too highly of myself. I desire to remain humble in Your sight and the sight of men. I know am nothing without You, and the things I accomplish are simply done by Your grace in my life. Lord, may I answer softly to those who would try to stir me to anger. Help me to be silent when I should not speak, and to speak up when I should. May my words be like Yours. I ask this in the name of Jesus. Amen.

God's Wisdom for Daily Living — *Betty Miller*
December 19 — *Day 353*

Proverbs 31:1-3 1 The words of king Lemuel, the prophecy that his mother taught him. 2 What, my son? and what, the son of my womb? and what, the son of my vows? 3 Give not thy strength unto women, nor thy ways to that which destroyeth kings.

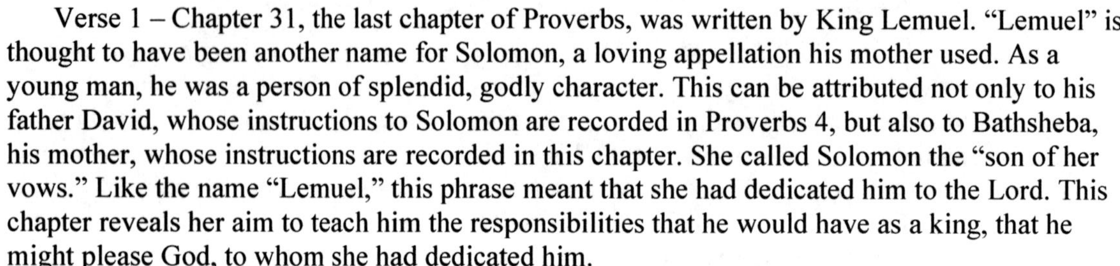

Verse 1 – Chapter 31, the last chapter of Proverbs, was written by King Lemuel. "Lemuel" is thought to have been another name for Solomon, a loving appellation his mother used. As a young man, he was a person of splendid, godly character. This can be attributed not only to his father David, whose instructions to Solomon are recorded in Proverbs 4, but also to Bathsheba, his mother, whose instructions are recorded in this chapter. She called Solomon the "son of her vows." Like the name "Lemuel," this phrase meant that she had dedicated him to the Lord. This chapter reveals her aim to teach him the responsibilities that he would have as a king, that he might please God, to whom she had dedicated him.

Verse 2 – Through the centuries, many mothers have dedicated their children to God and He has used those children mightily. Hannah, another great woman of faith and prayer dedicated her son to the Lord, and he was used mightily during a time in Israel's history when the light of God's revelation burned dimly. Her son was the great prophet, Samuel (1 Samuel 3:20-21).

More recently, we have the example of Susanna Wesley. God used her two sons, John and Charles, to touch the lives of many people for Christ. John Wesley founded Methodism, while his brother Charles wrote over 9,000 hymns and poems. John Wesley received much of his early spiritual and academic training from his mother. The year 2003 marked the 300th anniversary of John Wesley's birth. His life still influences people today, for which much credit is due his mother's faithfulness and dedication to teach her children the ways of the Lord.

Verse 3 – The prayerful woman who gives her children to the Lord will also instruct them in His ways. The first instruction that Bathsheba gave Lemuel was to reject loose women, bad companions and promiscuous ways. She realized the awesome responsibility her son would have as a king. She knew that if he were to please God, he must learn to fear the Lord. This would make him a man of integrity and help him to resist the three greatest temptations of those in authority: the misuse of wealth; yielding to pride; or yielding to lust. While these are especially tempting for those in authority, we all face the same temptations at various levels. We must remember, as Bathsheba did, our responsibility to warn our children of sin's dangers, and to teach them to walk in the reverence of God.

Dear heavenly Father, thank You for the many women over the years who have dedicated their children to the Lord, and have seen them come to serve You. May I, and all mothers, realize the awesome responsibility and opportunity we have to raise our children in the nurture and admonition of the Lord. Use our children in Your kingdom and cause them to become strong Christian witnesses. May they speak the Word of the Lord, even as we speak and teach it to them. Use them as Your humble servants and keep them from evil. I ask this in the name of the Lord, Jesus. Amen.

Proverbs 31:4-7 4 It is not for kings, O Lemuel, it is not for kings to drink wine, or for rulers to desire strong drink, 5 Lest they drink and forget the law and what it decrees, and pervert the justice due any of the afflicted. 6 Give strong drink (as medicine) to him who is ready to pass away, and wine to him in bitter distress of heart. 7 Let him drink and forget his poverty and remember his want and misery no more (AMP).

Verses 4-7 – David promised Bathsheba that her son would become king; so she wisely trained him for the enormous responsibilities he would face. She pointed out to him that drinking is an unbecoming indulgence for kings. Although drinking wine was the common practice of those times, she knew that her son would be accountable to God for everything he did. She warned him that wine was dangerous, for it clouds one's reason; causing one to forget the law, and to err in judgment. A king must be rational, so that he might remember God's laws and judge the people justly. He must always have a clear head.

According to these verses, the only cases in which the use of alcohol is recommended, are pain and extreme distress. In such instances, it can be administered medicinally. Paul reiterated this instruction to Timothy, directing the use of wine for his stomach and frequent ailments (1 Timothy 5:23). Even today, alcohol can be used medicinally, and we find it is an ingredient in a number of prescription compounds.

The affects of alcohol upon man have not changed through the millennia. It still perverts people's judgment. Long before one notices its effects, it slows one's responses. Because of today's high-speed travel, even the slightest slowing of a driver's responses can cause fatal accidents. Alcoholism also continues to generate great heartache for those enslaved by it and for their families.

The Bible tells us that we have been made a kingdom of priests to God. "And hath made us kings and priests unto God and his Father; to him be glory and dominion for ever and ever. Amen" (Revelation 1:6). As it was unfitting for Lemuel to indulge in wine, so it is unfitting for us, as God's royal family, to do so. We are responsible before God for those around us as well as ourselves. "For, brethren, ye have been called unto liberty; only use not liberty for an occasion to the flesh, but by love serve one another" (Galatians 5:13). As God's children, love should motivate us to abstain from anything that might cause someone to stumble.

Dear Father in heaven, what wonderful advice we find written in the pages of the Bible! May we all adhere to the wisdom that we find in it, and especially the wisdom given for kings. You have made us spiritual kings and priests. We need to act like kings and priests; with wisdom and holiness, so we can rule and reign in an evil world. Deliver us from all that would cause us to have poor judgment. Give us Your wisdom. May I live a righteous life before the world and be a faithful witness for You. I ask this in the name of Jesus. Amen.

Proverbs 31:8-9 8 Open your mouth for the dumb (those unable to speak for themselves), for the rights of all who are left desolate and defenseless; 9 Open your mouth, judge righteously, and administer justice for the poor and needy (AMP).

Verses 8-9 – Having warned Lemuel of the habits a king must avoid, Bathsheba instructed him on the actions a king must take in judging his people righteously. He must speak for those unable to speak for themselves, defend the helpless, judge both the poor and the rich without prejudice, and carry out justice for the poor and needy. It was his responsibility to investigate both sides of a matter brought to him and to speak for those unable to present their side, judging without partiality. "Ye shall do no unrighteousness in judgment: thou shalt not respect the person of the poor, nor honour the person of the mighty: but in righteousness shalt thou judge thy neighbour" (Leviticus 19:15).

We have seen that God's concern and love for the poor is expressed throughout Scripture. Psalm 140:12 states that God maintains their cause by raising up people to help them. Old and New Testaments instruct us to help the poor and to deal fairly with all people; poor or rich. Doing so honors God. Failing to do this was part of the iniquity of Sodom and Gomorrah, whose people spent their wealth and free time on self-indulgence. "Behold, this was the iniquity of thy sister Sodom, pride, fulness of bread, and abundance of idleness was in her and in her daughters, neither did she strengthen the hand of the poor and needy. And they were haughty, and committed abomination before me: therefore I took them away as I saw good" (Ezekiel 16:49-50). This verse gives us a description of their iniquity which fits most wealthy countries, particularly America: pride; being full because of an abundance of food; being idle; failing to help the poor; haughtiness; and committing abominations. When a nation exercises oppression and robbery as a way of life, and mistreats or ignores the poor and outsiders who need help, it will pay the penalty through reaping what it has sown.

"The people of the land have used oppression, and exercised robbery, and have vexed the poor and needy: yea, they have oppressed the stranger wrongfully. And I sought for a man among them, that should make up the hedge, and stand in the gap before me for the land, that I should not destroy it: but I found none. Therefore have I poured out mine indignation upon them; I have consumed them with the fire of my wrath: their own way have I recompensed upon their heads, saith the LORD GOD" (Ezekiel 22:29-31).

If those in authority do what is right and defend the poor and speak out for those unable to speak for themselves, such as unborn children whose lives are being ended in abortion, they will help their people turn from wickedness so that they might be blessed instead of cursed.

Dear Father, I am thankful that You are a compassionate Defender of the poor and needy. May we also be concerned about the poor. Thank You for blessing me with material things; may I reach out and bless those less fortunate than I with my goods. I want to share Jesus with those who are needy because when they know You, they will always have One to call upon who will never fail them. They can find peace, love, and joy in the midst of their circumstances and rise above their poverty, because You will never forsake them. I pray in the name of Jesus. Amen.

Proverbs 31:10-12 10 Who can find a virtuous woman? for her price is far above rubies. 11 The heart of her husband doth safely trust in her, so that he shall have no need of spoil. 12 She will do him good and not evil all the days of her life.

The remainder of Proverbs 31 records Bathsheba's instruction to Lemuel in choosing a wife. It is tragic that he failed to follow her advice. Solomon's wives did not know the Lord, and turned his heart from God to worship idols when he was old (1 Kings 11:1-13). Thus, a life that began magnificently ended miserably. The man who penned and preached a thousand wise things failed to practice the wisdom he taught. This chapter is not only advice for choosing a virtuous woman, but is also a spiritual type of the church (Christ's bride) who should demonstrate the qualities of the virtuous woman to the world.

Verse 10 – The first thing that is established is the price of a virtuous woman's worth. Like a costly jewel, she is not easy to come by. I believe every man needs God's help to find this kind of woman. We know that it is the Lord's will for a man to have a mate if he desires one, because after He had created Adam, He said: "...It is not good that the man should be alone; I will make him a help meet for him" (Genesis 2:18). God's favor rests on the man who prays and waits for the right mate, so that they can serve God together. God is delighted to answer such a man's prayer and will bring the right woman into his life at the appointed time.

Verses 11-12 – A virtuous woman is a comfort to her husband; encouraging him and doing him good all the days of her life. She never leaves or divorces him. Her husband can trust her completely, because she loves him for who he is and not for what he can do for her. Since he does not have to impress her with his ability to make money, he is not tempted to take anything by dishonest gain. A woman who marries a man for his money or for the security he provides does not marry for the right motives. When two people enter into a marriage with the idea of loving and serving each other, their marriage will be blessed because it is not based on selfishness.

In Day 102 and Day 122, we looked at the importance of being led by the Holy Spirit in choosing a mate and not allowing ourselves to be led only by our emotions. Love is much more than simply "falling" for someone and experiencing a sense of euphoria. The Lord certainly gives us wonderful feelings for the person we will marry. However, allowing feelings alone to guide us in the choice of a mate, can be disastrous. This description of a virtuous woman is a guide for choosing a spouse. The Lord delights to bring the best life partner to those who ask Him to do so and wait with patience and trust for His choice. What a glorious plan God has had from the beginning for both men and women!

Dear heavenly Father, thank You for sending me a wonderful husband. Let me always be a good and virtuous wife to him. I pray for all those who are seeking mates; that You will send them the right one in Your timing. I also lift up those who have troubled marriages and I ask that You heal them and restore their first love to them. Give them Your love for each other. Help them overcome selfishness, and heal each of them from the wounds that they have inflicted on one another through angry and hurtful words. You are the God of miracles; perform a miracle for those who need one in their marriages. I ask this in the name of Jesus Christ. Amen.

Proverbs 31:13-14 13 She seeketh wool, and flax, and worketh willingly with her hands. 14 She is like the merchants' ships; she bringeth her food from afar.

These verses describe the diligence with which a virtuous woman in Biblical times fulfilled her duties. Her chief responsibilities were the clothing and feeding of her family.

Verse 13 – Clothing a family was not an easy task in ancient times. Everything was made in the home from raw materials. "Ready-made" items were too costly for the common man. Wool and linen were the chief textiles. If her husband did not own his own flocks for wool or harvest his own flax, his wife would buy them at the marketplace. Flax had to be soaked in water before its fibers were ready for the distaff; and wool had to be carded. These were spun into threads, which were woven into fabrics. From wool, she made clothing and other household items. Linen was used to make sashes, nets, measuring lines, and finer garments. While the wealthy purchased dyed, fine fabrics from other countries, spinning, and weaving were still very important occupations even of wealthy women and queens. Thus, the first thing that Bathsheba described about a virtuous woman was her diligent labor in producing clothing.

Verse 14 – The other vital task of a virtuous woman was daily meal preparation. This also required much time and labor. Food was procured from one's flocks and lands or from a market. Bread was the staple food and baked daily. Women made flour by grinding grain on a small millstone, then crushing it in a mortar with a pestle. Milk was the chief food after bread. Women milked cows, goats, or sheep daily, and prepared the milk in sweet, sour, or curdled forms. They churned it to make butter and cheese. They gathered olives, grapes, dates, figs, vegetables, fruits and herbs from their fields. Most of their olives were pressed to obtain oil used for cooking and lamps. Eggs were gathered from their fowl. Salt, spices, and honey might be purchased at markets, often coming from afar. Although Bathsheba lived in a palace, she knew that one of the attributes of a virtuous woman was industriousness, for it expressed her love for her family.

Household tasks today differ from those of ancient times, but God's instruction still applies. Titus 2:3-5 instructs older Christian women to be examples to younger ones, by being holy, pure, and temperate; not gossiping or idle–and to teach them to love their families. This love is expressed by action and must be learned. As in ancient times, this involves keeping the house clean, doing laundry, and preparing meals. The home is a family's refuge. The wife is charged with its care and the husband with providing the means to maintain it. Younger women can spare themselves much heartache by heeding the advice of older, more experienced women. "Honour thy father and thy mother: that thy days may be long upon the land which the LORD thy God giveth thee" (Exodus 20:12).

Dear heavenly Father, thank You for instructing us, as women, in Your ways. Please teach me to love my husband the way that I should. I am asking You for Your love and grace; not only to love my husband, but my children as well. May I express Your love to them in the daily affairs of life. Give me the strength to be a good house–keeper and cook, along with my other duties as a wife and mother. Deliver me from selfishness and let me consider my family before my own needs. Lord, I know when I do this, that You will take care of my needs. I ask this in the name of Jesus Christ. Amen.

God's Wisdom for Daily Living — *Betty Miller*
December 24 — *Day 358*

Proverbs 31:15-16 15 She riseth also while it is yet night, and giveth meat to her household, and a portion to her maidens. 16 She considereth a field, and buyeth it: with the fruit of her hands she planteth a vineyard.

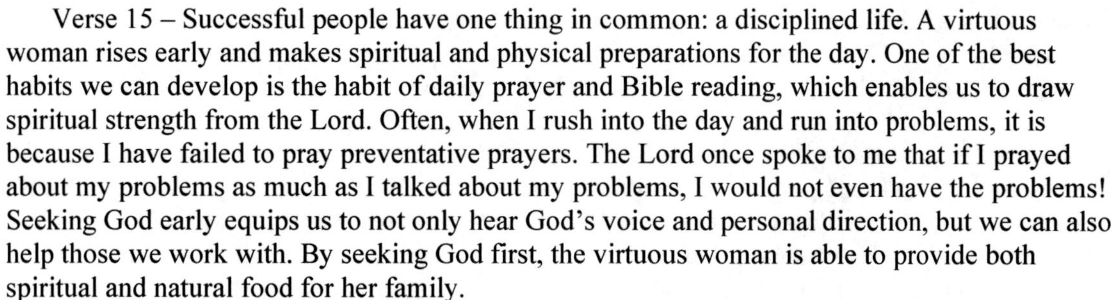

Verse 15 – Successful people have one thing in common: a disciplined life. A virtuous woman rises early and makes spiritual and physical preparations for the day. One of the best habits we can develop is the habit of daily prayer and Bible reading, which enables us to draw spiritual strength from the Lord. Often, when I rush into the day and run into problems, it is because I have failed to pray preventative prayers. The Lord once spoke to me that if I prayed about my problems as much as I talked about my problems, I would not even have the problems! Seeking God early equips us to not only hear God's voice and personal direction, but we can also help those we work with. By seeking God first, the virtuous woman is able to provide both spiritual and natural food for her family.

Verse 16 – A virtuous woman is also a capable businesswoman. Running a home is similar to running a business in many aspects, as it takes management skills to take care of the many domestic responsibilities. She executes business negotiations and invests her savings in profitable endeavors. Planning and organizing are both necessary skills to make any enterprise a success, but so is persistence and hard work. Once plans are made, we face the hard part of executing them. Many who are exuberant upon starting a new project lose enthusiasm along the way. One must consider whether one is able to invest the time and energy needed to a launch a new venture and make it profitable without neglecting the regular duties of hospitality at home and ministry to the needs around them, whether in the home or outside of it. "Be kindly affectioned one to another with brotherly love; in honour preferring one another; Not slothful in business; fervent in spirit; serving the Lord; Rejoicing in hope; patient in tribulation; continuing instant in prayer; Distributing to the necessity of saints; given to hospitality" (Romans 12:10-13).

The question of whether a mother should work outside the home has been much debated. It takes hard work and sacrifice to undertake a career in addition to caring for a family and home. Some mothers find it overly burdensome and become resentful. The ideal, especially when children are small, would be for a mother to stay home and rear her children, since that is when they are most impressionable. However, if her husband does not oppose it, and a woman can handle her household responsibilities and an outside job, Scripture certainly does not forbid her from doing so. The important thing is to follow the Lord's plan for one's life and do everything in love. When God is leading us to do something, He will provide everything we need to accomplish it. Like the virtuous woman, we need to "count the cost" before adding to our responsibilities and make sure that whatever we do, it is being done as unto the Lord.

Dear heavenly Father, thank You for giving me the grace and strength to accomplish all that You have called me to do. Please help me to be more disciplined, especially in my prayer life. Give me a love for Your Word so that I never neglect the reading of the Bible. Help me to hear Your voice so that I can follow Your advice in all of my affairs. May I also reflect Your nature in all of my business dealings. May kindness and consideration be a part of my nature. Give me the grace to reach out and help others and to be hospitable to all who enter my home. I ask this in the name of Jesus. Amen.

God's Wisdom for Daily Living — ***Betty Miller***
December 25 — ***Day 359***

Proverbs 31:17 She girdeth her loins with strength, and strengtheneth her arms. 18 She perceiveth that her merchandise is good: her candle goeth not out by night.

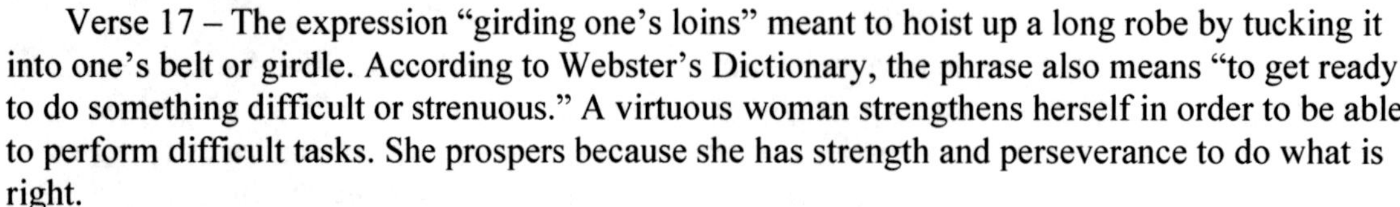

Verse 17 – The expression "girding one's loins" meant to hoist up a long robe by tucking it into one's belt or girdle. According to Webster's Dictionary, the phrase also means "to get ready to do something difficult or strenuous." A virtuous woman strengthens herself in order to be able to perform difficult tasks. She prospers because she has strength and perseverance to do what is right.

Man is composed of spirit, soul (comprised of will, intellect and emotions) and body. We all face physical, mental, and spiritual trials and need to be strong to overcome them. Since each part of our beings affects the others, we must strive to strengthen all of them.

Our physical bodies must have the right kind of diet and exercise to remain strong and healthy. We should be careful to discipline ourselves regarding proper eating habits and regular exercise. Even as we feed our physical bodies, we should also not neglect to feed our spirits by meditating upon God's Word. Obeying His voice exercises and strengthens our spirits. Our souls are fed by input and study that enlightens the mind and refines the emotions. Keeping the soul in correct balance also strengthens it. The will must rule the intellect and emotions. We must take the responsibility of choosing to think on what is edifying and reject what is compromising.

Our families depend on us. Jesus came to earth in a physical body as a tiny baby and His mother, Mary, cared for Him in the natural as well as provided the proper spiritual environment for Him. We must ask God for the strength to perform the important tasks before us. True strength is both moral and physical. It comes by taking care of every area of our beings. We are able to overcome when we are strong in body and soul, as well as in the Lord and the power of His might.

Verse 10 – A virtuous woman examines what she makes to be sure it is of good quality. She does whatever is necessary to achieve good workmanship. In the natural, this may mean working extra hours and "burning the candle" at night to complete a particular job. Spiritually, it means that her light of hope, faith and determination will not go out in the soul's night of trouble, fear or discouragement. She prevails because she has made herself spiritually, mentally and physically strong; ready to work hard and meet life's challenges.

Dear Father God, thank You for the good things You have given us. I am thankful to have work to do. May I always do excellent work at my job. Give me the grace to take care of my physical body properly, in eating and exercise. Help me make healthy choices regarding my food, so that my body is healthy. I need strength to do the things at my job, in my home, and most of all, in Your kingdom. Lord, may I also keep my spirit man strong by daily reading Your Word and spending time in prayer to commune with You. I desire to be like the virtuous woman in Proverbs 31. Thank You for sending your Son, Jesus, who came to earth, was born in a manger and grew into a Man who could relate to us on our level. Celebrating His birth brings joy to me. Thank You that His virtue is now mine. I ask this in the name of Jesus. Amen

Proverbs 31:19-20 19 She layeth her hands to the spindle, and her hands hold the distaff. 20 She stretcheth out her hand to the poor; yea, she reacheth forth her hands to the needy.

Verse 19 – Having prepared her flax and wool, a virtuous woman spun them into thread, the next step in making clothes. Drawing fibers from a quantity of flax held on her distaff, she used her spindle to twist them together into a continuous strand. As linen thread formed, she wound it on the spindle. So constant an occupation was spinning in the ancient world, that distaff and spindle became symbols of an industrious woman. These tools symbolized a woman's love and care for her family.

A spindle is a small rod, and a distaff a short staff. They bring to mind the shepherd's rod and staff, which symbolize his care for his sheep. Psalm 23 pictures the Lord as the Great Shepherd caring for us as His flock. This beautiful Psalm has comforted countless people over the centuries, for Christ's care and selfless love give even greater security than that of a mother. A good shepherd causes his sheep to rest and graze in green pastures. He leads them where they can drink placid water. Sheep are frightened of running water, since their heavy woolen coats render them incapable of swimming. He restores our souls with the spiritual food of His Word and the living waters of His Spirit. He leads us in righteousness. Even when we walk through the valley of the shadow of death, He is with us. This place is not called the valley of death, but the valley of the *shadow* of death. Shadows look ominous, but they cannot harm us. We need to remember this when faced with any threat of death from the devil. Jesus came to give us life, not death (John 10:10). He also prepares a table from which we may eat even with enemies around us. When we stay close to our Shepherd, we experience such wonderful victories that our cups run over. He anoints us with the Holy Spirit, who empowers us to triumph in all things. All the days of our lives, He follows us with His goodness and mercy. I asked the Lord one time why goodness and mercy "followed us," instead of going before us. He spoke to my heart that "goodness and mercy" were behind us to catch us when we fall down. He is there to catch us and lift us back up, so we can continue on the path of the Lord. We are promised that we shall live in the security of His house forever.

Verse 20 – Bathsheba described the virtuous woman as prosperous and compassionate. Sometimes giving money is easier than giving our time. Whether a kind word or deed, the virtuous woman gives from her own stores of faith and knowledge, as well as from her material goods. This is one reason Bathsheba described such a woman as blessed, for the Lord promises blessing to those who give to the poor. One of the most important things Christians do at Christmas to celebrate the Lord's birth is to assist the poor. There is more joy in this than in giving gifts only to family members. Honoring Christ by obeying Him and helping others is a gift we can present to Him any time of year.

Dear Father in heaven, thank You for the account of the woman in Proverbs 31. May we all be inspired by her virtue and love, being generous as she was. May we reach out not only to the poor, but to all those whom You lead us to help. Help me to give not only of my money, but also of myself. May I share my faith, my love, and my time with those who need encouragement and help. Lord, help me to be sensitive to the needs of those around me and not just walk by when someone needs the help that I could give. I ask this in the name of Jesus. Amen.

Proverbs 31:21-22 21 She fears not the snow for her family, for all her household are doubly clothed in scarlet. 22 She makes for herself coverlets, cushions, and rugs of tapestry. Her clothing is of linen, pure and fine, and of purple [such as that of which the clothing of the priests and the hallowed cloths of the temple were made].

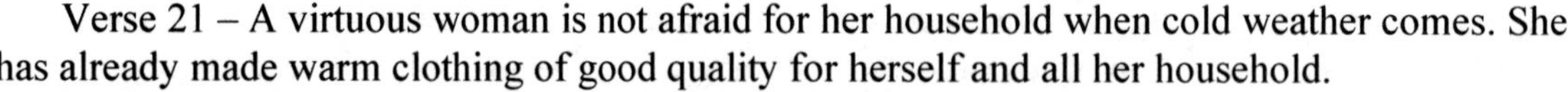

Verse 21 – A virtuous woman is not afraid for her household when cold weather comes. She has already made warm clothing of good quality for herself and all her household.

Clothing is a type of spiritual covering. The term "clothed in scarlet" also has a spiritual application. The blood of the Old Testament sacrifices represented the blood of Jesus, shed for the forgiveness of sins. Scarlet wool was used by the priests in connection with these sacrifices (Hebrews 9:19-22). Being "clothed with scarlet" is a picture of being covered by the blood of Christ. Under His covering, we are protected.

We find types of the saving power of Christ's blood throughout the Bible. Joshua 2 and Joshua 6 recounts that Rahab, a harlot in Jericho, who acknowledged the God of Israel and hid the messengers whom Joshua sent to spy our Jericho. When the army of Israel invaded, both her life and the life of her family were spared because she obeyed their instructions to tie a scarlet cord in the window of her house. The Israelites looked for the scarlet cord when they attacked Jericho, and brought Rahab and her family out to safety before destroying everyone in the city. The scarlet cord was a type of the blood of Jesus. Another type is seen in the Passover account of Exodus 12, as the Israelites' applied the blood of lambs to the doorposts of their houses in Egypt. When the Lord saw the blood on a house, He passed over it, not allowing the destroyer to slay their firstborn. Jesus, the Lamb of God, was slain on our behalf. When His blood is applied to our souls, God will not suffer us to be destroyed or go to hell.

Verse 22 – A virtuous woman also makes clothing from expensive, fine linen. This, too, has a spiritual application, for the bride of Christ is clothed in linen garments that represent her righteousness. "Let us be glad and rejoice, and give honour to him: for the marriage of the Lamb is come, and his wife hath made herself ready. And to her was granted that she should be arrayed in fine linen, clean and white: for the fine linen is the righteousness of saints" (Revelation 19:7-8). "I will greatly rejoice in the LORD, my soul shall be joyful in my God; for he hath clothed me with the garments of salvation, he hath covered me with the robe of righteousness, as a bridegroom decketh himself with ornaments, and as a bride adorneth herself with her jewels" (Isaiah 61:10).

We can all be dressed in this fine, white linen by accepting Christ. Only the scarlet blood of Jesus Christ can cleanse our souls from the stain of sin, and fit us for the clean white garments of righteousness (Isaiah 1:18).

Dear heavenly Father, I am grateful for the sacrifice Jesus made on the cross for my sins. Lord, I thank You for washing me clean by the blood of Jesus. Please give me the holy boldness to share what You have done for me with others, so that they too might know salvation and deliverance from their sins. Thank You that I can wear the robe of righteousness; may I never tarnish it in the sight of the world. Grant that I remain a faithful witness. I ask this in the name of Jesus Christ. Amen.

Proverbs 31:23-24 23 Her husband is known in the gates, when he sitteth among the elders of the land. 24 She maketh fine linen, and selleth it; and delivereth girdles unto the merchant.

Verse 23 – We may recall that in Biblical times, cities were enclosed by high walls with huge gates, where the elders met who presided over the affairs of the city. To be "known in the gates" meant that a man was a person of influence in the community. There is truth to the old adage: "Behind every successful man is a successful woman." A man and woman become one flesh when they marry (Ephesians 5:31-33). A virtuous woman is a crown to her husband. Her conduct and accomplishments bless and prosper him, and bring him honor. She will be an asset to him in every way. What we are and what we do influences others, especially those closest to us. How sad for a woman to disgrace her husband and family. "A virtuous woman is a crown to her husband: but she that maketh ashamed is as rottenness in his bones" (Proverbs 12:4). We also should always remember that we are Christ's bride and strive to always bring Him glory.

Verse 24 – The virtuous woman was so industrious and her work of such high quality, that she had enough garments both to clothe her entire household, and others to sell. She presented her products as a wholesaler to merchants who in turn sold them in the marketplaces. This was another way in which she gained money for her family. In yesterday's study, we saw that linen garments represent the righteousness that comes with salvation. Selling fine, white linen is a picture of sharing one's faith with others.

In addition to fine linen, the virtuous woman sold girdles, or sashes. The girdle was an important piece of clothing used in two primary ways: First, it enabled one to move freely when necessary. In ancient times, all people wore long robes. A girdle was worn to hitch the garments above the feet so that one could walk about freely when the task called for it. Certain activities might require the robes to be hitched higher than the ankles, in which case the sash was wrapped around the waist very tightly, and the garments pulled through the knees and tucked up into the girdle. This is where the expression "girding up one's loins" came from. The girdle was associated with strength. Wrapping it around the loins supported the back much as back supports do today. Second, the girdle provided a pouch for holding money and other items. Men also carried their swords or knives in their sashes.

Ephesians 6:13-17 tells us to put on the whole armor of God in order to stand against Satan's schemes. Part of that preparation is to "gird up our loins" with truth. When we embrace and walk in the Bible's truths, we will also walk in victory over the devil.

Dearest Father, thank You for my husband. May I always bring honor to him and to You by living my life in a godly manner. Lord, may I do the things in the natural to care for my husband and family, and more importantly, may I attend to the spiritual things that will cause them to know the plan of salvation and the Word of God. May I be mindful to put on the armor of God, so that I will be protected from the attacks of the devil. I want to remain steadfast in the cause of Christ. I ask this in the name of the Lord Jesus. Amen.

Proverbs 31:25-26 25 Strength and dignity are her clothing and her position is strong and secure; she rejoices over the future (the latter day or time to come, knowing that she and her family are in readiness for it)! 26 She opens her mouth in skillful and godly Wisdom, and on her tongue is the law of kindness (giving counsel and instruction).

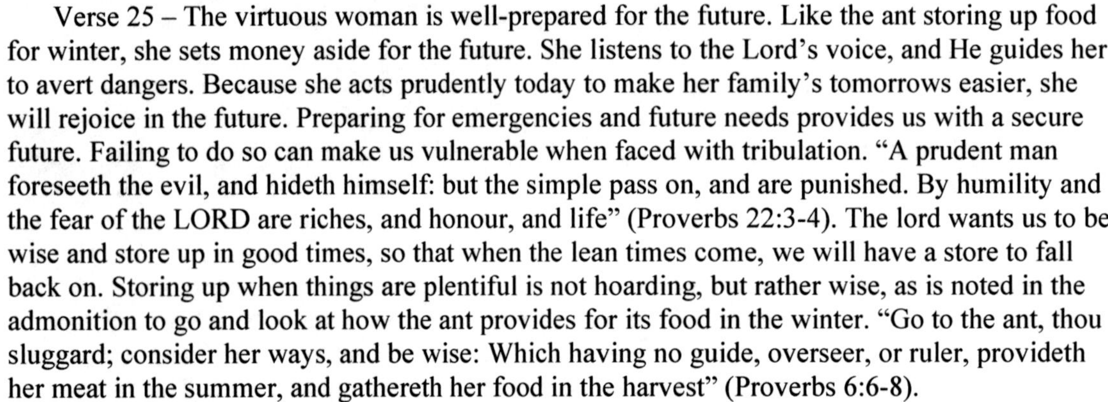

Verse 25 – The virtuous woman is well-prepared for the future. Like the ant storing up food for winter, she sets money aside for the future. She listens to the Lord's voice, and He guides her to avert dangers. Because she acts prudently today to make her family's tomorrows easier, she will rejoice in the future. Preparing for emergencies and future needs provides us with a secure future. Failing to do so can make us vulnerable when faced with tribulation. "A prudent man foreseeth the evil, and hideth himself: but the simple pass on, and are punished. By humility and the fear of the LORD are riches, and honour, and life" (Proverbs 22:3-4). The lord wants us to be wise and store up in good times, so that when the lean times come, we will have a store to fall back on. Storing up when things are plentiful is not hoarding, but rather wise, as is noted in the admonition to go and look at how the ant provides for its food in the winter. "Go to the ant, thou sluggard; consider her ways, and be wise: Which having no guide, overseer, or ruler, provideth her meat in the summer, and gathereth her food in the harvest" (Proverbs 6:6-8).

The virtuous woman is also described as full of strength and honor. Those who strengthen themselves in the LORD will receive honor from Him. "For who is God save the LORD? or who is a rock save our God? It is God that girdeth me with strength, and maketh my way perfect. He maketh my feet like hinds' feet, and setteth me upon my high places" (Psalm 18:31-33).

The Lord gives us feet like those of the deer who can leap upon the mountain's peaks. We are able to walk securely on the high places of intimacy with Him, above the storms of life and attacks of the enemy. God is our Rock, our high tower. When we take refuge in Him, our position is strong and secure. By humbling ourselves to worship and follow Him, we not only will escape destruction, but we shall receive the reward of riches, honor, and life. God will prosper us and honor us with long life, if we follow in His ways.

Verse 26 – A woman of character is kind and helps others to grow in the knowledge of God by her wise counsel and instruction. 2 Peter 1:4-8 tells us that we have been given great and precious promises. Through them, we can grow in grace by adding virtue to our faith; to virtue, knowledge; to knowledge, temperance; to temperance, patience; to patience, godliness; to godliness, brotherly kindness; and to brotherly kindness, love. These things sum up the characteristics of a virtuous woman or a godly man. By abounding in these things, we will always be fruitful in our knowledge of Christ, and able to help others.

Dear Father in heaven, thank You for the strength we have in You, enabling us to do all things that You ask us to do. May we grow in Your character, so that we are fruitful in the things of God. Lord, I thank You for Your guidance, so that we will make the right choices today, in order to avoid those things that would cause us to have future problems. I also thank You for daily provision, as well as provision for the future. Give me wisdom, so that I may take care of the things today that will bring me future security and blessing. I appreciate Your promises and I know that You will never forsake me nor leave me. Thank You for that. I pray in the precious name of Jesus. Amen.

Proverbs 31:27-29 27 She looketh well to the ways of her household, and eateth not the bread of idleness. 28 Her children arise up, and call her blessed; her husband also, and he praiseth her. 29 Many daughters have done virtuously, but thou excellest them all.

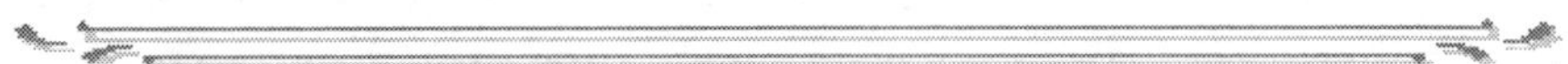

Verse 27 – A godly woman runs her household well and does not indulge in laziness. Satan uses tactics such as idleness to weaken a woman's character. Timothy was told to instruct widows under sixty to marry and keep house; otherwise they became busybodies (1 Timothy 5:13-15). Another tactic he uses is pushing women to either extremes in spiritual pursuits, or the opposite: extremes in their household duties. There should be a balance. If unequally yoked, some become overly spiritual and neglect their husbands. In such cases, she should remember that the way to a man's heart is through his stomach! She should take good care of her husband, cooking what he likes and doing special things for him. This should not be done as a bribe, but out of love for him and obedience to the Lord. He might then ask her the reason she has changed. She could humbly tell him that the Lord spoke to her about neglecting the home, and that God wants happy marriages. Knowing that God is interested in him draws a man to God.

Corrected priorities also frequently wins rebellious children. Many Christians show the love of Jesus to everyone outside their homes while their own families are starved for it, and are often crying out through their rebellion. We should certainly demonstrate Christ's love to others, but should show it first in our homes. Wives and mothers must recall that properly caring for their husbands and children is their primary responsibility. "That they may teach the young women to be sober, to love their husbands, to love their children, To be discreet, chaste, keepers at home, good, obedient to their own husbands, that the word of God be not blasphemed" (Titus 2:4-5). It is easy to become overly spiritual like Mary or overly practical like Martha (Luke 10:38-42). The Lord wants us to be balanced; to beware of becoming so "heavenly minded that we are no earthly good" and of being so practical that we miss the beauty of the Spirit.

Verses 28-29 – Bathsheba began the conclusion of her instruction by observing that a virtuous woman's care of her family is so excellent, that her children call her blessed and her husband praises her. Some of us may feel we fall far beneath this Biblical model, but we can aspire to her example by asking the Lord to help us in the areas where we are failing. As wives and mothers, we should examine our lives to see where we fall short, and ask God to help us be like the woman spoken of in these verses. Do our children call us blessed? What about our husbands? Are they praising us? Perhaps our children are rebellious at this time; maybe our husbands are far from the Christian ideal, and neither is praising or blessing us. Do we blame them, and insist that the Lord change them, or do we ask the Lord to turn the searchlight upon our own faults and failures, so that He might work a change in us? Our number one problem is not our children, our mates, our job, or our circumstances–it is *ourselves*. Until we are willing to change ourselves, the Lord cannot begin the needed change in our families.

How does God effect these changes in our lives? First of all, we must be honest with God and face our shortcomings and sins. We must come confessing: "God, I am resentful toward my husband and children. I don't want to be like this, but I can't help it. Please enable me to be the kind of wife and mother that will inspire them to bless me." When we do things out of love, without expecting anything in return, and ask the Lord for a loving and wise spirit to perform our daily chores, we will see changes in ourselves and those we love, since our seeds of love will bring a harvest.

Dear heavenly Father, thank You for the privilege of serving my husband and family. Lord, give me the grace to take care of my family in the manner that is pleasing to You. Although I may not be called to accomplish all the many things the virtuous woman of Proverbs 31 did, may I be faithful in my particular duties. You gift us in different ways. So, empower me to use my gifts to bless my family and bring glory to You. Give me Your love, so that I may serve out of love and not duty. Lord, may I turn my daily tasks into celebrations of love. I ask this in the name of Jesus. Amen.

Quotes About Strife and Anger

Whoever embraces hatred soon finds that this emotion cannot be confined to only our enemies, but it will spill over toward friends and break out against those whom one does not wish to hurt. --Day 61

To be right about the facts and yet act in a wrong manner undermines one's position. --Day 93

It is a man's honor to avoid strife, for this displays wisdom and strength of character. Any fool can take offense and argue with others. --Day 184

When two Christians cannot fellowship, it is because one or both of them are walking in darkness in some area of their lives. --Day 322

Quotes About Prudence

Major decisions should not be made quickly. It is easier to avoid getting into a bad situation than to get out of one. --Day 168

Developing a sensitivity and instant obedience to God's voice is prudent, because God will warn us of evils that we have no way of knowing about apart from Him. --Day 216

Saving prudently is not the same as hoarding. Hoarding has an element of fear and greed, while preparing for the future is wise. --Day 350

Proverbs 31:30-31 30 Favour is deceitful, and beauty is vain: but a woman that feareth the LORD, she shall be praised. 31 Give her of the fruit of her hands; and let her own works praise her in the gates.

Verses 30-31 – The conclusion of Bathsheba's instruction is that the fear of the Lord is our greatest asset, for it leads us to obey His commands and serve Him faithfully. We all reap the fruit of what we sow, and only what we accomplish for Christ through the Holy Spirit will merit God's praise. Everything else is vanity. It will perish and be forgotten.

Physical beauty is temporary, but the spiritual beauty of a good character will endure into eternity. When we are young and our whole lives lie ahead of us, we may not consider that we will grow old and die one day. What kind of legacy will we leave behind us? Will it be one like the virtuous woman whose works were praised by all who knew her? When we are older, we may not have the opportunities to serve God that we have today. Let us live each day by the wisdom found in Proverbs, so that we will not regret how our days on the earth were spent. This is the sum of Solomon's wisdom: "Let us hear the conclusion of the whole matter: Fear God, and keep his commandments: for this is the whole duty of man" (Ecclesiastes 12:13).

While these verses present a model for all women, it is also a spiritual type of the "Bride of Christ" and her relationship with her heavenly Bridegroom, the Lord Jesus Christ. Re-reading it with this in mind, we shall receive a wonderful revelation of what we can accomplish for the Lord when we are totally committed to Him.

Dear heavenly Father, thank You for including the Book of Proverbs in the Bible. Help me to heed its wisdom and apply it to my life. Teach me truth, and give me knowledge and revelation of Your Word, so that I might live an overcoming life in this earth. Guide me, so that I might daily walk in the Spirit and do the things that You have called me to do in my lifetime. May the contributions that I make to this world be those who are inspired by You, and come from Your heart. Let Your will be done in my life, both now and always. I ask this in the precious name of our Lord and Savior, Jesus Christ. Amen.

Post Note to My Readers: ***Thank you for taking this journey through the book of Proverbs with me. My prayer is that the wisdom of its pages will reside in you, guiding you into the fullness of all the Lord has for your life.***

Blessings,
Betty Miller

www.BibleResources.org

Topical Overview

Day 1: Proverbs 1:1-2
King Solomon, (who was the wisest of all men outside of Jesus) tells us how we can benefit from the wisdom and knowledge of God.
Day 2: Proverbs 1:3-4
Wisdom brings justice, judgment and equity.
Day 3: Proverbs 1:5-6
True wisdom increases our learning of Almighty God.
Day 4: Proverbs 1:7
The "fear the Lord," is defined as the starting place in attaining knowledge.
Day 5: Proverbs 1:8-9
We are instructed to listen to and respect the Godly advice and teachings of our parents.
Day 6: Proverbs 1:10-19
Young people are warned about the dangers of hanging out with the wrong crowd.
Day 7: Proverbs 1:20-23
Businesses and the marketplace will profit from following God's principles.
Day 8: Proverbs 1:24-33
A warning of calamity is given to those who refuse to listen to and yield to God.
Day 9: Proverbs 2:1-5
Bible study is an important part of our lives.
Day 10: Proverbs 2:6-7
If we desire to be wise, we must read the Bible.
Day 11: Proverbs 2:8
There are two sides of judgment; one for the wicked, one for the righteous.
Day 12: Proverbs 2:9
God's Word gives us understanding of righteousness, judgment and equity.
Day 13: Proverbs 2:10-15
When we have God's wisdom and discernment, we will not follow the path of evil.
Day 14: Proverbs 2:16-20
Divorce and sexual sin not only divide our homes, but also destroy the heart of a nation.
Day 15: Proverbs 2:21-22
This proverb reveals what makes a person upright and perfect.
Day 16: Proverbs 3:1-2
Keeping God's Word will cause one to live a long life.
Day 17: Proverbs 3:3-4
By allowing mercy and truth to rule our hearts, we will find favor with God and man.
Day 18: Proverbs 3:5-8
The Lord wants to bless us with healthy minds and bodies and spirits.
Day 19: Proverbs 3:9-10
When we honor God with the first-fruits of our labor, we shall have plenty and not lack.
Day 20: Proverbs 3:11-12
The Lord disciplines us so that we will not be destroyed. He corrects us as a good father.
Day 21: Proverbs 3:13-18
God's wisdom is more valuable than gold.
Day 22: Proverbs 3:19-20
The Lord God used His wisdom to create the earth and all the solar systems.

Day 23: Proverbs 3:21-24
If we honor wisdom and obey God's Word, it will produce the blessing of sweet sleep.
Day 24: Proverbs 3:25-26
We do not need to be afraid of evil things in the world. God promises to watch over us.
Day 25: Proverbs 3:27-29
Instructions are given in regard to repayment of a loan or a favor.
Day 26: Proverbs 3:30-32
We are to avoid strife. "Don't go picking a fight without a reason."
Day 27: Proverbs 3:33-35
A comparison is made between good and evil; blessings and curses.
Day 28: Proverbs 4:1-4
An admonition is given to young people to obey the godly instructions of their parents.
Day 29: Proverbs 4:5-9
Wisdom is to be sought and embraced as the principal thing. It brings beauty and glory.
Day 30: Proverbs 4:10-13
Honoring our parents will promote longevity and keep us from evil.
Day 31: Proverbs 4:14-19
We are to avoid the wicked path and not to go the dark way, but to walk in the light.
Day 32: Proverbs 4:20-22
We are to listen to and obey the Words of God, as they will bring life and health to us.
Day 33: Proverbs 4:23-27
We are to guard our hearts so that we do not yield to the things that would destroy us.
Day 34: Proverbs 5:1-13
Immoral appetites and sexual sins are tempting, but the bitter end of these sins is death.
Day 35: Proverbs 5:14-23
Pure water is like faithfulness in marriage, while adultery brings sorrow for the family.
Day 36: Proverbs 6:1-3
One who co-signs a note will be held accountable for it.
Day 37: Proverbs 6:4-11
Those who use excessive sleep as an escape from responsibility will end in poverty.
Day 38: Proverbs 6:12-15
Those who use scams and cons to mislead people are dishonest.
Day 39: Proverbs 6:16-19
Six things that God hates are revealed.
Day 40: Proverbs 6:20-22
Sons and daughters should listen to the words of their godly parents.
Day 41: Proverbs 6:23-29
Young men are instructed to avoid prostitutes.
Day 42: Proverbs 6:30-35
Tells how men in general react to a thief and an adulterer when he is caught.
Day 43: Proverbs 7:1-3
We are instructed to "lay up" the Word of God for the winter seasons of our lives.
Day 44: Proverbs 7:4-27
A description and warning is given on how a young man is seduced by a prostitute.
Day 45: Proverbs 8:1-11
We are directed where and how to find Wisdom.
Day 46: Proverbs 8:12
Through Wisdom and prudence people can discover witty inventions.
Day 47: Proverbs 8:13
Reveals to us that the "fear of the Lord" is to hate evil, pride and arrogance.

Day 48: Proverbs 8:14
We are warned to not seek counsel from fortune tellers, psychics, and astrology books.
Day 49: Proverbs 8:15-17
Good rulers in the earth will rule in the wisdom and justice that is recorded in the Bible.
Day 50: Proverbs 8:18-21
The possessor of God's wisdom will receive honor and material blessings.
Day 51: Proverbs 8:22-32
Wisdom is more than a wise method of doing things, but is the person of God Himself.
Day 52: Proverbs 8:33-36
If we refuse instruction and Wisdom, we will not be able to pass life's tests.
Day 53: Proverbs 9:1-5
True wisdom is to know Jesus and keep His commandments.
Day 54: Proverbs 9:6-9
Gives us instruction on how to relate to scorners and foolish people.
Day 55: Proverbs 9:10-12
Knowing God results in the understanding of everything else, and causes us to be fruitful.
Day 56: Proverbs 9:13-18
A warning is given of the deadly fate that awaits those who embrace a prostitute.
Day 57: Proverbs 10:1
A wise son's actions are compared with the actions of a foolish son.
Day 58: Proverbs 10:2-3
The riches that belong to the wicked will not help them in the day of death.
Day 59: Proverbs 10:4-5
We are instructed in the practical matter of work ethics.
Day 60: Proverbs 10:6-11
A comparison is made between the just and the wicked, according to their words.
Day 61: Proverbs 10:12-14
Hatred and foolishness are contrasted with love and wisdom.
Day 62: Proverbs 10:15-17
Righteous labor brings prosperity, while the sins that lead to poverty bring destruction.
Day 63: Proverbs 10:18-21
We are given advice concerning the words that we speak.
Day 64: Proverbs 10:22-26
The wicked rich man has sorrow with his wealth, while God's riches bring no sorrow.
Day 65: Proverbs 10:27-30
Instruction is given on how we can live a long life versus a shortened one.
Day 66: Proverbs 10:31-32
The words of the righteous are compared with the curses of the wicked.
Day 67: Proverbs 11:1-3
God loves integrity and hates the false balance of unrighteous dealings.
Day 68: Proverbs 11:4-6
Money cannot buy security in the day of wrath. Righteousness brings blessings.
Day 69: Proverbs 11:7-9
The lives of the righteous and wicked are contrasted. We are warned not to gossip.
Day 70: Proverbs 11:10-11
Individual righteousness, especially in leadership influences corporate righteousness.
Day 71: Proverbs 11:12
We can have good relationships with people by restraining from saying unkind things.
Day 72: Proverbs 11:13-15
We can avoid relationship problems by not being a talebearer or co-signing on a loan.

Day 73: Proverbs 11:16-20
A gracious woman and righteous man will bring honor to each other and their family.
Day 74: Proverbs 11:21-23
The actions of the good and evil people are contrasted.
Day 75: Proverbs 11:24-26
We are advised to give to the works of God and keep money for our living expenses.
Day 76: Proverbs 11:27-28
Doing good brings blessings, but seeking mischief brings a man trouble.
Day 77: Proverbs 11:29-31
We are warned against destroying the harmonious life that can be had in a family.
Day 78: Proverbs 12:1-3
Those who love instruction will love the knowledge of the Lord.
Day 79: Proverbs 12:4
A wife of good character brings honor to her husband, but a wicked wife causes him to become sick.
Day 80: Proverbs 12:5-7
Both sin and righteousness proceed from the heart and become good or evil deeds.
Day 81: Proverbs 12:8-9
A comparison is made between the righteous "wise" and the foolish "wicked."
Day 82: Proverbs 12:10-11
We are instructed to care for our animals and to be good stewards over our lands.
Day 83: Proverbs 12:12-15
The righteous are delivered from trouble, but the wicked are snared by their sins.
Day 84: Proverbs 12:16-19
We are not to give place to wrath, but to control our temper and refrain from telling lies.
Day 85: Proverbs 12:20-22
Ultimately, no evil will destroy the righteous.
Day 86: Proverbs 12:23-24
Prudence and diligence are contrasted against foolishness and laziness.
Day 87: Proverbs 12:25-26
Our goodness and encouragement can affect others in a positive way.
Day 88: Proverbs 12:27
We are given advice about hunting and killing animals.
Day 89: Proverbs 12:28 & Proverbs 13:1
Righteousness brings life, while the scorner's actions will lead to death.
Day 90: Proverbs 13:2-3
We shall reap the fruit of our lips, since the things we speak will affect our lives.
Day 91: Proverbs 13:4-6
We should flee from unrighteous business deals or activities that are promoted by greed.
Day 92: Proverbs 13:7-9
A comparison is recorded between rich men and poor men.
Day 93: Proverbs 13:10-12
We are told to avoid contention, how to attain wealth, and how the results of answered prayer will produce life.
Day 94: Proverbs 13:13-16
Those who keep the Word of God will be blessed, while those who despise it will be destroyed.
Day 95: Proverbs 13:17-21
Faithfulness produces accomplishments, versus good intentions which produce nothing.

Day 96: Proverbs 13:22-23
Righteous men reap material and spiritual blessings, and leave an inheritance to their children.
Day 97: Proverbs 13:24
Advice is given concerning child-rearing and corporal punishment.
Day 98: Proverbs 13:25
The fate of the righteous is contrasted to the fate of the wicked.
Day 99: Proverbs 14:1-2
A wise woman builds up her house with good words, while the foolish one will nag and tear the members of her house down.
Day 100: Proverbs 14:3-5
Foolish people can be recognized by their pride, laziness and bad witnesses.
Day 101: Proverbs 14:6-9
We must have a humble heart if we are to draw close to God and gain His understanding.
Day 102: Proverbs 14:10-11
The house of the righteous shall flourish, while the house of the wicked shall fall.
Day 103: Proverbs 14:12
We are warned to be careful about choices, as deception can lead one in the wrong way.
Day 104: Proverbs 14:13-14
Real happiness comes from knowing and serving God.
Day 105: Proverbs 14:15-18
The benefit of being prudent is contrasted to the folly of being a simpleton.
Day 106: Proverbs 14:19
Evil men cannot prevail against righteous men in the end.
Day 107: Proverbs 14:20-21
The rich and the poor are treated differently in this world. We should help the poor.
Day 108: Proverbs 14:22-25
Good people are blessed and evil ones are cursed, because of their own wickedness.
Day 109: Proverbs 14:26-27
The fear of the Lord brings life, while the fear of man will snare us.
Day 110: Proverbs 14:28-30
Rulers who are wise will serve the people, thus winning their favor and support.
Day 111: Proverbs 14:31
Our attitude toward the poor reflects our attitude toward God.
Day 112: Proverbs 14:32-33
The fate of a foolish, wicked man is contrasted to the fate of a righteous, wise man.
Day 113: Proverbs 14:34
Corporate righteousness will exalt a nation, while corporate sin will bring it reproach.
Day 114: Proverbs 14:35 & 15:1
The attitude of a servant should be respectful toward authority. Rebellion stirs up wrath.
Day 115: Proverbs 15:2-4
The wise are admonished to use a gentle tongue that will bring life and healing to others.
Day 116: Proverbs 15:5
A wise son heeds the correction given him by his father, while the fool despises it.
Day 117: Proverbs 15:6-7
The righteous have God's treasures, but the wicked have troubles, even with their money.
Day 118: Proverbs 15:8-9
The ways of the wicked are an abomination to God, but righteousness is His delight.
Day 119: Proverbs 15:10-12
The scorner hates the correction and reproof that keep a man on the right path.

Day 120: Proverbs 15:13-14
The differences between a merry heart and a sorrowful heart are compared.
Day 121: Proverbs 15:15
We can choose how we are going to react to our circumstances.
Day 122: Proverbs 15:16-17
"Little" is better with the respect of the Lord, than great treasures with trouble.
Day 123: Proverbs 15:18-21
A bad temper, slothfulness and dishonor to parents show a lack of wisdom.
Day 124: Proverbs 15:22-24
We are advised to get good counsel when needed.
Day 125: Proverbs 15:25-27
The wicked and his deeds are contrasted with the righteous and his deeds.
Day 126: Proverbs 15:28-29
The righteous are not quick to speak, but ponder how they should answer a person.
Day 127: Proverbs 15:30-33
We can tell what is in a person's heart by their countenance, as it reflects the attitude of the soul. People who are joyful bring joy to others.
Day 128: Proverbs 16:1-3
The Lord establishes the thoughts of those who commit their works unto Him.
Day 129: Proverbs 16:4
The origin of the devil is revealed.
Day 130: Proverbs 16:5-7
A man who pleases God will have even his enemies to be at peace with him.
Day 131: Proverbs 16:8-10
A little money with righteousness is better than having great wealth with injustice.
Day 132: Proverbs 16:11
God loves justice and equity as symbolized by a balanced scale.
Day 133: Proverbs 16:12-15
We are taught about the role of a king and his authority to rule.
Day 134: Proverbs 16:16-17
Wisdom and understanding are better than gold and silver. Pride is a dangerous sin.
Day 135: Proverbs 16:18-20
Those who become proud and arrogant are preparing themselves for a fall.
Day 136: Proverbs 16:21-24
Wisdom and understanding are increased by the words we hear and the words we speak.
Day 137: Proverbs 16:25
We can be deceived if we are not vigilant and discerning.
Day 138: Proverbs 16:26-30
A man should work for his own bread and avoid mischief and gossip.
Day 139: Proverbs 16:31
Unless an old man is committed to God, he will not have the Wisdom that reflects a crown of beauty and glory.
Day 140: Proverbs 16:32
A man who is slow to anger is one who can also rule his own spirit.
Day 141: Proverbs 16:33
Having God in our daily lives and activities will make a difference in our destiny.
Day 142: Proverbs 17:1
A little to eat in a household of peace is better than feasting in a household of strife.
Day 143: Proverbs 17:2
A servant who operates in wisdom has an advantage over a rebellious son.

Day 144: Proverbs 17:3
An analogy is made between the refining of silver and the refining of God's people.
Day 145: Proverbs 17:4-5
We should not give heed to a liar, nor should we mock the poor.
Day 146: Proverbs 17:6-7
God intended for parents and children to enjoy generational blessings.
Day 147: Proverbs 17:8-9
We are warned concerning bribes, gossip and unforgiveness.
Day 148: Proverbs 17:10-12
We are instructed to yield to reproof rather than being foolish to our own destruction.
Day 149: Proverbs 17:13-15
If we support an evil cause, it will bring evil back upon us.
Day 150: Proverbs 17:16-18
A fool cannot purchase Wisdom because it comes only to those who have a heart for it.
Day 151: Proverbs 17:19-21
Those who love to sin and enjoy strife are seeking destruction.
Day 152: Proverbs 17:22
Our attitude will affect the physical state of our body.
Day 153: Proverbs 17:23-25
Wicked men will lie and pervert judgment for a bribe.
Day 154: Proverbs 17:26-28
A man who holds is peace is wise.
Day 155: Proverbs 18:1-3
Those who seek to live without God are selfish, and refuse wisdom and good judgment.
Day 156: Proverbs 18:4
A man's words are as deep waters, and the wellspring of wisdom is like a flowing brook.
Day 157: Proverbs 18:5-8
Contentious fools will not only be self-destructive, but also bring destruction to others.
Day 158: Proverbs 18:9
A slothful person is kindred to one who is wasteful and a destroyer.
Day 159: Proverbs 18:10
There is power in names. The name of the Lord is like a strong tower.
Day 160: Proverbs 18:11-12
Men can suffer a downfall if they have a misplaced trust in riches.
Day 161: Proverbs 18:13-15
Making premature judgments will cause us to be ashamed if we are wrong in our suppositions.
Day 162: Proverbs 18:16
A man who presents a gift to someone will gain an audience with him.
Day 163: Proverbs 18:17-18
A case can be made for both sides of a discourse.
Day 164: Proverbs 18:19
When a person is offended, it is very difficult to win his favor again.
Day 165: Proverbs 18:20-21
Life and death are in the power of our words.
Day 166: Proverbs 18:22
A good wife comes from the Lord.
Day 167: Proverbs 18:23-24
The poor approach things differently than the rich do. A good friend sticks closer than a brother.

Day 168: Proverbs 19:1-2
There is great value in the virtue of integrity. We are not be hasty in making major decisions.

Day 169: Proverbs 19:3
Men who are resentful against God will not have a relationship with Him because they blame Him for their problems instead of seeing their own sin.

Day 170: Proverbs 19:4-9
Wealthy people will be sought out for their favors. Wisdom brings prosperity.

Day 171: Proverbs 19:10-12
It is not fitting for a foolish person to live in luxury. A man should control his anger.

Day 172: Proverbs 19:13-14
A man who has a foolish son and a contentious wife will suffer. A good wife is from God.

Day 173: Proverbs 19:15-16
Those who are lazy and idle shall go hungry.

Day 174: Proverbs 19:17
When we give to the poor, we are lending to God, and God Himself will reward us.

Day 175: Proverbs 19:18
We are never to discipline our children in our own anger.

Day 176: Proverbs 19:19-20
We are advised how to deal with rebellious people through the Wisdom that is gained by the counsel of the Lord.

Day 177: Proverbs 19:21
God is sovereign over the plans of men.

Day 178: Proverbs 19:22
God considers our character more important to Him than our circumstances.

Day 179: Proverbs 19:23
The reverential "fear of the Lord" leads to life and protects us from evil.

Day 180: Proverbs 19:24-25
Laziness is addressed, as well as instruction for dealing with scorners and reproving the teachable.

Day 181: Proverbs 19:26-27
A son who wastes his father and chases away his mother will cause his family shame.

Day 182: Proverbs 19:28-29
True judgment is addressed.

Day 183: Proverbs 20:1
The danger of drinking alcoholic beverages is presented.

Day 184: Proverbs 20:2-3
Civil authority has been given by God to rule over certain areas of the society.

Day 185: Proverbs 20:4-5
One who is slothful will end up with nothing because he refuses to work unless it is easy.

Day 186: Proverbs 20:6-7
The acts of prideful men without God are contrasted to the acts of righteous men.

Day 187: Proverbs 20:8-9
A good ruler is continually looking for ways to remove the evil in his domain.

Day 188: Proverbs 20:10
These scriptures deal with integrity versus cheating.

Day 189: Proverbs 20:11-12
Wisdom is given concerning the raising of children.

Day 190: Proverbs 20:13
Discipline must be cultivated in order to be successful in life.

Day 191: Proverbs 20:14-15
Trade and commerce policies are dealt with.
Day 192: Proverbs 20:16-17
We are advised to avoid a man who has a bad character.
Day 193: Proverbs 20:18
We should get counsel in order to establish our plans, especially in the matter of war.
Day 194: Proverbs 20:19-21
Wisdom warns us not to associate with unscrupulous people and not to curse our parents.
Day 195: Proverbs 20:22-23
We are instructed how we should react toward those who do evil things to us.
Day 196: Proverbs 20:24-25
We are instructed to know God, and to be careful about making promises to Him that we do not keep.
Day 197: Proverbs 20:26-28
Instructions are recorded for kings and rulers, as well as others.
Day 198: Proverbs 20:29-30
There should be no generational gap, as both young and old are needed.
Day 199: Proverbs 21:1-2
God is not only sovereign, but also omniscient and omnipresent.
Day 200: Proverbs 21:3-4
Doing right is more important than sacrifice. Man's pride and life without God is sinful.
Day 201: Proverbs 21:5-6
Certain virtues produce wealth, while evil virtues lead to poverty and death.
Day 202: Proverbs 21:7-8
The fate of violent thieves is contrasted to the fate of those who are pure in heart.
Day 203: Proverbs 21:9-10
We are given a strong admonition and warning to be careful about relationships.
Day 204: Proverbs 21:11-12
There are two ways to gain wisdom: through instruction and/or observation.
Day 205: Proverbs 21:13-14
We are warned to be sensitive to the needs of the poor and to avoid using bribes.
Day 206: Proverbs 21:15-16
The fate of those who pursue unrighteousness is contrasted with those who are just.
Day 207: Proverbs 21:17-18
The Lord turns things around, and blesses the righteous through the wicked.
Day 208: Proverbs 21:19-20
We are warned not to get into relationships with the wrong people and not to be wasteful.
Day 209: Proverbs 21:21
Seeking after righteousness is the secret of an honorable and overcoming life.
Day 210: Proverbs 21:22
A wise man can take a city and bring down the mighty stronghold of any enemy.
Day 211: Proverbs 21:23-24
We are to guard our speech and to resist being proud and haughty.
Day 212: Proverbs 21:25-27
The fate of those who make wicked sacrifices is contrasted with those who are generous.
Day 213: Proverbs 21:28-29
The wicked person will perish, while the upright man will be established in his society.
Day 214: Proverbs 21:30-31
No matter how well-prepared we may be for battle, the outcome rests in the Lord.
Day 215: Proverbs 22:1-2
Virtue is more valuable than material wealth.

Day 216: Proverbs 22:3-4
If we are prudent and seek the Lord with humility, He will give us discernment so that we do not go down a destructive path.

Day 217: Proverbs 22:5-6
Parents are instructed to train their children in the right way.

Day 218: Proverbs 22:7-8
The power of wealth gives the rich an advantage over the poor.

Day 219: Proverbs 22:9-10
A generous person will be blessed. Contention must be dealt with in order to maintain peace.

Day 220: Proverbs 22:11-12
Those who love purity of heart will have the king (Jesus) as their friend, and He will overthrow the words of sinners.

Day 221: Proverbs 22:13-14
Men are warned about listening to loose women.

Day 222: Proverbs 22:15-16
We are taught to discipline our children, and given instructions not to oppress the poor.

Day 223: Proverbs 22:17-18
When we submit to the Word of God, our lives will be pleasant for us.

Day 224: Proverbs 22:19-21
These verses are about knowing the Source of all truth.

Day 225: Proverbs 22:22-23
We are warned not to rob from the poor, as the Lord will take up their cause.

Day 226: Proverbs 22:24-25
We should avoid any friendships with habitually angry men.

Day 227: Proverbs 22:26-27
We are given advice in the area of pledging security for another's debts.

Day 228: Proverbs 22:28-29
We are to respect the boundaries that our fathers have set.

Day 229: Proverbs 22:29
Those who are diligent in business will receive an audience with kings.

Day 230: Proverbs 23:1-3
We are given advice about socializing and eating with those in prosperous positions.

Day 231: Proverbs 23:4-5
Our goal should not be to become materially rich, but rather to have the wisdom of God.

Day 232: Proverbs 23:6-8
Proper relationships are established by avoiding evil associations.

Day 233: Proverbs 23:9-11
Wisdom should not be shared with fools. God defends the fatherless.

Day 234: Proverbs 23:12
We are admonished to listen to the Lord's correction and to study the Word of God.

Day 235: Proverbs 23:13-14
We must correct our children by spanking them when they are disobedient.

Day 236: Proverbs 23:15-16
A father rejoices when his son has a heart of wisdom and speaks rightly.

Day 237: Proverbs 23:17-18
We are advised not to envy sinners; for our rewards will come when we respect the Lord.

Day 238: Proverbs 23:19-21
A father warns his son to stay away from the wild crowd of drunkards and gluttons.

Day 239: Proverbs 23:22
We are instructed to honor our parents and seek truth, wisdom, and understanding.

Day 240: Proverbs 23:23
Young people are admonished to honor their parents and bring joy to them.
Day 241: Proverbs 23:24-26
The Lord invites us to come to Him and learn of His ways
Day 242: Proverbs 23:27-28
A father warns his son to avoid the snare of being seduced by a whore.
Day 243: Proverbs 23: 29-35
A warning is given concerning what an addiction to alcohol will produce in one's life.
Day 244: Proverbs 24:1-2
We are warned not to be envious of wicked men and to stay away from their company.
Day 245: Proverbs 24:3-4
Through wisdom and understanding we can build and furnish our lives with precious things.
Day 246: Proverbs 24:5
Strength is gained by wisdom and knowledge.
Day 247: Proverbs 24:6
For the purpose of war, good counsel is a must.
Day 248: Proverbs 24:7-8
Those who do evil shall not stand among those who have the authority to judge them.
Day 249: Proverbs 24:9
Our thoughts can be sinful. A scoffer is an abomination to men.
Day 250: Proverbs 24:10
If we are unable to withstand adversity, we are weak and only have small strength.
Day 251: Proverbs 24:11-12
Our Christian duty is to rescue those who are in situations that will lead them to death.
Day 252: Proverbs 24:13-14
Eating honey is compared to the sweetness of godly Wisdom.
Day 253: Proverbs 24:15-16
The wicked man is warned not to attack the righteous man, nor his home.
Day 254: Proverbs 24:17-18
We are warned against rejoicing when our enemy falls, as the Lord is not pleased with that kind of attitude.
Day 255: Proverbs 24:19-20
We are not to fret about the wicked, for they will have no reward or light given to them.
Day 256: Proverbs 24:21-22
We are to respect authority--whether God's, or earthly rulers.
Day 257: Proverbs 24:23
The wise are told not to show partiality when sitting in a position of judgment.
Day 258: Proverbs 24:24-26
Judges are to execute their judgments in righteousness, and win the hearts of the people.
Day 259: Proverbs 24:27
We are to build our business before we build a new house.
Day 260: Proverbs 24:28-29
We are warned not to bear false witness against our neighbor, nor render evil for evil.
Day 261: Proverbs 24:30-32
The slothful person's property will be evidenced by obvious neglect and lack of care.
Day 262: Proverbs 24:33-34
Too much sleep will rob us our productivity and we shall come to poverty.
Day 263: Proverbs 25:1-3
Though God has concealed His wisdom from men, we can search it out and know it.

Day 264: Proverbs 25:4-5
Even as silver is refined, so wickedness is removed from the kingdom.

Day 265: Proverbs 25:6-7
We should not exalt ourselves in the presence of important people, but rather, take a humble position.

Day 266: Proverbs 25:8-10
We are warned to settle problems with our neighbor privately, rather than in court.

Day 267: Proverbs 25:11
A word that is wisely spoken is beautiful to those who hear it.

Day 268: Proverbs 25:12
As a gold earring is an ornament on an ear, so are the wise man's words of reproof.

Day 269: Proverbs 25:13
A faithful messenger is compared to the end of harvest.

Day 270: Proverbs 25:14
A comparison is made between a boastful liar and clouds that produce no rain.

Day 271: Proverbs 25:15
It will take much patience to persuade a ruler to change his mind, but it can be done if one is humble in their presentation.

Day 272: Proverbs 25:16
We should eat sweet foods in moderation, or we will become ill by over-indulgence.

Day 273: Proverbs 25:17
Over-extending a visit can destroy a friendship and turn into an invasion of privacy.

Day 274: Proverbs 25:18
A false witness affects someone like a sharp and heavy blow against them.

Day 275: Proverbs 25:19
If we put our confidence in one who is unfaithful, we will have a painful experience.

Day 276: Proverbs 25:20
We should be sensitive as to how we are to minister to those who are depressed.

Day 277: Proverbs 25:21-22
The way to overcome evil is to do good to our enemies. If we do so, the Lord will reward us.

Day 278: Proverbs 25:23-24
A backbiting tongue and quarrelsome woman will cause others to be angry with them.

Day 279: Proverbs 25:25
Hearing good news is compared to drinking cold water when one is thirsty.

Day 280: Proverbs 25:26
A righteous man who compromises is compared to a polluted spring.

Day 281: Proverbs 25:27-28
It is not good to boast of one's own accomplishments. One who cannot rule his own spirit is like a broken city wall.

Day 282: Proverbs 26:1
Honor bestowed upon a self-confident foolish person is not fitting.

Day 283: Proverbs 26:2
Curses do not come into someone's life by accident, there is a reason behind them.

Day 284: Proverbs 26:3
Some people will only be persuaded to obey, by receiving their instruction through punishment.

Day 285: Proverbs 26:4-5
These verses tell us how to address a conceited person who is acting foolishly.

Day 286: Proverbs 26:6-9
A fool can do great damage, if we allow it.

Day 287: Proverbs 26:10-11
God will justly reward fools, as they are like dogs who return to their own vomit.
Day 288: Proverbs 26:12
Pride and conceit are more deadly than the sin of a self-confident fool.
Day 289: Proverbs 26:13-14
A slothful person will never get anything done because of his fear of trouble.
Day 290: Proverbs 26:15-16
A lazy man refuses to even feed himself, but considers himself to be smarter than seven wise men.
Day 291: Proverbs 26:17
We are warned to stay away from strife, as we may make the problem worse.
Day 292: Proverbs 26:18-19
A man who deceives his neighbor, and claims it was a joke, is like a madman throwing firebrands and arrows.
Day 293: Proverbs 26:20-22
A talebearer will stir up strife, like wood added to a fire that increases the flames.
Day 294: Proverbs 26:23
Those who speak insincere words of love are like an earthen vessel covered by thin veneer of silver.
Day 295: Proverbs 26:24-26
One who speaks nicely, but is inwardly deceitful, will eventually be found out by all.
Day 296: Proverbs 26:27
Those who try to destroy others will find their own devices will trap and destroy them.
Day 297: Proverbs 26:28
Behind a lying tongue is hatred, and flattery will only work ruin.
Day 298: Proverbs 27:1
We should not boast about what we may do in the future, as we do not know what a day will bring.
Day 299: Proverbs 27:2
We should not brag about our accomplishments, but allow others to notice them and speak our praise.
Day 300: Proverbs 27:3-4
Jealousy and envy are greater burdens than the heavy weights of wrath and anger.
Day 301: Proverbs 27:5-6
True friendship includes honest rebuke, which is better than insincere compliments.
Day 302: Proverbs 27:7
A man who has an abundance of food will not even care for honeycomb; but a hungry person will find that even bitter food is sweet.
Day 303: Proverbs 27:8
A man who wanders from his home and wife, is like a bird that wanders from its nest.
Day 304: Proverbs 27:9-10
A good friend will be there for us in our day of calamity, even when our own family will not support us.
Day 305: Proverbs 27:11
A father charges his son to be wise.
Day 306: Proverbs 27:12
A watchful man will see the signs of impending danger and will plan how to avoid it.
Day 307: Proverbs 27:13-14
We can take advice in two areas: making known the risks of one who pledges things indiscreetly, and alerting us to be suspicious of those who go too far with flattery.

Day 308: Proverbs 27:15-16
A contentious woman is hard to deal with; it is wise to avoid marrying such a woman.

Day 309: Proverbs 27:17-19
Relationships are sharpened by godly friends sharing with one another, Faithful servants will be honored. Others will receive in their hearts what we reflect from ours.

Day 310: Proverbs 27:20
Those who yield to lust will never be satisfied, just as hell is never satisfied.

Day 311: Proverbs 27:21
As the refining of silver brings out impurities, so praise can bring out the impurities in a man.

Day 312: Proverbs 27:22
Bad character traits can be so deeply engrained that it is impossible to remove them even with drastic measures.

Day 313: Proverbs 27:23-24
We should not trust in riches and fame because that status can change at some point in time.

Day 314: Proverbs 27:25-27
Instructions are given for planning and managing our households and enterprises.

Day 315: Proverbs 28:1
The uncompromisingly righteous are as "bold as a lion," while the wicked flee in fear.

Day 316: Proverbs 28:2
When a wise man rules a nation it will produce stability.

Day 317: Proverbs 28:3
When a poor man takes advantage of the poor, he is like the destruction of a sweeping rain.

Day 318: Proverbs 28:4-5
Those who are rebels will praise the wicked; while the law keepers will contend with them.

Day 319: Proverbs 28:6-7
It is better to have character and be poor, than to be perverse and be rich.

Day 320: Proverbs 28:8-9
Those who make money unjustly will see their fortunes fall into the hands of those who will pity the poor and give to them.

Day 321: Proverbs 28:10-12
The wicked will fall into their own pit.

Day 322: Proverbs 28:13-14
He who confesses his sin shall have mercy, while the one who hides them will not prosper.

Day 323: Proverbs 28:15-16
A wicked ruler is like a wild, hungry animal that is looking to devour its prey.

Day 324: Proverbs 28:17-18
There is a penalty for murder; but there is a way even for a murderer to be saved.

Day 325: Proverbs 28:19-20
Those who are diligent will be blessed, but those who want to "get rich quick" will suffer.

Day 326: Proverbs 28:21-22
Showing favoritism is not good. The man who has an evil, covetous eye will reap poverty.

Day 327: Proverbs 28:23-24
A man who is honest and rebukes someone will find more favor than a deceitful flatterer.

Day 328: Proverbs 28:25-26
At the root of strife and self-confident foolishness is pride; but those who walk in God's Wisdom will be delivered and prosper.

Day 329: Proverbs 28:27-28
Those who give to the poor shall never lack, but those who look the other way will be cursed.

Day 330: Proverbs 29:1-2
Those who harden their hearts when they are reproved for their sin, will suddenly be destroyed.

Day 331: Proverbs 29:3-4
A son who loves godly wisdom will bring joy to his father's heart, while the son who visits harlots will grieve his father and waste his finances.
Day 332: Proverbs 29:5-7
A righteous man is a man free from guilt, therefore he can sing and is happy.
Day 333: Proverbs 29:8-9
A scornful person will incite others, but a wise man will bring peace among people.
Day 334: Proverbs 29:10-11
Murderers hate the righteous, but the righteous seek ways to save the souls of evil men.
Day 335: Proverbs 29:12-14
A wicked ruler has wicked officials around him, but a king who judges faithfully has a throne that is secure. The poor and wicked have this in common: both receive their light from God.
Day 336: Proverbs 29:15-17
Instructions are given for disciplining children, and the destiny of the wicked is revealed.
Day 337: Proverbs 29:18
When there is no vision and revelation from God, the people will perish.
Day 338: Proverbs 29:19-21
Instructions are given on how an employee should be treated. We should not speak hastily.
Day 339: Proverbs 29:22-24
Those with characteristics like anger, pride and thievery stir up strife and will be brought low.
Day 340: Proverbs 29:25-27
The fear of man is a trap, but those who put their trust in the Lord will be safe.
Day 341: Proverbs 30:1-4
These verses are the words of a man named Agur who is perceptive about the things of God.
Day 342: Proverbs 30:5-6
The Word of God is pure. We can confidently trust in it, and should never tamper with it.
Day 343: Proverbs 30:7-9
A prayer is given to be cleansed from all vanity, and to be supplied with basic needs.
Day 344: Proverbs 30:10
We should not accuse or scold another man's servant, as the servant's owner will curse you for adding to the burdens of the lowly.
Day 345: Proverbs 30:11-14
An exceedingly wicked generation of people is described.
Day 346: Proverbs 30:15-16
These verses record things that are destructive and are never satisfied
Day 347: Proverbs 30:17
The penalty for mocking, scorning and disobeying our parents is death.
Day 348: Proverbs 30:18-19
There are four things that are wonderful and mysterious: how an eagle flies, how a serpent slithers, how a ship sails, and how a man and woman are attracted to one another.
Day 349: Proverbs 30:20-23
An array of rebellious sinners is described.
Day 350: Proverbs 30:24-28
We are given an example of four things that are little, and yet wise in their actions. Among these are 3 insects and a small animal.
Day 351: Proverbs 30:29-31
There are four things that are stately in their stride: three animals and a strong king.
Day 352: Proverbs 30:32-33
We should not exalt ourselves, but guard our mouths from speaking evil.
Day 353: Proverbs 31:1-3
Motherly advice is given to a king to keep him from destroying his position.

Day 354: Proverbs 31:4-7

A mother gives advice to the king concerning wine and strong drink.

Day 355: Proverbs 31:8-9

A king should speak up for the cause of the poor and needy.

Day 356: Proverbs 31:10-12

A description is given of a virtuous and wise woman.

Day 357: Proverbs 31:13-14

The duties of the virtuous woman are listed.

Day 358: Proverbs 31:15-16

A virtuous woman is disciplined to rise early and make ready for the day at hand.

Day 359: Proverbs 31:17-18

A virtuous woman perseveres in the things that cause her business to prosper.

Day 360: Proverbs 31:19-20

A virtuous woman works with her own hands and ministers to the poor.

Day 361: Proverbs 31:21-22

The virtuous woman clothes herself and her household in beautiful garments.

Day 362: Proverbs 31:23-24

The virtuous woman's husband is well known among the elders in the community.

Day 363: Proverbs 31:25-26

The virtuous woman is one of strength and honor. She is well prepared for the future.

Day 364: Proverbs 31:27-29

The virtuous woman's children and husband praise her, and consider her to excel above all others.

Day 365: Proverbs 31:30-31

The greatest quality of the virtuous woman is that she worships and serves her Creator.

Other Books by Betty Miller

Overcoming Life Series:

Prove All Things - First in the Overcoming Life Series. Jesus warned that deception would be a sign of the end times. This book will give you clear Scriptural guidelines on how to discern the Spirit of Truth from the spirit of error.

The True God - Second in the Overcoming Life Series. This book will show you the character of God, explaining why He does certain things and why it is against His nature to do other things.

The Will of God - Third in the Overcoming Life Series. The first step to doing the will of God is knowing His will. Learn how to know the will of God for your personal life, your family, your ministry, and your finances.

Keys to the Kingdom - Fourth in the Overcoming Life Series. This book will show you how to gain authority in the Kingdom of God through prayer.

Exposing Satan's Devices - Fifth in the Overcoming Life Series. This is a powerful exposé of Satan's tricks, tactics and lies. Learn how to detect occult practices and deceptions. A list of cults and occult groups are included.

Healing of the Spirit, Soul and Body - Sixth in the Overcoming Life Series. Learn how to receive divine healing for emotional as well as physical problems.

Neither Male Nor Female - Seventh in the Overcoming Life Series. What is the woman's role in the church? Who is a woman's spiritual head and covering? Does God call women to the five-fold ministry?

Extremes or Balance? - Eighth in the Overcoming Life Series. Many Christians have hurt the cause of Christ through out-of-balance teachings and demonstrations. Learn how to avoid those areas and walk in balance.

The Pathway Into The Overcomer's Walk - Ninth in the Overcoming Life Series. This book provides the answers to the questions you will face as you press toward the prize of the high calling in Christ Jesus.

The End Times Series:

Mark of God or Mark of the Beast - This book sheds light on how we can be protected and delivered during the time we will live under the shadow of the Mark of the Beast.

Personal Spiritual Warfare - This book will show you how to obtain your personal victories in your financial, marriage, home, and emotional battles.

These books can be purchased online through the ministry bookstore at www.BibleResources.org

About the Author

Betty Miller and her husband, Bud, were founders of the Bible.com website and have now moved their ministry content to their newest website, **BibleResources.org**. They have served as pastors, teachers, and evangelists, with an apostolic/prophetic calling to proclaim the gospel through the Internet. Betty is a teacher of the Word of God, with a beautiful ability to present truth in a simple and understandable way.

She has authored 21 books, plus numerous articles and teachings posted on the BibleResources.org website. She attributes her gift of writing to the Lord. Through a miraculous event, Betty and Bud were able to obtain the Bible.com website in 1994 and then in 2012, in their senior years, have now founded another Bible based website called **BibleResources.org**.

God has used the Millers on the Internet to reach millions of people each month around the world with the Word of God. The new website, **BibleResources.org**, is devoted to helping people understand and grow in God by providing many Bible resources and tools free. The website offers an enhanced Bible search feature to help the user find what they are looking for in the Bible. The site also has an audio/video online Overcoming Life Church and Prayer Room, Bible Answers, Bible Teachings, Daily Devotionals, a Chapel Bookstore, plus many other Christian resources. *God's Wisdom for Daily Living* is also posted online at Bible.com for those who enjoy their devotionals on the computer or mobile devices.

Betty is a woman who shares her life as wife, mother, grandmother, great-grandmother, businesswoman, teacher and minister. Most of all, she shares her love of the Lord, whom she credits with making her life one of purpose and joy.

She and Bud live in the mountains of northern Arizona where she continues to write and minister.

About Christ Unlimited Ministries and its Internet Outreach - BibleResources.org

Ministry Goal: Christ Unlimited's Ministry goal is to strengthen the church worldwide and bring new converts to Jesus by making the Bible available in every format and language possible, along with furnishing Bible resources and sound scriptural teaching. Our desire is to honor Jesus and bring glory to God by continuing to share the gospel of the kingdom via the Internet as commanded of us in the Great Commission.

Mark 16:15: And he said unto them, Go ye into all the world, and preach the gospel to every creature.

Matthew 28:18-20: And Jesus came and spake unto them, saying, All power is given unto me in heaven and in earth. Go ye therefore, and teach all nations, baptizing them in the name of the Father, and of the Son, and of the Holy Ghost: Teaching them to observe all things whatsoever I have commanded you: and, lo, I am with you alway, even unto the end of the world. Amen.

Donation Information: If this book has blessed and helped you, you can help **BibleResources.org** continue its ministry to the world by donating to Christ Unlimited Ministries. (We are a 501(c)(3) tax-deductible non-profit ministry.)

Donate Online at: www.BibleResources.org

By Mail: Send your gifts to:
Christ Unlimited Ministries, P.O. Box 850, Dewey, AZ 86327

By Phone: Call with a credit card 1-888-BY-BIBLE (1-888-292-4253)

Christ Unlimited Ministries
P.O. Box 850
Dewey, AZ 86327
928-632-8005
Website: www.BibleResources.org
E-Mail: ContactUs@ChristUnlimited.com

CPSIA information can be obtained
at www.ICGtesting.com
Printed in the USA
FSOW02n1330230516
20651FS

9 781571 490223